cognitive development

The Dryden Press
Publications in Interpersonal Relations

GENERAL EDITOR
THEODORE M. NEWCOMB
UNIVERSITY OF MICHIGAN

Behavior

AND

Development

IN

Childhood

ALFRED L. BALDWIN

*Department of Child Development
and Family Relationships*

CORNELL UNIVERSITY

THE DRYDEN PRESS

NEW YORK

Preface

THE REASONS which led the author to add another text in child psychology to those which already exist stem basically from his convictions about the importance of psychological theory, both for the development of the field of psychology and for its teaching.

Child psychology is important because children are important, and also because childhood experiences influence later personality. The facts of child behavior do not, however, speak for themselves. Since each child is unique and has a unique history, it is essential to have an adequate theoretical system if we are to make predictions in real situations. The author has attempted to make explicit a theoretical framework which can be of help in predicting how children behave and how they develop.

In attempting to clarify these problems for the student, the author was forced to the basic distinction between child behavior and child development. One set of ideas describes *how the child behaves* in a specific situation. This is the psychology of childhood, the subject matter of Part I. A different set of ideas is required to predict *how the child's personality will change* and to identify the factors that determine the changes. This is the psychology of development, described in Part II. The author has found this distinction of very great help in clarifying problems. Perhaps the reader will also.

In the psychology of childhood particularly, the author feels that he has made some contribution to the science of psychology. The psychology of childhood is important as an applied science; its principles can help parents and teachers understand children. The behavior of children is also of basic importance for the science of psychology because it provides a rich store of data for comparative psychology. Whenever we attempt to describe individual differences in terms of any theoretical system, we usually find that the theory profits from the attempt. Psychology has profited greatly from studies of maladjustment and mental illness for just this reason. The comparison of children

v

with adults and the comparison of different ages within childhood offer similar possibilities for theoretical refinement.

In attempting to explain to the student how children differ from adults, the author has educated himself as well as the student. The fact that children are less competent and adaptive than adults is a commonplace, but the problem that this fact poses for psychology is perhaps not readily apparent: our theory of child behavior must predict and explain this fact. In his attempt to understand and to explain these problems of child psychology, the author believes he has developed some theoretical ideas which contribute something to the science of human behavior. All this, then, is one reason for writing this book and for writing a theoretical text.

A second reason for a theoretical text is an educational one. Students will understand children better and remember more of what they learn about children if they try to *explain* child behavior rather than merely to *describe* it. A theory offers a framework for memory as well as a deeper understanding of the behavior itself. This book attempts, therefore, to offer a consistent and coherent point of view. It attempts, also, to present other theoretical positions and to show the student by example that differing theorists can respect and learn from one another.

Although this text is theoretically coherent, it also attempts to capitalize upon the student's common-sense knowledge of human behavior. Thousands of instructive and fascinating incidents occur in everyday life; if we are alert and inquiring, we can learn from them and build hypotheses from them. This book tries to sensitize the student to the richness of everyday life. It is, in a sense, anecdotal. At the same time, however, it draws upon experimental evidence to establish relationships.

Although anecdotes are instructive, they do not constitute scientific proof. Common sense is a tacit theory, but, like other theories, it is erroneous in some respects and incomplete in others. It is important, therefore, to instill in the student a skepticism toward, as well as a respect for, current scientific theories and his everyday observations. We can do this by refusing to hide ignorance under platitudes, and by not trying to gloss over difficult problems on the assumption that students will be merely bored or confused.

Most important of all, we want the student to feel the excitement of inquiry and the importance of scientific understanding. This book attempts to do so by presenting the student with examples of steadfast efforts to understand and explain child behavior and development. Throughout this book the author has tried to approach each topic with but one objective—to make sense of it. If by so doing he motivates the reader also to try to make sense out of child behavior, he will be more than satisfied.

Like most books, this one involved more than its author. Friends, colleagues, students, and family all contributed. The author is especially indebted to the following people and wishes he could thank them more adequately. Professor Fritz Heider was particularly influential, and his ideas cannot be adequately acknowledged through usual bibliographic citations. Two students, Miss Lise Wertheimer and Mr. Aaron Hershkovitz, gave especially generously of their time, effort, and ideas. The family of a child psychologist is particularly important in his writing because it provides subject matter as well as assistance. The author's children have become very adept at recognizing the significance of his occasional pensive look. "Are you going to put that in your book?" they would ask. To his wife for manifold contributions, ranging from stimulating ideas, through tolerance of an author's eccentricities, to menial labor, the author is more than grateful.

Quotations from various sources are specifically acknowledged in the bibliography, but the author wishes to thank the following publishers for their permission to quote copyrighted material: *American Journal of Orthopsychiatry; American Journal of Psychology;* American Psychological Association; *Archives of Psychology;* Johann Ambrosius Barth; Basic Books; Child Development Publications; Bureau of Publications, Teachers College, Columbia University; Columbia University Press; The Commonwealth Fund; Doubleday, Doran and Co.; Duke University Press; Gustav Fisher; Harcourt, Brace and Co.; Harper and Brothers; Harvard University Press; Henry Holt and Co.; Houghton-Mifflin Co.; International Universities Press; The Journal Press; McGraw-Hill Book Co.; National Society for the Study of Education; Ronald Press Co.; University of California Press; University of Chicago Press; University of London Press; University of Minnesota Press; John Wiley and Sons; and Yale University Press.

Cornell University   Alfred L. Baldwin
April 1955

CONTENTS: AN OVERVIEW

(For complete Table of Contents, see pages xi-xviii)

Contents

PART ONE
BEHAVIOR IN CHILDHOOD

Behavior

IN

Childhood

1

The Field and Problems of
Child Psychology

THE STUDENTS who enroll in a course in child development or child psychology come into it with a variety of motives. Some of them actually work with children or plan to do so when they themselves become parents or teachers. Any first-hand dealings with children have a certain concrete "here and now" quality. It is important for those who do it to understand *children as children.* It is important because we do not want the child to throw a tantrum every time he has to wash his face, and we want him to respect the rights of other children, not to push them into the fish pond or off the jungle gym. These are immediate problems; they arise because the child does not behave in the same way in which the adult does. And the study of how a child behaves and how his behavior differs from that of the adult might be called the *psychology of childhood,* in contradistinction to the *psychology of development.*

But any class in child psychology will also include students whose primary interest is not so much in the child as such but rather in the child as "father of the man." Guidance workers particularly, although parents and educators must also be included, tend to look upon the child as the adult of tomorrow, and they are as much concerned with *what kind of adult he will become* as with what kind of child he is now. These students want the answers to questions about the effects of childhood experience upon the personality of the adult. Should children be weaned early or should they be allowed to take a bottle to bed with them as long as they wish to? Some parents follow the first practice; others, the second. Does it make any difference? This is not a problem in the psychology of childhood. The future consequences of early weaning is a topic which belongs in the psychology of child development.

Sometimes parents, teachers, and others may lose sight of one or the other of these points of view. The teacher may have a smoothly run and efficient schoolroom. Since she understands children, she uses the proper combination of humor, authority, and reasoning to reduce classroom friction to a minimum. She does not feel that she has any "problem children" because everyone behaves himself as well as can be expected, and there are no more than the inevitable number of failures. But many people nowadays, are suspicious of such well-behaved classes. They wonder whether their teachers are providing a favorable climate for the future development of intellectually alert participants in a democracy.

On the other hand, the teacher can be so focused upon providing the proper stimulation for future growth that she neglects the "here and now" problems. The nursery-school teacher pictured in a cartoon who found that Charlie, one of her charges, had hit another one with a hammer and had left him unconscious on the floor illustrates the point. Her first remark was, "We must be sure that Charlie does not develop guilt feelings."

The topics in the psychology of children differ, therefore, from those in the psychology of development. For the study of child behavior we need to see clearly how a child's behavior is different from an adult's. From this difference we can derive an understanding of the child's personality and can predict his behavior. For the purposes of the theory of child behavior, this personality may be assumed to remain constant; *i.e.,* we are not interested, at the moment, in the fact that his personality will change and mature as he grows. In the psychology of childhood are contained such problems as the nature of thinking in childhood. Is it logical or not? We also want to know the characteristics of interpersonal relations among children—what love, hate, shame, and guilt are like during childhood. We shall also discuss the nature of a child's wishes, goals, and needs. All these topics will be discussed, along with other topics in the psychology of childhood, in Part I of this book.

The psychology of development will be dealt with in Part II. Here we shall examine maturation, the process of becoming mature. Is this process predetermined at the time the child is born, or can it be accelerated by a challenging, stimulating environment? We shall also consider the effect of different societies on the child's personality, and on the kind of adult he becomes. We shall study how children learn and how they acquire their adult values. Finally, we shall examine a number of experiments on the effects of home environment on personality development.

The Intuitive Understanding of Children

Returning for the moment to the understanding of child behavior, we should note that skill in handling children and in appreciating how they feel is not the same thing as explaining their behavior. Intuitive understanding, although it is an important basis for building an explanation, is not the same as scientific explanation.

One of the difficulties we shall face in explaining child behavior is that most adults do not have the same intuitive understanding of children that they have of adults. Children are different from adults—not entirely so, but nevertheless different. Of course, children are not all alike; older children resemble adults much more closely than younger ones do, but, taken as a whole, a child cannot be expected to behave in a situation in the same way that an adult would. This is not to say that all adults behave alike, but, even though the behavior of an adult is not highly predictable, it almost always has a certain reasonableness about it which the observer recognizes and which enables him to understand the behavior he observes.

If an adult behaves in a way which is so unreasonable or irrational that it estranges him from his colleagues, they consider him peculiar, eccentric, or insane. If an adult is insulted in public by being called stupid, it is not unlikely that he will become angry. His anger may not be wise, but we feel that anger is natural and understandable in such circumstances. He may not openly display his anger, but instead he may try to show that the person who called him stupid is really the one who is stupid. He may stop talking, become sullen, leave the room, or, in extreme cases, he may even respond with a physical assult. An observer might well feel that these extreme responses are not fully justified by the circumstances but they are, nevertheless, within his ken. But if the adult's response to being called stupid were to chant, "Stu—pid, stew—pot, John—ny is a stew-pot," the observer might well feel that something not quite normal had taken place. Yet, such a response as this could occur quite readily if a child were placed in a similar situation.

Let us examine a much more complex situation showing how thoroughly we appreciate interpersonal relations between adults. The following are selected quotations from Shakespeare's *Othello,* in which Iago is trying to make Othello believe that Othello's wife, Desdemona, has been unfaithful to him. As Iago and Othello entered, they saw Cassio leave Desdemona. Then Desdemona pleaded with Othello to return Cassio to his favor. This request was granted by Othello, not because he was convinced of Cassio's worth but because Desdemona asked it. She has just left.

> *Iago:* My noble lord,
> *Othello:* What dost thou say, Iago?
> *Iago:* Did Michael Cassio, when you woo'd my lady,
> Know of your love?
> *Othello:* He did, from first to last: why dost thou ask?
> *Iago:* But for a satisfaction of my thought;
> No further harm.
> *Othello:* Why of thy thought, Iago?
> *Iago:* I did not think he had been acquainted with her.
> *Othello:* O, yes; and went between us very oft.
> *Iago:* Indeed!
> *Othello:* Indeed! aye, indeed; discern'st thou aught in that?
> Is he not honest?
> *Iago:* Honest, my lord!
> *Othello:* Honest! ay honest.
> *Iago:* My lord, for aught I know.

We cannot take the space to present the complete scene, but after Iago thus entices Othello into demanding his opinion, Iago gives a short lecture on jealousy, warning Othello not to be jealous. The effect of this is, of course, to make Othello very aware of the possibility of some illicit relationship between Cassio and Desdemona. Then Iago gives vent to his pretended suspicions, being careful to say that none of them has been proved. Then, to nail down the idea, he begs Othello *not* to be suspicious. Othello says, "I do not think but Desdemona's honest," to which Iago replies "Long live she so! And long live you to think so!"

Here we have an apparently paradoxical situation. Iago wants to make Othello believe something, and so he refuses to tell him. He has to be virtually forced to talk. He proclaims that he does not believe what he really wants Othello to believe. Yet, in reality, this behavior is not paradoxical or mysterious. It seems diabolically clever—"good psychology," in the common use of the term. Because of our intuitive understanding of our fellow man, we understand, as we read this passage, why Iago behaved as he did and why his tactics had the effect he wanted. This common-sense psychology is the soil out of which the science of psychology grows.

But with children we have much less feeling of intuitive understanding. Look at the following three examples:

A five-year-old was taken to see a performance of the passion play enacting the life of Jesus. The next morning he was asked about the play and replied, "A big black giant came and stole Jesus." As far as the adult could see, the cast included no "big black giant."

The second example comes from Louise P. Woodcock's description of two-year-olds: (1941)

A board was leaning against a block so that there was space underneath it. A boy pushed a hammer underneath the board so far that it stuck out the other side. He had pushed it so far that he could just touch it from the side he was pushing from. Then he wanted it out again and tried to get hold of it to pull it back out. Meanwhile it was actually protruding on the other side in easy reach. The teacher, thinking to help him solve his problem, called to him and asked him where the hammer was. He pointed to it, not underneath the board, but to the protruding portion on the other side. But when the teacher then asked him to get the hammer, back he went to his former position and tried again to reach it from the side from which he had pushed it in.

The third example, taken again from Woodcock (1941), is a conversation between a teacher and a two-year-old child:

Marcia asked the teacher, "Are you busy?"
Teacher: "Yes."
Marcia: "Not too busy?"
Teacher: "No."
Marcia: "Only one busy."

Depending upon one's experience with children, these anecdotes may seem unintelligible or only childlike. In either case they have a quality different from that of our experiences with adults, and we can understand them only after we have had sufficient experience with children to "get the feel" of child behavior. Even with such experience, they are not necessarily clear. Was Marcia, the two-year-old in the third example, really making a pun? Was it a joke for her? Was it a real mistake, confusion of "too" with "two"? Different nursery-school teachers would probably have different interpretations and different understandings of this behavior.

The point should be clear that some behavior of children is not easily understood by an adult, even when he has had considerable experience with children. On the other hand, children are sometimes crystal clear. A young child cannot hide his feelings as an adult can. A four-year-old is warned that a guest has only one eye and wears a patch over his blind one, and that he should not say anything about it or pay any attention to it because he might embarrass the visitor. He may try valiantly to keep from mentioning it, but he just cannot help staring at the patch all through dinner. We all know that the child is a very poor liar; if he knows he is lying, his whole demeanor reveals it. On the other hand, he can report the most outlandish events and apparently be convinced they are true.

How can children be so inconsistent—sphinxlike one minute, crystal clear the next? A child is heartbroken when someone takes away his favorite crayon, but one child, the sole survivor of an automobile wreck which killed both his parents, asked only one question after he heard that his parents were dead: "Who is going to take me to school in the morning?"

Interpreting Child Behavior from an Adult Point of View

Perhaps part of the reason that children seem so inconsistent to the adult observer is that he is likely to interpret their behavior from an adult point of view. If he does this, the child's behavior will sometimes make no sense at all. At other times it will make sense, but the adult must be careful not to misinterpret the significance of the child's behavior.

A preschool child once looked at a muffin tin holding a dozen muffins and, since there were four people in the family, said, "There will be three for each of us." His fond parent was amazed, and readily assumed that his three-year-old had divided 12 by 4 and arrived at the correct answer, 3. Upon closer inspection, it was observed that the muffin tin was arranged in four rows of three muffins each. What the boy probably did was to discover first that there would be one row of muffins for each person; then he counted the number of muffins in the row for each person. Even when seen in this way, it was certainly not stupid behavior, but it was much less mature than it appeared on the surface.

In order to understand children, there is no substitute for direct experience with them. In order to have as much experience with children as is possible within the covers of a book, we shall examine numerous concrete examples of child behavior. These examples give the flavor which comes from living with children and watching their delights and fears, their flashes of genius, their incredible blunders, their utterly charming moments and also their most obnoxious ones.

Although understanding children is very important and is an absolute prerequisite for dealing with them effectively, it is not sufficient. As long as we are satisfied with *understanding* children, we shall not be able to *explain* their behavior. We shall not be able to teach others to understand children except by letting them live with children. If, on the other hand, we can develop some explanation of child behavior which goes beyond intuitive understanding, we can effectively communicate our understanding and eventually even account for those aspects of child behavior which are beyond the present understanding of our wisest mothers and teachers.

Theoretical Conceptualization of Child Behavior

In order to make clear the difference between an intuitive understanding and an explanation of child behavior, let us return to one of the previous examples, that of the boy trying to retrieve the hammer from under the board (see p. 7). An intuitive understanding of this incident was revealed in the teacher's behavior. Her attempt to help the child solve the problem without telling him the answer was based on sound intuition. She called him away from his local view of the problem, got him to survey it as a whole, and then asked him where the hammer was. This might well have worked. Since it did not, she might have tried attracting his attention to something else for a moment, then asking him to run get the hammer for her. She might have tried setting up another similar situation, with the hammer protruding in the same way; then she could have asked the child to get her that hammer. If he obtained it by the short method, she could have returned him to his original problem.

If her understanding was completely intuitive—which is in fact very unlikely—she would have difficulty in communicating it. Her explanation would be in the form of analogies and metaphors. "You know how we can get so wrapped up in a problem we lose perspective," she might say. "We can't see the forest for the trees. I remember how I got locked out one Sunday when I went out for the newspaper. I pounded on the door for several minutes without thinking to see if the back door was unlocked."

Her intuitive understanding might lead her to make various changes in the situation to make it easier for the child to solve. But she could have done all these things and still be quite unable to put into words the psychological nature of the child's difficulty. When she tries to put the understanding into words, she speaks in metaphors and finds analogous experiences in her own life.

Let us now try to describe the child's difficulty in psychological terms, since this is the first step toward achieving an explanation of it. The science of psychology being what it is at the present time, we cannot be certain that our explanation is the only one or that other psychologists would agree with it, but we can try to formulate a small-scale theory.

One way to describe the child's difficulty is to say that he seemed to assume that he had to get the hammer out by the path through which he pushed it in. He did not—at the moment, at least—perceive that he could get back *by a different route* to the position from which he started. We can find other examples of child behavior which show the same principle. Another incident from Woodcock (1941) describes the behavior of Tammy, a two-year-old girl who was going with a boy to "paint" the roof. Each child had his pail of water with which he was going to paint. While Tammy had set down her pail and was not looking, the boy, Barton, stole the water from Tammy's pail. The teacher noticed the robbery; in a moment Tammy saw that she had been robbed; both gave chase and caught up with Barton as he neared his goal. The teacher told him to give back the water he had taken. Tammy now ran back to the exact place where the robbery occurred, put her pail down on the ground, and there waited for Barton to come back to replace the stolen "paint." Here is another example in which restitution of an act involves re-establishing in full concrete detail the circumstances as they had existed before the act took place.

Psychoanalysis has a word for this sort of behavior—*undoing*. As the child becomes more mature, his conception of going back to the starting point gradually changes. At first it must be an almost complete turning backward of time, a reliving of the behavior in reverse order. In maturity, as we shall see later, it is necessary only to re-establish the essential relevant conditions which were disturbed by the behavior which is being retracted. We shall see that the process of going back plays a role in such diverse behavior as starting a problem over again, making amends for an act, forgiving, or recapturing one's pride after a shameful incident.

We have seen how one aspect of the boy's problem of retrieving the hammer is his too-concrete definition of going back. A second is the fact that he was completely absorbed in getting it "back." What the teacher tried to do when she called him away from the task was to shake him loose from his narrow point of view. If she could get him to approach the problem afresh, to try to obtain the hammer as he would if he had never seen the situation before, he would almost surely reach it directly by the shortest path. She was trying to detach him from the problem as he had defined it, "getting the hammer back," and to redefine it as "getting the hammer." She failed, because even though he could take a new view when she asked him to point to the hammer, he went back to his original approach and was no better off than before when she asked him to get it. If this analysis is correct, then keeping him detached for a longer period of time might have succeeded, or presenting him with the identical problem in a different setting might have led him to see the problem from a new point of view.

In our analysis of his behavior, two concepts have emerged; *undoing* and *detachment*. The child tries to undo his behavior, whereas the adult in a similar situation needs only to re-establish the essential, relevant characteristics. The child is bound to his point of view. The adult is more detached from his point of view as it exists here and now—at least in this kind of impersonal problem.

Both of these concepts have a general applicability to other sorts of behavior; they are useful in explaining a variety of child behavior. Both of them are testable. We could design experiments which would present the subject with two alternative ways of returning to the starting point. One is a long, cumbersome retracing of his path. The other is a short cut. We should expect that older children would be more likely than younger ones to take the short cut.

Understanding vs. Explanation

This, then, is an example of the way in which a theoretical explanation of child behavior might be constructed. What is the difference between an intuitive understanding and a theoretical explanation? The first difference is that a theoretical explanation permits the behavior of the child to be deduced logically from certain stated assumptions or hypotheses. Once the analysis is presented, it is not necessary to have wide experience with children to make the prediction that children will have more difficulty than adults in finding a short cut back home. The prediction follows from the hypothesis.

A second difference is that a theoretical explanation applies to a wide range of child behavior which does not superficially resemble the original incident. There is no obvious resemblance between retrieving a hammer and forgiving an insult, but in terms of the theory some of the same principles apply. An intuitive understanding is more limited to actual incidents, although intuition is also generalizable to some sorts of new situations.

A third difference between an understanding and an explanation is that the explanation may be tested; it suggests further experiments. Although a prediction may be made on the basis of intuitive understanding, a correct prediction made on such a basis merely confirms the intuitive ability of the person who made it. If the teacher's predictions hold up, then we know that she is an understanding person. We cannot, however, detach her understanding from her personality unless she puts her predictions in the form of a theory. If a theoretical explanation holds up under testing, then the explanation is confirmed. The ability of the theory builder is also confirmed and our opinion of him is enhanced when his theory proves accurate, but this fact is incidental; it has nothing to do with the validity of the explanation.

In summary a theoretical explanation of child behavior offers three advantages over an intuitive understanding. First, it makes prediction a matter of logical reasoning rather than of insightful understanding. Therefore, the theory may be tested logically. (A test of intuitive understanding is a test of the person who has the understanding rather than a test of the understanding itself.) Secondly, a theoretical explanation offers the possibility of incorporating a wide variety of behavior into a single theory and enhances the possibility of seeing the relationships among apparently diverse behavior patterns. Thirdly, a theoretical explanation suggests new experiments and thus pushes the limits of our knowledge out into the unknown. Intuitive understanding is less likely to have this effect.

All these advantages of a theory over an intuitive understanding are valid, but they certainly do not indicate that intuitive understanding is wrong and theoretical explanation is right. In many cases the two do not even differ from each other. In fact, as we shall see in the next section, the process of theory building can most efficiently begin with an intuitive understanding of child behavior which is gradually transformed into a testable scientific theory.

Construction of Theoretical Explanations

The selection of a specific strategy for eventually achieving an adequate theory must partly depend upon the individual preferences of the scientist and upon his scientific background. This does not mean that all methods are equally satisfactory; surely they are not equivalent. It does imply, however, that there is no way to prove with strict logical rigor that one approach to the development of a theory is better than another. It is the author's conviction that scientific theory is best developed by building it upon an adequate intuitive understanding of human behavior, by trying to put this understanding into words, and by gradually integrating it into broader concepts until a consistent theory is achieved. Whenever it is possible to make an empirical test of a concept, it is important to do so, and to do so with all possible rigor; but it is equally important to demand an intuitive understanding of the behavior which corresponds to the logical prediction. Psychological theory is replete with examples of the error of trying to build a theory without basing it on an understanding of the phenomenon to be explained.

The effort to achieve an understanding of human behavior results in a definite attitude toward the data. Understanding is achieved by trying to put oneself in the shoes of the other person so that his behavior becomes understandable. We want to find out how it was possible for him to do what he did, how he felt, how the situation appeared to him.

Once the investigator feels that he understands the behavior, he must change his attitude toward the data. Thoughts and emotions of the other person are of no immediate use in formulating a theory because they are not objective. Instead of looking for such inner feelings, the theory builder searches for characteristics of behavior which are external and observable, and upon which different observers can agree. These consistently recognizable behavioristic characteristics are used to define the terms in which the psychological theory is stated.

The first step in transforming an understanding into a theoretical explanation is to put the understanding into simple everyday language. In beginning the analysis of retrieving the hammer, we started with the statement, "He seemed to assume that he had to get the hammer out by the path through which he pushed it in." This is a first attempt to describe in psychological terms what was taking place in the child's behavior. From then on, the argument proceeded to compare his behavior with other examples of child behavior and to introduce from psychoanalytic theory the concept of undoing.

The first step is very important. Depending upon the way the behavior is first formulated, the later development may or may not be fruitful. Suppose we had said that the boy trying to get his hammer out was stupid. In a sense this statement is correct, although he is no more stupid than other children his age. The trouble is that it does not lead any further.

Suppose that we had been led to the following speculation about the boy's behavior. Perhaps the boy had frequently lost objects in holes which had no opening on the other side. Therefore he could have learned that the only way to get an object out was to retrace the path by which it was pushed in. This answer would lead our search for an explanation in an entirely new direction. We would look to the history of the child for an explanation of his present behavior. This choice between a historical explanation and an explanation couched in terms of the psychological factors existing in the present is a fundamental one. The psychology of childhood is the result of looking at the present; the psychology of development results from looking to the past. Let us, then, examine these two types of explanation.

Historical and Systematic Causation

The distinction between child behavior and child development raises an important general question about the explanation of behavior. The general position tacitly assumed when we make the distinction between behavior and development is that it is possible to formulate the laws of behavior. These laws are expressed in such terms as motive, need, knowledge, or habit. Each of these terms is descriptive of the individual's behavior at a given moment, and, with them as a basis, a sound theory could predict the behavior of a person in the various situations which confront him in everyday life.

This assumption can be put into other words. The factors necessary to predict behavior can be measured and are assumed to exist at the time a person behaves. This is a statement of *systematic causation*. According to such an assumption, the statement that an adult is afraid of people because he was neglected and punished during childhood is incomplete. The causes of his fear of people, strictly speaking, lie in the present. To take a specific example, he may be afraid of people because he thinks they are hostile to him. Why does he think they are hostile to him? The reason for this may be described in terms of some personality characteristic which makes it easy for him to perceive hostility. Since we do not have an adequate theory of behavior, the precise nature of this personality characteristic is at present unclear.

Although it is possible to build an adequate theory of behavior without going outside the present, it is perfectly reasonable to ask about the history of this hypothetical person's fear of people. It is certainly true that it stems historically from earlier experiences and is in that sense caused by earlier experiences. Such causes are *historical causes*. The search for historical causes is completely legitimate, but since we make the general scientific assumption that there is some mechanism leading from a cause to an effect, then there must be a *systematic cause* which is a trace or consequence of the past experience and which transmits the influence of the past experience. In a complete explanation both historical and systematic causes play necessary roles.

An analogy will make the difference clearer. The floor of a house collapses. A systematic explanation would find the cause in the rustiness of the nails or the weakness of the boards. A historical explanation would find the cause in termites which invaded the house a year ago, in the water which soaked the floor in last spring's flood, and in the fact that the piano was moved to that spot a week ago. The termites, the flood and the action of moving the piano did not operate at a distance. They produced effects which have lasted, or they changed the properties of the floor so that, under some minor and unknown stress which occurred in the present, it collapsed.

Whether one looks for the historical antecedents of behavior or the systematic causes of it is partly a matter of choice, but in many cases the purpose of the investigation decides which sort of causative factors are investigated. Since the past cannot be changed, the search for a remedy demands an explanation in terms of the present situation. The only way to fix the floor is to make it stronger; one cannot prevent the termite invasion which happened a year ago. Even in psychoanalytic therapy, where so often the analyst helps the patient to uncover the childhood causes of his troubles, the assumption is made that these historical factors have their traces in the present personality and that it is the insight *now* into the historical roots of the difficulty that produces therapeutic changes.

If the aim is prediction rather than therapy, it is still generally easier to work on the basis of systematic rather than historical causes. The present situation is generally more accessible to measurement than the past history. In some cases, on the other hand, the collection of a case history is easier than the assessment of the present personality; hence it may be more fruitful to look for historical rather than systematic causation. For a complete explanation both are necessary.

The psychology of development clearly demands the search for the dynamics of the process of change which takes place in time. Childhood experiences are the historical causes of the adult personality. The practical goal to be attained, once an adequate theory of development is available, is to modify childhood experiences so that people will become more effective adults.

We see, then, that the distinction between the psychology of child behavior and the psychology of development has a sound scientific basis. Since, however, the historical causes of behavior must operate through modification of the individual's characteristics, and since these characteristics enter into a pattern of systematic causation, it is essential to discuss first the systematic causes of child behavior. Then the historical connections between the past and present may be described in terms of these systematic psychological factors.

Summary

In this chapter four main points have been presented:

1. The psychology of children deals wih the prediction of the behavior of the child. The psychology of development deals with the prediction of his later maturity and his adult adjustment. It involves a theory of growth and change.

2. It is important to have an intuitive understanding of child behavior similar to that feeling of communality we now have with other adults.

3. A theory of child psychology is not the same as a common sense understanding, but theory can develop out of understanding if we try to translate our intuitive grasp of child behavior into communicable principles.

4. In theories of child behavior and development, it is legitimate to search for contemporaneous systematic causes of behavior or for historical causes, but a historical cause operates by way of a mechanism that is represented in the present situation.

2

Maturity: An Introduction

SURVEY OF CHILDHOOD

THE CHARACTERISTICS OF MATURE BEHAVIOR

EXPANSION OF THE PSYCHOLOGICAL WORLD

SUMMARY

Survey of Childhood

The Neonate

WHEN A NEW BABY comes home from the hospital, probably the most impressive thing about him is his helplessness and fragility. "He's so tiny," a new mother may say, "I'm afraid I'll drop him." This helplessness of the new baby, although easily exaggerated, is not entirely a figment of the new parents' imagination. The newborn child is closer to the border between life and death than the older child. Many of his adjustments are inefficient and unstable. Whereas the adult, for example, has fairly efficient machinery for keeping his body temperature constant, the infant and even the young child of nursery-school age can develop an alarming fever in twenty minutes and recover equally rapidly. Even the breathing mechanism is not functioning very well in the newborn, as the two new parents who lie listening to the breathing of

17

the baby asleep in his bedside bassinet can testify. He breathes; then there comes a long pause which seems to last an hour; finally he breathes again. His breathing also exemplifies his instability and the variability of his responses. His breathing rate, for example, may typically be around 30 respirations per minute when he is sound asleep but may rise as high as 130 per minute when he is crying.

Just as helplessness is perhaps the infant's most obvious characteristic, the most obvious change as he grows up is an increase in competence and adjustment. Even his physiological mechanisms become more competent, and as a consequence his physiological adjustment mechanisms are better able to maintain the appropriate supply of oxygen, the proper balance of blood components, the proper body temperature, and other physiological states necessary for the normal functioning of the body.

We are not primarily concerned with this physiological maturing process in the growth of children. Except where it aids in understanding the behavior of children, a knowledge of physiology is irrelevant for the field of child psychology. Some kinds of behavior, however, especially in infants, are closely related to physiological changes. The ability of the child to look at an object—to point both his eyes in the same direction and to obtain a clear image of an object on the retina—is very important in his behavioral maturation. One of the major accomplishments of the first three months of life is the ability to look at objects—big ones, little ones, close ones, distant ones, and moving ones. A newborn child is not completely unable to follow a moving light, but it is sometimes startling to parents to see his eyes looking in two different directions at the same time.

Although the baby seems quite helpless, it is surprising how many adjustments to the external world he can make even at birth. He can suckle, for example—not too efficiently at first and in some cases only with considerable difficulty—but still most babies can get the food they need by nursing. He can sneeze and cough when his nose and throat are irritated. He can swallow and breathe alternately so that food doesn't get into his trachea. He can cry, and he has many reflexes which are not apparent except in a careful medical examination.

All these mechanisms of adjustment operate fairly well at birth; but it is important to note that they are all automatic responses to immediate stimuli. The newborn child never behaves in a way which seems to indicate that he is aware of the wider world around him. He is, for that reason, a rather disappointing person on whom to shower love and attention. Fathers especially, it seems, cannot become very excited about the tiny infant, and even mothers may describe the very new baby as animal-like. By the time he is three or four months old, it is common to hear the mother say that he is becoming a human being.

Probably the basis for this feeling of humanness is his new responsiveness to people and also the impression he gives of deliberately doing some of the things he does. He looks intently at his fingers, plays with his hands, even gets excited at new objects and strains toward them; when this behavior occurs, he seems to have some intention which exists previous to the behavior and determines it. Before this time there is a certain automatic quality in his behavior which does not fit our expectation of human behavior. His responsiveness to people also makes him seem more like a person. He begins to smile when smiled at—at least often enough to make his parents happy.

A little later, when he is five or six months old, he is generally a sociable creature. By this time he is not exclusively preoccupied with eating and sleeping. He can sit up in a chair if propped a bit; he watches what goes on; he can finger things; and he can pick up objects if they are not too tiny. He does not wait until food is given to him before responding; he anticipates food when he sees the bottle being prepared for him. At this age and for the next month or so he is the typical baby whose pictures decorate baby-food advertisements and who appears on the movie or television screen to excite a chorus of remarks of, "Isn't he cute." He is cute, and quite self-sufficient in many matters. Still, he is likely to reach for objects that are twenty feet away as well as for objects that are within grasp; he picks up objects with a whole-hand grasp rather than delicately with thumb and fingers in opposition (see Fig. 11.2, p. 289).

It is perhaps at this age that adults are most likely to attribute too much maturity to the baby, just as earlier they may have underestimated his capacities. Although his behavior looks as though it were intentional, his intentions cannot noticeably reach into the future. He cannot yet perform any activity as a means to a goal; each action pattern is still a unit in itself. He can follow an object within his visual field, but he is just beginning to be able to search for it after it has disappeared. He cries, and when his mother comes he is comforted; perhaps he stops crying at her appearance even before she has done anything for him; but it is doubtful whether he can "cry for his mother" in the sense of anticipating that if he cries she will come.

The End of Infancy

Advancing several months now, we take a look at the child of fifteen to eighteen months of age. He has come to the end of an era; he can walk around—not too steadily, but he can get there; he can—in our culture—eat with a spoon and drink from a glass, although he may go to sleep with a bottle. Whether he shows this precocity in his eating habits depends upon whether the parents feel it is important to teach him to eat in the adult fashion. There is no good reason to suppose that it hurts the child to be weaned this early, but neither is there any reason to think that drinking from a bottle at this age is harmful. By the age of eighteen months, he can say a few words, but most children are not yet at the point at which they really understand that objects have names and that language is used for communication with other people. Nevertheless, the child by this age comprehends a great deal of what is told him and what is asked of him.

By fifteen or eighteen months he is active and highly distractable. He is also very unpredictable; he may scoot from one object to another faster than the mother can follow. Give him a box of blocks and he can have them scattered all over the floor and be off to something else within ten seconds. From this time on, for many months his ability to move about and to manipulate objects far surpasses his judgment about where to go and where not to go, what to play with and what to leave alone. For a while it seems as though his good sense will never catch up with his physical agility.

At eighteen months he is hard to control. He is not particularly resistant to suggestions—this comes later—but telling him not to do something operates merely as an interesting suggestion of something to do. By far the most effective means of controlling his behavior at this time is to put attractive yet forbidden objects out of reach and to lure him away from dangerous activity by offering distractions.

At about this age it is common in our culture to begin toilet training. As we shall see later, we live in an unusual culture in so far as toilet training is concerned; in most other cultures toilet training is delayed until the age of three or four. It is not clear, however, whether any harm is done by this early toilet training; the method of toilet training is probably more important than the age of the child. We shall, in Chapter 22, discuss the various points of view about the effects of toilet training upon personality.

Preschool

Let us look now at the child of three or four, before he enters school but well after he has stopped being a baby. Now he can talk very adequately; he can express his ideas in such a way that his parents understand him. Indeed, it may seem to his parents that he talks more than adequately. After waiting anxiously for the first word and the first sentence and anticipating all the pleasure of having a child who is able to communicate, parents may feel that they have been flooded with an embarrassment of riches. It is as though every idea the child has must be expressed vocally; every fleeting thought, every absurd association, all must come pouring out in a steady stream. And the talking of the active nursery-school child does not seem to reduce his curiosity at all. He is still as active and curious as he was earlier. He can handle himself better and has judgment enough to avoid some obvious dangers, but he still has not learned to avoid all the forbidden things of the adult world. He is so brimming with energy and he gets into so many places that it would be surprising if some of them were not forbidden.

There is a story, which ought to be true, that a college athlete in excellent physical condition once tried to imitate all the activities of a four-year-old, minute by minute. After an hour the athlete was completely exhausted, but the child was still going strong. It is no wonder that the mother of the preschool child feels exhausted at the end of a day. The following record of three minutes of a three-year-old's life can perhaps illustrate the point better than any general words.[1]

> He suddenly picked up the cat from the couch where it had been lying. He slammed the cat into the truck [a toy truck], closed the door very hastily and sat for a moment with his hands on the door. He stretched way out putting his feet underneath the stove and leaning his back against the couch. He looked pensive and suddenly, however, he wiggled the truck vigorously with his left hand. He ate an apple with his free hand. He put the apple on top of the truck. Then he picked up a cigar box that was lying on the floor and moved it against the truck to secure the door and keep the cat from escaping. The cat stuck its head out of the truck, knocking the cigar box over. The cat got almost all the way out. Chuck saw the cat and grabbed for it in a sudden movement. He stuffed the cat back into the truck and slammed the door with a hard movement.

It is misleading to portray the three years of preschool life in a single picture, because the child changes in many ways during the preschool period. He becomes very negativistic at about two and a half or three; that is, he would rather not have something he wants than get it by conforming to a parental request. This negativism gradually subsides, although few parents would have any difficulty in finding examples of negativistic behavior even at the school-age level. In the course of the preschool period the child shifts from isolated play to play with other children. Frequently during the preschool period he begins to show exclusiveness. The childhood taunt "We won't let you play with us" makes its appearance. During this period he becomes capable of feeling ashamed of himself, and he also becomes mature

---

[1] From Roger G. Barker and Herbert F. Wright, *Dutton Thurstone,*

enough for his conscience occasionally to hurt him under appropriate circumstances.

School Age

Upon his entrance into school, the child's life suddenly widens in a remarkable way. He now must meet a stranger, the teacher, who is an authority over him. The parents find that their position of omniscience is lost. Now the child reports his teacher's statements as the gospel truth; if his father doesn't agree, that is just too bad.

The child must meet not only strange adult authorities but also many strange children. For the first time he has friends who are strangers to his parents. From these new friends he gets new ideas, such as going to the movies twice a week, riding bicycles downtown, going fishing alone, buying treats at the drugstore, or having an allowance of fifty cents per week instead of ten cents. Not all these ideas are welcome to the parent, who must now learn to meet the argument "Gee, mom, all the fellows do it."

Games make sense to the school-age child, and competitiveness becomes possible. Rules are gradually seen to be a social necessity, even though at first there are all sorts of rituals by which the rules of the game may be twisted to one's advantage. It is a rule in hop-scotch that if the rock which is aimed at one of the squares lands on a line, the player loses his turn. But for children this is not the end of it. If the one whose turn it is can say "Overs" before his opponent says "No overs," he may throw again; or if he can say "Liners" before his opponent says "No liners," the liner counts as good. It may be necessary to seal the ritual with some magic phrase such as "Overs, 1955 padlock." This is the age of incantations. One game, if it can be called that, is dependent upon the chance appearance of a Nash automobile. If the child says "Nash-no-strike-back-criss-cross," he is theoretically allowed to hit his companion without fear of righteous retaliation.

All this interest in games and appreciation of them is related to competitiveness. Perhaps it is also because of the public display of ability in the classroom that the child becomes aware of his position in relation to others. He can feel inferior or superior in a way which was not previously possible. He can practice persistently to become a skillful football player or maker of model airplanes. All of this focus on relative position is accompanied by self-imposed standards of behavior—albeit frequently not the adult standards of neatness or cleanliness.

During this same period of growth, the child learns something about social roles. He learns that certain behavior is expected of people in certain positions; that a regular fellow is no tattle-tale, that somebody has to protect the passer as well as be the passer, and perhaps even that a nine-year-old should pick up his own clothes. This understanding of the expectations of others implies a certain ability of the child to put himself in the other person's shoes.

By the time the child reaches adolescence, the point at which we shall leave him, he has become intellectually almost mature. He has learned many things about the real world and can think logically about them on the basis of information he receives. A young child can say, "A plumber is one who plumbs—he is the one who pulls out plums." But with age this sort of answer no longer occurs. Whether it is a matter of more knowledge or more logical thinking is one of the questions which must be discussed later. By the time the child is eleven or twelve he can, under favorable conditions, reason perfectly well. He is still immature in the sense of finding it difficult to remain logical under emotional pressure and to use his reasoning in interpersonal relations which are laden with emotion. The development of this emotional stability and self-acceptance is a task for the years of adolescence and young adulthood.

The Characteristics of Mature Behavior

We shall look again at these many aspects of child behavior after we have the tools for a better explanation of them. The purpose of this short survey of childhood is to depict the behavior of children at different age levels clearly enough for us to examine the question we face in the next few chapters—namely, "What are the differences between the child and the adult?"

Development in Different Cultures

We have seen, in our survey, many sorts of changes that come about in the course of growing up. For example, the infant is not very negativistic; the young child is frequently resistant to suggestions; the adult is not usually negativistic. We have said that school age is the age of incantations. It is obvious also that older children have much more knowledge than younger children; they know that 6 times 7 equals 42, that Columbus discovered America, that bubble gum costs a penny a chunk. Not all these differences are of the same kind. Some of them depend, for example, almost entirely upon the child's environment while growing up. The wisest adult philosopher of ancient Greece did not know the price of bubble gum, and many adults in other cultures would not know it today. Whether all children in the world become negativistic at about the age of three is a question that has not been

Fetal Posture
0 mo.

Chin Up
1 mo.

Chest Up
2 mos.

Reach and Miss
3 mos.

Sit with Support
4 mos.

Sit on Lap Grasp Object
5 mos.

Sit on High Chair Grasp Dangling Object
6 mos.

Sit Alone
7 mos.

Stand with Help
8 mos.

Stand Holding Furniture
9 mos.

Creep
10 mos.

Walk when Led
11 mos.

Pull to Stand by Furniture
12 mos.

Climb Stair Steps
13 mos.

Stand Alone
14 mos.

Walk Alone
15 mos.

Fig. 2.1 Stages in motor development. (From M. M. Shirley, *The First Two Years*)

finally answered but it seems doubtful that negativism is a universal characteristic of three-year-olds.

It might be very difficult to find any specific behavior pattern which is true of every child, no matter what his culture, all over the world, but nevertheless there are certain general characteristics that are probably universal for all human beings. It is certainly true, for example, that in every culture children are more helpless and less competent than adults. There is something about growing up that makes a child increasingly able to meet the problems of his culture, to solve these problems, and to exist as an independent person who does not need to be constantly cared for. Two ways in which this increased competence shows itself in our own culture are for the child to know the price of bubble gum and to know the multiplication table.

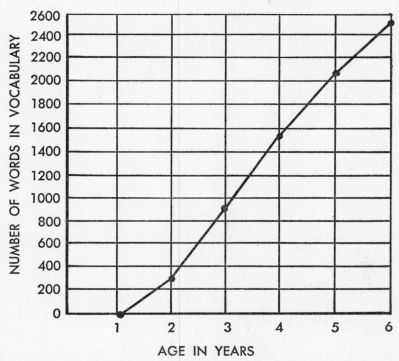

Fig. 2.2 Growth of vocabulary with age. (Data from M. E. Smith, *Studies in Child Welfare*, 3:5, 1926)

Development and Increased Independence

In our culture this increase in competence shows itself in many ways; in other cultures it may well show itself in some of these same ways but also in different ways. One of the most obvious is in the development of abilities. Look, for example, at Figures 2.1, 2.2, and 2.3, which illustrate the increase of three sorts of abilities. Figure 2.1 shows the development of walking. It is clear how walking makes the child more independent and better able to satisfy his needs. We do not know how the development of walking differs in different cultures—probably not very much. Figure 2.2 shows the growth of vocabulary, a development that is certainly different in different cultures. Figure 2.3 shows the size of type which is recommended for readers of different age levels. An increase in visual acuteness is shown in the fact that smaller type is readable by older children.

24-point type
for children under 7

18-point type
for 7-year-olds

12-point type
for 8-year-olds

11-point type
for 9-, 10-, and 11-year-olds

10-point type
for children 12 and older

Fig. 2.3 Type sizes suggested for readers of various ages. (After B. R. Buckingham, in National Society for the Study of Education, *Thirtieth Yearbook*, 1931)

It is quite clear that one big difference, probably the most obvious and important difference, between children and adults is the fact that the adult can fulfill his requirements for life more adequately than the child and that he can do so in a wider variety of circumstances than the child. He can get what he wants by adapting to many new and strange circumstances and to many different circumstances, whereas the child's adaptation is limited to a more special sort of environment maintained for him by other people.

Development and New Problems

In almost every area of behavior, age brings about improved adjustability, but age brings with it liabilities as well as assets. The process of growing up has other consequences besides the increase of the individual's adaptability. Sometimes the very condition that is necessary for a better adjustment to the realities of life brings with it new problems to which the child must adjust. For example, it is necessary to be able to compare oneself with others in order to behave realistically in social situations, but this very ability makes it possible for the child to feel inferior. The feeling of inferiority may be a problem which in turn motivates the child to a more adequate adjustment; but it does not inevitably happen that the child feels inferior about just those characteristics which he should try to improve. He may feel inferior about such irremediable defects as a club foot or about such unimportant characteristics as red hair. Furthermore, his shame may motivate him to adjustments that only make him worse off than he was before.

Children as they grow up become increasingly able to reach their major goals, but their goals grow up at the same time. All these new goals present new possibilities of frustration and unhappiness as well as of satisfactions. There are some childlike personality characteristics for which many adults yearn. The spontaneity and relaxation of the child are attractive to those of us who are burdened with the necessity for continual striving and effort. Even when we realize that the striving is not entirely necessary, it is not always easy to relax and be contented with what we have. The curse of "keeping up with the Joneses" is one pressure that the young child does not experience.

The import of this discussion is that children in all cultures change in certain predictable ways as they grow up. Some of these changes—e.g., the increase in acuity of vision—are probably part of the developmental process. Perhaps some of them take place merely because the child grows up in an environment that contains other people and that contains inanimate objects which follow certain constant physical laws. Such changes as these will be quite general. They will appear in many cultures. Even when the exact content of the mature behavior is a function of the specific culture, its general features may be universal.

Perhaps some of these changes take place merely because the child grows up in an environment which contains other people. Since people universally do not like to be hurt, children in every culture learn some rules which prohibit unrestrained hostility toward others. Still other universal aspects of development may depend on the fact that the physical laws of nature do not vary from culture to culture. Unsupported objects fall to the ground; people drown if submerged too long in water; strong winds can blow down houses. Developmental changes which are caused by these common environmental circumstances as well as those which are inherently part of the growth process itself will be found in many cultures. Even when a specific manifestation of mature behavior is unique to a specific culture, its general features may be universal. Contempt is expressed in different ways in different cultures—e.g., sneering, thumbing one's nose, flicking the fingernail on the teeth. But the meaning of contempt is essentially the same regardless of how it is expressed.

One important consequence of these changes is that the child becomes more adjustable and adaptable. The mature person in any culture is able to reach his objectives despite some changes in the circumstances. This consequence is not, however, the motivating factor for the change in the individual child. He does not become mature in order to become adaptable. His growing up follows certain general principles whose operations result in more competence and greater adaptability. Some of the other consequences of these same developmental principles may be vulnerability to unnecessary pressures, acceptance of inappropriate values, repressions, personality defenses, and other attitudes which may eventually lead to maladjustment.

The task of the rest of this chapter and the next three is to describe these general principles. We shall not, in this portion of the book, discuss the processes of development and growth, for such discussion belongs in Part II. In Part I we shall merely describe the changes that occur as the child matures. We shall indicate four general principles which distinguish the behavior of children from the behavior of adults without considering how the change takes place.

The first of these principles involves the greater content of the adult's psychological world, the increase in the number and variety of external situations which are within his ken. The second principle involves the adult's greater ability to recognize the constant and objective properties of the external world, regardless of the fact that any such characteristic may appear in many different contexts. The third involves the increase in the differentiation and flexibility of the individual's behavioral response to situations as he matures. The fourth involves the increased emotional stability of the adult, his greater resistance to the disruptive effects of stress.

These principles can be noted in everyday examples of child behavior when it is contrasted with the behavior of older children or adults. They represent a first step in the analysis of the psychological factors underlying the greater adjustability and skill of the adult compared with the child.

The remainder of this chapter will be devoted to the expansion of the psychological world. First, the principle will be depicted in everyday behavior; then it will be restated in a more careful, scientific fashion.

Expansion of the Psychological World

With maturity, the child's psychological world expands. The term *psychological world* includes everything that the child takes into account in his behavior. The newborn child responds to many features of the world, but they are all quite close to him. They impinge more or less directly upon his sense organs. The adult, on the other hand, responds to many aspects of the world that are perceptible only indirectly, through elaborate sets of cues or signs.

When a child, arriving home a half hour late for dinner, is greeted with stern, reproving looks, he is very likely to say, "I didn't hear you call" or "I didn't hear the clock strike six." To the parent, who has perhaps been bellowing from the back porch, it seems that this statement could not be true. But frequently it is true; one of the characteristics of the immaturity of the child is his relative inability to respond to a wide variety of stimuli, especially when he is intently interested in some activity. It requires maturity to pay attention to one activity and nevertheless to be sensitive to other aspects of the environment.

Another example illustrates a different aspect of the constriction of the child's psychological world. When a baby of three or four months is in his crib fingering some toy, a rattle perhaps, and accidentally drops it over the edge, it seems surprising to the adult that he makes almost no effort to see what happened to it. Except for a brief moment, he hardly seems to know that it is gone. When an object is no longer directly perceptible to the young infant, it seems to him to have dropped out of existence.

By the time he is eight or ten months old, on the other hand, he peers after objects which have disappeared. If his mother disappears into another room, he may watch the spot where he last saw her and wait for her to return. But the child of one or two years is not likely to wait long or grieve long over the disappearance of a loved one. It is a common experience for parents going out to a party to leave their child in tears while the baby sitter tries to comfort him. Upon their return they frequently hear that the baby cried for just a few minutes after they left and then was perfectly happy. The same experience is reported by nursery-school teachers; the child, despite his grief at parting, finds something to interest him soon after his mother leaves.

Other examples point to another aspect of the narrowness of the child's world. Children are notoriously not very foresighted. In trying to look into a pan on a high counter, the toddler dumps a whole dish of chocolate pudding onto his face. The six-year-old, all dressed up for Sunday school, chooses just that time to change a tire on his bicycle—forgetting that he has his best clothes on. Children have difficulty in anticipating the consequences of their actions. They often fail to take into account the future results of behavior. There is, of course, no magic change from heedlessness to foresightedness at any age. Some consequences are easily perceived; others are obscure. Even babies of eight months can anticipate some obvious consequences, whereas the most foresighted adult will sometimes fail to look ahead.

The child's psychological world expands in another direction—to include more abstractions. The nursery-school child is likely to want concrete goal objects—candy, toys, mother, or a frisky puppy—but the ten-year-old child can have goals which are much more abstract. He can want to ride a bike with no hands, to be president of his club, to be a good baseball player. A subscription to a child's magazine often makes a poor gift for the five- or six-year-old. A magazine that will come every month for twelve months is not so impressive as a toy that gleams brightly under the Christmas tree. Similarly, it is not easy for children to be satisfied with a vacation trip instead of a Christmas present. They may accept it when it is offered, but the disappointment in their faces on Christmas morning is only too obvious.

A practical consequence of the increase in the scope of the child's world is the necessity to give him more room and more freedom as he grows older. Although the six-month-old baby can be quite contented in a play pen, the eighteen-month-old child needs a play yard, the five-year-old needs a square block, and the school-age child may demand several square miles of free movement to keep him contented. It may seem that the two-year-old peering through the picket fence at his ball lying just out of reach would be as frustrated as the older child. Perhaps he is at the moment, but he can, nevertheless, spend a whole happy morning in an area which the older child would find very confining.

The term *psychological expansion* can be seen from these examples to include many superficially different changes which occur with maturity. Underlying them all is a common psychological core; the narrow, meager, concrete world of the young child becomes the broad psychological world of the adult.

Of the four general principles of maturity described in the preceding section, we have discussed only the first, the expansion of the psychological world. This is perhaps the most superficial of the four; it *describes* one of the changes that does occur as the child grows up but it is not in itself *explanatory*. There is nothing in the principle as stated that indicates what objects the child can respond to and why; there is only a statement of the fact that expansion occurs.

The principles to be discussed later are explanatory. They point toward psychological conditions which are necessary for an object to be included in the psychological world. Before moving on to these principles, however, we should state this first principle more carefully, in words that will enable us to relate it to the later conceptual explanations. There are two aspects of the principle of expansion of the psychological world that need better definition. First, the term *psychological world* is not clear. Secondly, there are many kinds of expansion which have been described. They need to be classified and delimited more carefully.

The Psychological World

The concept of the psychological world of the child which we have described comprises the things he knows about, the objects that he is aware of, the things he notices and keeps in mind as he goes about his daily life. Such a concept of the psychological world is in many ways quite correct, but for the purposes of scientific explanation of child behavior it is not adequate. There are two defects in it: First, it restricts the term to include only the objects of which the child is conscious. Secondly, it is difficult to determine its contents because we know only as much of what is in his consciousness as the child can tell us. If the psychological world is defined in terms of what the child is aware of and thinks about, there is no way of using the concept in describing the behavior of infants. Even the adult is not able to report all the factors which ought to be included in a description of his psychological world. It is possible not to hear a call to dinner and unlike the boy in the example, nevertheless obey it; at least it is possible to be unable to remember hearing it. Perhaps it is an experience peculiar to absent-minded professors, but I have on several occasions been absorbed in a book, put it down, and wandered into the dining room, still completely absorbed in what I have been reading. When I arrived there I found that dinner had been called. Presumably I heard it and responded in an absent-minded way, but it was not a conscious experience.

It is necessary, therefore, to examine the meaning of the term *psychological world*. It has been used to describe the behavior of children. How can it be defined so that it is an observable phenomenon which does not necessitate any speculation about the child's conscious awareness of the objects in his environment?

Fortunately, it is possible to define the term objectively. The child's psychological world comprises all the objects—the term *objects* including such abstract states as skillfulness or the presidency—to which the child is able to adjust. If the child adjusts to an object, he changes his behavior to suit the changes in the object. Let us analyze a concrete experimental example illustrating the ability of the eight-month-old baby to respond to an object that is out of sight (Piaget, 1952). A watch is held out toward the child so that he can see it. Then it is placed underneath a cloth lying on the floor in front of the child. If he reaches for the cloth, pulls it aside, discards it, and reaches for the watch, he has demonstrated his ability to respond to an object that is out of sight.

This statement can be tested. Suppose someone claimed that the baby were merely playing with the cloth and, having moved it, discovered the watch underneath it. Then the baby should perform the same action with the cloth whether or not he had seen the watch go beneath it. If he pushes the cloth aside only when he has seen the object put beneath it, he is responding to the object, not the cloth.

By this method the psychological world can be described behaviorally; that is, its contents can be determined merely by observing the behavior of the child, without any necessity for determining his conscious awareness. The principle of expansion of the psychological world describes the fact that the child becomes increasingly able to respond and adjust to objects in the world, and that these objects may become more abstract, or less obvious, or more remote, as the child increases in maturity. When the child learns to anticipate the consequences of his actions, he is responding to the remote future. He is behaving in such a way that the attainment of his future goals will not be endangered by his present behavior.

If this discussion clarifies the meaning of *psychological world,* we may now continue to a more systematic description of the different sorts of objects which the child is able to incorporate into his psychological world as he increases in maturity. One important variety of goal object that is possible only after the child has come to have considerable maturity is the abstract goal. A concrete goal object can be perceived directly, even though it need not always be perceived directly at the moment that it is functioning as a goal object. Abstract goals are not perceivable directly; they are recognized only through the appearance of a complex set of relationships. One's own position of power is perceivable only through the fact that other people do what one wants them to do and that other people may be hurt or helped if one wishes. Thus, power is not nearly so obvious or so easily perceivable a goal as is a new tricycle.

The other important aspect of the expansion of the child's psychological world as he grows older is the inclusion of objects that are relatively more remote. This can be illustrated by many examples. Adults have long-range goals that extend forward for years. Such goals as becoming a lawyer, discovering a cure for poliomyelitis, or establishing a world federation are obviously more remote than the goal objects of childhood. Nevertheless, it is not easy to encompass all aspects of remoteness in a single definition.

Four Aspects of Remoteness

As the child matures, his psychological world expands to include objects which are more and more remote in four ways: (1) temporally, (2) spatially,

(3) logically, and (4) mediationally. Temporal remoteness is perhaps the most obvious of the four and has already been illustrated in the discussion of long-range goals and the anticipation of consequences.

Spatial remoteness in many cases coincides with temporal remoteness. If the goal is to reach a distant object, then the object is spatially remote but the goal is temporally remote. Children show confusions, however, in relating themselves to distant objects, even when there is no temporal element present. It is difficult, for example, for them to keep track of the various turns and bends in a path as they walk along it. If, after hiking through the woods for a short while, the child tries to point in the direction of home, he is likely to do so quite inaccurately. If the trail crosses another trail, he may not know which turn leads in the general direction in which he desires to go. Adults, too, can have this difficulty, but not to the same extent to which children have it.

A seven-year-old going from New York to Kansas City asked whether on the way he would visit his grandmother, who lived in California. The spatial relationships had been explained to him several times; he had previously gone to California from Kansas City, leaving it in the opposite direction. In other words, he had had the information and experience which would establish for an adult the spatial relationships involved. A five-year-old who lived in Stamford, Conn., once asked, after the family had been traveling for two days, whether they were out of Stamford yet. She, too, had visited neighboring towns and had had ample experience which would have made the spatial relationships clear to an older child.

Logical remoteness can be illustrated readily. If A implies B, and B implies C, and C implies D, then A implies D. To trace this chain from A to D and thus be able to respond to D—that is, to know what to do to achieve D or avoid D, as the case may be—is to be sensitive to logically remote aspects of the environment. A good chess or checkers player frequently wins from an inferior player because he is able to anticipate more moves and trace out the logical consequences of each move for more steps than his weaker opponent. It is not the actual temporal distance that makes the anticipation difficult; the whole game occupies only an hour or so of actual time. It is the number of logical steps that helps make the consequences difficult to anticipate.

The fourth kind of remoteness is concerned with the way in which we get information about the external world. In order to understand mediational remoteness, it is necessary, first of all, to clarify what is meant by *mediation* (Heider, 1953). When some external event starts a chain of consequences eventually resulting in some sensation, the connecting chain *mediates,* or conveys, information about the event which started the chain. All information which comes to the organism is mediated. To take a simple example, air waves mediate sound; the sound mediates the meaning of the words; the meaning of the words mediates the opinion or intention of the speaker; the speaker may himself be mediating or transmitting the decision of some authority.

For the transmission of information there may be cues which mediate information only because they connect the present situation to some past experience. In the experiment demonstrating the ability of the child to respond to an absent object, the sight of the cloth indicated or mediated the presence of the watch. This mediation occurred not because the watch physically affected the way the cloth looked but because the appearance of the cloth identified it to the child as "the cloth that I saw put on top of the watch." This recognition of the identity of the cloth is an essential step in obtaining the watch; it is a cue to its presence. If there were no such cue, the child would have to be clairvoyant to divine the existence of the hidden watch.

There are good media and poor media. One of the characteristics of a good medium is that it transmits the information or the influence unchanged. When a medium is good, such as air or light, we do not generally even notice its existence, and we can easily perceive "through it" to the object which is the source of the causal chain. When a medium is poor, however, it takes more discernment to be sensitive to what it is transmitting. A high-fidelity record player is a good medium, for it transmits the original sound without distortion or the addition of new, irrelevant elements. Similarly, actions mediate the intentions of people, but it requires maturity to be sensitive to the intention rather than to the action. Children find it difficult, for example, to consider a crime to be more reprehensible if it is deliberate than if it is unpremeditated (Piaget, 1932). They are likely to judge misdemeanors exclusively in terms of the external consequence rather than the intention of the person (see p. 54).

A second example of a relatively poor medium can be observed when one person must transmit the decision made by a higher authority. It is difficult, even for adults, not to treat the person as though he were responsible for the decision. It is difficult, for example, to avoid becoming irritated by the refusal of a clerk to accede to our request even though he tells us that there is a rigid company rule that would prevent his helping us if he wished to.

Thus, a general principle can be stated that with maturity the child is able to respond to sources of action rather than to the more immediate cues which are merely mediators of the remote object, and that he can perceive through poor media as well as good ones.

Summary

This chapter has introduced the concept of maturity. In a preliminary glance at the general psychological characteristics of children at several age levels, we noted that the most obvious comparison between the young child and the older one can be made in terms of competence or adaptability. In order to describe some of the psychological factors underlying this increase in the competence of the child, four aspects of maturity were listed. The first of these, expansion of the psychological world, comprises the child's ability to notice obscure objects, to anticipate consequences, to strive for abstract goals as well as concrete ones, and to strive toward a remote future goal. There are four kinds of remoteness: temporal, spatial, logical, and mediational.

3

The Attainment of Objectivity

THE ESTABLISHMENT OF PERMANENT IDENTITY

CONSTANCY OF PERCEPTUAL PROPERTIES OF OBJECTS

THE ATTAINMENT OF VALUE CONSTANCY

LOSS OF EGOCENTRISM

THE ACHIEVEMENT OF INDEPENDENCE FROM FIELD
ORGANIZATION

SUMMARY

THE PRECEDING CHAPTER discussed the expansion of the psychological world of the child and pointed out that, as he matures, the child becomes able to respond to more and more objects and more kinds of objects. The hypotheses outlined in the present chapter offer a partial explanation of the expansion of the psychological world. In order for the child to be able to respond to an object, he must be able to perceive it clearly; he must recognize it as the same object in a variety of contexts. In order to know what he can do with it, he must know what its objective properties are.

It is not uncommon for a mother to be forced to leave her young child for a few days. Since most babies are born in hospitals, the arrival of a new sibling (a word meaning either a brother or a sister) necessitates the absence of the mother from the home. When she returns, having been lonesome for her child during her stay in the hospital, the mother of an 18- or 24-month-old child may be in for an unpleasant surprise. She is greeted not with smiles of welcome but with shyness, as though she were a stranger. Her baby has forgotten her! The person who now confronts the child has for him no psychological identification tag that makes him respond to her as his mother. This shortness of the child's memory is one aspect of his lack of objectivity; because of it, he cannot take as much advantage of his past experience as can the adult. Consequently, he has more difficulty in knowing what to expect of situations which confront him.

In other examples of behavior, the child may not fail to recognize an object, but rather he may fail to perceive that an object is usable as a tool when such a use is not one of its common functions. A child of five once lost the cork from his pop gun behind the piano. Since he could not reach it with his hand, he began looking for a stick. The gun in his hand would have served as a perfectly satisfactory stick, but its customary function somehow prevented the child from seeing its sticklike character.

The adult may also have this difficulty when he solves a problem. In one experiment (Scheerer and Huling, 1952), the adult subject is casually asked, when he first enters the experimental room, to hang a "No Smoking" sign on the wall. The sign is to be hung from a nail by a loop of string. Then the subject is given a problem whose solution can be achieved if there is an additional piece of string available. In the instructions the subject is specifically told that he may use any object in the room to solve the problem; yet it is surprising how many adults fail because they do not recognize the use to which the string holding up the sign might be put. When a piece of string is simply left hanging from a nail, the solution is reached quite rapidly.

A slight variation on this theme is familiar to teachers of arithmetic. The same process, addition, looks different to school-age children when it is required in the problem, "$7 + 5 = ?$" and when it is required in the problem, "John had 7 apples; Jim had 5. How many did they have altogether?" To recognize the applicability of addition to the latter problem requires the child to have somehow abstracted the essential nature of addition out of its specific concrete setting. A more extreme example of the same difficulty in abstraction is reported of a mentally defective adult patient who worked in the furnace room of a hospital. He could add 3 loads of coal and 2 loads of coal to obtain the correct sum, 5 loads. He could not, however, perform the same operation if the objects in the problem were loaves of bread instead of loads of coal (Goddard, 1919).

In a final set of examples, let us examine this same kind of immaturity in interpersonal relations. To be a good judge of people, one must be able to perceive their objective personality characteristics by observing their behavior in specific situations. When the child is persuaded by some eight-year-old confidence man to pay thirty-five cents for a piece of worthless scrap iron, which he afterwards regrets purchasing, we would expect him to learn something about his friend's character. Yet, as often as not, the same friend will sell him another bill of goods a few days later. The child's belief in the value of the item he is buying depends only upon the persuasiveness of the friend's language, not upon an evaluation of the friend's honesty or on his own appraisal of the object itself.

In a much more common situation, the preschool child may be unable to conceive that his mother forbids him to play with knives because she does not want him to be hurt. Despite all the evidence that the parent loves the child, the good times together, the cuddling, and the gifts, it is almost inevitable that the child will be angered by such a prohibition. The child's response at the moment is determined by the momentary situation and does not depend upon whether the parent actually is kind or is cold and hostile. In other words, the child does not perceive the permanent personal warmth of the parent. Parents sometimes feel in these circumstances that the child is ungrateful for all the kindnesses he has been shown. It is not ingratitude but rather immaturity that he is exhibiting.

These various examples of the child's failure to perceive the objective properties of the situation have included a number of different types of objectivity. We must now return to a more careful discussion of the separate trends of maturation: first, the development of the ability to recognize the identity of objects; secondly, the ability to perceive the properties of objects.

The Establishment of Permanent Identity

The Difference Between Objects and Images

Perhaps the first requirement for attaining objectivity is to be able to conceive of objects. This may seem to be a very simple ability that would be present as soon as the child could perceive at all, but actually it is more complex than it seems. Some of the things we look at are assumed to have a permanent identity; others are assumed to be created anew each time they appear. When the movie is finished and the lights in the theater go on, we do not ask where the picture has gone. Such a question is meaningless. The shadow that forms the picture on the screen does not have a permanent identity; it appears and disappears, depending on the circumstances, but does not exist when the house lights come on.

Most objects, however, do have a permanent existence. When a friend disappears into his home, we do not think that he goes out of existence at the instant he goes out of sight. We assume that he is inside the house, that he still is the same person we were talking to a moment earlier, that we could talk to him on the telephone, or that we could go into the house and find him. Our psychological environment is full of objects which are not immediately perceptible but which we assume are still existent.

The child must learn to make this distinction between pictures that appear and disappear without any existence between appearances, and objects that go out of view but not out of existence. The child, moreover, does not merely make a mistake, as the adult might do. When we are watching a play and see one of the characters go out of the room, we attribute to him a permanent existence even though that character has completely disappeared while the actor is off stage. Adults can make mistakes like this, but the infant does not even conceive of the possibility that any object can have existence except when it is actually perceived. Thus, we noted (p. 29) that when an infant loses an object over the edge of the crib, he makes no effort to find it. For him it is gone, completely gone.

Development of the Object Concept

As we shall see in Chapter 13, there are stages in the development of this assumption of permanent identity. Merely to recognize that an object is there to be looked for when it is out of sight is one step. To recognize that it may have made a specific motion while out of sight and to anticipate where it will reappear is something else again. This requires a sort of reconstruction of invisible actions as well as invisible objects. One observation related to this ability was made by Shinn (1909), one of the early workers in the field of child development. One part of a very detailed diary she kept of the development of her niece describes the behavior of the baby at about the age of twelve months when the mother disappeared behind a screen. At this age the baby looked to the opposite side of the screen where her mother would emerge.

Not only must objects have some psychological permanence, but the parts of the object that are momentarily invisible must also have permanent psychological existence if the child is to respond adequately.

Piaget has made a number of observations concerning the development of identity of the baby's bottle (Piaget, 1954). He observed, for example, that if the bottle is presented to the eight-month-old baby with the nipple visible, the baby takes it, turns it, and puts the nipple into his mouth. If, however, the bottle is presented to the baby in such a way that he cannot see the nipple, he tries to suck from the bottom of the bottle. The fact that the baby tries to suck the bottle might be taken as evidence that it is "a bottle" to him. But since babies at the age of eight months will frequently suck on any object that can be put into the mouth, we cannot be sure. To turn the bottle around, however, so that the invisible nipple becomes visible, as the child can do a few months later, implies something more. Such behavior constitutes evidence that the bottle is treated as something that has a nipple, even when the nipple cannot be seen. Thus, it is justifiable to say that constancy of the object has been attained. The bottle, regardless of how it is presented, is behaviorally identified as an object which has a suckable portion.

Thus, we see what the concept of permanent identity implies in regard to inanimate objects. First, the object must be assumed to exist even when it is imperceptible. Secondly, its parts must be assumed to exist even though they are invisible. Thirdly, the possibility of invisible movements must be conceived of.

The Recognition of Objects and People

We have seen one prerequisite for the child's ability to identify objects, the development of an object concept. A second one is the learning of the cues which identify a particular object. It is not uncommon for a young child to fail to recognize a familiar person when he is not dressed in the customary manner: the baby fails to recognize his mother in party clothes.

We should realize first of all that when the child fails to recognize a familiar person, he does not necessarily think that that person has gone out of existence. Even after the basic idea of the permanence of objects is achieved, the child or adult must still recognize which object is which and connect each appearance of an object with the previous appearances of that same object. This is a matter of learning the identifying cues which mark each specific object or person. Since most inanimate objects do not change their appearance very often, the identification problem is not ordinarily difficult. Furthermore, it is frequently not important. If I need a lawn mower, it is not essential for mowing the lawn that I identify which one I used last time and be sure to use it again. If someone has exchanged mowers with me it would probably be a minor matter. Any one will do. It is only rarely that the precise identification of an object is essential. To prove that a specific bed is the one George Washington slept in or that a specific gun fired the fatal bullet requires exact identification of an object.

In adjusting to people, it is both more important and more difficult to identify them accurately. People do not like to be mistaken for somebody else. Personality characteristics are not very obvious; it is usually best to judge the personality from one's previous experience with a person, which requires recognizing him again. Recognizing a person is made more difficult by the fact that he may change clothes, comb his hair, get his face dirty, and unintentionally disguise himself in many little ways. It is not surprising, therefore, that children can get confused and fail to recognize the small number of essential cues that are valid indicators of the identity of an individual. Rather, it is surprising that they do as well as they do.

The development of the ability to conceive of a permanent object and to identify an object or person even though it may appear in different circumstances, or from different perspectives, is thus seen to be a major achievement of the child. This ability, furthermore, can be seen to underlie the ability to respond to absent objects as described in Chapter 2.

Constancy of Perceptual Properties of Objects

Size Constancy

Even though the child recognizes the permanence of objects and can identify them, the objectivity of perception is not complete. He must also develop the ability to recognize the objective properties of objects. He must be able to compare the sizes of two pieces of pie, if he is to avoid being cheated by his brother. The problem the child faces in comparing a piece of pie on the plate in front of him with his brother's pie on a plate across the table is more

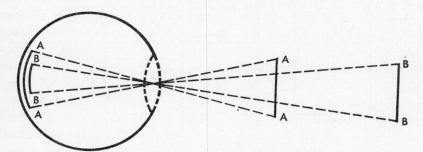

Fig. 3.1 Change in the size of the retinal image with distance. Objects A and B are the same size. Object A is half as far away from the viewer as Object B. The retinal image of A is twice the size of the retinal image of B. (The eyeball has been drawn disproportionately large.)

complex than it appears at first glance. The difficulty arises because the size of the image of an object upon the retina of the eye depends upon how far away it is as well as upon how large it is. The retinal image of the pie which is at his own plate is, of course, much larger than the retinal image of the piece of pie across the table. If retinal images were the only basis for size judgments, each child would be convinced that his own piece of pie was much the bigger. In this case such a delusion would make for peace at the dinner table, but in many other circumstances such a failure to judge the true size of distant objects would be a serious handicap. The ability to make accurate judgments of the size of objects despite the fact that one of them is farther away than another is called *size constancy*.

It has been experimentally demonstrated that size constancy improves with age. The usual experiment for the study of this constancy involves two objects at different distances from the subject, who must report which of the two looks larger. In other experiments the subject alters the size of one object until it appears to be the same size as the other. In the experiment (Brunswick, 1930) whose results are shown in Figure 3.2, the standard object is a disk 100

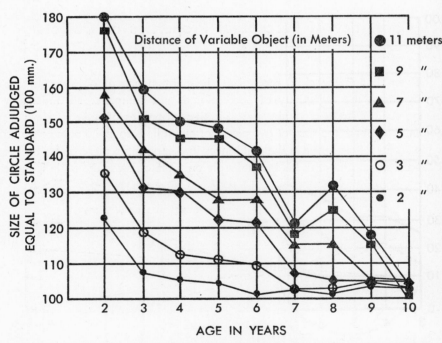

Fig. 3.2 Change in size constancy with age. The variable circle at various distances is adjusted so that it appears to be the same size as the standard circle, which is always 100 mm. in diameter and one meter distant. (After F. Beyrl, *Zeitschrift Psychol., 100,* 1926, 365, Table 10)

mm. in diameter, placed at a distance of 1 meter. The comparison disk, whose size may be adjusted, is farther away. If the subject, when he is asked to adjust the size of the comparison disk until it looks equal in size to the standard, reports equality when the comparison disk is actually the same size as the standard (*i.e.,* 100 mm.), perfect constancy is indicated. Figure 3.2 shows that, for young children, the farther disk must be more than 100 mm. in diameter to look equal in size to the standard. With increasing age, constancy is approached.

Other Perceptual Constancies

Size is not the only property of objects which shows increasing constancy with age. Two other varieties of constancy frequently studied are brightness and form. The perceived brightness of an object (*i.e.,* whether it is white, gray, or black) depends partly on how much light it reflects but also on whether it is seen as brilliantly illuminated or as only dimly lighted. The perception of the illumination depends upon the brightness of the surrounding field. A piece

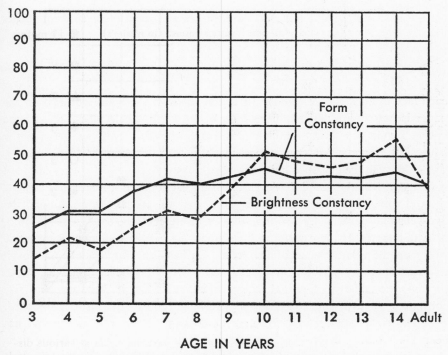

Fig. 3.3   Change in form and brightness constancy with age. (Data on brightness constancy, from E. Brunswik, *Zeitschrift Psychol., 109,* 1928. Data on form constancy, from S. Klimpfinger, *Archiv. f.d. gesamte Psychol., 88,* 1933)

of black paper in strong sunlight can actually reflect more light than a piece of white paper in deep shade, yet it is not perceived as whiter than the white paper, provided that the observer can also see some of the background.

Brightness constancy can be studied in much the same way as size constancy—by asking subjects to judge whether two stimuli are the same objective shade of gray when one of them is in a brighter illumination than the other. If they judge the two to be the same shade when they actually are, there is perfect, or 100-percent, constancy. If they judge the two to be the same shade when they are reflecting the same absolute amount of light, there is no constancy (0 percent). In Figure 3.3, the solid line shows the change in the brightness constancy with age. The exact values depend, of course, upon the amount of difference in illumination and other factors.

Form constancy describes the ability of an observer to judge the objective shape of a figure when it is turned so that he does not have a full front view of it. In the perspective drawing of the cube in Figure 3.4 we perceive

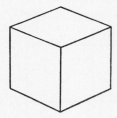

Fig. 3.4   A cube, showing how three different shapes are all perceived as squares.

each face to be square, although the actual shape of the figure outlined on the paper is not square and is different for each of the visible faces. The dotted line in Figure 3.3 shows the change in form constancy with age. Again, the figures are expressed in percentages of perfect, or 100-percent, constancy.

Although the evidence indicates quite clearly that constancy does improve with age, it must be noted that even the youngest children in these experiments showed some constancy. In the size-constancy experiment, for example, the two-year-olds perceived a 180-mm. disk at 11 meters to be equal to a 100-mm. disk at 1 meter. If there were no constancy—i.e., if the judgment were made solely on the relative sizes of the retinal images—the far disk, being eleven times as far away as the near one, would have to be eleven times as big to produce the same-sized retinal image. In other words, if there were no size constancy, an 1100-mm. disk would have been judged equal to the standard.

The psychological mechanism leading to perceptual constancy has not been satisfactorily determined, and there are numerous unanswered questions about its factors. The role of past experience in the process is not clear. It can be seen, however, that perceptual constancies result from some sort of analysis of the immediate stimulation into two factors, one representing the properties of the object and the other the properties of the setting in which the object appears. The pattern of light coming from an object in the brightness-constancy experiments is eventually perceived as an object with a certain brightness illuminated by a light of a certain brilliance. Cues necessary for such an analysis may be present in the brightness of the background of the immediate situation. In other situations familiarity with the object may furnish the information which permits an objectively correct judgment to be made. This way of looking at the problem of perceptual constancy shows that it is representative of a large class of judgments which also depend upon the analysis of incoming information into two parts. Some properties are attributed to the object, others to the setting (Heider, 1953).

Constancies in Social Perception

The foregoing pattern of analysis leading to perceptual constancy also operates in the perception of social situations. Suppose that I found a wallet full of money and asked several people who its owner was. If a man claimed it was his and proved it, I would not be led to perceive him as a truthful person. I would attribute his telling the truth to the motive presented by the situation, not to a personality trait of the person. If, on the other hand, the same person voluntarily told me that he had dented the fender on my car, I would now perceive him as truthful. I would not even make him prove that he was actually telling the truth. The situation is so structured that all its pressures are against telling the truth; hence, a person who tells the truth despite these pressures must be a truthful person. This is a perfectly sensible judgment to make, because what is meant by a personality characteristic of truthfulness is the willingness to tell the truth even when there are no ulterior reasons for doing so. To tell the truth when there are ulterior reasons for lying is excellent evidence of such a personality trait.

Similarly, a perception of cowardice does not depend solely upon the behavior of running away. A person is not a coward unless he runs away from a situation that is not dangerous or from a dangerous situation when there are good reasons, sufficient for most people, for staying despite the danger. Cowardice implies either an escape response that is provoked by very mild danger, or a motivation to escape that is so strong when provoked that it overpowers all other motivation.

Such judgments as these, which distinguish between the pressures of a situation and the characteristics of the person in the situation, are commonly made by adults and are an important basis for our intuitive opinions of other people. Sometimes our judgment goes astray because we fail to distinguish between the properties of the situation and of the person—*e.g.,* when we dislike the person who plays the role of villain in a movie—but most of the time we show a reasonable amount of constancy in our perception of personal traits.

Just as the child shows improvement in size constancy and in form constancy as he grows up, so his ability to make the proper analysis of social situations also increases with maturity. If a child asks his mother a question and receives no answer, he may react as though he thought it was his mother's intent to be secretive and to frustrate him. He may nag at her persistently and annoyingly. The mother's refusal to answer the question may have been due, however, to her having to watch the cake in the oven very carefully—that is, it stemmed not from her own secretiveness but from the demands of the situation. To perceive the demand of the setting through the behavior of the mother requires maturity.

Constancy in social perception also requires that sufficient cues be present to permit such a perception. Knowledge of the context of an action is necessary for anybody's judgment, and adults are not infallible. There is a joke illustrating this point. A visitor to the combat zone was being guided to his destination by a soldier. His guide whispered directions to follow him, to turn to the right, to duck his head, and the visitor responded with soft whispers of assent. Finally the visitor whispered to his guide, "How far away are the enemy?" "Ten miles," came back the whispered answer. "Why are you whispering, then?" the visitor asked. "I have a bad cold," said the guide.

Perceptual Constancy in Relation to Mediated Perception

Let us see how our description of the mechanism of perceptual constancy is related to the ability to perceive through a poor medium (see p. 34). It is difficult to respond to objects when all the information about them comes by way of mediators, because the mediators' own properties distort the information they transmit. Thus, the illumination of a room is conveyed by the brightness of the walls and other surfaces in the room. But the surfaces have their own objective color and shade, and these properties influence the amount of light reflected. What is achieved in brightness constancy is truly amazing. All this distorted information, the resultant of some unknown illumination shining upon surfaces of unknown reflectance, is somehow analyzed in a perception that the room is brightly lighted, that it has dull gray walls, and that it contains a black desk and an aluminum radiator. Simultaneously with recognition of the color of the wall, radiator, and desk comes perception of the illumination, a mediationally remote property of the situation. The objective properties of objects and the remote object whose properties they mediate are both perceived when perceptual constancy is attained.

Perception of Area

In some cases, the objective perception of one property of an object is difficult to achieve because of the interference of other properties of the same object rather than because of the influence of its setting upon the appearance of the object. For example, the area of a rectangle depends upon both its height and width. Because both linear dimensions are easier to perceive accurately than is the area, the areas of two rectangles are difficult to compare when one of them is very long and narrow and the other is nearly square. Our perception tends to be influenced too much by the length or by the width and thus leads us to overestimate or underestimate. Most people tend to underestimate the amount of metal in a thin wire a mile long.

Even when there is a basis for a correct judgment of such a property, the perceptual problem may distort the judgment of children. Piaget (1952) has performed experiments on children to study their perception of the way in which height and width both affect the area of a surface. He showed the child a tumbler partly filled with small beads. Then he poured the beads into another vessel that was taller and thinner than the first and asked the child whether the number of beads had changed. Children of four or five, even though they agree that no beads have been added or taken away, believe that the number of beads has changed. They do not all agree on whether there are more or fewer; some say more because the pile of beads is higher, others say fewer because the pile is thinner, but children at this age level do not coordinate the two dimensions so that a decrease of one can balance an increase in the other.

The Attainment of Value Constancy

The discussion thus far has been concerned with the perception of objective properties of the external world—identity, size, causal relations, and the like. In this section we shall consider perception of the desirability or value of the objects of the external world. Values are clearly not objective in the same way that size is. One child may like milk; another may dislike it. Milk is not inherently likable but is objectively white. To perceive milk as green would be sufficiently peculiar to raise doubts about one's visual normality, but to believe that it tastes bad is nothing more than an idiosyncrasy.

We cannot, therefore, discuss the value of objects in exactly the same way that we discussed their more objective properties; but there is, nevertheless, a sense in which values can be distorted. We are shocked and horrified when we see a serious automobile accident in which people are hurt; yet, we can read in every day's newspaper about serious accidents without being shocked and horrified. Seeing the accident gives it more psychological impact than merely reading about it. This is a distortion of values. If it is horrifying for people to be hurt in an accident, it ought to be just as horrifying whether we happen to witness it or not.

The following incident illustrates value distortion. A boy of twelve decided to raise chickens in order to earn money. He bought some day-old chicks and raised them carefully and tenderly, meanwhile looking forward eagerly to his profits. Finally the time came to take them to market, and he was faced with the task of killing them. But they had become almost pets, and he found the task abhorrent. He finally solved his problem by building a miniature guillotine, on which he tied down a chicken with its head under the ax. The blade was released when a string was pulled. Placing the guillotine on one side of a bush, he ran the string over the bush to a point from which he could not see what was happening, and then he was able to achieve sufficient emotional detachment to pull the string. After the deed was done he could go back around the bush and take care of the dead chicken he found there.

There are several examples of value distortion in this single anecdote. The first one occurred when he bought the chickens. He knew that they would have to be killed before he could realize his profits, but he failed to appreciate how much he would dislike that task. Probably if he had then realized how he would feel, he would not have chosen chicken raising as a means of earning money. The repulsiveness of the task of killing the chickens was minimized and not accurately perceived, presumably because the task was so remote. Thus, a goal object may be perceived as less attractive or repulsive when it is in the remote future than when it is immediately at hand. When this occurs, the person makes decisions which he is not happy about afterward.

The second value distortion occurred when he found that he could not kill the chicken in a face-to-face relationship, so to speak, but that he could perform the same act if he did not have to watch. In other words, the attractiveness or repulsiveness of the event was reduced if it was not immediately perceptible, even though the act itself was the same. We are, of course, making no assumption that it is either good or bad to kill chickens. What is considered a distortion in this incident is that the psychological repulsiveness of the task did not depend upon any permanent property or value of the act but was influenced by objectively irrelevant factors, such as the temporal or the spatial remoteness.

Conflict Between Immediate and Remote Goals

TEMPTATION   We have in our culture an excellent word to describe the problem of choosing between a less valuable goal whose psychological impact is heightened by immediacy or obviousness and an intrinsically more valuable goal whose psychological attractiveness is reduced by remoteness or obscurity. We call such choices *temptations*. The college student who is trying to decide whether to go to a dance or study for a course is said to have yielded to temptation if he goes to the dance and to have resisted temptation if he studies. What is the psychological structure of this special type of conflict called temptation which distinguishes it from other types of conflict situations? Temptation occurs only when there is a conflict between two alternatives, one of which is more immediate or more concrete or more impressive and the other more remote, or abstract. The temptation to go to the dance is stronger when the examination in the course is a long time away. Indeed, the tendency to go to the dance may so completely overpower the motivation to study that there is no conflict and no feeling of temptation in the usual sense. As the date of the examination comes closer, the conflict changes. It is much easier to forego a movie or dance tonight to study for an examination tomorrow morning than to forego it to study for an examination two weeks away. The term *temptation* is usually applied to conflicts which, if both alternatives had equally immediate consequences, would be resolved unquestionably in one direction, but which are so structured that the intrinsically more important consequence is remote.

In children the compelling character of immediate goals can be seen even more strikingly. The child who has been told and clearly recognizes that if he takes a piece of candy or touches a blown-glass swan he will be punished may, nevertheless, be unable to resist the temptation when he actually meets it face to face. If a child is offered a plate of cookies from which he may select one, he has great difficulty. He sees one and seems compelled to touch it before he looks at any others; after he has touched one, however, he does see another and then he must touch that one. To look at them all with his hands behind his back before choosing one seems almost impossible for the preschool child.

This proverbial inability of children to resist temptation can be accounted for by the hypothesis that the psychological potency of immediate and remote factors is very unequal in early childhood but becomes more nearly equal with an increase in maturity.

PROCRASTINATION   Another common problem of children—dawdling—may perhaps be explained in similar terms. When a child is faced with a task which is an unpleasant duty, he often delays starting it and even after he does begin, he may proceed slowly and with many interruptions. When an eight-year-old comes in from a football game and is told to take a bath, he doesn't find the prospect very enticing. He perhaps agrees that he should have a bath; he probably knows that he must take one; he may even realize that the longer he puts it off the more he will be reminded, nagged, and coerced. Still, all these consequences are rather remote. Hence, many immediate things attract his attention: he sees the newspaper and sits down to read the comic page; he notices a rubber band on the floor and fiddles with it for awhile. In his room, where he undresses, there are hosts of interesting objects to be played with, twisted, rolled around. Numerous feats of skill offer themselves to his mind, and he practices them all. By the time he has run this gamut of distractions, probably with some parental remonstrance, he may have consumed an hour and a half. Then, of course, he wonders why there is no time left to do what he wants to do.

The procrastination of the college student in getting started on a term paper is not essentially different, but at this level of maturity the whole process occurs on a grander scale. It is when the paper is weeks away that the adult procrastinates, whereas the child procrastinates about activities that are fifteen minutes away. In an ultimate state of complete value constancy, the individual's choices would be made with full regard for the intrinsic value of each consequence undistorted by its immediacy or its remoteness. The attractiveness or "valence" of an activity would depend upon its intrinsic properties, which are not changed any more than its size is changed by its distance or its setting.

We must not be confused by the restriction of the term *temptation* to those cases in which the immediate goal is the attractive one. Negative consequences are sometimes more immediate than positive ones and, again, their negative affect is enhanced by the immediacy. To take a bad-tasting medicine in order to get well is difficult, but more so for children than for adults. The repulsiveness of the medicine is more potent because it has to be taken now, whereas the good consequences of taking the medicine are more remote. That adults are not entirely free from this effect of immediacy can be seen in the reluctance of people to go to the dentist to prevent a toothache. Frequently it is necessary for the toothache to become immediately present before they are willing to pay the dentist a visit.

A second possible source of confusion lies in the fact that the choice of alternatives is not entirely determined by the value of the goal object. The amount of work involved in achieving the goal and the probability of obtaining it may enter in to modify the choice; and these may be affected by the immediacy of the goal. It is frequently true, for example, that remote consequences are actually less likely to happen than immediate ones. The passage of time may carry with it the possibility of avoiding the bad consequence entirely. Hence, there may be good reason in specific cases to prefer the immediate good thing to the remote good thing. These factors cannot account, however, for the general tendency of people to be more governed by the immediate than by the remote.

Approach and Avoidance Gradients

The greater potency of immediate than remote events has been studied experimentally under the term *approach* and *avoidance gradients*. The existence of such gradients has been demonstrated in several ways, but they all point to the fact that the tendency to approach a goal increases as the distance to the goal decreases and that the tendency to avoid a danger increases as the distance from the danger decreases. Hull (1938), for example, has shown that the speed of a rat running in a straight alley increases as he gets closer to the end of the alley where the food is. Hull called this increase the "goal gradient." If the rat is harnessed and is momentarily stopped in the course of his run, he will pull toward the goal. This pull can be measured on a spring scale and it has been found that he will pull harder if he is stopped close to the goal than if he is stopped close to the starting point. Similarly, if a rat is shocked at one end of a runway, he will pull harder if he is close to the shock than if he is far removed from it (Brown, 1940).

In this way it can be shown that there is a gradient of approach tendencies and another gradient of avoidance tendencies. One of the empirical findings from such studies is that the avoidance gradient is steeper than the approach gradient. In other words, if a goal is painful or dangerous as well as desirable, the tendency to approach it can be indicated by the dotted line in Figure 3.5. Similarly, the tendency to move away from it can be indicated by the solid line.

The avoidance gradient is steeper than the approach gradient and crosses it. When the rat is still far away from the combination goal and punishment, the avoidance tendency is weaker than the approach tendency and the animal comes closer to the goal. As he gradually comes nearer to the object, the two tendencies become more nearly equal, finally being equal where the gradients cross. Beyond that point, the avoidance tendency is stronger than the approach, and the animal moves away from the object. Thus, the prediction would be that the animal would hover at the spot where the two gradients cross. Actually, the animal does vacillate about that point, never getting much closer to or farther away from the object. These experiments demonstrate clearly that for rats the psychological effect of either a threatening object or a goal object is stronger when it is more immediate and weaker when it is more remote (Miller, 1944).

It has not been experimentally shown that children or adults behave any differently from rats in such a situation. We can think of everyday examples in which such behavior does occur, but also of examples in which adults, at any rate, behave differently. The adult may decide at a choice point either to

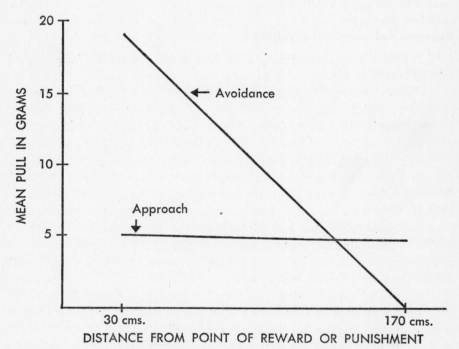

Fig. 3.5 Gradients of approach and avoidance. (After N. E. Miller, in J. McV. Hunt [ed.], *Personality and Behavior Disorders,* p. 434)

take the punishment to get to the goal or not to take it, but he does not necessarily hover in the middle of the path. If he is not emotionally involved, he probably either makes his choice before he starts or else goes quite close to the punishment to see how severe it is. In other words, the adult in some situations is not more repelled by the punishment the closer he gets to it. For such situations, value constancy is almost completely attained in adult behavior.

On the other hand, the boy who is very bashful but very much in love may worship a girl from a distance but be unable either to give her up completely or actually to ask her for a date. Here is behavior which seems analogous to hovering in the middle of the path. Adults are not free from the effects of immediacy, but we see that the gradual approach of maturity involves the development of value constancy.

Loss of Egocentrism

One of the factors which hamper the perception of the objective properties of the external world and which distort the perception of value is *egocentrism*. The practical joker who urges his victims to be good sports but who
loses his own temper completely when he is himself a victim of a practical
joke is displaying egocentrism. The meaning of the joke becomes completely
different when it happens to him.

Numerous examples show that the child is unable to perceive a situation
from the point of view of somebody else. The seven-year-old may intensely
dislike being bossed by older children but still be indignant when his younger
sibling shows resentment of his bossiness. It may make no difference to the
preschool child whether another child hurt him accidentally or deliberately—
i.e., he gives no significance to the intentions of the other child—but when
he himself hurts somebody, he is quick to excuse himself by saying that it was
only an accident.

Egocentrism basically depends upon the fact that at any one moment the
object or action in the external world appears from only one point of view,
that of the observer. Thus the right hand of a person facing the child is, from
the child's point of view, on the left. It is difficult for children to conceive of
another point of view (Piaget, 1928). In one experiment (Piaget, 1948)
children were shown several common objects. Each child was asked how these
objects would look to a doll that was placed so that it viewed the objects from
a different perspective. The youngest children, less than four years of age,
could not conceive that there would be any difference. As another example,
a child was asked how many brothers he had. He answered correctly, "Two,
Paul and Henry." Then he was asked how many brothers Paul had. The
response was that Paul had one brother, Henry. Piaget (1928) found that in
no group younger than ten years of age were 75 percent of the children able
to answer this question correctly. In order for the child to recognize that he
was himself a brother of Paul, he had to look at himself from the point of
view of Paul. His failure was due to egocentrism.

Egocentrism shows itself in several further ways, as Piaget's ingenious
experiments have demonstrated. For example, Piaget (1929) showed that the
young child believes that when he walks the moon follows him. This belief
is in harmony with the apparent movement of the moon in the direction of
the motion of the individual. Later the child no longer believes that the moon
follows him. In one striking incident, not taken from Piaget, the role of social
relations in the decentering process was obvious. A boy first perceived that the

moon did not follow him by wondering, when he and a friend were walking toward each other, whether the moon could follow both of them and realizing that it could not. Here an appreciation of the point of view of another person is clearly significant in affecting this belief.

Egocentrism can not only prevent the child from taking the point of view of some other person, but it can also prevent the child from taking any point of view that he has never experienced himself. Thus, it is difficult for children to answer questions about what would happen if some untrue premise were true, or some nonexistent state existed. When Piaget (1930) asked a child of eight whether a fan would make a breeze in the room even if there were no air, the child answered, "Yes." The conversation continued as follows:

> *Experimenter:* Why?
> *Child:* Because there would be air in the room.
> *Experimenter:* But suppose there were no air in the room at all. Would there still be a breeze?
> *Child:* Yes.
> *Experimenter:* Why?
> *Child:* Because there would still be a little air in the room.

In another type of experiment the child is not asked to assume anything that is impossible but merely to accept the arbitrary premises of a problem in logic. He is to solve the following problem, which is adapted to the Parisian environment in which Piaget employed it. "If I have more than one franc, I shall go by taxi or train. If it rains, I shall go by train or bus. Now it is raining and I have ten francs. How do you think I will go?" Clearly there is no obvious reason why the man should not take a taxi if it is raining, but when adults are given a puzzle they do not worry whether the premises are true or not. They accept the premises as true and reason from there. Piaget (1928) found that children seven to ten years old answered along the following lines: "He will go in the train because it is quicker"; or "He will go in the bus because it is nicer in the bus"; or that he would go in the taxi because ten francs was not too expensive. In other words, children are bound to the concrete problem of a man standing in the rain with ten francs in his pocket trying to decide how to make his trip. This inability to ignore any concrete fact even though it is irrelevant to the solution of the abstract problem is a sign of egocentrism.

A final example of egocentrism is found in the moral judgments of the child. In one of his experiments Piaget (1932) asked a child which of two actions in a story was the worse. In one story, for example, two little boys are each asked by a stranger for directions for reaching some well-known place in town. One of the boys makes a mistake in his directions and the stranger gets lost. The other purposely misdirects the stranger but the stranger finds his way anyhow. Which of the boys behaved worse? Younger children tend to think that the first boy is worse because the stranger lost his way. In other words, it is the ultimate consequence, not the intent, that counts. Older children base their judgment on intent. The same difference appears between older and younger children when they are asked to compare the crimes of two children. One of them in trying to help her mother dry the dishes, breaks twelve of them; the other, just for fun, breaks one.

We have examined various examples of how egocentrism affects various judgments and hampers logical thinking. We have noted that at any one moment the child can directly perceive only one view of an event. He can see only as much of a cube as is visible from one side; he can perceive directly only the effect that an event has on him. As long as his judgment of an object or event is limited to the information that is immediately evident (Piaget expresses this fact by saying that the child is completely egocentric) the child cannot conceive of an object that is not visible; he cannot react to a part of an object that is on the side away from him; he cannot anticipate future consequences that are not immediate consequences. Egocentricity in this extreme form involves response to only the immediately perceptible stimuli.

The child loses some of this egocentrism by the end of infancy. He becomes able to recognize objects and react to the invisible as well as the visible portions of them. He can even respond to a hidden object that he has seen hidden. Now egocentrism shows itself in other ways. The difficulty the child has in assuming an impossible premise lies in the fact that he cannot imagine a situation that he has never experienced. In order to understand what would happen in a new situation, the child must have some principles to guide his perception of how the new situation would be similar to and how different from what he knows. To know that a fan would make no wind if there were no air, he must grasp the fact that wind is air in motion, and he must not be bound by his own experience in which fans always produce a wind. Then he can think through the problem and see what aspects of a fan's behavior would be affected by the lack of air and what aspects would not be affected. To do this, the child must first have the necessary knowledge, and second he must be able to analyze the problem to separate different aspects of the fan's performance. As long as the child thinks in terms limited by his own experience, he cannot solve such problems.

Finally, egocentrism obviously hampers social adjustment because social adjustment requires that one be able to make decisions that involve other people. And if these decisions are to have the expected effects on other people, the feelings of the other people must be judged accurately at the time the decision is made. It is Piaget's (1928, 1950) contention that the child gradually loses his egocentrism and attains a more realistic point of view because he develops several important abilities as he grows up. He becomes able to integrate his past experience with his present perception and to anticipate future experiences in such a way that he can effectively assume different points of view at the same time and thus form accurate judgments. Also, he becomes able to communicate with others and to receive communication from others. It is only through such communication from others and through their actions that the child learns that other people see things in ways different from his own, and gradually he is thus able to appreciate their point of view.

The Achievement of Independence from Field Organization

Let us pause for a moment to take stock. With each step we have been plunging deeper into the psychological causes of child behavior. Our first definition of maturity involved only accuracy and competence. One of the elements that bring about accurate perception and realistic behavior is the ability to take into account many aspects of a situation, remote and immediate, obvious and hidden.

Our next step was an attempt to describe one of the conditions necessary for adjusting to other people and to objects—namely, objective perception. Unless an object is recognized when it is seen, the individual cannot respond to it intelligently. Unless the individual perceives the objective properties of an object, he cannot use that object as a tool. Unless the individual can conceive how a situation would appear to somebody else or from a different point of view, he cannot very well predict how other people will behave and he cannot anticipate the consequences of his actions without actually testing them out.

We are now ready to take one further step—namely, to describe one condition that prevents the perception of objective properties and that hampers the anticipation of consequences. This condition involves the way in which the stimuli in the immediately perceived situation are organized and related to one another. In so far as their organization is rigidly determined by certain laws called the *laws of field organization,* the perception of the situation is rigidly fixed and inflexible. With maturity, the individual becomes more independent of these laws and thus his perception may become more realistic.

The first step in clarifying this process is to understand the function of the immediate situation in the perception of the external world.

Function of the Immediate Situation in Providing Cues

To understand how the organization of the stimulus situation may prevent objective perception, it is important to note how the immediately perceived situation provides information about remote and hidden aspects of the situation and thus guides behavior to remote goals.

Even though we are quite familiar with a house, when we try to find our way through it in the dark we can bark our shins on a chair or run into the side of a doorway. This ineffective behavior does not necessarily imply that we do not know where the doorway is in the house, nor need it be due to the fact that the chair is in an unfamiliar place. Such mistakes may occur because in the dark we may not get enough cues to tell us exactly where we are in the house. This example shows how dependent we are upon the immediately perceived situation for cues to guide behavior. Knowledge may be useless unless we get enough cues to utilize our knowledge. Any condition—darkness, visual defect, or social blindness—that reduces the number of cues in the immediate situation must hamper our adjustment, even though our knowledge of the external situation is quite accurate.

Thus far, we have considered only the absence of or blindness to cues as the basis of inadequate or unclear perception. Without being unclear, or fuzzy, however, the immediate situation may be so organized that it does not provide us with the information we need. The picture shown in Figure 3.6, for example, contains a hidden figure. The easily perceived portion of the picture depicts the tomb of Napoleon Bonaparte. Beside the tomb there is a hidden figure of Napoleon standing in his characteristic posture. There is nothing unclear about the picture but, because of the way in which it is organized, the figure of Napoleon is not easily seen. If for some reason the hidden figure was an important cue to guide our behavior, the organization of the picture might prevent us from responding to it. Any factor, then, which reduces or rigidifies the perception of the immediate situation will influence the adequacy of the behavioral adjustment.

The figure in this picture is not easy to see because objects which are in some way clearly segregated from the rest of the background are much easier to perceive than those which are not distinct. The stimuli that actually strike the retina from two different objects are not necessarily distinct from one another. In order to perceive two objects, the individual must receive enough cues from each of them to recognize them, and he must also separate the cues that refer to one object from those that refer to the other.

Some of the objects that must be separated are not spatially separate from each other. This is most obvious in the separation of figure from ground. When we see an object against a background, we cannot actually receive stimulation from the ground that lies directly behind the object, but because of the continuity of the background from one side to the other, we "see" the ground extending behind the object. Thus, the difficulty in perceiving Napoleon in Figure 3.6 can be explained. The white space between the two trees is seen merely as sky, continuous with the sky on either side of the two trees; all the

Fig. 3.6 Can you find Napoleon standing beside his tomb? (From S. S. Fernberger, "An Early Example of a 'Hidden Figure' Picture," *Am. J. Psych.*, *63*, 1950, 448)

sky is perceived as one single background. If we are to perceive Napoleon, we must perceive the space between the two trees as an object in itself.

The Effect of Field Organization upon Perception

We have seen how the organization of a field may influence the accurate perception of a situation. One aspect of maturity is to be able to perceive complex stimuli—*e.g.*, adults should have less difficulty than children in finding Napoleon in the picture. Now let us investigate the principles that determine how a perceptual field is organized. Then we shall attempt to formulate this general characteristic of maturity.

The laws of field organization describe the relations among stimuli in the immediate perceptual field that lead to their being organized in one way rather than another. These psychological principles state the conditions that will make one stimulus stand out and be obtrusive; furthermore, they describe the conditions that cause two stimuli to be perceived as a unit or as related to each other.

A recent advertisement of television sets contained pictures of two sets— a very large picture of a set near the center of the page and another, smaller picture near the bottom. Attention was attracted to the large central picture, which was, naturally, much the more attractive model. Also printed on the page were two prices—one, the price of the smaller, lower-priced model, in very large type, and the other, the price of the large model, in much smaller type. It was inevitable that upon first looking at the advertisement one would take the price printed in large type to be the price of the set whose picture occupied the large space in the center of the page, and the price in smaller type would be perceived as related to the less conspicuous picture. Thus the reader was led to believe that the expensive model was selling for the lower price. In very small type under each price was a statement that indicated by model number the set to which the price really referred. This advertisement illustrates both the laws of attention-getting and the laws describing the perception of relationship.

THE CAPTURE OF ATTENTION   The attention-capturing characteristics of the external world have been investigated by students of perception and also by those interested in the psychology of advertising. Objects which are large, centrally placed, unusual, or strikingly differentiated from the rest of the field, or objects, whose meanings evoke strong attitudes, are likely to capture the attention of the observer. When such an object does capture the attention, it may provoke behavior that does not take the unnoticed environment sufficiently into account. The young man who almost gets run over because he is watching a pretty girl can testify to this fact.

We should note that there are two classes of characteristics listed above. Some characteristics describe the physical location and properties of the stimuli that make them highly noticeable. The others describe the effect of the meaning of a stimulus in terms of the attitudes and values of the observer. A discussion of the effect of values upon perceptual sensitivity will be deferred to a later chapter; at this point it is sufficient to note that advertisers, when they are trying to appeal to children, regularly display such valued objects as baseball players, pursuit planes, ponies, and ice cream.

Some of the principles of attention-getting do not, however, depend upon any specific meaning; any object which is large, brightly colored, and centrally located tends to attract attention. All these conditions can be subsumed under a general term—*perceptual segregation*. If one part of the field is segregated from the rest, either through physical separation or through dissimilarity, it tends to be distinct, obtrusive, and noticeable. Thus, bright objects, colored objects, and isolated objects all tend to be obtrusive, provided that the field is not entirely composed of objects that are equally bright, or similarly colored, or equally isolated from one another.

With maturity, the obtrusiveness of these perceptually segregated objects becomes less compelling. The adult can ignore the obtrusive things that tend

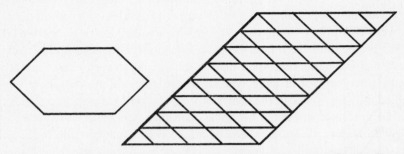

Fig. 3.7 The figure at the left is embedded in the larger figure. Can you find it? (After K. Gottschaldt, *Psychol. Forsch., 8,* 1926, 261-317)

to attract his attention. It is a requirement of effective adjustment for the person to be thus freed from these primitive perceptual laws. Because small and apparently insignificant aspects of the perceptual field can in fact be cues to extremely important remote objects and events, well-adjusted behavior cannot be geared only to the obvious aspects of the situation. The downtown street at night may be full of big red flashing lights, but the driver must be sensitive to the relatively unobtrusive red light on the traffic signal. The child who keeps on teasing after he is no longer amusing may do so partly because he fails to notice the little cues that indicate that his victim is getting angry. The child is easy for the magician to fool because the magician is an expert at misdirecting attention in order to hide the true causal structure of the trick he performs.

The following incidents of child behavior, quoted from Woodcock (1941) further illustrate how one part of a behavior sequence may be so much more noticeable than the rest that the child adjusts to it alone.

Jean, when asked to step over rather than on another child's block building, became so intrigued with the stepping-over process that she repeated it several times, but always from the original side and walking on the building each time as she returned to the starting point.

A striking example is seen in the one-piece snow suit problem where for some unfathomable two-year-old reason the sitting-down feature seems to hold a position of special clarity or interest that wipes out attention to intermediate steps.

To remove this kind of a suit, it is simplest for the child to sit on the floor while leggings are pulled off over his shoes. In practice. however, the youngest may sit down before even the sleeves are off; many will sit down of their own accord as soon as the sleeves are off, and only the most mature, those approaching three can see the whole process clearly enough to recognize that they must push the suit below their hips before they sit down since otherwise they will sit on it, making it impossible to remove.

The fact that children have more difficulty than adults in segregating a figure which is embedded in the background has been demonstrated by Witkin

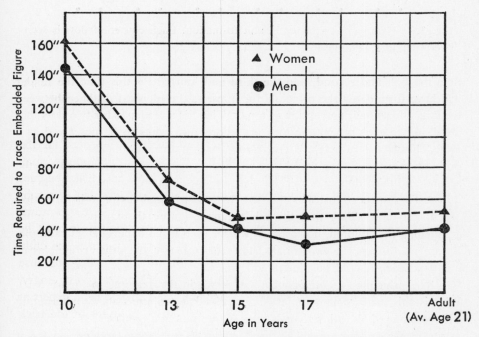

Fig. 3.8   Time required to discover embedded figures at various chronological ages. (After H. A. Witkin *et al., Personality Through Perception,* p. 124)

and his colleagues (1954) through the use of a hidden-figure test. The subject is told that he must locate in the complicated drawing shown at the right of Figure 3.7 the simple figure shown at the left. His success in doing so and the time required to trace out the hidden figure are his scores on the test. Figure 3.8 shows in graphic form the scores of children of different ages on the embedded-figure test. As we see, the scores improve until about the age of fifteen.

Perception of Relationship

We have spoken thus far only of the factors that make it easy or difficult to isolate or segregate one part of the perceptual field from the rest. The field organization also influences the ease with which the relationship between two objects may be perceived. The principles describing the influence of field organization upon the perception of relationship have been described by Wertheimer (1923) in his research on perceptual unit formation. The following configuration of dots, for example, will be perceived as several pairs of dots; the first two are perceived as a pair, the next two as another, and so forth. Why are they not perceived so that the second and third form a pair, rather

• •   • •   • •   • •   • •   • •

Fig. 3.9   Nearness as a factor in unit formation. Each cluster of dots is seen as a group or perceptual unit.

than the first and second, and the third and fourth? By this time the reader will have formulated the principle for himself: the physical distance between the dots affects their perception as a pair. There is a tendency for two dots that are closer to each other than they are to any other dots to be perceived as a unit. This is the principle of *proximity* in unit formation. The reader will probably also have discovered that when the suggestion was made to see the second and third dots as a pair, he was able to see them as a pair by trying to do so. This further illustrates the fact that these principles of unit formation are not so compelling that the adult cannot ignore them. They are more compelling for children, however, as will be seen in an experimental example. Before we discuss the experiment, however, some of the other principles of unit formation should be illustrated.

The principle of *similarity* can be shown in the example in Figure 3.10. Why is this arrangement of letters perceived as columns of *a*'s alternating with columns of *b*'s rather than as rows of alternating *a*'s and *b*'s? If all the elements in the array were alike, there would be no strong tendency to see it

a	b	a	b	a	b	a	b	a
a	b	a	b	a	b	a	b	a
a	b	a	b	a	b	a	b	a
a	b	a	b	a	b	a	b	a
a	b	a	b	a	b	a	b	a
a	b	a	b	a	b	a	b	a

Fig. 3.10   Similarity as a factor in unit formation. Because of similarity, the figure is seen as columns of *a*'s and *b*'s.

either as columns or rows. If the members of a column are all similar and the members of a row are not all similar, the columns tend to become perceptual units.

A third principle, *good continuation,* is illustrated in Figure 3.11. This figure contains two lines crossing. Each of the crossings might conceivably be seen as two angles point to point, but because the upper left-hand line and the lower right-hand line make a good continuation of each other, as do the upper right-hand line and the lower left-hand line, they are perceived as two lines crossing each other.

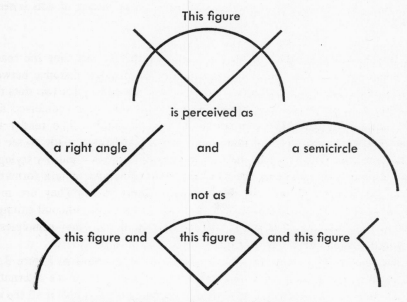

Fig. 3.11   Good continuation in unit formation.

In everyday life these unit-forming factors make it easier to perceive some relationships than others; also, they hamper the perception of an object as isolated if it is tied into a unit by proximity, similarity, or good continuation. An earlier example (see p. 37) described the failure of the subject to use the string from a "No Smoking" sign for solving a problem that involved a piece of string. One way to state the psychological nature of the difficulty is that the string and sign made a good psychological unit, so that it was difficult to perceive the string as isolated from the sign.

Unit formation also influences the individual's judgment of causal relations. Michotte (1946) has shown, for example, how unit-forming factors may influence the perception of causality. If the subject in an experiment is shown an animated motion picture in which one disk moves toward another and hits it and then the other disk moves away, the time interval between the moment of impact of the two disks and the moment when the second disk begins to move determines how the event is perceived. If the second disk begins to move at the moment of impact and the velocity of the two movements is the same, so that the motions of the first and second disks are essentially continuous (principle of good continuation), the event is seen as one ball striking another and making it move. If there is a clear pause between the two movements—*i.e.,* if the second disc does not start moving until a moment after it is hit—the two movements are seen as independent. If the second disk begins to move at the moment of impact, as in the first case, but much more rapidly than the first disk, the event no longer looks like the impact of two inanimate disks; instead it looks as though the second disk were alive and as though it jerked away from the first as soon as it was touched.

The influence of these unit-forming factors upon the perception of causality in a much more complex situation can be seen in the principles derived from studies of the magical beliefs of various cultures. In many cultures, for example, there is a belief that contact with an object somehow transfers some of its properties. To eat the heart of a lion makes one lion-hearted. This effect of physical contact can be seen occasionally in our own culture. The man who did not wash the hand that had shaken the hand of Abraham Lincoln was somehow behaving as though the contact would wash off.

A second principle of magic is similarity. The destruction of an image or statuette of an enemy is a standard practice among sorcerers who wish to destroy the enemy. The effect of this can be seen in ourselves also. We would be reluctant, for example, to prick the eyes of a photograph with a pin— especially if the photograph is one of a close friend.

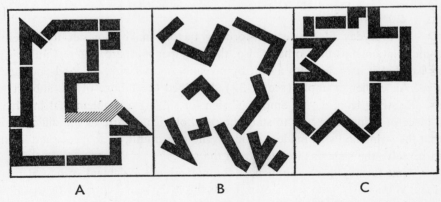

A   B   C

Fig. 3.12   Block patterns like those used to study the effect of organization on perception. (After H. Volkelt, *Ber. u. IX Kong. f. Exp. Psychol.,* 1926)

INFLUENCE ON CHILDREN OF UNIT-FORMING FACTORS   That these unit-forming factors are more compelling for children than for adults is illustrated by an experiment of Heiss and Sander (1930) on the ability to isolate an object from a perceptual unit. They presented to children of various ages the block arrangement shown in *A* of Figure 3.12. The shaded block was missing and had to be selected from a group of available blocks. In some cases the available blocks from which the needed block was to be chosen were arranged haphazardly, as shown in *B*. In other cases they were arranged into the closed figure shown in *C*—which would, according to the principles of unit formation, have many unit-forming factors. As would be expected, it was more difficult to find the correct block in *C* than in *B*, because it is necessary to ignore the unit in *C* in order to isolate the block with the correct shape. This was true of all children up to the age of nineteen, the oldest group in the experiment (see Fig. 3.13). The relative difficulty of the two conditions changed, however, with age. As shown in Figure 3.13, the three- and four-year-olds took twice as long in condition *C* as in condition *B*, whereas the nineteen-year-olds required only a few seconds longer for *C* than for *B*.

The significance of such unit-forming factors in behavior is that the cues which refer to a single object or event may or may not be close to or similar to

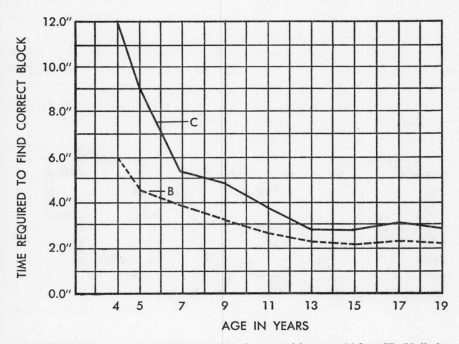

Fig. 3.13   Change in strength of field forces with age. (After H. Volkelt, *Ber. u. IX Kong. Exp. Psychol.*, 1926)

one another. With maturity, these unit-forming factors can be ignored, if necessary, in order to recognize the perceptual field in such a way that it reflects the causal structure behind it. The light switch and the light do not form a perceptual unit. Furthermore, it is necessary to differentiate many kinds of relationships among objects—*e.g.,* next to, in communication with, similar to, sign of, cause of, etc. Not all objects that are close to one another or similar to each other have the same relationship.

The Effect of Field Organization on Interpersonal Relations

These principles of unit formation have been extended by Heider (1953) to interpersonal relations. Unit formation, when extended to social relations, explains the fact that the individual can perceive people as belonging together in a unit and that he can perceive himself in a unit with other people. This kind of unit formation can be shown to follow the principles previously stated. For example, two Americans, one from Chicago and one from Oregon, might not ordinarily feel that they had much in common, but if they happened to meet in Africa where they were the only Americans, they would feel much more communality. Their similarity to each other is so much greater than the similarity of either of them to other people in the area that unit formation would probably occur.

In the same way the principle of proximity can be seen in social relations. People who are thrown together, especially if they are separated from other contacts, tend to form a unit and to show the characteristics of units. This is not inevitable, to be sure; there can be disrupting factors that prevent proximity from causing unit formation. This is also true of unit formation in visual perception, but, as a first approximation, the assumption that proximity brings about unit formation in social groups is probably sound (Homans, 1950). The importance of contact and proximity can be best illustrated by the perennial desire of children, especially nursery-school children, to sit next to the teacher, to sit next to company at the table, to be close to the important people in the child's life.

Another of Heider's extensions of Wertheimer's principles to interpersonal relations deals with the relation of liking and disliking to unit formation. Liking is a unit-forming factor—a uniquely social one. Its relationship to unit formation can be illustrated by many examples. We want to be close to the people we like and separated from the people we dislike. (Liking tends to lead to proximity.) If we like someone, we tend to become similar to him even in irrelevant ways. Frequently we take on the mannerisms of our close friends; children openly copy their friends. Conversely, similarity fosters unit formation and feelings of belongingness; this is one reason for the adoption of a standard dress by various cults. Birds of a feather flock together.

The simultaneous presence of unifying and disrupting factors in social groupings leads to frustration, tension, and unhappiness, which can be completely resolved only by some sort of adjustment that reconciles the conflict. If people who dislike one another are in the same group, unhappiness is generated. If they can form separate groups, there is less tension than if they are forced to stay in the same group despite their mutual dislike. To perceive that a friend has performed a disliked action—has become a unit with it—causes tension and unhappiness. There are three logical alternatives for resolving the conflict: (1) The friendship may be broken. This now leads to a harmonious situation: disliking a person who has done a disliked thing. (2) His action may come to be seen as not so bad after all. Now the attitude toward the act is harmonized with the attitude toward the person. (3) It may be impossible to believe that he really intended to do it. Perhaps it was an accident or he was forced to. This breaks the unit comprising the person and the act. Each of these resolutions of the conflict leads to what Heider (1953) calls a harmonious situation, in which all the unit-forming factors exist among the same objects and all the disrupting forces exist among objects in different units.

As he reads these descriptions, the student is likely to feel that something about them rings true but that they seem oversimplified. He will certainly think of exceptions to each of the principles—of twins who hate to dress alike, of enemies who do remain in the same group, of associations composed of specialists who are all different rather than alike. These exceptions are true; the basic principles, like the perceptual ones described earlier, are modified in the adult, mature person. As an individual becomes mature, he can tolerate his friend's doing things with which he disagrees. These principles that embody the primitive laws of interpersonal relations are especially compelling to children. They have their effect upon adults also but are less simple and compelling in their functioning.

The compellingness of similarity can be illustrated by studies of contagious behavior. Redl (1949) offers the following illustration:

> Eighty rather disturbed children between the ages of eight and fourteen are in a large camp mess hall. Johnny, in a fit of temper against one person at his table, throws a plate at him. A minute later, plates fly all through the air, and the place is in an uproar, even though Johnny neither contemplated nor planned any such effect and is otherwise a rather inconspicuous figure at the camp—without any leadership role.

We shall examine later some of the factors determining who initiates contagious behavior. For the moment we are concerned only with the fact that behavior is often contagious. To follow the fad, to imitate blindly, to feel uncomfortable when different, are all characteristics that mark children's behavior more than adults'.

The influence of field organization can be summarized in the following statement: The factors that have been described—attention-getting and unit-forming—are properties of the psychological field. To the extent that they operate, they induce the individual to perceive, to feel, to like, and to imitate. The compellingness of these factors in children is one aspect of immaturity.

Summary

With this chapter we come to the end of a section primarily devoted to a description of the principles underlying the child's perception and knowledge of the external world. His psychological world expands; his perception of the properties of the external world becomes more objective. Finally, we have seen how one of the factors hampering this expansion and objectivity is the compellingness to the child of the laws of field organization. These laws describe the conditions that tend to make a stimulus noticeable and obtrusive and the conditions that tend to make two stimuli be perceived as part of a psychological unit or as related to each other. In so far as the cues to important external events are easily noticed, the child has little difficulty in adjusting. But important cues are not always obvious, and the important relations are not always paralleled by perceptual unit formation; thus, the ability to adjust to the real world depends upon being free from these laws of organization. This freedom gradually increases as the child matures.

4

Maturity: Differentiation

CRITERIA OF DIFFERENTIATION

DIFFERENTIATION

SUMMARY

THE PRECEDING CHAPTERS have been concerned with the adequacy of the child's view of the world and with his attainment of accurate, objective perception. The present chapter is concerned with maturity as it affects the adequacy of the individual's response. Objectivity is necessary for well-adjusted behavior, but a well-controlled behavioral adjustment is just as necessary.

The child who is learning to play baseball must learn to recognize the situations that require the infield players to play close to home; he must learn that a left-handed batter is more likely than a right-handed batter to hit to right field. Such knowledge of the external reality is important, but, having properly located himself in right field for a left-handed batter and having learned to judge where a fly ball is going to land, he must also learn to catch the ball. The accuracy of his perception is of no avail unless his behavior takes advantage of it. Differentiation is a concept that describes primarily the characteristics of well-controlled behavior, although we shall see that it is also useful in describing some aspects of the perceiving process.

The term *differentiation* has been taken into psychology from other biological sciences because there seems to be a similarity between behavioral development and maturation and biological development and maturation. In order to clarify the use of the term, it might be well to describe it first in its biological setting.

A fertilized egg consists of a single cell. The first step in the development of the embryo is the splitting of this single cell into two, then four, then eight, then sixteen cells. This is a very concrete example of differentiation; at first there are no easily distinguishable parts of the fertilized egg; after the splitting process the organism has sixteen easily distinguishable parts.

These sixteen cells of the early embryo are all alike in appearance and function. They are essentially indistinguishable from one another. Before long, however, certain groups of cells in the embryo begin to have different functions and different properties: some of them form the inside layer of the hollow ball-like organism and become stomach and intestines; some of them form the outside layer and become nervous tissue; still others, form the middle layer and become muscle tissue. This is another sign of differentiation: the cells become distinguishable from one another in appearance and in function.

Criteria of Differentiation

Child psychologists, trying to understand the essential nature of development, perceived a similarity between this differentiation process in embryological development and the behavioral development of the child. This similarity is quite clear, for example, in the development of emotions. The newborn child seems to have one detectable emotional state—excitement. When he is not excited, he is relaxed, and this is a state of non-emotionality. Bridges (1932), who propounded this concept, observed that by the time the child is three months old two kinds of excitement may be discerned—distress and delight—but there are still times when the child's emotional state seems neither distress nor delight but is best described merely as excitement. Later, different sorts of distress appear; *e.g.,* fear and anger separate themselves from generalized distress. Figure 4.1 shows Bridges' entire scheme of the development of emotion. Such a scheme excellently illustrates the concept of differentiation. Situations which at a later age arouse a variety of emotions at an earlier age produce the same undifferentiated emotion. This is the basic concept of differentiation. When, in the course of an individual's development, we can observe the appearance of distinguishable patterns of behavior which were previously not distinguishable, we can say that his behavior has become more differentiated.

When we say that fear and anger are distinguishable at the age of six months but are not distinguishable at the age of two months, we do not imply that all of the expressive behavior of the two-month-old child is of a single pattern. Even at birth, children cry in different ways at different times. When we say that fear and anger are differentiated, we mean that the differences in the child's crying can be systematically related to different situations. In

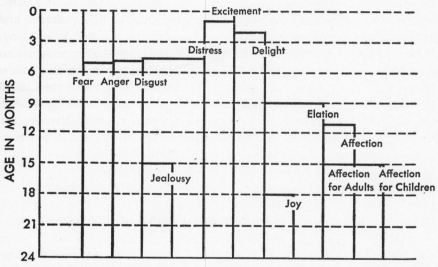

Fig. 4.1 Differentiation of the emotions. (After K. M. B. Bridges, *Child Devel., 3,* 1932, 340)

situations in which he is blocked or frustrated, he shows one sort of crying, whereas in situations in which he is overpowered or frightened, he shows different behavior patterns. For the child to show differentiated behavior, then, he must discriminate between different situations and make a different behavioral response to each class of situations. Discrimination is thus one criterion of differentiation.

Another aspect of differentiation is *independence,* or the ability to perform two or more activities at the same time. It is sometimes necessary, for example, in playing the piano, to play ⅔ time with the right hand and ¾ time with the left. In one measure the right hand strikes two evenly spaced notes while the left must strike three evenly spaced notes. This task is not easy for the beginning student, because it requires the two hands to function independently. If one part of the body can behave in a fashion that is uninfluenced by the behavior of another part, then the two parts are independent. If, on the other hand, one aspect of behavior is rigidly determined by another aspect of behavior, the two are not independent and to that extent are undifferentiated. Independence is thus a second criterion of differentiation.

The third and final criterion is *articulation*. When young children are first learning to sing, they have difficulty in going from one note to another without sliding. If they try to sing two notes an octave apart they tend to slur through all the notes in between rather than to stop one note sharply and then start the other one. In an articulated behavior pattern, each unit of behavior appears at its proper position in the pattern and is limited to its proper position. The difficulties the child has in saying, "She sells sea shells by the seashore" illustrate disarticulation.

There are, then, three indications of differentiation—*discrimination*, *independence*, and *articulation*. Our hypothesis is that when the behavior of the child becomes more differentiated it becomes better controlled, more adaptable—in a word, more mature. Each of the three criteria will be discussed in turn. They are arranged in the sequence above for several reasons. Discrimination is more closely related than the others to the discussion in the preceding chapters. Discrimination describes another ability that is essential for accurate perception, whereas independence and articulation are characteristics of behavior rather than of perception—they are easily observable and objectively measurable. Following the discussion of these three criteria, we shall return to the general problem of differentiation to see how we shall use this concept in explaining the difference between child and adult behavior.

Discrimination

It is sometimes embarrassing for a young man walking down the street with his date on his arm to hear himself hailed as "Daddy" by an unknown two-year-old. He is, in such a situation, the victim of the child's lack of discrimination. The two-year-old, when he uses the word "Daddy," may not discriminate between the man who is his father and all other men. The fact that the child may not discriminate in his use of the word does not necessarily imply that he treats all men as though they were his father. He can still be shy with a strange "Daddy" but warmly greet his own father.

PERCEPTUAL DISCRIMINATION   Children show in many other ways their deficiency in discriminating. At birth, children respond to a light of a certain degree of brightness; they respond to sudden changes of light intensity. There is evidence that newborn babies are quieted by a moderate light but are more active in darkness. On the whole, however, they are relatively insensitive. We cannot be certain, but it may be that newborn babies do not have any color vision at all. Certainly they do not make the color discriminations of which older children are capable. Staples (1932) found that by the end of the third month infants looked at colors longer than at gray stimuli, but it was not until the child was six months of age that his behavior indicated any discrimination among different colors.

The child's perception of weight also becomes more discriminating as he matures. The ability to discriminate between small differences in weight improves until approximately the age of twelve. The fact that infants may try to grasp objects that are far beyond their reach indicates their lack of spatial discrimination, but by the time children are in school their accuracy of depth perception seems to be as good as it will ever be (Updegraff, 1930).

In the more complex discriminations of visual forms and visual patterns, there is clear evidence that discrimination improves with age. One way of

Fig. 4.2 The Seguin form board used to study form perception.

investigating form perception in children old enough to manipulate objects involves the use of a form board. A form board has a number of holes of various shapes, into which the properly shaped blocks may be fitted, as illustrated in Figure 4.2. The ability to select the properly shaped block increases with age between 2 and 6 years (Baldwin and Wellman, 1928).

In still more complex form perception, it is apparent that the inability to discriminate among patterns having the same form but differently oriented in space is one of the difficulties in learning to read. To distinguish among *p, q, b,* and *d,* is quite difficult for many first-grade pupils. The printed letters differ only in their orientation. For the same reason *was* and *saw* are frequently confused by children learning to read; one is the reverse of the other. To know one's right from one's left hand also requires a discrimination in terms of spatial orientation and is not generally learned until late in the preschool period.

One more illustration of the improvement in discrimination is interesting in terms of the social relations of the child. In studies of discrimination of the facial expressions, Buhler and Hetzer (1928) has shown that the infant under the age of six months smiles just as readily at an angry face as at a smiling one. In studies of the ability to identify facial expressions in pictures, it is found that children do not perform so well as adults. Curiously enough, children find a scornful expression quite difficult to identify, although for adults it is one of the easiest expressions to recognize (Gates, 1923).

SPREAD OF EFFECT   A somewhat different sort of failure to discriminate is illustrated in the following behavior. Children, particularly young ones, find difficulty in discriminating between the object in their environment that is responsible for an effect and all the irrelevant objects in their environment. The baby who is pricked with a needle in a series of inoculations provides an example of this. Some children, after such an experience, become afraid of doctors, nurses, white uniforms, the doctor's office, the office building, etc. These children are in some sense failing to discriminate between the painful needle prick and all the surrounding stimuli. Adults may resent the needle prick, but they are not so likely to fear all the rest of the situation as is the child.

Watson and Raynor (1920) have performed an experiment classic in child psychology showing how such fear reactions may be established. They believed that all acquired fears are learned by this spread of effect. Albert, the subject in this experiment, was a baby of eleven months. The experimenters first made sure that Albert did not already have some fear of furry animals. Then they conditioned him to fear a white rat. They handed one to the baby, and, just as the baby reached for it, one of the experimenters loudly banged an iron bar. This made such a noise that it was frightening to the baby. After only three such experiences of being frightened by the loud noise just as he reached for the rat, Albert showed definite symptoms of fear whenever he saw the rat. With repetition of the situation, Albert became obviously afraid of the white rat, and his fear spread to other similar objects—small furry animals, and even woolly material. This behavior of Albert reflects his immaturity, his inability to perceive the situation clearly, and his failure to discriminate among different stimuli in the same situation.

The adult in most such situations would not respond in this undiscriminating way; instead, he would discriminate the aspect of the situation which was frightening from the aspects which were not. Under certain conditions, however, adults seem to show a similar lack of discrimination. Some adults, for example, never feel comfortable in a town in which some personal tragedy occurred, despite the fact that other aspects of the town may be quite pleasant.

ANIMISM   There are many examples of lack of discrimination in the interpersonal behavior of children. We shall now discuss an example of poor discrimination that is important in the child's social adjustment, and has received much attention from psychologists. This is *animism,* or the attribution of life to inanimate objects. The term *animism* was first used by anthropologists to describe the fact that in many primitive cultures stones, stars, the sun and moon, and other objects of the physical world are endowed with life, with the ability to perceive, and with manlike intentions.

There are numerous anecdotal examples of animism in children. Scupin, (1907) one of the early observers of child behavior, has told how his own child asked his parents to "make the mean old smoke go away" when he saw steam rising from his cup of hot milk. Another adult remembers how as a child she thought it must be tiresome for a stone to stay in one place all the time, so she moved them around to give their lives some variety (Queynat, 1920). Piaget (1929, 1930) observed similar behavior in children. One child of six, for example, was asked why the wind blows. He answered, "When it is going to rain so as to break off branches for a fire." Another belief of six-year-olds, Piaget found, is that clouds are alive and know that they are moving.

Piaget described four stages of animistic thinking. In the first one, all objects that are active in any sense, *i.e.,* moving or movable are thought to be alive, even though at the moment they are stationary. At this stage stones can be alive. In the second stage only objects that can move, such as wagons, bicycles, or clouds, are considered living. In the third stage the concept of life is limited to those things that move by themselves. Vehicles such as wagons are thus excluded, but the sun and moon are thought to be living. In the fourth stage life is restricted to plants and animals.

Russell and Dennis (1939) (1940) have investigated animism systematically by asking large numbers of children and adults whether certain objects were alive. In addition, the experimenters asked for the reasons for the belief. In different experiments they used somewhat different objects, but in general they included such objects as a match, a lighted match, a watch or clock, the sun, the moon, clouds, rivers, and the ocean. These experimenters generally confirmed Piaget's findings on children, but they obtained similar results with adults. This last fact raises serious questions about the results of all these verbal procedures for investigating animism.

Dennis (1951) found for example that about 40 percent of a sophomore psychology class, thought some one of these objects was alive. It is very difficult to believe that any college sophomore really thinks that a lighted match or a clock is alive. It is important, therefore, to determine just what he means when he answers in this way. Adults' reasons, as reported to Dennis, were the same as those given by children. A clock, for example, was considered by a middle-aged adult to be alive because the hands moved by themselves. In another study, Zambrowski (1951) found some physicians giving animistic answers. One of them, for example, said that the sun was alive because it was born, it developed, it died, it gave birth to other suns, and it interacted with its fellows.

It seems possible that some of these adult subjects were using "alive" in a figurative sense—as in a "live" coal. Others were perhaps being facetious; it is not uncommon for college sophomores to pull the experimenter's leg when they are asked what seems to them a ridiculous question. The physician may have been trapped by his own scientific rigor. He knew that life is very difficult to define scientifically and perhaps he approached the task by first establishing a set of criteria for what he meant by "life." When an example— like the sun—fit the criteria, he stuck to his guns and called it alive, despite his common-sense judgment.

If all these questions of interpretation arise in understanding what an adult means when he calls something alive, then such questions must also be relevant for deciding what the child means when he calls the sun alive. Since children's use of language is notoriously loose, such questions of interpretation must be answered before the results can be clear.

ANIMISM AS A CONFUSION OF SOURCE AND MEDIATOR   There is, however, another approach to the problem, a more behavioral one, which may actually give us more important information about the child than we would obtain by further questioning. It is obvious that our behavior toward people differs from our behavior toward inanimate objects. We attribute to people a set of abilities that objects do not have. We assume that people can perceive and respond to what they perceive; objects only react to the influences that impinge on them. We assume that people can act spontaneously, that they can initiate action as well as respond and react to stimuli. We assume that people have intentions and goals and that they direct their behavior toward these goals.

When we ask, however, how we discriminate behaviorally between living and nonliving objects, we encounter difficulty. We do not respond much differently to plants from the way we do to objects. We do not feel more sympathetic when a tree is cut down than we do when a charming old house is torn down. We do not assume that plants can perceive, that they can initiate action, or that they have goals. The difference between plants and people is almost as great as between objects and people. Animals fall halfway between. We do assume that animals can perceive, that they behave spontaneously, and most of us assume that animals show goal-directed behavior.

If we want to approach the problem of animism behaviorally, therefore, we must recognize that the classification of plants with animals and people is more or less arbitrary and probably is learned by the child. Of more significance is the child's discrimination between sources of action and mediators of action.

Sources of action are the people who are responsible. If we wish to influence a person who is a source of action, we must change his attitude or his intentions. We ask, beseech, bribe, threaten, or persuade him. We do none of these things when we are dealing with objects that are mere instruments or impersonal links in a causal chain. If someone throws a rock at us, we ward off the rock or dodge it, but we become angry and threaten the person who threw the rock. If someone gives us a gift, we feel friendly toward the person, not the gift.

From this, it might appear that people are always sources of action and objects are always mediators. But this is not entirely true. Objects, of course, can never be sources of action, but it can happen that a person is a mediator or tool rather than a source.

We do not ordinarily become angry with the postman who brings bad news; and we do not feel that a person should take the blame for actions that he is forced to do at the point of a gun. If we do attribute responsibility to a person who is only a mediator or instrument, we are not being animistic in the strict sense of the term, but we are making a similar sort of error.

When we look at the problem of animism as one of failing to discriminate between sources of action and mediators, we shift the problem somewhat from its original formulation, but it becomes a much more understandable and significant aspect of adjustment. It is of only academic interest that a child or adult thinks a lighted match is alive, but it is of very great importance for the child to recognize that his parents are not the source of all the rules that he resents. It is essential for us to recognize the responsible person behind the events that we experience, whether he uses an inanimate object or a person as a tool.

Looking, then, at the broader problem, we find that there is some research, although not enough, on the failure of the child to discriminate between sources and mediators of action. Piaget (1952) reports, for example, that if, during his first year, the baby grasps an object held by the experimenter, he will at first merely pull on the object. After he is able to coordinate more than one means to an end, he will push on the experimenter's hand while pulling on the object. He has perceived and responded to the immediate cause of the object's not moving, but he is responding to the hand in much the same way that he would to a clamp.

During the second year, however, he begins to respond to the person who frustrates him. Piaget does not report further development of the experiment, but in a slightly different experimental situation Maudry and Nekula

(1939) report that the child responds to the person behind the action. (See p. 158 for the details of this experiment.) This is one discrimination: between the origin of action and the mediation of action. When the child is sufficiently mature to respond to the person rather than to the action, it seems that he is prone to respond to many inanimate objects as though they were responsible sources rather than inanimate causes of action. This is the time when he first becomes angry at chairs, calls them naughty, and punishes them after he bumps into them. With further maturity his animism gradually declines.

STIMULUS CONFIGURATIONS PERCEIVED AS SOURCES   In order to understand why children are likely to perceive many inanimate objects as sources of action, we must examine the relationships among stimuli in the external world that tend to make an object be perceived as a source. The question might be put in the following concrete form: If, in an animated motion picture, a number of objects, such as squares, circles, and triangles, moved around the screen, what pattern of motion of an object would make us perceive it as animate—i.e., moving under its own power toward goals of its own? Heider and others have performed this experiment, and we shall examine their findings.

In the first place, we must recognize that the experience of the individual plays an important role in what he perceives to be animate. If we saw a chair on the screen, standing perfectly still, we would perceive it as inanimate. If we saw a person on the screen, also standing perfectly still, we would perceive him as animate. We have learned that in other circumstances people show animation and that our culture calls them living objects. This recognition of other properties of stimuli is an important factor in our perception of them. We should also remember that this is partly a matter of convention. If we were from a different culture, we might perceive the same object differently— i.e., we would perceive a river as living if that were the cultural belief. Our beliefs about what is alive are not entirely dependent upon the immediate stimulus.

When we try to analyze the characteristics of the stimulus situation that tend to make us perceive action as animate rather than lifeless, we find that the concept of animism involves several properties. One of these is *sentience:* living objects feel stimulation and respond to it. In the discussion of Michotte's experiments (see p. 63), we noted that the movement of an object after it had been touched gave under certain conditions the impression of being mechanically caused and under other conditions the impression of being the response of a living object to a stimulus. Probably the most important general condition for the perception of a response as living is the disproportion between the stimulus and the response. In most kinds of mechanical causation, the effect is generally proportional to the cause, but the response of a living organism to a stimulus may be much more intense than the stimulus.

A second condition that leads to the perception of animation is reported by children when they are asked why objects appear to be living. They say that objects that can move by themselves are alive. The apparent *spontaneity* of action is certainly important in determining animistic perception. The Walt Disney cartoons provide examples constantly. Mickey Mouse throws a skillet at Donald Duck. Donald dodges it successfully, but the object, having missed on the first try, makes a U-turn in mid-air and comes zooming at Donald again. At the moment of the U-turn it suddenly stops being an object and becomes a living thing.

Not only does the object make a U-turn spontaneously, but it makes it so that it is again headed toward Donald. This gives us the strong impression that it has not only life but also a goal—to hit Donald. Here we have a third characteristic of animated action—namely, *goal-directed behavior*.

Whenever a response contains a sequence of different actions all producing the same result, these different actions appear to be alternative means to the same end, which is characteristic of goal-directed behavior. This factor can be seen in situations in which adults perceive intentionality. Suppose you were in a room with five doors. As you went toward each one, it slammed shut and automatically locked. When the first door slammed, you might not assume that somebody was trying to lock you in, but by the time the fifth one had slammed, you would be convinced that there must be some intention guiding such concerted action. No animism in the usual sense is involved here— merely the perception of some agent with an intention.

When the golfer hooks the third or fourth golf ball into a pond, there is this same convincing convergence upon a single result. It may lead to animistic perception. The convincingness is increased because the golfer cannot perceive how anything *he* did produced such a result, and it certainly was not *his* intention to hit the balls into the pond. The factors of stance and muscular set that actually produce the hook are obscure; hence, it is inviting to perceive the club as the origin of the action and as the responsible agent. The frustration of the golfer, which makes him less mature and more irritable, contributes its share, with the result that he breaks the club in two or throws it into the pond after the balls. When the convergence of actions upon a result is especially striking, not only may intentionality be perceived but an imaginary object may be conjured up to carry the intention. The man who suffers a long series of reverses may feel that "fate" is against him.

We have seen that an object may be perceived as alive for three reasons: because it shows sensory responsiveness, because it moves spontaneously, or because its behavior appears goal directed. Most living objects display all three of these characteristics although not necessarily at the same time. A wriggling worm on the ground displays spontaneity but neither sentience nor goal directed behavior. The increased wriggling when it is put on a fish hook displays sentience. Because of these bases for the perception of animation, we sometimes find that children report that an automobile is alive but they deny that it can feel anything when we kick it. These different criteria of life probably underlie some of the confusion in the results of experiments on animism.

SUSCEPTIBILITY OF THE CHILD TO ANIMISM   We can see, therefore, how difficult it is to interpret what a person—child or adult—means when he calls something alive. Depending upon how he is questioned and upon the circumstances, he may use the term in different senses. If he is presented with a stimulus situation containing all the conditions for the perception of animateness—responsiveness, spontaneity, and goal-directedness—either a child or an adult is likely to perceive the action as stemming from some living source.

There are reasons, however, why the child will be less able than the adult to detect whether or not an action is animate. One reason is that he does not have as much knowledge of the variety of mechanical principles. It seems likely that the perception of animation comes only when the action cannot be easily explained in some other fashion. The second reason is that the child does not perceive through mediators to the causes of action as well as does the adult. Therefore, he will be more likely than the adult to see mediators as sources. When he bumps into a chair, he is likely ot become angry at the chair, whereas the equally irritated adult will ask, "Who left this chair in the middle of the doorway?" thus showing that he perceives a person as responsible for the position of the chair.

Probably the fact that so many of the events in the child's life do have a personal source tends to facilitate his attribution of life to the whole class of events that, for him, are as yet undifferentiated. Furthermore, he may be led by the form of the question to give animistic answers. If he is asked, "How did the mountains get here?" or "Why do clouds move?" the phraseology of the question is conducive to the perception of an origin. Therefore, it requires unusual maturity to deny the very existence of an origin and to say that the movement of clouds or the formation of rivers was caused by something he does not know about.

We have spent considerable time on this final example of discrimination. We shall apply these principles later, but we can indicate now, to show their significance for everyday life, one role they will play in our later discussions. If a parent is authoritarian, he makes himself the source of the orders and the pressures to which the child must conform. If the child resents this pressure, he will tend to feel resentful toward the parent, whom he sees as the source of the pressure. Actually, the parent is not the source of all rules. Many of the rules are dictated by reality: knives cut and will hurt the child; automobiles are dangerous; stoves are hot and will burn. Yet, if the parent merely orders the child to leave the knife alone, to stay away from the road, and not to touch the stove, he is making himself the source of the rule. Another sort of parent will explain the reasons for rules. When he does this, he is trying to make the child understand that the source of the rule is not the parent. He is trying to make the child recognize that the parent is merely an interpreter or mediator of the external world. If he succeeds, the child's resentment is lessened and is turned away from the parent.

We have noted, in this discussion, that the child discriminates more poorly than the adult. We have examined a few examples of this difference; in the later discussion of child behavior we shall find numerous other examples of the same general principle.

Independence

The second property of differentiated organisms is the independence of functions. The various behavior patterns are more separable and independent of one another in differentiated than in undifferentiated organisms.

Before attempting to describe independence, let us consider why independence of different behavior patterns is important for adjustability to the environment. Suppose the three actions involved in writing the word *cat* were all dependent. Instead of the letters C, A, and T being independent actions, each one usable in any word, the letter A could be written only following the letter C, and T could be written only following CA. It is obvious that this would make writing an enormously difficult task. Actually, of course, we can combine any letter with any other letter and any word with any other word as the situation requires it.

Each of us has a large repertoire of actions, such as hitting, grasping, lifting the foot, wrinkling the brow, smiling, closing the eyes, etc., etc. In order to achieve the necessary flexibility of adjustment to the environment, it is important for us to be able to combine these actions into many different patterns. But if we are to combine them at will into new patterns, they must be independent of one another. We must look carefully, therefore, at the way in which independence develops, so that we can later understand how the child comes to have this flexible use of his behavioral repertoire, combining his different behavior patterns in a wide variety of ways.

Dependence of two activities is perhaps best illustrated by the difficulty of doing two things at the same time. A favorite stunt of the adult who wishes to show off his prowess before children is to pat his head and rub his stomach simultaneously. Most adults find it only slightly difficult, but children find it very difficult to do. This does not mean that the child cannot distinguish between patting and rubbing. Rather the two activities influence each other so much that the child tends either to rub both his head and stomach or to pat both, depending upon which activity he happens to be concentrating upon.

RIGIDITY OF PATTERN   The dependence of different parts of the body upon one another may result in their behaving in the same way at the same time. If a young baby likes the sugar water he has been fed, he may strain toward it. When he is fed lemon juice, he dislikes it and pulls away from it. In each case his limbs and body all function homogeneously—they all point toward the sugar water and they all retreat from the lemon juice.

This homogeneity of action in the different parts of the body of the newborn and the participation of the entire body in his activity has been called *mass activity*. Irwin (1930), observing the movements of newborn infants during the first ten days of life, found that the great preponderance of their activity was mass action, in which the entire body, including the limbs, participated. In studies of the development of the ability to reach for an object, it has been shown that reaching with two hands precedes reaching with one hand.

The same generalized participation of other parts of the body when one part is engaged in a specific action may be observed in the first-grader learning to write. As he laboriously forms the letters, his whole body squirms, he screws up his face, his tongue may protrude, and his legs cross and uncross. When the adult first tries to wiggle his ears, he finds that he too moves many parts of the face besides his ears.

In learning any new motor skill, it is not uncommon to find that the early movements are hampered by dependence among different parts of the body. In playing the piano, for example, it is sometimes necessary to play two separate keys (say C and E) simultaneously and to alternate this pair with another pair one note higher (D and F). This requires that the thumb and middle finger hit keys simultaneously, followed by the index finger and fourth finger. It is surprisingly difficult to do this rapidly—the fingers fall all too easily into the 4-3-2-1 order and it is not easy to move the fingers rapidly in a different order. This difficulty stems from a primitive sort of dependence of the motion of one finger upon the motion of another.

This last example indicates that dependence of one part of the body upon another does not always mean that the parts must function homogeneously and simultaneously. Frequently there is symmetrical functioning in which both hands reach together or both eyes blink at the same time, but there are also actions of the very young infant which are asymmetrical. The *tonic neck reflex* is such an action. Gesell has observed that when a baby less than three months old is lying on his back, he tends to adopt a posture in which one arm is outstretched, the other arm flexed, and the head rotated toward the side of the outstretched arm. This posture is sometimes called the fencing position (see Fig. 4.3). Just why this position is naturally preferred is not at all clear, but it undoubtedly reflects some neurological state.

Fig. 4.3 The tonic neck reflex in infants. (After A. Gesell, in L. Carmichael, ed., *Manual of Child Psychology*)

It is not, therefore, the homogeneity or the lack of it that marks the dependence of two functions; rather, it is their inseparability. If it is not possible for one aspect of an action to occur without the occurrence of the entire pattern, then the parts of the body are dependent on each other. When some sequence of actions is automatic, so that one action automatically follows another, then this pattern also shows dependence.

From this description it can be seen that many automatized habitual behavior patterns show dependence among their parts. When removal of one shoe is automatically followed by removal of the other, the two actions are dependent. Much adult behavior shows this habitual character, but it remains automatic only so long as the individual is not paying attention to what he is doing. If the adult thinks about it, he is quite capable of taking off his shoes in the reverse order from his usual habit. This distinguishes habitual behavior from the automatic sequences of behavior in early infancy.

SPREAD OF TENSION Sometimes, although the behavior of the child does not show any rigid patterning, there seems to be tension throughout the entire body when only one part of it is actually functioning. When the three-year-old reaches for something just out of reach, he does not lie down and point with all four limbs, but both arms reach up and the rest of the body wiggles and dances. This dancing is not purposeful jumping but a generalized restless activity. It is as though the muscle tension spreads to the entire body.

Adults show this spread of muscle tension also, but it is particularly noticeable in periods of stress and frustration. An experiment by Arnold (1942) on the effects of stress illustrates this. A group of stenographers were given dictation at a gradually faster and faster rate until they finally were unable to keep up. The degree of muscle tension in both the right and the left arm was continuously measured. A high level of muscle tension in the writing arm and a low level of tension in the nonwriting arm was characteristic of efficient operation. When the tension in the nonwriting arm began to increase rapidly, the breaking point was near. Spread of tension to nonparticipating parts of the body is symptomatic of, or perhaps causes, inefficient performance (see Figs. 4.4a and 4.4b).

An experiment by Kounin (1941) deals with the interdependence of activities in a slightly different way. He was interested in the effect of satiation

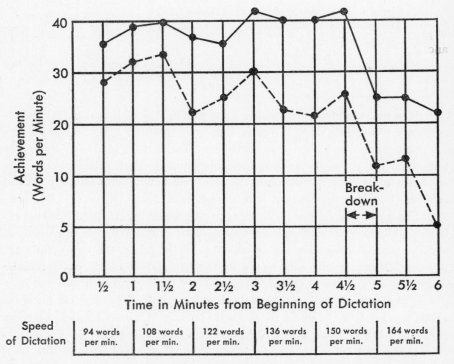

Fig. 4.4a Speed of shorthand as dictation rate is increased. (After M. B. Arnold, *J. Gen. Psychol.*, *26*, 1942, 328)

with one activity on the rapidity of satiation with some other activity. His procedure for producing satiation was to ask a child to draw a cat, not a complicated, lifelike cat but a very schematic one (see Fig. 4.5). The child continued to draw cats line after line and page after page until he finally was so bored with the activity that he refused to continue. Then he was asked if he wanted to draw bugs. Most of the subjects did, and they then continued drawing bugs until they were satiated with that task. It took a shorter time to become satiated with drawing the second figure. After the second task the subjects were asked if they would like to draw turtles, and they were allowed to continue that task until they were bored with it—usually not a very long time—and then were asked whether they wanted to draw rabbits. The satiation time for this task was then measured.

If a subject took just as long to become satiated with the second task as he did with the first, then the two activities are completely independent in so far as satiation is concerned. Satiating one of them has no effect upon the other. If, however, after becoming satiated with the first task, a subject re-

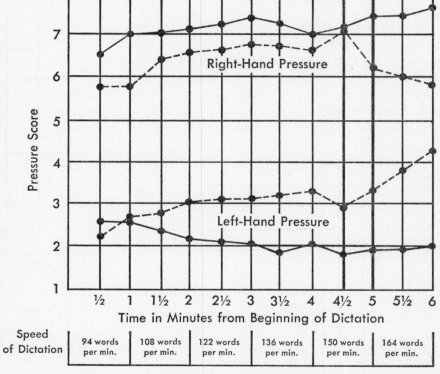

Fig. 4.4*b* Pressure on pencil during rapid dictation. (After M. B. Arnold, *J. Gen. Psychol.*, 26, 1942, 328)

fused to start the second—*i.e.*, he was already satiated with it—then the two tasks are highly dependent in the sense that the satiation with one of them has the effect of producing satiation with the other also.

Kounin's hypothesis is that the older the child, the more these activities are independent of each other. In order to vary only the chronological age of the subject, he compared three groups who all had the same mental age, about seven years. One group consisted of normal seven-year-old children; the

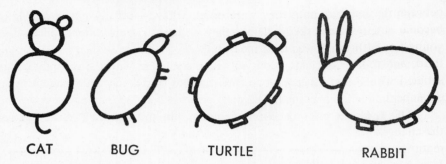

CAT   BUG   TURTLE   RABBIT

Fig. 4.5 Drawings used in the study of satiation. (After J. S. Kounin, *Character and Personality*, 9, 1941, 251-272)

second consisted of feeble-minded adolescents with a mental age of seven; the third consisted of middle-aged feeble-minded patients, again with a mental age of seven. Thus the mental age was kept constant while the chronological age was allowed to vary. The results confirmed Kounin's hypothesis (see Fig. 4.6). The middle-aged feeble-minded patients showed hardly any difference

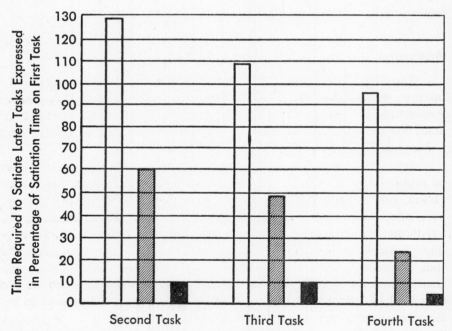

Fig. 4.6 The effect of satiation with one task on satiation with later tasks at various maturity levels. (After J. S. Kounin, *Character and Personality*, 9, 1941, 251-272)

between the satiation times of the different tasks; in fact, they took longer to become satiated with the second task than with the first. In contrast, the youngsters of normal intelligence, aged seven, were satiated with the second, third, and fourth tasks in about one tenth the time it took them to become satiated with the first task. In other words, the tasks were, for them, highly dependent.

This is almost the only experiment that attempts to distinguish between the changes due merely to increasing age and those due to increasing mental maturity. In normal childhood both growth processes occur simultaneously. It may be that some of the criteria that have in our discussion been connected with maturity are actually connected with age. Without more evidence, it is not possible to do more than raise this interesting distinction between age and maturity.

In this section, the first of those dealing with the characteristics of behavior patterns, the term *independence* has described the relationship that may exist between different parts of the same pattern. Dependence leads to inflexibility because one aspect is rigidly determined by another. Independence, on the other hand, allows the combining of a repertoire of actions in many different patterns, thus permitting flexibility.

Articulation

The third criterion of differentiation is articulation. Its opposite, diffuseness, is characteristic of immaturity and the lack of differentiation. Articulation is more difficult to conceptualize than either discrimination or independence. It can be best explained by illustrations; then we shall attempt a more formal definition of it.

Since articulation is a word commonly used in describing speech it may be illustrated in the sounds uttered by infants. The first sounds are vowels (Irwin, 1941). Vowels are produced by air passing over the vocal cords and proceeding unimpeded through the mouth and nose. The contours of the mouth and throat and the position of the tongue determine which vowel is thus produced. If these factors are gradually changed, the vowel sound can slide smoothly from one to another—e.g., *a-a-a-a-e-e-e-e-o-o-o-o*. If this transition occurs rapidly, the sound produced is a diphthong. The sound of long *i,* for example, is the diphthong *ah-ee*. A consonant is produced by interrupting or sharply impeding the flow of air, as in *mama* or in the *f* sound. These sounds demand more articulation and occur in infant speech later than the simple vowels.

Articulation can be seen, therefore, as the breaking of a sequence or pattern of action into sharply distinct units. Trying to talk with a mouth full of oat-meal results in diffuse rather than articulated speech. The sounds do not have sharp beginnings and ends, and one sound is not made distinct from another. The early infant speech is diffuse in this same way; sounds slide from one to another to produce patterns that are almost indescribable and unreproducible. When the child is about six months old, he can speak some syllables. This requires more articulation. In his babbling, which becomes very marked in the latter part of the first year, he combines two syllables in sequence. At first these combinations are repetitive, such as "ma-ma-ma-ma-ma" or "ba-ba-ba-ba-ba." Later, when he combines different sounds into a pattern, still more articulation is present. The ability to combine different sounds at will to match a model involves not only articulation but also independence of one sound from its predecessor.

Articulation may thus be seen to involve the establishment of sharp and distinct boundaries between different parts of a pattern. That is the reason that, in singing, a slide from one note to another is less articulated than a sharp change of pitch.

The infant shows diffuseness in areas of behavior to which the terms *diffuse* and *articulated* are not usually applied. The newborn does not, for example, drop off to sleep and wake up with any distinctness (Gesell, 1954). He moves gradually from being awake to being asleep and to being awake again. One of the accomplishments of the first year is to move suddenly from being asleep to being awake.

Another example of the shift from diffusion to articulation appears in laboratory studies of *apparent movement*. In the usual apparent-movement experiment, two lights separated by a space are presented in fairly rapid alternation. Instead of appearing as two alternating lights, they will, under these conditions, appear as a single light moving back and forth from one position to the other. Some of the warning signals at railway crossings operate in this way; the two lights flash alternately and at the proper distance give the impression of a swinging light like the old-fashioned wig-wag signal. This perception of two lights as a single moving one is a diffuse perception: the sharp boundary separating the two lights from each other is blurred under the effect of rapid alternation. Research has shown that children perceive move-ment at a slower rate of alternation than do adults (Meili and Tobler, 1931). In other words, the children are less able than adults to articulate their per-ception under these conditions of rapid alternation, presumably because their perception is more diffuse.

Just what is meant by diffuse perception? This is a central problem in understanding young children and is one that we have hardly begun to solve. We should like to know how the world looks to the young child, but we can say much more about what the child is unable to perceive than we can about what he does perceive.

The difficulty is pointed up by the fact that the child, generally speaking, shows less discrimination and less detailed perception than adults. But we find that occasionally the child responds to differences that most adults miss. It is not uncommon for a child to remember details, such as the color of a person's dress or some detail of an experience, that adults did not remember. Nevertheless, on the whole the child has a less adequate memory than adults. What

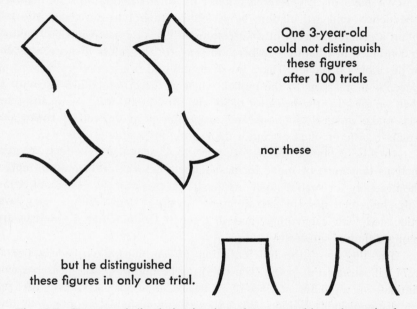

One 3-year-old could not distinguish these figures after 100 trials

nor these

but he distinguished these figures in only one trial.

Fig. 4.7   Perceptual discrimination in a three-year-old, as determined by Crudden's experiment. (After H. Werner, *Comparative Psychology of Mental Development*)

we do not know is just what sort of things stand out and are easily perceived by the child and what sort of things are more difficult for him. This is well illustrated in an experiment by Crudden. A three-year-old boy was trained in distinguishing between a pair of forms. Three such pairs are shown in Figure 4.7. The child was unable to distinguish between the figures in either of the first two pairs after 100 trials, but the third pair was differentiated after the first trial. In all three cases the same forms are involved; only the orientation is changed. A reasonable interpretation would seem to be that the global character of the figures was largely determined by the top part, so that the presence of the notch in the one figure was differentiated only in the third case. This hypothesis should, of course, be subjected to further tests. All such examples point to the need for more experimentation to formulate a general theory of diffuse perception.

Differentiation

We have discussed three criteria of differentiation: discrimination, independence, and articulation. Now, let us attempt to put them together to obtain a general concept of differentiation. The discussion in this section will be continued in Chapter 6, where we shall try to present a theoretical model for describing behavior. There we shall find that it is necessary to have more concepts, more parts to the model, when we describe mature behavior than when we describe the behavior of infants. In other words, we must, as scientists, make more distinctions and articulate more theoretical constructs to explain a differentiated organism than an undifferentiated one.

In this section, therefore, we shall look at a few examples of the distinctions that must be made for an adequate description of mature behavior. The necessity for such distinctions lies in the fact that the criteria of differentiation are met, namely that different aspects of behavior are independent, articulated with each other, and that the individual makes discriminations among different situations.

The theory of the differentiation of emotions described earlier (see p. 71) illustrates this point. The child, as he matures, becomes able to discriminate among different kinds of emotional situations and to respond to each in a distinguishable fashion. What these distinguishable emotional states are called, and what relation they have with one another, are matters of psychological theory. The discussion of differentiation will, therefore, consist of a description of some of the distinctions that the scientist must make in his theory about child behavior. In so far as the necessary distinctions become more numerous as the child becomes more mature, the hypothesis that differentiation increases with increased maturity is justified. In order to prove that these distinctions are necessary, we must show that the maturing child makes more discriminations and responds differently to situations which were once equivalent to him. We must show that different acts become more independent of one another, that they can be combined into various patterns, and that his behavior shows sharper boundaries or differentiation among its different aspects. In other words, the three criteria of differentiation demonstrate the necessity for distinguishing between one psychological characteristic and another.

The Distinguishability of Sense Modalities

In addition to the differentiation of emotions, there is evidence that the senses—vision, hearing, and the rest—are, in the young child, much less distinguishable from one another than in adults. One phenomenon that has been found in some adults—*synaesthesia*—has been shown to be much more common in children (Révész, 1922). The commonest type of synaesthesia is colored hearing, a state in which the individual experiences color when he is stimulated with a sound. He hears the sound, but he experiences a color sensation as well. Snyaesthesia may exist between any two modalities, not necessarily only between vision and hearing. The usual reports on synaesthesia come not from children but from older people, who are able to describe their experience more accurately than a child. One blind boy, for example, reported that when he heard a tone from a piano he experienced a brilliant white if the tone was high, a bluish gray from a medium-pitched tone, and a dark gray from a low tone. The tone from a cornet seemed to be a very bright golden yellow color. His responses remained essentially constant when retested more than two years later (Wheeler and Cutsforth, 1931).

This striking sort of failure to discriminate between tones and colors is not common; it is much easier to demonstrate that the perception of a color is influenced by sounds that occur simultaneously, and that perception of sounds may be influenced by vision. Several people assert that they hear better over the telephone when they are wearing their glasses. Some of them even interrupt the person at the other end of the line to say, "Wait until I put my glasses on." One little boy of six began telling something to his mother who was lying on the couch resting. He stopped and said, "Now, open up your eyes or you won't hear what I'm saying."

These examples would carry little weight if there were not experimental evidence indicating that such statements are not mere imagination. Zietz (1931), for example, showed that colors that were exposed for a very short time (1/100 second) were influenced by the pitch of a sound occurring simultaneously. A red stimulus, for example, was perceived as bluer when accompanied by a low pitch but more orange when accompanied by a high pitch. These experiments were carried out on adults to show that even with maturity there is still some interaction and dependence of vision and hearing.

DISTINGUISHABILITY OF COGNITION, MOTIVATION AND ACTION   In our most intellectual activity we feel a clear separation between our looking at the external situation, judging and appraising its properties, and anticipating the consequences of various lines of action, and then (here is where the separation comes) deciding what action to take. We obtain a clear picture of the objective situation, anticipating the future as much as possible. This picture of the situation, including our judgments about aspects of the world that are not immediately perceptible, is called a *cognitive map*, and the act of formulating that map is the process of *cognition*. (The word is derived from the Latin and means *knowing*.) We act upon the basis of our cognitive map, our knowledge of the situation. The acting is separated from the cognition by a voluntary choice.

In some kinds of behavior, there is no such separation. If, for example, a doctor taps the knee tendon, the leg jerks. Here the process leading from stimulus to response is undifferentiated. There is no act of appraising the tap, then deciding to jerk the leg; the entire process is involuntary. One hypothesis, which we shall employ again in subsequent pages, is that the early behavior of the child is undifferentiated, roughly analogous to the knee jerk, but that maturity brings the gradual development of a distinction between the perceiving, judging, anticipating process—*i.e.*, cognition—and the action. When the action is thus differentiated from cognition, the action itself will be said to be voluntary and cognitively guided.

We cannot yet thoroughly explore this concept, but it is possible to present some examples showing how the young child seems to discover the properties of the external world only through acting toward them. Werner (1940) describes objects at this stage as "things of action." Shinn (1909), who observed very carefully the development of her niece, reports the following incident.

> She was very fond of drawing our hair through her fingers; and on the 181st day, getting a chance to try her uncle's, which was visibly unpullable, scolded with comical disappointment at finding the close shorn ends could not be seized. This happened again on the 185th day. On the same day she was given a round cracker for the first time. She turned it about carefully, as she was accustomed to do with a square one, seeking the corner to bite.

The baby apparently found the corner of a square cracker a particularly good spot to chew; perhaps it helped her try out her teeth. When she was given a round cracker she did not visually perceive that it had no corner; instead, searched with her mouth for it. In other words, the square cracker was not visually perceived as having a corner, but in chewing on it the child enjoyed the tactual contact with the corner. The round cracker was apparently equivalent to the square one in so far as visual properties were concerned; its difference was perceived only by the child's being unable to behave toward it in the familiar way. Whatever the child's perception of the cracker was, the cracker is better described as "chewable" than as "square" or "round."

Not all adult behavior is marked by a differentiation between cognition and action. The feelings aroused in us by tragic or depressing or comic situations are states that do not display the full separation of cognition and action. We do not decide to feel sad; instead, sadness captures us. At the same time, sadness is not like a perception—it is a feeling we experience rather than a property that we perceive in the world. In children, this differentiation is less complete; feelings and perceptions blend together more than they do in adults. Thus, one two-year-old cried out, "Poor zwieback" when his biscuit was broken in two. Another spoke of a cup lying on its side as "Poor tired cup." A third child said that a fog was "like whispering." In these cases perception is not a detached activity conveying information from the objective situation but partakes to some extent of the quality of feeling and emotion. Werner (1940) calls this *physiognomic perception*.

Adults may also experience physiognomic perception. We speak of a threatening cloud or an angry sky, and, in the presence of an overwhelming force, we may experience to some extent the feeling of being weak and threatened. At times, of course, such a feeling of being threatened is quite realistic and is an appreciation of the fact that the oncoming storm may actually put us in danger. But even in the safety of our home we may still call the sky angry and threatening. Adults may also use such words to convey to the listener or arouse in the reader the feeling that they are experiencing. Thus, the person trying to convey his feeling of joyful anticipation while he opens a present may describe how the knots of gay ribbon "tease" as they "stubbornly cling" to the package. This deliberate use of metaphor may reflect either a genuine physiognomic perception or the conscious selection of words in order to create an effect.

Summary

This chapter has described and illustrated the various aspects of differentiation. Differentiation is a theoretical concept describing some of the changes that occur as the child matures. It may be defined in terms of three criteria: (1) the increased ability of the child to discriminate among various situations as he matures; (2) the independent functioning of different aspects of a behavior pattern; and (3) the appearance of articulation, sharp changes in behavior, and distinct boundary lines.

These criteria justify the psychologist's making distinctions among different concepts and building a complicated model to describe behavior. The increase in the complexity of behavior is described by the general term *differentiation*.

5

Maturity: Emotional Stability

DAN WAS A SHY, RETIRING SOPHOMORE. He had never been very much interested in girls, but early in his sophomore year he noticed a girl on campus with whom he was quite taken. She was pleasant and friendly, with a face that liked to smile, and, since she was generally alone or with other girls, Dan's competition didn't seem too severe. He began to muster his courage to ask her for a date, but he had great difficulty. Once, when they both got to class early, he almost made it; but just as he was about to speak, someone else came in. Since he could not talk to her right out in public, the golden opportunity was lost. Dan's roommate tried to encourage him. "Go ahead and talk to her; she won't bite you." But Dan could not quite do it, even near the end of the first semester. One day he and his roommate were walking along the campus talking about her when Dan saw her coming toward them—with a boy! "Well," he said, "I'm glad I didn't ask her for a date if she's that fickle."

Dan was a college sophomore, clearly able to think logically and to respond to remote goals—that is, he was in many ways mature. Yet, with regard to this girl and under the stress of these circumstances, he responded in a way that was clearly immature. He was somehow assuming that by merely thinking about the girl, he had put her under obligation to him. The immaturity of his behavior is indicated by the fact that some nine- or ten-year-old children can, if told this story, see what is absurd about his comment.

Many people, like Dan, are capable of mature behavior but do not always behave maturely. In this chapter we shall discuss the factors that prevent a person from operating on his maximum level of maturity. Furthermore, we shall see that the ability to maintain one's level of maturity in the face of frustration and stress is itself a characteristic that increases with maturity.

Stress and the Level of Maturity

People do foolish things when they are under severe stress, *i.e.*, when frustrated, in danger, or in almost any highly emotional state. The unfortunate golfer who became so angry at hooking four successive balls into the lake that he threw the clubs in after them does not habitually attribute motives to inanimate objects. One of the factors making it possible for him to perceive a diabolical purpose in his golf club's actions is the emotional state induced by seeing his score mount, his expensive golf balls disappear into the lake, and his ineptness publicly displayed.

Children are usually upset even more easily than adults. Isaacs (1930) reports an incident about Conrad, one of the six-year-olds in a private school. Conrad broke the glass in which he kept his toothbrush by accidentally striking it against the faucet in the lavatory. He immediately said to Miss D. (one of the assistant teachers), "It doesn't matter—it's mine." Then, however, he burst into tears and said, "It's your fault, you made me break it, you horrid thing," despite the fact that Miss D. was nowhere near the scene of the accident. In ordinary circumstances he would not have been so immature as to attribute responsibility for the mishap to someone who had no connection with it and had not even witnessed it.

Frustration and Regression

The effect upon maturity of the kind of stress resulting from frustration has been experimentally demonstrated by Barker, Dembo, and Lewin (1941). The subjects of this experiment were nursery-school children in a play situation. Each subject was first introduced to a room in which a number of toys were available. For a half-hour period, the child was allowed to play with the toys. His play was rated by observers on a constructiveness scale, constructive play being generally defined as having an organized structure showing behavior toward long-term goals—*e.g.,* building tracks in order to play with a train that would carry blocks from one point to another.

After the child had played with the toys for the half hour, a curtain that had heretofore formed one wall of the playroom was raised, revealing behind it a much more attractive set of toys, including more elaborate versions of the same sort of toys. Instead of a toy fishing rod, for example, there was a fishing rod and a pool of real water to fish in. Such additions kept the play roughly comparable, although the toys were more attractive. The child was allowed to play in this paradise for a period of time; then he was taken back to the original playroom and a screen made of wire netting was lowered in place of the original opaque curtain. This screen provided an excellent view of the tantalizing inaccessible toys. Furthermore, it was equipped with a door forbiddingly padlocked, which served to increase the frustration by attracting the child's attention to a possible route through the blocked barrier. All in all, the arrangement was well designed to produce frustration, and it succeeded admirably.

The object of the experiment was to see whether this stress reduced the constructiveness of the play with the toys with which the child had played before being introduced to the more attractive ones behind the screen. One difficulty with measuring the constructiveness of play was that the child, when he was returned to the original set of toys, did not play much at first, but instead spent his time trying to get behind the screen, trying to get through the door, and pleading with the experimenters to unlock the door. Even when the child played with the toys, he frequently did so with one eye on the screen, so to speak. But enough time was spent in apparently concentrated play for the constructiveness to be measured, and it proved to be lower. Twenty-one out of twenty-eight children showed a drop in constructiveness. In other words, the child under the stress of frustration played at a lower level of maturity than he did before the stress.

The data resulting from this experiment are quite clear, but their interpretation is less so. What we do not know is just what it is about the stress situation that made the child's play less constructive. One hypothesis suggested by the experimenters is that the frustration made the child less differentiated, so that he was unable to play as far into the future or to conceive of plans elaborate enough to obtain a high score on constructiveness. It is probably true that frustration can be so intense as to lower the child's capacity for planned action, but this experiment cannot prove this point. The experiment investigated the constructiveness of activity that was irrelevant to the frustrated motive—*i.e.,* activity that could not help the child to get back to the toys behind the barrier. To be constructive in this situation, the child had to have not only a capability for constructive activity but also an ability to seal himself off from the frustration situation and to prevent the frustration of his motivation from interfering with his play behavior.

Child and Waterhouse (1953) have suggested that this experiment measures the effect of interference more than it does the effect of frustration. Their hypothesis is supported by the fact that some children who were not constructive in free play were, nevertheless, extremely ingenious in trying to reach the better toys. One of them, for example, fished in the fishpond by poking his pole through the wire screen.

This second interpretation seems reasonable. The lowered constructiveness of the child's play depends partly upon the fact that he was not entirely involved in his free play. Even when he was apparently absorbed in his free play and was paying no attention to the better toys behind the screen, the impulses and ideas connected with the goal behind the barrier still interfered with his play. He could not really lose himself in his play activity. This may well be one way in which frustration reduces the maturity of behavior, particularly the maturity of behavior that is not directed toward solving the frustrating problem. It also seems likely that the emotional state of the child made him more vulnerable to these distracting and interfering stimuli. The child who is not frustrated is able to ignore many distractions. We cannot, then, be sure just how frustration results in a lowered maturity; probably it has several different effects. The essential finding, however, that frustration tends to reduce the level of maturity of behavior is valid.

Stimulation and Regression

It is not only frustration that produces regression to less mature modes of activity. Leitch and Escalona (1949) have shown that in infants less than one year old stimulation—or, it might be better to say, overstimulation—can produce regression. They have produced overstimulation merely by presenting an infant with one toy after another, keeping him active and interested. Eventually he begins to show signs of less mature behavior. He is not tired in the usual sense; he is not cranky and cross. He is alert, interested, and having a wonderful time, but he is, nevertheless, overstimulated. If he ordinarily reaches for a dangling ring with one hand, in a fairly well-controlled fashion, he may regress to reaching with both hands symmetrically. When he is trying to execute a motion, he may show uncontrolled movement.

The possibility of producing regression in older children by this sort of overstimulation has not been demonstrated experimentally, but everyday experience with children strongly suggests the same phenomenon. Anyone who has had to supervise a birthday party for nursery-school children has seen excitement mount. All the children are very pleased and happy; the situation could by no stretch of the imagination be called frustrating. Nevertheless, the party moves gradually to a higher pitch until children are running through the house at breakneck speed. The loudness of the voices is deafening. Curiously enough, children are much more easily upset when they are excited even though the excitement is of this happy variety. A hurt that might otherwise be taken stoically can produce streams of tears at a birthday party. Tantrums are not uncommon when the parent tries to extricate his child from the group to take him home. We tend to think that the child is having such a good time that he hates to leave and that this is why he makes such a fuss about going home. It may not be that the party is so attractive but rather that the child is over-stimulated. Through overstimulation he may lose his perspective. What he wants he wants intensely, not because it is so pleasant but because his perception is so narrowly focused that he cannot see the attraction of other activities.

The Concept of Tension

The concept that we shall use to describe the general characteristic common to all kinds of emotionality is *tension*. The children at the birthday party are made tense by the succession of exciting stimuli to which they are exposed. The frustrated person is made tense by being unable to reach a goal he wants. Generally speaking, the longer he is so exposed, the more tense he becomes.

Since the concept of tension is an important one and will be used in subsequent discussion, let us clarify its meaning fully. It is appropriate to say that a state of tension exists in a person whenever in everyday language we could call him tense. We have all experienced symptoms of a state of high tension: being keyed up, being too sensitive to noise and distraction, being too restless to sit still. The child laboriously trying to write shows symptoms of tension. The person carefully placing the fifth or sixth story on a house of cards is tense. The superstitious child whistling as he walks by the graveyard is also tense. Tension exists in many different circumstances and may be a facet of many different emotions.

Tension is a condition produced by any sort of stimulation that requires adjustment. An even, monotonous level of stimulation may exist as a background and apparently produce no tension at all; if anything, such stimuli are relaxing and sleep-producing. Intense, attention-capturing, changing, or unfamiliar stimuli, however, are exciting and tension-producing. Certain sorts of situations are especially powerful in arousing tension. Frustration raises the level of tension; so do situations that require care and effort. Situations that intrude or impose some pressure on us or those that challenge our abilities produce a state of tension.

Effects of Tension in Infants

What are the consequences of tension? Some are general; others depend upon the degree of tension; still others depend upon the specific context in which the tension occurs. We can obtain a clear preliminary picture of the effects of tension from an analysis of the behavior of the newborn infant. The baby who is asleep is at a low level of tension; he is relaxed, unresponsive, and quiet. His low sensitivity is demonstrated by the fact that his reflex responses are less easily evoked than when he is awake (Wagner, 1937).

When the infant is awake, he is more tense—*i.e.,* more sensitive to stimulation and more active. His alertness may however be nonselective or focused. Similarly the alert infant's behavior may be focused in a response to a specific stimulus, or it may be merely restlessness.

Looking first at focused behavior we find it particularly evident during nursing. Nursing behavior is elicited by a special sort of stimulation of the infant's lips and mouth; his sensitivity to this stimulation is high, but at the same time he is markedly less sensitive to other kinds of stimulation. During nursing, his threshold to pain rises; his other reflexes become less active (Wolowik, 1927). In short, other stimulation may have no effect. On the other hand, other stimulation may, when he is focused upon nursing, increase the intensity of sucking instead of evoking its customary response. Mothers utilize this fact when they stimulate the baby by nudging him or pinching him to keep him sucking. The same experiment has been performed under controlled conditions (Jensen, 1932). When the infant has the nipple in his mouth but is not sucking on it, a pinch on the leg may evoke sucking, or if he is sucking lazily, it may evoke more intense sucking activity (see Fig. 5.1).

In other words, the individual can be focused upon some stimulation so that he is either unresponsive to irrelevant stimuli or responds to them with intensification of the directed activity. It is, of course, possible for such extraneous stimuli to become strong enough to break up the behavior pattern and evoke a different one. If the baby has the colic or a pin is sticking him, the pain may be intense enough for him to feel it while nursing, despite his

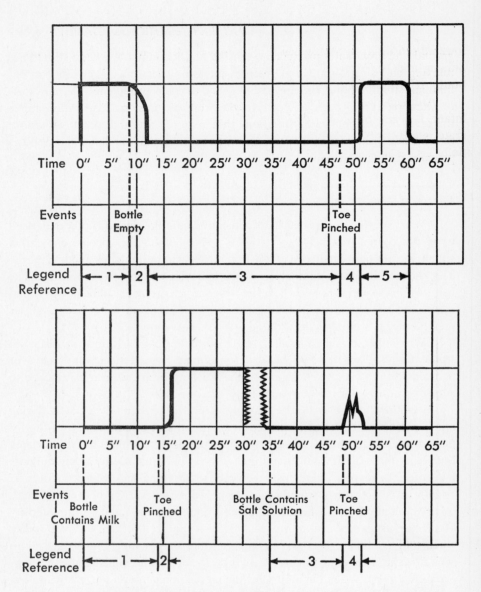

Fig. 5.1 The effect of stimulation on sucking activity. The upper graph shows that (1) sucking on milk at 40° C. continued until the bottle was empty; (2) the infant quickly discriminated air from milk and refused to suck; (3) after the infant had refused for 35 seconds to suck on air, its toe was pinched; (4) in four seconds the infant began to suck; and (5) the infant continued to suck for nine seconds. The lower graph shows that (1) after the infant had refused for 14 seconds to suck, its toe was pinched; (2) two seconds later, the infant began to suck; (3) after the infant refused to suck the salt solution for 14 seconds, its toe was pinched; and (4) immediately after the infant's toe was pinched, slight mouth movements occurred. (After K. Jensen, *Genet. Psychol. Monogr., 12,* 1932, 454)

lowered sensitivity to such stimuli. If he does feel it, he will in most cases stop nursing and begin to cry. At this point he is unresponsive to the breast or bottle. If it is poked at his mouth, he turns his head away from it.

Although sucking is the clearest example of focused behavior in the infant, it is not the only one. When stimulated by a prolonged sound of moderate intensity, the infant may become quiet and "listen." Under these conditions his responsiveness to irrelevant stimulation is reduced (Weiss, 1934).

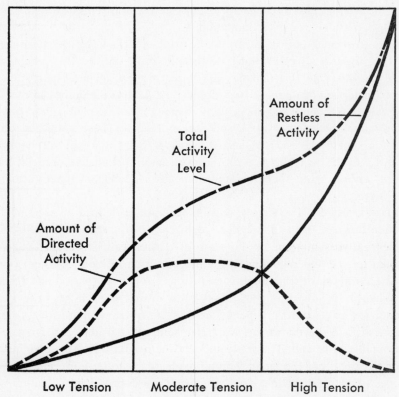

| Low Tension | Moderate Tension | High Tension |

Fig. 5.2   The effects of tension on the behavior of young infants.

This phenomenon of focused sensitivity to an external stimulus occurring with a directed response seems to be most characteristic of mild states of tension. With further increase in tension, the sensitivity to stimulation increases, but the response loses its differentiated character. Instead of a directed response, the baby shows an undirected restlessness, crying, and general mass activity.

These relationships can be schematically represented by the graph in Figure 5.2. The main points to note are that: first, activity increases with tension; secondly, sensitivity to stimulation increases with tension; and thirdly, focused activity is characteristic of the middle ranges of tension. Below the middle range, there is too little responsiveness to be focused; above it, the responsiveness is high but generalized.

Effects of Tension in Adults

Many of the symptoms of tension in the young infant have their counterpart in the feelings and the behavior of the adult who is tense through frustration, disappointment, or overstimulation.

The frustrated person seems to be well described by the term *tense*. Indeed, he describes himself thus. He feels he must do something; he cannot tolerate passivity; he is afraid he will "blow his top." These symptoms are most characteristic of a severe frustration. Less serious difficulties in reaching one's goal are frequently experienced as challenging in an exciting sort of way. The individual feels active, alert, and well mobilized. These symptoms correspond roughly to the focused and directed activity in infant behavior and represent a lower degree of tension. Stimulation and challenge occur at lower levels of tension, emotional disequilibrium and a feeling of inner turmoil at higher levels.

RESTLESSNESS   The state of tension need not be defined in terms of these subjective feelings, even though the word *tension* in common usage denotes them. Objective symptoms of this state of tension can be observed and are important for the understanding of the process of frustration.

One symptom of frustration is an increase in muscle tension and restlessness. When it spreads through the body, this muscle tension has been shown to reduce the effectiveness of behavior. A more overt symptom of tension is restlessness. The person who is frustrated tends to be fidgety and nervously active, unable to sit still. The restlessness of the person trying to solve a problem, or the pacing of the father waiting for his baby to be born, are everyday examples of restlessness in a frustrating or tension-producing situation.

Lewin (1935) has studied the restlessness of a child who is separated from some desired object by a circular fence. The object is in the center of the circle; the fence is continuous around it. The child tries to get through and over the fence, searching for an opening, but after finding none he begins to show restless activity. It is significant that his restlessness does not move him away from the goal. The fence prevents his going closer to it, and his motivation prevents his going away from it. Consequently, the only direction that the activity can take is one that keeps the goal the same distance away all the time. The child begins to circle the fence, no longer looking for an opening but merely moving. His pace increases until finally he is going at a dead run in a circle just outside of the fence.

IMPULSIVENESS A second symptom of tension is somewhat different from these directionless symptoms of restlessness. The individual who is tense is impulsive. After a severe disappointment, children may show that they are upset by weeping. In ordinary circumstances a person can have reasonable control over his tears, but under tension they come easily. People who are normally quite reticent may, under the pressure of frustration, reveal their innermost feelings to some sympathetic listener. After the tension has passed, they may again feel reticent and be quite ashamed of having exposed themselves while they were "not themselves."

One type of impulsiveness, irritability, is especially marked when the tension is due to frustration. An irritable person is hostile and easily provoked to anger. Irritability is so marked during frustration that it is necessary to hypothesize that frustration specifically leads to hostility. In frustration, the increase in sensitivity to irritating situations and in readiness to be hostile is greater than can be accounted for merely by impulsiveness.

The hostility may, of course, be directed against the frustration. If a child's mother tells him he must practice his music instead of playing hop-scotch, the hostility may be directed toward his mother—unless he feels that it is unsafe to be hostile toward his mother. When a frustration is seen as a deliberate action intended to be hostile, the evoked hostility is not so much an expression of irritability as of the motive to retaliate. But in addition to such "sensible" hostility, the frustrated individual frequently shows an irrational sort of irritability. He may become very angry at people whose only crime is to invite hostility or to be mildly provoking.

The following anecdote, though somewhat extreme, illustrates the point. It concerns the unfortunate predicament of a college student who had to get up for an eight-o'clock class. He didn't like to get up early, but it was a required course. One morning everything went wrong. He broke a shoelace and couldn't find a new one. His hot plate didn't work, and so he had to shave and dress without even the consolation of hot coffee. He hoped to take time for a cup of coffee at the corner restaurant before his bus came, but as he rounded the corner the bus was just pulling up to the bus stop. Away he dashed down the street, yelling to attract the driver's attention, but the driver pulled away, leaving him stranded. It was too much. A man happened to be standing near by, leaning over to tie his shoelaces. The sight of him in such a posture was too tempting. Our frustrated student ran over and kicked him in the appropriate spot, justifying himself by shouting, "You're *always* tying your shoelaces!"

This increased implusiveness and irritability is more frequently displayed in the overt behavior of frustrated children than in that of adults, because adults are better able to exert self-control. When the adult finds self-control difficult, he may overdo it by inhibiting all expressiveness and acting with great care. It is not uncommon to see frustrated, anxious people become "deadpan" in their effort to keep themselves under control. This is similar to the phenomenon of the intoxicated person who does things very deliberately and carefully because he feels slightly befuddled. After he has imbibed still more liquor, he may give up any attempt at control and his behavior may become suddenly and markedly uninhibited. Similarly, in severe frustration, the self-control may be finally broken by some minor incident that causes the frustrated person suddenly to show completely uncontrolled impulsive behavior. He "blows his top."

INCREASED SENSITIVITY TO STIMULATION The impulsiveness of the person under tension is one aspect of the general increase in sensitivity to stimuli that accompanies an increase in the level of tension. Children, when they are excited, are much more distractible than when they are placid. They are much more susceptible to contagious behavior, much more likely to imitate unthinkingly. Not only does their behavior show their sensitivity to stimuli but the sensitivity makes for a further increase in tension. Stimulation produces tension; tension makes the child more susceptible to stimulation; this susceptibility makes the tension increase still further; this in turns leads to still greater sensitivity. Thus, the increase in tension is a self-feeding process that tends to grow more and more rapidly until it gets out of control.

Frustration shows this effect. The tension produced by frustration tends to increase spontaneously as long as the individual is frustrated. Unless he can exert strong control over his reactions, the mounting tension can lead to a highly emotional state. If anger is the most marked feeling of the frustrated person, the end state can be a tantrum in which the person angrily smashes things, rips up what he is trying to do, and gives in to his feelings completely. If fear is the most marked characteristic of the frustration, the end state can be panic. Ordinarily the person does not reach panic because he runs away from the danger, but if his pride, or social rules, or external constraints force him to face the danger, then he may eventually go into panic.

To be in an emotional state is itself a source of unpleasantness and possibly fear. It can be fearsome because the individual is afraid of losing control over himself; he may not know to what lengths his emotional behavior will lead, and in addition he may feel that it is improper to display emotions. Boys especially are taught to feel that they are sissies to cry or to show fright. All of this fear about self-control adds to the tension and increases the emotional pressure.

In so far as the behavior in these states of high tension is focused, the individual becomes extremely sensitive to those stimuli that are relevant and quite insensitive to others. Thus there is a narrowing of the perception to exclude stimuli that are not immediately relevant. The child who is very angry and very near to a tantrum may get even angrier if he is subjected to additional frustration, but he is insensitive to other kinds of stimuli. Such a state is immature in the sense that the child's psychological world has contracted to include only a few objects. When the end state is actually reached, the individual apparently becomes insensitive to almost all stimuli. We have seen this in a child's tantrum; but it is equally obvious in the panic of a crowd trying to get out through the door of a burning building, or in that of the drowning man who clings so tightly to his rescuer that he drowns them both. If any irrelevant stimulus is to reach the man in a panic, it must be strong. The person in other emotional end states is equally difficult to reach; a sharp slap may be required to stop an attack of hysterics. The behavior in one of these end states seems to involve only the most primitive expression of the feeling that completely overwhelms the victim's consciousness. The child in a tantrum kicks away all restraints; the drowning man clings to any object. Even in the end state the behavior reflects the quality of the emotion, but it is displayed in a very immature impulsive fashion in that recognizable state.

Tantrums

One of these overwhelming emotional end states is a tantrum. Since tantrums are not uncommon in childhood and especially since they are not always genuine, we shall digress slightly from our main theme to discuss them specifically.

A tantrum is a state of violent excitement and tension arising from anger and frustration. Such tantrums are quite common in infancy; in fact, most of the expressions of anger in children less than one year old are explosive, undirected tantrums. As the child grows older, he becomes able to feel hostility toward people and objects that frustrate him and he may express such hostility by trying to hurt the person at whom he is angry—that is, his hostility becomes focused and directed (see p. 157). He may still, however, have a tantrum occasionally. If he is sufficiently frustrated in enough ways and is quite powerless, he may finally brust into tears, lose all control, bang doors, throw things, lie in the middle of the floor kicking and screaming, and be completely impervious to all attempts to soothe him. If he is in a genuine tantrum, he will not even respond to the words that tell him that he can have his own way. He is truly incommunicado.

When such a tantrum occurs, the best procedure is to leave the child alone, isolate him, and let him recover from the attack. There is no point in trying to reason with him or explaining why he cannot do what he wants, or threatening him with dire punishment if he does not stop screaming. It is probably better not to touch him, because any restraint merely adds fuel to the flames.

There is no question that such tantrums can occur and can be genuine. There is, however, another sort of tantrum that is almost a voluntary action, relatively superficial and designed to coerce the parent into complying with the child's wishes. The emotionality in such a case is an exhibition of childhood histrionics. These deliberate tantrums are marked by a very fast recovery when the child sees that a tantrum will not work or when the parent gives in. The unbiased observer can see the child watching out of the corner of his eye to observe the effects of his tantrum.

Between these two extremes are tantrums of almost every possible degree of genuineness. One variety that is fairly genuine occurs merely because the child does not try as hard as he can to control himself. He is genuinely tense; he might, however, by strenuous effort early in the build-up of tension, prevent the tantrum and keep himself under control. Whether or not he does so depends upon the motivation for him to keep control. Such tantrums are genuine but preventable; the child's unwillingness to prevent them is the only voluntary aspect of them. More like the simulated tantrum are those that have some sincerity but are exaggerated at every point. The child is sufficiently aware of what is going on around him to get perverse pleasure out of being excessively miserable.

The wise policy in dealing with children who have tantrums must depend upon how much the tantrums are tools by which the child controls his associates and how much they represent real inability to maintain emotional control. In the latter case the symptom is probably more serious in its implications if the child is at an age at which most children can maintain adequate control.

Maturity as the Maximal Level of Behavior

The discussion thus far has shown how stimulation, tension, and frustration may reduce the maturity level of an individual's behavior. The adult under tension behaves in a less mature way than when he is not under tension. In so far as maturity is concerned, he behaves like a younger person.

We can see that the criteria of maturity discussed in the last few chapters are statements of maximum ability—i.e., the maturity of which the individual is capable of under favorable circumstances. It is not to be expected that the adult will act at his maximum level of maturity every minute of the day.

One of the factors that may prevent the behavior at one moment from being as mature as other samples of behavior of the same individual is, as we have seen, the tension under which the person is operatiing. Another factor is, of course, that the situation in which he is involved at the moment may not require his maximum maturity. An adult asleep is not demonstrating any more maturity than a child asleep; an adult sitting under a shady tree lazily watching his float dance on the ripples while he waits for a fish to bite is not displaying more maturity than a ten-year-old doing the same thing. Situations that are unstimulating do not demand maturity, and situations that are too stimulating prevent maximally mature behavior. There is an optimum amount of stimulation that evokes behavior at a maximal maturity level, and it is this maximal level that usually increases with age.

Resistance to Regressive Effects of Tension

Because of the effects of tension, a person may momentarily be unable to behave as maturely as he would in more favorable circumstances. There are, however, individual differences in the ability to resist the pressure of tension. Some people can operate almost as well under severe tension as they can under favorable conditions; others are seriously hampered by tension. The ability of the individual to keep his maturity of behavior close to his maximum even if the circumstances are overstimulating or frustrating we shall call *emotional stability*. Emotionally stable people make good pinch hitters—they can think on their feet; they can meet emergencies.

We can now examine the final criterion of maturity. Adults, in general, show more emotional stability than do children. As the child grows up, not only does his maximum level of maturity increase but a larger proportion of his everyday behavior displays nearly maximal maturity. The vicissitudes of the child's behavior are truly amazing. He can be completely adult while on a trip in the company of one adult. Upon his return, as soon as he begins to play with his younger siblings, the maturity of his behavior may drop to the level of that of the youngest child present. It is a great relief to parents to discover that their children have the reputation among their adult friends of being well-behaved, cooperative visitors—so mature. The parents who see the child only at home, where he makes little effort to be mature, may listen to such compliments with amazment. They seldom get the benefit of this occasional maturity.

As the child grows older, this discrepancy between his "best behavior" and his everyday, run-of-the-mill behavior gradually disappears. Throughout childhood there is an increase in emotional stability. There is some evidence to indicate that the achievement of emotional stability, in the sense in which we are using the term, is one of the few aspects of maturity still to be attained in adolescence. Most studies of intellectual functioning have found little difference between the early adolescent and the adult. On standard intelligence tests, a mental age of fourteen years is average for adults. After this age the

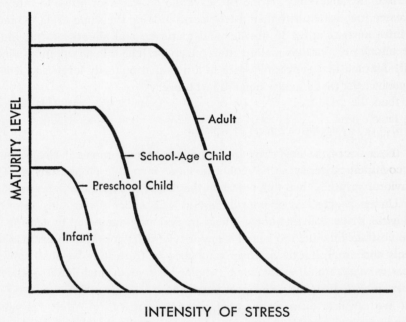

Fig. 5.3   The hypothetical relation between maturity and stress at various age levels.

child gains more information if he lives in an environment that provides it, but more significantly he gains good judgment—*i.e.,* he becomes able to function maturely under conditions of stress.

Figure 5.3 presents this hypothesis concerning the relation of maturity to emotional stability. The vertical dimension measures maturity, and the horizontal dimension indicates day-to-day variability of maturity. With increasing maturity, an increasing proportion of behavior is near the maximum, even though the possible range of maturity continues to reach to the minimum values found in the emotional end states of panic and tantrum.

Summary

With this chapter we complete our analysis of the concept of maturity. Our task has been to describe the differences between child and adult behavior. We have found that the most striking difference lies in competence, adjustability, and adaptability to a wide variety of circumstances. We have discussed the differences between children and adults in order to show the processes that underlie the greater adaptability and adjustment of the adult. We must keep in mind, however, that the processes that make maturity possible also have other results that are not necessarily signs of a good adjustment. The mature organism is vulnerable to pressures to which the child is insensitive; the adult has many goals that make his life richer and more complex than the child's but do not make him any better adjusted; the adult, in fact, lacks some childlike traits that he wishes he might recapture.

The characteristics of maturity can be divided into two main classes: (1) those concerned with the accurate, complete, and objective perception and cognition of the external world, and (2) those that make the organism's behavioral response flexible, adjustable, and adequate.

Under the first of these classes, we find that *the adult has a larger psychological world than the child*. He perceives and cognizes more objects and more abstract relations than does the child, and he can adjust to more remote objects and events. Chapter 3 and part of Chapter 4 are concerned with the processes underlying the large psychological world of the adult. One such process is *objective perception*. The child, in his progress toward objectivity, must first of all recognize that external objects do not appear and disappear depending upon whether or not he is perceiving them. Then he must recognize which object is which when he does see it, and he must know what he can do with it. He must be able to recognize an object even when he sees it in different surroundings. He must be able to recognize a property of an object, such as its size, even though the retinal image is larger when the object is close than when it is far away. The ability to perceive through the immediate stimuli to the objective properties of an object is called *perceptual constancy*. The child must achieve perceptual constancy of physical properties, such as shape and color, and also of personality traits, such as generosity or reliability. Furthermore, his evaluation of future events, which determine his choices and his preferences, must depend upon these stable properties of objects; otherwise he will find that what appeared attractive in prospect may be distasteful when it is actually experienced. This is *value constancy*.

Three conditions hamper objective perception—namely, *egocentrism, bondage to the laws of field organization,* and *lack of discrimination. Egocentrism* is the inability to appreciate how a situation looks from some point of view other than the one the person now has. In its most extreme form, egocentrism prevents even one's own past experiences with an object from being integrated into the present perception. In the less extreme forms, it makes reasoning from suppositional or arbitrary premises, recognition of the arbitrariness of social convention, and appreciation of the point of view of another person difficult or impossible.

The *laws of field organization* describe the conditions that tend to make certain stimuli stand out and be noticed, and also the conditions that tend to put objects in the same psychological unit. The principles of *proximity, similarity,* and *good continuation* lead to the formation of perceptual units that are segregated from the rest of the field. Such *segregation* makes the unit as a whole obtrusive. These laws are very compelling in childhood, but with increased maturity the individual becomes able to disregard them when necessary.

The inability to make fine discriminations has a certain logical connection with the objectivity of perception. The failure to discriminate prevents the individual from responding differently to situations that are sufficiently similar to be apparently identical but are in reality different.

Two concepts, *independence* and *articulation,* describe mature behavior. The adult is capable of thousands of different actions; the child can perform only a small number. It is not the number, however, so much as the organization of these actions into complex behavior patterns that makes possible the complicated coordinations and skillful manipulations of which the adult is capable. In order for the person to behave flexibly, he must be able to combine his repertoire of actions in many different ways. The series of actions that make up a pattern must not be so inextricably linked together that they cannot occur separately or be integrated into a different relationship. This flexibility of behavioral adjustment is achieved because many of the adult's actions are independent of one another and combinable in any desired way.

Futhermore, each component of the behavior pattern must appear in its proper place, and each action must be linked smoothly to the action that should accompany it or follow it. This is described by the term *articulation.*

As we have seen, not all adult actions are independent and readily articulated with each other, just as no adult's perception is completely objective. Independence and articulation are important for flexibility, however, and whenever flexibility of response and adjustment to new behavioral demands is essential, rigidity of behavior is a handicap. When flexibility is unimportant, rigidity is not a serious defect.

Not only must different *actions* be independent, but various *functions* of the organism must be independent and articulated for maximum flexibility and adjustability. Cognition must be independent of action, because adjustment sometimes requires that we make different responses in the same situation. The selection of goals and the instrumental actions that achieve goals must be independent, because the same instrumental act will not achieve the same goal in all situations. Flexibility, independence, and articulation of function are described by the general term *differentiation*. With maturity, behavior becomes more differentiated.

Stimulation or frustration produces a state of *tension,* one of whose consequences is reduction in the level of maturity. The final characteristic of maturity is *emotional stability,* the ability to maintain a high level of maturity in spite of stress and strain. Because of emotional stability the adult functions near his optimal level a much larger proportion of the time than does the child.

Now we shall look at child behavior from a somewhat different point of view. Instead of being primarily concerned with its adequacy or its competance, we shall try to understand it, regardless of whether it is well or poorly adjusted. What we are striving for, of course, is a theory of behavior. If we succeed completely, we shall be able to predict every aspect of a child's behavior whether or not it is relevant to his maturity. We cannot expect to develop a complete theory of child behavior, but we shall find that many aspects of everyday child behavior can be understood and explained.

6

A Model of Human Behavior

GENERAL CHARACTERISTICS OF A MODEL OF
MATURE BEHAVIOR

GOAL SELECTION

COGNITION

GOAL-DIRECTED BEHAVIOR

SUMMARY OF MODEL OF VOLUNTARY BEHAVIOR

WE HAVE THUS FAR DISCUSSED MATURITY and attempted to present a picture of the important differences between children and adults. It may have seemed as though maturity was the only significant characteristic of a person, but this is not true. Maturity describes one set of characteristics of a person, but if we are to understand his behavior we must know much more than his maturity level. We can easily see that to label an action as immature does not provide an explanation for it.

One night a family was having a special dinner, with candles lit to make the occasion more festive. In the course of the meal, the eight-year-old son reached for the butter and brought it back past the lighted candle. Almost automatically the butter dish came to rest directly above the candle flame and remained there for a long instant. Suddenly the boy came to with a start, and looking exceedingly sheepish, hastily withdrew the dish.

Why would an eight-year-old hold a plate of butter over a candle at the dinner table? If we try to understand this behavior in the light of the discussion of maturity, it is quite obvious that such behavior is immature. It is shortsighted; it seemed somehow forced upon the child. He certainly did not stop to think about it; his disgust with himself as soon as he had realized what he had done makes it clear that he had not decided to do it. He literally discovered himself doing something very foolish. The incident illustrates immaturity, but to say that it was immature does not explain why the act was attractive. To account for such impulsive behavior we must consider the problem of motivation. What conditions impel or motivate an individual to act in a certain way?

Let us look at a second example of immature behavior that will illustrate some of the other factors necessary for an understanding of human behavior.

One summer evening, after two families had spent a pleasant day together, their six children, three from each family, wished to spend the night together. Their parents refused because it was not practicable. The matter seemed settled. When time to leave finally came, however, none of the children could be found. After the adults had first searched the neighborhood, then combed a whole section of town, they finally called the police for help. The six children were found at ten o'clock at night at least two miles away from home. What had happened was that the children were determined to spend the night together; they had started to walk to a farm that they had recently visited to sleep in the haystack. The only thing that stopped them seemed to be that the little ones—who were only three—became too tired to walk the whole distance, and the biggest ones—who were only seven and eight—were too tired to carry them.

Here, as in the preceding example, there is no question that the behavior is immature, but recognizing its immaturity is not sufficient. What we need to know is what led the children to behave as they did. Why did they feel so strongly about being separated? What gave the notion of sleeping in a haystack so impelling a quality that they broke well-established rules to try to achieve it?

Our task in this chapter is to present an outline of the factors that are important in the explanation of human behavior. We must see how perception and cognition fit into a theory of human behavior. We must discover the factors that arouse motives and establish the goals in the immediate situation. We must also discover the factors that inhibit some motivation and permit other motives to be realized in overt action. Finally, we must see how the specific behavior that is directed toward a goal is chosen, and how it is guided toward goal attainment.

In the present chapter we shall merely outline these problems and leave the details to be discussed in the remainder of Part I. At the same time, this chapter is a summary of the preceding chapters, because in it we shall examine a model of human behavior that is designed to describe mature behavior— objective, differentiated, and goal-directed. The model will be an idealistic one, in that no actual behavior can fit it precisely. It will represent an extreme of maturity. As we examine it we shall see how immature behavior differs from the behavior described in the model. In this sense, therefore, the chapter is a summary of the section on maturity, because it illustrates the implications of the concept of maturity for the description of human behavior.

General Characteristics of a Model of Mature Behavior

Before examining the model in detail, let us take an over-all view of it (see Fig. 6.1). There are three main sections in the model: cognition, goal selection, and goal-directed behavior. We assume that one necessary step in behaving is to obtain a map or picture of the external world (see p. 92). Since

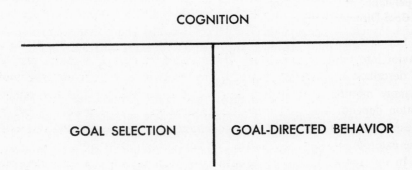

Fig. 6.1   A schematic division of voluntary behavior.

behavior is adjusted to the external world, the individual must have some picture of it. We know that the unknown is frequently disconcerting, especially to young children during the last part of the first year and throughout early childhood. We know that a certain proportion of adult behavior is specifically directed toward discovering what the external world is like. Curiosity is a common human trait. The first section of our model of behavior, therefore, is concerned with the process of knowing or cognizing what the situation is like. Cognition includes perception of the immediately perceptible aspects of the environment and also processes of making judgments or inferences about remote parts of the situation.

The second section of the model is concerned with the process of goal selection. An individual does not constantly have the same goals. In some situations the college student wants to pass an examination; in others he wants a date with his best girl; in still others he wants the football team to win its big game. In any specific situation one or several motives may be aroused. We must therefore discover what situational factors tend to arouse what kinds of motives. Not all motives are realized in overt behavior. Some are inhibited; others are ignored because they are unimportant; others are too difficult even to try to satisfy. Some motives, however, do establish a goal that the individual tries to attain.

The third section of the model is concerned with goal attainment or goal-directed behavior. Once a goal is set, there are often alternative ways of trying to achieve it. The selection of the means to a goal, the carrying out of that means, and the guidance of the ongoing behavior toward the goal are all involved in goal-directed behavior.

These three sections of the model are schematically represented in Figure 6.1. Later figures will fill in some of the details in each section.

Independence of Cognition from Goal Selection and Goal-Directed Behavior

Let us consider for a moment the reason for our having split up human behavior into these sections. One of the characteristics of maturity that has been described in an earlier chapter is objectivity in perception and cognition. The more mature an individual is, the less is his cognition of the external situation dependent upon his immediate situation, his immediate mood, his wishes, hopes, and fears. Objective cognition is determined by the properties of the external situation and not by the perceiving individual.

In our model of human behavior we shall assume that the individual constructs a picture or map of the external environment. Objectivity requires that this picture of the external world be accurate and that it be uninfluenced by the individual's motivation. To the extent that we see the world as we want to see it, or as we fear it may be, we are unable to respond to it as it really is.

Thus, in our model of mature behavior, cognition of the external world is independent of motivation. The cognition may determine the motives that are evoked and especially the motives that are acted upon, but cognition is not *determined by* the motives of the individual.

This condition is not always fulfilled in actual life. We shall see later how needs may influence perception; we all know from everyday life that our understanding of a situation may be influenced by our hopes and fears. In the model, however, we separate the process of goal selection from cognition because increasing maturity brings with it an increasing differentiation of motivation and cognition.

We assume, furthermore, that cognition and motivation are independent in another sense. Many aspects of the situation that are not relevant for goal selection or for goal-directed behavior are nevertheless cognized. The batter concentrating on hitting the ball may not be paying attention to the fact that the sky is blue, that the right-field grandstand is filled, that a bird is flying overhead, but a surprising number of these irrelevant details do apparently register. It is also true that many irrelevant details are probably not cognized; the narrowing of cognition to include only the objects of immediate relevance is especially common under strong tension. A broad unselective cognition is, however, one mark of mature behavior.

In these two senses, therefore, cognition and behavior are independent when maturity is at a maximum. For that reason they are distinguished in this model. If the distinction is made, the lack of differentiation of the two can be shown in terms of the dependence of cognition upon motivation or the narrowing of cognition by strong motivation; if the distinction is not made, it is very difficult to describe voluntary behavior in which the two are most nearly independent.

Independence of Goal Selection and Goal-Directed Behavior

Just as cognition is distinguished in the model because it functions independently, so the distinction between goal selection and goal attainment depends upon the fact that they function independently. One of the important characteristics of adult human behavior is that we can use many different abilities to attain the same goal, and that we can use the same ability to attain many different goals.

To illustrate this independence of means and ends, we have only to think of some skill, such as swimming. If a person knows how to swim, he can swim for fun, he can swim to save a life, he can swim to get across a stream. The ability to swim is a skill that is acquired only once; it can function as a means to various goals or as a pleasure in itself.

It is obvious, also, that we may attain our goals in more than one way. To get to the store we may walk, drive, take a bus, or ride a bicycle. Many skills and many goals seem to be completely independent; any one of a repertoire of skills may under appropriate conditions be used in order to achieve any one of a number of goals. There is nothing in the make-up of the person himself that dictates that one goal must be reached by a certain means;

it is only the external circumstances that determine the means required to reach the goal.

When this complete independence exists, then, motives and behavior are differentiated from each other, and this differentiation is one characteristic of mature behavior. Not all behavior of the adult is completely independent from goals; for the child the dependence is much greater; and in some of the instinctive behavior of animals we find almost no independence.

To note these various conditions of dependence, let us examine several behavior patterns. Crying, for example, is not differentiated from motivation in most adult behavior. We cannot cry voluntarily in the same way that we can walk voluntarily. We cannot cry every time crying would help us to achieve our goal. One of the traditional beliefs in our culture is that many women can cry as a means to an end. They can apparently let the tears stream under complete control. Whether this is true of all women is unimportant. Certainly good actors can train themselves to cry upon demand. Most of us, however, can cry only when we have certain feelings and motives.

Children may show a lack of differentiation and independence in some behavior patterns that are quite voluntary and independent for adults. Piaget reports, for example, that one child was able to clench her fist only when reaching for an object and could not clench it independently in imitation of someone else. That action had not yet become an independent act, under voluntary control and usable in the service of various motives. Children are less able to lie convincingly than are adults. To make a statement merely as a means to an end without regard for its truth requires a certain differentiation.

Some of the instinctive behavior of animals clearly demonstrates behavior patterns that are rigidly dependent upon the stimulus conditions that elicit the instinct and are unusable as a means to any other goal. The honeybee, for example, performs a very intricate dance that informs the other bees in the hive about the location of food, but as far as anyone knows, this dance is never used to communicate the location of other objects, such as an enemy. When the behavior pattern depends completely upon the conditions that elicit an instinct, it would be useless to make the distinction between motive and behavior. But there are all degrees of dependence of behavior upon motive, ranging from the rigid instinctual acts to the planned voluntary activities of the adult.

Since so much of the adult's voluntary behavior does exhibit this independence between goals and the behavior patterns that attain goals, we incorporate the distinction in the model and shall discuss separately the selection of a goal and the choice of behavior to attain it.

Thus, we see the basis for dividing the model into the sections previously described. We shall now examine the details in each of these sections, beginning with motivation rather than cognition because motivation clearly illustrates a general relationship between external stimulating factors and internal factors that is present in the other sections.

Goal Selection

In the picture of goal selection shown in Figure 6.2, we note first that several motives are indicated. This is necessary to represent the process by which the individual chooses among competing wishes, but for the purposes of the present section we shall consider only the process by which one motive is evoked.

The Distinction Between Motive and Need

In Figure 6.2 a line connects each motive to cognition and another line connects each motive to some personal characteristic, or need. This same pattern of interrelation holds for every motive. The individual is made to want something partly by the external situation as he perceives it and partly because he has some personality traits which make him susceptible to the influence of the external situation. The external factor which arouses a motive is called an instigation. The internal factor which determines the individual susceptibility to instigation is called a need.

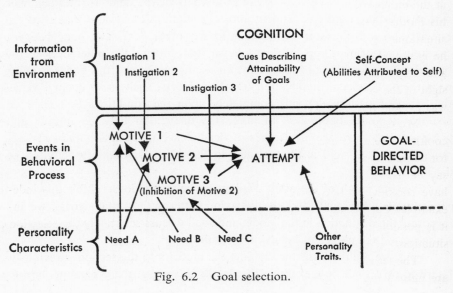

Fig. 6.2   Goal selection.

Let us look at a concrete illustration of this process. If we perceive a five-dollar bill lying on the sidewalk, our cognition of that money instigates a motive to stop and pick it up. The motive is determined, however, not solely by the external situation but also by our individual needs. If money were not valuable to us, the sight of money would not evoke the desire for it.

The psychologically active wish which is aroused in the immediate situation is called a *motive,* to distinguish it from a *need.* The selection of names for these two concepts is troublesome. The terms *motive* and *need* are not entirely satisfactory, because both words have been used by other authors in other senses. The reader should be warned that the terminology in the field of motivation is very confused and confusing; some authors use the words *need* and *motive* interchangeably.

A boy comes home from school intent upon changing his clothes so that he can play football. As he enters the kitchen door, he discovers that his mother has made a big batch of chocolate cookies. The sight and smell of the cookies motivate him to take one. His wish for a cooky is a motive. It is an active wish that affects his behavior—*i.e.,* he takes one. Even if for some reason he does not actually take a cooky—perhaps his mother says not to touch them, because they are for her bridge club and she is not sure she has enough—nevertheless, the boy has a motive to take a cooky, and that motive affects his behavior. In this case it makes him complain, it makes him feel frustrated and perhaps makes him give up football for the afternoon so that he can wait around to see if any cookies will be left over after the bridge party.

If we consider the difference between the boy's psychological condition at the moment just before he discovered the cookies and at the moment after his mother has told him not to touch them, we can see that objectively the situations are the same; he is without a cooky. Before he sees them, however, he is not at all frustrated; he is thinking about football. After he sees them and wants them but is *then* prevented from having one, he is frustrated. The sight of the cookies was an instigation that evoked a motive; until that motive was evoked he could not be frustrated by the lack of cookies.

We can say that even before the boy saw these specific cookies, he liked cookies. This statement is just as true before as after he saw them. His liking for cookies is not, however, an active psychological want or motive. When we say he likes cookies, we mean that if he were to be given an opportunity to have cookies, he would seize the opportunity. This liking for cookies is an example of a *need.* Saying that the boy has a need is equivalent to saying that it is possible to evoke a motive by presenting him with the proper instigating situation.

The term *motive* describes the wishes that are present at any moment and are influencing the individual's behavior at that moment. The entire life of a person may be described as a series of episodes of motivated behavior. During one episode, a boy may be trying to get the right answer to a long-division problem. Then he becomes puzzled and raises his hand—now he is trying to ask the teacher a question. He notices that it is recess time, and now he wants to hurry to reach the baseball diamond so that he can have the first turn to pitch. In this way, a minute-by-minute record of his behavior can be divided into episodes (Barker and Wright, 1955). During one episode—playing baseball, for example—the motives that existed in preceding episodes are not necessarily influencing his behavior.

There is, however, in the sequence of episodes of motivated behavior, a pattern that reflects the personality of the individual. One boy may have many more episodes of playing baseball than another, and fewer episodes of reading comic books. The *need* concept is necessary to account for the fact that there is consistency and structure in the various episodes of motivated behavior that occur in the life of the individual. Thus, the appraisal of the needs of an individual is based upon the observation of consistency in recurrent episodes of motivated behavior. The appraisal of the motives of an individual is based upon the analysis of his behavior within one episode of motivated behavior.

We can all discover in ourselves some persistently recurring wishes that we recognize as being somehow characteristic of us. Some of us want prestige; we find that again and again in our daily life we behave in the way we do in the hope of gaining more respect and applause from our associates. Some of us want money—a need that manifests itself in various specific wishes for a raise in salary, for inheritance, and for other gains.

Despite the fact that we experience money-directed motives repeatedly, however, almost nobody is constantly and perpetually motivated to make money. There are at least some moments in the life of everyone when his behavior seems irrelevant to needs for money. To go to a movie, to play with the children, to read a book—these are not generally an expression of the need for money. On such occasions the motive to make money is not present psychologically; that is, it is not affecting behavior.

Some less central needs show this phenomenon even more clearly. If a man likes to play tennis, he is not continually playing or continually seeking a game; much of his time he spends working, walking home from work, or engaging in other activities that are irrelevant to playing tennis. Yet, in a sense, it can always be said that he likes to play tennis. When he is looking for a partner, or driving to the courts, or buying new tennis balls, his motivation to play tennis is active and is directing his behavior.

A motive is an active wish for something, a present psychological force toward some goal. A motive is behaviorally identifiable because it is a factor affecting behavior "here and now." This does not mean that a motive always produces movement in the direction of the goal; there may be a conflicting motive that is stronger. Even when it is not being displayed in goal-directed behavior, a motive nevertheless affects behavior. It may be the weaker side of a conflict, as we have just suggested, but in that case it is revealed in the existence of the conflict itself, which results in tension symptoms or in disturbances of the behavior that is directed toward the stronger goal. A motive is psychologically active and affects behavior.

A need, on the other hand, is a personality characteristic which can be described as a state of sensitivity or susceptibility. A motive is easily evoked if the need is strong. The person with a strong need for money can easily be motivated to get money. Thus, needs influence behavior not directly but only by predisposing the person to specific kinds of motives. Needs cannot be frustrated; only motives can be frustrated. When a motive is present but the individual is not moving in the direction of the goal, he is frustrated. Since a need is merely a state of susceptibility or sensitivity, it cannot be frustrated. Even though a person has a strong need to make money and is therefore easily and frequently motivated to make money, he is not frustrated during the time that he is motivated toward some goal other than money. If, however, he were motivated to make money and could not move toward that goal, he would be frustrated.

We have discussed in detail the relation between motive and need because it illustrates a general pattern that will characterize other sections of the model as well. Certain of the terms in the model are actual *events* that take place in the course of behaving. A motive is such an event. These events result from the interaction of two sets of factors: one, stimulus conditions that are necessary to evoke the event; the other, the characteristics or dispositions of the individual that permit the external stimuli to be effective in evoking the event. The motivating situation, or instigation, is external, the needs are internal characteristics of the individual. The instigation will evoke a motive if the appropriate needs are strong enough.

Let us now see how this interaction affects the resolution of various motives and inhibitions that determine which goal the individual attempts to achieve.

The Distinction between Motive and Attempt

Returning now to the model (see Fig. 6.2) we find the next concept in the chain is labeled *attempt*. It is necessary to distinguish between the motive and the attempt, because not all motives necessarily lead to action. The selection among the various motives and the decision to act upon any one motive is a part of the process indicated by the term *attempt*.

There are several types of situations in which the motive does not automatically lead to action. The first occurs when two or more motives are simultaneously evoked. The external situation may evoke several motives. In some cases these motives are compatible; that is, they are all satisfiable by some one course of action. In other cases they are in conflict with one another; satisfying one of them will, of necessity, mean frustrating the others. When irreconcilable motives are evoked the individual may choose one and disregard the others, or he may try to satisfy each of them in turn, or he may be unable to come to any decision and take no action. All these modes of behavior would be described in our model under the concept of attempt.

Motivation may also not be realized in action when the motive is prevented from producing action by some sort of inhibitory factor. In Figure 6.2 motive No. 3 is an inhibiting motive and prevents the expression of motive No. 2. These inhibitory factors may be of several sorts. A motive may be inhibited because the individual foresees the consequences of satisfying it—e.g., the temptation to steal may be inhibited by the knowledge that the act will be punished. There are innumerable situations in which knowledge of consequences inhibits the open expression of the motive.

Inhibition may also occur because the individual respects a rule against such behavior. Many times we do not yield to temptation even when we could realistically avoid punishment. When control over motives takes this form, psychologists say that the inhibition has become internalized. It is not dependent upon actual punishment for its effectiveness.

There are other situations as well in which a wish does not lead to action. The wished-for goal may be impossible of attainment; in such cases we sometimes do not even try. Many people have wished to see the other side of the moon, but almost no one has made the slightest effort to achieve this goal. A motive likewise does not lead to action when it will be satisfied without action. A schoolboy in the dull days of February may fervently wish that summer would come, but the wish does not lead to any goal-directed behavior.

The difference between the motive and the attempt can be expressed by the terms *wanting* and *trying*. When a boy wants a new bicycle, the motive is active. His wanting the bicycle affects his behavior: he may be restless; he may talk about it. But none of this behavior can be called an attempt to get the bicycle. Sometimes, but not always, the boy does more than just want a bicycle; he tries to get one. In this case, the attempt is actually made. Some combination of circumstances—the intensity of the motivation, the availability of a means to the end, the perseverance of the child—may lead to an active effort to achieve the goal.

This distinction between the motive and the attempt implies a measure of maturity. The weighing of several motives and the decision to act on one of them is most characteristic of deliberate voluntary behavior. When behavior is impulsive, as much of the behavior of young children is, then the distinction between motive and attempt does not exist. The model of impulsive behavior is less differentiated than the model of deliberate voluntary behavior. It is the fact that in voluntary behavior it is possible for a motive to exist without being acted upon that justifies the distinction between the two concepts in the model.

Now that we have examined the concept of attempt and noted how attempt differs from motive, let us consider the factors that determine when a motive will provoke an actual attempt and which one of various motives will be chosen in case of conflict. Among these factors are the strength of the motive, the possibility of success, the self-confidence of the person, and his ability to make a choice and renounce other motivations. Some of these factors are external and depend upon cognition. Others are internal; they are personality characteristics that predispose a person to be susceptible or insensitive to inhibitory influences.

One cue from the cognitive map is the self-concept, a picture of the person himself as he sees himself. A person who believes he is lucky, strong, and unable to fail will take action on motivation that a more timid person who sees himself as weak would not try to satisfy. The decision to act or not to act frequently reveals a great deal about how a person perceives himself.

Thus, we see that each step in the behavior process is like every other one in its general character. It depends upon certain characteristics of the external situation, as perceived or cognized by the individual, and it depends upon certain characteristics of the individual.

Cognition

Returning now to cognition—the formation of a cognitive picture or map of the external situation—we find the same sort of interaction between internal and external factors that marked the relationship among instigations, needs, and motives.

Suppose that a little girl is playing with her dolls in her bedroom when she discovers that she must have a needle to mend her doll's dress. She can directly perceive the objects in her room: the walls, doors, furniture, etc. Now, surrounding this immediately perceived space there is another area of known space. She knows (cognizes) the position of her parents' room, the hall, and the stairs leading down to the front hall. She may remember that there is a needle on her mother's dresser. Her cognitive picture contains the needle, and in the picture it is located on the dresser. We do not need to assume that the girl actually imagines the dresser with the needle on it; but she knows where the needle is located and how to get to it. At the moment her cognitive map includes only the part of her environment relevant to her behavior. However, if she wanted to go to school, she could easily extend her cognitive map to include the neighborhood, the streets, and the paths leading to school.

Like a motive, this cognitive map is a psychologically active event, occurring because the little girl is thinking about the needle and its location. There are many other things that the little girl knows but that are not part of her cognitive map. For example, she knows that $3 \times 5 = 15$; she knows that a knife can cut her finger. This sort of knowledge is different from the contents of the cognitive map because it is not connected with her present situation. There is no knife cutting her finger, or threatening to. She does not anticipate that a knife will cut her. Her knowledge about knives influences her thoughts and her anticipations—*i.e.,* her cognition—only when she is doing something with a knife. In the same way she knows that $3 \times 5 = 15$, but there are no three things taken five times in her present cognitive map. This knowledge is important—in the appropriate circumstances it could help her to decide on the number of cookies to take on a picnic for five people—but at the moment it is not related in any way to her immediate situation.

Here we can see the resemblance of cognition to motives. Both cognition and motives are psychologically active; they exist "here and now"; they influence behavior here and now. Cognition is what a person is thinking about; motivation is what a person is wanting.

How is the individual's cognition of a situation constructed? On the basis of the information immediately available in her room, how is the little girl able to construct a cognitive map of the entire house? As we see in the model shown in Figure 6.3, the external stimuli set the basis on which the cognition is formed. These stimuli must provide the information for the perception of external objects, or in some way cue the individual's knowledge so that it can be employed in the construction of a cognitive map. In the example we have been describing, the little girl's knowledge of her house enabled her to recognize where she was on the basis of the available stimuli, and thus she could extend her cognitive map beyond the borders of the immediately perceptible area on the basis of that knowledge.

We see that cognition, like motivation, is the result of interaction between external stimuli and internal characteristics. These internal factors—characteristics of the person that contribute to the cognitive map—are quite varied. In some cases mere knowledge or memory is sufficient. In other cases problem-solving ability is necessary if one is to make the correct inferences about what is in the invisible part of the environment, or what the future consequences of action will be. In Chapter 13 we shall see that some kinds of cognition require that the individual have an appropriate set of tacit assump-

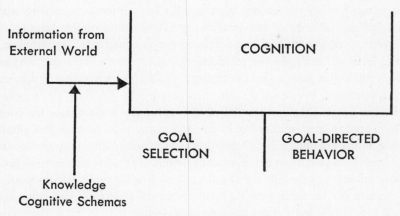

Fig. 6.3 Cognition.

tions about the properties of the external world. He must, for example, recognize that the number of objects in a group is not changed if the objects are rearranged. Another example of such a schema, as Piaget calls it, is the conception of objects as permanent and independent of one's perception of them (see p. 39). These tacit assumptions are not quite the same as knowledge, but they are part of the equipment of the individual that enables him to construct an accurate cognitive map on the basis of external stimuli.

The cognitive map is a characteristic of maturity in that it implies objectivity of perception. The map is an objective picture of the situation surrounding the person, representing objects with their objective properties and their relationships with one another. Perhaps most important of all, the person himself is represented in the map; and the properties that the individual believes himself to possess constitute his self-concept. We have already seen how this self-concept influences the individual's decisions.

We conceive of cognition as the first step in the chain of events that leads from the external stimuli to the behavior of the individual. The cognitive map, then, influences goal selection and guides goal-directed behavior. We can identify certain properties of the cognitive picture that arouse motivation: these are instigations. We can identify other aspects of the cognitive picture that do not evoke motivation but guide the person in his attempt to attain his goal. These features of the cognitive map are cues. Sometimes, of course, an instigation may be a cue, as when the individual is motivated by an opportunity to obtain something he has long wanted. The same stimulus that arouses behavior also guides it.

In Figure 6.3, all these features of the cognitive map are represented. The external stimuli are shown on the left. They interact with knowledge, ability, and probably other personal characteristics. Out of this interaction a cognitive map of the individual's surroundings is constructed, containing external objects, the self, and the relationships among them. This cognitive map furnishes both the instigation of motivation and the cues that guide goal-directed behavior.

Before concluding the discussion of cognition, we must note that cognition is a process that makes goal selection more reliable and goal-directed behavior more adequate. Like other processes underlying mature behavior, however, cognition may become a goal in itself. The term *curiosity* describes a motive to know something, to have a clear and accurate cognition of unknown parts of the environment. In many cases, therefore, the behavior of the individual is guided toward the goal of providing him with a more accurate cognitive picture of his environment. We can see that a search for knowledge and an interest in truth imply a level of maturity in which cognition is already well developed.

Goal-Directed Behavior

Now let us discuss the third section of the model, the guidance of behavior. The specific behavior pattern the individual uses to *attain* his goal is not an involuntary one, fixed by the *selection* of the goal. The behavior is determined by the external conditions, particularly by the position of the goal in relation to other external objects. Whether climbing or swimming or driving a car is used to reach a goal object depends upon whether the goal is on the other side of a fence, the other side of a stream, or the other side of town. *Guidance of behavior* is our term for the process by which these cues from the external world affect behavior so that it does attain the selected goal.

Let us first determine what is guided behavior. We can think of many examples of unguided behavior. The knee-jerk reflex, for example, is not guided. When the doctor taps your knee, the leg moves. There is no guidance of the behavior because there is no consistent result of the behavior. The knee does not jerk in such a way that the foot hits anybody, or misses anybody, or accomplishes any consistent result. The stimulation comes from the tap, and from then on the behavior runs its course regardless of consequences.

Coughing is not guided behavior. It is stimulated by an irritation in the throat or trachea but is not guided toward any particular goal. It may happen that the coughing expels some dust particle or other irritant in the throat. If that happens, the stimulus for the coughing is removed and the individual stops coughing, but if the cough does not dislodge the irritant, the stimulus persists and the person continues coughing. Here we have a mechanism that is unguided but that nevertheless has an adaptive function. The behavior of coughing may remove a certain class of objects. It is unguided behavior, however, or at least very poorly guided, because the irritation may not be removable. The coughing may, in fact, only increase the irritation and produce a coughing attack that is functionless and painful.

From this discussion we can see what the term *guidance* implies. Before a behavior pattern can be considered to be guided, there must be stimuli that indicate how close we are to attaining the goal and that can evolve behavior to bring us still closer. When an infant just learning to reach puts out his hand for an object, he can look to see the relationship between his hand and the object. He can move his hand so that the distance between his hand and the object decreases, and he can continuously check on his progress, changing the direction of the movement when the distance increases. When the hand covers the object, movement stops. If the reader tries to trace a figure using mirror vision only, he can perceive the nature of guided behavior.

The general principles of guidance of action have been studied recently by physicists who are developing guided missiles and other sorts of automatic control mechanisms. They speak of a system that is self-directed toward some end point as having "negative feed-back," because a stimulus indicating inaccuracy of the performance feeds back and affects the control of the system. By this they mean that there is some stimulus that indicates how far the system is in error. If the system is designed to keep an airplane headed north, then there must be some stimulus that indicates how far the path of the plane deviates from north. If a guided missile should be traveling toward a target object, there must be some stimulus that indicates how much the path of the missile deviates from the target. The guided system is designed so that this stimulus activates controls which reduce the stimulus. When the stimulus indicating error is reduced to zero, then the controls of the system are held fixed to keep the error at zero.

In a thermostat set to keep the house at 70 degrees, the error is indicated by the relation of the actual temperature to the thermostat setting. If the temperature is too high, the heating system is turned off until the temperature falls to the proper level. If the temperature is too low, the heat is turned on.

The results of the heating system are fed back to control the system. This is another example of negative feed-back, the effect of the feed-back being to reduce the "error."

Nobody knows how closely the guidance of human behavior resembles the control mechanisms of such physical systems, but the general idea is the same. For human behavior to be guided, there must be some indication of how far the person is from his goal. This indication of error must stimulate the person to behave in such a way that he comes closer to his goal.

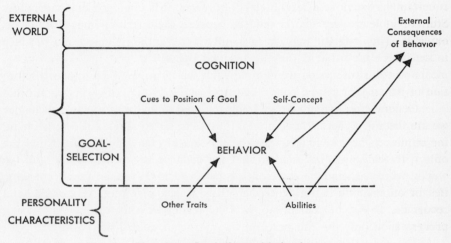

Fig. 6.4   Goal-directed behavior.

Even in the behavior of newborn infants, there are some mechanisms that result in guided behavior in the sense in which we have been using the term. When the young infant fixates on a light, for example, the process is guided so that the eyes move to place the image of the light in the center of the retina.

As the child matures, more and more of his behavior is guided behavior, directed toward the attainment of some goal. As we shall see in Chapter 12, the guidance of complex behavior toward remote and abstract goals requires the development of an objective and broad cognitive picture of the environment. In Figure 6.4, the guidance of behavior by cognition is indicated by the lines connecting the behavior to the cognitive picture.

Skills and Abilities

Behavior, although guided by external cues, is not determined solely by the cognitive picture. The actual behavior and its success are determined also by the skills and abilities of the individual. The individual may know where he wants to go and what he will have to do to get there but he may nevertheless be unable to attain the goal because he lacks the strength or skill to execute the behavior required. For people with different skills, therefore, different behaviors may be required to achieve the same goal.

Some of the abilities of children have been extensively studied and tested. The abilities investigated have not been limited to those that determine success or failure in the execution of a specific action. Some skills, particularly motor skills, are of this sort; but general intelligence, probably the most thoroughly studied ability, plays a role in many aspects of behavior. Intelligence is certainly related to the accuracy of the cognitive map of the external world. Stupid people are more apt to have an inaccurate or incomplete picture of the external world than are highly intelligent people. Intelligence also plays a role in the determination of the goals the individual will try to achieve, and of the means to these goals. Thus, we find that intelligence enters into the determination of behavior at many points.

General intelligence is also related to the ability to learn. In the model we are discussing here, the problem of learning is completely ignored. Learning implies a change in behavior over a period of time; here we are concerned only with the momentary factors that determine behavior in a situation. The way in which experience may cause changes in the knowledge, needs, or abilities of an individual will be discussed in Part II of this book. We should recognize, however, that some abilities have their effects on the learning process as well as on behavior itself.

Summary of Model of Voluntary Behavior

The entire model is put together in Figure 6.5. We have seen how this model, which describes deliberate, voluntary, goal-directed behavior, incorporates many of the criteria of maturity that were discussed in earlier chapters. The breadth of the cognitive map describes the size of the individual's psychological world. The fact that the cognitive map represents the objective properties of external objects and the fact that the content of the cognitive map is not determined by needs of the individual imply that the cognition is objective. It is not distorted by the emotions of the individual or by his position. The differentiation of the model is shown in many places. The independence of needs and cognition, of goals and the means to goals, of motive and the attempt to satisfy a motive—all constitute evidence for differentiation, and this differentiation is required for behavior to be mature.

This is, of course, an idealized picture of behavior. Nobody's behavior fits this model completely. Our perceptions are not completely independent of needs, although with increase of maturity the independence increases. For none of us are goals and means completely independent. The nature of the goal makes some difference in our goal-directed behavior; nevertheless, it is approximately true that for voluntary behavior, means and ends are independent.

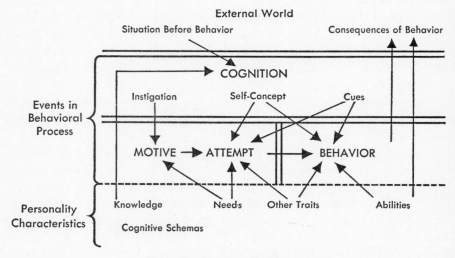

Fig. 6.5 Voluntary behavior.

Taking this model to represent mature behavior, we now face the task of describing less mature behavior. If the concepts in this model are necessary for describing adult, voluntary behavior, how then should we describe the behavior of infants?

To provide what answers we can to this question is the task of the next several chapters. We shall discuss each of these concepts of mature behavior and show how it appears in the behavior of children at various levels of maturity. We shall see that such processes as goal selection and cognition, which are independent in mature behavior, are far from independent in child behavior. We shall see that it is difficult to conceive of true cognition in young infants. We shall see how control over motivation gradually develops during childhood.

7

The Instigation of Behavior
in Childhood

THE INSTIGATION OF BEHAVIOR IN THE NEONATE

INSTIGATION BY OPPORTUNITY

MOTIVATION EVOKED BY IMPOSITION

INSTIGATIONS TO BENEFIT OTHER PEOPLE

PUBLIC EXPOSURE OF BEHAVIOR AS AN INSTIGATION

SUMMARY

THE MODEL OF MATURE BEHAVIOR presented in the preceding chapter contained three sections: cognition, goal selection, and goal-directed behavior. We shall begin our description of child behavior with the section on goal selection, and this chapter will be devoted specifically to the description of the various kinds of external situations that provoke behavior.

We shall begin with external situations because the behavior of the newborn infant cannot be divided into cognition, goal selection, and goal attainment, but seems, instead, to be direct, impulsive response to stimulation. Since the instigation of impulsive behavior becomes, in the mature organism, the instigation of motives, we begin with the process of goal selection. Then we shall see how cognition, control of impulses, and guidance of behavior are added to the picture.

The Instigation of Behavior in the Neonate

Let us turn, then, to the study of the newborn child (or, to use the technical term, the "neonate"). How does the neonate act, and what stimuli provoke his behavior? The activity of the young infant falls into two classes. Some of his behavior is patterned; it is provoked by certain sorts of stimulation and is predictable. Some of his behavior, on the other hand, is generalized, unpredictable, restless activity. The restless movements appear to be completely random. Sometimes they are provoked by some stimulus, but they are not consistently elicited by a specific stimulus, and often it does not seem to make much difference what the stimulus is. Much of the random wriggling of the young infant cannot be clearly related to any specific stimulus. This random, mass activity resembles the restless, fidgety behavior of the older child or adult. We know very little about what provokes it, but we do know a little about the conditions in the organism that make mass activity likely. We shall speak of those conditions in Chapter 9, in which other internal conditions will be discussed.

Turning now to the patterned behavior of the neonate, which is the root out of which later goal-directed behavior will develop, we find that his behavioral repertoire has been described in detail. Table 1 lists some of the dependable responses to stimulation of which the neonate is capable.

TABLE 1

THE BEHAVIORAL REPERTOIRE OF THE NEONATE*

EYES

1. The closing of the eyes to a flash of light.
2. The contraction and expansion of the pupil of the eye as the amount of light increases or decreases. The two eyes operate together. Shining a light in one of them produces contraction of both pupils.

FACE AND MOUTH

1. The turning of the head toward the point of stimulation of the mouth region.
2. Opening and closing of mouth may occur spontaneously or as a part of the "search" movements which may accompany sucking.
3. Pursing or pouting when lip is tapped.
4. Sucking an object in the mouth.
5. Swallowing substances in the mouth.

* Selected items from W. Dennis, *Psych. Bull., 31,* 1934, 5-22.

TABLE 1 *(continued)*

6. Rejecting substances from mouth with a grimace and turning lower lip when satiated.
7. Frowning.
8. Yawning.

THROAT

1. Crying.
2. Cooing.
3. Sobbing.
4. Sneezing.
5. Coughing.
6. Gagging.
7. Holding breath.
8. Hiccoughing.
9. Vomiting.

HAND AND ARM

1. Closing hand upon object pressed into the palm—palmar reflex.
2. Arm withdrawal to sharp tap or prick of hand.
3. Rubbing of face.

SEXUAL RESPONSE: Erection of penis.

FOOT AND LEG

1. Knee jerk.
2. Stepping movements when the child is held upright with feet touching surface.
3. Babinski and plantar reflexes. When the inner sole is stroked the toes are bent downward (plantar response) or the big toe is extended while rest are flexed (Babinski reflex).

RESPONSES INVOLVING COORDINATION OF MANY PARTS OF BODY

1. Startle response. To a sudden intense stimulus the arms separate with fingers spread, the head is thrown back, and the legs are extended.
2. Tonic neck reflex (fencing position). Head is turned toward one side, the arm on that side is extended, and the other arm is bent.
3. Nursing posture. The arms are bent so that the fists come against the chest, the legs are extended.

This is a surprisingly long list of behavioral activities, despite the fact that it is not complete. It does not make the infant seem so primitive or so helpless as we sometimes consider him. Many of these activities are clearly functional, in the sense that they help the baby adjust to the world. The first two reflexes, closing the eyes and contracting the pupil, are protective. They continue essentially unchanged into adult life. The eyeblink of the adult occurs involuntarily when a light is flashed into the eyes or a puff of air is blown into the eye, although the adult can also close his eyes voluntarily even when there is no such stimulus.

The first five responses listed in the section devoted to the face and mouth are all concerned with nursing. In the neonate, feeding is not a single reaction; it is necessary to distinguish three or four responses, each of which is stimulus oriented. The first of the feeding responses is the movement of the head in response to tactual stimulation of the face around the mouth. If one cheek is stroked, the mouth opens and the head moves in the direction of the stimulation. Under appropriate conditions these head movements result in the baby's mouth touching the nipple. This effect stimulates a second response: when the lips are touched there is a pursing of the lips, or a pouting, which fits tightly around the nipple and makes sucking effective. The sucking itself is a response to stimulation of the inside of the mouth and is followed by swallowing. The swallowing is stimulated by the presence of liquid in the mouth and is coordinated with breathing, so that the infant does not choke. Of these neonatal responses, only the swallow reflex continues into adult life more or less unchanged, although the adult can exert some voluntary control over swallowing. The other aspects of the nursing response disappear and are superseded by voluntary eating behavior.

Sneezing, coughing, gagging, hiccoughing, and vomiting are reflex activities that are quite rigid and continue unchanged through the individual's life. Crying comes under some kind of voluntary control but is not completely volitional. Cooing is not, strictly speaking, a reflex at all. It is a pattern of behavior that requires the coordination of several sets of muscles, but it is not elicited by any specific stimulus.

The same thing is true of the tonic neck reflex. In some animals it is a reflex response to turning the head. If the head is turned, the two forefeet take up the fencing position as illustrated in Figure 4.3 (p. 83). In the infant this patterned behavior occurs, but not in response to any specific stimulus. Frequently the young infant is found lying with the head turned, one arm extended, and the other flexed; in later life his posture is not so predictable.

Some of these responses of the infant are clearly adaptive; others do not seem to have any function in the adjustment of the baby to his environment. The grasp response is an example. When the baby grips an object that is thrust into the palm of his hand, he may be displaying the vestige of a response that was once functional. The tight grasp of the infant monkey as it clings to its mother is very functional. Although the grasp response does not help the infant adjust to his environment, we shall see later that very important voluntary activities, such as grasping and reaching, develop out of this originally automatic response.

Rigidity of Infantile Responses

It is not strictly correct to speak of all of these responses as reflexes. Some of them, such as coughing and pupillary contraction, are quite rigid and automatic and are invariably elicited by the appropriate stimulus in every neonate whose nervous system is normal. Other responses in the neonate's repertoire, however, are much less rigid. The various nursing responses serve as a good example.

The observed nursing behavior of children shows some variability. On the one hand, the "reflex" does not operate efficiently in all cases; on the other hand, the behavior seems to be slightly modifiable to fit individual circumstances. Some observations of how neonate behavior is both less efficient and more intelligent than the idealized instinct have been made by Jean Piaget, a Swiss psychologist at the J. J. Rousseau Institute at Geneva. He has developed a number of ingenious experiments to test the development of conceptual thinking in children, which we shall examine later, but at the moment we are more interested in his observations of infant development.

The subjects for these observations are Piaget's own three children (called Laurent, Lucienne, and Jacqueline in his reports). He spent many hours watching their spontaneous behavior when they were infants and observing how they reacted to various chance stimuli. When he observed some interesting bit of behavior, he would devise an experiment on the spur of the moment to study it more carefully. We shall see that his experimental material is far from orthodox; it is likely to consist of handkerchiefs, blankets, boxes, hats, coat pockets, and other things that were available when the experimental opportunity arose. Probably the least reliable information from these experiments is the age of the child. There were only three subjects, and in all probability they were more advanced than normal in their development. We should examine these observations, therefore, not with the idea of determining norms but to understand the processes underlying infant behavior.

Piaget made a number of observations of nursing behavior. How, he asked, do the nursing responses of the young infant deviate from the usual picture of a reflex, and of what significance is this flexibility for later development? The first deviation from the idealized picture of a rigid reflex is that the sucking response may not function perfectly at first. Some few days may be required for its development. Jacqueline, for example, let go of the nipple during nursing and, despite the fact that all the conditions for stimulating the reflex were present, she did not take hold again spontaneously. When the nipple was pushed into the mouth itself, she began to nurse. This behavior can be noted many times in a hospital nursery. The inadequate sucking response is more common among prematurely born children but may occur after a full-term pregnancy. There is no evidence that it is indicative of general retardation.

A second deviation from the idealized picture is the presence of spontaneous sucking movements in the absence of any mouth stimulation. Piaget describes such sucking by Laurent immediately after birth. His movements were not full-blown sucking movements but included pursing of lips, movements of tongue, and some sidewise movement of the head. If one of the baby's hands touched his lips or cheek by accident, the sucking reflex appeared very clearly and strongly and he began to suck his finger. Children have been known to be born with thumb already in mouth.

A final complication of the picture of nursing is the very rapid change that may occur even in very early infancy. On the third day of Laurent's life, for example, when his lips touched the nipple or the breast tissue near the nipple, the searching head movements began, but they were not necessarily limited to the side that was stimulated. By the twelfth day, however, the search was limited to the stimulated side. On the twentieth day, when his lips were deliberately touched to the breast but not at the nipple, he sucked the skin for a moment, stopped, moved a little, and sucked again until he accidentally touched the nipple with the outside skin of one of his lips. Even this did not strongly stimulate the sucking response. When a moment later, however, he touched the nipple with the inside of the lips, he immediately began nursing.

Already we can see some very primitive kind of recognition. At this level of maturity, recognition is only a certain discontent with the skin of the breast —because it does not feel quite right—that leads to the discontinuation of sucking. The nipple does "feel right," and sucking is continued.

The adequacy of Laurent's search and the apparent maturity of his nursing depended partly upon how stimulated he was by hunger. When he was very hungry a large area on his cheek was sensitive enough to a touch to elicit searching movements. When, on the other hand, he was not very hungry, the sensitive area decreased in size.

Nursing behavior is not the only neonatal behavior that is not so rigid and fixed as the term *reflex* is intended to indicate. The grasp reflex, too, is not altogether automatic. Fixation of the eyes can occur in early infancy, but it does not always occur. Commonly enough the baby's eyes gaze around independently of each other.

It is interesting to note that these responses which are not completely rigid even at birth are the ones that develop into voluntary activity. Whether the early plasticity is a prerequisite for development is not known.

Instigation by Opportunity

In the mature individual one of the most important instigators of motivation is opportunity. If an individual can achieve some goal, the opportunity instigates a motivation to do so. On the other hand, the impossibility of attaining some goal is a very effective dampener of hopes and wishes.

We find the beginnings of this pattern of instigation very early in life. Perhaps the best example is the presence of an object as an instigation to reach for it. If a red ring is dangled in front of the face of a baby four to six months old, he will reach for it (Gesell and Thompson, 1934). This is goal-directed motivated behavior. The motivating situation is the presence of the ring in front of his face. If the ring is moved behind a screen, he will, at this age, no longer reach for it. Thus, the situation has lost its motivating power. Not only does he not reach for the invisible object, but there is no evidence that he is frustrated by his inability to reach for it. The behavior and the impression it gives to the observer are quite consistent with the statement that the infant no longer wants the ring when he cannot see it. This behavior of reaching for a dangling ring is so predictable that it is used as a test of ability to reach. It is not used as a test of the child's motivation to reach for rings; its motivating power is taken for granted.

The instigation that elicits this reaching behavior is merely the sight of a noticeable and obtrusive object that attracts the baby's attention. Furthermore, it seems that the object is somehow more attractive by virtue of its not actually being in the child's grasp. When the baby of four months or older already has a cube in his hand, his attention shifts immediately when a new cube is presented. Between the ages of four and six months, he is likely to drop the first cube when his attention is drawn to the second (Gesell and Thompson, 1934). The sensitivity of the child at this age to the fact that an object is not in his hand can be seen in his response to its gradual approach. If a shiny cup is held in front of the child until it captures his attention and then is gradually brought closer and closer, he becomes more and more excited as it approaches. Once he has captured the object he may finger it and mouth it, but his attention and motivation seem more easily turned elsewhere after he has obtained the object than before.

These observations suggest that the most primitive characteristics of this sort of instigation are (1) the noticeability or obtrusiveness of the object, and (2) its separation from the individual. In other words, we tend to want anything we notice that is not in our possession. If this were the only factor in motivation, it would make no difference what the object was. There would be no selectivity, no preference for one object rather than another. Obviously, adults have such preferences; even the young infant has some selectivity (as we shall see in Chapter 10), but one of the important facts about the behavior of the young child is that, within wide limits, he shows relatively little selectivity; he is motivated to approach almost any noticeable object that he does not possess. Obtrusiveness of an object tends to make it a goal.

The power of these factors can be seen even in children of nursery-school age and older. The difficulty of keeping toddlers' hands off knick-knacks, books, and the radio is all too familiar to the parent of the eighteen-month-old child. Even during the nursery-school period, there seems to be very little selectivity, provided the object is obtrusive enough.

Adults, too, can be motivated by mere opportunity. A few years ago the postal authorities were trying to decide how to prosecute the man who put the following advertisement in the paper: "LAST CHANCE TO SEND YOUR DOLLAR TO P.O. BOX 221." He presumably collected several hundred dollars merely by offering an opportunity without giving the slightest hint of what the opportunity was.

Such behavior as this is sufficiently uncommon in adult life to make an unusual story. Very frequently, however, if two valued objects are available, the individual will be motivated toward the one that is more clearly suggested by the situation. If an adult wanted either a new television set or a new washing machine, he might find his choice influenced by seeing an advertisement for one rather than the other. In adult life, therefore, the obviousness of the opportunity or the obtrusiveness of a goal object frequently determines which motive out of a number of possible ones is evoked. Only infrequently, however, does the mere presence of a very clear opportunity to do something make the adult want to do it unless he already considers the goal valuable.

In children, on the other hand, the importance of the situation is so strong that it is possible to create a motive merely by offering the child a very clear and obvious opportunity. When the child will reach for any noticeable object that is dangled in front of him, his motive cannot be thought of as dependent upon the value of the object for him. The object becomes a goal merely by being offered to him. When the teacher says to a group of first-graders, "The first one finished may deliver this letter to Miss Jones," she is more likely to make everybody want to be the messenger than if she says, "Jack, you deliver this letter to Miss Jones." By her phrasing, she makes the letter delivery an opportunity rather than an imposition and thus creates positive motivation rather than resistance.

The noticing of an object by the child seems to be a common instigator of motivation. Usually, but not always, the situation indicates an opportunity for the child to obtain the object. Some objects that are directly perceptible are, in fact, impossible to obtain; and there are many objects not directly perceived which the individual can obtain by trying. In the course of maturation, it seems that the conditions that instigate motivation gradually change. The possible goals of the mature person are not limited to those things he can see, or even to those things that may come to mind under the stimulation of a specific situation. The mature person's range of possible goals may include anything that he can achieve. Which goal in this possible range he is actually motivated to obtain and which one he tries to obtain depend upon his likes, his preferences, and his needs.

Nevertheless, the physical presence of an object, or some clear reminder of it that makes the individual cognize it, continues even for the adult to make one opportunity clearer or more obvious than another and therefore to incline his motivation in the direction of the obvious opportunity.

What situations serve to remind the person of a possible goal object? Its visible presence is certainly one of the clearest reminders of it and ensures that it will be cognized. Other situations also ensure that the individual will think of a goal object and thus be motivated by it.

Habitual Motivation

The existence of a situation that has, through learning, become associated with a specific goal activity will motivate the individual. Perhaps the development of thumbsucking illustrates this point as well as any other. As Piaget describes it, thumbsucking occurs at first only when the child accidentally gets his thumb into his mouth. Later, if his thumb happens to touch his face, he is able to control his hand movements enough to get the thumb into his mouth. Still later, the child can bring his thumb to his mouth no matter where his hand happens to be. At that time the child may begin to suck his thumb in certain customary situations. Some children regularly suck their thumbs while they go to sleep. Other children suck it as soon as the bottle or the breast is removed. A confirmed thumbsucker seems to have his thumb in his mouth anytime the hands are not busy with something else and he is not intent on some other activity.

Let us consider the child who sucks his thumb whenever he is put to bed. There is nothing about the situation of being put to bed that makes thumbsucking an especially clear opportunity. Some children, but not all, have formed the habit of thumbsucking in this situation. For a child who has the habit, the act of going to bed instigates a motive to suck his thumb. Thus, through the process of learning, some situations may suggest certain kinds of activities that are not particularly obvious from a superficial observation of the situation itself.

We see the same mechanism in many other situations. A child may have, on his first visit to a certain house, played with some special toy. He is very likely to ask for that toy again on his next visit, even if it is not visible. A certain child may be teased and bullied so frequently that the mere presence of that child immediately suggests teasing and aggressive activity to his playmates. Thus, customary activities may occur even when many other opportunities are objectively present.

Prolongation of an Interesting Activity

Not only may an activity become habitual in a specific situation, but the suggestion for any activity may remain for a period of time after the activity has ceased. Piaget describes one incident in which a child lying in a crib was able to make a doll suspended above his head move and jiggle by rhythmically shaking his body and making the crib jiggle. Watching the doll move was obviously intensely interesting to the child. When it stopped, he would shake the crib to make it move. Very often children repeat an action in order to resume some activity that has just stopped. There are many other opportunities possible for instigating another motive, but the end of an activity does not immediately erase it from the child's cognitive map. That activity may remain a goal and thus instigate behavior to re-establish it. This requires a certain level of maturity, of which the child of three or four months is capable, because it involves a short period of memory. One of the criteria of development evolved by Buhler (1930) for the six-month-old child is the attempt to restore a contact that is broken off.

At approximately twelve months of age, the child can remember an interesting event long enough to be motivated to repeat it when the same circumstances arise again. In another of Buhler's tests of infant development (Buhler and Hetzer, 1935), for example, the child is given a rubber ball with a toy chicken inside that can be made to pop out by squeezing the ball. The experimenter allows the child to play with this ball for a short time, being sure that he succeeds in making the chicken appear. Then the toy is removed for a few minutes before it is given back to the child. The experimenter does not, in fact, return the same toy that the child played with; instead, he substitutes one that is superficially like it but does not contain the chicken. The child is expected to squeeze the ball and to show some sign of surprise that the chicken fails to emerge. We see in this experiment that the child of that age can be motivated by the presentation of an object that has previously proved interesting.

Summary of Motivation by Opportunity

Let us summarize the development of the ability to be motivated by opportunity. At first the only situations that instigate approach behavior, such as reaching, sucking, and looking, are those in which the goal object is physically present. The child cannot perceive another sort of opportunity until he is able to respond to absent objects. After cognition expands to include objects that are momentarily out of sight, a situation can instigate a wider variety of motives because it presents more opportunities. Even at this stage, however, some possible goals are more obvious than others because they are more easily perceived. The child's motives are determined by what the situation suggests rather than by what realistic opportunities it offers. A child's motive for candy can be as strongly instigated by a picture of the candy as by an invitation to take a piece out of a box.

Even in adult perception and cognition, the obvious aspects of a situation are probably overemphasized, but as maturity increases the realistic attainability of different goals becomes increasingly important in determining the goal selected. Furthermore, selection among the numerous opportunities presented by a situation—even if they are all realistic—comes gradually to depend upon the enduring needs of the individual.

The behavior of adults when they have an important decision to make illustrates clearly the dominant role of needs. In the face of a significant decision, the individual tries to scan every opportunity. He strives not to miss any just because it is hidden or obscure. He tries to decide by determining which goals are intrinsically valuable and which goals are attainable; he no longer selects a goal merely because it is obvious. Thus the development of maturity brings with it a change from instigation by obviousness of a goal to instigation by realistic opportunity to attain a goal and by its intrinsic value.

Motivation Evoked by Imposition

One class of instigations to motives is opportunity. Let us now discuss a second type of instigation to motivation—namely, imposition. To preview briefly the course of the discussion, we shall first discuss the general concept of imposition to derive a definition of it. Then we shall see that, unlike opportunity, imposition tends to evoke emotional responses as well as specific motives. One aspect of development is, in fact, the gradual shift from a purely emotional reaction, when the young child is imposed upon, to the directed behavioral response of the older person when he responds to impositions. Finally, we want to observe some of the kinds of motives that may be instigated by imposition.

The Concept of Imposition

Any parent who has tried to cut a child's fingernails, remove a splinter, or comb his little girl's hair knows that it is far less unpleasant for the child to do something painful to himself than to have someone else do it to him. It seems curious that it should make any difference whether we hurt ourselves or are hurt, but passively suffering pain at the hands of another person is harder to bear than inflicting it on ourselves.

The important events in a person's life can generally be classified into one of two categories. They may be events that the person himself causes, or they may be the results of the actions of someone else or of natural processes (Angyal, 1941; Heider, 1953). Insults, promotions, earthquakes, and good weather all happen to a person without his having much to do with their occurrence. We shall call this second variety of events an imposition. The illustration of removing a splinter exemplifies the fact that the psychological impact of the same event differs according to whether or not it is an imposition.

The two classes, autonomous events and impositions, are not completely distinguishable. Some events depend upon both the individual's own actions and the actions of other people. A sale, for example, must have both a buyer and a seller. Since either party can reject or accept the transaction, it is an imposition on no one. A kind of event difficult to classify is one that results from a person's own actions but that he did not intend to produce.

Opportunities are not impositions. No matter how strongly one's behavior is invited or sought for, no imposition is implied so long as one feels free to accept or refuse the invitation. If an opportunity is forced upon a person, it is no longer an opportunity. The motives that are elicited by opportunities lead the person into activities that are enjoyable in their own right. When we are free to choose, we do the things we like to do. As we have seen, the child's freedom is actually restricted by his inability to think of all the possible activities that he might engage in. But since this restriction is not felt by the child, it is not a psychological imposition.

Emotional Response to Impositions

Since opportunities do not impose anything on a person, the motives that are instigated are often accompanied by no emotional reaction or perhaps by only a mild sort of pleasure. The reaction to an imposition is different. Most of us respond to impositions with an emotional reaction. We may become angry with the person who imposes; we may be very grateful to a rescuer; we may be frightened at a danger which can overwhelm us. These same impositions may also evoke motives—to retaliate, to repay, to resist, or to escape.

The differing responses to impositions and opportunities appear in early infancy. The infant who is shown a shiny toy may show some pleasant sort of excitement, but often his attempts to reach the object are carried out very soberly. When the child is imposed upon, however, the situation is different. An emotional state of anger, panic, grief, or anxiety is the result of an imposition. The child's response to impositions has from the very beginning, therefore, a different quality from his response to opportunity or suggestions. An important characteristic of the behavior elicited by impositions is its accompanying emotional state.

The young infant's response to some impositions seems to be a purely emotional one. When the baby is screaming from colic, he is displaying an emotional response, not motivated behavior. Similarly many of the anger, distress, and fear responses of the infant are emotional rather than motivated reactions. In some situations, however, the infant's response seems to be a mixture of purposive behavior and emotional response. The infant who does not like to have his face washed may respond emotionally when the washcloth covers his eyes or probes into his ears, but his behavior seems also to have a certain direction to it. He turns his head away from the stimulus; he may push the washcloth away from him. His behavior seems to be both emotional and motivated.

Several factors determine the degree of directedness of the infant's response to an imposition. One factor is the structure of the external situation. The imposition may be clearly perceived and easily responded to. The washcloth is an object which impinged immediately upon the child. It has a specific location and the child can make a directed response to escape it. Not all impositions, however, even intensely painful ones are easily located and responded to. When the baby has a wet diaper or a stomach ache, he becomes restless but he cannot respond in a clear, directed fashion as does the infant who withdraws from a pin prick or rears back away from the spoon which has lemon juice in it. In order to elicit either withdrawal or resistance, the stimulus must be sufficiently well localized that the child can cognize it and move away from it. Thus the infant can turn his head away from the bottle if he does not want it; he can spit out milk which is heavily salted; he can remove his hand from a piece of cold metal.

The situational factors that produce clear withdrawal rather than a generalized emotional response are in some ways just opposite to factors that elicit reaching and other approach responses. In both cases the object must be clearly perceptible and easily located. To produce an approach, the object must be separated from the child himself. It must be perceived as "out there" in space. The stimuli which produce withdrawal are those which are clear and obtrusive but not separated from the child. They are too close; they impinge too strongly; they impose on the child. The shiny ring is immediately perceptible, but it is separated from the child. The effect of the reaching behavior is to bring it closer. The pin prick or the lemon juice is immediately perceptible but it is not segregated from the child; that is just the trouble—it is already too close, and the child withdraws to be separated from it.

Thus we see that impositions that are clearly structured can elicit directed behavior even in young infants and are just opposite to the situations which elicit approach behavior. Many impositions are not clearly structured, however. There is nothing within the infant's limited psychological world to react to. When this occurs, the infant's response is more generalized and less focused. As the infant matures, his psychological world expands and situations which he was unable to perceive clearly at an earlier age may become understandable. With maturity, therefore, directed responses may be elicited by situations which earlier provoked a purely emotional reaction. We shall see several examples of this sort of development in later sections.

Having examined the general reactions to imposition, especially the distinction between the generalized emotional response and the directed behavioral response, we turn now to a more detailed discussion of the various motives instigated by an imposition. One such motive is resistance. We frequently fight back against an imposition, trying to prevent it or to turn it back. A second reaction may be to escape it or withdraw from it. This motive is frequently accompanied by fear, but not in every case. A third motivation instigated by imposition is reciprocation. When some other person imposes upon us, we frequently want to return the imposition. We like to retaliate injury and to repay favors.

Resistance to Imposition

No one seems to like to be imposed upon. We are all more easily led than pushed. Nevertheless, most people do not have too much difficulty distinguishing between an imposition that is intrinsically unpleasant and one that is unpleasant only because it does impose on us. It is one of the signs of maturity to be able to respond not to the mere fact of imposition but to the specific change that is imposed. Children, however, may show a very strong unselective resistance to all impositions.

NEGATIVISM: The unselective resistance against all impositions is called *negativism*. Young infants are not very negativistic because they are not very sensitive to subtle kinds of impositions. If the parent tries to order an eighteen-month-old child to do something or not to do something, the child does not make any special response to the fact that it is an order. Klein (1932) reports that it is easier to obtain obedience to a positive command— a command for the child to do something—than to a negative one—a command for him to refrain from doing something. She also found that children could not, before the age of two, be obedient when an authority was not present, but that they could, if caught in the act of disobedience, show emotional reactions indicating that they knew they were doing something bad.

Both of these findings seem reasonable in terms of the conceptualization that we have been developing. Ordering the child to do something has the effect of offering him an opportunity. By thus directing his attention toward that activity, the adult has constructed the appropriate conditions for creating a positive motive. This is particularly true for activities that are not intrinsically repulsive or frightening. There is no evidence that the child at such an early age will overcome his fears and do things that frighten him, even if commanded.

Ordering the child not to do something, on the other hand, is frequently tantamount to making him want to do it. This reaction is not necessarily resistance or negativism but merely a display of impulsiveness. By directing the child's attention toward what he should not do, we establish the conditions for making him want to do it just as surely as if we had told him to do it. Under the influence of the motivation of the immediate situation, the child of such a level of maturity can do very little resisting.

As the child becomes older, however, he recognizes more accurately situations in which other people are trying to make him do something. During this period the occurrence of negativism, or resistance to suggestion, gradually increases. The development of resistance has been studied by Reynolds (1928) and also by Rust (1931). It seems to make its first noticeable appearance at about eighteen months and usually increases to a peak at about thirty months or perhaps as late as thirty-six months. From then on, it declines.

During the period when negativism is increasing, the child seems to become more acute in recognizing whether he is being invited or commanded. An invitation he usually accepts; a command he usually refuses and counteracts. Even matter-of-fact statements are frequently structured as impositions—

e.g., "The table must be clean before we can eat dinner."—"No!" Gesell and Ilg (1942) list some "key" words that they recommend for phrasing one's requests to children who are sensitive to impositions. Such phrases as "It's time to," "you forgot," "new," "different," "surprise," "secret," and "guess what" are all designed to make the future inviting and to lessen the feeling of being compelled. All these phrases are in harmony with the principle of evoking motivation by structuring the situation as an opportunity to change the present situation. Invitational phrasing of requests is effective before the age of thirty months, but, because of the child's relative insensitivity to compulsion at an earlier age, the phrasing is not so critical.

With still more maturity, the individual again becomes less sensitive to phraseology. He knows, more or less, what he wants to do. Pleasant tasks are not so likely to lose their attractiveness merely because he is commanded to do them. That the phraseology of commands never completely loses its effect is indicated by the fact that many effective propaganda techniques depend upon skillful phrasing.

Negativism is sometimes said to be a demonstration that the child has a mind of his own, but sensitivity to impositions need not be a voluntary action. When the child refuses to sit down until he is told to stay on his feet, his resistance can be just as automatic an impulse as any positive response. It is only after the child does what he wants to, whether commanded or invited, that he has a mind of his own. The sensitivity to commands that marks negativism indicates, however, that the child is becoming sensitive to the conflicting instigations of many motivating situations. Thus, the conditions for the development of choice exist. At the same time, his contrary behavior undertaken against the pressure of the environment probably enhances the child's feeling of voluntary action. Negativism can be seen, therefore, as portending the development of choice and volitional behavior.

Thus far we have examined two of the common instigations of childhood. First, the presence of an object or the opportunity to obtain an object tends to make the object a goal and to evoke motivation to obtain it. The second instigation, an imposition, evokes resistance. These instigations can exist in either social or impersonal situations.

INSTIGATION BY CHALLENGE   A second example of the role of resistance in the motivation of child behavior can be observed in the child's response to challenge. Some situations manage to be both inviting and imposing at the same time, so that the two instigations apparently reinforce each other and make the motivation even stronger. A challenge offers an opportunity but at the same time places serious difficulties in the way of carrying it out. It invites us, but at the same time it threatens us with failure. A challenging situation is even more potent in evoking motivation than a situation that offers no obstacles, and it is certainly more motivating than a situation in which the task is obviously impossible. Instigation by a challenge can be illustrated by several experiments.

EFFECT OF BARRIERS ON MOTIVES   An interesting illustration of the way in which a challenge motivates behavior is the effect of barriers upon motivation. A barrier, if it is not too difficult to overcome, enhances the attractiveness of possible goal activities. The effectiveness of motivating a child's behavior by saying, "You can't do this," is well known, as is the strong effect upon curiosity of saying, "I know a secret." The phrase does not suggest a specific goal object, but it emphasizes the fact that, whatever it is, the child does not have it. "Grass is greener on the other side of the fence" is a proverbial statement of this principle.

The effect of barriers upon motivation can be shown in experimental situations such as that used in H. F. Wright's (1937) study of the behavior of cafeteria waitresses. In the cafeteria he observed the customer gave his order to a waitress, who then went through a cafeteria line to fill the order. When the waitresses selected a piece of pie for a customer, they tended to take the nearest one. On the other hand, when they selected a piece of pie for their own meals, they were more likely to take one from a back row of pies, which was 12 inches farther away than the front row on the counter. Each of us has probably scanned the array of pies on a cafeteria counter and decided that the one in the far corner was the largest. How many times has the nearest, most convenient one looked largest?

Whereas a barrier may enhance the strength of a motive, a conspicuous absence of any difficulty or barrier may reduce the strength of a motive. There are numerous examples of motive reduction by the fact that the goal is so easily obtainable that it seems as good as present. It is well known, for example, that if a family moves to a new area abounding with scenic and historic spots, it will put off visiting them. "We can see them any time, why now?" On the other hand, visitors who can spend only a few days in the region will not perceive these sights as so obviously available; hence, they will make an effort to see them. The permanent resident's motivation to see these spots is reduced by the knowledge that they are there all the time even though he has never actually seen them.

Similarly, there is experimental evidence from rats and from athletes that as the goal is neared the motivation to reach it increases until it is approached very closely. Then, for some reason, it seems psychologically to be as good as reached, even though it has not been reached in reality. Runners have to be trained to keep running at full speed until they are past the finish line; otherwise, they are likely to slow down during the last few feet.

The motivating effect of the perception of the barrier depends upon two factors: (1) the clarity with which the barrier segregates or separates the end result from the present situation, and (2) the interpretation of the barrier as a kind of imposition that threatens a contemplated action—a threat that reinforces the motivation established by the perception of the goal itself.

LEVEL OF ASPIRATION   The response to challenge shows an interesting development. The first signs of it occur in the play of the young infant. Piaget in his numerous observations of his three children repeatedly reports on the quality of the child's motivation as he gradually acquires a new behavior pattern. Often, although not always, the first appearance of the pattern is accidental. Then, however, the child begins to pay very close attention to his behavior; he is deadly serious and extremely intent. Once he has the new behavior under some control, it suddenly becomes great fun. It is during this stage that the baby may repeat the same behavior over and over and over again. Finally, when the new activity has become easy and automatic, it is no longer fun. The child then performs the activity whenever there is reason to, but it is no longer a source of pleasure for its own sake. During the period when the activity is possible but difficult, the child shows the strongest motivation to perform it.

Later in the child's life, toward the end of the preschool years but especially during the school years, the child begins to restrict his behavior by rules whose effect is to make a task more difficult; he tends to choose slightly difficult tasks in preference to easy ones.

The level of aspiration can be seen as a further example of instigation by a challenge. Whenever we challenge ourselves to achieve some goal not by just any means but in some especially difficult way, we have demonstrated a level of aspiration. To a young child the idea that the golf ball must be hit into the cup with a club is incomprehensible. If he wants the ball in the cup, he simply drops it in. If we are dissatisfied with our golf score, we struggle harder to break 100 or break 80. Why not be satisfied with the score we have? We cannot easily resign ourselves to a poor score because a level of aspiration is not easily reduced. In this section we shall see how the ability to have a level of aspiration is one element of the maturity of the school-age child.

In the usual experimental studies of the level of aspiration, the subject is given some task upon which he can be scored. A large variety of tasks have been used—penetrating mazes of various degrees of difficulty, playing pin-ball games, stringing paper clips into a chain, or putting pegs into holes. Before he attempts this task, the subject is asked to estimate what his score will be. This, too, may be done in various ways. In the maze problem, for example, he may choose the difficulty of the maze he will try to solve. In other tasks he may merely predict his score. This prediction is called his level of aspiration. It is the individual's attempt to measure the level of performance that he has set as his goal—the score that should separate feelings of success from feelings of failure. If he reaches or exceeds his level of aspiration, he should feel successful. If he fails to reach it, he should be dissatisfied with his performance. The subject's prediction of his score may not correspond pre-

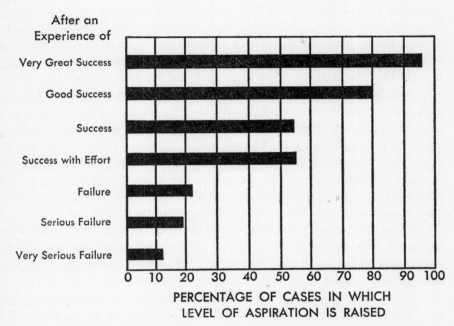

Fig. 7.1 Frequency of raising the level of aspiration after various degrees of success and failure. (After K. Lewin *et al.,* in J. McV. Hunt [ed.], *Personality and the Behavior Disorders*)

cisely with his true goal for the test, but it is one objective value that can be obtained from the subject.

The effects of many different kinds of factors on the level of aspiration have been measured. It has been found, in general, that if the individual reaches or exceeds his estimate, he is likely to raise the estimate for the next trial. If he fails seriously to reach it, he will probably lower his estimate for the next trial. The level of aspiration generally is maintained a little above the individual's level of performance (Gould, 1939). If the individual is given some social norms for the performance, these affect his level of aspiration. Jucknat (1937), studying a group of 500 eleven-year-old children, obtained the results shown in Figure 7.1. These results have been confirmed by others.

In a sense, the level of aspiration is arbitrary. What difference does it make whether or not a person reaches his level? Why should he not be satisfied with his performance whatever it is? Why should he keep his level of aspiration above his performance level? One factor is competition with one's associates. Anderson and Brandt (1939) have shown the effect of this factor on fifth-grade children. The task used was a series of cancellation tests, in which the subject is presented with a long list of letters or symbols of some kind and asked to cross out some specific letter whenever he comes to it. His score is the number canceled within a given time limit. Before each test the subjects in this experiment were asked to write down privately the score they thought they could make. Then after each test the true scores were posted. No individual was named, but each child could tell where he stood in the group. The experiment showed that the children tended to set their goals so that their aspirations were closer to the average level of the whole group than was their actual performance. The students in the top quarter of the class set a goal that was on the average 5.8 points below their performance. For students in the lowest quarter of the group, the level of aspiration was 13.6 points above their performance. In other words, the estimates were more closely clustered about the group level than were the performance scores.

DEVELOPMENT OF THE LEVEL OF ASPIRATION   One of the characteristics that come with maturity is the ability to set goals for oneself that are slightly challenging rather than easily attainable. This may be done by being dissatisfied with a score or an achievement or by trying to reach a goal the hard way rather than the easy way. The child has always responded to goals that are challenging in the sense that they lead to goal-directed action. Such goals stimulate tension and are responded to with pleasure and excitement. It is only when the child sets his own challenges and determines for himself a goal that is not implicit in the motivating situation that it is possible to speak of a level of aspiration. The motivation to achieve a difficult goal is not in itself a level of aspiration.

Two experiments, one by Fales (1940) and another by C. Anderson (1940), show the development of the level of aspiration. Fales was interested in the young child's striving for independence. When a child refuses help in tying his own shoes or in taking off his snowsuit, he is displaying the first beginnings of a level of aspiration. It is not merely the end result that is the goal, but the manner by which the result is achieved. Fales found that the child refuses help on easy tasks more frequently than on difficult ones. Furthermore, it was found that praising the child's independence, or training and encouraging his independence in some specific area, tends to increase his level of aspiration. He will, as a consequence, more probably refuse help in the other tasks he meets.

Anderson studied the maturity of the level of aspiration of children in a ring-tossing game. Three groups of children, aged three, five and one half, and eight, were shown how they could throw the rings onto a peg to make a score. Two criteria of maturity of the level of aspiration were employed. The first was the manner of throwing. Younger children tend to place the rings on the peg. They can understand only the concrete goal of getting the rings in the proper place. With increasing age the child tends to drop the rings on the peg or to toss them on from a distance. The second criterion was the way in which the child behaved when he missed. The youngest children deal with each ring separately. If one ring misses the peg, it is immediately retrieved and rethrown. The older children rethrow the entire set of five rings after they have all been thrown once. They see the five rings as a single unit. To rethrow them at all before counting the score is, of course, a sign of immaturity. The oldest children tend to accept the result without rethrowing.

The score obtained from this analysis led to a maximum value of 9. The scores for the eight-year-olds averaged 8.54; for the five-and-a-half-year-olds, 6.34; and for the three-year-olds, 2.13. Anderson showed that by the age of eight the child's level of aspiration closely resembles the adult's. He aspires to different goals, of course, but his level of aspiration responds to the factors usually found in adult level-of-aspiration experiments. Jucknat also found that there were no differences in her experiment between eleven-year-old children and adults. The development of a level of aspiration seems, therefore, to occur at elementary-school age.

Let us consider what is required for a level of aspiration besides an ability to be motivated by a challenge. If he is to maintain a level of aspiration, the child must possess, first of all, the ability to organize a series of goals in the form of some continuum ranging from low to high. Secondly, he must recognize one task as more difficult than another and see the more difficult one as a greater achievement. He must be able to conform to arbitrary barriers to success because he is focused upon the quality and difficulty of his achievement rather than only upon the concrete results of the activity. Anderson showed that if the concrete results are emphasized by offering a reward, the maturity of the child's behavior declines. It does not decline for the youngest group because they are already so focused upon the external result that the level of aspiration cannot decline. But for the older groups there tends to be a regression to less mature patterns of aspiration, indicated by placing a missed ring on the peg or rethrowing it to obtain a better score.

Escape from Imposition: the Instigation of Fear

We have noted that imposition or the threat of it instigates resistance and the motivation to overcome the imposition. Imposition may instigate other motivation as well, particularly when the force behind the imposition is very powerful. It may instigate fear and the motivation to escape rather than to resist.

Fear, like resistance to imposition, is a motivation that is usually accompanied by affect and emotion. Thus, the behavior of the fearful person is not only purposive behavior, directed toward escaping from danger, but is also expressive behavior displaying the state of fear. The difference between mature and immature manifestations of fear is that the mature person identifies the source of the fear-producing stimuli and directs behavior away from the danger. The fear of the infant is not directed toward an object, and the behavior is not clearly avoidant, although, as we have seen, the infant does have some avoidance responses. Curiously enough, these are not the ones that are usually conceived as expressing fear.

Fear in infancy seems to be closely related to the startle response. Fearful people are more easily startled than those who are less timid. When a person is in a dangerous situation, he is more easily startled than when he feels completely secure. It seems probable that a careful observational study of infancy would show how the startle reaction forms the historical antecedent of the fear response in later life.

The startle response itself is present from birth. It has been found by Landis and Hunt (1939) to be a highly predictable reflex response to all kinds of sudden stimuli—a loud noise, a sudden drop or jar of the body, or a bright flash of light.

Investigations of later infancy have not succeeded in describing precisely the difference between the situations evoking fear and those evoking anger. The suddenness of the startling stimulus is one important difference between the two types of stimulation. Both types of stimulation impose on the child; both produce crying and distress. Gradually, with maturity, the fear becomes a withdrawal response to overpowering situations; the anger becomes an attack response to frustrating situations. Before these properties are clearly distinguished, the differences are quite subtle, and in many situations the observer would probably be unable to decide whether a child was angry or afraid. In clear-cut situations, however, one or the other type of behavior seems to be clearly displayed. The startling situation is one in which fear is obvious.

The fears of children during infancy and later have been surveyed and tabulated by Jersild and Holmes (1935). They found that throughout infancy the most frequent fear-provoking stimuli are sudden noises and noisy objects. Strangeness and unfamiliarity, however, are close seconds. Strange objects, situations, and persons tend to make the baby afraid, although there are wide individual differences in the susceptibility to fear of the unfamiliar. Thus, the shyness of the baby less than a year old when confronted with strangers might well be called fear; his shyness leads to withdrawal. Fear continues to lead to withdrawal throughout life. The prevalence of other sources of fear is shown in Figure 7.2.

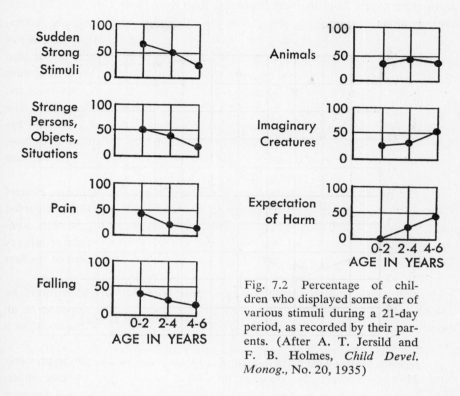

Fig. 7.2 Percentage of children who displayed some fear of various stimuli during a 21-day period, as recorded by their parents. (After A. T. Jersild and F. B. Holmes, *Child Devel. Monog.*, No. 20, 1935)

An experiment by Arsenian (1943) shows the fearsomeness of a strange situation for many children, and it further demonstrates clearly how the presence of the mother or some other familiar person allays children's fears in a strange situation so that the children are less inhibited and less emotional.

The children were placed in a strange room that was empty except for toys and other available play objects. The children, who ranged in age from eleven months to thirty months, were all able to walk around, so that their movements might be recorded.

There were two groups of children in the experiment. One group was composed of children who were accompanied into the experimental room by a mother or some very familiar person; the other group faced the new situation alone. Figure 7.3 shows the security scores for the two groups. The security score is a composite score involving the emotionality of the child and the degree to which his actions were inhibited in the experimental situation.

Two results are quite clear. When the children returned to the experimental room on several successive occasions, it became familiar, and their security increased. Secondly, the children who were accompanied by mothers were more secure from the very beginning than were those children who were entirely alone.

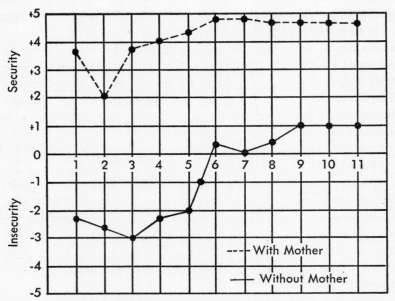

Fig. 7.3 The effect of the presence of a familiar person on a child's security. (After Jean M. Arsenian, *J. Abn. and Soc. Psych., 38,* 1943, 236)

When we contrast these fear-provoking situations with situations that are fear-provoking for adults, we can see that the instigation to fear in the adult is more specific and object-oriented than for the child. The threat of a powerful imposition that cannot be resisted, but that can perhaps be escaped, evokes fear in an adult, and he feels secure when he is safe from danger.

In the behavior of the young child we can detect the early beginnings of this fear response. The strong startling stimulus has some of the characteristics of a strong imposition. The reduced fearfulness of the child when he is not alone in a strange situation suggests that he views his mother as a protector and that her presence makes him secure.

Thus, we can see in the shyness of the baby toward strangers and his liking for familiarity the roots out of which the more mature fear responses gradually develop and differentiate. The unknown continues to be slightly frightening because we cannot be sure in the unknown situation that we shall not find ourselves helpless in the face of danger. But we gradually differentiate the probably dangerous unknown situations from those which are not threatening, and we respond to the latter with interest and curiosity. We continue to be momentarily frightened of a startling stimulus, but we quickly survey it and decide whether or not it is frightening.

The differentiation of security feelings develops similarly. Whereas, for the young infant insecurity is unfamiliarity, with differentiation insecurity comes to be equated with vulnerability to danger. Some familiar situations are insecure—the dentist's chair, for example; some unfamiliar situations are secure—such as a trip to a new place. Whereas the presence of the mother probably makes the child feel secure merely by making the situation more familiar, the presence of protectors makes adults feel secure in accordance with the power and influence of the protectors. Some indication of the further development of this feeling of security comes from a finding of Klein (1932) that the child of fifteen months will seek specific help from an adult and will turn to the adult for protection.

To summarize, this discussion suggests that security or insecurity is a possible psychological state after the fifth month. With maturity, this state gradually becomes more and more differentiated out of generalized distress; it comes to indicate the individual's perception of his power relative to that of environmental events, and at the same time his expectation of harm. To determine the age at which these dimensions of security become well developed will require further research.

The Reciprocation of an Imposition

We have seen that imposition and opportunity may stem from the inanimate environment or from the social environment, and that escape or resistance may be directed toward people or toward objects. There is another general principle of motivation, however, that by its very nature can exist only in a social setting. When another person is the source of an imposition, the imposition instigates reciprocation. There is a tendency for people to want to return smiles with smiles, to repay favors, to benefit the people that benefit them, to revenge injuries, to dominate people who try to dominate. To put it abstractly, if another person imposes some event upon us, we are motivated to impose that same event on him. We shall begin this discussion with the smiling response because it is one of the earliest social-behavior patterns that the child develops.

SMILING   The earliest social response that has been studied is smiling. As we shall see, the smiling of the infant is not truly a social response, but it is closely related to the presence of other people.

It has been found that the situation that most frequently evokes smiling from the infant is being smiled at. One research study has investigated the exact stimulus situation that is necessary to evoke a smiling response on the part of an infant of four to six months (Spitz and Wolf, 1946).

Spitz and Wolf were concerned first in determining how widespread the smiling response is in infancy and especially whether it depends upon which person presents the stimuli. Studying a group of 145 infants between the ages of two and six months, they found that smiling could be evoked in 142 of them by the following stimulus: the experimenter presented to the child a smiling and nodding face, in a full front view so that the child could see both eyes of the experimenter simultaneously. When the experimenter turned his profile to the child, the smiling stopped. In other words, the smiling response is rather indiscriminately evoked by a full front view of a nodding or smiling face. In contrast to these findings on children less than six months old, Spitz and Wolf found that children over the age of six months do not respond to this stimulus indiscriminately. They smile, but only at certain people.

The purpose of the next part of the experiment was to determine whether the pleasant expression of the face—pleasant from the adult point of view— was essential. The experimenter cultivated his ability to make faces; he put on an extremely sardonic expression which could hardly be interpreted as pleasant. He presented this expression to the infant, nodding his head simultaneously, being sure that both eyes were visible to the child. Of the 142 infants who smiled in the first experiment, 141 smiled also at this exaggerated expression. Turning to the child the profile rather than the full front view again stopped the smile. When one eye was covered, smiling also stopped. This experiment showed that the infant is responding not to the emotional attitude that the face represents but rather to a specific stimulus pattern.

The experimenters next attempted to narrow down the stimulus pattern to its essentials by wearing a Hallowe'en mask over the face. The child again saw a full front view, and either the head was nodding or the tongue was being rhythmically protruded and withdrawn from the mouth of the mask. Of the 142 cases, 140 smiled at the Hallowe'en mask. In the final experiment of the series, the child was presented with a life-sized puppet whose face was the Hallowe'en mask. The head of the puppet was nodding when the child saw it. Again 140 out of 142 infants smiled. A number of control experiments were performed to try to evoke smiling in some completely nonhuman way. Flashlights of various intensities were used, bells of various intensities were rung, and other control stimuli were used in an effort to provoke a smile, but all the responses were negative.

These experiments show that some behavioral patterns require (except under highly unusual experimental situations) human beings as the stimulus object. Nevertheless, the lack of discrimination of the infant reveals that his behavior is evoked by a limited set of stimuli and is not dependent upon the recognition of friendliness, kind intentions, or any of the usual conditions that make adults feel like smiling at another person.

Gradually the child develops more discrimination. Spitz and Wolf report that by the second half of the first year the infant discriminates among different people in so far as smiling is concerned. This finding is a generally accepted one, confirmed by many experimenters. At about the sixth or seventh month the child begins to respond to his mother with smiling and pleasure, whereas he may be shy and sober with strangers.

The child also becomes more discriminating in his response to facial expressions. Whereas the four-month-old infant smiled in response to a horrible grimace with a waggling tongue, a child of six or seven months, Buhler and Hetzer (1927) report, responds differentially to a scowl and a smile on the face of the person who is looking at him. When the mother smiles at him, the child responds positively with smiles, but when the mother frowns, he may cry, scowl, or become inhibited.

Here we find perhaps the earliest example of reciprocation, although we cannot be sure that this is true reciprocation. Does the infant return a smile because he in some sense recognizes friendliness and positive feeling and is expressing it reciprocally, or is the smile of the six-month-old imitative or sympathetic? We cannot answer these questions for the young infant, but by the time the child is two, there seems little doubt that positive approaches to him are reciprocated.

The later developments in children of reciprocation of positive actions have not been studied. We have almost no idea of when a child is mature enough to want to return a favor. We do not even know whether the wish to return favors stems from a feeling of obligation or is a spontaneous impulse stemming from friendliness.

THE INSTIGATION OF ANGER AND RETALIATION   It probably indicates something about the interests of the psychological profession that we know so little about the dynamics of the motivation for returning benefits but have studied anger and hostility in considerable detail.

Hostility seems to be developed, partly at least, from the angry, tantrum-like emotional behavior of infancy. The development of hostility is partly a process of directing this anger toward an object; usually it is directed toward the person who provoked the anger. Hostility does not develop solely from tantrum behavior; it involves such acquired behavior patterns as hitting, kicking, and pushing. Perhaps they are crystallized out of the violent thrashing about of an infantile temper, but they can be learned in other situations in which anger is not present.

Not only does the motivation to hurt another person develop out of anger, but it is commonly accompanied by anger even in adult behavior. To hurt somebody when one is not angry is to hurt him in cold blood. There are people, of course, who deliberately hurt other people as a means to a goal; there are even people who apparently enjoy the suffering of others, and who hurt them just for the pleasure of hurting. But since these hostility patterns are relatively uncommon, our discussion of hostility can concentrate upon the appearance of the retaliation motif during childhood. By the time a child is in nursery school he is provoked to retaliate or reciprocate whenever he is hurt by another child, although he may be too fearful to do so. We shall, in this section, examine the course of events leading up to this motivational pattern and see what happens to it during childhood.

According to Bridges (1932) (see p. 71), anger and fear are two emotions that become differentiated out of a less differentiated emotion of distress. These two varieties of distress continue to be closely related; fear can change into anger, and anger can change into fear. After the middle of the first year of life, however, the two emotions are quite clearly different.

Despite the fact that anger occurs during the first year, we are not justified in assuming that it means that the child wants to hurt another person. The situations that provoke anger and the way in which it expresses itself seem to suggest that at first it is quite diffuse and undirected; only later does it become directed hostility.

The situations that seem to provoke anger during the first year are "impositions," especially those that prevent the child from moving. Goodenough (1931) reports in her observations of two infants less than one year old that anger was frequently aroused during the routine of bathing and dressing. Mothers know how difficult it is to clean the baby's ears and nose. This routine, which necessitates holding the baby's head motionless and probing rather vigorously, seems to be especially irritating. Goodenough also found that anger could sometimes be provoked by breaking off a social contact with the infant.

In early infancy, anger is a violent explosive crying, like a tantrum. It is not directed behavior. Even though the infant may push away the intruding object (the cotton swab or the spoon), his behavior is better described as a removal of an unpleasant stimulus than as an angry attack upon the irritating object. It may be that these "pushing away" actions are the early behavior patterns from which hitting and attacking develop, but at this early age level there is no evidence that the infant is hostile toward anything. He is just angry.

For further developments in the child's ability to be hostile, we can turn to the experiments by Maudry and Nekula (1939), who studied ninety-two children, ranging in age from six to twenty-five months. Two children were put into a play pen together and left for four minutes. This period was used as a control to see what kind of reactions would ensue when there was no play material available. Then each child was given a block and a third block was placed on the floor between the two children. After another four minutes, a bell was given to one of the children and the observers concentrated upon the behavior of the other child, the one who did not have the bell. In a third period, a drum was given to the two children and each child was given a drumstick. Finally, a ball was given to the two children and they were shown how to roll it back and forth between them.

By these devices the children were placed in a situation that might be expected to stimulate competitiveness and frustration, and also in one that offered an opportunity for cooperation. According to Maudry and Nekula's observations of the youngest children, six to eight months of age, the partner was generally ignored; for that matter, the play material was frequently ignored also. The observers noted that the new material was more likely to be attended to if it were given to the partner but that no hostility was thus evoked; when the child's attention was drawn to the material, his approach to the partner was positive.

At the next age level, nine to thirteen months, the play material was much more quickly and frequently responded to. If the partner had the material, the attitude was negative—i.e., the child was unfriendly rather than friendly—but his behavior was directed toward obtaining the material rather than attacking the partner.

The children in the next older group, fourteen to eighteen months, showed a shift of interest from the material to the partner, but usually after the desire for material was satisfied. If the child had what he wanted, he might lose interest in it and make a partial approach to his partner, but if the partner had the material which the child wanted, he still tended to be focused upon the material. Even when the child was focused on the material, his fights to get it were not so socially blind as they were in younger children.

In the oldest group, nineteen to twenty-five months of age, there was interest in the partner, although it was still outweighed by interest in the material. At this age level the material could be used as a medium for establishing social contact; it was not solely an alternative to social contact.

This research suggests that, as the child matures, he stops reacting solely to the goal to which access is not permitted and begins to react to the frustrating agent. This reaction to the frustrating agent is a hostile attack.

The most important instigation to hostility throughout the preschool period is conflict over material possessions. This may be the reason that there is less quarreling in play situations involving a dramatic theme in which each child has a part than in situations involving material possessions.

EFFECTS OF MATURITY ON HOSTILITY   The effect of maturity upon feelings of hostility can be described in terms of (1) the perception of hostility in a wide variety of situations; (2) the ability to maintain hostility for a long time; (3) the perception that hostility is the intent to hurt.

Because of his increased sensitivity, the preschool child can be hurt or frustrated in many ways that were not possible when he was less mature. Scolding, for example, may not be effective as a disciplinary technique, but the child, because he has become more sensitive, can be hurt by it and may become angry and hostile because of it.

A second example of the sensitivity of the preschool child is the fact that he can be hurt by feelings of inferiority. People who do better or have more than he does may be perceived, therefore, as appropriate objects of hostility. He may fight for the biggest hammer or the best tricycle, whereas formerly the "biggest" would not be an important characteristic. Finally, the fact that he can feel guilty may make him hostile toward the people who blame him or even toward an innocent bystander. When he makes a mistake, he may tell his mother, "You made me do it." (See p. 351 for another example.) She was not the cause in any clear way, but his need to blame someone rather than himself may evoke hostility toward the nearest person, toward a customary scapegoat, or perhaps toward any weak person.

In view of the fact that the child's hostility can be aroused in more ways as he matures, it might be expected that the frequency of hostile reactions would increase with age. But this is clearly not true. In several studies that have analyzed the frequency of quarreling in nursery school (Jersild and Markey, 1935; Green, 1933), a consistent finding has been that the frequency of quarreling decreases with age. This is further indicated by the fact that in quarrels between two age levels, the initiator is usually the younger child— although it is generally the older child who wins the quarrel.

Although the frequency of quarrels decreases with age, their length increases. This may result from the fact that the child is not easily distractable from the object about which he is quarreling. Furthermore, he is more capable than he was earlier of a permanent hostility toward another person (see p. 201). This ability to hold a grudge is not very pronounced, however, at the nursery-school age. Even the longer quarrels of preschool children are, as a rule, quite short and depend upon relatively superficial factors, such as frequency of contact and the probability of interference. Thus, there is more quarreling than average between good friends. This finding probably depends on the fact that close friends are usually together a great deal and thus frequently want the same thing.

A similar indication of the dependency of quarreling upon chance conflict rather than long-term hostility is the fact that there is more quarreling indoors than outdoors; there is, in fact, a general relationship between the amount of space per child and the frequency of quarrels within a play group.

With maturity the child comes to appreciate the intention behind hostile behavior. A clear illustration of this perception of intent is a common reaction of the nursery-school child to punishment or to hostility. When he says, "Aw, that didn't hurt me," his remark can mean only that he recognizes the intention of the other person to hurt him and, furthermore, that he recognizes that his failure to acknowledge hurt frustrates the other person's intention. He may pretend he is not hurt even when he actually is because he wants to frustrate the aggressor's intention.

When he selects a retaliation that has nothing to do with his punishment or with the deed for which he was punished, the preschool child also recognizes that the aim of aggression is to hurt another person. When the child is frustrated or hurt by the parent, he may proceed to violate some completely different rule. If the parent says that the child cannot have a visitor, the child may say, "All right, I won't pick up my toys." The dynamics behind such behavior is the recognition that the parent is the source of the rules, and that breaking any of them hurts the parent by frustrating his wishes. The child is punishing the parent, not trying to compensate for having no visitor. We should recognize, incidentally, that parental punishment is frequently equally unrelated to the act of the child. The parent who punishes the child for getting into a mud puddle by sending him to his room or by not letting him have his dessert is demonstrating the equivalence of widely varying means of punishing the child.

In general, then, the child's hostility shows definite maturational changes during childhood. It becomes more differentiated, it persists longer, and, perhaps most significant, it reflects the ability of the child to perceive the intent of other people and to respond to the intent itself rather than to the physical action.

Competition and Dominance

Competition and hostility are so closely related that they are at times indistinguishable. Both of these motivations are excellent examples of the principle of reciprocation. Two people in competition are each trying to triumph over the other, just as two fighters each try to injure the other. Furthermore, it is difficult at times to distinguish between trying to win and trying to hurt. On the one hand, almost any victory does have the effect of psychologically hurting the loser; it is not surprising that he is easily motivated to get his revenge. One of the difficulties in learning to be a good sport is to be a good loser and to avoid becoming angry with the victor. Competition, therefore, is easily transformed into hostility. On the other hand, some hostility seems to be as much competition as aggression. The object of most fights is in one sense to hurt the opponent, but the end of most fights comes when one person gives up. After the loser has admitted defeat, it takes a very vindictive opponent to keep on inflicting pain, despite the fact that this is exactly what he was trying to do up to that moment. In this section we shall look at what evidence we can find to elucidate the development of competitive activity.

VARIETIES OF COMPETITIVE SITUATIONS   The most primitive cause of a competitive situation is probably the existence of an unsharable goal object. If there is only one toy for two children, the existence of rivalry and competition is facilitated. If the competitive situation is of this type, it is clear that competition may engender hostility between the competitors. Each one must frustrate the other in order to reach his own goal. Competitive behavior may frustrate another person in two ways. The first is truly accidental or incidental, in that the winner frustrates the loser only by winning. In a second situation, harming another person is a means of winning. In shuffleboard, for example, one has the choice of trying to put one's own puck in a high scoring area or knocking the opponent's puck out of a high scoring area or into a penalty area. Both procedures are aimed at winning, but the second is much more likely to provoke hostility in one's opponent. It requires considerable maturity not to feel hostile toward any competitor, but more self-control is required when one's own good performance is destroyed than when it is merely surpassed.

Competition in adult life is by no means always forced upon the participants as a result of finding themselves in a situation containing a realistically unsharable goal. Games with unsharable goals are invented so that there can be a winner and so that competition can occur. Many adults compete with their fellow men even when there is no realistic demand for it.

Competition is greatly facilitated by the existence of a status dimension. A continuum that has a desirable end, on which people may be located, sets up a possible competitive situation. Since very few pairs of people are at the same position on a continuum, there is an ever-present possibility for any difference in positions to arouse competition. Suppose, for example, that a man has a need for money. His position on the dimension of wealth may be determined. If his level of aspiration is influenced largely by the wealth of his contemporaries or his friends, his motivation may be only indirectly related to his needs for the things money will obtain. If, because he sees the situation competitively, he is motivated to move other people lower on the dimension— i.e., to reduce their wealth—as well as to move himself higher, his need for wealth and prestige may arouse essentially hostile and antisocial motives.

COMPETITION DURING THE PRESCHOOL PERIOD   Turning now to the appearance of competitiveness in the preschool period, we should look first at the situations that present an unsharable goal. The fact that two young children both want an unsharable goal makes the situation objectively competitive, but it is not psychologically competitive unless the children are aware of each other as people. In the study by Maudry and Nekula (see p. 158), the behavior of the youngest children who wanted the same toy was described as socially blind. Near the age of two, the activities and competition of the children became directed more toward the partner and less exclusively toward the material. In a sense, such play is competitive.

Greenberg's study of competitiveness in preschool children employed a somewhat similar technique (1932). Each child was paired with an experimental partner, and the two were allowed to play with blocks. The competitiveness was introduced by suggestions made along the way. Sometimes the experimenter would ask the children to compare their block constructions, "Which of these is the prettier?" or "Let's see who can build the prettier house." In this situation, it is important to note, competitiveness has taken a different form. There is no unsharable goal object; instead, competition is reflected by the relative position of the two partners on some scale of value, such as prettiness or size.

Greenberg found that competitiveness in this more mature sense was not apparent in the behavior of children below the age of three. Sometimes the younger children competed in the sense that both grabbed for the same block or one might take blocks away from the other's construction. Neither member of the pair, however, paid any particular attention to the construction of the other child. The interest was focused upon the material. The three- to four-year-olds were also not very competitive. They were much more aware of the other child than at the age of two, but their sensitivity was social rather than competitive. Greenberg found that from the age of four to six, the oldest age in his study, high competitiveness could be easily stimulated. Gesell and Ilg (1942) confirm the fact that bragging and comparisons between the self and other people are more prevalent at four than they are earlier.

Once a child is mature enough to be competitive, further maturity brings about a more realistic evaluation of accomplishment. The younger children in Greenberg's study, when asked whose construction was the prettier, always replied that their own was. Among the oldest group, however, some children appreciated the beauty of another's construction.

Another sort of change in the nature of competitiveness may also be expected with increased maturity. Since competition depends upon the child's sensitivity to the competitor as well as to the task, it is to be expected that even though a four-year-old does compare his finished work with other people's or boasts beforehand that he will build the bigger house, he can easily become so involved in the activity that during its progress he is not at all sensitive to the competition. Or if he does watch the other child at work, he may lose interest and become distracted from his own work. Thus, for competition to affect the child's motivation continuously throughout a task, the child must be mature enough to keep at his own task and at the same time be aware of his competitor. Leuba (1933) found such results with children who were paired in a task of putting pegs in holes. He compared the performance of each child when alone and when paired with another child. The two-year-olds were not affected by the social situation. The three-year-olds and four-year-olds were competitive, but competition lowered their performance. The five-year-olds, on the other hand, showed increased production when placed in the competitive situation.

Instigations to Benefit Other People

We have been mainly concerned, thus far, with the less pleasant side of child behavior: hostility, resistance, fears. Children may also be instigated to be friendly and helpful to others.

At least two types of situations tend to evoke the response of helping other people. One is the rendering of a favor or benefit. If someone benefits us, we are motivated to benefit him. This reciprocation of friendly actions has been discussed only briefly because of the absence of reliable information about its origins and development. A second instigation to nurturant or helping behavior is the presence of another person in trouble or distress. A sympathetic response is to do something that benefits the other person and relieves him of his trouble.

Sympathy among children has been studied extensively by Murphy (1937), who observed children in a nursery school as various opportunities arose for sympathetic response. She also observed children in an experimental situation. A two-year-old was put in a play pen with no toys. This helpless child without toys was intended to instigate a sympathetic response. The subject of the experiment was brought into the room to see whether he would show some sympathetic response toward the child in the play pen. If he did not do so within a few minutes the experimenter asked such questions as "She hasn't got any of her things, has she?" or "What do you think she wants?" Later the experimenter started to lift the young child out of the play pen but pretended that she was having trouble doing so, in order to see whether the subject would help her. If no help was forthcoming within ten seconds, the experimenter asked for help. This was the strongest instigation employed in the experiment.

The general findings of this study show that children become more responsive to distress as they mature but that individual differences within an age level are greater than average differences between age levels. The study also showed that more obvious and spectacular distress was required to evoke sympathetic response from younger children than from older children. Children of two or three do not recognize black-and-blue swellings and bruises as signs of distress but may respond sympathetically to conspicuous bandages and to flowing blood. Older children may respond not only to signs of physical injury but also to the subtler forms of distress, such as deprivation of food or toys or mother, confinement, or interference with physical activity.

Public Exposure of Behavior as an Instigation

We have in our adult life a number of attitudes related to the privacy of behavior. We have laws to protect privacy; exhibitionists and Peeping Toms are prosecuted. The exposure of one's defects generally brings shame with it and instigates a motive to hide or conceal the defect but children are quite unpredictable when they are in the limelight. A child playing in the living room before guests may yell, stand on his head, or perform any silly antic that is necessary to steal the limelight and get attention. He basks in it and is exhilarated by it. Then a half hour later in a different setting, the child happens to make some remark that everybody finds amusing. At the burst of laughter, the child may dive out of sight under the table or behind some furniture and refuse to emerge. The preschool child may appreciate the focus of attention when he seeks it, but he does not like it very much when it is thrust upon him.

Let us try to discover the factors that produce this shyness or embarrassment. Because the child, when he turns shy, tends to hide himself and to get out of sight, we suspect that one cause of discomfort for him is the fact that he is visible—highly visible—when everyone turns his attention upon him. It is this conspicuousness that seems to be uncomfortable when it is suddenly imposed upon him.

The degree of visibility may vary from one situation to another. When the child acts in concert with others, when he is just one member of a group, he is—from his own point of view—psychologically less visible than when he is alone before an audience. Therefore, he feels less conspicuous and uncomfortable as a group member. The size of the group of spectators also affects the feeling of being exposed. As the number of spectators decreases, there seems to be a corresponding decrease in feelings of being conspicuous. We all feel that a *faux pas* is in some way less serious if committed in a small group than before a large audience.

We must keep in mind that shyness depends on *feeling* conspicuous. If the child becomes completely absorbed in what he is doing, he may not know or realize that he is being watched. His psychological feeling of being visible may disappear entirely. Possibly this is what occurs sometimes when the child voluntarily remains in the limelight, but this hypothesis alone cannot account for the positive pleasure that he sometimes derives from being the center of attention.

The reaction of an adult to being the center of attention seems to depend partly upon whether he is confident that he is making a good appearance. If he feels that a weakness is being put on exhibition, he feels embarrassed and ashamed. If, on the other hand, he is confident that he is making a good appearance, he may seek the limelight. It is not easy to determine whether these same feelings of self-confidence or doubt motivate the young child who seeks the center of the stage or who retires out of sight. A child of two or three can hardly have the same clear feeling of weakness or strength that an adult has, but such a self-image may nevertheless be present in a less differentiated form.

There is a certain weakness implied in the mere fact of suddenly being made conspicuous through no choice of one's own. More important in the feeling of shame, however, is the exposure of one's clear weaknesses and defects. People can be ashamed of any sort of weakness—disfigurement, defect, error, or sin. When they are ashamed of something, they try to hide it. It is important to recognize that in the evocation of shame it may make little difference whether or not a defect is of vital importance to one's functioning. A scar, for example, which has no realistic effect upon one's abilities, may nevertheless be a source of great shame and embarrassment. It also makes little difference in so far as shame is concerned whether the defect is something for which one is responsible; accidental blemishes or inherited defects may be the source of as much shame as errors committed through heedless lack of foresight. All these considerations suggest that shame is a primitive, undifferentiated feeling of being degraded and unworthy.

Having one's weaknesses nakedly exposed, especially when they are made the center of attention, tends always to produce shame, but the nature of the audience makes a great deal of difference. A third factor affecting the feeling of shame is the status of the spectators—taken in relation to the status of the person who is being exposed. Some characteristics produce shame only when they become visible to one's superiors. Being exposed to people of inferior status may not evoke shame at all. People accustomed to servants may behave just as though the servant were not there. If the spectator discovers that someone he greatly admires is really not admirable, the person whose defect is thus exposed may feel ashamed even if the spectator is of low status; the alcoholic who is ashamed when his children see him drunk illustrates this point.

The reaction to being shamed can be logically deduced from this conceptualization of shame. The first reaction is to get out of sight. This is the immediate reaction because the visibility is frequently the most painful part of an embarrassing situation. The tendency to hide also illustrates the primitiveness of the feeling. One is ashamed when other people know of a defect; there is actually little point in hiding because one cannot wipe out the knowledge other people have acquired by merely disappearing from their field of vision. Nevertheless, invisibility is highly attractive. Once some shameful fact is exposed, it is possible for the shame to be renewed more strongly than ever by any sort of public appearance even if the defect is subjected to no further exposure. Shame may be elicited when the defect itself is not visible; it is evoked in the person who feels defective whenever *he* is conspicuous. People may not feel comfortable when their ill-gotten gains are made public even if the fact that they are ill gotten is well concealed. This fact further illustrates how undifferentiated a feeling shame is.

A second reaction to being shamed is to become hostile toward the spectators. Since the visibility is painful, those who watch are, in a sense, those who inflict the pain, and they become, therefore, the object of hostility. This hostility may be strongly reinforced by a desire to degrade the spectators. If those who watch are not worthy of one's respect, the shame is reduced. Therefore, attempts to be contemptuous of them, to show up their defects, and to degrade them are attempts to adjust to the situation.

Summary

We have in this chapter discussed the conditions that instigate a number of motives. One group of motives thus far neglected—those of compliance, conformity, the sense of duty or obligation, the motivation to act the way other people wish us to, and the various motives associated with guilt, retribution, and self-punishment—will be discussed in Chapter 10, on the social control of behavior. In addition to this cluster of motivations, we have omitted many ramifications of interpersonal motivation because so little is known about it.

We must not minimize, however, the importance of what is known about motivation in childhood. As we have seen, one important distinction among instigations is the distinction between opportunities or invitations and impositions. There are some events that the individual himself brings about; he is the cause, the source, and the responsible person. There are other changes in the individual's environment which happen to him, which he suffers or undergoes rather than causes. These impositions are important instigations to motivated behavior and they are also the situations that evoke emotional responses.

Some instigations invite motivated behavior by presenting to the person a reminder or an opportunity for some behavior pattern. We have seen that this sort of instigation gradually comes to depend on opportunity rather than mere suggestion, and we shall see in the next chapter how the selection among opportunities depends upon the needs of the person.

The instigations that are impositions tend to evoke emotional responses as well as motivated behavior. These motives develop with the differentiation of the appropriate emotion out of undifferentiated excitement. When the emotion first occurs in the infant, the accompanying behavior is restless and undirected, apparently merely an expression of one variety of tension. As the child matures, this undirected emotional behavior gradually becomes directed. This process requires the cognition of the source of the emotional provocation and the development of an appropriate motivated response to this provocation. In some cases the effect of the motivated behavior is to reduce or eliminate the provocation—e.g., escape or resistance to threat of imposition. In other cases, the instigated behavior is retaliatory, compensating, or some response more complex than a mere avoidance of unpleasant emotional tension. These complex responses occur far more frequently in interpersonal situations than in the reaction to impersonal instigation.

We have described and exemplified four general patterns of interpersonal instigation of motives. The first is the response to opportunity in an interpersonal situation. This may be illustrated by the procedures for studying sympathy. A person in trouble offers an opportunity to be nurturant. Weakness instigates a variety of different motives because it presents an opportunity to impose any sort of action the person wishes. Cold-blooded cruelty or sadism is instigated by weakness; dominance and bullying behavior may be instigated by weakness; so, of course, may kindness and nurturance.

The second general pattern is resistance to imposition. This has been exemplified by negativism, as well as by the motivation to hide, which is instigated by exposure. If the imposition takes the form of frustration, the resistance is seen as an increase in the strength of the frustrated motive. This was illustrated by the effect of barriers on motivation by the studies of level of aspiration, and by the strong instigations provided by a challenge that offers both an opportunity and a barrier.

The third general pattern of response to imposition is straight avoidance or escape. This occurs especially when the imposition is powerful and sudden, and is often accompanied by fear.

The fourth pattern is reciprocation. There is a tendency to reciprocate all sorts of impositions, whether they are intrinsically pleasant, unpleasant, or neutral. The hostile attack upon the source of an imposition is, in some cases, a way of avoiding or warding off the threat; but when the motivation occurs after the injury is done, it is called revenge or retaliation.

It is obvious that there are many alternative motives that may be instigated by the same situation. The details of the instigating situation may determine, in some cases, which response is the most likely; but the most important factors that determine which motive is actually instigated are the needs of the individual, his susceptibility to various instigations, his preferences for various types of activity, and his attitudes toward other people. The next chapter will be devoted to the discussion of his needs.

8

The Needs of Children

A NURSERY-SCHOOL TEACHER is not surprised to find that on some occasions all her children are engaged in the same activity. When two or three children begin some very noticeable, exciting activity, such as marching in single file in and out the various rooms, each pulling some wheel toy after him, it is not uncommon for others gradually to join in the game until the entire three-year-old group is playing follow-the-leader. This unanimity illustrates the compelling motivating power of a clear suggestion from the environment.

On the other hand, not many of the games in nursery school are so contagious. The schoolroom usually contains several groups, some children building with blocks, some in the doll corner, some playing with wheel toys,

170

and a few isolated children here and there intent on their own affairs. Yet all these children are offered the same opportunities and the same suggestions. The same nursery-school situation does not evoke the same motives from all of them because each child has his own individual preferences and dislikes, his own needs. The task of this chapter is to describe the properties of needs and how they change with maturity.

The actual behavior of the child when confronted with a concrete situation is the result of the interaction of two factors: (1) the strength of the various instigations that the situation offers and (2) the sensitivity of the child to these various instigations. If one opportunity is very clear and none of the others is obvious, then even if the child is not especially sensitive to that opportunity, it is likely to evoke the motive because of its clarity. Although the schoolroom situation still contains the opportunity to play with dolls, build with blocks, listen to records, etc., the children marching with wheel toys make that opportunity much clearer than others. Unless the child likes much better to play with dolls than to march, he will probably be motivated to join in the game. When no single activity is obtrusively presented, the various opportunities are about equally clear, so that the child's choice of activity is more likely to reflect his play preferences.

The specific likes and preferences for one activity over another are examples of needs, to be sure, but not all needs can be described so specifically. Any psychological condition that makes the child more easily motivated by one instigation than another must in our terminology be called a need. Irritability, for example, is a need. When the seven-year-old has been told he is too little to play football with the gang, he continues, of course, to be motivated to play football. He may also try to retaliate by spoiling the game for the others. The frustration makes him irritable. If, when he arrives home, his sister is playing with dolls on the front porch, he may see in this situation an invitation to wreck her playhouse. It is one opportunity offered by the situation; another one would be to play house with her; and there is, of course, nothing stopping him from doing many other things irrelevant to doll play. The opportunity to spoil her game is the one that evokes a motive, not because he has a strong dislike for his sister or for doll playing but because he "has a chip on his shoulder." Even if he were not so irritable as to seek out a fight, he might be more easily provoked than usual. A mild request to burn the trash, which would ordinarily be responded to willingly or at worst grudgingly, now may provoke a tempest of anger. These temporary periods of susceptibility to irritation, which are called moods, are short-lived needs because they temporarily sensitize the child to one kind of instigation more than to other kinds.

The fact that such psychological states as moods are classified as needs makes it clear that there is no one-to-one correspondence between motives and needs. A catalogue of an individual's needs is not a list of every possible motive he may have. Some very specific likes and preferences correspond closely with possible motives. A strong preference for classical music is most obviously revealed in the motivation to listen to it, but less specific needs often have no single corresponding motive. Great admiration for the President of the United States is equally relevant to many different motives—to vote for him, to support his proposals, to attack his critics. The lack of one-to-one correspondence between needs and motives also indicates that a need is not an unborn motive awaiting the proper conditions to be transformed into a motive. Instead, the need is a condition of the organism that makes it susceptible to a certain pattern of stimulation. The need does not change into a motive; it is an entirely different sort of concept.

Before entering into our full discussion of needs, we should also clarify one further possible confusion. Children's needs are sometimes thought of as the things children require for good health and good development. It is perfectly true that babies need a mother's love or that babies need an adequate supply of Vitamin D. The requirements for healthy development are numerous, but many of these requirements are not needs in the special sense in which we have been using the term. The infant has no psychological need for Vitamin D. He is not more easily motivated to eat foods containing Vitamin D than foods of other sorts. Similarly, there is no evidence that the young infant needs a mother's love. He does not miss it or seek it out if it is absent. Mothering is very important for the proper development of an infant, but the baby of four or five months does not need it in our meaning of the term. Later, after the child is a year or so old, he may strongly miss his mother if she is absent; he may call for her. Now he needs his mother in the special sense of the word which we have adopted.

The Varieties of Needs in the Mature Person

With this general introduction to the concept of need let us locate the concept in the model of human behavior. If we look back at the model described in Chapter 6 (see p. 130), we find that there are many characteristics of the individual listed along the bottom of the diagram. Needs constitute one class of personal characteristics; skills or abilities form another class; knowledge and cognitive schemata constitute still another.

For our present purposes it is essential to be clear about the differences between needs and skills. When a man sees a drowning person, he is motivated to help him. How he helps him depends partly upon his skills. He may throw a life preserver, he may swim out to him, he may row out in a boat. The personal characteristics that determine his motivation to help the drowning man are needs. His skills determine which method he selects and how successful he is. Needs are the characteristics that determine which motives will be instigated by a situation; skills are the characteristics that determine which behavior patterns he can and cannot perform in a particular situation. Irritability, sympathy, favorable attitude toward Negroes, honesty—these are examples of various sorts of needs. Strength, small-muscle coordination, ability to manipulate numbers—these are examples of skills or abilities.

We have seen that in mature behavior the selection of a goal and the specific behavior that attains the goal are independent in the sense that the individual may employ the same instrumental action to attain different goals and may employ any one of a series of behavior patterns to reach a specific goal. This independence of goal selection and goal-directed behavior implies that the needs underlying goal selection and the skills underlying goal-directed behavior are independent also.

Although mature behavior may show this independence, we have seen that goal selection and goal-directed behavior are not independent in young children. Thus, we shall find that needs and skills are not necessarily differentiated in children. The smiling behavior of infants does not indicate merely an ability to smile; it also reflects the social responsiveness of the child. But it is not purely a measure of social responsiveness; the smiling of the young infant is evoked by a specific stimulus, not by all social stimulation. We cannot distinguish in the young infant the need to smile from the ability to smile. Neither term is entirely appropriate.

We shall find, therefore, that the description of the personality characteristics of a young child requires us to take his level of maturity into account. Before plunging into these difficulties, let us consider for a moment the varieties of needs that characterize mature adults. Then we shall see how some of these needs develop out of the more general characteristics of young children.

General Needs; Sensitivity to a Class of Instigation

One type of need exhibited by the mature person is illustrated by such general personality traits as orderliness, nurturance, cowardice, or fastidiousness. What does such a trait as nurturance imply for the behavior of a person?

Nurturance is the need underlying the motivation to help other people, to take care of them when they are in trouble, to do things for them. A nurturant person is more likely than a nonnurturant one to take care of a lost child, to find out where he lives and to take him home.

We have seen in the preceding chapter that one class of instigations is described as "a person in distress." We have seen how nursery-school children may be motivated to help another child who is in trouble. But Murphy (1937) found wide individual differences among children. Of the eighteen children whom she studied, five were consistently unsympathetic. These differences could be described in terms of the general need of nurturance. Some children are less sensitive than others to the instigation to help others.

In order to distinguish a general need from the other varieties of need, it is important to see that a general need is not very selective in terms of who is helped or what the consequences are. A person who is very sympathetic or highly nurturant is motivated to help anybody in distress. No matter who the person is, the motive is evoked by the instigation "person in trouble."

There are other general needs besides nurturance. A general need implies a sensitivity to a certain instigation but does not imply any selectivity within it. A sadistic person is generally thought of as one who enjoys hurting others. He is instigated by an opportunity to hurt somebody—anybody. An irritable person is one who responds to any interference with hostility and aggression. An orderly person is one who is made uncomfortable by disorder. He takes any opportunity to make a situation neat and orderly, regardless of whether it involves his own possessions, or whether there is any objective reason for orderliness.

This picture of a general need appears more rigid and extreme than it actually is because we have looked at a need in isolation. In real life nobody is completely and unselectively responsive to a general class of instigation, because other needs, such as attitudes and objectives, interact with general needs, and also because some of the motives instigated by general needs are inhibited. General needs, therefore, describe the sensitivity of the person to a variety or class of instigations with no selectivity within that class; it makes no difference what person is involved or what the consequence of the specific action may be.

Attitudes; Sensitivity to People in Situation

Not all needs are defined by the instigation alone, as are general needs. The definition of an attitude is more complex. Attitudes depend upon the presence of a specific person or a specific class of people toward whom the attitude is felt. To like someone is to have an attitude toward him. Whenever one person likes another, the attitude affects his response to instigations that involve the object of his attitude. Liking a person means that we want that person to be happy, that we want good things to happen to that person. If, therefore, we see a person we like in distress, we are motivated to help him. Whereas the general trait of nurturance describes a sensitivity to any person in distress, a favorable attitude describes a selective sensitivity to the person who is the object of the attitude. If he is in trouble, we help him; if we have an opportunity to benefit him, we are motivated to do so; if we have an opportunity to be with him, we take advantage of it. If he wants us to do something, we are motivated to accede to his wishes. In other words, liking a person implies that we are responsive to a variety of instigations but only because that person is involved.

An unfavorable attitude toward, or a dislike for, a person also implies sensitivity to a variety of instigations that involve the disliked person. We are not inclined to help the disliked person in distress; we are strongly motivated to win if we compete against a person whom we dislike. We avoid contact with people we dislike; we think up excuses to escape from their presence.

Liking and disliking are not the only attitudes, although they are the commonest ones and the ones that have been studied most thoroughly. Admiration, for example, is an attitude which is similar to liking but more specific. Admiration especially sensitizes us to accept the other person's opinion as true, and to try to make the admired person like us. A general attitude of liking has these same effects to some degree, but admiration emphasizes some specific characteristics of the general attitude more than others. In like manner, contempt and hatred are both similar to dislike, but each emphasizes a specific set of sensitivities and minimizes others. Rivalry with another, envy for another, jealousy of another—all these are more specific attitudes describing groups of sensitivities to instigations that involve the object of the attitude.

The object of an attitude is not always a single person; there can be attitudes toward classes of people—for example, Jews, Negroes, Catholics, foreigners, or scientists. There can be attitudes toward institutions, such as the church, the Communist party, or one's college. One can feel an attitude toward inanimate objects, especially those to which he has some sentimental attachment. We can see that there is a border line where it is difficult to distinguish between an attitude and a general need. To hate everybody is virtually equivalent to a general need to be hostile.

Objectives; Sensitivity to the Consequences of an Action

We have discussed general needs, which are relatively unselective, and attitudes, which select our instigations on the basis of what people are involved in a situation. Now we shall discuss a need that is selective, but selective on a basis different from that of an attitude. A person's *objective* determines his responsiveness to instigations in terms of the outcomes of the action. If a boy has the objective of becoming a doctor and has no other need, he will prefer certain opportunities to others. Opportunities to attain his goal are strongly instigating; other opportunities are ineffective. He strongly resists impositions that threaten his career, but he does not resist a command that will further it. He will be selective about people, but not because he likes or dislikes them. People are tools for advancement. He may help someone in distress if by doing so he will be more likely to attain his objective, but not otherwise. The focus of this sort of need is upon the possible outcome of any action. For such a person only two instigations are patent—opportunities to achieve his objective and impositions that hamper his progress. A person with no other variety of need than this would not like anybody for his own sake, and he would not respond to any general class of instigations, such as people in trouble or people who hurt him. All his behavior is instrumental—*i.e.,* it is a means toward an objective, not an end in itself.

Obviously, no person like this exists, but it is worth while to imagine such a single-minded person to see how objectives guide behavior. We all have some objectives, but not one only, and not to the exclusion of all attitudes and general needs. In order to strive consistently for a single long range objective, a person must have many of the characteristics of maturity, but mature people need not be cold blooded or single minded. Such a person is a good example of the fact that maturity is not always admirable or desirable.

In order to understand some of the varieties of adult motivation, we must point to some distinctions within the general class of result-oriented needs. We must distinguish among various sorts of objectives.

One sort is the long-range goal. The unpleasant medical student whom we just described has a long-range goal—*i.e.,* he is trying to bring about a desired state of affairs. His objective is definite; his goal-directed behavior will eventually come to an end if he is successful. As long as there is a definite objective, the term long-range goal is appropriate. Once the goal is reached, the individual is no longer able to be motivated by situations that had previously been motivating. Once the boy has the bicycle for which he has worked and saved so long, he can no longer be motivated by opportunities to obtain a bicycle.

His need is not necessarily lessened, however, as can be clearly seen in his strong resistance to any attempt to take his bicycle away from him. This need to maintain the status quo or to ward off threats might be called a *maintenance need.* Because there is no further achievement possible in so far as this goal is concerned, the only situations that instigate motives are threats to dislodge the individual from his position. These may be overt threats, such as those met by the leader of the wolf pack who must periodically fight upsurgents, or they may be perceived as obligations and duties. The judge, or the teacher in a small town, or a social leader, has certain obligations that he must meet to maintain his position.

A maintenance need requires more maturity in some ways than do long-range goals, because the result of each episode of motivated behavior is merely the same state that preceded it. No opportunity to change is offered; therefore, the situation is not intrinsically a strong instigation. When the child is taught manners he is at first highly praised for being mannerly. After awhile, however, it is expected that he will say "please" when he wants something from somebody. He will be reprimanded for not saying it, but he gets no special reward when he does say it. From the time he no longer feels it is an achievement to be mannerly, it stops being fun. From then until the actions finally become automatic and habitual it is an unrelieved chore for the child to remember his manners, and it is not surprising that he often forgets. The behavior of many dignified civic leaders and college professors when they get away from home at a convention testifies to the weariness that accompanies the continual maintenance of a position.

Having discussed long-range objectives and the change in the character of a need once the objective is reached, we now turn to long-range objectives that have no definite end point or goal. The accumulation of money is such an objective. It is possible for a nursery-school child to refuse the offer of a dime because he already has one, but after a certain appreciation of money is achieved no such satiation with money occurs. Many of the needs of older childhood and adulthood have this interminable quality. A collection is never too big, one never has too many friends, he is never too skillful, he never has too much knowledge. Such needs as these seem to require more maturity than do long-range concrete objectives, because there is a certain abstractness about the goal of "having money" that is not true of the goal of "having forty-five dollars for a bicycle." It is for this reason easier to save for something definite than to save for the sake of saving, and it is a common practice of parents to introduce the practice of saving by motivating the child to save some money each week toward a concrete goal.

Combinations of Needs

We can see that the motives that are instigated in a situation may be a complex result of various needs. If a person is rather negativistic, for example, and dislikes being ordered around, but at the same time is very fond of a friend of his, the impact of his friend's telling him to do something is a complex one. Both motives are evoked. He is in conflict, motivated to resist and also to conform to the friend's wishes. It might be that he follows the friend's suggestion as long as it is not put in too domineering a way, but he does not exhibit the deferential characteristic of the attitude as strongly as he does the nurturant, which fits in with his need to be autonomous and to do something on his own volition that helps his friend out of trouble. It might be that his attitude changes if his friend is very domineering; but here we come to changes of needs, which will be discussed in Chapter 19.

To summarize, we have found three general classes of needs: first, general needs determined by the pattern of instigation, regardless of the people involved in it and regardless of the more remote consequences of the motivated behavior; secondly, attitudes determined by the person or class of people who are involved in the instigation; and thirdly, objectives, which are the ultimate consequences of a motivated action; the motivation that any situation instigates depends upon what will be the consequences of the behavior.

Objectives require the most maturity of these three varieties of needs and include most of the instrumental behavior that is characteristic of everyday behavior. There are different sorts of objectives, however. First, there are long-range goals that have a definite end point. Secondly, there are the maintenance needs of the person who has reached his goal but must continue to behave appropriately to maintain his position. Thirdly, there are objectives that represent long-range goals, but that have no clear end; an individual can continue to be motivated by opportunities to make money, for example, regardless of how much money he already has.

Needs in the Behavior of Neonates

Let us now examine the behavior of children for evidence of the development of needs. We begin with the behavior of the young infant.

Tension

In the behavior of the newborn child, sensitivity to environmental stimuli exists in two forms, both of which lead to the development of needs in the more mature organism. First, there is alertness, or awakeness, a very general state that involves an indiscriminate sensitivity to any and all situations and stimuli. We will speak of this sensitivity as a state of tension. People of all stages of maturity differ in this general level of alertness, and the level of alertness or vigilance differs from one time to another. It describes a general sensitivity to stimuli that exists in the young infant as well as in the adult.

Tension, despite its generality, may result in a sort of selectivity which regards a stimulus as either an invitation or an imposition, depending upon

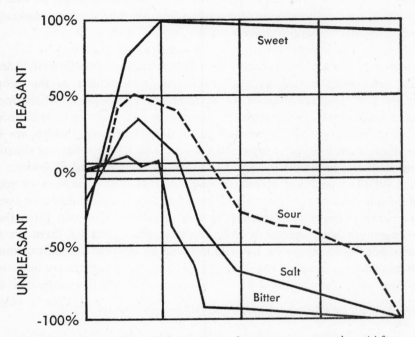

Fig. 8.1   The relation of pleasantness of taste to concentration. (After Robert S. Woodworth, *Experimental Psychology*, p. 498. Data from R. Engel, 1928)

the level of tension at the moment. We can easily see how this comes about. If the stimulus from an object is too intense, it causes the baby to withdraw, whereas a similar stimulus of lower intensity evokes an approach. For example, a shiny metal cup is ordinarily attractive, partly because it reflects light in a noticeable way, but a bright light shining into the child's eyes can be so intense that it evokes withdrawal, turning the head away and closing the eyes. Engel (1928) has shown that many ordinarily unpleasant stimuli are pleasant if mild enough. Figure 8.1 shows this effect for some taste stimuli.

In a state of high tension the child is very sensitive to stimuli. Stimuli that would ordinarily be attractive may, therefore, be too intense if the infant is already overstimulated. He may turn away from or push away objects which he reached for when he was less tense.

One type of personality difference among children is in the level of sensitivity to stimuli. Escalona and Bergman (1949) have described several cases of young children who were unusually sensitive to external stimuli. Such a child may be disturbed in his sleep by noises that do not ordinarily disturb other children. He may startle to sounds that are not intense enough to be startling to most children. He may wince as though moderately intense stimuli are actually painful. He seems to be vulnerable to stimuli that do not have any particular impact on most children. Escalona and Bergman describe it as a weak barrier between the stimuli of the external world and the child himself. They suggest that such a child must protect himself against the overwhelming stimulation from the external world and consequently may withdraw more than the usual child, the withdrawal in some cases resulting in the development of serious maladjustments.

We have spoken of this sensitivity as though it were unselective—as though the child were equally sensitive to sounds, lights, tastes, smells, etc. There is no reason, however, why the threshold of the child to all stimulation should be the same. Some children may be especially sensitive to tactual stimuli; others may have very acute hearing. Escalona (1953) has studied a number of neonates in an attempt to catalog some of the qualitative differences among infants. She has observed different patterns of sensitivity among infants, but we do not as yet have information to suggest the implications of such individual differences.

Reflex Activity as a Source of Individual Differences

The mechanism underlying tension is, therefore, one characteristic of the newborn child that makes him responsive to stimulation. Because of temporary changes in the level of tension, the baby may at one time accept stimuli that he would reject at another. The tension mechanism provides one source for individual differences among infants.

The second mechanism underlying the behavior of the newborn child is his repertoire of reflexes. Each reflex is an innate selective mechanism. It determines that he will respond to a specific stimulation—e.g., contact with the lips—differently from the way he responds to other stimuli. In Chapter 7, where we listed many of the innate behavioral responses of the baby, we were trying to describe the various stimuli that instigated behavior. In this chapter we should examine the same sort of behavior as indicative of the child's personality and note the changes in this responsiveness as the child develops.

There are individual differences in the responsiveness of the various innate mechanisms of the infant. Some babies respond eagerly to the stimuli that evoke sucking; others are more lethargic and may not exhibit any nursing behavior for a short time after birth. If this responsiveness were general— *i.e.,* if a low responsiveness to sucking stimuli were always accompanied by an equally low responsiveness of the grasp reflex and the visual reflexes—we would see the whole pattern as merely another example of low tension level or insensitivity. There seem, however, to be individual differences in the patterns of reflex responsiveness among children. Some children are more oral than others; their responsiveness to sucking stimuli is greater than the sensitivity of other reflex activities. Such children spend more of their time in oral activities—mouthing objects, sucking the thumb, empty sucking—than they do in other sorts of activity. On the other hand, some children may have a more active visual responsiveness; they spend more time looking and examining objects visually.

What is the reason for these differences in the kinds of activities in which an infant engages? The evidence suggests that these reflex activities are pleasurable. Perhaps they are innately so; perhaps they become so through use. But, in any case, such activities as sucking, looking, grasping, listening, phonation, are all apparently fun for the child. Furthermore, activity that is learned may in turn become a source of pleasure.

The best indication of the fact that reflex activities may be rewarding is that the infant learns behavior whose only consequence is to activate his reflex behavior patterns. Grasping can be the reward that reinforces learning to reach for objects.

Thumbsucking as a Source of Satisfaction

We can see the pleasure of sucking in the following series of observations of the development of thumbsucking made by Piaget (1952).

Observation 16. At 0;1(1) Laurent is held by his nurse in an almost vertical position, shortly before the meal. He is very hungry and tries to nurse with his mouth open and continuous rotations of the head. His arms describe big rapid movements and constantly knock against his face. Twice, when his hand was laid on his right cheek, Laurent turned his head and tried to grasp his fingers with his mouth. The first time he failed and succeeded the second. But the movements of his arms are not coordinated with those of his head; the hand escapes while the mouth tries to maintain contact. Subsequently, however, he catches his thumb; his whole body is then immobilized, his right hand happens to grasp his left arm and his left hand presses against his mouth. Then a long pause ensues during which Laurent sucks his left thumb in the same way in which he nurses, with greed and passion (pantings, etc.). . . . .

Observation 17. At 0;1(2) Laurent in his crib cries with hunger. He is lifted to an almost vertical position. His behavior then goes through four sequential phases quite distinct from one another. He begins by calming himself and tries to suck while turning his head from left to right and back again while his arms flourish without direction. Then (second phase) the arms, instead of describing movement of maximum breadth, seem to approach his mouth. Several times each hand brushes his lips; the right hand presses against the child's cheek and clasps it for a few seconds. Meanwhile the mouth is wide open and unceasingly attempts to grasp something. The left thumb is then caught and the two arms become rigid, the right arm against the chest under the left arm which is held by the mouth. During a third phase, the arms again wave about in space without direction, the left thumb leaving the mouth after a few minutes. During this time the child becomes angry, his head thrown back and his cries alternating with attempts to suck. Finally a fourth phase begins during which the hands again approach the mouth which tries to seize the fingers which touch it. These last attempts meet with no success and crying ensues.

Observation 19. At 0;1(4) after the 6 P.M. meal Laurent is wide awake (as was not the case at the preceding meals) and not completely satisfied. First he makes vigorous sucking-like movements, then his right hand may be seen approaching his mouth, touching his lower lip and finally being grasped. But as only the index finger was grasped, the hand fell out again. Shortly afterward it returned. This time the thumb was in the mouth while the index finger was placed between the gums and the upper lip. The hand then moves 5 cm. away from the mouth only to reënter it; now the thumb is grasped and the other fingers remain outside. Laurent then is motionless and sucks vigorously, drooling so much that after a few moments he is removed. . . .

Observation 20. At 0;1(5) and 0;1(6) Laurent tries to catch his thumb as soon as he awakes but is unsuccessful while he is lying on his back. His hand taps his face without finding his mouth. When he is vertical, however (held by the waist, his arms and torso free), he quickly finds his lips. . . . At 0;1(9), for example, Laurent sucks his thumb while lying on his back. I take it out of his mouth and, several times in succession, he puts it back into his mouth again almost immediately (having at most groped between nose and mouth) and only grasping the thumb, his other fingers remaining outside the mouth.

This sequence of observations, which takes place within a week, shows the gradual improvement of thumbsucking. Notice how at first an apparently accidental touching of the cheek stimulates more directed head motions. Later, the directed portion of the action seems to begin even before his hand hits his face. Finally, by the end of the week, Laurent initiates the entire action and can suck his thumb without much fumbling. By the end of the sequence he apparently wants to suck his thumb; sucking is no longer a mere accidental result of random activity. Piaget calls this process the expansion of the schema. The sucking pattern has expanded so that it includes the actions that bring the thumb to the mouth as well as the actual sucking behavior.

Notice that, at first, sucking is evoked only by a posture which has been closely related to the experience of nursing. Then with further development the sucking behavior may begin in a variety of postures. This makes it more usable in the service of the child's motivation.

Notice, thirdly, that thumbsucking seems to be preferred to finger sucking. From the very first observation it seemed as though finger sucking did not provide Laurent the kind of stimulation that reduced his restlessness. Thus, on the first day the finger did not stay in the mouth. Perhaps it was not as "suckable" because it did not provide the same pattern of stimulation on the inside of the mouth as the mother's breast. Later during the same day, when the thumb rather than the finger happened to find its way into his mouth, Laurent's restlessness ceased. Since he did not move, the thumb stayed in position; this prolonged the sucking experience. The fact that thumbsucking reduces restlessness has the effect of keeping the thumb in the mouth once it gets there and contributes to the learning of the thumbsucking behavior.

Sucking an object makes it stimulate the inside of the mouth, which in turn is the stimulus for sucking. Thus, sucking is a circular, or self-perpetuating, action. When the child is actually nursing, the gradual ingestion of milk accompanies this circular reaction. Because the child is hungry, the ingestion of food reduces the intensity of stimulation from hunger and lowers tension, so that the child goes to sleep and his sensitivity to the stimulation in the mouth disappears. We might expect, however, that the reaction in thumbsucking should continue forever because it results in the repeated stimulation of sucking responses without reducing the sensitivity through appeasing hunger.

What seems to happen is that thumbsucking itself becomes a satisfying activity. In Piaget's observations, for example, the baby sucked his thumb *after* a meal, and it is common to see babies go to sleep sucking a thumb. This finding implies that thumbsucking has become satisfying as well as stimulating.

It is hard to escape the conclusion that sucking is a pleasurable activity whether or not it satisfies hunger. When the child succeeded in getting his thumb in his mouth, restlessness ceased. The activities that lead up to this end result were learned. The best explanation seems to be that they were rewarded by a pleasurable experience. Thus, we see thumbsucking established as a behavior pattern that may occur at any time, after as well as before a meal.

We have no way of telling, of course, whether the fact that thumbsucking is innately pleasurable is the basis for the learning to put the thumb in the mouth; or whether the thumbsucking became a source of pleasure because the child became used to it and grew to like it. Perhaps the two processes go on together; the child learns to suck his thumb and also learns to enjoy thumbsucking.

It seems difficult to believe that sucking is innately pleasurable. There certainly are some reflex activities which are not pleasurable—for the adult at least. The knee jerk, for example, does not seem to be any particular fun. There is no reason to suppose that for the neonate, one reflex is innately more pleasant than another, although, of course, we cannot be sure that such is not the case.

Another possibility is that sucking becomes rewarding because it is a part of feeding behavior, and feeding is a rewarding experience from the very beginning. The trouble with this view is that other kinds of reflex behavior patterns also appear to become pleasurable. Piaget has shown how the child learns to grasp an object through the fact that the grasping behavior is pleasurable and serves to reward actions that produce it. Similarly, control of the eyes is learned through looking; control of the voice comes because of the pleasure in making vocal sounds.

A third possible explanation for the pleasure connected with some reflex behavior and not others comes from the fact that only certain reflexes are characterized by modifiability and by circularity. If a reflex is a circular response—i.e., if it restimulates itself—then it tends to become repeated much more frequently than a reflex like the jerk or the eyeblink, which does not reactivate itself. Thus the child can learn to like such behavior through becoming accustomed to it. The fact that a reflex is modifiable makes it a suitable basis for learning and for development into more complex behavior patterns. The problems of learning and the factors that change needs will be discussed more fully in Chapter 19.

Regardless of how it happens that some reflex activities are fun for the infant and others not, it is clear that such differences do exist. It is not surprising, therefore, that children differ in their patterns of activity. If for some reason thumbsucking and putting other objects in the mouth develops more easily or earlier than some other behavior pattern, we might well expect it to be a source of especial satisfaction and to be engaged in more frequently than the less developed behavior patterns. Escalona (1953) has observed many such individual differences among the patterns of activity of very young infants. These differences in activity are the earliest examples of preferences and needs in child behavior.

We can note how closely this picture of infantile activity fits some of the assumptions of psychoanalytic theory (see p. 539). Freud assumed that oral activity is more satisfying, more pleasurable than any other activity during early infancy. For this reason he said that the young infant is in the oral state, at the same time he recognized that other activities, such as looking and feeling, are also sources of pleasure, and he called them partial instincts. We do not know yet whether it is true that all infants find their most important source of pleasure in oral activity. There is some evidence against such an assumption, but there seems little doubt that oral activity is one important variety of infantile activity and that it is the reward behind important adjustments and learning processes.

Physiological Needs

The most obvious primary needs are physiological, such as hunger, thirst, and pain. It is obvious that a newborn child can feel the pangs of hunger, or the pain from an upset stomach. In this section we shall see how such influences affect the behavior of the baby.

Infants who are hungry or in pain show signs of the fact. They cry, they cannot sleep, they fidget, writhe, and often bend backward rigidly. The effects of such internal stimulation can be described as follows in the concepts we have employed: The infant is stimulated by these pains, and the stimulation increases his tension level. If the proper remedy is applied, the stimulus disappears, the tension level is lowered, and he will become quiet.

Before we can classify such internal stimuli as needs—using the term need in the special sense we have employed—we must show that the effect of each of these types of stimulation is to produce some special sensitivity that results in selective behavior, in responsiveness to some instigations but not to others. If the hungry infant is more sensitive to the stimulation of the mouth and lips that evoke sucking than he is to other stimuli, and if the hungry infant is more sensitive to such stimuli than is the infant who has the colic, then it is obvious that being hungry leads to a specific kind of stimulus sensitivity. If, however, hunger cannot be distinguished from other physiological conditions by observing the behavior of the infant when he is placed at the breast, then it would appear that hunger pangs are not yet distinguished from any other sort of pain and that its effect is merely to increase the general level of tension.

The crucial experiments have apparently not been performed. From casual observation of infants, however, it seems that hunger is an unpleasant stimulus, but so vague that it is experienced not as a localized stimulus but rather as a generally unpleasant state of affairs. What effect does this state of hunger have on the infant? It makes him alert, responsive, cross, and cranky, and it makes him cry. Because he is alert he is sensitive to stimuli and will suck readily, but not necessarily more readily than any other active infant. The baby who wakes with some other indefinite pain will also suckle readily.

When a baby does cry, whether from hunger or because of a wet diaper, his behavior seems to indicate that he does not recognize very well the locus or cause of the unhappiness. Any change, a change of diaper, cuddling, straightening of the bedclothes, or offering him the breast, are all likely to be gratefully received and frequently have a temporary effect of stopping the crying. Unless, however, the change really removes the basic cause of distress, these ministrations have no permanent effect; the tension-producing stimulation continues and the baby returns to his whimpering and crying.

The best interpretation we can make, without further precise information, is that the young infant feels the pain or other type of stimulation accompanying these physiological needs, but that the stimuli are so vague and difficult to locate that they do not evoke any patterned response; they merely increase the level of tension. The one clear exception to this generalization is the withdrawal behavior evoked by a painful stimulus on the hand or arm.

Before these internal stimuli representing physiological needs can instigate specific motivated behavior, the baby has to learn some behavior patterns that have the effect of removing the stimuli. We cannot judge how easy it is for the child to learn that eating relieves hunger, that turning over relieves the prick of a diaper pin, or that crying relieves all these pains (it does so by bringing the mother to the rescue, but it is not necessary for the baby to be clear about the mechanism). In many ways it seems doubtful whether the pain from hunger is readily recognized, or whether its relief occurs quickly enough after eating to be a reward effective in establishing learned behavior.

No matter how easy or how difficult it is to learn the meaning of hunger pangs, we know that the state of hunger in the older child or adult may make the individual want food. Probably the stimuli that hunger produces tell the individual himself that he is hungry and remind him of eating. Thus, hunger is sometimes experienced as a wish for food, not as an internal state. To perceive it so requires maturity, however, and it is beyond the ability of the infant to perceive hunger in this way. Even the four or five-year-old child frequently does not know that he is hungry. He comes into the house sullenly, he is irritable and mischievous, but he does not ask for food. The wise mother gets dinner onto the table quickly, and all is well.

Whenever there is a physiological basis for a need, there is an automatic production of stimuli that become more and more obtrusive and noticeable with increasing need strength. After the person has learned the effective responses, such needs automatically provide reminders of the goal object. Thus, physiological needs such as hunger, thirst, and bladder tension automatically result in motivation and in goal-seeking behavior.

Except that they are accompanied by stimuli, these physiological needs are like all others. They sensitize the individual to potential goal objects. Just after a Thanksgiving dinner, no food is tempting. With increasing deprivation, the need becomes stronger; the individual goes through the stage where he can be tempted by some especially delectable morsel to the stage where he can enjoy a meal, and on to the stage where he will actively seek out food because the appropriate internal stimuli remind him that he is hungry. If his need remains unsatisfied for a long enough period, he will eat almost anything edible and even some things that are not.

Nonphysiological needs do not automatically produce the stimulation that serves as a cue. Even when they are strong, some external suggestion is required to evoke motivated behavior, but there is generally no lack of such external stimulation. Almost anything can remind the homesick person of home and evoke the motivation to return. All the familiar scenes remind the jilted lover or the recent widow of the now absent loved one and evoke active mourning and longing. The six-year-old who would like a bicycle finds no lack of reminders to keep his motivation active. In actual practice, therefore, a very strong need makes the evocation of the motive almost inevitable, whether or not the need has a physiological basis. It is probably true, however, that it is easier to distract the child whose motive is based on a nonphysiological rather than physiological need. A movie may take the child's mind off his wish for a new bicycle even if he wants it very badly. If he needs to go to the toilet, however, the stimuli intrude even upon his enjoyment of Roy Rogers.

To summarize our discussion of the needs of the neonate, we have suggested two mechanisms. The level of tension provides some crude selectivity, because it makes the infant painfully sensitive to stimuli that would be attractive to an infant who is less tense. The most important selective mechanism of infancy is the reflex activities. These mechanisms, which operate from birth, may or may not be innately pleasurable, but at any rate some of them become sources of pleasure early. It is difficult to say how important are the basic physiological needs in infant behavior. The young infant has some behavior mechanisms of withdrawing from painful stimuli, but it seems likely that hunger, thirst, and most internal stimuli do not instigate specific behavior patterns, and it seems unlikely that they are very effective rewards to reinforce learning. The question is an open one, however, and can be resolved only by further information.

Susceptibility to Emotions: the Origin of General Needs

We turn now to the development of needs during later infancy and childhood. We saw in Chapter 7 that there is a period during infancy and early childhood when impositions evoke an emotional response, but not necessarily a goal-directed motivated behavior pattern. During this period the susceptibility of the child to provocations that arouse a specific emotion is a characteristic that is probably a forerunner of a general need. A general need in the adult is, we recall, a personality trait marked by a sensitivity to one type of instigation but without selectivity within that class of instigations. Irritability, for example, is an easily aroused hostility whenever the person is frustrated or interfered with.

As soon as the child becomes mature enough for the various emotional patterns to be distinguishable, we can begin to describe his personality in terms of the ease of arousal of these emotions. As the child's response to these provocations gradually matures, the behavior that is instigated becomes more directed and purposeful, and the emotional susceptibility of infancy becomes what we have called a general need. This does not mean that the child who is easily startled as an infant must necessarily become a fearful child when he matures. Needs can appear, disappear, or change over time, as we shall see in Chapter 19. Nevertheless, there is some evidence indicating the identifiability of later personality characteristics from the behavior of the infant. To the extent that there is a constancy of such traits, we would expect that the easily startled, easily frightened baby would become the older child who tries to escape rather than resist impositions. Mary Shirley (1933) found, for example, that one child in her study who was distinctive for his "timorous crying" was later described as apprehensive. He hid behind his mother and was shy with strangers.

One of the earliest recognized temperamental characteristics is irritability, or fussiness. When mothers are asked to describe the behavior of their new infants, they are likely to use some general term such as "quiet" or "fussy." As we have seen, the differences in mood and personality of infants can perhaps all be described in terms of a general level of tension, although more data will be necessary to establish such an overall hypothesis.

As soon as various emotions become differentiated, more specific traits, such as fearfulness, hostility, etc., may be distinguished. Certain general conditions, however, have been found to be related to susceptibility to these emotional states. These conditions are perhaps at the root of individual differences in general needs in childhood.

Fearfulness

Susceptibility to specific fears can often, of course, be traced to frightening experiences, although sometimes the connection is not obvious (Jersild and Holmes, 1935). More generally, studies have found that fearful children are frequently those who have been severely punished or threatened, or who have been encouraged in their fearfulness through the example of their parents. These findings will be dealt with in some detail in Part II of this book, but they are interesting at this point because they point to two characteristics that might cause a general fearfulness. One is the person's perception of himself as weak; the second is his perception of the environment as dangerous. Since a weak person is, in fact, more vulnerable to danger than a strong person, any circumstance that leads an individual to consider himself weak frequently makes him believe that he is faced with danger. It is reasonable, in the light of these considerations, that weakness or physical handicap would predispose an individual to be fearful. Pintner and Brunschwig (1937) and Boutinier and Henry (1946) have found that deaf children and blind children are more than normally prone to be fearful.

A second source of general fearfulness is one's evaluation of the total environment. People are more fearful in situations that are generally dangerous. A stimulus that would not be fearsome at all if it occurred on a calm evening in some suburban town might be frightening to almost anyone on a battlefield. Thus, it is reasonable to find that children who are raised in homes in which the parents constantly warn them of danger and disaster are more likely to be apprehensive than children whose home environment is not so highly protective.

Anger

Some conditions temporarily make any child, and even the neonate, more irritable—*e.g.*, fatigue, slight illness, or hunger. When the baby is slightly under the weather, he is likely to be cross and cranky, fretful and easily provoked.

This could well be due to a higher than normal general sensitivity to stimuli. Since imposition and restraint arouse anger, and since an increased tension level makes the child more sensitive to stimulation, moderate stimuli that are ordinarily inviting may, for the tense child, be too strong for comfort and thus provoke withdrawal, crying, and anger. If the baby's tolerance is low, more of the stimuli of everyday life will be impositions because they are too strong to be tolerated.

We also have evidence from everyday life that a series of frustrations, especially when the child has not been able to show his anger, may make him very irritable (see pp. 470ff.). He seems to be so well prepared to be angry that it takes very little imposition to provoke it. Another interpretation of the same phenomenon is that a series of frustrations makes the child feel that other people are imposing on him. If he enters a situation with the expectation that other people will try to impose on him, he may interpret as impositions actions that under other circumstances would not seem restricting. This same pattern could be the basis of a more enduring trait of irritability. If we expect that other people are looking out only for themselves, that they will cheat us if they have a chance, that they have no consideration for our feelings—if, in short, we mistrust other people—we may perceive their actions as impositions when they really are not.

In contrast to fearfulness, anger depends upon a certain assumption of strength. A weak person is more likely to flee from an imposition, whereas a strong person would become indignant and resist it. Thus, experience that contributes to a feeling of strength or a belief that resistance will succeed will predispose the individual to be angry rather than afraid. We find, for example, that children whose parents have given in to tantrums or to angry outbursts are more likely to become angry at an imposition than to conform.

It has been repeatedly found that boys show more hostility than girls. They show more of it in their fantasy life (Sears, 1953), they have more fights in free play situations (Green, 1933). This may be due to the fact that anger is more acceptable in boys than in girls. It may be due to more basic differences in strength or activity level. Several people have found that active children show more aggression than passive ones (Bender and Schilder, 1936), but they may show more of all types of outgoing activity. Whether there is a special relationship between activity and aggression has not been established.

Attitudes in Childhood

An attitude, we recall, is a need that is focused upon another person or class of people. It is marked by a responsiveness to a variety of instigations in which the object of an attitude is involved, but not unless he is involved. The first examples of an attitude are the child's special feelings about his parents, especially his mother. The first part of this section will be devoted to a description of the changes in the nature of love and hate as the child matures.

Love and Hate in Infancy

When the mature person loves someone, he shows it in a variety of ways. He is motivated to be close to the loved one; he wants the loved one to be happy and to enjoy good things; he wants the loved one to agree with him; he is inclined to agree with the opinions of the person he loves; and he becomes angry with people who threaten a person he loves. Dislike, for the mature person, is the opposite of liking, and implies the opposite of each of the above characteristics. These characteristics of love are not found in infancy; they are the results of a long developmental process.

The first sign of an attitude of any sort is the infant's selectivity with respect to people. Spitz (1946) found in his study of smiling in infancy that below the age of five months the children smiled indiscriminately at any person who provided the minimal stimuli. Beginning with the last half of the first year, the child smiles selectively at his mother or at familiar people. At about the same time the child shows his desire for social contact by becoming angry when an adult stops playing with him and by pulling at the adult or his clothes to attract his attention.

If we call this behavior the first sign of love of which the child is capable, love, in the infant, might be described as merely social contact and physical proximity with the love object. We must not take this to mean that the infant longs for the presence of the loved one, because we have already seen how short-lived is the grief of the infant when he is left alone. The baby's love is recurrent rather than permanent. It is evoked when the adult is present and lasts for a short time after he has disappeared, but it does not seem possible for the infant to long for an absent person for any length of time.

It is interesting to see that even at this age love demands reciprocation. The child pays attention to his mother and wants her to pay attention to him. To be ignored is frustrating, although the infant is not always aware that he is being ignored.

The relationship between love and physical proximity is illustrated by another finding by Mrs. Arsenian (1943), who studied the reactions of young children in a strange situation (see p. 153). One of the groups in that experiment was composed of children accompanied by their mothers. The mother sat quietly in a chair and did not interfere with the child's activity in any way. She was present but did not participate. When the observers recorded the movements of the children in this group, they found that the mother was a sort of magnet. A child would cling to her closely, or if he played with the toys, his playing took place in an area surrounding the mother. This area could be plotted from an analysis of his movements, and it was found, interestingly enough, that the "region of security" extended farther in front of the mother than behind her. Being visible to the mother seemed to make the child more secure than being out of her field of vision. The relevant observation for the present section is, however, that proximity to the mother was important for the child.

The child's love for his parent during the second year includes more than merely wanting to be close to her. In the second year the demand for contact becomes more specialized and focused on the people who are familiar and well known to the infant. He is sharper in his demands for attention and frequently becomes angry with the parent who fails to pay attention to him.

The most significant development of the second and third year, however, might be described as the process by which love becomes the opposite of hostility. During infancy this relationship between the two feelings does not exist. Love is related entirely to contact; the infant wants to be close to his loved objects. The opposite of this feeling is to want to get away from disliked objects. Shyness, withdrawal, and perhaps fear are, therefore, the opposites of love during the period of infancy. In adults the opposite of loving is hating, and although hating includes a desire to have no contact with the disliked object, it encompasses much more. The central motif of hate or hostility is to hurt the disliked person. We have a positive wish to frustrate the person we hate. At the same time love, in adult life, includes more than wanting to be close; it also includes wanting to benefit the loved one. It is this aspect of loving that is opposite to hatred.

So our theory of child development must explain this change in the meaning of love—the desire to benefit the loved one as well as to be close to him. With this addition, love becomes a feeling that is opposite to hostility.

Since there is almost no information about the details of this change in the meaning of love, we can do little more than speculate upon the factors that bring it about. By the time the child has come to love the parent, albeit in an infantile way, the parent is important to the child. He is in a position to threaten the child with loss of love and to punish him by denying love. This pressure on the child is not possible until his love for the parent is well established. Love-oriented disciplinary techniques, *i.e.,* threats of loss of love, are very potent; we shall see later (see p. 576) how effective they can be in enforcing the parent's wishes.

If the parent uses this pressure, he is teaching the child something about the meaning of love. He is making his love contingent upon the child's obedience—*i.e.,* doing what the parent wishes him to do. Also, he is reinforcing the idea that not to love the child is equivalent to punishing him. His disciplinary techniques generally include both denial of love and physical punishment. The parent consistently pairs the two, and thus teaches the child that to be loved is to be safe from punishment and that punishment goes along with not being loved.

The relation between love and hate is also apparent in other ways. If the child is attacked by someone, either a powerful parent or another child, the aggression will instigate the child's wish to hurt the aggressor, but it will also make the child be afraid and run away. The combination of fear and hatred of a powerful person is a very common occurrence in interpersonal relations. Thus, it is not unreasonable that their opposites should also combine; benefiting another person and being close to him might thus become parts of a single attitude.

INTERRELATIONSHIPS AMONG LOVE, HATE, AND FEAR Regardless of the factors that bring it about, there develops, by the time the child is in the early preschool period, a characteristic triad of relationships among the three attitudes of love, hate, and fear.

Karen Horney (1945) has proposed a very useful scheme for classifying the basic character of an individual's interpersonal relations. There are three alternative directions of action: (1) moving toward people, (2) moving against people, and (3) moving away from people. Heider (1953) has shown how these three alternatives are logically interrelated; he has stated the relation explicitly, whereas Horney implies it. The present conceptualization is adapted from Heider.

Love, or moving toward another person, is a state characterized by two motives, wanting to be close to the loved one and wanting to benefit the loved one. It is a state of security implied by the trust that the other person is kind and wants to return the benefits.

This state has two opposites, depending upon whether the wish to be close or the wish to benefit the other is taken as the reference point. The opposite of the wish to be close is the wish to be away or distant. In its most extreme form this is a fearful attitude, the result of feeling weak and overpowered. While the desire to be alone or detached is not always based on fear, it is frequently rooted in a fear of the other person. The opposite of the motive to benefit the other person is the motive to hurt him; this is hate. In order to be hostile with safety, it is necessary to be strong, but neither hostility nor fear is an especially secure psychological state, because both have as backgrounds the expectation of harm from the other person. For that matter, moving toward others is sometimes a sign of weakness. If the person's desire is to ingratiate himself and to placate a powerful figure by obedience, toadying, and bribery, he does not truly love. These relationships are diagrammed in Figure 8.2.

According to Horney, the person's basic attitude toward other people can be described in these terms and will determine the way many of his interpersonal relations develop. Certainly the intuitive understanding of the relationships among love, fear, and hate and the relation of them to the individual's power is an important basis for effective interpersonal relations. The fact that nearly all people somehow understand the relations among these attitudes but that almost no one in ordinary life is clearly aware of them is an excellent example of our observation in Chapter 1 that many of the bases for understanding our fellow man are intuitive but that psychology must try to make the relationships clear and explicit if it is to explain human behavior.

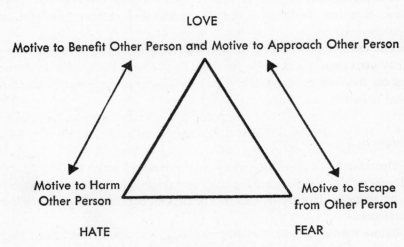

Fig. 8.2 The interrelation of love, fear, and hate.

The Character of Love in the Preschool Period

We have seen that by the time the child is of preschool age, his liking or love for another person means both wanting to be in contact with him and wanting to benefit him. In early childhood his intentions to benefit the people he loves may be sound enough, but unfortunately his ability to benefit the parent is hampered by his immaturity. He exhibits his wish to benefit the parent by giving the parent gifts, by hugging and kissing him. But he is still quite egocentric; he cannot see a situation from the parent's point of view and therefore cannot realistically do what the parent wishes. If the parent is telephoning when the child is smitten with affection, it would be of real benefit for the child to keep quiet until the conversation is over. But this demands more maturity than he has.

These actions gradually become less self-centered; they come to be expressions of love and not so completely demands for love; but the essential characteristic of immaturity that blocks the full development of this altruism is that the child is egocentric, and therefore he cannot see the situation from the parent's point of view.

One of the significant childhood developments pertaining to love and hate is, therefore, the gradual reduction of egocentric orientation. A consequence of lessened egocentrism is that the child's love and hate become more effective. When he can understand what it is that other people really do want, he is better able to express his love. He is also better able to express his dislike and aggression. It is very amusing to listen to the threats of a nursery-school child. On the one hand, he threatens to kill, maim, drop bombs on, and destroy his opponent utterly. In the same breath he threatens not to invite him to his birthday party. Throughout it all, one gets the feeling that the child is primarily describing the things that would be bad for him, with very little appreciation of what is bad for his opponent.

Technique of Visible Suffering

There is no doubt that this increased objectivity is necessary for the child's development, but it does make the child vulnerable to a new set of pressures, and the parent's unthinking use of his new powers may have unfortunate consequences.

Before the child has a clear idea of what it is that makes the parent happy or sad, there is little point in the parent's trying to capitalize on the child's love for him. It is not effective for us to try to influence the two-year-old to conform to parental standards by telling him how happy it will make us if he keeps his food on the table, and how disappointed we shall be if he deliberately spills it.

After he truly appreciates what it means to hurt a loved one, the situation is quite different. Now he can be led to do things that his mother wants because she wants them and because it is an expression of love to satisfy her wants. At the same time, to frustrate her wishes and especially to hurt her put the child in a serious psychological dilemma. He is in the position of having hurt the person for whom he cares. This may provoke guilt feelings and self-punishment.

Whether the child's hostility to the people he loves does result in guilt feelings depends upon how the situation is structured. If the mother responds to disobedience or hostility with punishment or revenge, then the child quickly loses his feeling that the mother is the victim. She is the aggressor. After the punishment, he has been hurt. He and his mother are quits; indeed, he may feel he is the injured party.

If, however, the mother responds in such a way that her victimization is very clear to the child, if she cries or openly expresses how much she is hurt by the child's action, if she is dramatically disappointed and accuses the child of not loving her, then the child is put into a guilt-producing situation. This technique of producing guilt might be called *visible suffering*. It is a very effective technique to secure conformity from the child, provided he is mature enough to be susceptible to it.

Visible suffering need not be insincere or a deliberate technique. The discussion of parent behavior in Chapter 20 will show that parents actually are hurt and disappointed and ashamed when the child violates cultural standards. The overt expression of their disappointment is genuine, and it frequently has the consequences outlined above—*i.e.,* it produces conformity by making the child feel guilty.

One experiment on college students gives some indication of the importance of this technique. In this experiment, carried out by MacKinnon (1938), the students were assigned certain problems. The experiment was so designed that the answers to the problems were lying on the table beside them. It was permissible for the subject to look up the answers to certain of the problems, but not to others. Yet the answers to them all were easily available. The student was left to himself but was watched through a one-way screen. As would be expected, some of the students cheated and others did not.

The students were then interviewed to discover their personality characteristics. Those who did not cheat were found, in general, to be more susceptible to guilt feelings than those who succumbed to temptation. Furthermore, when the subjects were questioned about the kind of discipline their parents had employed, it was found that those who had not cheated and who were more susceptible to guilt had been more frequently subjected to what MacKinnon calls *psychological discipline*. By psychological discipline he means the same technique that we have called visible suffering—the overt expression of disappointment, regret, and shame by the parent. The results were not entirely clear-cut. For reasons not readily understood, it was psychological discipline by the father rather than the mother that seemed to differentiate the conformers from the violators. Since the subjects were boys, it is undoubtedly important that they were more sensitive to the father than the mother in this respect, but the precise implication of this fact is difficult to determine.

This type of discipline has been described by other child psychologists, usually under the term *threat of loss of love* (Sears *et al.,* 1953). In other words, it has not been differentiated from the discipline exemplified by such phrases as, "Mama doesn't like boys who hit their little sisters." It is true that parents who are hurt and disappointed by the misdemeanors of their children may feel hostility toward their children (see p. 531). From the point of view of the child, however, it is debatable whether the psychological effectiveness of visible suffering is dependent upon the threatened loss of love.

A person at the maturity level of the child will probably perceive any punishment as a threat of loss of love. When the parent spanks the child, for example, he is deliberately inflicting pain. Although the child at the moment is probably more focused upon his own painful position than upon the parent's feelings, he must, if he perceives their feelings at all, perceive them as hostile. When the parent deprives the child of a privilege or sends him away to his room, the child probably perceives that also as loss of love.

As we have described them here, denial of love and visible suffering are different techniques; they depend upon different characteristics of the child, and have different impacts upon him. Denial of love capitalizes upon the child's need for love and arouses anxiety. Visible suffering is essentially an accusation that the child does not love the parent. It capitalizes upon the child's love for the parent and evokes guilt feelings.

Jealousy

We have seen how some of the characteristics of mature love gradually develop during childhood. Let us now look at a somewhat different aspect of the love relationship—its exclusiveness. To be jealous is to assume that love is exclusive and unsharable. The traditional pattern of jealousy is, of course, the triangle. Two people are both in love with one person; each is jealous of the loved one and each hates the other. The assumption tacitly present is that the love relationship is an exclusive one, that a person's love is not something that can be enjoyed by more than one. In our culture heterosexual love is presumed to have this quality, but there is an equally clear cultural insistence that other kinds of love—mother love, for example—must not be exclusive. The mother is expected to be able to love all her children, and they are in turn supposed not to demand exclusive love from her. Favoritism in a parent or teacher is seen as unfairness and arouses hostility toward the teacher and towards "teacher's pet" as well.

An analysis of the structure of interpersonal relations suggests that exclusiveness is a natural consequence of love (Heider, 1953). If there are three people in a group, it is easy for it to split into a pair and one person outside the pair. Any tendency on the part of one of a group of three to like one of the others better than he does the third is likely to provoke reciprocal feelings on the part of the preferred person. At the same time, it is likely to provoke hostile feelings in the rejected one, which in turn evoke return hostility. The result of all these tendencies is the splitting of a threesome into a pair and an outcast. Many mothers know the danger implicit in groups of three and try to invite one less or one more. Gesell and Ilg (1942) report the difficulty of obtaining congeniality in a group of three children until they are seven or eight years old. If the threesome is well matched, it is unlikely that the same person becomes scapegoat every time, but if one is actually different in some noticeable way, the same person may repeatedly become the outcast until his friendship with the other two is permanently broken. It is amazing to see three almost identical triplets split into a pair and an outsider on the basis of some minute difference, but it does happen.

In the play of children there is a great deal of exclusion of one person from the relationship between two other children. There is the same unwillingness to share friends that there is to share toys, and the reasons in the two cases are much the same. For the other child to have a favorite toy creates the motivation to want it back. When young children give gifts, they often demand them back immediately. Gesell and Ilg (1942) report social exclusiveness from about the age of three and one-half. This corresponds with the time when special friendships are developing.

One final factor in the problem of jealousy in our culture is the exclusiveness and the seclusiveness of the husband-wife relationship. A common example of jealousy in children can be seen in the reaction of a child to his mother kissing his father. This sort of situation immediately makes the child want to join the party. The parents may view this behavior as an intrusion or an imposition and they may reject it, even though they do so in a kindly fashion. Almost no parents are completely open about their sexual relationships in front of the child. It is almost inevitable that the child's curiosity as well as his jealousy is aroused.

The secrecy that the parents maintain about their sexual life perhaps reflects their own feeling that it is in some sense shameful, although most married couples would deny such feelings of shame. Nevertheless, they may react to the child's probing curiosity with the same mixture of embarrassment and hostility that normally accompanies the threatened exposure of a shameful secret. If so, the child is likely to perceive the secret activities as shameful. His reaction depends upon a variety of other factors, but it may be intolerable for him to accept the possibility of his parent doing something shameful. It is difficult to appraise the significance of these feelings in normal personality development.

Some *avant-garde* parents conclude from these facts that they should be very open about their sex life and permit the child's curiosity to be fully satisfied. Such a course may work out well; nobody knows for sure what consequences it has. On the other hand, some parents may try to help the child distinguish between privacy and shame. They may show him that some relationships are too intimate to be shared or exposed, but that they are not necessarily shameful. This differentiation, if accomplished, must certainly require a great deal of maturity. It is probably facilitated if the parents do not treat the child as though all his secrets were shameful by forcing him to expose them.

SIBLING RIVALRY   The feeling of a child toward his siblings, especially toward that sibling who is next in age to himself, has been customarily viewed as an example of jealousy. In some respects it is, but in order to understand the problem we must look at it in its totality rather than merely as an example of jealousy. We should consider separately the feeling toward a newly arrived sibling, the feeling toward a sibling who is in the toddler stage, and the feeling toward a sibling who is two or three years younger when both siblings are near school age.

When a new sibling is born, especially when the second child is born, there is a real change in the household. Baldwin (1947) has shown, for example, that the behavior of the parent toward a child changes when the mother becomes pregnant and continues to change until after the birth of the sibling. The child-centeredness of the home is the variable that shows the greatest decrease, although it is not the only one. How would this change be expected to affect the child? The first question to be answered is whether or not he notices it. It may be that the sudden and dramatic leave for the hospital and the flurry and bustle in the return home have more psychological impact upon the child than the more gradual, even though more basic, change in parent behavior.

If the child notices the change, what is its psychological significance? In order for the child to feel jealous and to feel rivalry toward the baby, he must attribute the change to the new sibling and perceive him as the cause. That such feelings are sometimes present is undeniable, but they demand considerable maturity. A considerably easier reaction—i.e., one that is possible at a much lower level of maturity—is for the child to be discontented and upset in a generalized, undifferentiated way. The consequences of such a feeling would be a heightened irritability, easily aroused tension, regression in terms of accomplishments, and an active tendency to seek overt affection from the mother. This common pattern of behavior in children who are disturbed by the arrival of a sibling need not signify a feeling of competition or jealousy toward the new sibling, even though he is the cause of the disturbance. Because such a child is irritable, it is not surprising if he sometimes displays hostility toward inoffensive objects, including the new sibling.

Which kind of behavior actually occurs when a sibling is born depends, among other things, upon the level of maturity. If the displaced child is about a year old, no reaction should be expected. If the child is slightly older, then general symptoms of disequilibrium and disturbance should be manifest. If the displaced child is sufficiently mature, the new sibling might be resented personally, although it is also possible for such a mature child to perceive the sibling as an opportunity to be protective and superior. Many children who are old enough seem to enjoy taking responsibility for heating the baby's bottle, for helping with his bath. They make baby care a joint enterprise with the mother. Sewall (1930) found that the intensity of symptoms of jealousy toward the newborn sibling are strongest when the older child is between the ages of eighteen months and three and one-half years, with a peak around three. Sewall did not, however, differentiate generalized symptoms of unhappiness from directed symptoms of hostility.

Hostility between siblings is not ordinarily at its most intense when the new sibling is born. It is between older siblings that most of the bickering and fighting takes place. The relationship between the siblings at the time the younger is reaching the stage of running around produces an abundance of reason for hostility. The younger child is into everything, including the possessions of his older sibling. He may interfere with block building, tear up model airplanes, and generally make a nuisance of himself. Since the older sibling is no paragon of patience, he feels hostile and expresses it. He may well express his hostility so forcefully that his parents must interfere in order to protect the younger sibling, despite the fact that he instigated the trouble. This is unfair, and although the parents recognize the justice of the older sibling's complaint, it is difficult to explain their attitude to him. Thus, fuel is added to the fire. In these situations the hostility is directly provoked and requires no special maturity.

For the relation between siblings aged five or older, when each is sensitive to the other one and near enough of an age to be competitive, the term *sibling rivalry* is very appropriate. Now they compete for the biggest dessert, the latest bedtime, the first turn at the bathroom. Every acquisition of the older one—a bicycle, a watch, a privilege—is immediately demanded by the younger. If it is not granted, he is unhappy and feels discriminated against. If it is granted, the older one feels that it is unfair because, "I had to wait until I was eight to get a bicycle. Johnny gets it when he's only six."

Thus, it can be seen that any single explanation of the attitude of siblings toward each other is likely to be inappropriate if applied indiscriminately to all age levels. There may or may not be any relationship between the amount of hostility at one age level and the amount at a later age. Whether the children who are most upset when the sibling is born are the ones who later display the most rivalry when the sibling is of school age is a question that has not been answered. It seems quite conceivable that there is little relationship in the intensity of rivalry and hostility at different age levels. If so, the importance of the child's being displaced as a cause for his feelings of rivalry may be seriously overestimated.

The Development of Enduring Attitudes

Inconstancy of the Infant's Love

After noting the various characteristics of attitudes as they develop throughout childhood, let us now see how attitudes become longer lasting and enduring. When the two-year-old's behavior is observed, it is important to remember that his love is not a constant thing. Like other motives, the wish to be close to the mother may disappear under the influence of distractions. Thus, the child may wander around the house, playing first with one thing, then with another, apparently without any thought of being close to his mother. Then, sometimes quite suddenly, he is reminded of her presence; the fact that he is out of her sight and she is out of his suddenly hits him. A noise in the kitchen where she is working may be the reminder. At other times it is not possible to decide just what awakened him to the fact that he was away from her. But, all at once, he will dash back to where his mother is.

Another possible interpretation of this sort of behavior is that the child may be testing his growing independence by going away from the mother. It makes some difference which interpretation is accurate. If, for example, this is true independence and autonomy, then the child might be aided in his efforts by being encouraged to stay away from his mother for short times. If it is not truly autonomy, then such encouragement would merely instigate his wish to be close to her.

Although it is doubtful whether the child is testing his autonomy, we cannot assume that he is not learning through such behavior to be autonomous. It seems very reasonable to assume that each such experience that ends with finding the mother still close at hand has a reassuring effect and makes the child more easily led into independent activity for longer periods of time.

On the other hand, attempts to make him independent of his mother and able to play by himself may backfire. Keeping him in a play pen and not letting him be near his mother when he wants her can well have the effect of making him more sensitive to her absence and less able to stay interested in his own activities for long stretches. Of course, if the mother goes away for a long time, say a period of several days, then because the child is not periodically motivated to be near her, he can forget her with surprising quickness.

In other respects also, loving is not at this stage a permanent feeling that tempers all actions. The child who is absorbed in his own activities is at that moment neither loving his parent nor not loving him. Love is irrelevant to his behavior of the moment. Thus, he may not show any of the characteristics that we have ascribed to love.

In adults, love is a need, a state of permanent sensitivity, not merely a recurring motive. Thus the adult, even when absorbed in some irrelevant activity, can remain sensitive to the feelings of the people he loves. The fond father, even when absorbed in answering his professional mail, will notice a new stamp and save it for his stamp-collector son. A considerate husband will remember not to invite guests on the night when his wife has a meeting, even though he feels free to do so on other occasions. He will not do things that would hurt a loved one even in connection with some completely separate motivation, because his sensitivity to the wishes of the people he loves arouses motivation to avoid hurting them. When this sensitivity fails, we do not say that he is hostile, but that he is inconsiderate. The child, because of his immaturity, is frequently inconsiderate.

The Duration of Friendships in Childhood

As we saw in the discussion of hostility in Chapter 7, quarrels during the the preschool period tend to be very short, to last only one round. Gradually, however, the length of a quarrel increases and lasts from one incident to another. The duration of friendships seems to increase similarly. There are very few data on the basis or the length of friendships during the early childhood years, but friendships in later childhood have been studied. The general conclusion from such studies is that friendships, even in early adolescence, are based upon many external factors, such as nearness and chance contacts, just as much as upon personality characteristics, and that the duration of the typical adolescent friendship is quite short.

At the sixth-grade level, for example (Thompson and Horrocks, 1947), the most frequent reason given by children for their choice of friends is frequent contact with them. This might be expected, because nobody can become a friend of someone with whom he has no contact. However, the necessity for the maintenance of this frequent contact in order to keep the friendship intact is indication of the ease with which even relatively mature children follow the rule, "out of sight, out of mind."

It was found that with eleven-year-olds only about half the friendships lasted as long as two weeks. This does not mean that friends became enemies, but the choice of the person who was the best friend of an eleven-year-old had barely a fifty-fifty chance of being the same as the choice two weeks

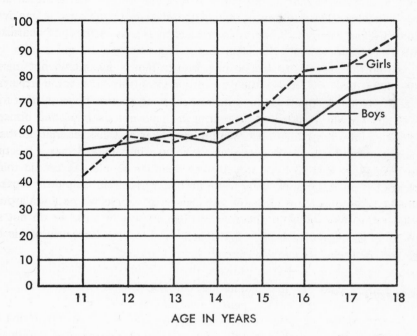

Fig. 8.3 The relation between age and stability of friendships. The graph shows the percentage of children of various ages who chose the same person as a best friend on two occasions two weeks apart. (After G. G. Thompson and J. E. Horrocks, *J. Genet. Psych., 70,* 1947, 53-63)

earlier. The stability of friendships increases steadily with age until, by the age of eighteen, about three-fourths of the friendships last two weeks or more. The results for the various age levels are shown in Figure 8.3.

It was found that the most frequent reason for change was not a quarrel, but merely the lack of recent contact. The second most frequent cause for change was a quarrel. The data do not indicate whether the lack of recent contact meant a real move so that contact became impossible, but it fits our general knowledge of children of this age level to assume that for more or less chance reasons the pair did not happen to get together for awhile, and before long some other friendship had taken its place.

Attitudes Toward Classes of People

The difference between liking or disliking an individual and exhibiting an attitude toward a class of people is merely that the broader attitude influences behavior whenever any person of the class is encountered. If an individual dislikes Negroes, he tends to treat each Negro as though he disliked him. If people were entirely logical this statement would be quite valid, but it is within the capacity of human unreason to like many individual Negroes and still to dislike Negroes. Such an attitude controls behavior when some issue arises that demands action with respect to the entire Negro group.

Thus far, in speaking of attitudes, we have not distinguished between justifiable and unjustifiable ones. We all have likes and dislikes that are more or less appropriate—*i.e.,* that lead us to behave in a realistic way. We may also have unreasonable likes and dislikes of other people. Attitudes toward a class of people are more likely to be unrealistic than an attitude toward an individual, because there are very few classes of people who are sufficiently similar to justify a single attitude toward them all.

For this reason we usually find that it is not actual experience with the members of a class, such as Negroes, Jews, Catholics, or foreigners, that is the sole basis of one's attitudes toward them. Various emotional factors may enter. People who are fearful and insecure in general are more likely to develop social prejudices than people who are more self-confident (Gough, *et al.,* 1950). We also find that many prejudices are the result of a total acceptance of the attitudes of the child's peers and parents. For this reason many prevalent social attitudes do not appear early in life.

The increased conformity to social and cultural norms as the child grows older can be well illustrated in the development of racial attitudes. Criswell (1939) studied the tendency of white and Negro children in the elementary grades in New York City to prefer a member of their own race over a member of the other race when choosing with whom they would like to associate. Each child named the person whom he would choose as a companion. The number of Negroes chosen by whites, whites by Negroes, Negroes by Negroes, and whites by whites was computed. The results are presented graphically in Figure 8.4. It is important to notice that white children were in this study more restricted in their choices than were Negroes. In kindergarten, where this difference was particularly marked, there were more Negro children who expressed a desire to associate with some white child than there were white children who included some Negro child in their preferences. With increasing age the two races became substantially the same in the degree of self-preference. By the fifth and sixth grade there was essentially no crossing over the race line in the selection of preferred associates. This does not necessarily indicate that either group had no *wish* to associate with the other race, but the cultural segregation was sufficiently recognized to prevent the selection of members of the other race as preferred associates. This finding is generally confirmed by other studies. Among young children race is no barrier to association, but with the gradual development of the child's sensitivity to

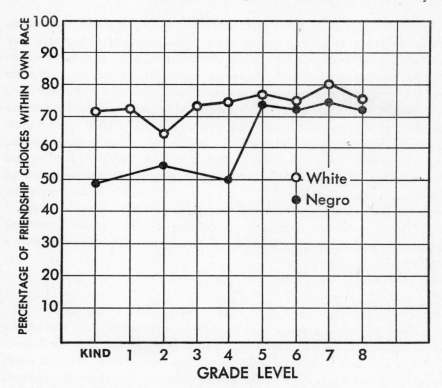

Fig. 8.4 Friendship choices of Negro and white children. (After J. H. Criswell, *Arch. Psych., 33*:235, 1939)

cultural expectations, especially when these expectations are specifically emphasized by the parents, the child comes to accept and believe in the policy of social segregation.

The Objectives and Interests of Children

The discussion of maturity in Chapters 2 and 3 demonstrated that the child's behavior is more and more oriented to the consequences of his actions as he matures. He develops objectives and long-range goals instead of merely responding to the impulse of the moment. We need not discuss the general concept any further, but we shall review in this section some of the investigations of the specific nature of children's goals and interests.

Play Preferences of Children

One of the earliest kinds of preference which a child can show is his choice of material in a free play situation. One characteristic of preferred play materials among young children is the obtrusiveness of it; bright colors, for example, are preferred. But with maturation there is also a trend away from toys that primarily require active muscular activity toward more sedentary toys. Blocks, locomotor toys, and other objects to carry and manipulate are well liked at the preschool level (Bott, 1928). Somewhat later, small-muscle activities become enjoyable, and scissors, paper, pencil, and crayons become popular. At still higher age levels there is a rise in make-believe play, and then a rather sharp decline in make-believe games with the approach of adolescence. The tendency toward sedentary activities continues with the popularity of reading, and with the increased tendency among adolescents to be spectators rather than active participants in games. The trends are obscured by sex differences. At every age boys prefer more muscular, active kinds of play than girls.

Interests of Children

One study by Jersild and Tasch (1949) investigated the interests of school children by asking them what they liked best about school. The results, shown in Figure 8.5, indicate a different trend from that of play activities. The children in the first three grades reported that they liked best the academic side of school. It is not clear to what this refers, but certainly many young children find it very exciting to learn to read and write and do arithmetic. For older children, from seventh grade on, the reported interest in games and sports increased sharply. It is also very interesting to look at the things the children reported they disliked the most. Dislikes are not just the opposite of the likes. Young children do not report very frequently that they dislike games. The most commonly disliked activity for young and old alike is school work. For young children the most significant thing about school is school work. They report it either as the most liked or most disliked activity; most of them like it. Later, the other areas become more prominent and appear more frequently in the likes and the dislikes of children.

Another way to investigate the interests of children is to study their choice of reading, and radio and television programs. It is one of the indisputable facts of recent years that the introduction of television has influenced markedly the leisure-time activity of young children. Some children spend twenty hours a week watching television, nearly as much time as they spend in school. This time might otherwise be spent in more active pastimes. Radio

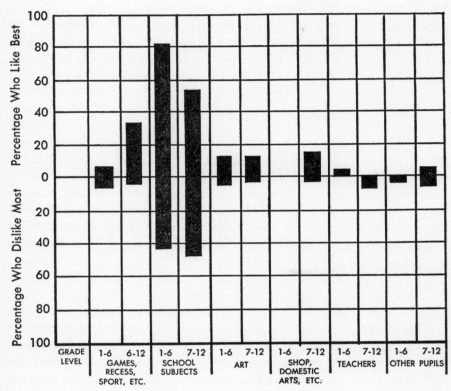

Fig. 8.5 Liked and disliked school activities. (After A. T. Jersild and R. J. Tasch, *Children's Interests*)

listening has dropped off sharply since the advent of television, but it has had effects on reading time and other leisure activities. There does not seem to be much evidence, however, that television has changed the nature of interests. The popular television programs are similar to the plots of popular books. Television only makes such stories more absorbing.

Lazar (1937) found that adventure, action, thrills, mystery, and such stories were very appealing to children, but that among older children biography and factual material are often well liked. These results are probably true today.

Still another indication of the objectives of children is their expressed vocational choices. The general trend of the findings is that younger children are more likely to express vocational aims that are picturesque: to be a cowboy, or a pilot, or an army nurse. With increase in age, the choices become more varied; they include more mundane professions, such as law or teaching. Furthermore, they become more realistic. Early choices are likely to be high-status choices: doctor, lawyer, etc. Toward the end of high school many choices may be more down-to-earth: secretary, stenographer, clerk, etc.

In general, we can say that the objectives of children are active and striking and that as the child matures he becomes more sedentary, more realistic, and more conforming to the norms of our society.

Summary

In this chapter we have discussed the needs of children and the appearance of various sorts of needs at different levels of maturity. We first saw that three sorts of needs can be readily distinguished in terms of the model of human behavior presented in Chapter 6. General needs are those that sensitize the individual to a type of instigation. Sympathy and negativism exemplify general needs. Attitudes are needs that are focussed upon a certain person or object or class of people. What instigation the individual responds to depends upon who is doing the instigating. Objectives or long-range goals, another class of needs, selectively sensitize the child to instigations according to what consequence will be brought about. He will resist impositions if they lead him to do something he does not like, but will not resist them if they lead to his doing something he does like.

We have seen that the personality characteristics of infancy do not fit any of these precisely, but that there are characteristics of infants that form the basis upon which later personality characteristics may develop. We have seen that the various reflexlike behavior patterns in infancy that are modifiable and self-stimulating become the preferred behavior patterns of the infant. Our general thesis has been that the needs of childhood become more selective and specialized with maturity. The earliest personality traits are, therefore, general needs; they appear first as susceptibilities to various emotions. Attitudes and long-range objectives appear later.

We have studied the appearance during childhood of the general needs and some of the characteristics that predispose the child to anger or fear. We have examined in detail the development of attitudes in childhood, especially the development of love or hate toward another person. Finally, we surveyed the interests and objectives of children.

9

Social Controls over the Behavior of Children

A RATHER precocious eight-year-old once said to a four-year-old, "It isn't fair for you to hit me because I am bigger than you and it isn't fair for me to hit little kids." This statement, revealing incidentally an unusual lack of egocentrism on the part of the eight-year-old, presents one principle of fairness. It is not fair to attack or hurt another person when some factor beyond his control prevents him from retaliating. The person who has a need to be fair will be prevented from behaving in ways that are unfair. Such a need will cause some motives to be evoked in specific situations and will inhibit the expression of others. A person with such a need, for example, is motivated to achieve a balance of power if he sees that his opponents in a game are clearly outclassed.

This is one illustration of social control over behavior, and with it we enter into the next area of the model of human behavior described in Chap-

209

ter 6. We are still in the section concerned with goal selection, but we are now at the stage in which some motives are realized in an overt effort to gratify them and others are inhibited or overpowered by competing motives. Since conflict with social rules is an outstanding reason for children to inhibit motives, we shall begin our discussion with the mechanisms by which social controls over motivation are attained.

Let us preview the course of the discussion in the next two chapters. First of all, we must attain a clear picture of what social rules are like and how they are related to the structure of society. We must also describe some of the differences among rules: some rules are concerned with behavior itself, some rules require or forbid certain objective consequences of behavior but do not put any restriction or prescription upon the means by which these consequences come about; still other rules seem to be concerned primarily with the motivation of the person rather than with any specific behavior pattern or consequence of his actions. The characteristics of social rules will occupy the first portion of the chapter.

Next we must see how social rules bring about conforming behavior. A great deal, but not all of social conformity is achieved through a psychological process of compliance to rules. The individual's own motives may coincide with social rules, or he may conform to a social pattern because he is motivated to be like other people. In order to adjust to these rules the child must understand the nature of rules and recognize that other people expect him to fulfill the requirements of his social role.

Reward and punishment are not the only mechanisms for obtaining conformity to social rules. The person may comply with a rule because he has a need to comply. When he perceives that another person wishes him to behave a certain way or expects certain behavior of him, this perception instigates a motive to comply. We must see how and when the need to confirm appears in child behavior. A social rule may also be thought of as a duty or obligation, as something which the individual feels he ought to do. The sense of duty operates even without external enforcement; the individual enforces these rules for himself. We shall see what is known about a sense of duty in children.

The third section of the discussion of controls of behavior, to be found in the next chapter, will be concerned with the actual process by which an impulse may be inhibited. We shall examine some of the ways that a child can regulate the strength of his motives so that they do not get out of control. We shall see also that he may control the strength of the inhibition rather than the strength of the impulse so that he does what he wants without experiencing a conflict.

Lastly, we shall examine personality defenses in children. These defenses differ from controls over motivation in that controls function after a motive has already been evoked and is pressing for action, whereas defenses function to prevent the evocation of motives which, if aroused, would be frustrated, require control, and cause conflict. Thus defenses are preventions of conflict and frustration; controls are adjustments to conflict and frustration.

Social Rules and Roles

One of the important developments in sociology and social psychology in the last fifteen years is the concept of social role. This concept is a bridge by which we can understand the structure of a culture on the one hand and its impact on the individual on the other. A number of sociologists and anthropologists have developed this idea, but the presentation we shall use is patterned after that of Newcomb.

Newcomb (1950) has shown how society can be viewed as a structured set of positions. Positions are the places in society that must be filled by people. Associated with each position are certain more or less rigidly prescribed modes of behavior and certain functions to be performed. The positions of minister, policeman, governor, and businessman are all examples of such places to be filled. For whoever occupies each position certain behavior is required, other behavior is permitted, and still other behavior is forbidden. The minister must ordinarily preach on Sunday, and visit his parishioners. He is expected to forego some secular pleasures in which laymen may indulge. The behavior that is expected of a person occupying a certain position is his *role*. The position is the label assigned to the person, and the role is the description of the behavior that is expected of the person in that position. Every person is subjected to certain rules of behavior. These rules are not matters of choice; they describe the requirements of the roles the person has.

Varieties of Roles and Rules; Universality of a Role

There are many different rules and different kinds of roles that determine the behavior of people. Let us consider first the number of people to whom a certain rule applies or, to put it another way, the number of people in a role. Some rules are almost universal; this implies that they define a role that almost everyone in a society has. The nearly universal rule against killing in our society applies to everybody except possibly the youngest children. On the other hand, there are rules that apply only to children, to schoolteachers, or to some other restricted group. There are rules that may apply only to one single individual. A certain boy may have to wash the car every Saturday before he can play. That rule may apply to no one else in the world.

Generality of a Role

Rules and roles may not only vary in terms of the number of people to whom they apply but also may be restricted in terms of the situation in which they apply. There is a rule against driving 50 miles per hour in the business district, but not in the open country. It is forbidden to shout during prayer in church but not during a football game. A minister may have to preach a sermon in church on Sunday but not in the drug store on Monday. On the other hand, there are very few situations that permit stealing.

Thus, we see that there are rules that apply to all people in all situations (the rule against killing is almost completely universal). There are rules that apply to all people but only in specific situations (no one may walk on the grass in parks). There are rules that apply only to some people, but for these people they operate in all situations (Roman Catholic priests must not marry). Finally, there are rules that apply only to a restricted group of people and in a restricted set of situations (Boy Scouts should wear the Scout uniform to troop meetings).

Permissiveness of a Rule

Thirdly, a social rule may be more or less mandatory. When we describe the role of father, for example, we find that there are some things a father must do—*e.g.,* support his children. There are some things he must not do. There are some things he ought to do but is not required to—*e.g.,* spend some time in recreation with his children. There are things he would be disapproved of for doing but they would not be forbidden. There are some things he may do but is not required or expected to—*e.g.,* spank his child. There are some aspects of his behavior as a father that are entirely voluntary—*e.g.,* to play parcheesi with his children.

Ascribed and Achieved Roles

Thus we see some of the ways in which social roles may vary. In addition, sociologists and anthropologists distinguish between ascribed roles and achieved roles. Ascribed roles are those that the individual cannot choose to accept or reject; they are imposed on him. If a six-year-old is required to go to school, this is an ascribed role. Nobody can choose whether he is six or not. Roles that depend upon parentage, age, or sex are all ascribed. Other roles do not automatically fall on any person. He may choose the role or not—at least, he may choose to try to achieve that role. The marital role is an achieved role; people are not required to marry in our society, and not every person who does want to marry can succeed in finding a spouse.

Rules Oriented to Behavior, Consequences, or Personal Traits

Now let us consider the impact of a rule upon a specific person, regardless of its breadth. It is important to distinguish among three sorts of requirements that a rule may make. It may prescribe or proscribe a behavior pattern—*e.g.,* courtesy demands that a person not eat with his knife. The rule may require or forbid a certain consequence—*e.g.,* we must not do things that might hurt others. Thirdly, the rule may require a specific ability or need of the person— *e.g.,* we should not be unkind.

This last requirement may not be easy to understand, but it is quite important. A good example of a rule that is not oriented to the consequence of actions but rather to the motivation for the action can be found in our society in the rule concerning exposure of the body. This rule seems very confusing and inconsistent if we look for some fixed behavior or some fixed consequence that is to be avoided. Children are taught that it is proper to undress before other members of the family, especially if one is young. In fact, if the child is young enough, he is permitted to appear in a state of partial undress before guests. As he becomes older (although the transition is not sharply defined) more modesty is appropriate, especially in the presence of the opposite sex. Even so, considerable exposure is permitted within the family. Even though exposure is permitted, however, it is usually considered wrong to make a point of looking at another member of the family who is undressed or deliberately to attract attention to one's nakedness. Furthermore, a little girl may not be reprimanded for allowing her brother in the bathroom when she is in the tub, but she may be reproved if while sitting in the living room she does not keep her skirt down in front of the same brother. She should keep her skirt down in public, but she may wear a bathing suit, which is even more exposing. She may appear in public in a bathing suit, but to appear in underwear is disgraceful. On the other hand, if the house is on fire, she should not hesitate to run outdoors even though undressed.

Through all these superficially contradictory conventions there runs a consistent core. What is basically forbidden is to be motivated to expose oneself or to be motivated to look at another person who is exposed. A person who has such motives is immoral. Most of the conventions are sensible and not contradictory if they are viewed as rules that prevent one from appearing to have the immoral motives of exhibitionism or voyeurism. To be careless about one's clothing, for example, or to undress in front of a window without pulling down the blind, or any failure to take the easy and obvious precautions against being seen exposed makes it appear that one wants to be seen. If, on the other hand, there is a good reason for exposure, such as participating in athletics or escaping from a burning house, the fact of being exposed does not imply that the exposure was the goal of the action. If one were to express in general terms the logic behind these proprieties, it might be phrased, "Do not be a person who is motivated by exhibitionism."

A second illustration of the differences among the various orientations of a social rule can be found in the varying interpretations of what constitutes lying. A lie might be defined as a statement that is untrue or inaccurate. This is a simple behavioral definition, easily applied, and one that children usually learn at an early age. Children may call fairy tales lies when they apply this definition. If lying were so defined, the rules about lying would be behavior oriented. It is a characteristic of the words of a statement that they are either accurate or inaccurate.

Or on the other hand, lying might be defined in terms of its consequences. A lie is a statement that induces another person to have a false or inaccurate belief. According to such a definition, fiction is not a lie because in our culture it is not accepted as factual. Usually there is in the front of the book a statement that any resemblance to reality is purely coincidental. Tall stories are generally not lies, according to this definition, because they are not believed. If we accepted this definition, however, it would be lying to present facts that are literally accurate but that are misleading. Many advertising claims are misleading and do mislead people even when they are not outright falsehoods. According to this rule an unintentional misstatement would be a lie. Whether a statement is a lie would depend upon the actual consequences, not the intent.

A third definition might be that a lie is a deliberate attempt to induce a false belief in another person for purposes of one's own gain. According to this definition, an attempt to deceive is a lie whether it succeeds or not. It would exclude "white lies," even though they are attempts to deceive, because they are motivated by kindness rather than by selfishness. If lying were so defined, it would be oriented toward the motivation of the liar rather than toward behavior or consequences.

If we ask how lying is actually defined in our society, we run into difficulty, because there is no complete agreement on it. Probably the third definition comes closer than either of the others. The third definition is, in fact, the dictionary definition of fraud. Only intentional deception is called a lie in this society, and the deception must be intentional to be punished.

Rules about hurting other people are, however, consequence oriented in our society. We have punishments for people who accidentally injure others. We must not only refrain from intentionally injuring other people, but we must also guard our behavior so that we do not accidentally hurt anybody by our actions. Only when the injury could not have been foreseen or prevented is it genuinely excusable. The rules concerning injury are, therefore, more oriented toward consequences than are the rules about lying, although neither is wholly oriented in a single direction.

Impact of Various Rules on Child Behavior

The significance for the problems of child psychology of all these distinctions among social rules is that different rules put quite different demands upon the child. Rules that are universal, for example, do not require much flexibility. As we shall see (p. 439), an adequate adjustment to such a rule may be automatic and can be learned even when the child is immature. Those rules that depend upon the situation are more demanding. If the child must follow one rule in one situation but another rule in another situation—*e.g.*, one behavior pattern if he is chairman of a group, another if he is a member— he must have a clearer, more flexible adjustment. If he must change his pattern of behavior as he moves from one role to another, he cannot succeed with a rigid mode of adjustment.

The various orientations of rules are important for the same reason. Rules oriented to behavior alone are usually simple; obedience can be learned easily and early. Rules oriented to consequences and rules oriented to the characteristics of the person, however, demand more maturity. Of these two, probably the most demanding rule is one that is focused upon the needs or abilities of the person. An adequate understanding of this sort of rule requires more maturity than any other.

To summarize, a role is the set of rules of behavior that governs the behavior of a person who occupies a certain position in the social structure. The role may be a unique or idiosyncratic one, or it may be one occupied by many people. The role may prescribe behavior in all situations or only in a limited set of situations. Even if the role governs all situations, a single rule may apply to many situations or to only a few. The role prescription may be mandatory—*i.e.*, absolutely require behavior patterns or absolutely forbid some behavior—or it may encourage or discourage, or it may leave the individual free to choose. Generally, a role requires some behavior patterns, encourages others, leaves some freedom, and discourages or forbids still other behavior.

Finally, we see that the requirements of a role may be focused upon behavior, consequences, or personal characteristics. One rule may require a certain behavior pattern, regardless of the consequences of the behavior in a specific situation. Another social rule may be focused upon certain consequences and require or forbid any behavior pattern that brings about these consequences. Or a social rule may be focused upon the characteristics of the person and require or forbid him to display certain characteristics.

The Social Roles of Children

We now turn to the rules that apply especially to children in our society. In every society the newborn infant is not expected to behave in the same fashion as the adult in the culture. For a period of time after birth, he is permitted to do things in the natural infantile way. He gets his food by sucking, he has no specified duties, he is not required to conform to any especial rules. Whiting and Child (1953) have called this the period of initial indulgence.

Then, at some time in the life of the child, the rules that apply to adults in the society are applied to him. Weaning is an example of such a process. He is prevented or discouraged from nursing or is encouraged to eat in a more mature way. This begins the period of socialization. Socialization is not begun simultaneously for all aspects of behavior; the length of the period of initial indulgence varies for different aspects of behavior.

Comparison of Our Society with Other Cultures

Whiting and Child are primarily concerned with the socialization of behavior in five systems: oral, anal, sexual, aggressive, and dependent. The oral system has to do with eating; weaning marks the end of the period of initial indulgence. Toilet training is the end of initial indulgence in the anal system. The introduction of rules against sex play in children is the corresponding point for sexual behavior. Rules against aggression and rules requiring independence and responsibility mark the end of initial indulgence in aggression and dependence.

These authors have compared a large number of cultures in these variables and in the severity of the socialization process. A severe socialization is one in which the child is expected to shift rapidly from infantile to mature behavior; it is generally accompanied by punishment for infantile behavior. A gentler socialization occurs when the child is slowly led into more mature behavior by reward and encouragement for the new behavior patterns, but without punishment for lapses into the earlier pattern.

By and large, our society is one of the most severe, according to these findings. We cannot speak of our culture as a whole; the judgments used in this study are actually based upon the description of the way middle-class parents raise their children, as reported by Davis and Havighurst (1946).

WEANING   With respect to weaning, Whiting and Child have ratings on 51 cultures. The age of weaning was rated for each one on a scale ranging from a possible low of 3 to a high of 21. The actual range of the 51 cultures was from 6 to 18. The earliest weaning took place among the Marquesans, as described by Linton (1939). There was almost no nursing of children among the Marquesans when Linton observed them. The women thought that nursing spoiled the beauty of their breasts. The child was fed a sort of thin gruel that was slapped upon his mouth while he lay on his back. He sputtered and choked but gradually got some of it into his stomach. This is the most extreme culture, but the American middle class is the next earliest. Not only the early weaning, but also the rigidity of scheduled feeding during infancy, which may make the child cry for the twenty minutes or the forty-five minutes left before the time for the next bottle, accounts for the low rating of our society. In terms of severity of weaning practices, the middle-class home is not so extreme. It is more severe than the average of the other cultures studied by Whiting and Child, but is not at the very top. It is about half way between the middle and the upper extreme.

TOILET TRAINING   Initial indulgence in anal behavior is concerned with the restrictions upon anal activities during infancy and with the age of beginning toilet training. There are only two cultures more severe than the American middle-class group in their treatment of infantile urination and defecation. The severity of toilet training depends upon how rapidly training is expected, and how much punishment is employed to make the child change his habits. In this respect the American middle class is equal to the most severe of the twenty cultures for whom Whiting and Child obtained reliable ratings. In contrast to the practice in our society, the Siriono, a primitive South American tribe reported by Holmberg (1950), are the most lenient in toilet training. The Siriono make essentially no effort to train the child until he can walk, and then they proceed very gradually. The child learns entirely by imitation; by the time he reaches the age of three, he has learned not to pollute the house. The mother still helps the child, however, and not until he is six does he take care of his defecation needs entirely by himself.

SEXUAL RESTRICTIONS   Regarding restrictions on sexual behavior in infancy and childhood, the American middle class is again rather severe.

When rated on the freedom allowed sexual activities, it was quite extreme. Only two societies are less indulgent of sex play in childhood. In terms of the severity of punishment for sexual activities, our society is not at the very extreme, but falls about half way between the middle and the upper extreme.

DEPENDENCY   In comparing the American middle class with other cultures on the indulgence of dependency of the young child, we find that, although we do not begin specific independence training at a very early age, we do not permit our infants to be as dependent as most other cultures do during the period of initial indulgence. Among the Kwoma, for example, who have been studied by Whiting (1941), the child is in physical contact with his mother almost all the time until he is weaned. She gives the child her breast whenever he cries, and if that does not help, she tries to discover the source of the trouble. Judging from the Davis and Havighurst data on the middle class, our society is below the middle, but not at the lower extreme in indulgence.

AGGRESSION   In aggressiveness training, there seems to be little justification for a separation of initial indulgence and severity of socialization. The child is not capable of aggression until he is old enough to be socialized, so that few societies have a definite period in which he is allowed freedom to be aggressive. Our society is rated slightly above the middle on severity of socialization of aggression, but not close to the upper extreme.

OVER-ALL SEVERITY OF SOCIALIZATION   When all these measures are combined into a general judgment about the indulgence of a society and its severity in training children to take on adult behavior patterns, we find that the middle class is at the lower extreme in indulgence, tying with two primitive tribes, and in severity of socialization it is close to the top, tied for second place. We should note that severity of socialization in our society is expressed in number of demands for conformity and length of learning period for conformity. One gets the impression that the actual severity of punishment in our society is not extreme.

Observers of the American middle-class culture have frequently suspected that we are unusually demanding in our treatment of children, that we make these demands while the child is quite young, and that we require very rapid training. These suspicions have been confirmed by the comparisons just reported. The common conclusion to such a finding is that it is no wonder there is so much maladjustment in our society. It is not at all obvious that such a conclusion is justified. Certainly we do not wish to justify unnecessary severity in training children, but we shall see when we look at the factors in development how difficult it is to assess the full consequences of our child-training practices.

Sex Differences in Social Roles

These findings were concerned with only a few of the roles assigned to children in our culture. There are others, of course—talking, reading, going to school—that are more specific in their demands. Different roles are assigned to the two sexes in our society even when boys and girls are very young.

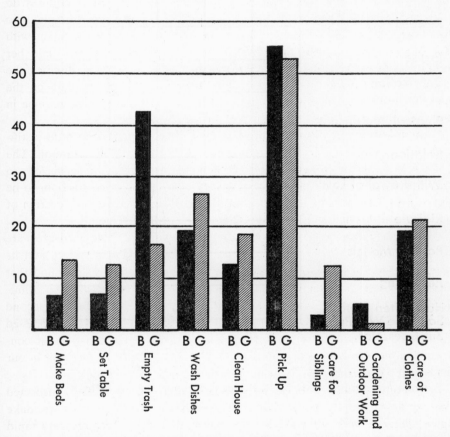

Fig. 9.1 Differences in chores assigned to boys and girls by mothers. (Data from an unpublished study by R. R. Sears, E. Maccoby, H. Levin, *et al.*)

By and large, girls are not encouraged to be so active and aggressive as boys; they are permitted to display their feelings more readily; they are expected perhaps to be more mature in the sense of being "little ladies," whereas the corresponding pressure on boys to be "little gentlemen" is not so strong.

Anthropologists have remarked that boys in our society are almost encouraged to have a double life. One mother, for example, reprimanded her son's swearing by calling it "barn language," as though recognizing that it was appropriate in its place. In recent times in some rural communities (West, 1945) adolescent boys were expected to go through a period of wildness when they sowed their wild oats, whereas girls were strictly forbidden the same activities.

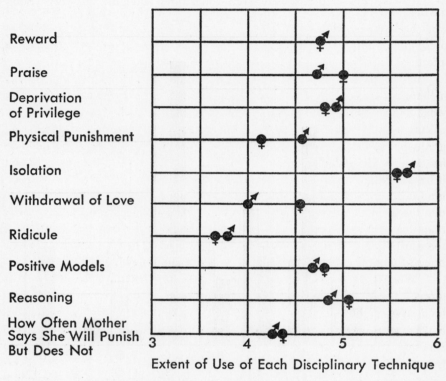

Fig. 9.2 Differences in disciplinary methods used on boys and girls. (Data from an unpublished study by R. R. Sears, Eleanor Maccoby, H. Levin, *et al.*)

The difference in the sex roles of children in our society can be seen in the differences in the way boys and girls are reared. Figures 9.1 and 9.2 show some comparisons of methods used in rearing boys and girls in a sample of American homes.

Other Aspects of Social Roles in Childhood

Another role in our society that changes with age is the assignment of responsibility to the child. Babies are obviously considered to be irresponsible in our society. We do not know whether or not other cultures are similar. The young infant, even when he is being trained to drink from a cup, for example, is not culpable if he fails. He is not blamed for it, and the parent does not feel justified in becoming angry at him even though she may punish him to train him. By the time the child is three years old, however, and in the middle of his negativistic period, he is frequently blamed for his misdemeanors. We tend to assume that he is wilfully disobedient, that he is deliberately misbehaving, whereas at an earlier age we believe that he does not understand what he is supposed to do. Parents, therefore, may become angry with young preschool children although they do not feel justified in being angry with an infant.

Is the parent justified in taking a different attitude toward the misdemeanors of the older child? To some extent he is, because the child must learn what it means to be responsible. We must recognize, however, and in this culture we do partially recognize, that responsibility can be acquired only gradually. In fact, the child is never assumed to be completely responsible for his actions. His parents continue to be legally responsible through childhood; if he commits a crime he receives a very different kind of treatment from the kind accorded an adult. Juvenile courts explicitly operate on the philosophy that the delinquent is the product of his environment and needs therapy, rather than that he is responsible for his own actions and deserves punishment. Thus, the attribution of responsibility does not occur at some moment in an all-or-none fashion; it appears gradually throughout childhood.

When we try to classify the social rules imposed on young children in terms of whether they are behavior oriented, consequence oriented, or focused upon the needs and intentions of the individual, we find no information beyond our everyday knowledge. Since behavior-oriented rules are more concrete and easier to understand, the rules for young children are more frequently of this type. On the other hand, parents try very early to get the child to appreciate the importance of intentions. They succeed, apparently, because preschool children frequently defend themselves by claiming that their misdemeanor was an accident.

Before leaving the discussion of social rules and role prescriptions, we should indicate that much of this discussion could be applied equally well to any sort of pressure on the child, regardless of whether or not it is a general social rule. An authority's wishes constitute a social pressure, usually one that is limited to one person or one situation; but this type of pressure can be oriented toward behavior, consequences, or motivation, just as general social rules can. We have limited our examples to cultural rules merely because they constitute perhaps the most important and consistent social pressure on children.

Social Conformity in Children

We have been describing the social rules of our society and comparing our society with others in its demands upon children. Now we shall examine the psychological mechanisms that bring about the individual's conformity to social rules. These mechanisms underlie the conformity of both children and adults, although we shall see that some processes require more maturity than others.

If we examine the model of human behavior, especially the section describing goal selection, we can see that social rules might have their impact at different points in the process of goal selection. On the one hand, the rules may be part of the individual's cognitive picture of his environment. He perceives that there is an external pressure to which he must adjust. For example, the speed limit on a stretch of road is usually known to the driver. Knowing the speed limit may not make him obey it, but if he does obey it he is complying to an external pressure. We will use the term *compliance* to describe all conforming behavior in which the individual explicitly obeys a rule. Not all the behavior that does, in fact, conform to social rules represents a psychological process of complying with the rule. There are two kinds of social conformity that do not depend upon complying to a perceived rule or standard.

Harmony of Motives and Social Rules

In one case, our own motives are in accord with the rules. For example, there are rules in our society against eating human flesh. We all obey those rules, but the fact that we are prohibited from being cannibalistic never enters our minds. Human flesh is repulsive to us, not innately, but through our childhood training and experience; so we have become people who do not like human meat. The social rule exists, but it has been instilled in us in such a way that we do not refrain from cannibalism because we recognize and obey the rule, but rather because we are not motivated to be cannibalistic.

In our model of behavior the dislike for human flesh is a need just like the dislike for burnt potatoes. It has a different history, but it functions the same way in its mechanism of affecting behavior. We shall see in Part II (pp. 467-470) the processes underlying the development of such needs and values and the factors leading to the complete acceptance of social pressures as one's own motivation, but at present we shall regard such needs as the needs described in Chapter 8.

Conformity to Group Patterns

A second basis for social conformity that does not depend upon one's compliance with a cognized rule is through contagious behavior, imitation, or following the fashion. Most of us want to be like other people—not entirely like them and not like all of them, but still not completely different. When a yo-yo fad sweeps through a school, every child wants a yo-yo. He would not be a social outcast if he did not have one, but he wants one anyway. This process depends upon the fact that another person's behavior instigates a motive by suggesting a pattern of behavior that is like the other person's. If this were all that is involved, then such an instigation would actually evoke behavior only when the individual found the suggested pattern of behavior attractive in its own right. The essential feature of the motivation to copy or conform to a fashion is the fact that there is a need to be like other people or like certain other people. Thus, other people's behavior instigates the motivation to imitate.

IMITATION   Imitation occurs during very early infancy, perhaps as early as three or four months, but it is difficult to be sure how early it can occur. According to Piaget (1951), the basis for imitation in young infants is the similarity of some model that the child perceives to one of his own behavior patterns. At first the only actions that the child imitates are those for which the perception of the model corresponds to the child's perception of one of his repertoire of actions. He cannot imitate facial grimaces, for example, because he has never seen himself make faces, but he can imitate sounds in his repertoire because he hears the model and also hears his own sound. This early imitation is somewhat automatic; he does not act as though he is trying to imitate.

With increasing maturity the child imitates actions that he cannot perceive himself doing as he perceives the model, and finally he is able to imitate actions that he has never performed before. In this last stage the child gives every appearance of trying to copy the model. In other words, the model can instigate the motivation to copy it. Copying and imitation are very common among children, and the sight of one child performing some new or noticeable action is almost sure to provoke some of the watchers to try it also.

The child's selectivity about what and whom he imitates gradually increases with age. During the first year and perhaps most of the second, the child's imitation is unselective. He tends to imitate any interesting activity. By the end of the second year, however, the child imitates some people more than others; usually he imitates the people who are most important to him and whom he likes the best.

Valentine (1946) reports that his child, at the age of two, preferred to imitate his mother rather than anybody else. In one case, the child not only imitated the mother, but insisted that everybody in the entire group of adults also imitate the mother's actions.

CONTAGIOUS BEHAVIOR   Among older children imitation or contagious behavior has been investigated by Lippit, Polansky, and others (1950; 1952). They recorded instances of contagious behavior—*i.e.,* imitation of one child by another when there was no attempt by the first to influence the second— in the spontaneous play behavior of groups of children. They also recorded deliberate attempts of one child to influence other people, and obtained by in- terview procedures a score for each child on a group of variables that are highly correlated to social influence.

They found some interesting results. First, as we might expect, the chil- dren who are imitated tend to be those who are influential. This was true whether the judgments of influence were studied or the actual success in in- fluencing other children was taken as a measure of influence. They did not find, however, that the children who most readily imitate others are the unin- fluential children. Instead, it seems that one characteristic of the powerful child is spontaneity of action. As a result, they are somewhat more open to con- tagion than the average. They are also better able to withstand social pressure.

In this experiment, susceptibility to contagion requires some spontaneity and willingness to act. If we could watch a fad sweep through a group, it would be interesting to see who would take it up early, who would wait until it was already quite popular before following the fashion, and who would resist the fashion until the very end. It would not be surprising if the influential children took the fashion early while the more passive ones would wait until it was already popular, but not withstand the pressure to the end.

Not only actions, but also opinions and values may be imitated. The process of accepting another person's opinion is sometimes voluntary and de- liberate. If I admire somebody, I will tend to accept his beliefs as true and his values as valid. Therefore, I will tend to agree with them and thus come to have the same convictions and attitudes. Because this process is clear and de- liberate, it is possible for full-blown, well-organized opinions to be transmitted and accepted. Such well-organized opinions as that labor unions should stay out of politics or that acquired characteristics cannot be inherited may be adopted in this fashion. The coherent system of beliefs of the admired person is accepted in such a way that it retains its coherence.

One may also adopt the attitudes of another person merely through ex- posure to them. The fact that the other person is liked or is important or powerful makes us more influenced by exposure to his attitudes than to those of other people who are less significant in our life. Such an adoption of attitudes needs not operate through the cognitive acceptance of a belief. It is taken in through a sort of "osmosis"; consequently the acceptance may be quite uncritical and may even be contrary to one's own cognitively clear beliefs. A totalitarian country, by restricting news, continuously exposes its people to only one set of attitudes. Even if one tries to be unbiased, it is difficult to combat such exposure over a long period of time.

The things that are accepted in this unclear fashion are more likely to be vague general attitudes or involuntary mannerisms than coherent systems of belief. Very few people acquire an Oxford accent because they admire Oxford and believe that the proper way to talk is with an Oxford accent. Yet many people acquire such an accent from exposure to it. Whether or not they acquire it probably depends to some extent upon how favorable is their attitude toward Oxford. In more important matters than accents, the tacit unrecognized assumptions of a society or a person are likely to be transmitted through exposure, and, once acquired, they may color the interpretation of all other experiences.

The child's imitation of the parent results, even at an early age, in the acquisition of many mannerisms, habits, and generalized attitudes through mere exposure. Thus the soundness of the advice to set a good example for your child. Many a mother has been shocked to hear her little girl scold a doll harshly, only to recognize it as an imitation of her own language toward the child. With increasing maturity the child may accept his father's clearly formulated beliefs and defend them stoutly to his friends. "I'm going to vote for Eisenhower," he may say. His father may find, however, that the teacher supplants him as the final authority on all questions. If the teacher says that Australia is an island, it is useless to try to tell the child that some people call it a continent.

Mechanisms Underlying Compliance to External Rules

We have seen two sorts of social conformity that do not depend upon the perception of a rule and the motivation to comply with it. One is the presence of motives that correspond with a social pattern; the other is the motivation to imitate actions and follow a fashion. Now let us turn to the processes underlying compliance—i.e., conformity through explicit obedience to rules.

Compliance to a required course of action, whether it is socially required or whether its wisdom is indicated by some other consideration, results from constraints on behavior. Some constraints, such as stone walls or fences, actually prevent behavior from occurring. The English language describes such barriers to action by saying that these are the things we "cannot" do. Other constraints do not actually prevent the behavior but make us regret it afterwards if we do not comply. These are the things that we "may not" do.

As long as conforming behavior is actually coerced—if the person cannot do anything but conform—the problem of control is simple. He could not violate the rule if he tried. This is the kind of conformity established by prison walls. At the other extreme, conformity occurs through the individual's own motivation. If he wants to do the things he is supposed to do, then again there is no problem of control.

Between these two extremes the problem of control arises. When one wants to do something that he ought not to do, but is not physically prevented from doing, then he must exert self-control.

There are three requirements for self-control. First, the individual must understand the rule so that he can recognize when he should and when he should not do as he wants. This understanding makes it possible for there to be the instigation for the motivation to comply. Secondly, he must have some sort of need that interacts with the instigation to result in the actual evocation of the compliant motive. Thirdly, he must have the self-control to be governed by the compliant motivation, even though the goal is remote and abstract, rather than by the impulse that it is necessary to inhibit.

In the remainder of this chapter we shall consider the first two of these factors and look at some of the empirical evidence on the gradually developing social compliance of children. The following chapter will be entirely devoted to the problems of self-control and personality defenses.

The perception of a social rule is the instigation that may evoke a motivation to comply. Whether there is any real motive to comply depends upon the presence of appropriate needs, and any one of three sorts of needs may underlie a motive to obey the rule.

FEAR OF PUNISHMENT Some social rules are enforced by rewards and punishments. If this is the only basis for compliance, the person complies because of fear of punishment or a desire for reward. The consequences may be physical ones. Children may obey through a fear of physical punishment; some adults refrain from criminal activities through fear of fines or imprisonment. More commonly, however, the consequence that people fear is social. They fear social disapproval; they fear public exposure. The child may fear the denial of love. Social abandonment and loss of the respect of one's fellows is more fearsome for most people than physical restraints or punishments.

Fear of external consequences alone is not very effective in enforcing social rules, because the effectiveness of such a rule depends upon the violator's being detected. Whenever a person believes that he will not be detected, the fear of punishment, social or otherwise, loses much of its force. Increasing the severity of the punishment does not great influence the effectiveness ot the rule, inasmuch as very few people violate a rule because they decide that the crime is worth the punishment. Probably nobody feels that speeding is actually worth even a five-dollar fine, although five dollars may mean very little to some people. This is illustrated by the fact that most speeders slow down when they see a policeman. Most casual violations of laws stem from becoming so involved in behavior that the consequences are momentarily lost sight of.

Fear of punishment is more effective with children than with adults, primarily because children are not realistic about the probability of getting caught. Children seem frequently to believe that parents are all-seeing and omniscient. Parents can, in fact, tell a great deal about what a child has been doing by the way he acts, and thus do detect misdemeanors in a way that must seem miraculous to the child. Violations of rules in childhood practically always stem from lack of self-control and from forgetting about the rule in the excitement of the moment. Deliberate breaking of rules may occur when the child is very angry and takes that means of taking revenge.

It is a common belief, justified by a little evidence, that fear of loss of love is more potent than fear of punishment. It is not easy to see why this would be true. It is hardly likely that the effectiveness stems from the mere fact that loss of love is a more severe punishment. More likely, it stems from the fact that the loss of love is not an event that happens and is done with. If the child really feels psychologically abandoned, or feels threatened with abandonment, he may be constantly haunted by a state of anxiety. This uncertainty about his acceptance keeps him looking out of one corner of his eye to see how his parent is reacting to what he does. Thus, the authority behind the rules is more frequently in mind. He is trying not only to avoid further disapproval, but also to gain approval, so he is inhibited into conforming more of the time. The child's reactions to accusations of his failure to love the parent (or *visible suffering,* as we have called it) are similar. If he is mature enough to be susceptible to it, his guilt feelings have the same vagueness and haunting quality that anxiety has.

NEED TO COMPLY A second need, besides fear of consequences, may lie behind compliance to rules. The mere perception of a wish or an expectation from somebody else may instigate the motivation to fulfill it. We shall call the need that describes a person's sensitivity to such instigation the need compliance, or need to acquiesce.

This need is present to some degree in all of us. Nearly anyone will lend a match to a stranger or tell the time if he is asked. Some of us have great difficulty in saying no to salesmen. An essential characteristic of loving someone is the need to acquiesce to his wishes; usually it is done with no feeling of sacrifice, but because we are easily motivated to do what a loved one wants. Those who try to explain away all altruistic motivation argue that this is merely fear of disapproval. There is no reason to accept such a position, although it is certainly true that some acquiescence is motivated by fear.

SENSE OF DUTY   A third need that leads to conformity is the responsiveness of the individual to duties and obligations. Some people are strongly motivated toward a course of behavior as soon as they see it as their duty, whereas other people are much less bound by their obligations. This is the sense of honor that is behind such statements as, "His word is as good as his bond." This sense of duty produces behavior that is apparently motivated by the desire to exhibit or display—although not necessarily to the public—a personal integrity and sense of honor. A person who keeps his promise through thick and thin is often not influenced by the actual consequences of his behavior. He may keep a promise to a person now dead with the same integrity with which he keeps his promise to a person who can react to him. He is not apparently motivated to make others believe that he is honorable, because he may carry out his promises secretly. A man with a strong sense of obligation must be honorable in his dealings in order to live with himself. His own self-esteem demands behavior that lives up to his values and his sense of duty.

Despite the fact that a sense of duty or obligation is self-enforcing, so that it does not require any external pressure to bring about conformity, it is still an external duty in some sense. It may be onerous to the person; he may feel a conflict between duty and pleasure. He may feel that he wants to do one thing, but ought to do another. In a real sense, it is not his own motive but an obligation that governs his behavior. Freud developed the concept of *superego* to describe this control over behavior. The superego represents the rules of the society that one has learned and *internalized*. By *internalized* is meant that the individual enforces the rules on himself. Notice, however, that such a sense of duty is not so internalized as those social rules that are felt by a person to be his own motives rather than any sort of external demand.

To summarize, we have examined three needs that are especially relevant to compliance with social rules. The first, the fear of punishment, includes all the needs that may be involved in the consideration of the consequences of our actions, and especially the desire for social approval. The second is a more positive need—*i.e.,* it underlies a wish to comply or to acquiesce rather than a fearful avoidance of nonconformity. The third is a sense of obligation or duty.

The Development of Compliance in Children

Three factors in the development of compliance in children have been extensively studied. The first is the development of games during childhood. Since games involve rules, the child's changing reaction to games tells us a great deal about his conception of rules. The second factor is the development of moral values in children, especially honesty. The third is the understanding of social values and social rules, and along with it the understanding of social roles.

CHILDREN'S GAMES   Many of the problems of conformity can be easily studied in the games of children, in which there is a necessity for establishing rules that everybody follows.

We find that there are no clear rules in the play of preschool children. When a large number of children are brought together, as in a nursery school, the types of play relations that may be found change with the age of the child. Parten (1932) has described six different types of play activity found in nursery school.

The first type is not play at all; the child is unoccupied. Second, some children may be found in solitary play. Their play shows no influence of the presence of other children. As far as the play is concerned, the child could just as well be in a room by himself. The third type of play is spectatorship. The activity of the child shows his sensitivity to the other children, but he does not interact with them in any way. He merely watches. A fourth type of play activity, slightly more active, is parallel play. In parallel play the child copies or imitates what other children are doing; he plays along with them but without any interaction with them. When the parallel play is accompanied by interaction among children—talking back and forth, discussing what each is doing, perhaps specifically doing something together—then it might be called associative play. This can still be distinguished from cooperative play. In cooperative play the children are not necessarily doing the same thing at the same time. If one child plays the housekeeper while another one delivers mail, then the two play roles dovetail and complement each other. This is cooperative play. If the two children both played mother, each to her own doll, it would be more associative than cooperative. Figure 9.3 depicts the changes with age in nursery-school play. It will be seen that associative and cooperative play rise with age, while solitary play declines.

Notice that Parten found no competitive games in nursery school. The three- or four-year-old cannot, psychologically speaking, play a competitive game. He may observe the behavior of other people in what is called a game, but for him only the superficial aspects of the behavior are meaningful. Because he does not understand the game in terms of its purposes, he has no way of knowing what is essential about it and what is arbitrary. The young child, Piaget (1932) finds, believes the rules to be absolute and fixed. Marbles is a

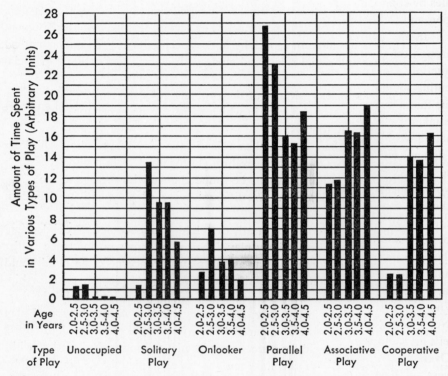

Fig. 9.3 Age changes in type of play in nursery school. (After M. B. Parten, *J. Abn. and Soc. Psych., 27*, 1932, 243-269)

game played with marbles and a round circle. It would not be right if the circle were a square. At the same time, the behavior of the child is not at all determined by the rules. When three-year-olds play marbles, they throw the marbles around, they draw the circle, but nobody wins and nobody loses. If a three-year-old is asked who won, he may say that he did or that both people did. In any case his reply is unrelated to the actual game.

With the development of competitiveness he begins to have some appreciation of what winning and losing mean, but during late preschool and early school age his understanding is still quite superficial and is defined only in terms of who has the most marbles at the end of the game, regardless of how they were obtained. For the game to be a game in the adult sense of the word, it is necessary for the child to recognize the existence of rules that determine the permissible methods of obtaining marbles. Furthermore, it is necessary to recognize that the rules operate for both participants in the game. When this is fully realized, the child follows the rules of the game because otherwise there is no game. At the same time he will recognize that the rules are only rules by common consent, and that any set of rules that both participants agree upon and follow is fair.

In the course of achieving this adult view of a game, the child goes through the period of making new rules to fit the demands of the immediate situation. Generally these so-called new rules are merely means for circumventing some rule that, at the time, happens to be oppressive. In checkers, the rule that a man must be played if touched and that once it is played it may not be taken back seems very burdensome to the child who has just made a play that allows his opponent to take two men. The immaturity of the child makes it difficult for him to anticipate the consequences of his play; but that is what the rule demands. Once the mistake is made but quickly discovered, then the two opponents are in a position in which one of them dislikes the rule and the other, of course, wants it. One of the common solutions that children arrive at, although not in a planful way, is to permit "overs" if the other player has not yet made his move. The rule about "overs" may, however, depend upon whether one child can say "overs" before the other says "no overs." A new game is beginning to be built upon the old one. Quarrels arise in the new game. Each child may say his magic words almost simultaneously with the other. Who was first? We can imagine the resulting argument. "I said it first"— "No! I said it first"—"All right, let's try it again. Overs"—"That wasn't fair! Let's do it this time. No overs"—"That doesn't count. Overs"—"No overs"— "Overs, overs, overs, overs, overs"—"No overs, no overs, a thousand times no overs"—"A million times overs"—"A zillion no overs"—"A zillion zillion overs, 1955 padlock. Anybody that says 'no overs' again is a big fat toad!"

The words may vary, but the general tune is the same for such wrangling among school-age children. On the one hand, they want really to play the game. They are not satisfied unless there is a real winner. On the other hand, they cannot appreciate the requirements of a game—*i.e.,* that both parties must accept and conform to the rules. With more maturity such wrangling as we have just described declines. The older child recognizes the rule as arbitrary but also recognizes that rules make the game a good one or a poor one. Although a game about who can say "overs" the faster may be possible, it makes checkers into a very different game from the one it started out to be. In later life changes in rules are made ahead of time and with the aim of improving the game, not merely trying to gain a temporary advantage.

HONESTY IN CHILDREN Honesty can be investigated relatively easily because it is not difficult to devise tests that appear to allow the child an opportunity to cheat but that are in fact designed so that the dishonesty of each individual can be determined. The classical study in this area was carried out by Hartshorne and May (1928), who studied the honesty of school children in twenty-one different situations. They were able to obtain honesty scores for each child, but the most striking finding from their research was the apparent specificity of honesty. One child might be honest in one situation but dishonest in another, whereas a second would show just the reverse pattern. One child might illegitimately increase his grade on an arithmetic paper if he graded it himself, but would not cheat in the game of "pin the tail on the donkey" if given an opportunity to peep. Almost no child was completely honest in all situations.

The temptation to cheat varies in different situations. One study (Howells, 1938) found that children cheat more when the examination is difficult than when it is easy. Another study (Gross, 1946) found that children are more likely to change an answer on their papers if the error is a little one rather than a large one. Another factor that probably influences the occurrence of dishonest behavior is the involvement of the child in the situation. It has been shown, for example (Slaght, 1928), that dishonest children are more excitable and impulsive than honest children. One of the characteristics of impulsive people is that their behavior depends more on the conditions of the moment than upon enduring principles of action. It is this impulsiveness of children that would lead us to expect inconsistency in honest behavior. Dishonest behavior does not imply, for the child, a consistent philosophy of trying to get away with as much as he can. It is a weakness of control in the face of impulses rather than a philosophy of life. Some dishonesty in adults, especially in criminals, does probably signify a consistently dishonest, antisocial attitude. Honesty is probably also a more consistent determiner of action for adults than for children. We can all recognize, however, that we are more likely to be honest with friends than with enemies, more honest in dealing with individual people than in dealing with impersonal organizations, such as insurance companies or the Bureau of Internal Revenue.

One of Hartshorne and May's findings seems surprising, but it is probably correct, because it has been confirmed by other investigators. Older children tend to be less honest than younger ones. Slaght (1928) found that younger children were more likely than older ones to condemn such principles as "cheat if you can" or "lie to keep a secret." The factors behind such findings as these are complex, and we cannot be sure what they are. In so far as honesty depends upon the child's fear of being caught, it would be expected to decrease with age. Very young children sometimes believe their elders are omnipotent; older children are more realistic about the probability of being detected in cheating. If honesty does increase with age, it depends upon the value's being inculcated in the child. Our own society is not one that sets a good example of honest behavior—we preach honesty more than we practice it—and so it is not surprising if children become disillusioned. Still a third factor may be that the older children in the Hartshorne and May study were in the period of preadolescence in which peer values are more important than the values of the home and parent. If they saw honesty as an adult value, they might rebel against it.

The period of preadolescence, roughly nine to eleven, is marked in our society by a rejection of adult standards. Unruliness in school is likely to be at a peak at the ages of nine to eleven, fourth to sixth grades. Jones (1939) reports that teachers frequently complain about such behavior problems as teasing, scuffling, rebelliousness, carelessness, untidiness, and disobedience during this period. Piaget found that this is the time when the child begins to recognize the importance of accepting rules, but at the same time the rules are not accepted from authority without question. Rules become a matter of agreement among peers. It is as though the child achieved this mature understanding of social rules only by rejecting the authority-based standards that were potent at an earlier age. He must now acquire these values for himself by discovering their validity in social interaction.

THE UNDERSTANDING OF SOCIAL RULES   We have seen that the changes in the child's conformity to social rules are accompanied by changes in his understanding of the social values of his elders. Gesell and Ilg (1949) report that feelings about being good or bad are very marked at six and seven. This concern with being good is a sort of ethical level of aspiration, but goodness is defined in a childish way. A child at this age level may do a kindness for somebody or resist some temptation, because such behavior signifies that he is a "good" child. In other words, he is concerned with how he is evaluated by others or perhaps with his own self-esteem but not with the objective fact that a kindness is required because the other person is in trouble or that resistance is necessary because the tempting activity would have objectively bad effects. The egocentricity of the child's desire to do a good turn is well illustrated by the Cub Scout who asked his mother if she would come outside and cross the street so that he could do his good deed by "helping an old lady across the street."

Another sign of immaturity is the child's difficulty in recognizing the importance of assessing intentions in evaluating the goodness or badness of an act. Sin is defined in our society largely in terms of the motivation of a sinner. We saw earlier (see p. 54) the reaction of children when asked to evaluate two crimes, of which one had worse objective consequences and the other had less effect but was accompanied by bad intentions. Younger children call the boy who broke twelve plates by accident worse than the boy who broke one on purpose, whereas older children evaluate the two children in the reverse way.

Gesell and Ilg (1949) report that at about the age of nine, the child is much concerned with fairness. Such a concern can be just as egocentric as a concern with goodness, but when the child begins to sympathize with another person who is treated unfairly, he is showing a shift from an egocentric morality to more objective ethics. He is beginning to feel that unfair situations should not exist, regardless of who is responsible for them and regardless of his own personal involvement in the situation. To be motivated to right a wrong or to remedy an ill merely by the presence of the injustice is to feel that certain objective states of affairs "ought" not exist.

In the development of a sense of fairness, it has been suggested that there are transitional steps (L. P. Holt, 1951). One of the early concepts of fairness might be called equalitarianism—the demand that everyone should be treated exactly alike. Thus, the child at this time may demand complete equality of desserts, of gifts, or of privileges. This is the time that makes parents despair of ever making the children happy. If father brings a different gift for each child when he returns from a trip, each child may feel he is treated unfairly, because the other received something different. This is the time when desserts are inspected microscopically to detect any possible difference in the sizes of the helpings. It is at this age that each boy on a baseball team demands his turn to be pitcher, regardless of which one is actually the best pitcher.

The child at this age may, however, demand equal treatment for others as well as himself. He begins to appreciate the point of view of the other person but is very concrete in his evaluations. There are good psychological reasons for this tendency. If objects are matched concretely, they are easy to compare and evaluate. Cookies can be counted, cake can be measured, ice cream can be dished out in standard-sized spoonfuls.

In a further development fairness becomes more differentiated. Benefits are adjusted to fit the needs and desires of the individual and later the welfare of the group. Such a concept of fairness demands more maturity and more sophisticated judgment to determine whether dissimilar benefits are fairly divided. When group welfare enters into consideration, serious ethical dilemmas may occur. There may be cultural values placed upon certain positions that do not correspond to the objective value of the position. The acclaim given the backfield man because he is conspicuous is an example of the public's valuing only what it notices. The hard-working linesman must, therefore, have considerable maturity to accept a position which is essential for the team, but which is not likely to receive public acclaim.

In many offices the secretary literally is as important for the functioning of the organization as are the executives. She may be appreciated by those who work there, but she gets less salary and less prestige despite the amount of skill and judgment that she may display. It is not fair, and she must have a certain selfless loyalty to stay in such a position without resentment.

With maturity, fairness gradually shifts from a more concrete demand for equality to a flexible judgment that takes into account the needs and abilities of the various people in a situation as well as the objective demands of the situation itself. It represents an objectification of ethical principles and a trend away from the egocentricity of earlier childhood.

LEARNING SOCIAL ROLES   Undoubtedly the most important problems in the development of roles come with adolescence. The problem of adolescence has sometimes been described as the problem of shifting from the role of the child to the role of the responsible adult despite cultural pressure to delay such a shift. Nevertheless, the problem of roles has arisen before adolescence. The individual may not know just what his eventual role is going to be until he is grown, but even as a child he has certain roles and is expected to conform to them.

In the preschool years it seems that the child has almost no understanding of roles, especially the role he himself must play. The young child knows that he is, because of his age, forbidden things that are permitted to an older child; therefore, he wants very badly to grow up. Still, he does not easily shift from one role to another. As he gradually learns what are appropriate topics of conversation at home and how they differ from appropriate topics away from home, he is meeting an isolated aspect of shifting roles. The nursery-school child may act differently as a guest than at home, but generally not because he recognizes that he is a guest. It is more because he feels strange or excited and stimulated away from home. He also has some recognition of the fact that when there is company he gets away with behavior that is not ordinarily permitted.

Perhaps the sex role is the most clearly defined for the child, but even here, the perception is fuzzy and undifferentiated. The nursery-school child does not generally treat boys very differently from girls. He is aware of the fact that boys and girls are different and shows considerable interest in sex differences. Gesell and Ilg (1949) report that at the age of four there is some tendency for play groups to split along the sex line. As we have seen, there are some differences in the play of preschool boys and girls. Boys are more aggressive, for example. But all of these social role differences become much more pronounced during the elementary-school years. Real antagonism between the sexes, for example, is not uncommon in the pre-adolescent years.

The patterns of cultural expectations that are called roles are not unlike the rules of a game. They are based upon common consent and have some ties to reality, but, nevertheless, are arbitrary in many respects. When cultural expectations are defended in the face of criticism, it is frequently difficult to find any good reason for the custom except that it is just done that way. It is difficult to find a logical reason that the president of a club should vote only in case of a tie, or that the mother should carry the burden of child care. Despite the lack of logical reasons, the individual's recognition of these expectations gradually becomes a feeling that role behavior is *demanded* by the position and that the role behavior *ought* to be performed, because other people depend upon the person to fulfill the role that accompanies his position. Nevertheless, the roles are arbitrary; they could be organized differently.

The acceptance of roles requires, therefore, much the same kind of maturity as the acceptance of rules. There must be sensitivity to the expectations of others, because others are acting on the assumption that the role behavior will occur. At the same time the role cannot be defined in a completely rigid fashion. The basis of a position is the function it plays in the smooth operation of a group. It is this function which must be the goal. To the extent that the function rather than the behavior is the goal, flexible adjustment is possible. This focus upon the function of a position gives the behavior an objective orientation as well as a social orientation. It is the effect of the behavior in group operation that ought to be the criterion of role fulfillment. Here, as in other cases, the danger lies in either a too-rigid behavioral definition of role behavior or in a too-irresponsible unpredictability of behavior. The balance must be drawn with wisdom.

The school-age child is gradually learning these things. He learns that the second baseman should primarily cover second base, that he should be prepared to cover first in the case of a bunt toward first base, that he should be prepared to relay a ball in from the outfield. This is his role behavior. The primary object, however, is to put the opposing team out. If he can do that by varying from his role, he is playing better than average baseball, provided that he can still be depended upon to play his role. When the manager tells a player to bunt, he may become angry if the batter hits a home run despite the good consequence of a home run.

What the school-age child grows into, therefore, is not a clear perception of his eventual role in society, but an understanding of the way roles operate and interact with each other. At the same time he is learning the content of literally hundreds of roles, so that he has the background to recognize his own position eventually, and to choose his role in so far as he has the choice.

Summary

This chapter has dealt with some of the problems of social control of motivation. First, we discussed the variety of social rules and roles, their range of applicability, whether they are ascribed or achieved, and their possible orientations to behavior, consequences, or personal traits. Then we looked at the actual social rules that apply to children and compared them with comparable pressures on children in other societies. In general, ours is one of the most severe cultures; we indulge children less than almost all others and put heavy requirements on them.

Then we examined the psychological processes underlying social conformity. Some of the psychological mechanisms that result in conformity do not appear to the individual himself to involve his complying to an external rule. He is motivated to follow the social pattern through imitation, or he has incorporated social rules so that his own motivation is in accord with them. Most conformity, however, comes about through compliance with external rules.

There are three prerequisites to compliance. First, understanding of social rules and roles must develop during childhood. Secondly, the needs underlying a motivation to comply must exist. These needs may be fear of punishment, a need to acquiesce to the wishes of other people, or a sense of duty. We have seen how some of these needs gradually appear during childhood. The third requirement is the ability to control impulses. This is the topic of the next chapter.

10

Self-Control in Childhood

THE ADJUSTMENT TO FRUSTRATION OR CONFLICT

METHODS OF ACHIEVING SELF-CONTROL

THE CONSEQUENCE OF INSUFFICIENT SELF-CONTROL

PERSONALITY DEFENSES

SUMMARY

IN THE LAST CHAPTER we examined the various controls on his own behavior that the child must learn to exert before he can be adjusted to this complicated social world in which we live. We saw that he must learn what he ought to do, no mean feat in itself. Furthermore, he must gradually develop the motivation to conform. This is not sufficient, however. Like the girl in *Oklahoma,* the child may feel that he "can't say no."

In this chapter we shall examine four factors in the problem of establishing control over motivation. First is the adjustment to frustration. The frustrated person simply wants something he cannot have. There is ordinarily no moral issue involved, and the barrier in the way of satisfying his motive is often a physical one. No self-control is required to keep the person from satisfying his motivation; the external barrier prevents gratification. The adjustment of the frustrated person consists, then, in giving up his unattainable goal. We find in his adjustment a good example of some of the processes of control over motivation.

Secondly, we shall study the development of self-control itself. How may a child gain control over his own motivation? What mechanisms can reduce conflict when a person tries to do something he does not want to do? Thirdly, we must examine the dilemma of the person who has not resisted temptation and who now faces the consequences. He, too, is frustrated, because he is suffering or is about to suffer an experience he dislikes. The fact that he may feel he deserves it does not appreciably help his frustration. His feeling may be one of fear, anxiety, shame, or guilt. He may adjust to these feelings by some of the same mechanisms that he uses in adjusting to frustration. Finally, we shall see how, by means of personality defenses, some of these dilemmas are avoided, perhaps at the expense of good adjustment.

The Adjustment to Frustration or Conflict

Reviewing briefly the discussion of a frustration situation as a cause of tension (see p. 98), we recall that frustration raises the level of tension. The increased tension has several consequences: (1) it produces restlessness; (2) it increases irritability and hostility; (3) it makes the individual more impulsive; and (4) it increases his susceptibility to further increases in tension. Because of this last characteristic, the individual who is exposed to frustration for a long period may become more and more tense and emotional until he is reduced to some very primitive emotional state, usually a panic or a tantrum. We have seen that children are more vulnerable to frustration or conflict than adults; all of these problems are more severe for the child than the adult.

Frustration and conflict situations are essentially alike in their emotional characteristics, so we shall use frustration as an example throughout. The main difference between a frustration and any other conflict is that the frustrated person cannot satisfy his motivation. He is blocked by some impenetrable barrier. In a conflict situation, he is caught between two apparently incompatible motives. The barrier in the way of satisfying each motive is not a physical one, but is, instead, the other motive. We shall see that this structure of a conflict does differ in some ways from a frustration, but in their main features frustration and the struggle to resolve a psychological conflict are alike. How, then, can the individual caught in a frustration face the insoluble problem and at the same time avoid being caught and tossed in an emotional storm?

Problem Solving

The obviously best solution is to somehow circumvent the original frustration by problem solving. Perhaps he can get through the barrier or satisfy both conflicting motives. As long as the situation is challenging and exciting, the individual tries to solve the problem. In fact, his problem-solving ability may be increased by this mild state of challenge (Deiter, 1951). When the tension becomes high and the motivation very strong, however, his ability may be reduced by the increased motivation and by the state of tension.

Various experiments show that animals are less able to solve a detour problem under high motivation than under moderate motivation (Köhler, 1924). A too-strong motive seems to prevent the animal from exploring or perceiving a path to the goal that requires his moving away from it in order to get to it. Deiter (1951) has studied the effect of three levels of motivation upon the ability to discover a short-cut solution to a problem when an obvious but long and laborious solution is available. The subjects were asked to translate a great mass of material into a coded form by means of a substitution code—each letter of the alphabet to be systematically substituted for some other letter. One method of performing the task was to look at a letter of the message, look up in the code the proper substitution, write down the code letter, and then repeat the process again and again. If, however, the subject discovered the fact that there was a system to the code (each letter being replaced by the one three letters before it in the alphabet), he could perform the task much more simply and easily. Deiter found that subjects under the lowest motivation and under the highest were less likely to find the short cut than those under moderate motivation. The highly motivated subjects doggedly persisted in the obvious procedure, trying to go as fast as possible. The very ability required to solve a problem may be lost if the tension reaches high enough levels.

If the solution demands only effort, strength, or persistence, high tension may be a help rather than a hindrance. People who perform superhuman feats of strength and endurance in an emergency are examples. If, however, judgment, delicacy, or finesse is demanded, it is only by exerting self-control that the individual can maintain efficiency in problem solving. The self-control itself may have deleterious effects upon some sorts of problem solving. Furthermore, the attempt to solve the problem requires that the individual remain psychologically involved in it (see pp. 459-461). This state of involvement enhances the psychological effect of frustration and increases the tension.

Resignation

To resign oneself to failure or to renounce both conflicting motives is another solution to the problem posed by being exposed to frustration. The problem here is to understand how resignation can occur when it accepts the failure to reach the goal, and it is failure to reach the goal that caused the frustration.

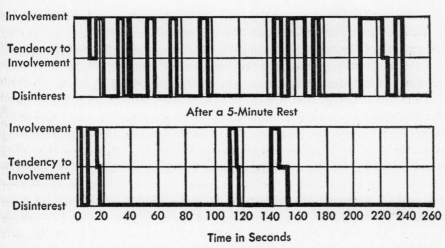

Fig. 10.1 The temporal course of resignation for a child aged 47 months. (After S. E. Fajans, *Psych. Forsch.*, *17,* 1933, 283)

The effect of resignation is to reduce the frustration by decreasing the motivation to reach the goal. The frustration situation is sufficiently unpleasant that the individual prefers not having the goal to remaining in the state of tension that accompanies continued efforts to reach it. People do not resign themselves easily and oftentimes only temporarily. Fajans (1933) has investigated the sequence of events leading up to complete resignation. He presented a child with an insoluble problem. At first the child works steadily on the problem. Then, as he becomes frustrated, his attention wanders, and he spends less and less time in contact with the problem. If, after he has once given up, he is allowed a five-minute rest before he is again presented with the problem, he again becomes engaged in it, but this time he leaves it more rapidly than he did after the initial presentation. In Figure 10.1 the horizontal dimension measures time. The type of behavior is indicated by the level of the graph. When the graph is high, the child was actually involved in the problem. When the graph is on the middle level, the child's activity was less clearly directed toward solving the problem but not clearly directed away from the task. The lower level indicates time spent away from the task. The child whose record is pictured in Figure 10.1 spent the first 15 seconds involved in the problem; then he lost interest slightly for 4 seconds, returned to it fully for 2 seconds before losing interest completely for 14 seconds. This child loses interest very easily by comparison with other children in the study.

Adjustment Through Reduction of Instigation

It is not usually easy to resign oneself. Resignation is made more difficult if the external situation continually restimulates the motivation, as can be shown in the following experiments. The first experiment, by Barker, Dembo, and Lewin (1941), has already been reported in Chapter 5 in another connection, but it is also relevant here. The children in this experiment, it will be remembered, were allowed to play with toys, then introduced to much more attractive toys; but after a tantalizingly brief play period with them they were taken back to the first toys. The barrier between the subject and the attractive toys was a transparent chicken-wire screen, so that every time their glance roved around the room the children could see what they were missing. This visibility of the goal as well as its proximity maintained the instigation that evoked the frustrated motivation. After the children were removed from the more attractive toys, they spent much of the time vainly trying to get back to them. They pulled at the screen, tried the lock, appealed to the experimenter, became emotional, and generally demonstrated without any doubt that they were frustrated. In each case, however, the child eventually became absorbed in the available toys.

In an experiment by Reed (1952), the Barker, Dembo, and Lewin experiment was repeated except that the stimulus presentation of the attractive toys behind the barrier was changed. After the child had played with the attractive toys, he was taken out of the room and down the stairs to the usual nursery-school situation, where his behavior was observed. When the child was asked to leave the toys, he protested, but once he was back in the regular play room there was no sign of emotionality, no attempt to get back to the room with the attractive toys, no appeal to the experimenter. There was no apparent increase in muscle tension or activity level, though these were not specifically measured. To the ordinary observer these children showed no signs of frustration or emotional tension. There was, however, a marked drop in the constructiveness of play and some increase in the amount of aggressive play.

This experiment suggests that frustration did occur; there was evidence of it in the subjects' protests when they were asked to leave the nice toys and also in the fact that constructiveness decreased. The evidence also indicates, however, that the overt signs of frustration were reduced by taking the children away from the attractive toys so that the original motivation was not continually restimulated and frustrated all over again by the enticing presence of the inaccessible toys behind the screen.

The importance of the presence of the instigation in maintaining a motive can be seen in many everyday examples. One of the frequently observed consequences of frustration is *leaving the field* (Lewin, 1935). It has been found in many frustration experiments that the subject, after he is frustrated, tries to leave the experiment; he may suddenly remember an appointment, or get tired, or develop a headache. The experimental situation, although it contains the only possibility of his reaching the goal, nevertheless becomes distasteful. There is no logical reason why the subject cannot give up his aspiration and resign himself while he stays in the room, but it is difficult to stay in the physical presence of the experimenter, the goal, and the barrier without remaining motivated and therefore frustrated. If he can separate himself physically from the situation, he can forget about the whole business.

A more extreme form of leaving the field, which shows the importance of stimulus contact with the goal object, has been described by Lewin (1935) as *encapsulation*. His example of it is a little boy who is being teased by his older sister. She dangles the boy's toy in front of his face but just too high for him to reach it. Whenever he loses interest in the game she lowers it so that it is directly in front of his face. When he turns away, she moves the toy so that it is still in front of his eyes. He is like the dog in the cartoons who has a frankfurter dangling in front of his nose from a stick fastened to his back. The boy's final defense against this persistent teasing is to kneel down and bury his face between his hands and legs. Now it is impossible for his sister to make him look at the toy he wants so much. He shuts himself off as completely as possible from all external instigation in order to escape the tension-evoking situation. We occasionally see similar behavior in children who hide their eyes or crouch down behind the seat at the most exciting part of a movie.

Distraction

A slightly different mechanism for reducing the strength of the frustrated motive is to establish a competing motive through distraction. It may occur spontaneously in child behavior, as does leaving the field, but the best examples of it are found in the parent's deliberate use of distraction as a technique for helping the young child weather a serious disappointment or to keep him from continuing undesirable behavior. By attracting his attention to something else, "giving him something better to do," the motivation toward the original goal is reduced.

For young children the distraction can be made psychologically effective by making it physically prominent, by putting it in front of the child and by saying to him, "Look here. See what I have for you," or words to that effect. The mother comforting her crying child searches the environment for something unusual. "Look, that doggie wonders why you're crying" or "Listen, did you hear the fire siren?" When the child is older, his attention cannot be diverted so easily or quickly. The mother may then try to think of some interesting activity if her child is badly disappointed. "Would you like to help me make cookies?" or "Why don't you play with your electric train?"

Self-distraction as a defense against the presence of unpleasant motives can frequently be seen in adult behavior. If one is preoccupied with grief or anxiety or some exciting anticipation, it is difficult to keep from thinking about it and paying attention to it. It may be possible to think about something else instead. Adults read absorbing books or go to the movies while waiting for some important news to come. Some people grieving over the loss of a loved one can immerse themselves in the exacting, attention-capturing details of housework or a clerical job or skilled labor requiring minute attention, to gain a measure of relief.

Substitution

Still a fourth kind of adjustment to frustration—which may or may not be actually adjustive—is the activation of motives toward substitute goals. The idea of substitute goals is important because it is implicit in many theories about the development of personality. A group of children may make a scapegoat of some unfortunate victim. They turn against him, blame him for anything that goes wrong, and may actually drive him entirely out of the group.

This phenomenon has been explained by some psychologists as the substitution of another object of hostility for one that is more invulnerable or inaccessible. The original object of hostility in this case might be the parents or the teacher. Other psychologists believe that hostility can accumulate from the numerous frustrations the children have endured. The present hostile behavior is one of many alternative expressions of this hostility.

A neurotic symptom is frequently described as the appearance in a disguised form of a motive that has been frustrated. Not all the behavior that may appear to be a substitution of one goal for another is necessarily best interpreted in that fashion, but some substitution of goals certainly does occur in human behavior.

First of all, it is necessary to distinguish clearly between substitute goals and substitute means. To find an alternative means to the goal when access to it by the more easily perceived paths is blocked is a successful solution to the frustrating situation. What can serve as an alternative means is, of course, dependent upon the specific situation, but the only characteristic that it must have is the property of allowing access to the goal. In all other respects, it may be quite different from the original means. As a *means* of getting downtown, an automobile is generally preferable to a streetcar. As long as a child's goal is to be downtown, he will not care which means, automobile or streetcar, he uses. If, however, the child has never ridden on the streetcar, his goal may be to ride the streetcar. In this case an automobile ride is no substitute goal. All means that reach the same goal are equivalent except as they differ in speed and efficiency.

SUBSTITUTE VALENCE   The substitutability of goals is a different matter. If a boy plans to play baseball but is prevented from doing so by rain, he is faced with a situation that permits very few alternative means. If there is no way for him to play baseball, he must accept a new goal. He may put off the game until tomorrow and read a book. The book is not a substitute for baseball; it is another goal for which a need already existed before the baseball was rained out, and its strength is not affected by the inability to play baseball. If, however, he decides to play electric baseball, an indoor board game that is a sort of "pretend" baseball game, it is likely that he would not have played electric baseball at all except for the fact that the motive to play baseball was activated and then frustrated. When true baseball was prevented, the simulated baseball game became attractive as a substitute.

This property of some activities to become attractive because some other motive was frustrated is called *substitute valence*. *Valence* is a technical word for *attractiveness*. In the previous example the game of electric baseball had substitute valence, but reading a book did not. The reason that reading a book is not said to have a substitute valence is that it was already an attractive thing to do, although not quite so attractive as playing baseball. If the boy turned to it when frustrated, he was taking his second choice. The game, however, is said to have *substitute* valence because it *became* attractive only because real baseball was prevented; therefore, its attractiveness is the attractiveness of a substitute for baseball.

SUBSTITUTE VALUE   Now let us assume that the boy did play electric baseball as a substitute for real baseball. The next question to be asked is whether he wants to play baseball just as much after he finishes the indoor game as he would have had he read a book instead. If the need to play real baseball is reduced, partially satiated, by playing electric baseball, then it has *substitute value*. If the need to play real baseball is not reduced, then the game has for this boy no substitute value.

Because the young child rarely engages in an activity purely as a means for attaining his goal, most of his activities are as much goal activity as means activity. For this reason most frustrations cannot be met by finding an equally good means. When substitution occurs, it is probably substitution of goals. The child, because he does not consider a glass merely a non-leaking container of milk, is in a worse spot than the adult if his favorite milk glass is broken. He wants that specific glass, and if a substitute is to satisfy him it must be a substitute "favorite glass," not merely a substitute "functional glass"—in other words, a substitute goal, not a substitute means. If the adult does not appreciate the kind of frustration that faces the child, he may say, "but this other glass is just as good." This is something like telling an adult that a thirty-five-cent pocket edition of Poe's short stories is "just as good" as his precious first edition, because it has all the same words in it and may be more clearly printed and easily read.

Several experiments on substitution of goals have been performed in order to determine what properties of a substitute goal give it substitute value. The original experiment dealing with this question was performed by Lissner (1933). She established a need by involving the subject in a task and then frustrated it by interrupting him. (An earlier worker had already shown that interruption of a task motivates a person to resume it [see p. 459f.].) She could then study the effects of different substitute activities upon the tendency to resume the original task. She used three types of tasks: puzzles, riddles, and translations. First, a task was interrupted, and during the interruption the subject was given another task to do. In every case a puzzle was offered as a substitute for a puzzle, a riddle for a riddle, and a translation for a translation. In order to determine the effectiveness of different sorts of substitutes she employed four substitute tasks: ones that were easier than the original but similar in type, ones that were more difficult but similar, ones that were easier and of a different type, and ones that were more difficult as well as different. After completing the substitute task, the subject was given an opportunity to resume the interrupted task. Without any interpolated task there would be a strong tendency for the subject to resume the interrupted task. The index of the effect of the substitute was the *substitute value,* measured by the ratio— the tendency to resume when there is no substitute divided by the tendency to resume when there is a substitute. To take a concrete example, if a given task tended to be resumed 85 percent of the time when no substitute was interpolated but only 50 percent of the time when there was a given substitute interpolated, then the substitute value of that interpolated activity is .85/.50, or 1.7. A complete absence of substitute value would be indicated by a value of 1.0, since there would be just as much resumption with the interpolated activity as without it, thus indicating that the substitute had not had any value in satisfying the need to resume the task. Figure 10.2 shows the average substi-

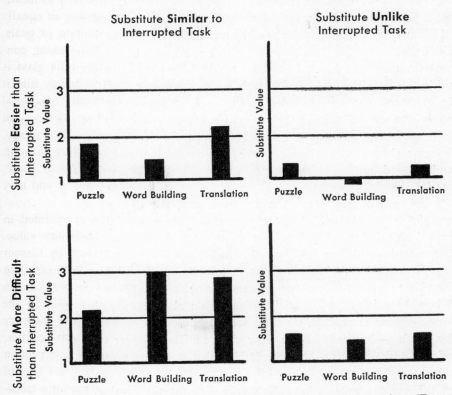

Fig. 10.2 The effect of similarity and difficulty upon substitute value. (Data from K. Lissner, *Psych. Forsch., 18,* 1933, 218-250)

tute value of the various types of substitutes for each task. The height of the bar graph in each cell indicates the substitute value. It will be noticed that similar tasks have more substitute value than different ones, and that easy tasks have less substitute value than difficult ones. In establishing a substitute value, similarity seems in this experiment to be more significant than difficulty.

The factor of difficulty in substitute value suggests that the goals of the subjects in this experiment were not all the same. For some of them, the goal was to solve the specific puzzle or riddle or translation that was presented. For others the goal was to demonstrate (either to the experimenter or to the subject himself) the ability to do the task. Some subjects might well have had both goals. In so far as the goal was merely to demonstrate ability, any equally difficult or more difficult task would be equivalent to the original. In so far as the goal was to solve the specific problem, the only task with substitute value would be very similar to the original, not only in difficulty but in other properties as well. Actually, the similar tasks in this experiment were almost identical to the interrupted tasks. Had the original tasks in this experiment been presented as a test of ability, it would be expected that the effect of difficulty on substitute value would have been much greater than the effect of similarity.

On the other hand, had some attempt been made to ensure that the subjects wanted to perform each specific task, the effect of similarity should be enhanced. One way to select tasks that function as specific and concrete goals is to select those that the subject likes to do. Enjoyment of a task tends to be more dependent upon its concrete properties than upon its membership in some abstract class. Henle (1942) has found that tasks which are liked and enjoyed by the subject have fewer possible substitutes than those which are less liked.

In another experiment the concreteness of the goals of young children was shown, together with its effect upon substitute value. Adler (1939) interrupted a task but offered as a substitute a task that was identical to the interrupted one. When the first task, "building a house for Mary," was interrupted, then the task, "building a house for Johnny," had little substitute value for either younger (about seven years) or older (about ten years) children. When the original task was described in an abstract way that emphasized housebuilding in general, then the second house was an excellent substitute for the first—but only for the older children. The younger ones still saw the original task in such a concrete fashion that not even a replica could have substitute value.

These experiments have dealt only with substitute value. No effort was made in Lissner's experiment to see whether the substitutes became attractive to the subject as a result of the frustration. Experiments on substitute valence show that a much wider range of activities have substitute valence than substitute value (Sliosberg, 1934). Under conditions of very high frustration some of the activities that become attractive seem very bizarre. An experiment by Dembo (1931) showed this clearly. Subjects were given a very difficult task of throwing ten rings over the necks of two distant bottles. The task was hardly possible, yet not obviously impossible. After subjects had been kept in this frustrating situation for a long time and not allowed to give up, they occasionally performed in very bizarre ways. They would, for example, throw the rings over two bottles that were much closer although they knew that this was not permitted and did not constitute any success. Some of them even threw the rings over a coat hook. All of this substitute behavior took place while the subject was presumably trying to accomplish his task, and of course it had no substitute value. As a matter of fact it made the subjects even more emotional to find themselves doing these futile substitutes.

The relative immaturity of the person when seriously frustrated is exemplified by the wide range of activities that may have valence but not value. One of the characteristics of maturity is the ability of the organism to have a clearly structured long-range goal and be insensitive to those goals that may be similar to or close to the desired one, but that do not really satisfy the individual's motivation. Children are less able than adults to resist the attractions of substitutes which they discover later have no value.

Methods of Achieving Self-Control

We have observed that the adjustments to frustration are methods for controlling the strength of a motive without satisfying it. None of them, with the exception of problem solving, actually reaches the goal. By leaving the field or reducing the stimulus support, the motive is reduced in strength; by distraction a competing motive is increased in strength; by substitution—when it has substitute value—an alternative goal is chosen.

The fact that the adjustment to frustration reduces the strength of the frustrated motive means that these same adjustment processes may also function in the control of motivation. When a person is tempted to do something that will be punished, or that he feels he ought not to do, the strength of the temptation obviously depends upon the strength of the motive. A reduction in the motivation makes it easier to resist temptation. Thus, escape from the field can be not only an escape from frustration, but it can also be an escape from temptation. Mowrer (1940) has shown something like this in experiments on rats. When he first taught the rat to push a lever in order to get food, the sight of the lever became an instigation to the motive to push it. Then he wired the lever so that the rat was shocked when he touched it. Now the lever was a fearsome object. When the rat came close to the lever, he was motivated to push it and also motivated not to push it. In some cases, Mowrer observed a very remarkable reaction: the rat ran to the opposite end of the cage. One interpretation of this reaction is that the sight of the lever instigated the conflicting motives, the conflict was unpleasant, and the rat escaped the conflict by running away from the stimuli.

Not only escape from the field, but also distraction and substitution may be used to resolve the conflict between temptation and duty. In fact, any adjustment that makes the motive less strong prevents the individual from giving in to the temptation. The little boy, snowball in hand, watching a man in a tall silk hat walk by would do well to restrain or reduce the strength of that impulse which is about to get him into trouble. The achievement of the ability to control such motives, either because they would lead to trouble or because they are being frustrated, is one aspect of achieving self-control.

There is another side to self-control as well—the ability to do things that are very distasteful. Here the problem is not so much to decrease a motive as to increase it. The girl who must give her first piano recital would be much happier if her motive to do so were stronger. The techniques people use to get themselves to do the things they ought to do should also be classed under self-control.

One factor that makes self-control more necessary and yet more difficult is a high level of tension. The higher the tension, the more sensitive is the person to instigation and the more compelling are his impulses. Anything, therefore, that contributes to the general level of tension, whether or not it adds to the attractiveness of the impulsive goal, adds to the need for self-control. Fatigue, excitement, external stimulation, or frustration may all increase impulsiveness and make self-control more difficult.

The Advantage of a Prior Decision

When parents anticipate a difficult situation for a child, they frequently try to prepare him for it before it happens. If, for example, the family is planning a visit to a home containing an excitable and exciting child, the parents may try to discuss ahead of time the problem of not becoming too boisterous. The idea behind this preparation is that the child can, in advance of the stress situation, prepare himself to be controlled when he would be quite unable to make that decision under the stress of the moment.

This example illustrates the fact that there are two meanings to the term self-control: one is the ability to make wise decisions under difficult conditions; the other is to carry out actions that have been decided upon in advance. The latter is the more easily done. The earliest examples of self-control, therefore, involve merely carrying out a predetermined action in the face of situations that hamper self-control. Later developments of self-control permit decision-making in situations in which one line of action is strongly suggested and is very attractive.

The fact that decisions can be more easily made ahead of time can be understood through a consideration of the properties of motivating situations. We described temptation as the situation where a less valuable goal is more immediate than a more valuable goal, so that its psychological impact is enhanced by its immediacy or its immediate perceptibility (see p. 49). Suppose a child earned a dollar toward buying a pet. On his way to deposit it in the savings account he went into a drug store and saw the display of comic books. If he were at that moment given the choice of buying ten comic books or saving his dollar, he would find it very difficult not to choose the comics. The difference in the immediacy of the two goals is very great. If, however, the choice were presented three or four days in advance, the psychological effect would be very different. If before the money was earned he

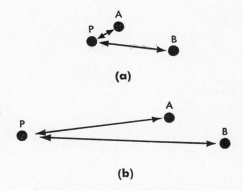

Fig. 10.3 The effect of advance decision upon the relative immediacy of goals. If the decision is made when the person (P) is close to A and B, as in (a), there is a large difference between the relative distances of A and B. If the decision is made when P is distant from A and B, as in (b), there is little difference between relative distances of A and B.

(a)

(b)

was asked, "Would you rather spend your dollar on comic books or save it for your puppy?" both goals would be relatively remote. Under these conditions the intrinsic desirability of the two alternatives would be more likely to determine the choice.

Figure 10.3 illustrates this point schematically. If the decision to take alternative A or B is made at the point where the two paths branch in Figure 10.3a, it can be seen that A is much more immediate than B. If, however, the branching of the paths comes earlier, as in Figure 10.3b, the relative difference in immediacy is much less. The difference in immediacy is less important and the intrinsic value of the goals is relatively more important, therefore, when the decision is made while both are remote.

A second reason that it is easier to make a wise decision ahead of time is that the advance decision may be made in relative calm, unhampered by tension and excitement. If the individual can foresee that a later decision will, of necessity, be made under conditions of excitement, he may try to make the decision in advance. The young baseball player is often urged to decide before the play begins what he will do if the ball comes to him.

All these considerations point to the fact that decisions made ahead of time can generally be made more wisely. The danger in advance decisions is, of course, that the situation may change unexpectedly to negate the wisdom of the prearranged action. It should also be understood that to make a decision ahead of time requires considerable maturity, an ability to picture a situation that has not yet occurred, and an ability to make accurate predictions about what decision will be wise.

Carrying Out a Decision

After a decision has been made, one sort of self-control can be achieved by an external manipulation of the environment so that the external factors in the situation will be in harmony with the advance decision and encourage or even coerce the behavior. For example, when a boy knew he was going to be left on his own responsibility in a situation that would tax his self-control—*i.e.,* he was to be left alone in the house with his younger sibling, with whom he found it difficult to stay on good terms—he went to his room, closed the door, and played by himself. He decided to stay out of trouble-making situations since he had no confidence that he could restrain his temper if it were provoked. This decision could be made in the calmness preceding the test of his self-control, and he could thus prevent a temptation from arising. People who are afraid to talk publicly sometimes accept an invitation to do so. They can decide six months ahead of time to make the speech and, by so doing, initiate a chain of events that externally forces them to carry through with the decision. In the public situation itself, such a person might be entirely incapable of volunteering a single remark.

With more maturity, it may not be necessary to manipulate external circumstances so that they prevent temptation or enforce the proper behavior. It may be sufficient merely to make the decision ahead of time to ensure ample time to screw up one's courage. The "one for the money, two for the show, three to make ready, and four to go" routine before popping the medicine in the child's mouth illustrates a way of easing the situation for the child. Many fictional stories have described how people have decided in advance to do something which they fear upon a certain signal. In *The Red and The Black* (Stendahl, 1830), Julian Sorel was very shy but very determined to gain the love of Madame Renault. One evening when they were talking he vowed he would take hold of her hand upon the last stroke of the clock as it struck ten. By this device he was able to make himself do something that he was afraid to do.

This "resolving" is a type of self-control that makes it possible for remote consequences of greater intrinsic value to exert more psychological influence upon the behavior than an immediate attraction. Once the decision has been made, the individual can to some extent increase the potency of the remote end by fixating his mind upon it, by devaluing the immediate goal, and by a much more intangible process called "exerting will power." The crucial time is at the beginning of the action; once it has begun, the motivation to continue is aroused, and by that time the decision may be irrevocable.

Vigilance

Fortunately such will power is only rarely necessary, because such behavior requires tremendous effort and is performed at great cost. If the conflict is less extreme or the organism more mature, self-control may require not resolution but merely watchfulness. The individual is able not only to carry out a predetermined action but even to make a wise decision on the spot. Only a constant *vigilance* is required. This is, of itself, effortful and demands a deliberately conscious effort to look ahead to the remote consequences of all the alternatives before acting. The feeling of the person walking through high grass and rocky ground where rattlesnakes are common exemplifies an attitude of vigilance. In one experiment, designed to lure the subject into a habitual type of response so that he would miss an obvious solution to a problem, it was possible to obtain entirely different results merely by printing upon the answer sheet, "Don't be blind" (Luchins, 1942). Such an admonition did not tell the subject how to avoid the trap but merely made him watchful.

We sometimes describe a child in this state of vigilance as "being on his best behavior." Such vigilance is likely to be aroused by strange or awesome situations. Thus, it is common for a child to be well controlled when visiting, especially if he is on his own without parents present. He can become vigilant partly by deciding to be, partly through the mere feeling of being responsible for himself. He is also prone to relax his vigilance quickly when he returns home, reflecting the fact that vigilance is effortful. The relaxation that comes with having no longer to be vigilant is frequently called "letting off steam," because in children it seems to be accompanied by noise, whistling, running, jumping, and generally impulsive, nondirected behavior.

A state of high vigilance is common in people for whom self-control is not easy. Anyone is usually vigilant in situations that require significant decisions, or in states of insecurity in which any straying from the correct path is viewed as extremely dangerous. "Walking a tightrope" is the way in which some such people describe it. The state of vigilance is characterized by a tension that frequently interferes with the individual's other activities.

The Consequence of Insufficient Self-Control

It is the lot of everyone to give in to temptation on occasion. Even when there are good reasons to comply with a social rule, all of us are sometimes found lacking sufficient self-control. For every time this happens to adults, it occurs ten times in a child's life. He is frequently too little and too late in his self-control.

Fear, Shame, and Guilt

Once a rule has been broken, provided the child is mature enough to know the consequences of his crime, he finds himself in a state of fear, shame, or guilt, or perhaps in some undifferentiated combination of them all. If he really understands the rule, the violation of it is sufficient to bring him back to the full realization of the enormity of his offense. Before the crime, while self-control was not operating, the child's thoughts are completely filled with the desirability of the temptation. With the gratification of the tempting motive it declines sharply in strength and loses its savor. The child is left holding the bag, anxiously contemplating the consequences.

If the consequences are clearly external, if punishment is entailed and the child knows it, then it is appropriate to describe his emotion as fear. He is afraid of a specific future event: a whipping, a loss of privilege, or some punishment.

Oftentimes, the punishment is not so concretely pictured. What may be most potent is the child's fear of his violation's being exposed to other people. This fear of ridicule or exposure, the fear of being compared publicly to other children, the fear of being debased or degraded in the eyes of the people he values, is all encompassed in the child's feeling ashamed of himself. We have already seen that shame is a very unpleasant emotion evoked by the exposure of a defect or a weakness to people whose good opinion is important. Shaming is often employed for disciplining children for just this reason. When a parent shames a child, he generally points out that the child's behavior is immature or babyish. He says, "What would people think?" By doing so, he emphasizes the possible exposure of the child's behavior and tries to make him ashamed of it. He may compare the child to other children, pointing out how he has failed by comparison with his siblings or friends.

Still a third emotional state that may be evoked by violation of rules is guilt. Since in our culture guilt and shame occur so frequently together that the distinction between them is often lost, we should scrutinize the differences between them.

The differentiation of guilt from shame can be best illustrated if we consider the situations that are shameful and embarrassing but not guilt producing. One can be ashamed of a facial scar, a lack of skill, or stupidity. It is not necessary to feel guilty about such defects, and most people do not do so. Those things concerning which one is guilty are the situations for which one accepts responsibility. The more a crime is premeditated and deliberate, the more likely it is to evoke guilt. The distinctions among premeditated murder, murder on the spur of the moment, and accidental killing are explicitly formulated in criminal law.

Another difference between guilt and shame lies in the absolutistic quality of sin and guilt, which is not so true of shame. A sin is a sin whether or not anybody knows about it. Guilt can be hidden and private; shame depends much more upon the public knowledge of the behavior. An act can be shameful if public but not if private. Although a sin is a sin, regardless of publicity, it is sinful only if the deed is voluntary, not if it is coerced or unavoidable.

The distinction between shame and guilt is not drawn so sharply in everyday language; in our culture sin is degrading and, therefore, something to be ashamed of if exposed. Guilt is applicable to a portion but not all of the states that are shameful, but there are very few acts, if any, that can evoke guilt and not shame. Guilt probably develops later in childhood than shame because it requires more maturity. It is difficult to obtain empirical evidence about the first appearance of guilt feelings, a sense of responsibility, and the feeling that one deserves punishment. Gesell and Ilg report the appearance of the first signs of self-evaluation and standards in their description of the child of four (1949). Concern with goodness and badness, they report, is still more prominent in the child of six. They do not, however, distinguish between guilt and shame, so we cannot be certain from their description that this concern is a feeling of guilt.

Adjustment to Fear, Shame, and Guilt

The child's reaction to having violated a rule depends partly upon whether fear, shame, or guilt has been evoked. But some of his adjustments are the same for all three emotional states.

UNDOING Probably the first reaction is a wish not to have committed the crime, whatever it was. This may lead to an attempt to undo the act, to restore the situation to what it was before the rule was broken. Levy (1937) observed this reaction in children who were subjects in an experiment on sibling rivalry. He used a doll-play situation for the study. The child, after he had come into the experimental room, was allowed to play with dolls. Two of the dolls used were a mother doll and a baby doll. The mother doll's breasts were made of clay so that they could be smashed if the child wished, and the baby doll was put to the mother's breast to nurse. This situation was designed to evoke indications of sibling rivalry in the children. They were allowed to do whatever they wanted with the dolls, and some of the children smashed them, especially the baby doll. They were not reprimanded or punished for this, but in many cases the children showed signs of distress as soon as they had broken the doll. Some of them tried to put the doll back together, to undo the breaking.

We saw, in an example in Chapter 1, that a child who had been robbed of a bucketful of water required that the boy who stole the water return it to her in the exact spot from which it was taken. This illustrates that undoing is an immature, concrete form of re-establishing the status quo.

SELF-PUNISHMENT In contrast to this concrete undoing is the complex reaction to guilt feelings. One way of relieving guilt is to undo the crime and bring back a previous state of affairs, but the adjustment is much more devious. There are, in fact, two sorts of actions that re-establish the status quo after a crime has been committed. One is punishment. The guilty person is absolved of guilt feelings after he has been punished and has paid for his crime. Another is compensation to the victim; but if the victim of a crime exacts revenge, the perpetrator is no longer expected to repay.

Relieving one's guilt by punishment is one reason that people may wish to harm themselves. Self-punishment is one of the most difficult actions to understand; it seems to go directly contrary to our most basic motives. But one's guilt can be so great that a guilt-relieving punishment may actually be welcomed. One little girl of eight years came running in to her mother in great distress and begged to be spanked. She had smoked a cigarette and was overwhelmed by guilt over the action. "Mommy, you've got to spank me." The mother was not actually distressed over the girl's smoking—she took a philosophical attitude about the occasional stolen cigarettes of childhood—but she wisely decided that she should spank the child under these circumstances, and the child was much relieved.

This is unusual behavior. More commonly, children who feel guilty about some action may exhibit their willingness to be punished by not trying as strenuously as they might to avoid punishment. An even milder symptom of the guilty child's recognition of his guilt is his lack of resentment toward the punisher. The difference in the child's feelings when he is punished unjustly and when he receives a deserved punishment is tremendous. An unjust punishment can rankle for years and be the source of real hostility; a deserved punishment, even if he does not like it and tries to escape it, is not often resented provided that it somehow matches the severity of the crime. Farber (1945) found a similar sort of reaction in prisoners. Many prisoners felt, that because they had committed a crime and had been caught, society was justified in a punishment of a certain length. They owed a certain number of years in prison. Then, at some point, a prisoner might suddenly come to feel that he had paid enough. From then on, society was in his debt. Likely as not, this point did not correspond to the end of the sentence, but the prisoner from that time on was more resentful and hostile, and felt that he was being treated unfairly.

Undoing, then, is one adjustment to all sorts of violations of rules, but the process of making amends or expiation is central to the feeling of guilt. When fear or shame are primarily evoked, then concealment of the crime is a very common reaction. Concealment prevents the punishment and also prevents the exposure that would be so shameful.

ESCAPE FROM INSTIGATION   Still another adjustment to fear, shame, or guilt does not really solve the problem. It stems from the fact that these emotional reactions depend upon instigations, just as motives do, and they can be reduced by the same adjustments that reduce the strength of motives. People can escape from guilt or shame by escaping from the stimuli that evoke guilt and shame in the same way that they can escape from temptation by leaving the field. A person feels more guilty if he must look at the consequences of his crime than if he can run away and stop thinking about it. Distraction also can ameliorate fear, guilt, and shame, just as it can help assuage grief or frustration.

These adjustments are especially effective in dealing with guilt and shame because the stimuli that evoke these feelings do not necessarily become so intense that they force their way into awareness. A child can perhaps look away from the signs of approaching punishment, but he can hardly remain unmoved by the punishment itself. He can, however, look away from social disapproval and ignore it. Social disapproval rarely intrudes as obviously and as intensely as actual punishment. He can escape from the situations that remind him of his guilt and actually escape from his guilt feelings. A child can sometimes be seen holding his hands over his ears while he is being reprimanded. He can encapsulate himself against these socially oriented emotions as well as against other types of motivation. Mowrer (1950) emphasizes the importance of this sort of adjustment in the neurotic personality. Neurotics are believed by many people to be overpowered by a too strict conscience, but Mowrer claims that it is deafness to the voice of conscience more than a too-great sensitivity to guilt that is at the root of neurotic behavior.

Personality Defenses

All of the adjustment processes described thus far have been concerned with the adjustment and control of motives after they have been instigated. In terms of the model, these adjustments occur between the evocation of the motive and the actual attempt to gratify it.

Now we return to a discussion of one additional aspect of the individual's needs: the needs that may prevent the evocation of motives that would be doomed to frustration, would lead to violation of social rules, or would require strenuous self-control. These same defense mechanisms can also prevent the evocation of shame or fear or guilt when the individual has behaved antisocially.

We shall consider only two defense mechanisms in this section: repression and reaction formation. Repression is probably the most important single defense mechanism. In this section, we shall discuss it entirely in terms of how it defends the personality against frustrations, conflict, and danger. Later, we shall discuss some of its other consequences in behavior (see pp. 444-445).

Repression

Repression is a defense first elucidated by Freud (1900) and believed by him to be one of the foundation stones of personality development because it describes the way in which dangerous or unpleasant ideas, perceptions, memories, feelings, or wishes are made unconscious. Something like repression occurs in the forgetting of disagreeable chores, in forgetting the names of people we dislike, or in forgetting that some good idea is not our own but was taken over from somebody else. The utility of repression as a defense is quite obvious. It operates as a defense to prevent motives in much the same way that removal of a motive's external instigation reduces the strength of an already present motive. Repression is, therefore, a selective insensitivity that results in the failure to perceive or cognize situations that would instigate dangerous or unpleasantly frustrated motives. The material that must be repressed is, in some cases, immediate stimulation, as when the child does not notice his rival's new bicycle but does notice his rival's new black eye. In other cases it is a remote goal that must not be cognized, as when the child does not perceive the hostile motive behind his being a "tattletale." In still other cases it is a memory whose recall would re-evoke frustration. Freud argues that the forgetting of the experiences of infancy is due to repression because so much of the infant's experience is concerned with matters that are disgusting and anxiety provoking to the adult.

The repression may serve either of two functions. It may prevent the evocation of a dangerous motive—*i.e.,* one that would, from the point of view of the child, result in danger if it directed overt behavior. Thus, temptation can be prevented if the tempting situation cannot be perceived. Refusal to perceive such a situation prevents not only the impulsive behavior but also the tension and anxiety that would occur if the individual tried to prevent the behavior by other means. The tempting situation is anxiety producing because the impulse that it arouses is powerful and leads to dangerous consequences. It has the properties of immediacy and compellingness. The repression prevents the anxiety as well as the impulsive behavior.

In other situations the repression may not prevent impulsive behavior at all, but rather prevent the shame of failure, the fear of punishment, or guilt feelings. The awkward child may, for example, forget his dancing class. It is not that the class situation evokes dangerous impulses, but that it forces the child to expose his weakness. If he remembered his class but stayed away although he felt pressure to go, he would be in conflict. In this case, the repression functions to prevent the build-up of the tension state that the evocation of the motive and its subsequent frustration would produce.

The existence of such a defense has been well established in a variety of situations, both clinical and experimental. It has been observed repeatedly by psychotherapists after it was first described by Freud.

The following case, quoted from Maslow and Mittelmann (1941), illustrates the sort of clinical finding that has provided much evidence for repression:

> A patient developed attacks of palpitation together with periods of depression about six months before applying for treatment. When he was first asked what the circumstances were under which these complaints started, he said nothing unusual. He thought hard about the circumstances, discussed them repeatedly, and again he said, "Nothing distressing occurred at that time." After repeated interviews he remembered that about that time he had had a quarrel with a friend of his over money matters, following which they had not seen each other for some time. The quarrel was patched up but they never really became good friends again. To check up on his memory, the patient asked his wife about the time of the quarrel. She confirmed the fact that the quarrel had occurred just before the onset of the patient's depression.

This is not a very dramatic case, nothing to be compared with the ones presented in the movies, but in many ways it is typical of the inability of the person to remember the significant things about his difficulties.

The same phenomenon has been investigated more objectively under controlled conditions. Malamud and Lindner (1931) showed to a number of psychotic patients several pictures for 30 seconds each. The patient was to report everything about the picture that he could remember. It was found that in a number of cases the report of the patient omitted details of the picture that had some meaningful relation to the patient's problem. To substantiate the hypothesis that the omission was due to repression, the patients were asked to report their dreams the following night. In a number of the cases, it was found that the dream content contained the omitted details of the picture from the day before. The fact that it was dreamed is not important for our purpose, but it is evidence that the unreported material had not completely disappeared but could affect such behavior as dreaming. An example of the type of material reported in the Malamud and Lindner experiment follows.

A woman who was depressed over the death of her infant was shown a picture, "The Immaculate Conception," in which the main figure was surrounded by cherubs. These cherubs were left out of the patient's report about the content of the picture. The next day she reported that she had dreamed that she was surrounded by cherubs.

The evidence for repression comes also from purely experimental studies upon normal subjects rather than patients. In these experiments the intent of the experimenter is to induce feelings of guilt, shame, or something that is sufficiently intense to cause repression. One of the emotions that has been successful is shame over a poor performance. Rosenzweig (1933) and later Glixman (1949) presented two groups of subjects with jigsaw puzzles of comparable difficulty. One group was told that this was an intelligence test; the other was told that the experimenter needed their help in determining how well the experimental material worked and how it should be classified. For each subject, half of the tasks were interrupted. After all of the tasks had been done, the subjects were asked to recall as many of them as they could. The second group in this experiment was a control group on whom a familiar experiment was being repeated. Generally, there is a better memory for the tasks that are not finished than for those that are completed (Zeigarnik, 1927). In the case of the group that was told these tasks constituted an intelligence test, the interruption was interpreted by the subjects to mean failure. This group remembered more of the tasks they had finished than those they had not. The results of Glixman's experiment are shown in Figure 10.4.

Reaction Formation

One of Shakespeare's characters said, "Methinks the lady doth protest too much." An unduly vehement and especially an unnecessary denial of a statement is often taken as evidence for its truth. A child may, for example, see a friend on whom he has played some trick talk to the teacher. Despite the fact that the conversation may have nothing to do with the trick, the guilty boy may rush to his own defense. "I did *not* let the air out of his tires." He

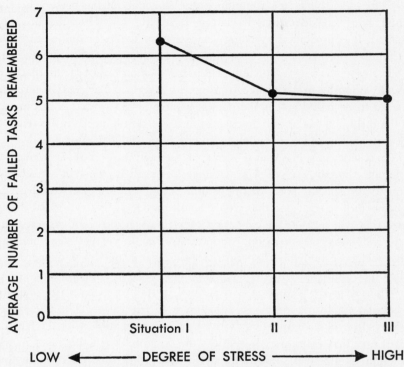

Fig. 10.4   The effect of failure on recall. (Data from A. F. Glixman, *J. Exp. Psych., 39,* 1949, 281-295)

feels guilty about the act and wants to hide it. Because of his sensitivity, he is likely to believe that the conversation between the other child and the teacher is concerned with his prank. His strong motivation not to be found out leads him to an overt defense of his innocence that the truly innocent person would not feel called upon to make. The inappropriateness of the defense is particularly apparent if most people would not feel guilty about the act even if they had done it.

This sort of vehement statement that is the opposite of the truth resembles the personality defense called *reaction formation*. Reaction formation is the phenomenon of behaving strongly and insistently in exactly the opposite way from what one is impulsively inclined to do. To be studiously polite to a person one dislikes is an example of almost conscious reaction formation. Because it is almost conscious, this careful courtesy serves as a good example to analyze. The dislike is a dangerous need, dangerous in the sense that it may lead one into hostile behavior that will make for unpleasantness, that would be socially disapproved, and that would result in retaliation. By being carefully polite—*i.e.,* by saying complimentary things about the person, by showing him every consideration, by letting him have his way—the hostility is prevented. It is prevented by being very sensitive to opportunities to be kind and friendly—in this case not spontaneously friendly but deliberately friendly. The sensitivity to these opportunities represents another need, one that is diametrically opposite to the dislike. This need is, therefore, a *reaction formation.* The need to be polite makes the person behave in a way that is incompatible with the dislike. Thus, it is a defense against the hostile need in the sense that it prevents that need from leading to unwise impulsive behavior.

To restate this in general terms, a reaction formation is a need that counteracts the dangerous need. A dangerous need is one that sensitizes the person to the specific sorts of opportunities and threats that would evoke a dangerous motive, *i.e.,* one that would lead to anxiety, frustration, or disaster. A need that will prevent the evocation of such dangerous motives must sensitize the individual to other opportunities and threats, so that some competing motive will be established that on the one hand is not itself dangerous and on the other hand prevents the dangerous motive from appearing.

When reaction formation is described in this way, it can be seen to be very similar to distraction as an adjustment to frustration. The effect of distraction is to evoke a competing motive that is incompatible with the frustrated motives and that consequently reduces the frustration. In the cases in which distraction is effective, some other opportunity that the concrete frustrating situation happens to offer is utilized to evoke the competing motive. If a wagon is present, it may be used to distract the child from his wish to go down the slide. The only requirement for an effective distraction is that it be different from the unattainable goal and that it be obvious enough to evoke motivation readily.

When a need, however, is to function as a defense against another need, it must have some very specific characteristics. It must sensitize the person to opportunities and threats that will be present whenever the dangerous motive is evoked. If for some reason it were necessary, for example, to build a defense against wanting to go down slides, a liking for wagons would not be very effective, because there would not be wagons available whenever slides were. Therefore, even if the liking for wagons was much stronger than the liking for slides, the motivation to slide would be evoked whenever a wagon was not available.

It is this necessity for the defensive need to be evocable in tempting situations that makes the opposite need particularly effective as a defense against a dangerous need. Because so often opportunities can be seen as impositions, and impositions can be seen as opportunities, many situations that instigate one motive can also instigate the opposite motive. Thus, for example, kindness can be a defense against hostility. If a boy had strong needs to be hostile, he would be motivated to be hostile whenever he found an opportunity; he would find such opportunities in the weakness and vulnerability of others. Such a need would also make the boy sensitive and touchy. He might take offense at unintentional slights and hurts. He would certainly become angry at clearly hostile acts.

If this hostility in himself becomes a threat to him; if it makes him anxious and fearful, there might develop a defense against it that would prevent the hostility. For this purpose, the development of a strong need to be kind and nurturant and forgiving would be effective because the same situations would motivate kindness that motivate hostility. A weak person who offers an opportunity to be hostile is also attractive to a kind person who, because he sees the other person as vulnerable to danger, is motivated to protect him. Insults that are effective instigators of hostility are also opportunities to turn the other cheek or to return good for evil.

For another example, dominance can be defense against dependence. Those situations that offer opportunities to be dependent, such as a meeting with a strong dominant person, are threats to dominance; therefore, the defensive need for dominance can evoke motivation to take the lead in the same situations where dependence would lead one to follow.

What is the function of the concept of "reaction formation"? If a person is kind, it is clearly true that he is not hostile, because the two are incompatible. Why, then, say that the kindness is a defense against the hostility? Why not say that the hostile person is changed so that he is now kind? If there is no way to distinguish between a kind person and one whose kindness is a defense against hostility, then such an argument is convincing; there is little point in calling such personality changes defense mechanisms.

It is certainly a widely held belief, however, that a reaction formation can be identified, that such defensive needs have a certain insincerity about them, that the kindness that is a defense against hostility is distinguishable from kindness that is not performing this defensive function. Frequently the defensive character of a need can be seen in its inappropriateness. Thus, a reaction formation against hostility is likely to appear as mildness and gentleness under circumstances that would ordinarily provoke hostility, but the mildness may not appear in situations that generally evoke kindliness and nurturance. For example, some Caspar Milquetoast characters do not resist the dominance of powerful superiors; instead they almost go out of their way to understand and submit and not to resent dominance. In the face of milder and more objectively presented opposition, such a person may, on the other hand, be intolerant and aggressive. Turning the other cheek is a mark of very great gentleness and human understanding only if the individual is equally kind and understanding of weak and unfortunate people. If unfortunates are treated brusquely or condemned, then turning the other cheek becomes hypocrisy and cowardice.

Identification of a defensive need may also be possible because the dangerous need may affect behavior overtly in fantasies, dreams, or projective tests, although it is well defended in real life. Such symptoms are commonly taken by clinical psychologists as evidence of the need behind the defense.

Finally, it should be said that needs that perhaps once existed as a defense may operate so effectively that eventually they can no longer be called defensive. Defensive needs are perfectly genuine needs, and the labeling of them as defensive does not imply that they are not needs but rather that something about their intensity or their inappropriateness leads the observer to believe that they are protecting the person from the dangers of an opposite need.

Righteous Indignation as a Defense

It should be noted that two of the needs that commonly serve as defenses are not necessarily opposite to the dangerous need that requires a defense. These two needs are hostility and self-esteem. In each case there are special factors accounting for the presence of the need. Hostility is prominent as a defensive need because temptation of any kind, if it arouses dangerous motives, is a threat. Therefore, regardless of what motivation is evoked, the tempting object can be seen as a threatening object. To hate and destroy this threat or to fear and avoid it is, therefore, a defense against any temptation. Thus, a militant hatred of alcohol, bars, and liquor interests can be, although it is not necessarily so, a defense against the temptation of drink. Prudishness, including the hostile condemnation of sexual activity, can also be a defense against temptation.

Self-esteem becomes involved through a different mechanism. Most of the motives that lead to dangerous consequences are those that are disapproved in this culture. The dangerous consequence frequently is the punishment and disapproval of other people. The defense against such motives is therefore good, and thus the defensive need increases self-esteem and the feeling of being right. When a child has just acquired some desirable control, the resulting halo is clearly visible in his self-righteousness. The feeling of righteousness and hostility can go together despite the fact that hostility is not approved of in the culture. The perception of an object as bad because it is tempting may lead not only to the hatred of it but also to the feeling that the hatred is right.

No one is a severer critic of the table manners of others than the child who has just developed his own. This fanatical hatred with the conviction of righteousness behind it may be much more serious than the childhood example just cited. It can be a very dangerous combination of motives in a society, leading to witch hunts, revolutions, and war.

In summary, reaction formation is the development of a need that defends the individual against a dangerous need by leading to his being motivated in a way that is incompatible with the dangerous motive. For this purpose the diametrically opposed need is especially suitable. We sometimes describe this reaction formation as "leaning over backward" to avoid a dangerous motive.

Summary

With this chapter we complete the discussion of goal selection, one section of the model of human behavior. Chapter 7 dealt with the instigation of motives. Motives are instigated by the cognition of appropriate external situations. We saw first that motives might be instigated by the presence of goal objects or other objects that suggest or remind the person of a goal. Gradually, the goals that are realistic opportunities for the person become more powerful instigators. In the light of our recent discussion of defenses, we might look upon the increasing power of opportunity to investigate motives as a sort of defense. Unattainable goals—*i.e.,* goals which are suggested but which there is no opportunity of attaining—are traps that lead to frustration. To the extent that the individual is motivated only by opportunities, he is protected against one source of frustration.

There are other sorts of instigation of motivation. Impositions are especially strong instigations. They make the person want to resist the imposition—*i.e.,* to prevent it, or if it has already occurred, to reestablish the original state of affairs changed by the imposition. If another person is the source of the imposition, if he imposes on us, we want to reciprocate and to inflict the same imposition on him. We want to do so, too, if the imposition was intrinsically pleasant—that is, we want to return the favor.

In Chapter 7, these were the main instigations discussed. Later, we have noted some other instigations, especially the instigations to conformity. Another person performing an activity instigates imitation, especially if the other person is liked and admired. A whole group of people is even stronger instigation to conform to the group pattern.

In examining the appearance of these instigations during childhood, we have seen the importance of the various emotions. Anger is evoked by the same sort of impositions that instigate resistance and retaliation. Anger, however, appears at an earlier age than directed resistance or retaliation. With maturity the child becomes able to identify the source of the imposition, to attack that source as a means of resisting imposition, and to retaliate against the source of the imposition. Fear is evoked by the same sort of impositions that instigate escape; with maturity the motivation becomes more directed. In connection with the discussion of violations we have seen how the emotional states of shame and guilt are evoked. These also accompany their own motives. They instigate specific motives to hide or to conceal one's defect in the case of shame, and self-punishment in the case of guilt. These unpleasant emotional states may also be perceived as impositions and thus instigate other motives, such as hostility against the spectator, against the accuser, or even against the victim if he keeps evoking guilt by his presence.

As we saw in Chapter 8, instigations do not by themselves evoke motives. The person must have a need that makes him sensitive to the instigation. There are a number of different kinds of needs describing different patterns of sensitivity to instigations. General needs, for example, are needs that sensitize the person to one class of instigations, regardless of what the outcome of the motivated behavior is, and regardless of who is involved. Attitudes, on the other hand, sensitize the person to instigations depending upon the presence of the person who is the object of the attitude. An objective, a third variety of need, is a sensitivity to opportunities to attain a specific goal, regardless of whether it involves submitting to or resisting impositions, and no matter who is involved. We saw that general needs, in a primitive sense, are found in the susceptibility of infants to fear, anger, and other emotions. Attitudes develop out of the infant's early discrimination between the familiar and the unfamiliar and go through a long developmental process before they resemble the adult's attitudes of love and hate.

Next, we discussed the social controls over motivation. We saw that social rules can be viewed as the requirements of certain social roles in society. We saw also that these social rules (1) may require mere behavioral conformity, (2) may be focused upon the consequences of the action rather than the action itself, or (3) may be focused upon the motivation for the action. Many rules have all three requirements.

Three conditions must be met before the child can conform to rules. First, he must understand them. In children's games we found a good example of the development of an understanding of rules and their bases. Secondly, he must be motivated to comply in the face of temptation. This last topic is discussed in Chapter 10. We have seen how the child can adjust to frustration or conflict and reduce the strength of motives, even without satisfying them. This permits him to control his behavior when satisfaction of the motive is impossible. It also permits him to reduce the psychological impact of fear of punishment, shame, and guilt, and thus to behave antisocially. As so often happens, the maturity required for well-adjusted behavior can also foster certain sorts of maladjustment. Finally, we have seen how these adjustments may occur in advance to prevent motivation rather than control it.

This, then, completes our discussion of goal selection in childhood. We shall return to these problems when we discuss the factors that develop or change needs and thus bring about the various individual differences that are apparent in describing child behavior. Now, however, we must move on to the section of the model concerned with goal-directed behavior. After the goal is selected, how does the person select a means to his goal—*i.e.,* a behavior pattern that will attain the goal? And how is the behavior guided toward the goal? This is the topic of the next few chapters.

11

The Abilities of Children

GENERAL INTELLIGENCE

PRIMARY MENTAL ABILITIES

THE REALIZATION OF MENTAL ABILITIES

MOTOR SKILLS AND THEIR DEVELOPMENT

LANGUAGE SKILLS

SUMMARY

THE SECTION of the model of human behavior dealing with goal-directed behavior is concerned first with the organism's selection of the best means to attain its goal. The individual must survey the situation, interpret the cues that are available, and decide how to attain the goal. This decision must be made in the light of the external situation and also in terms of the abilities of the individual himself. Then, after the behavior is initiated, it may be continually guided and controlled so that the goal is actually achieved. The ability of the individual to perform this entire process is encompassed in the term *general intelligence,* the concept with which we begin our discussion of goal-directed behavior. We will then discuss some of the more specialized abilities of children.

General Intelligence

Like many theoretical problems in the study of human beings, the problem of understanding intelligent behavior began with a practical request. Schoolteachers have had to face the fact that some children do well in school and others do poorly. Some children do so poorly and seem so very stupid that they are removed from the regular school system and given special training or in some cases are put in homes for the feeble-minded. The practical problem of determining which children in a school could profitably continue in the course of instruction and which ones were not able to profit from school experience was faced by the school system of France in the early part of this century. The Minister of Public Instruction commissioned Alfred Binet to devise a test to identify mentally defective children. This test, which he constructed and published in 1908, was the first of a series of intelligence tests, of which the most popular example in present-day use is the Stanford-Binet Test of Intelligence.

The Construction of a Test of General Intelligence

Looking back upon the history of intelligence testing, we can see that one important factor in the measurement of mental ability is that intelligence was first tested in children. The fact that children grow and obviously become more able and competent makes it very convenient to measure their level of maturity. The first tests of intelligence were really attempts to measure the maturity level of a child, especially those aspects of his maturity that were important for his school performance, by comparing him with children of various ages. If a child could pass more items in a test than the average child of his age, he was judged to be of more than average intelligence. If a child of five years of age could pass as many test items as the average child of seven years, he was judged to be as intelligent as the average child of seven. We can, in other words, use the average performance of children of various ages as a scale against which any one child can be compared. Bright children are precocious; they perform as well as the average child of an older age. Dull children are retarded; they perform no better than the average child of a younger age level. Behind this procedure is the quite reasonable assumption that the average child increases in general intelligence as he grows up.

MENTAL AGE   A test of general intelligence of children can be constructed on the following basis: First, we select a group of test items. Then we give those items to a large number of three-year-olds, four-year-olds, five-year-olds, and so on, to find the average performance for each age level. We can make the test more refined by including more age levels—three and one half, four and one half, etc. Now, when we test a specific child, we give him this test and find out how many items he passes. If he does as well as the average five-year-old, he has the intelligence of a five-year-old. If he does better than a five-year-old but not as well as a six-year-old, we can give him a score somewhere between five and six years, perhaps 64 months. His performance on the test is called his *mental age*. In the Stanford-Binet test, his mental age is measured in months. A child's mental age is the age of the average child who can pass the same number of items that he does.

I.Q.   Obviously, the child increases in mental age as he grows up, but for some purposes we are concerned with how well he does in relation to the average child of his own age. A four-year-old with a mental age of five years is obviously brighter or more intelligent in some sense than the six-year-old who has a mental age of five years, even though they have the same mental age. The measure of relative brightness is the I.Q. (Intelligence Quotient), the ratio of a child's mental age to his chronological age. If a child of four has a mental age of five, the ratio of 5/4 is 1.25. For purposes of pure convenience this number is multiplied by 100 to avoid the decimals. The I.Q. of such a child is 125. The six-year-old who has a mental age of five has an I.Q. of $5/6 \times 100$, or approximately 83. So we have really two measures of intelligence: mental age, indicative of the level of performance, and I.Q., indicative of the child's advancement or retardation relative to his chronological age.

We have not yet discussed a number of important problems in the selection of test items and in the selection of the group of children on whom the test is standardized; but, before going into those issues, let us look at a concrete example of such a test of general intelligence, the Stanford-Binet, which was first developed by Terman in 1917 and later revised by Terman and Merrill in 1937.

THE REVISED STANFORD-BINET TEST   The 1937 revision of the Stanford-Binet contains a group of tests at each year level from two to fourteen. In addition it contains a group of tests for the two-and-one-half-, three-and-one-half-, and four-and-one-half-year age levels, because the child's ability increases so rapidly at these younger ages that we need tests for every six months. It also contains groups of tests for average adults and superior adults of various levels. These depend upon a somewhat different logic from the tests for the lower age levels.

The following summary of the items in the test will illustrate the kinds of performance that are demanded by the test. The items at half-year age levels are omitted.

TABLE 2

OUTLINE OF THE REVISED STANFORD-BINET INTELLIGENCE TEST,
FORM L*

YEAR II

1. Three-hole Form Board. (The child must place three differently shaped blocks in the properly shaped hole within a time limit.)
2. Identifying Objects by Name. (There are six objects—e.g., button, cup, engine, spoon. The child must point to the correct one as each is named by the examiner.)
3. Identifying Parts of the Body. (The child must point to the parts of a doll as each part is named.)
4. Block Building: Tower. (The child must built a tower of blocks after the task has been demonstrated.)
5. Picture Vocabulary. (The child must name common objects when he sees their pictures.)
6. Word Combinations. (The child's spontaneous use of word combinations in his conversation with the examiner is recorded and scored.)

YEAR III

1. Stringing Beads. (Strings beads while watching demonstration.)
2. Picture Vocabulary. (Names objects from card in response to "What's this?")
3. Block Building: Bridge. (Makes bridge following demonstration.)
4. Picture Memories. (The child must recognize an object when it is presented among others.)
5. Copying a Circle. (Subject is asked to make a circle like the sample.)
6. Repeating Three Digits.

YEAR IV

1. Picture Vocabulary. (Names objects in response to "What is this?")
2. Naming Objects from Memory. (The child must tell which of three objects has been hidden.)
3. Picture Completion: Man.
4. Pictorial Identification. (The child must point to correct picture when asked to "Show me what. . . .")
5. Discrimination of Forms. (Finds forms to match sample.)
6. Comprehension II. (Responds to "Why do we have . . . ?")

* Adapted from L. M. Terman and M. A. Merrill, *Measuring Intelligence: A Guide to the Administration of New Revised Stanford-Binet Tests of Intelligence,* Boston, Houghton Mifflin, 1937, pp. 75-132.

TABLE 2 *(continued)*

YEAR V

1. Picture Completion: Man.
2. Paper Folding: Triangle. (Imitates tester.)
3. Definitions. ("What is a . . . ?")
4. Copying a Square. (Is asked to "Make one like this.")
5. Memory for Sentences II. (Repeats sentence after tester.)
6. Counting Four Objects. (Tells "How many.")

YEAR VI

1. Vocabulary. (The child must define five words from a prescribed list.)
2. Copying Bead Chain from Memory I. (Different kinds of beads in alternation.)
3. Mutilated Pictures. (Tells what is missing in picture.)
4. Number Concepts. (Gives tester requested number of objects.)
5. Pictorial Likenesses and Differences.
6. Maze Tracing. (Indicates shortest way through maze.)

YEAR VII

1. Picture Absurdities I. (Tells what is funny or foolish about pictures.)
2. Similarities: Two Things. (The child must say in what way certain objects are alike.)
3. Copying a Diamond.
4. Comprehension III. (Answers common sense questions in the form of "What's the thing to do when . . . ?")
5. Opposite Analogies.
6. Repeating Five Digits.

YEAR VIII

1. Vocabulary. (Defines eight words.)
2. Memory for Stories. (The child must remember essential facts in a short anecdote.)
3. Verbal Absurdities I. (Tells what is foolish about statements.)
4. Similarities and Differences. (Tells how certain objects are alike and how they are different.)
5. Comprehension IV. (Tells what to do in certain circumstances.)
6. Memory for Sentences III. (Sentences longer than for V-5.)

YEAR IX

1. Paper Cutting. (Makes drawing to indicate how a piece of folded paper from which a hole has been cut would look if unfolded.)
2. Verbal Absurdities II.
3. Memory for Designs. (Designs must be drawn from memory.)
4. Rhymes. (Tells the word that rhymes with certain other words.)

TABLE 2 *(continued)*

5. Making Change. (Tells how much change would be left after certain transactions.)
6. Repeating Four Digits Reversed.

YEAR X

1. Vocabulary. (Defines eleven words.)
2. Picture Absurdities II.
3. Reading and Report. (Tells what he has read after reading a given story.)
4. Finding Reasons I. (Tells why certain acts should be performed, etc.)
5. Word Naming. (Names as many words as possible in one minute.)
6. Repeating Six Digits.

YEAR XI

1. Memory for Designs. (Draws from memory.)
2. Verbal Absurdities III.
3. Abstract Words. (Definitions.)
4. Memory for Sentences IV.
5. Problem Situation. (Tells why people performed a certain act related to him.)
6. Similarities: Three Things.

YEAR XII

1. Vocabulary. (Defines fourteen words.)
2. Verbal Absurdities III.
3. Response to Pictures II. (Tells all he can about a picture exposed to view.)
4. Repeating Five Digits Reversed.
5. Abstract Words II.
6. Sentence Completion. (Provides missing words to complete meaning of sentences.)

YEAR XIII

1. Plan of Search. (Tells what plan he would follow in finding object lost in a certain situation.)
2. Memory for Words.
3. Paper Cutting. (Draws diagram to show how folded paper from which hole has been cut would look if unfolded.)
4. Problems of Fact. (Explains incidents in narrative.)
5. Dissected Sentences. (Rearranges words to form sentences.)
6. Copying Bead Chain from Memory. (More complicated than at Year VI.)

YEAR XIV

1. Vocabulary. (Defines sixteen words from list.)

TABLE 2 (continued)

YEAR XIV

2. Induction. (Discovers rule to predict number of holes in papers folded various numbers of times.)
3. Picture Absurdities III.
4. Ingenuity. (Reasoning problem.)
5. Orientation: Direction I. (Tells in what direction one would be going if he made certain turns from a given direction, etc.)
6. Abstract Words III.

AVERAGE ADULT

1. Vocabulary. (Defines twenty words from list.)
2. Codes. (Writes given message in code.)
3. Differences between Abstract Words.
4. Arithmetical Reasoning.
5. Proverbs. (Tells meaning.)
6. Ingenuity. (Reasoning test.)
7. Memory for Sentences V.
8. Reconciliation of Opposites. (Tells in what way certain opposites are alike.)

SCORING THE STANFORD-BINET TEST   When this test is actually administered to a child he is not given every item in the whole test. It would be very time-consuming and would be boring to a seven-year-old child to give him all the items that would be entirely too easy for him, and also those at the top of the scale that would be too difficult. Instead, we try to find the child's *basal age*. This is the age level at which he passes all of the items. A seven-year-old may not pass all the seven-year items, but perhaps he does pass all of the six-year level. His basal age then is six years. We assume that he would have passed all the items below that age level. It is a reasonable assumption, and as long as we follow the same procedure for the standardization group, we do not on the average affect the score even if the assumption is wrong. Then the child is given each item above his basal age until we come to the age level at which he fails all the items. Perhaps our seven-year-old passes some seven-year items and some eight-year items, but fails the nine-year level completely. At that point we stop the examination even though he might pass some more difficult items. Suppose that the child we are using as an example had the following record:

Year Level	Items Passed	Mental Age Credit
6	6	72 months (basal age)
7	4	8
8	1	2
9	0	0
		Total 82 months

To calculate the mental age, we begin with the basal age of six years or 72 months. To this we add credit for the four items he passed at the seven-year level. Since the six items would accumulate 12 months' credit if they were all passed, each item counts 2 months' credit. Passing four of them thus gives a credit of 8 months. The one item at the eight-year level counts 2 months' credit. These credits are all totaled, giving a mental age of 82 months. Since the child is 84 months old, his I.Q. is $82/84 \times 100$, or 98.

THE SELECTION OF ITEMS IN AN INTELLIGENCE TEST   An inspection of the items in this test make it clear that not every kind of performance that improves with age is included. For example, there are no items that are likely to indicate the fact that the child's motor skills improve with age, although some of the items involve a certain amount of motor skill. The trouble with the procedure of including all behavior that improves with age is that we suspect that not all abilities improve at the same rate. Some children are advanced in baseball playing but retarded in reading. We have to decide what items should be included in a test of general intelligence and what ones should be reserved for a test of motor development or a test of social development. This decision demands a theory about the nature of intelligence.

Binet had a specific problem to solve—the selection of children who could not profit from school. Although he had some theories about intelligence, he devised a test primarily of the abilities that contribute to school success. This practical use of intelligence tests has continued to influence the selection of items, but each person who has constructed a test has to some degree been guided by his conception of the nature of intelligence. Terman felt that the ability to carry on abstract thinking and to use abstract symbols was perhaps the focus of intelligence. Thus, his tests, especially the 1917 version, contain many items involving vocabulary and use of symbols. Other people feel that an intelligence test should not be overloaded with such items, and they include more items that do not require verbal skill. We shall see later how Thurstone (1938) has tried to approach this problem.

Even when the general type of item is selected, there are good items and poor items to include in a test of intelligence. For a test like the Stanford-Binet, in which the items are arranged in groups, it would be ideal if an item at the five-year level were passed by very few people below the age of five and by nearly all people above that age. Certainly it ought to be an item that is passed more frequently by each higher age level. An item that was passed oftener by four-year-olds than by four-and-one-half-year-olds and then passed still more frequently by five-year-olds would be a poor item for a test. Figure 11.1, showing the percentage of children of various age levels who pass a specific item, illustrates the characteristics of a good item.

THE STANDARDIZATION OF AN INTELLIGENCE TEST   After items have been selected, it is then necessary to find out how well the average child of each age level performs on the test. This is called the *standardization* of the test and enables the scores of other children to be interpreted. The problems to be solved in standardization are very knotty ones. The first question involves

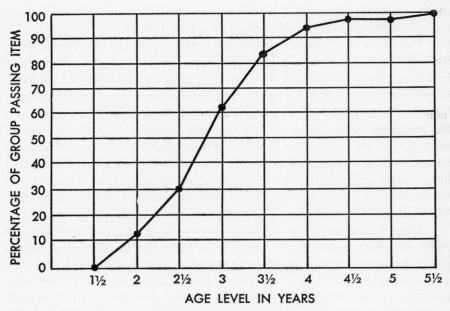

Fig. 11.1 Percentage of children of various ages who pass a test item (copying a circle) at the three-year-old level. (Data from Quinn McNemar, *The Revision of the Stanford-Binet Scale,* p. 90)

a decision about what group will be tested with the test and for what group can the test be valid. If the psychologist who devises a test wants it to be applicable to all children all over the world, children from different cultures, using different languages and with widely different background, he must somehow find items that are passed more and more frequently by older age levels among all these groups of children and he must then include a representative sample of all such children in his standardization. Nobody has attempted such an ambitious project; it may well be an impossible task. Terman wanted to make his standardization group representative of children in the United States. To do this he went to great pains to sample children from different parts of the country, children in rural and urban areas, children in public schools, children in private schools, children out of school for some reason, children from various socioeconomic levels. Even when he could not obtain a representative sample of children, he could determine how his sample was atypical and make corrections in his test norms to allow for the fact that a representative sample would have more children from a certain area than his standardization group did.

Developmental Norms

When parents of a two-year-old child read in some child-psychology book that the average two-year-old has a vocabulary of 272 words and their child uses only a small number of words in his conversation, they may worry unnecessarily. In the light of such experience it sometimes seems that it is a disservice to the public to discuss such norms of development. The psychologist who wrote the book would, of course, tell such parents not to worry. He would point out that one child differs a great deal from another in the development of language. He would also indicate that children who are developing one area of skill may lag in another area. Furthermore, he would emphasize the necessity for drawing no conclusions about the retardation of a child on the basis of only one index of development. And he would point out that the predictability of future language development on the basis of the size of the vocabulary at the age of two is not very high. He would cite cases in which language development was retarded but the child became unusually fluent in the use of language as he grew older.

A great deal of research in child psychology has gone into the standardization of developmental norms. These facts about the expected age of appearance of various behavior patterns are, despite the problems they present, very important for both practical and theoretical reasons. The function of such norms is to permit the objective appraisal of a child's developmental level. For that reason the tests that have been developed emphasize objective behavioral symptoms that efficiently mark the developmental level of the child. Very useful predictions can be made by the trained psychologist or pediatrician who uses these norms to make decisions about a child. Such tests of development as those published by Gesell (1928) or Psyche Cattell (1942) or Buhler and Hetzer (1935) are routinely administered before a baby is placed for adoption, because the adopting agency does not wish to place a child in a home for which he is too bright or too dull.

The early utilization of such tests may, for example, enable the pediatrician to recognize the presence of *cretinism,* a condition resulting from the inadequate functioning of the thyroid gland. If cretinism is discovered early enough, the administration of thyroid may prevent an otherwise serious mental deficiency. These examples show that, in the hands of the trained person, tests of developmental progress are invaluable.

Even for parents, developmental norms are extremely valuable guides despite the fact that they are at the same time sources of untold needless anxiety. Whenever the parent is concerned about some especially annoying habit that his child has developed or is worried because he seems so stupid, it is very reassuring to find that such behavior is only natural for a child of his age and that he can be expected to grow out of his difficulty. If it were not for developmental norms, there would probably be much more misunderstanding of children than exists now.

On the other hand, it is very difficult for a person who has not been trained in test procedures and their interpretations to appreciate how variable child behavior can be. Despite anything that psychologists can say, it is very difficult for parents to accept calmly the fact that their child does not walk yet even though "the book" says that it is to be expected at his age level. Similarly, it worries parents if their child is still negativistic when "the book" says he will have outgrown it at a certain age.

All of this is to warn and reassure those readers who might be inclined to take too literally the statements reported in experiments about the age at which various kinds of behavior occur. Even the best standardized tests of development are difficult to interpret properly, and many of the findings reported in experiments are not even intended to be accurate statements of the age at which the behavior *normally* occurs. In some studies the children used in the experiment are selected from a certain socioeconomic level by virtue of the fact that they are enrolled in a nursery school, and because of this selection the performance of the children is atypical. In many experiments such factors as this are reported in order to avoid an uncritical acceptance of age levels.

Primary Mental Abilities

Criticism of General Intelligence

Some psychologists have quarreled with Terman's approach to testing intelligence. His procedure is sound enough if there is good reason to suppose that there is an ability which can usefully be called general intelligence. Some people have felt, however, that there are different types of intelligence. Most tests of general intelligence emphasize the kinds of ability required for school-work, but perhaps other children have abilities that have just as good a right to be called intelligence, but that are not measured by the usual intelligence test. If it is true that some children are high in one type of intelligence and other children are high in another type of intelligence, then the best a general intelligence test can do is to measure both abilities and average them in some way. Thus, children who are high in both types receive the highest scores, children who show primarily one or the other type receive moderate scores, and children who are low in both receive low scores. It is argued that it would be much more useful to measure the different types of mental ability separately, so that each child would receive several different scores rather than a single general score. Thus, the child who had a great deal of two sorts of ability would receive two high scores, and the children who had only one would receive a high score and a low score.

If we look at the actual test records, it is quite clear that some children accumulate their mental age score by passing certain items and other children who have the same total score pass other items. It is frequently found that one child does well on the verbal items but somewhat less well on the nonverbal items, whereas another child performs most successfully on the nonverbal items.

We might think that the best solution would be to consider every item a separate ability. A vocabulary test might be one ability; drawing a picture of a man might be another. Certainly they seem superficially to require quite different skills. If we carried this point of view to its extreme, we would describe a person in terms of all the activities he could perform. For every single behavior pattern—running, adding, drawing, reading, etc.—there would be a separate ability. There are several difficulties in separating abilities in this way. First, it would make the description of a person's abilities very cumbersome. We would much prefer to assume that the same ability might underlie several different behavior patterns. Perhaps a good memory contributes to such activities as finding one's way through a region that has been seen only once, to the ability to memorize poetry, and also perhaps to debating. Perhaps piano playing and typewriting have something in common. If there are abilities that contribute to different performances, we are better able to predict performance than if we have to test for each of the many thousand behavior patterns that might be distinguished.

A second difficulty is that the arguments against the unity of general intelligence might be applied to each behavior pattern. Some people may add well because they recognize the figures rapidly, others because they quickly recall the sum of two numbers, others because they can keep a total in mind while they add new figures to it. That a behavior pattern appears as a single activity does not mean that it represents a single ability.

Criterion of an Ability

How, then, can we decide whether or not two activities require the same ability? One way is to find whether success in the two activities is correlated.

If two activities require exactly the same ability, then anybody who succeeds at one of the activities will succeed at the other, and anybody who fails at one will fail at the other. If tennis and badminton require the same skills, good tennis players will do well at badminton and poor tennis players will also be poor badminton players. If two activities do not require exactly the same ability but require some of the same abilities, then there will be a tendency for people who succeed at one to succeed at the other. Good tennis players may not always be good badminton players, but they may be more likely to succeed at badminton than poor tennis players. This could happen if badminton skill overlapped with but did not exactly coincide with tennis skill.

This tendency for success in one activity to go along with success in another may be measured by the correlation coefficient. The correlation coefficient may take any value from $+1.00$ to -1.00. A correlation of $+1.00$ means that there is perfect correlation; high scores on one test are made by exactly the same people who make high scores on the other. A correlation of -1.00 means just the opposite—the higher the score a person makes on one test, the lower will be his score on the other. A correlation of 0 means that there is no relationship between the two scores.

Selection of Primary Abilities

Many psychologists have analyzed the correlations among performances on various sorts of activity in order to discover what abilities are required for each one. The task is a difficult one and contains many technical problems. Furthermore, two analysts may take the same data and analyze them into different patterns of abilities. There are no final conclusions, therefore, about the primary abilities of people. The set of hypothesized primary factors for mental abilities that is most popular in the United States has been developed by Thurstone (1938) from his analysis of a large battery of mental tests. He believes eight abilities can be clearly identified: (1) verbal ability, (2) number ability, (3) perceptual speed, (4) rote memory, (5) inductive reasoning, (6) deductive reasoning, (7) word fluency, (8) ability to visualize objects in space. British psychologists (Vernon, 1950) are more inclined to think that a general factor of intelligence underlies all mental tests but that two additional factors, one verbal and another relating to practical, mechanical, and spatial abilities, can be distinguished among different groups of intelligence tests.

Not only is there a difference of opinion about what mental abilities should be considered primary, but there are equally great differences of opinion about the theory of what a primary mental ability is. Some people look upon an ability as a unitary concept that contributes to a number of different kinds of performance. The strength of the arm muscles is a factor that plays a role in many actions, such as lifting, pulling, and throwing. An ability might be conceived of in similar terms. We do not know anything about primary mental abilities in terms of their physiological functioning, but we can think of an ability as a property of the organism that functions in some performances and not others. It may be very important or relatively unimportant in different behavior patterns. According to such a conception, the function of an ability is to carry out a behavior pattern successfully. The more the ability, the more difficulty can be overcome. The unity of the ability accounts for the correlations among different activities that involve the same ability.

This is not the only basis for conceptualizing about abilities. The mere fact of correlation between two activities need not indicate that they have any ability in common. It may be that the same environmental influences that develop one activity develop the other also. If it happened that in the entire school system of a country children memorized "Paul Revere's Ride" at the same time they learned to ride a bicycle, we would find in this country a high correlation between success at reciting the poem and success in riding a bicycle. Children who could do one would tend to succeed on the other, and children who failed one would fail on the other. From this correlation we might be tempted to assume that the ability to recite "Paul Revere's Ride" involved the same abilities as bicycle riding. This absurd illustration merely points out the dangers of interpreting correlations. There probably are sets of activities that are taught simultaneously to groups in this country. The correlation between arithmetic and language tests is probably enhanced by the fact that good schools teach both and teach them effectively, poor schools probably do a poor job on both, and children who are outside the school system probably are taught neither. The correlation could arise from the environment rather than from the characteristics of the growing child.

Correlations Among Abilities of Children

The abilities of young children might throw some light upon this question. If the correlations among different activities primarily depend upon their having been taught together, then the various activities of young children would be less correlated than those of older children. If, on the other hand, an ability is a property of the organism, then the correlations among activities would appear as soon as the activities themselves make their appearance. Here also the evidence is unclear. When we think of the behavioral repertoire of the newborn infant, we find it hard to think of abilities in the usual sense at all; certainly we do not see signs of primary mental abilities. By the time the child is five or six years old, however, it is possible to test for five primary abilities: verbal, number, perceptual, motor, and spatial (Thurstone and Thurstone, 1950). These abilities are not completely independent of each other. There is a tendency for scores on the various abilities to be correlated, and the correlations are generally higher for children than for adults.

In the light of this finding, one hypothesis that has been advanced is that abilities differentiate with age. The very young child may have only one general ability, but as he grows up it may become possible to separate out different sorts of ability. The evidence for this hypothesis is not very clear. The intercorrelation of the primary mental abilities at young ages is in agreement with such a hypothesis, but other studies using different tests have not consistently found a differentiation of abilities (Vernon, 1950). Many studies have found that the organization of abilities and their interrelationships is not constant; it changes with age but not in a clearly predictable fashion. There are many technical problems in these studies that stem from the assumptions underlying the statistical analysis of the data, so that it is not possible as yet to come to any clear conclusion of the question.

We do not yet have a theory about the functioning of abilities that would suggest the type of research required to decide among these various alternatives. When we do have some theories about ability, we can utilize all these data to build up a truly adequate picture of the abilities of human beings. Meanwhile, the situation is not so chaotic from the practical point of view as it is from the point of view of a theory. We have good tests to predict many kinds of skills. These tests are constantly used to help children decide what courses to take and what vocations to prepare for, and to help teachers give the most effective aid they can to children who are having academic trouble. The various ways of looking at primary mental abilities, as well as the proposals about what are the primary mental abilities, have their practical uses. As in other branches of science, much practical benefit can come about without an adequate theory, but when we do develop a good theory of abilities, we will then be able to solve many additional practical problems that are at present beyond our skills.

The Realization of Mental Abilities

One further problem in the analysis of the abilities of children can be illustrated in the study of mental abilities. By and large, the mental testing programs in the schools have been successful. Many children who would not profit from a regular classroom program have been discovered and assigned to special classes. Many others who have had trouble in school have been tested so that the cause of the difficulty might be more readily ascertained.

Discrepancies Caused by Motivation

There are always children, however, who do not conform to the predictions made for them by various intelligence tests. One common variety of misfit is the child who shows up well in an intelligence test but does very poor schoolwork in spite of it. He is the underachiever, the one who does not live up to the potentialities indicated by the test results. Very often such a child is found to be failing for emotional reasons. He may not be motivated to perform well in school; he may not care enough to study. As we can see in our model, ability will show itself only when the child is trying to attain a goal that requires the ability. It is often amazing to see such children, after having done poorly in schoolwork, suddenly bloom when they become interested in school activities or when they see how schoolwork fits into their own motivation.

There are other cases of underachievement that are not obviously the result of poor motivation but, instead, reflect the fact that school may be frustrating and build up tension. Children who are very tense behave less maturely than they would if they were more comfortable. School examinations may send a child into a panic, whereas the more relaxed atmosphere of an intelligence test may not make him tense. There are a variety of reasons for underachievement, all of which show that ability cannot be measured or cannot be realized unless the proper conditions are present.

Even more surprising, perhaps, are the children who overachieve. They do better in real life than their performance on a test would indicate. In some cases this is the result of poor motivation in the test situation. If the child does not try on the intelligence test, he may not make as high a score as he could under more favorable conditions. Examiners are well aware of the need for engaging the child's interest and motivation in the test and often do not consider a test valid when they feel that the child is disinterested. It is the intent of the examiner to obtain the child's best performance on the test, because it is only under good motivation that the maximum ability is displayed.

Lack of Differentiation of Needs and Abilities

There may be a more fundamental reason for either overachievement or underachievement, however. In order for an ability to be readily testable it needs to be under a sort of voluntary control. One item on the Stanford-Binet, for example, calls for repeating several digits. Unless the child can voluntarily try to remember them, unless the ability to memorize is usable as a means to many different goals, then the test may be quite unable to evoke the child's ability. Probably by the time this item is required in the Stanford-Binet, its difficulty does not lie in the child's being unable to memorize voluntarily, although some of the errors of young children on this item suggest that this may sometimes be the trouble. When a child is asked to repeat 4-8-2 and answers 4-5-6, it seems that he remembered the first one but then was carried off by a more familiar habit of counting. This is considered a failure on the test and does not necessarily affect its validity, but if we concluded that the child could not remember three items, we might be wrong. We are not sure that his trouble was his failure to remember. In a real-life situation in which the child heard his friend's telephone number and was not trying to memorize it, he might find that he knew the number the next time he wanted it.

We can state this point in more general terms. Before an ability is testable outside of the situation in which it is used, it must be independent of a specific motive and a specific situation. It must be usable as a means to many different goals. In fact, it should probably not be called an ability unless it can contribute to the attainment of more than one isolated goal. To say that the newborn child has the ability to jerk his leg because he does so when his knee is tapped is rather misleading. It could just as well be called a need to jerk his leg as an ability: neither term is appropriate. It is very important that the child cannot voluntarily jerk his leg until somewhat later. When a specific stimulus elicits a specific fixed response, there is little point in trying to decide what is the means and what is the goal, or what is the need and what is the ability. The terms are not useful until the individual shows some degree of differentiation.

Those abilities that have been most thoroughly studied—motor skills, intellectual abilities, and language skills—are the behavior patterns that have become most clearly differentiated from motives by the time the child is usually tested. We can reasonably expect that if the child adds correctly on a test, he will add correctly in any other situation in which he tries to add correctly. Similarly, he can run just about as fast after a streetcar as he can on a race track.

When we come to the study of social skills, however, and especially skills in interpersonal relations, the independence of ability and need is not nearly so clear. It is very hard to be friendly to a person we do not like. If a child cannot hide his feelings, is it proper to say that he does not have the ability to be friendly? Certainly if we put the child in a test situation in which we tell him to be as friendly as he possibly can and then score his performance, we will very likely not get a true picture of his friendliness. Many children would "overachieve," because they would be very friendly and outgoing in real life even though they were completely inhibited when they were told to "be friendly."

Not only are many of the behavior patterns of interpersonal relations not differentiated from specific motivations and attitudes, but we would mistrust them if they were. We find it hard to be comfortable with a person who can turn his charm on and off like an electric light, because we are accustomed to using friendly behavior as a symptom of a friendly attitude. We count on the dependence between the behavior and the motive. We can, however, become accustomed to something different. We do not assume that a person who is walking is a person who enjoys walking; he may well be walking because he wants to get where he is going, although he may actively dislike the walk.

To summarize, we have seen some of the reasons that tests may not be accurate in their predictions about the individual's performance outside of the test situation. Ability is not the only factor in performance; motivation is equally important. Poor motivation in a test performance may fail to reveal an individual's true ability; or poor motivation in everyday life may not realize his tested ability. Finally, we have seen that unless motives and behavior patterns are relatively independent—*i.e.,* unless the behavior pattern can be used as a means to several different goals—the predictability of behavior from a test situation is often very poor. Most test situations can test only those abilities which are differentiated and usable in the service of a variety of motives.

We have used mental abilities as an illustration of the general problems of studying ability—the problems of test construction, of the isolation of primary abilities and the distinction among them, and of the pitfalls in the prediction of real-life behavior from performance in a test situation. We might have used motor abilities or some other area equally well. Let us turn now to a review of the empirical findings on the development of some other sorts of ability without repeating in detail these general problems.

Motor Skills and Their Development

If we examine tests of development for infants, we find that many of the items are descriptive of motor development. Since it is motor development that increases most obviously and rapidly during infancy, these items are naturally the ones appearing in the norms. Table 3 gives a summary of the items of motor behavior that are characteristic of various age levels during infancy (Griffiths, 1954).

Table 3

Motor Behavior During Infancy*

First Year

First Three Months

The baby:
1. Lifts his chin up slightly when lying in the prone position (first month).
2. Pushes with both feet against the examiner's hands (first month).
3. Holds his head erect for a few seconds (second month).
4. Lifts his head well up when lying prone (end of second month).
5. Kicks his feet vigorously when laid down (end of second month).
6. Is active in his bath, kicking his feet, etc. (end of second month).
7. Lifts his head up slightly when in supine position (third month).
8. Can roll from side to back (third month).

Second Three Months

9. Holds his back firm when held in the sitting position (beginning of fourth month).
10. Lifts his head and chest up when lying prone (fourth month).
11. Holds his head erect continuously (fourth month).
12. Lifts his head and shoulder when in dorsal position (fifth month).
13. Can roll from one side right over to the other (fifth month).
14. Plays with his toes (sixth month).
15. (First crawling reaction.) Pushes on hands, draws up knees, etc. (sixth month).
16. Sits with slight support—e.g., can be left sitting among pillows in pram or cot (end of sixth month).

Third Three Months

17. Can roll over from back to stomach or from stomach to back (seventh month).
18. (First stepping reaction.) Moves feet alternately as if dancing when held up (seventh month).
19. Tries vigorously to crawl, using both hands and feet (eighth month).
20. Sits alone for a short while (eighth month).
21. (Stepping reaction.) Moves feet definitely one in front of the other (ninth month).

* Ruth Griffiths, *The Abilities of Babies,* University of London Press and McGraw-Hill, 1954. Reprinted by permission of University of London Press. The scale was standardized on a population of 600 London children between two weeks and two years of age.

The baby:

22. Can turn himself around when left lying on the floor (ninth month).
23. Can be left sitting on the floor (end of ninth month).
24. (Crawling.) Makes some progress, forwards or backwards (end of ninth month).

Fourth Three Months

25. Stands when held up (tenth month).
26. Sits well in a chair (end of tenth month).
27. Can pull himself up from crawling or sitting by grasping the furniture (eleventh month).
28. Can stand holding on to furniture (eleventh month).
29. Creeps on hands and knees, or gets about freely by some other method, e.g., bear walk (eleventh month).
30. Side-steps around inside cot or playpen, holding on to railings, etc. (twelfth month).
31. Can walk when led, adult holding one or both hands (twelfth month).

SECOND YEAR

First Three Months

32. Climbs onto a ledge or step when crawling (thirteenth month).
33. Can stand alone (thirteenth month).
34. Walks alone, at first unsteadily (end of fourteenth month).
35. Can kneel on floor or chair. Balances in this position (end of fourteenth month).
36. Climbs the stairs, climbing up but not yet down (fifteenth month).
37. Likes to walk pushing a wheeled toy (fifteenth month).

Second Three Months

38. Trots about well (sixteenth month).
39. Can stoop to pick up a toy without overbalancing (seventeenth month).
40. Climbs into a low chair (seventeenth month).
41. Can walk backwards (eighteenth month).
42. Likes to walk pulling a toy on a string (eighteenth month).

Third Three Months

43. Can climb stairs, up and down (nineteenth month).
44. Can jump. Child gives a little jump when standing if pleased, with both feet off the floor (nineteenth month).
45. Runs (twentieth month).
46. Can now walk up stairs (twentieth month).
47. Climbs and stands up on a chair (twenty-first month).

Fourth Three Months

The baby:

48. Can jump off a step, both feet off the ground together (twenty-second month).
49. Can seat himself at table, placing chair first (twenty-second month).
50. Walks up and down stairs; has abandoned climbing, but still holds adult's hand or the banisters (twenty-third month).
51. Can kick a ball (twenty-fourth month).
52. Can be trusted on stairs alone (twenty-fourth month).

One of the important accomplishments of the infant is the control and integration of various portions of his own body. One sort of motor control is the control of looking. A second is the development of reaching and grasping. A third is the development of erect posture and walking. A fourth is the development of motor control. The muscles involved in speech will be discussed in the section on language skills (see p. 292), because learning to talk involves much more than motor control.

Looking and Grasping

Gesell lists the development of control over fixation of the eyes as one of the important accomplishments of the first three months. Even at birth the child fixates on a light most of the time. But he easily loses track of a visible object if it moves at all rapidly, and especially if it moves in a vertical direction. By three months, however, the child can successfully look at the things he wants to and does spend much of his time inspecting his surroundings. Even after three months, looking may not be entirely under voluntary control; the nursery-school child has difficulty in not looking at objects that are noticeable and interesting. The development of the ability to look voluntarily has not been empirically investigated.

The development of grasping is well illustrated in Figure 11.2, taken from the studies of Halverson (1931). At first the child cannot contact an object. Later, contact is made but no grasping. Then we see in the succession of pictures the gradual development of the grasp from a whole-hand squeeze to a grasp with the whole hand to a grasp with the fingers only. Chapter 12 contains more details about the voluntary control of grasping in connection with visually controlled reaching.

Locomotion

The development of crawling has been studied by Ames (1937). Figure

11.3 shows the fourteen stages of prone progression that she identified, together with the approximate age at which each occurs.

The development of erect posture and walking has been studied by several investigators. Figure 11.4 pictures the development as described by Mc-Graw (1940). In the stage first pictured we see the reflex stepping movements of the young infant. When he is held so that his feet just touch the ground, he makes stepping movements but is quite unable to support his weight. Then gradually he begins to keep his legs stiff when his feet touch the floor and to push against the pressure on the soles of his feet until finally he can bear

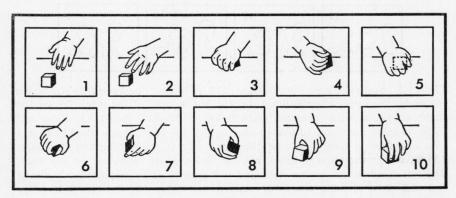

Fig. 11.2 The development of grasping. (1) *Aged 16 weeks:* The child reaches for the cube when it is presented to him but does not even touch it. (2) *Aged 20 weeks:* The child can touch the cube when he reaches for it but is unable to retrieve it. Sometimes he "corrals" the cube by pulling it against his body or his other hand (3: "primitive squeeze"), but he cannot actually grasp it. (4) *Aged 24 weeks:* The "squeeze grasp." The child approaches the cube from the side, enveloping it in his hand and pressing it with his fingers against the heel of his hand, but without using his thumb. (5) *Aged 28 weeks:* The hand grasp. Like the squeeze grasp (4) except that the hand approaches the cube from the top rather than from the side. (6) The palm grasp is the earliest grasp involving the opposition of thumb and fingers. The thumb presses the cube against the palm from one direction; the fingers—especially the index and middle finger—press it from another direction. The cube rests in the palm toward the heel of the hand. (7) *Aged 32 weeks:* Superior palm grasp. Like the palm grasp except that the cube rests in the palm closer to the thumb and forefinger. (8) *Aged 36 weeks:* Inferior forefinger grasp. The thumb and forefinger are on opposite sides of the cube, which is held between them, not pressed into the palm, resting close to the base of the thumb and first finger. (9) *Aged 52 weeks:* Forefinger grasp. Like the inferior forefinger grasp except that the cube is held well out toward the tips of the thumb and forefinger. The cube is picked up by first resting the hand on the table. (10) The superior forefinger grasp. Like the forefinger grasp except that no hand rest is necessary; the cube is picked up while the hand hovers in the air above it. (After H. M. Halverson, *Genet. Psych. Monog., 10:*2-3, 1931)

Fig. 11.3   Stages of prone progression. (1) Thrusting one knee forward beside the body: the upper chest is lifted slightly, but the rest of the trunk lies on the floor; weight is on the forearms, and one knee is thrust forward. (2) Knee and thigh forward, inner side of foot pressed against the floor: this is like (1) except that one foot is turned so that the inner side is pressed against the floor. (3) Pivoting: the chest is lifted, but the abdomen and hips are on the floor. The left hand moves to the right and the right knee is simultaneously thrust forward, thus pivoting the body toward the right. (4) Inferior low creep position: the left side of the body is in contact with the floor; the right knee is thrust forward, as in (2), but the child cannot bring his other knee forward in order to get his body off the floor. (5) Low creep position: the child is stomach downward, with nose, forehead, shoulders, and chest against the floor. Abdomen and hips are raised. The knees are thrust forward underneath the body, one at a time, but without any actual locomotion. (6) Crawling: the head and upper chest are raised from the floor by the forearms, with the rest of the body resting on the floor. The arms lift the forepart of the body, then push backward or forward so that the body slides. (7) High creep position: the child assumes a creeping position on his hands and knees but does not actually progress. (8) Retrogression: the child goes into a high creep position (7), then pushes backward and extends his legs so that locomotion is backward and he becomes prone. (9) Rocking: while in the high creep position, the child rocks on his arms and legs without making any progress. (10) Creep-crawling: the child assumes the high creep position, then falls forward to a prone position. This sequence is repeated regularly and permits considerable progress. (11) Rhythmic hands-and-knees creeping: the child lifts his right hand and left knee together. (12) Creeping with one foot exhibiting a near-step pattern: this is like creeping except that while one knee moves forward the other foot rather than the knee almost touches the floor. (13) Creeping on hands, one knee, and one foot: this is like (12) except that the foot rests on the floor, substituting for the knee in bearing the weight of the body. (14) Quadrupedal progression: creeping on hands and feet rather than hands and knees. (After Lois B. Ames, *Genet. Psych. Monog., 19,* 1937, 409-460)

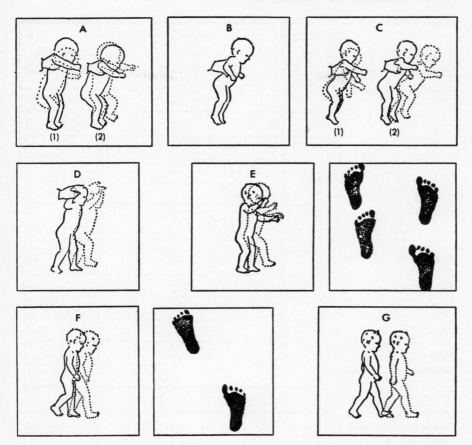

Fig. 11.4 The development of walking. *A. Newborn or reflex stepping:* **When the infant is supported so that his feet barely touch the floor, he sometimes lifts both feet (1) and often makes actual stepping movements (2).** *B. Suppression of stepping movements:* In the months immediately following phase *A,* stepping movements are inhibited. *C. Transition:* If supported as before, the child may keep his feet in one position but move his body up or down (1), or he may stamp in one spot, or make stepping movements (2). *D. Deliberate stepping:* If the child is held by his hands, he may make voluntary stepping movements which bear his weight. *E. Independent stepping:* The hands and arms are used, and the child's feet are wide apart. *F. Heel-to-toe progression:* The arms are more relaxed and the body more erect than in *E. G. Integrated walking:* The arms swing rhythmically; the movement of each arm is associated with the movement of the opposite leg. (After Myrtle B. McGraw, *The Neuromuscular Maturation of the Human Infant* and *Growth: A Study of Johnny and Jimmy*)

his weight. He must also develop balance before he can stand upright by himself. Then he begins to walk, at first hesitatingly, spending more time on one foot than on the other (see Fig. 11.4), with the feet spread out to make as broad a base as possible. Then gradually the gait evens, the balance improves, and the walking becomes typical of the older child and adult.

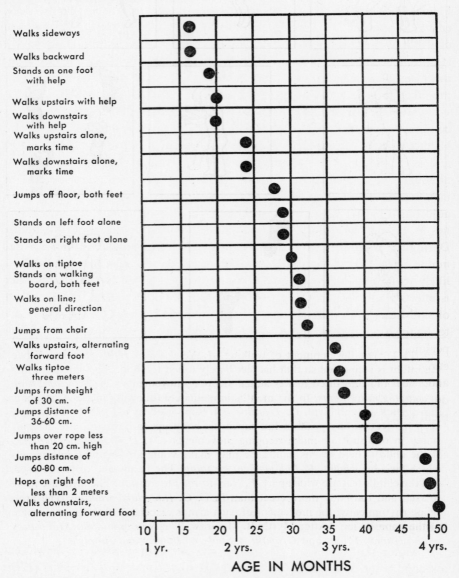

Fig. 11.5   Motor skills in childhood. (After N. Bayley, *Soc. for Research in Child Devel. Monog.*, No. 1, 1935)

Motor Skills

By the end of infancy the child can walk reasonably well and can reach for and grasp objects quite well, but many motor skills are beyond him. In Figure 11.5 we see the age at which some of the more complicated skills emerge. These data were obtained by Dr. Nancy Bayley (1935) of the Institute of Child Welfare at the University of California. The Institute conducted a long-term study of a group of children from Berkeley, testing their development and personality from birth to maturity. The data shown in Figure 11.5 are taken from tests made during the first four years of their lives.

After the preschool period the speed and accuracy of all these activities continue to increase, and the child acquires new behavior patterns that require balance and coordination. In these skills there are large individual differences and sex differences. We should not think that motor skill is unimportant; although our society does not require as highly developed motor skill of its members as do some of the primitive societies, it is essential for the child's adjustment to our culture. In later childhood the importance of motor skill lies in the fact that it is a source of recognition and popularity in the group. During the preadolescent years, boys especially value athletic proficiency and motor skill. H. E. Jones (1949) has shown that boys who are awkward are likely to be unpopular and socially maladjusted. Which is cause and which is effect is not clear as yet; probably there is a circular effect, in which lack of skill tends to isolate the child from his peer group and the isolation tends to hamper the development of motor skills and to encourage undesirable personality patterns. Among girls, motor ability is not so important. Beginning early in adolescence, girls tend to perform motor tests less well than boys, and, what is probably more important, they are not so strongly motivated to do well. They do not try so hard, probably because it is less important for them to do well.

Language Skills

Prelinguistic Sounds

Motor skill represents one line of development of ability in childhood; a second is the development of language skills. At first, of course, the sounds made by the infant cannot be called language, but they nevertheless are important for his development. The prelinguistic sounds gradually change their character from birth until the child truly begins to talk. The most important work in this area has been done by Irwin (1941), who recorded the speech sounds of ninety-five infants during the first thirty months of life. At first the infant's sounds are rather restricted in variety; he utters more vowels than consonants. There is an increase in the variety of both vowels and consonants, but after the age of one year the number of consonants is greater than the number of vowels.

There are also developmental trends in the various kinds of vowels and consonants. Irwin found that at very young ages the predominant type of vowel is the kind that is articulated in the front of the mouth such as *ee* or *ay*. By the time the child is thirty months old, the back vowels, such as *oo,* have increased markedly, although they still do not outnumber the front vowels. Just the opposite trend appears in consonants. The earliest sort of consonant sounds are glottals like *g,* which are articulated back in the throat. The proportion of glottals steadily declines, and the proportion of dentals, postdentals, and labiodentals increases. These are sounds like *t, d,* and *b,* which are formed up in the front of the mouth.

All of these trends represent developmental trends. Children who are retarded in other respects also tend to show a pattern of speech sounds that is characteristic of younger children, whereas precocious children proceed through these developmental sequences at an above-normal pace (Irwin, 1941). The effect of stimulating environment can be detected from the quality of prelinguistic speech sounds.

It does not seem, however, that these speech sounds are specifically learned from the speech of the adults who surround the child. It is typical that in the course of infancy the baby will cover the gamut of sounds, including many that do not belong to the language he will eventually learn. The infant in the English-speaking home may utter umlaut sounds like those which he will have so much trouble recapturing when he tries to learn German in high school or college. This suggests that the sounds that become part of the child's language are not specifically taught but rather selected out of a rich repertoire of infant sounds. This is not entirely true, because some sounds are so difficult that the child does not acquire them until after he has begun to talk. By the time the average child is thirty months old he will have used all the vowels distinguished in the phonetic alphabet but only about two thirds of the consonants he will eventually learn.

As the child's babbling becomes more mature, he repeats many sounds over and over again, just as he repeats many of his other actions over and over again. The sounds he repeats and babbles over may be picked by chance or by imitation. In the next chapter we shall see how imitation develops when we observe how these skills are coordinated into goal-directed behavior. At about the age of ten months the child uses his first word. Probably he babbles it, and his parents recognize it and identify it. There is no reason to suppose that the first words are communications that the child makes to the parent, or that they have a meaning in the adult sense of the word. They are probably actions, just like other actions of the child that are interesting, are encouraged by parents, and become part of the child's repertoire of actions.

Before long, these words—again like other actions—are tied into goal-directed behavior to become one-word sentences. *Mama,* for example, is frequently used in situations in which the child wants his mother. It is a request for help in the same sense that the baby's holding out his hands to his mother is a request to be picked up.

Vocabulary

Probably the most important step in language development is the child's discovery that words have meaning. The discussion of this topic must be deferred to the chapter on cognition because we need to develop some other

TABLE 4

INCREASE IN SIZE OF VOCABULARY IN RELATION TO AGE

Age		Number of Words	Age		Number of Words	Age		Number of Words
Years	Months		Years	Months		Years	Months	
0	8	0	2	0	272	5	0	2072
0	10	1	2	6	446	5	6	2289
1	0	3	3	0	896	6	0	2562
1	3	19	3	6	1222	8	0	3600
1	6	22	4	0	1540	10	0	5400
1	9	118	4	6	1870	12	0	7200
						18	0	15000

ideas before we can understand the process of attributing meanings to words. This discovery occurs close to the end of infancy and marks the beginning of a tremendous growth in language. Table 4 summarizes two studies (Smith, 1926; Terman, 1917) on the size of the vocabulary of children of various ages. Notice that from ten months to eighteen months the child acquires an average of only twenty-two words, but from the eighteenth to the twenty-first month he acquires almost one hundred. Over 150 new words are added in the period of the twenty-first to the twenty-fourth months.

Further growth of language skill can be shown in many different ways. There is an increase in the clearness of articulation, for example, as children grow older. One study (Wellman, Case, Mengert, and Bradbury, 1931) reports that when the child is two, only about 32 percent of his sounds are correctly articulated. By the time he is three, this figure has become 63 percent, and the later values continue to increase: 77 percent at four years, 88 percent at five, 89 percent at six. Another study (Davis, 1937) found that about 70 percent of five-and-one-half-year-olds make no errors in articulation and 91 percent of six-and-one-half-year-olds have essentially perfect articulation.

Another aspect of growth in language skill is the integration of words into sentences. Nice (1925) outlines several stages of the development of sentence structure. The first stage is the use of a single word before the age of one year. Following this is the early sentence stage. The sentence may contain only a single word, but the child uses it in a meaningful way in interpersonal interaction. This occurs on the average at eighteen months and lasts from four to seven months. It is marked by a heavy preponderance of nouns and a lack of connectives, such as articles, conjunctions, and prepositions. What Nice calls the short-sentence stage comes next. In it the typical sentence has three or four words and there is still a predominance of nouns, although the child's speech at this stage is not as overloaded with nouns as it was earlier. Tenses, comparatives, and other inflections are not yet mastered, and there are very few (2 to 4 percent) compound or complex sentences. The complete sentence arrives at about four years, on the average, and is marked by sentences of six to eight words, fair use of inflections, and a generally more definite and precise use of language.

As we saw in the discussion of primary mental abilities in children, there are eventually two kinds of verbal ability, one usually labeled *verbal ability* and measured by the size of vocabulary and competence in filling the blanks in incomplete sentences. The other verbal ability is *word fluency* and is measured by such tests as thinking of as many words as possible that end in *-tion*. There is nothing in the research on the development of language ability that suggests how this division comes about or to what it is related.

Summary

In this chapter we have examined several types of ability found in child behavior and have looked at the general problem of describing ability. Ability is a personal characteristic that makes it possible for the individual to respond to cues in such a way that he attains the goal that has been established by the processes of goal selection. If ability is to be a useful concept, it is important that there be fewer abilities than there are actions. In other words, the same ability should contribute to various behavior patterns. We have seen the difficulties in deciding when two activities require the same abilities and the differences in opinions about what constitute the primary mental abilities.

Furthermore, we have seen the importance of the differentiation between abilities and needs. Until behavior is independent of goal selection, there is no reasonable way to distinguish between an ability and a need. The reflex activities of the neonate are examples of behavior that could be either need or ability, depending upon the point of view. In those areas of our behavior, especially interpersonal relations and expressive behavior, in which the differentiation of behavior and motive is incomplete, we find great difficulty in obtaining a valid test of ability and poor predictability outside the test situation.

Finally, we have looked at the measurement of mental abilities and the problems to be faced in test construction and in the standardization of a test of general intelligence. Without going into the same detail, we have surveyed the empirical data bearing upon the development of motor and language skills.

12

Goal-Directed Behavior in Childhood

PIAGET'S FORMULATION OF INTELLIGENT BEHAVIOR
IN INFANCY

THE MECHANISMS OF INTELLIGENT BEHAVIOR

SUMMARY

IN OUR MODEL of human behavior, abilities correspond roughly to tools that are available for a job, but the tools are of no value unless the person can use them at the proper time to get his work done. As we have surveyed some of the child's skills and discussed the methods of testing his abilities, we have been primarily concerned with the description of the skills themselves. Now in this chapter we want to pay especial attention to the way these skills contribute to the attainment of the child's goals.

We shall first obtain data by examining some concrete observations upon the development of goal-directed behavior during infancy. Then we shall describe the various mechanisms by which the organism's behavior brings about an adjustment to the demands of the environment. It may be done through continued random activity, through a preset organization of habits, or through a special sort of cue that guides behavior toward its goal. In the more complex examples of guided behavior, the cognitive map of the situation serves as the guide. We shall then look at some of the special problems of guided behavior, including the difficulty presented when a detour is required and the guidance of imitative behavior. Finally, we shall discuss the general characteristics of cognitively guided behavior that distinguish it from non-guided behavior in order to see how it represents a more adequate adjustment to the vicissitudes of everyday life.

Piaget's Formulation of Intelligent Behavior in Infancy

Piaget made many observations, with his own children as subjects, on the development of intelligent behavior in infancy, employing the concept of *stages* of development. The term *stage* does not imply that behavior develops in sudden steps. In some cases there does appear to be a sudden emergence of a new pattern, but many of the stages described by Piaget are merely periods of development that merge gradually into the next stage.

The six stages of infancy may better be thought of as six basic achievements that mark the progress of the child during the period of infancy. During the first, or neonatal stage, only a limited amount of adjustment to the external demands of the environment is possible. With each succeeding stage, new types of behavior become possible for the child. He can still, however, exhibit behavior appropriate for an earlier stage; the characteristics of earlier stages do not disappear. Not every situation that confronts the child requires the most mature adjustment of which he is capable. Furthermore, a new stage is not attained simultaneously in all aspects of the child's behavior. He may be advanced in so far as reaching and grasping are concerned, but may not be at the same stage in his vocalizations.

It is possible that when any new area of motor skill emerges, regardless of when this new skill appears, it may show a fore-shortened development through all the stages. Thus, when the child first learns the skills involved in playing a pinball machine he may have to build up that skill through various stages of development which his more customary abilities went through much earlier.

The Schema

One other anticipation of the later discussion may clarify it. Piaget uses the term *schema* (plural, schemata) throughout. A schema is a unitary behavior pattern. Piaget does not believe that every action that the child makes is one that can be reliably repeated. In order for an action to be a schema, it must be a repeatable action pattern that occurs in essentially the same way every time it reoccurs and is consistently evoked in some predictable way. A knee jerk is, for example, a schema because it is repeatable every time the knee tendon is tapped with a hammer. Sucking is a schema; so is the child's turning his head toward a source of sound; so is reaching or grasping. Crooking the index finger is not necessarily a schema even though it occurs in the course of grasping an object. In order for it to be a schema it must be possible to evoke it independently. We shall see several examples in which development brings with it the independent existence of actions that were previously bound into a larger unitary pattern.

We shall also see new schemata develop from the uniting of previously independent schemata. The independent elements do not stop being schemata when they are integrated, because they can still be evoked independently, but it may be that the action when it becomes part of a larger schema is not the same as the action when it occurs independently. The thumbsucking schema, for example, is integrated with the grasping schema to permit the child to put other objects than his thumb into his mouth. Still, there are subtle differences in the hand motions when the thumb is to be sucked or when the hand is bringing an object to be sucked. Incorporation of a schema into a larger organization frequently results in a new schema that does not contain the exact schemata that entered into the combination.

Stage 1—The Neonatal Period

The first stage of infancy has already been described (see pp. 132-137) The behavior of the child is limited to the reflexlike activities that existed at birth, plus the random, restless, mass activity indicative of tension. During the first weeks following birth, some consolidation and perfection of the schemata occur. Sucking, for example, becomes more efficient and leads more rapidly to the ingestion of food (see p. 135).

Stage 2—Primary Circular Responses

A *circular response* is a behavior pattern that is self-stimulating. Sucking behavior, for example, is a response to stimulation on the inside of the mouth. If the thumb is in the mouth, it stimulates sucking. At the same time, the sucking does not get rid of the thumb, but, on the contrary, by pressing the thumb against the roof of the mouth, it makes the thumb stimulate the mouth even more intensely. The behavior results in the further intensification of the stimulation, which thus evokes a more intense response, and therefore the response is called circular. Circular responses result in the persistent continuation of some action.

The central feature of stage 2, according to Piaget, is that the child develops new behavior patterns that continue the existence of stimulation. He can, for example, during the latter part of stage 2, move his hands so that an object in them stays in view of the eyes—*i.e.,* so that he can continue to look at it. Another characteristic of the second stage is that the child learns to bring about the stimulation that starts a cycle of circular behavior. We described earlier (see p. 181) the way the child learns to put his thumb in his mouth. At that time we were interested in this behavior because it showed that thumbsucking was pleasurable activity. Now we can look at the same behavior as an example of stage 2 in infant development. The child learns a behavior pattern, thumbsucking, that initiates a circular response.

PREHENSION Let us turn to a more complicated behavior pattern that develops during stage 2: the child's ability to reach for and grasp an object when he sees it. This ability is worth a close look because reaching is considerably more important than thumbsucking in the child's later adjustments, and also because the development of prehension is an excellent example of the way various aspects of the infant's behavior gradually become coordinated.

Visually guided reaching and grasping an object seem to depend upon three more elementary schemata that must be perfected before visually guided prehension is possible. These three basic behavior patterns are: first, thumbsucking; secondly, grasping an object that touches the hand; and, thirdly, looking at an object. The first of these has been discussed. It may seem peculiar that thumbsucking has anything to do with prehension, but it does, because as soon as he has grasped an object in his hand the child commonly puts it in his mouth. This sucking of objects seems to play an important role in the development of prehension. The grasp reflex of the newborn child, an automatic grasping of an object that is pressed into the palm, is at first the same sort of circular response exemplified by sucking. Piaget has observed that even at this early stage there is a certain focus upon the grasping. Putting an object in the child's hand may stop his crying and focus him upon the new stimulation.

The first sign of progress is the gradual development of the ability to grasp an object that touches the hand, whether or not it is carefully placed in the palm. Thus, when the child accidentally touches an object, his hand movements change until he hits the object with the palm of his hand; then the grasp reflex goes into operation. The amount of fumbling gradually diminishes with further growth and practice. Finally, he is able to turn his hand and grasp an object immediately upon touching it with any part of the hand.

It is at about this point, Piaget believes, that looking enters into the picture. Looking has itself undergone a development somewhat similar to grasping. The child at first can fixate upon a light and even follow it as it moves slowly across the visual field. He exhibits a sort of focused behavior (which Piaget calls an "interest" in the light). Gradually the child learns to look at other objects, to explore contours visually. New sights continually attract his visual attention.

At this point the child begins to look at his own hands. As yet there is no evidence that looking at his hands influences hand movements; he does not move his hands so that they can be seen. Nevertheless, we see the beginning of an interaction between looking and hand movements.

At the same time thumbsucking has developed so that the child can put his hand into his mouth. This prepares the way for the coordination of grasping and sucking. The next step, as described by Piaget, appears when the child can grasp an object and put it in his mouth as soon as he touches it with his hand. This is prehension, but it occurs only when it is evoked by tactual stimulation of the hand, not by visual perception of the object. Throughout this period the interaction of looking and hand movements increases. The child still cannot guide his hands visually, but looking at his hands may increase their activity or, in other circumstances, he may be able to hold his hand still while he looks at it.

We are now ready for the coordination of the *looking-hand-movement* schema with the *grasping-sucking* schema. This first appears, according to Piaget, in the child's being able to reach for and grasp an object that is visually presented to him, but only when his hand is in the same visual field as the object. If the child sees his hand next to an object he is now able to guide his hand movements visually until he touches it; then the grasping-sucking schema takes over and the object goes into the child's mouth. The two actions do not remain separate but rather become a single reaching schema. Finally the last step is taken. The child can reach for an object anywhere in his visual field even if he cannot see his hand at the moment.

We have looked only at the high points in this process of learning to reach. The details show a much more gradual progress from one accomplishment to the other. To illustrate the slow, laborious development, let us review Piaget's observations of his son Laurent as he gradually moves into the stage of being able to direct his hand movements visually toward an object. In the case of Laurent—and Piaget emphasizes the individuality of the development of different children—this seems to have taken place through the mediation of a schema we have not yet mentioned, the mutual fingering of the hands. Laurent, like most other children, enjoyed touching his hands together, and it was one of his earlier accomplishments. After this schema had been consolidated, Piaget held an object so that the trajectory of the two hands as they came together would cause them to hit the object. Then the *grasping-sucking* schema was activated. At this point the schema of bringing his hands together was not consistently evoked by seeing an object in front of him; but by placing an object at the proper spot while Laurent was engaged in bringing his hands together, Piaget taught him to bring his hands together when he saw an object. If the object was located at the proper place, bringing his hands together resulted in his grasping it. If, however, the object was too close or too far, it was missed. Laurent gradually learned to modify his hand movements in accord with the visually perceived location of the object until he could reach for it no matter where it was.

To summarize, stage 2 is marked by an extension of the primary circular reactions. The child learns to prolong some sorts of activities and he learns to bring about such circular reactions as grasping, sucking, or looking, even when the original stimuli that evoke these reactions are not present. Before moving on to stage 3, we should notice that these observations are all further illustrations of the fact that these early schemata are just as much needs as they are skills. The circular reactions seem to be pleasurable in the sense that they reward and reinforce a process of learning.

Stage 3—Secondary Circular Reactions

In stage 2 we have seen the development of circular responses whose effect is to prolong certain types of reactions—looking, sucking, grasping, and the like. All of these responses exist in the child's repertoire of behavior patterns from birth. The primary circular responses merely make such activities the end point of various actions that the child learns.

At approximately four months of age, according to Piaget, the child acquires a new type of circular response whose effect is to prolong or to reenact some interesting new happening that is not in itself an innate activity. Suppose, for example, the child accidentally hits a suspended toy and makes it swing violently. This occurrence, the swinging, captures the child's attention and he learns to produce such swinging by hitting the suspended object. The end result of this new schema is something new in the child's repertoire. Whereas the end result of a primary circular response is some action like sucking, which the child already does, the end result of the secondary circular response is an external event that the child has never produced before. It is important to note that the "goal" of the secondary circular response is more external and remote than the end result of earlier schemata. The goal, if it can be called that, is not an activity of the child, but rather an external event.

The following observations illustrate the formation of secondary circular reactions (Piaget, 1952). When Lucienne was just over three months of age, she jolted her crib by kicking her legs violently. Some cloth dolls that were suspended from the top began to swing as the crib was jolted. Lucienne looked at them, smiled, and soon was kicking violently again. Piaget concluded that Lucienne did not begin to kick the second time in order to make the dolls move. He felt instead that she was merely being exuberant. That evening while Lucienne was lying quietly, Piaget made the dolls move gently. This immediately brought about violent kicking, but again it was impossible to say whether Lucienne was repeating the behavior which caused the movement or was merely kicking as one part of her expressions of delight.

On the next day the response was somewhat different. Piaget showed Lucienne the dolls. She immediately began the movements but without any accompanying smile. Her interest was intense and her behavior seemed purposeful. Two days later Piaget observed Lucienne busily making her dolls swing to and fro by regular leg movements. This time is seems clear that the movements are regular and intentional. An observation made when she was 3 months, 16 days, is especially clear. As soon as Piaget suspended the dolls, Lucienne began to shake them, without any smile. She made definite rhythmic thrusts of the legs with a fairly long time interval between thrusts.

About a month later, age 4 months, 17 days, a further development occurred. Piaget hung a doll above Lucienne's head; it immediately evoked the now well-established schema. This time, however, one of her legs accidentally hit the doll directly. This produced an especially violent movement that Lucienne watched delightedly. Piaget reports that Lucienne then looked at her motionless foot intently; then began the usual movements. He could tell that she was not controlling her foot because her eyes remained fixed on the dolls and she did not modify her foot movements when her father changed the position of the doll. Lucienne did, however, move her foot very slowly as though she were groping for the doll. Hereafter there seemed to be two schemata, a generalized reaction that was first established, and a more specific leg movement which occurred later but which could not yet be called a kicking schema. One observation is interesting in that it shows that more generalized behavior accompanied high excitement. When the doll was at a distance, Lucienne began the specific leg movements, but when Piaget moved it closer and closer to her face, the movements became more violent and excited and less differentiated. Beginning at five months, Lucienne seemed to be beginning to establish control over her leg movements. Even at 5 months 1 day she seemed to change her movements to accommodate to the position of the doll, but by 5 months 18 days she accommodated clearly to various positions of the doll although she was not uniformly successful in kicking it. The schema had by that time become almost a true kicking schema.

Here we see a schema actually being formed. Unlike sucking or looking at a light, it is not part of the child's original equipment. Instead it is a schema acquired by the child after the sequence is accidentally produced. There has not been sufficient research to determine just what conditions are required for such a circular reaction to be established. We can, however, understand something of the psychological meaning of such behavior when we see that the event, the movement of the doll, is obtrusive and noticeable. The stopping of the interesting and exciting movements is a kind of imposition. The presence of the doll is a suggestion or invitation. This state of affairs stimulates a child of sufficient maturity to repeat the action that originally produced the movement.

This is the first appearance, in the child's life, of a strategy for problem solving that is very frequently used later. If an adult notices that he has produced some interesting event, or especially if he suddenly finds that he has solved a problem, he will often repeat the action that he has just completed. In more complex situations we often repeat the action that solved a problem on an earlier occasion. The infant does deliberately repeat an action in order to produce a result, but the strategy probably has its origin in these simple secondary schemata. The infant is capable of this sort of behavior only under very simple conditions. Lucienne repeated her behavior when the results of the action occurred almost immediately upon beginning the behavior and stopped quite soon after the behavior ended. Had there been more delay between action and effect, or a longer period after she stopped moving her legs before the doll stopped moving, it is unlikely that a new schema would have been created. Under the right conditions, however, a new schema is created. This new schema is a repeatable, consistent response to a specific situation.

These schemata of early infancy may be used inappropriately. Lucienne capitalized on this behavior pattern in many situations, but she seemed to generalize it entirely too far. On a later occasion she began to make these leg motions after she had seen her hand move in front of her eyes. On still another occasion, she went through these same motions in front of the jack-in-the-box that had just popped out at her. Such behavior clearly shows that she did not understand the real basis of her action. She did not know how the leg motions produced the movement. It is not easy to see, however, just why she used these actions when she did and not at other times.

The question is an important one. Some actions must be detached from the situation in which they first occur in order to be useful. Hitting, kicking, looking, grasping, and similar schemata can be applied to many different objects. If the child had to make a separate discovery that each new object could be grasped, grasping would not be as usable a skill as it is. Some actions depend upon very special circumstances, on the other hand, and to perform them in inappropriate situations is only frustrating. It is clear that learning what schemata are appropriate in what situations is important, but it is not clear just how the process takes place or why the child makes the errors he does.

Stage 4 — Means-End Behavior and the Utilization of Already Established Schemata as Means to New Situations

In the next period, which may begin at about six months and which extends to approximately the end of the first year, the child shows a number of advances demonstrating an increase of the scope of his psychological world to include past and future events. He also shows the ability to employ one schema as a means to a goal. Furthermore, he begins to "explore" a new situation by applying a whole series of schemata to it.

A clear example of means-end behavior was discussed in Chapter 2— namely, reaching for an object that is hidden behind a screen (see p. 31). The appearance of one complete schema as a means to another, even when the stimuli that would evoke the second schema are not visible, is good evidence for goal-directed behavior.

The following observations (Piaget, 1952) show the sequential development of Laurent's ability to remove an obstacle in order to reach an object.

Until the age of 7 months, 13 days, Laurent had never succeeded in removing an obstacle. Piaget had tried on two previous occasions to test his ability to do so. He had shown the six-month-old infant a box of matches but had put his hand in front of them so that it blocked Laurent's reaching for the box. Laurent could see the box and reached for it but did not try to remove his father's hand. Just after the age of seven months, he showed a similar response.

At 7 months and 13 days, however, Laurent behaved quite differently. Piaget again used a box of matches as the goal and put his hand in front of it so that Laurent could not reach for the box directly. Laurent began to hit at the hand as though to knock it down or make it go away. Piaget tried the experiment again but used a pillow as a barrier. This was soft enough that it would give if Laurent hit at it. Laurent immediately hit at the pillow, lowering it until he could reach for the match box. Here is a clear example of one behavior pattern occurring as an instrumental action. Furthermore, it is interesting to note that the instrumental act itself had already been established as a schema. Laurent had already learned to hit objects to make them move; always before, however, the hitting was its own goal.

At 7 months, 28 days, Laurent used another schema as an instrumental action. Piaget presented a small bell behind the cushion. Laurent first hit the cushion as before, but then held it down with one hand while reaching for the bell with the other hand. He did the same thing to his father's hand when it was a barrier. Even when this behavior was clearly established, Laurent could not push away his father's hand when the hand was holding the goal object rather than merely blocking the way to it. At 9 months, 15 days, however, when Piaget held one end of Laurent's toy, Laurent pushed back the hand with one hand and pulled on the toy with the other.

DIFFERENTIATION OF ACTION FROM MOTIVATION What psychological changes are indicated by the ability to utilize a schema as a means to a goal? The significant change is the detachment of the schema from its original motive. This detachment appears in two different ways. First, it is possible for a schema—such as the hitting schema in the example—to be evoked although the child does not want to hit things but, instead, wants to obtain the watch. Before this time, the conditions that evoked the schema of hitting at an object involved some motivation to make the object move. Now, the hitting schema is sufficiently independent of such motivation that it can be evoked in a situation in which the motivation is to reach the object behind the obstacle.

Another sign of this detachment of the hitting schema from the customary motivation is the fact that hitting the pillow did not evoke the continued hitting of it as in a circular reaction. If hitting had set up a circular reaction, the action of hitting the pillow would have begun a repetitive activity. The behavior of hitting would have distracted the child from his original goal had there been no detachment of the action pattern from the motivation.

This separation of action and motivation is not complete, and it never becomes entirely so. In many examples of child behavior we can observe the child being distracted by an action that he began as a means of getting to some distant goal.

COMPREHENSION OF A NEW SITUATION There is additional evidence in stage 4 of the differentiation of motives from actions. Piaget (1952) reports that the child during this stage may, when he meets a new object, run through his repertoire of schemata.

Observation 136. At 0;8 (16) Jacqueline grasps an unfamiliar cigarette case which I present to her. At first she examines it very attentively, turns it over, then holds it in both hands while making the sound *apff* (a kind of hiss which she usually makes in the presence of people). After that she rubs it against the wicker of her bassinet (habitual movement of her right hand, Obs. 104), then draws herself up while looking at it (Obs. 115), then swings it above her and finally puts it into her mouth.

A ball of wool: She looks at it, turns it over, feels it, squeezes it, then lets it go, accidentally. I rest the ball on her stomach. Jacqueline draws herself up three or four times while looking at it, then feels its surface again, pulls the string while staring at it, shakes it in all directions and finally again goes *apff*.

A tin box: Jacqueline grasps it, examines it all over, feels it, then goes *apff*. Afterward she shakes it, then hears a sound when striking it. She then strikes indefinitely, then draws herself up while looking at it and striking it. Then she examines it at length from the side while holding it in the air and going *apff*. Afterward she emits some sounds such as *adda, bva,* etc., while brandishing it and turning it in all directions. Finally, she rubs it against the wicker of the bassinet again going *apff*.

At 0:9 (4) she looks for a long time at a straw table mat, then delicately touches the edge, grows bold enough to touch it, then grasps it, holds it in the air while slowly displacing it, shakes it and ends by tapping it with her other hand. This behavior is accompanied by an expression of expectation and then of satisfaction. Jacqueline finally expresses her feelings by going *apff*. Then she rubs the object against the edge of the bassinet, etc.

Originally all these schemata were evoked in specific situations in which each produced some effect that was sufficiently noticeable to be interesting and motivating. Now, they have become so detached from any one stimulus situation that in a new situation they can all appear in succession. This independence of a schema from a specific motive is a mark of maturity.

We can also see in this behavior the foreshadowing of a kind of observational curiosity that characterizes later behavior. The behavior takes place not merely to achieve some definite result, but to find out about the environment. At this time we may not be justified in calling it curiosity about the unknown, because the child's behavior may be merely the exercise of his schemata. We cannot be sure that he is showing a curiosity about the properties of the object.

Whether or not it signifies curiosity, such a sequence of schemata does provide the child with a sort of concrete functional definition of the object as suckable, throwable, or shakeable. Through the application of all these schemata to an object, its possible use as a means is enhanced. He discovers what the object can do and what he can do to it.

The consequence of the development of means-end behavior is that very complicated schemata can be developed through the combination and integration of heretofore independent schemata. Schemata can be utilized in situations quite unrelated to those in which they were first established, and in the absence of needs tied to each specific schema.

At the same time, we can see that each new schema represents a possible source of enjoyment that did not previously exist. This is most obvious in the child's playful activities when he performs an action over and over again. He seems most likely to exercise a schema that he has recently acquired, probably to consolidate the ability.

Stage 5—The Discovery of New Means by Active Experimentation

The next developmental stage, according to Piaget's analysis of infant behavior, is marked by two types of advance. First, the child deliberately varies his behavior even though the situation remains unchanged; he is interested in trying out new variations of his schemata. A second closely related ability is to discover in the course of problem solving new schemata that he had never before displayed.

The first type of advance is illustrated when Laurent is given a slippery can that accidentally falls from his hands (Piaget, 1952). Laurent, age 10 months, 2 days, began by turning the can around this way and that, passing it from one hand to the other. Because it was slippery he dropped it several times. Laurent seemed to become interested in this accidental event and began to repeat it. It was not easy at first to tell whether he was intentionally releasing the can or dropping it by accident, but gradually the dropping became more regular and frequent, making it clear what Laurent was doing.

At first he seemed to be interested in variations on a theme of letting go of the object. He opened his hand and let the can roll off. Then he turned his hand so the can fell between the thumb and index finger. Later he turned his hand palm downward, opened it and let the object fall.

At the age of 10 months, 10 days, Laurent played with a tiny chunk of bread, letting it fall many different ways. He even detached crumbs from it and let them fall one at a time. During this observation he seemed less interested in the act of letting go than in the actual fall of the object. The next evening while lying on his back he played in a similar way with other toys. At one time he held his arm up vertically to drop a toy; another time he held his arm up obliquely in front of him or behind him. When the object happened to fall in a new and interesting spot, on his ear for example, Laurent repeated that drop several times.

What characteristics are implied in Laurent's behavior? First, it is clear that the schema has become even more detached from the stimulus situation than it was in stage 4, although the major step in detaching a schema from a specific stimulus situation took place when the child became able to use a schema as a means to an end.

Secondly, this behavior shows that Laurent's goal has changed. Now, in this playful sort of situation, he is motivated to do something different from his former behavior. Play, in the earlier stages, has the basic form of practice play; schemata are repeated numerous times, apparently just for the fun of it. Newly acquired schemata are especially attractive for this sort of play. Although this form of play continues to appear throughout childhood, play in stage 5 can encompass modifications as well as repetitions of schemata. Whereas previous modifications of the schema took place under the pressure of accidental events that changed the situation, now they occur spontaneously. In other words, the child is beginning to be bored by the familiar and to explore the unfamiliar.

This is not a completely new characteristic; the child previously has been coming in contact with new things and has not been upset by them. In a sense, the playful repetition of a newly acquired schema is already a kind of enjoyment of the new. But in stage 5 curiosity and exploration seem to be more clearly expressed.

We remember that in the previous stage the child ran through his repertoire of schemata in a new situation. We could not be sure from those observations that the child was actively finding out about the properties of the external world. In stage 5, on the other hand, his curiosity is clearly evident.

THE COMPREHENSIVE SCHEMA   A consequence of this deliberate variation of behavior is to accelerate the development of a comprehensive schema closely attuned to the environment. This sort of schema is, in its final form, so different from earlier schemata that it deserves a close examination. We have seen that the earliest schemata were very specifically activated by just the proper stimulus situation and the behavior was rigid, predictable, and reflexlike. Then, as accidental variations in the results of the behavior occurred and were assimilated, new schemata appeared that were slightly different from the original. These new schemata were different with respect to the stimulus that evoked them and also different in their results.

To take a completely hypothetical illustration of such an organization of schemata, we might examine the process of tossing a ball into boxes at different distances. Because we, as adults, can empathize with the problem, it perhaps serves as a better illustration than would a more realistic example of child behavior. Suppose that we first learned to toss a ball into a specific box, a specific distance away. Then, when we saw the box at a different distance, we responded in the customary fashion and this time, of course, the ball did not fall into the box. If we tried repeatedly, however, we might accidentally succeed in hitting the box because the schema is not completely rigid—i.e., the actual throw of the ball varies somewhat even when the same schema is operating. Thus, by accident, it might be thrown more strongly and fall into a more distant box. If this were taken in and assimilated, then there would be two schemata, one resulting in a slightly more energetic throw than the other, and these would be evoked by different stimulus situations, the stronger one by a more distant box, the weaker one by the closer box. There would be considerable overlap because of the variability of the individual schema.

We might conceive of the development in this fashion of a series of independent schemata, each activated by a box at a different distance. Such a set of schemata would enable us to toss a ball into any box regardless of distance and to adjust the strength of the throw to the perceived distance of the box.

But the adult schema does not seem to have this character. It is very doubtful that we have separate schemata for throwing a ball every possible distance. Instead we seem to have a sort of comprehensive, flexible, and adjustable schema in which there is a correspondence between the continuum of distance and a continuum of strengths of throws.

When we actually perform this task as adults, we adjust the first throw to the perceived distance, then we modify our next throws in terms of the error first made. When we finally get it just right, then we say that we have the "feel" of it. From this time on, our behavior is less determined by the perceived distance of the box and is more an attempt to repeat the previously successful performance. As long as the box stays in one place we can "get in the groove." This getting into the groove is developing a separate schema that is independent, to some extent, of the comprehensive schema of adjustments to distance. It is marked by attention to the feel of the arm movements and the attempt to reproduce the feeling of the proper throw.

In other words, there is a sort of broad correspondence of throws and spatial distance. Differentiated from this general schema, there is, in addition, an especial kinaesthetic movement with an individual identity that distinguishes it from other specific throws for other specific distances. It is the broad system of movements adjusted to the continuously varying demands of the external space that was, historically, first called a schema (Head, 1921). In the adult there are many such schemata that mediate many of our adjustments—*e.g.*, pointing to any desired object that is in the visual field, motor control of all sorts, and the action patterns that mediate general locomotion from one point to another.

We can see some origins of these comprehensive schemata in infant behavior. The schema relating intensity of throwing to the distance of the object requires a proportionality between one aspect of the stimulus situation and one aspect of the response. Infants show quite early the beginnings of a sort of proportionality between the situation and the response. Laurent, for example, during stage 4, was imitating his father (Piaget, 1951). When Piaget said, "Papa," Laurent said, "Papa." When Piaget said, "Papapa," Laurent responded, "Apapa." Piaget found that as he increased the number of syllables, the child could correctly imitate him until there were four or more. When Piaget increased the number of syllables from three to four, the response was "Papapa," and for all larger numbers the response was "Papapapa." Two syllables were always repeated correctly; three or four were likely to be confused and responded to as "Papapa"; more than four were all treated alike. Such behavior reminds us of the number systems of some primitive tribes who have a word for *one,* for *two,* and then a word for *many* (Werner, 1948).

Another example of a comprehensive schema is the "body image." One of the characteristics of adults is that they keep track of their position in the external world. The schema is not infallible—a person may lose his location in the world—but people do a surprisingly good job of keeping track of their location. Yet, they do not continually think, "Now I am turning right, now I am moving forward, now I am turning left." Instead, they automatically keep track of their location and frequently know which direction is north without the necessity for any calculation.

In the same way we know surprisingly well the boundaries of our body. When we go around a corner we seldom bump into it despite the fact that we have not mentally calculated that we should head toward a point a foot away from the corner in order for our hips to clear. One of the requirements of learning to drive skillfully is to have a sort of "body image" of the car that functions like the body image itself. When this is achieved we can park the car so that the wheels are a few inches away from the curb, we can turn corners without bumping the back wheels over the curb, we can judge pretty well whether or not a parking space is too short.

Although the integration of specific schemata into a broad adjustable flexible schema is not well understood, the ability of the child in stage 5 to make slight variations in his actions and to observe their effects exhibits the transitional process of interrelating previous schemata into a broader system and, furthermore, speeds the process along by integrating many of the little variations that would not occur so soon by chance.

PROBLEM SOLVING THROUGH ACQUIRING A NEW SCHEMA This same ability to vary actions spontaneously also permits the child to develop new schemata to fit the demands of a new situation. Although the situation may at first activate schemata that are not entirely appropriate, the child can actively experiment by modification of the schema until a new modification does achieve success. It is this same characteristic that makes it possible for the child at this stage to imitate actions that he has never before done. Up to this stage, his imitation has been limited to his own repertoire of schemata.

The following observations (Piaget, 1952) illustrate the development of adaptation to a new situation:

This series of observations was concerned with Laurent's solving problems in which he had to pull a goal object toward him by pulling on the object on which the goal object rested. Until the middle of the eleventh month Laurent had failed such problems. Piaget tested him several times by showing him some object that was itself out of reach. It rested on a pillow which, however, Laurent could reach. During these tests Piaget observed that when Laurent could not reach the goal object he would frequently seize the first object his hand touched. Sometimes this was the pillow, but just as frequently it was the bedclothes in front of him.

At the age of 10 months, 16 days, however, Laurent solved the problem for the first time. Piaget put his watch on a large red pillow and put the pillow directly in front of the child. Laurent first tried to reach the watch and then grasped the pillow. When the pillow moved, Laurent apparently noticed for the first time that the watch moved with it. Now he moved the pillow back and forth, watching the watch move with the pillow. He concentrated on watching the two objects move together without reaching for the watch.

To check upon Laurent's insight into the problem, Piaget immediately arranged a more complex problem. He put two identical pillows in front of Laurent. The second was placed just beyond the first, but overlapping it a little. Piaget ironed out the overlap with his hand so that it would not be too obvious that there was a separation between the near and far pillow. As soon as Laurent saw the watch, he seized the first pillow and pulled it. But then he noticed that the watch did not move. He examined the contact point between the two pillows, and then he reached for the more distant pillow, pulled it to him by one corner, and thus attained the watch.

In these observations the child, partly because he pays attention to the objective situation and partly because he can initiate some changes on his own, is able to solve the fairly difficult problem of the relation of an object to its support. It is important to realize that as long as the child is not beyond the fifth stage, he must actually manipulate the pillows and observe the consequences before he can discover the relationship. It was only after the watch did not move that Laurent became intent upon the second pillow. The circumventing of the necessity for this overt trial-and-error procedure through anticipation depends upon visualizing the consequence of an action without actually performing it. This is one of the achievements of stage 6, which will be discussed in Chapter 13, dealing with cognition in children.

The Mechanisms of Intelligent Behavior

The title of the book in which Piaget makes these observations of the adaptive behavior of infants is *The Origins of Intelligence in Children*. When we think about intelligent behavior in adults we commonly think of problem solving. If the adult is trying to attain some goal, he uses his intelligence to plan his course of action, to circumvent obstacles, and to utilize the available tools most effectively.

Such a description of intelligent behavior presupposes considerable maturity. It assumes that the motive is already established and that the methods of attaining the goal are all that remain to be selected. When we look at the behavior of infants, it is immediately apparent that motives and the means for satisfying them are not distinct, and that we cannot find situations in which the child plans out his methods of attaining his goal. The young infant is not trying to suck his thumb or devising a method for getting his thumb into his mouth. Our usual way of thinking about intelligent behavior is too adult-centered to be meaningful when we try to describe the behavior of young children.

At the same time, the infant does have problems that he copes with in his fashion. The crying baby has a problem; when he settles down contentedly to nurse or suck his thumb he has solved it. There are some situations that stimulate the child's behavior so that the behavior changes the situation. There are other situations that do not stimulate behavior or else evoke behavior that prolongs or extends the same situation. Circular reactions are self-repetitive and self-prolonging. When the child becomes engaged in the circular reaction, he seems to be contented. He learns behavior patterns that bring him into a circular reaction. Later, he seems obviously to enjoy the repetition of a schema over and over again. These stable or repetitive situations seem to be satisfying or enjoyable, as well as we can judge from the child's behavior.

Intelligent or adaptive behavior is, therefore, the behavior that brings about one of these stable, satisfying states of affairs. Sometimes problem-solving behavior is clearly a process of escaping from pain or high tension or something unpleasant. The stable state attained by escape or avoidance of unpleasantness may be sleep or passivity. The situations that evoke a behavior pattern are not, however, always obviously unpleasant, and the stable end-states brought about by behavior are not always passive. We need a label for these stable conditions that will include both the passive ones when tension is low and the active ones that are circular and repetitive, and apparently enjoyable. Let us use the term *adaptation* to describe the condition of a person in a stable state. Now, intelligent behavior is adaptive behavior, and if it is successful it brings about a state of adaptation.

The first problem in understanding adaptive behavior is to discover the mechanisms that underlie adaptive behavior. What we ordinarily think of as problem solving or planning is merely one of these mechanisms, and a very mature one. There are at least four different adaptive mechanisms that we can observe in child behavior; if they were all conscious and deliberate, we might call them four strategies of problem solving.

Strategies of Problem Solving

The first of these is continuous random behavior until the instigation is removed, the tension is reduced, and the child is quieted. The second is a fixed predetermined behavior pattern that is released by a definite stimulus. It may be an innate response, developed in the species through processes of evolution. Coughing as a means of getting rid of a throat irritation is an example. The fixed response may be learned by the individual through the processes of habit formation, but once the habit is automatized it functions in the same way that instinctive behavior does. A third is repetition of a previously successful action. This resembles the second, of course, but is a more deliberate, voluntary kind of problem solving. The fourth is guided behavior. We shall speak of two varieties of guided behavior; first, simple feed-back, in which a single stimulus in the situation guides behavior toward the stable end-state. Fixation of the eyes, for example, or pointing the finger toward an object are examples in which a single stimulus indicates the error of adaptation and stimulates action that reduces this error. A second sort of guided behavior is cognitively guided. Here the individual has a cognitive picture of himself in relation to the goal and behaves so that he moves toward it. Since the cognitive map is based on a variety of cues, there may be cognitive guidance even when no single external stimulus is available to guide behavior from beginning to end.

Let us now look at these mechanisms individually and see how they function in the adaptive behavior of children.

Continuous Random Behavior until the Cause of Tension Is Removed

In the discussion of the concept of tension, we saw that it is evoked by stimulation and at a high level produces general undirected mass activity. Since the infant's tolerance of stimulation is not very high, a great deal of infant behavior is general restlessness.

An excellent example of this sort of random behavior is found in an observation made by Piaget reported earlier in another connection (see p. 181). The child, Laurent, is being held by his nurse just before a feeding. His mouth makes sucking movement, his head rotates and turns continuously, his arms are waving vigorously and constantly. As a result of these arm movements, his hand eventually comes into contact with his face. This contact stimulates his head to turn in that direction, but his hand does not happen to get into his mouth. Even when it does happen to get into his mouth, the arm waving does not stop immediately and he loses his thumb. Finally, however, he does capture the thumb securely and lies quietly, sucking vigorously.

The restless activity is not directed, but its continuation makes it possible for the child accidentally to reach an adjustment. The random movements eventually stop when the child finally becomes engaged in some satisfying consummatory activity, which either removes the stimulation, or at least focuses his behavior and reduces his responsiveness to the stimuli that provoked the tension.

There are innumerable illustrations of this sort of accidental success in the everyday life of children and adults. It is truly an accidental success many times, although it occurs only if the organism is. stimulated into random restless behavior. At other times, we see a more restricted sort of random movement that is not guided toward a goal, but that does increase the probability of accidental success. Thus, in another observation on Laurent (see p. 182), we saw that after he had once gotten his hand in contact with his mouth, the restless movements became less vigorous so that his hands stayed close to his mouth. Now the probability of an accidental contact is increased, so the thumb gets into his mouth sooner than it would have otherwise.

Habitual or Instinctive Response to Instigating Situation

A second sort of mechanism that may bring about the achievement of an adapted response is a fixed automatic response to some stimulus pattern. The phrase used by some animal psychologists to describe this sort of behavior is very apt. They say the response is "released" by the stimulus. This phrase suggests that the behavior pattern is predetermined. The stimulus releases it but it does not guide it or affect the form of the response. Many of the behavior patterns of young infants illustrate this mechanism. The pursing of the lips when they are touched is one example. The grasp response is another. Later, when the infant repeats an action that has produced an interesting result, the response is predetermined. It is not guided to produce the result but is released by the appropriate stimulus. Despite the fact these responses are not guided by the stimulus that evokes them, they frequently lead to adaptation. The releasing stimulus occurs many times as part of the situation to which the fixed response is an adjustive pattern of behavior. But the response occurs just as inevitably when the releasing stimulus occurs outside of the situation in which the response is appropriate.

Some of the most striking examples of this sort of instinctive behavior are described in Tinbergen's (1951) observations of the behavior of animals. The female goose, for example, responds to a certain sort of noise ordinarily made by a gosling in distress by attacking the intruder. The goose also responds to certain stimuli that indicate a different species by attacking the stranger. Lorenz (1952) reports that he observed a mother goose respond to the distress call of a young goose of a different species. The distress call evoked protective behavior. The goose came flying to the rescue, attacked the invader, and saved the life of the young bird. Then the mother goose turned and looked at the young bird. Now the stimuli for "stranger" became effective; and the goose attacked and killed the young bird that she had just defended.

The behavior can thus be seen not to depend upon an actual cognition of "my baby in danger." It was obvious even when the mother was coming to its defense that the young bird was not of the same species. Instead, the defensive behavior is evoked by a specific key stimulus and is not modified by other perceptible aspects of the situation. Later, the attack behavior was released by a different key stimulus.

The effectiveness of such a mechanism depends upon the fact that in the natural habitat of the goose the distress call is a reliable indication of the goose's own young in trouble. Only rarely is this automatic response maladaptive in a natural environment. Of course, psychologists investigating response mechanisms constantly plot to make instinctive behavior maladaptive. They may evoke elaborate courting behavior in a male fish by presenting him with a crude wooden stick that has a bulging red protuberance. The red bulge is the releasing stimulus and is ordinarily found on a receptive female (Tinbergen, 1951).

The automatized habit of the human being strongly resembles the instinctive mechanism, except that it is the result of learning. Much human behavior is habitual; even behavior that is originally guided and goal directed may become automatized (see p. 454). Each of us habitually puts on the same shoe first. In terms of the end result of getting both shoes on, either one could come first as well as the other. Nevertheless, each man customarily takes just one of the two possible sequences. The concept of habit describes this rigidity.

The common-sense idea of habit has never been better described than by William James (1890):

The marksman sees the bird, and before he knows it he has aimed and shot. A gleam in his adversary's eye, a momentary pressure from his rapier, and the fencer finds that he has instantly made the right parry and return. A glance at the musical hieroglyphics, and the pianist's fingers have rippled through a shower of notes. And not only is it the right thing at the right time that we thus involuntarily do, but the wrong thing also, if it be an habitual thing. Who is there that has never wound up his watch on taking off his waistcoat in the daytime, or taken his latchkey out on arriving at the doorstep of a friend? Persons in going to their bedroom to dress for dinner have been known to take off one garment after another and finally to get into bed, merely because that was the habitual issue of the first few movements when performed at a later hour. . . . In action grown habitual, what instigates each new muscular contraction to take place in its appointed order is not a thought or a perception, but the sensation occasioned by the muscular contraction just finished. A strictly voluntary act has to be guided by idea, perception, and volition, throughout its whole course. In habitual action, mere sensation is a sufficient guide. . . .

James puts his finger accurately on habit's distinguishing characteristic: it seems to be a response to a limited aspect of the situation without any guidance toward a goal. He also indicates another characteristic of the habit: it is action performed in the usual, customary way.

An example from child behavior of the functioning of habitual response when the behavior ought to be guided by the immediate situation sometimes occurs in one of the common intelligence tests. The child is asked to repeat digits, perhaps 4-2-5-9-3. Some children will respond 4-2-5-6-7. The digit 5 seems to set off the habitual counting behavior, 5-6-7-8-9, so that the memory of the last two numbers does not guide the response of the child. It is almost as though some button had been pushed and the counting automatically occurred. The response was not guided by the requirements of the situation, as in goal-directed behavior, but instead the appropriate stimulus, 5, released a fixed sequence of responses that were not relevant to the demands of the test.

A habit may contain within it guided behavior. It is an automatic response to some releasing stimulus, but once released it may then be directed toward a goal. The example James used of the marksman was habitual in the sense that the sight of the bird released the behavior, but was guided in that the pointing of the gun was accurately governed by the position of the bird in space. People may end up in bed when they start out merely to change clothes for dinner, but they accurately guide their behavior within the sequence—the coat is placed on the hanger, the hanger is guided to the rod in the closet, the person reclines accurately on the bed.

REPETITION OF A SUCCESSFUL ACTION   Habits are learned because they are reinforced—*i.e.,* they lead to success. But habit formation is usually a lengthy process requiring a number of repetitions. It can happen, however, that a person immediately repeats an action that resulted in some reward. We saw excellent examples of this sort of behavior in the secondary circular reaction (see p. 303). We also saw, when Jacqueline bounced in front of her jack-in-the-box (see p. 305), that such behavior may go astray. Here we have behavior that is not guided toward a goal, but nevertheless is not an automatic response to certain simuli. The child frequently follows the pattern of repeating successful actions even when the situation requires something different from the customary behavior. He is prone to repeat some phrase or action that worked once, without looking to see if it still will work. A six-year-old loves to tell jokes and ask riddles; he also loves just as much to ask the same riddle over and over again. Somehow the idea that the riddle is worn out once the answer is known doesn't seem to impress him.

Simple Guidance of Behavior

The third mechanism that may underlie the achievement of an objective is true guidance of behavior. In order for guided behavior to occur, there must be some cue in the situation that indicates how far the individual is from achieving his goal; furthermore, this cue must be a stimulus that can evoke behavior that brings the individual closer to achieving his goal. Instead of a fixed response released by a stimulus, we see here a system of responses—learned ones—in which the external cue controls the choice of response. The system functions in such a way that the response furthers the state of adaptation.

We can see examples of this sort of guidance in Piaget's description of the development of prehension (see p. 301): *e.g.,* the child can reach for the object only when he can simultaneously see his hand and see the object. Here the perception of the hand in relation to the object presents a clear stimulus that can serve as the guide to behavior. If the child reduces the distance between the hand and the object, he will eventually reach it. He cannot reach for the object without seeing his hand because he does not yet have his tactual space coordinated with his visual space. He doesn't know what it feels like to put his hand at a point that is visually indicated. That coordination is achieved in the next stage.

Visually guided prehension is not the earliest example of simple guidance. There is probably true guided behavior when the child can put his thumb in his mouth, regardless of where the thumb is to begin with; and when he can fixate and follow a slowly moving light, his behavior is apparently guided by stimuli. We do not know just what these stimuli are or how the mechanism functions.

Cognitively Guided Behavior

SIMPLE FEED-BACK VS. COMPLEX COGNITIVE GUIDANCE   The goal-directed behavior illustrated in the development of visual prehension is a case of simple feed-back. There is some immediately perceivable cue that indicates the relation of the person himself to his goal. In this case it is the distance between the hand and the object.

The more complex varieties of guided behavior demand more maturity because there may be no single stimulus to guide behavior from beginning to end. When we go from one room in a house to another, the stimuli that guide one portion of the path may be quite different from those that guide other portions of it.

It seems, instead, that we have a cognitive map of the entire house and that we have located ourselves in that map. As we move along we can, at any point, indicate our position in the cognitive picture. Thus, we are provided with a cognitive indication of the relation of the self to the goal object. This cognitive indication is based upon numerous cues, not the same ones at each point. In other words, there is no single guiding stimulus feed-back; instead, there is a cognitive picture that integrates the many stimuli to provide a cognitive guide for action.

When does cognitive guidance first appear in the life of the child? One indication of it is means-end behavior. When the child first removes a barrier and then reaches for the hidden toy, the guidance of the first part of the action depends upon one set of cues; the guidance of the last part of the behavior depends on other cues. Any behavior guided toward an invisible goal must be an example of complex guidance.

THE DETOUR PROBLEM   Kohler (1926), in one of his experiments with animals, placed the animal inside a U-shaped fence close to the bottom of the U, as shown in Figure 12.1. Food was placed on the other side of the fence, which was transparent but impassable. The animal could see the food, but the only way to get to it was to go around the end of the fence. This meant that the animal had to move away from the food in order to get to it. This problem was impossible for some species of animals. The problem becomes more difficult if the animal is quite hungry; he seems to be psychologically compelled to remain physically close to the food and unable to move away from it, even though he can obtain it only by moving away.

The difficulty in a detour problem is related to problems of guidance. We might say that the simple guidance of behavior governed by sight of the goal object is in conflict with a more complex cognitive guidance of behavior. In many sorts of guided behavior the guiding cue is actually the same as the cue that brings information about the goal object. In other words, the guiding cue to behavior is also the stimulus that instigates motives. The path by which

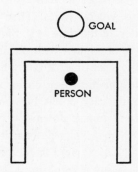

Fig. 12.1 A detour problem.

information reaches the individual corresponds to the path he can follow to reach the goal. The nearer the goal object is, the stronger the instigation.

When, therefore, the goal object is very close and the individual is strongly motivated, but when the path to the goal does not correspond to the direction of the goal object, the problem is difficult. The person is strongly impelled to follow his visual path to the goal; but if his behavior is guided by a correct cognitive picture, he will go around the detour even if this takes him further away from the goal momentarily.

Children often have difficulty with detour problems. Woodcock (1941) gives the following example:

A similar example is the habit of the younger Two's on arriving at the closed playroom door, to cluster as near to it as possible, usually pressing both hands against it, a move making necessary the herding back of the whole group before the door can be opened. It is only the older members of the group who early get in mind that this familiar door opens toward them and they must stand a little distance back from it to allow it to swing open.

This situation is different from the original experimental situation in that the door is not transparent. In other words, the pressing against the door to get through it is behavior directed toward a remote object, the playroom invisible behind the door. Yet, despite this sign of maturity, the children delayed their eventual entrance into the room by crowding so close to the door that it could not be opened. There was something compelling about the straight-line pathway into the room.

An amusing variation of the detour problem was observed by Lewin

(1935) in a nursery-school play group. This is the problem of a young child discovering how to sit down on an object (a stone, in this instance). His difficulty in sitting down on a predetermined spot lies in the fact that he must turn around so that he faces away from it in order to sit on it. In his first attempts the child marches up to the stone and then goes into a sitting position but does not contact the stone. He tries this several times. Then he tries to back up to the stone, looking over his shoulder all the time at it. Since his neck will not twist a full 180 degrees, the direct visual contact with the stone makes him sit down at one side of it. This happens several times. Finally he discovers a way to make the visual line between him and the stone correspond to the behavioral path that sets him on it. He bends over, looks between his legs, and thus is able to back up directly to the stone and sit down.

This behavior illustrates the difficulty in making a detour; it also illustrates the need for visual guidance of motor activities. Here the detour demands not the moving away from the goal but the looking away from it. It is like the original detour experiment in that it was the fact that the goal was visually close which made the detour difficult. Visual contact does not seem to be properly distinguished from behavior contact with the goal (see p. 72).

Another kind of behavior frequently observed in children illustrates the importance of this visual contact. A boy was waiting for relatives to come for a visit. They were expected momentarily. They would come around the corner at the end of the block on which the boy lived. For at least fifteen minutes before they could be reasonably expected, he was stationed at the window looking in the direction from which they would come. Then, as the time for their arrival came closer, he became more and more fidgety, finally leaving the house and going down to the corner where they would turn. From this vantage point he could see their car while it was still a block or two away, probably one minute earlier than he would have seen it had he remained at the window. When they did come, he was half a block away from the house, so that by the time he had run back to the house, the rest of the family had already greeted the visitors at the car. Here again is a substitution of visual contact for a more realistic sort of contact with the expected guests. This tendency was very compelling; the mild teasing the boy received to the effect that his watching would not make the guests come more quickly was accepted but had no effect upon his behavior.

To summarize, we see in the detour problem a conflict between a simple and a more complex guidance of behavior. Much of the goal-directed behavior of the young child is merely a matter of reaching out for goals or going directly after them. All of these depend upon simple guidance. Problem solving in more complicated situations, however, demands detours, patience, and other characteristics of maturity.

Guidance of Imitative Behavior

The goal-directed behavior described thus far has been primarily concerned with obtaining an object. Many of the goals of ordinary life are quite different. The child tries to screw a jar lid onto a jar, to add a column of figures, to hit a baseball with a bat. Here the attainment of a goal is not a matter of approaching it physically but, rather, one of performing an action in the proper way. Some of the problems of guiding behavior can be seen in observations about imitation. In order to imitate an action, the child must make his behavior conform to a pattern.

It is not easy to determine just how early imitation can occur, because even in earliest infancy crying is a contagious behavior. The crying of a baby in the hospital nursery frequently stimulates general crying by many babies. Probably the reason for the contagion is that all the babies are on a similar schedule; when one is awakened by hunger, the others are nearly ready to awaken also. The first cries of one arouse the others and soon they all cry, not in imitation of the first but each because of his own tension. Piaget observed that contagious crying during stage 2 is not only started when another baby begins crying but also may stop when the other baby quiets. He also noted other kinds of vocalization in response to noises.

The child in stages 2 and 3 is able to imitate only those actions that he himself has done and that he has perceived himself doing. If a child has a certain schema and has perceived it in action, the perception of a pattern that closely resembles his perception of his own schema is sufficient to evoke that schema. All that is necessary is that the performance of the action by the child himself produce stimuli that are perceived by the child in the same way in which he perceives the model.

The following pair of observations illustrates the point (Piaget, 1951):

> At 0:6(22) J did not imitate the gesture of opening and closing a hand.—at 0:7(22) she imitated a general movement of the fingers with the hand kept still but she neither imitated a new individual movement of the fingers such as raising the forefinger nor the action of opening and closing the hand. The reason appears to be that she often moved her fingers spontaneously whereas she only opened and closed her hands as part of more complex activities such as grasping. Similar reactions at 0:8(1).
>
> At 0:8(13) I observed that she alternatively opened and closed her right hand, watching it with great attention as if this movement, as an isolated schema, was new for her. I made no experiment at this point, but the same evening I showed her my hand as I opened and

closed it rhythmically. She thereupon imitated the movement, rather awkwardly, but quite distinctly.

The necessity for the child both to have isolated the schema and to have seen it in action is indicated by these observations. This theory, incidentally, does not originate with Piaget. It has previously been developed by Allport to account for learning words (1924). The child hears the word he says and it sounds like the word the parent says when some object is present. The fact that each of us can hear his own voice in much the same way that he hears other people's voices makes it much easier to learn to talk. The difficulty in teaching a deaf child to talk shows how great is the handicap of not being able to hear one's own voice.

Stage 4 is characterized by the ability to imitate actions that are already in the child's repertoire of schemata but that are not perceivable by him in the same way that the model is perceived. The laborious way the child moves from the known to the unknown is shown in the following observations (Piaget, 1951):

> At 0:8(4) J was moving her lips as she bit on her jaws. I did the same thing and she stopped and watched me attentively. When I stopped, she began again, I imitated her, she again stopped and so it went on. . . .
> At 0:8(9) I put out my tongue in front of J, thus resuming the experiment interrupted at 0:8(3) which up till then had given only negative results. At first J watched me without reacting, but at about the eighth attempt, she began to bite her lips as before, and at the ninth and tenth she grew bolder and thereafter reacted each time in the same way.
> At 0:8(12) same reaction. At 0:8(13) she put out her tongue biting it as she did so. When I imitated her she seemed to imitate in return, watching my tongue very carefully. But from the next day onward until 0:9(1) she again began to bite only her lips when I put out my tongue at her without her having done so. Biting the lips thus seemed to her the adequate response to every movement of someone else's mouth.
> At 0:9(2) however, J put out her tongue and said ba-ba at the same time. I quickly imitated her and she began again laughing. After only three or four repetitions, I put out my tongue without making any sound. J looked at it attentively, moved her lips and bit them for a moment, then put out her tongue several times in succession without making any sound. After a quarter of an hour, I began again, and then about half an hour later. Each time she again began to bite her lips, but a moment later put out her tongue.

The process by which Jacqueline discovered the movement that copied the model is quite clear from these observations. It was difficult for her to separate biting her lips from sticking out her tongue. The sound, "ba-ba," however, because it was perceivable by the child, was easily differentiated from sticking out her tongue and was quickly eliminated when Piaget put out his tongue without making the sound.

With the later part of stage 4 and stage 5, the child becomes able to imitate new models, which do not correspond to any schemata that have been previously differentiated out of the child's own behavior. This ability to imitate corresponds to the previously described systematic variation of a schema so that new adjustive schemata can be developed in the face of a problem.

Effectiveness of Cognitively Guided Behavior

In the more complex kinds of goal-directed behavior and in the imitation of a complex model that requires a new coordination of the parts of the body, some sort of cognitive guidance of behavior seems to be necessary. In order for cognitive guidance to occur, the cognitive picture has to be clear, objects must be differentiated from each other, and parts of the body must be cognitively distinguished from each other. The person must recognize what specific combination or sequence of actions is required by the situation; he must also be able to perform his repertoire of activities in any combination or sequence that the situation demands.

Cognitively guided behavior is not always more effective than the more automatic and reactive type of behavior based upon guidance by single stimuli or upon habitual behavior patterns, but it does have certain characteristics that are highly advantageous in certain circumstances. Let us first look at a few examples of behavior that are not cognitively guided and that are more effective than they would be if they were not automatic.

The details of a motor performance are rarely cognitively guided. Good athletes can seldom tell in precise terms what they do. To some football players it seems as though they just hold out a football and kick it. The detailed coordination that makes such an athlete a good punter may be unknown to him, and he may even lose coordination if he pays too much attention to these details.

Many of us can tie our ties quite adequately, but we may have great difficulty in visualizing just how the tie turns and bends if we trace it through the knot. How many people know whether the part of the knot that is visible is closer to the narrow end of the tie or to the wider end?

These examples show behavior that is efficiently performed but, in its details at any rate, is not cognitively guided or cognitively clear. In contrast, we can think of many types of behavior that are quite clear cognitively. Where is the light switch in your living room? Where is low on your car's gear shift? If eight boys had seven apples each. how many would there be altogether?

The behavior that is required to answer these questions is ordinarily quite clear. Most of the behavior that we deliberately decide to carry out is cognitively clear. Automatic behavior and the detailed sequence of actions within units of behavior are usually unclear and not cognitively guided.

Requirements for Cognitively Guided Behavior

Having seen several examples of action based upon cognitively unclear cues and, on the other hand, several examples of cognitively guided behavior, we can now state the distinction in more formal terms. When the external situation is clearly perceived and clearly understood, it seems that the relationship of each part of the situation to its causes and its effects is itself clearly recognized. If some part of the situation is a cue or a sign, its relationship to what it signifies is clear. In other words, our cognitive map (see p. 123) of the situation contains many separate parts; the function each part plays in the whole is represented in our cognition of the situation.

Take, for example, the difference between a cognitively clear and unclear understanding of the same problem. If we drive a car up a slope in icy weather, it may slow down and barely creep along. Most of us have but little understanding of the physical principles underlying this phenomenon. In our usual driving, the slowing of the car to five or ten miles per hour makes us want to shift to second. This is usually correct because when the car is going so slowly we need more power to speed up; this power is obtained by shifting gears. This is not to say that the relationship of power to gears is cognitively clear; we automatically shift gears when the speed gets too low. On ice it happens that this adjustment is not the correct one. The car's slow speed on an icy hill signifies not that there is too little power, but instead that the wheels are skidding. What is needed is to get the wheels rolling instead of skidding. Too much power on the wheels only makes them skid more. What we must do is to put so little power on the wheels that it will not reduce the very small friction between the tires and the ice. The car should just barely creep along and very, very gradually increase in speed. For the person to whom the situation is cognitively clear the cues indicating skidding have a definite meaning. The power on the wheels and the friction of the wheels on the ice are both included as elements in his cognitive map, as well as the relation between the two. He can reason what to do. For the rest of us, to whom these cues are not clearly related to their meaning, the situation as a whole makes us want to shift gears and step on the gas.

To take another example of the difference between cognitive clearness and unclearness, we might contrast the perception of the sound of a symphony orchestra by the usual listener and by a skilled symphony conductor. To the usual listener, the sound is a totality. He can recognize that different instruments are playing and in some parts of a symphony can recognize a specific instrument. To the conductor, however, the picture is much clearer. Even when the entire orchestra is playing simultaneously, he can recognize the various sections and know what theme is being played by each. He can perceive the parts distinctly separated from each other, perhaps as distinctly as most of us perceive each piece of furniture in a room.

We have seen that cognitive guidance is not always efficient. We must, however, recognize two important characteristics that distinguish it from impulsive or automatic behavior and that make it efficient under some circumstances. The first is that cognitively guided behavior is less rigid and more amenable to relearning than is behavior that is not guided by cognitive understanding. The second is that a clear cognitive picture can be put into words and verbally communicated to other people. Therefore, cognitively guided behavior can be learned through verbal instruction. You cannot produce or change a conditioned response through verbal instruction.

Flexibility of Cognitively Guided Behavior

If our picture of the external world is clear, if all the details are represented, then we shall recognize any lack of correspondence between the picture and the reality it supposedly represents. Furthermore, the aspects of our expectation that do not correspond to reality will be identifiable.

Let us return, for a moment, to the example of the symphony orchestra. Suppose the bassoon section were making a mistake that should be corrected. The usual listener is, in the first place, not so sensitive as the skilled conductor to the fact that a mistake is being made. If all he hears is the total sound, the effect of one small part may not be very noticeable. Even if he recognizes that the music does not sound exactly right, how could the untrained listener know what to do about it? He could say that it was not right, but he could not describe even to himself what about it was wrong. It would take him a long time to isolate the difficulty. The conductor who heard the same music in a well-differentiated way would, however, be able to point to the bassoon section and know that the trouble lay there. He could correct the mistake much more rapidly.

In general, the person whose behavior is determined by the "feel" of the situation finds it difficult to do anything other than follow his feelings. Even when he has made a mistake and thus knows that his intuitive grasp is in some way inadequate, he still has no notion of how to change his behavior except as he laboriously relearns and achieves an intuitive feel of the changed situation. In contrast, the person whose behavior is clearly cognitively guided finds it much easier to diagnose the difficulty and change his behavior appropriately.

The importance of cognitively clear understanding for the flexibility of response to new situations has been experimentally demonstrated. One of the classical experiments on the transfer of training was performed by Judd (1908). He trained two groups of boys to thrust a stick at the bull's-eye of an underwater target. Because of the distortion of the water, this task required some learning. In the first part of the experiment the target was 12 inches beneath the surface. One group of boys was given practice on the task without any instruction. The other group was told about the principles of refraction. The two groups were allowed to practice to a prescribed level of efficiency. There was not much difference in the rate of learning of the two groups. When, however, the task was changed so that the target was only 4 inches under water, the group that had not been taught the general principle showed a marked decrease in accuracy; it took them almost as long to learn the new task as to learn the original. The group who had been taught the principles, on the other hand, relearned the new task quickly. Many other experiments along this general line have shown the importance of a clear understanding of the objective situation for effective transfer to a changed situation.

The amenability of cognitively guided behavior to verbal instructions is well illustrated in an experiment by Deiter (1954). He studied the emotional response of subjects to various stimuli through the galvanic skin response. If a person becomes apprehensive or expectant, the resistance of his skin to an electric current decreases, and this change can be measured electrically. This decrease is called the galvanic skin response and is denoted by GSR.

Deiter based part of his experiment on a previous one by Lazarus and McCleary (1949). He showed the subject twelve nonsense syallables, one at a time, and repeated this procedure over and over again as many times as was necessary. Six of these twelve syllables were "shock" syllables. Every time a shock syllable was presented to the subject, he received an electric shock that was strong enough to be noticeable and perhaps cause apprehension. Gradually, the subject began to respond to the shock syllables with a galvanic skin response even before the shock was applied. We might say the galvanic skin response was conditioned to the six shock syllables. Or we might say that the subjects recognized the syllables, expected the shock when they saw the shock syllables, became expectant or apprehensive, and produced a GSR. After this GSR to shock syllables was very stable and consistent, the subject then proceeded to the second part of the experiment.

In this part of the experiment the twelve syllables were presented to the subject, but, instead of being clearly visible, they were presented for a very small fraction of a second. In some cases the exposure time was so short that the subject could not say what the syllable was. Deiter found, as had Lazarus and McCleary, that even when the subject could not read the syllable, he would show a greater GSR to the shock syllables than to the non-shock syllables. In other words, the GSR was a response that could be evoked even without a clear cognition of the syllable or a conscious awareness of what syllable it was.

Deiter, however, made one change in the experiment. Before he began the second part of the experiment, he gave the subject verbal instructions that contradicted the preceding experience. He told the subject that from that point on, he would receive a shock only on the syllables that had previously been non-shock words and would not receive a shock on the syllables for which he had previously been shocked. He was interested in whether the previous conditioning or the verbal information would determine which syllables would elicit the GSR. What he found was that the response depended upon whether or not the subject could clearly perceive the syllable. When the syllable was presented so quickly that the subject could not read it, he responded to the previously shocked syllables with a GSR. On the other hand, when the subject could read the syllable (*i.e.,* when it was cognitively clear), his GSR appeared on syllables that he had been told would be shock syllables. Thus, in this experiment, behavior that is based upon a clear cognition of the situation is more amenable to verbal instruction than is a response that occurs without clear cognition of the situation.

Communicability of Cognitively Guided Behavior

The second characteristic of a clear cognitive picture is that it is much more communicable than is one's intuitive appreciation of a situation. When the parts of a field and the relations among the parts are all clearly cognized or represented in the cognitive map, they can be given names. The verbal description contains the same differentiations as the cognition itself. When the cognition is vague it is almost impossible to put it in words; the most effective way of communicating the idea is to give a concrete example that embodies the discrimination that is to be conveyed.

We have evidence of the vagueness of children's cognition when we listen to their attempts to communicate their understanding to another person. Piaget (1926) investigated this problem by showing a child the diagram of a stopcock shown in Figure 12.2. He explained it to the child as follows:

1. Look, these two pictures (I and II) are drawings of a tap.

2. This here is the handle of the tap.

3. To turn it on, look, you have to do this with your fingers (move the finger on diagram I and show the result on diagram II). Then it is like this (diagram II).

4. You see when the handle is turned on like this (point to *a* and make horizontal movement) then the canal (point to *b*, call it also the little hole, door, or passage) is open.

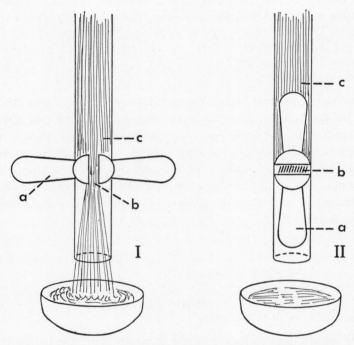

Fig. 12.2 A typical drawing of a stopcock used to test communication between children. (After J. Piaget, *The Language and Thought of the Child*)

5. Then the water runs out (point to *b* in diagram I).

6. It runs out because the canal is open.

7. Look here (diagram II) when the handle is turned off (point to *a* and make a vertical movement) then the canal (point to *b*; can also be called the hole or door or passage) is also shut.

8. The water can't get through, you see (point to *c*). It has stopped.

9. It can't run out because the canal is closed.

Here is one boy's (age 6 years, 3 months) explanation to another child (Piaget, 1926):

> You see this tap, when the handle is straight like this (*a*, Diagram I) lying down, you see the little pipe has a door and the water can't get through (He has moved to diagram II by this time) then the water doesn't run, the door is shut. Then you see here (Diagram I) you find the little door and then the water comes into the basin and then the two sides of the handle (*a*) are like that then the water can run and then the pipe is like that (*b* in diagram II) then there is no little door then the water can't find the little door. Then the water stays here (*c*, diagram II). When the tap is on there is a little pipe, then the water can get through and the handle, oh well the handle is lying down (*a*, diagram I) whereas here the little pipe is straight, (diagram II) the handle is straight and the little pipe (*b*) is lying down.

Obviously this boy's understanding is not completely vague. He has some idea of the function of the "little pipe." For him it seems that the relations *straight* and *lying down* are vague and interchangeable; yet it is upon the distinction between the two that the whole explanation depends. We should point out that vague cognition is not the only reason for children's confusing explanations. Part of the trouble is his lack of knowledge of words and part of it is his failure—through egocentricity—to appreciate how the explanation sounds to a listener.

Summary

This chapter has been concerned with the processes by which a child reaches a goal. In early infancy a motive cannot be distinguished from the behavior that satisfies it, but gradually during infancy the child becomes able to select a goal and to try out various methods of attaining it.

The stages of goal-directed behavior during infancy have been described by Piaget. During stage 1, the infant's behavior consists only of innate reflex mechanisms. Stage 2 introduces primary circular reactions, and the child behaves in a way that prolongs them. These circular responses seem to be primitive sorts of goals, and the child in stage 2 learns how to attain them. In stage 3, we find secondary circular reactions; the child learns how to repeat an action that produced some interesting, exciting result. In this fashion new schemata are constantly established. In stage 4, we find the first combining of schemata so that one is a means to the other. In stage 5, there are spontaneous variations of schemata, and the child can invent or discover a new schema as a means to solving a problem. At this stage, however, trial and error are still overt.

In these observations we can see four mechanisms of adjustive behavior: (1) continuous random activity until the cause of tension is accidentally removed; (2) a fixed response released by some stimulus present in the situation (this mechanism may be innate or it may be habitual); (3) repetition of a previously successful action; (4) behavior guided by cues from the goal. Guidance may be simple, as in the reaching or eye fixation of infants, wherein some stimulus serves as a guiding cue. When there is no single external stimulus to guide action, the individual's cognitive map may integrate all the external information in the situation in order to guide goal-directed behavior.

We have seen that some goal-directed behavior actually consists of physically approaching a goal. Other kinds of goals occur, however. When the child is trying to imitate a pattern, his goal is to make his behavior conform to the pattern. Here the details of the guidance of behavior are more obscure, but the same general mechanisms can be described.

We have examined the characteristics of cognitively guided behavior. It is not always a more efficient behavior pattern in a stable situation, but it does have the advantage of being flexible in changing situations, and a cognitively clear understanding can be communicated. Cognitively guided behavior can, therefore, be acquired through verbal instructions.

13

Cognition in Childhood

COGNITION IN INFANCY

CONCEPTUAL THINKING IN THE
PRESCHOOL PERIOD

LANGUAGE DEVELOPMENT

SUMMARY

WE HAVE LEFT to the last what is perhaps the most complex problem of child behavior, the child's perception and cognition of the external world and his understanding of the nature of the physical and social environment that surrounds him.

Let us return for a moment to the description of cognition in Chapter 6. A cognitive picture is a representation of the external world. In it the objects of the world are represented, their relations to each other in space are pictured, and their properties are indicated. Also, the person himself is pictured in the cognitive map. We saw in the last chapter that cognition of one's own person is necessary for guided behavior of the more complex varieties.

This cognitive picture is one's conception of the situation confronting him at the moment. At this moment I cognize the typewriter in front of me, the desk to one side, the window beyond. Further, I can fit this room into the broader picture of the world. In my cognitive map are routes to distant places, other parts of town, other towns, and other countries. All of this, if present, is my cognition of the present situation.

I have other knowledge as well that is not represented in my present situation. I know, for example, that if I dropped a ball from a tower it would fall. I can picture that fall in my imagination. Such a picture is not part of my cognition of the present situation, because I do not know where a ball is being dropped from a tower. It is not connected with my present situation. Not all my mental pictures are part of my cognitive map. This knowledge about how balls act when dropped, the relation between the various numbers in the number system—all such knowledge is not useless. It plays an important role in the formation or construction of my cognitive map, and it may on occasion contribute to my cognitive map. If I see a ball dropped from a tower I search for it on the ground beneath. My cognitive picture of its location is partly determined by my knowledge or understanding of the fact that objects fall to the ground.

Thus, we see that the cognition of the situation is a resultant of the physical stimuli from the external world acting upon an organism that has certain properties that make an accurate cognitive picture possible. Some of these properties are the perceptual sensitivity of the person, his visual acuity, his maturity, and his understanding of the properties of physical space, cause and effect, and interpersonal relations. We cannot list all the properties of the person that are relevant to his cognition.

In this chapter we shall emphasize three sorts of development during childhood. First, we shall examine what little evidence there is about the perception of young infants and see how the child's perceptual acuity and sensitivity changes. Secondly, we shall see how the infant develops his understanding of physical space so that he perceives objects as located in space, how he recognizes that they are independent of his own person and have a permanent existence even when he is not perceiving them. In addition, he comes to recognize that external objects are subject to external cause-and-effect relationships. This development corresponds roughly to the period of infancy and parallels the development of goal-directed behavior as described in the preceding chapter. Thirdly, we shall examine the development in the older child of concepts and understanding of the abstract properties of classification and number. The school-age child can recognize that a dozen of eggs always contains the same number of eggs, whether they are arranged in three rows of four, piled in a heap, or distributed one to a nest. His acquiring of this concept of number will illustrate the process of understanding the external world that is behind so much of the complex problem solving and goal-directed behavior of adults.

Cognition in Infancy

The Perception of the Neonate

People have frequently speculated about what the world looks like to the newborn child. Some have pictured perceptual apparatus as a camera that accurately records the incoming stimuli. The child may lack understanding of the picture, his actions may be immature and poorly coordinated, but the reception is clear. Others have pictured the baby's view as a "big blooming buzzing Confusion" (James, 1890). Still others have pictured the child's world as a sort of vague totality in which sights and sounds and touches are indistinguishable; objects are not separated from each other; everything is fuzzy and unclear.

The evidence for any view about the qualities of the child's subjective experience is almost impossible to obtain. It is more realistic to ask how the child's perception affects his behavior rather than how the world looks to him. We can study his discriminations and the behavioral adjustments that depend on cognition.

Sensitivity of the Neonate to Stimuli

There is no doubt that the newborn child can see, but it is not at all clear what he can see. His ability to distinguish colors is doubtful. It is even more doubtful whether he can distinguish forms. For one thing, there are frequently hemorrhages of the retina that cloud vision, and the eyeball is so shaped that clear vision is unlikely. It also seems that the accommodation mechanism to permit clear vision of objects at various distances is not functional at birth. He can respond, however, to different intensities of light. There is considerable evidence to show that the neonate is quieted by moderate light as compared with darkness. It suggests that the presence of a visual stimulus focuses his responsiveness and leads to a decreased responsiveness in other respects.

Although there is still some doubt about the sensitivity of the neonate to sound, the existence of hearing has been reasonably well demonstrated. Possibly there is some relative insensitivity during the first few days. It is doubtful whether he can discriminate among pitches of sound. He does, however, respond differently to different intensities of sound. Just as with vision, the baby responds to the beginning of the sound stimulus, but, as the sound continues, his activity level gradually declines. This has been described as "listening."

Smell and taste, especially smell, are difficult to investigate. It is doubtful whether neonates respond to any odors as such. Some substances irritate the mucous membrane of the nose and produce facial grimaces, but probably the smell receptors are not involved. It has been shown, however, that the sucking behavior of the neonate can be modified by introducing salt into his milk. It is doubtful if he can detect other tastes, such as sweet, sour, and bitter. At any rate infants are less able to discriminate among tastes than are adults.

Infants respond to the temperature of the milk and show in other ways that they are sensitive to temperature. They definitely respond to touch, movement of the body, and posture. Since none of these external factors accounts for all activity and since all action is assumed to be evoked by some stimulus, it is generally assumed that neonates are responsive to internal stimuli.

The infant's sensitivity does not tell us anything about the organization of his perception. If an adult looks at a black circle on a white field, the black area is localized in the white, the contour is sharp, and the shape of the black figure is distinguishable. The adult can distinguish between a circle and a triangle. Are these same statements true for young infants?

The best evidence we have is indirect, coming from the reports of adults who have been blind since birth and obtain their vision in adulthood (Senden, 1932). These adults have developed quite adequate understandings of the properties of objects from the other senses; furthermore, their visual apparatus has developed as much as it can without external stimulation. It may even have atrophied or become abnormal through lack of stimulation. The congenitally blind may have lost sensitivities that they once possessed. Nevertheless, we can make a reasonable guess that infant perception is no better than the visual perception of these people.

They report that some aspects of visual organization are present when they first recover sight. They can distinguish between one area of the visual field and another. If a black figure on a white ground is presented, they can tell which is which. On the other hand, they have tremendous difficulty in distinguishing one shape from another. Although it is immediately obvious to the normal adult that a triangle has corners, these people have to search and search to discover whether or not a figure has a corner. It takes them several months of visual experience to begin to make these obvious discriminations. Another curious difficulty they experience is in transposing learning. If they learn to name correctly a square made of white cardboard, they may be unable to recognize it when it is colored yellow, despite the fact that they have little trouble distinguishing colors and learning to recognize them.

So we see that it is not surprising that infants take so long to develop some of the simple ideas of space that we take for granted. They do not at first even have the clear information that would make it possible to identify the properties of objects. The development of form perception has been studied in some detail. It seems that by perhaps six months of age, the child can distinguish forms. He cannot verbally name them, of course, but his discrimination can be tested by rewarding one type of choice to see if he can learn to solve the problem. In this experiment (Ling, 1941) two forms are presented to the child. The incorrect one is fastened down, whereas the correct one is removable and if sucked gives a sweet taste because it has a small amount of saccharin on it. The child not only distinguishes these forms but continues to distinguish them if the forms are turned around or made larger and smaller. This is one type of transposition that persons with recently obtained vision have difficulty in performing.

The Development of Cognition of Space

Before we can truly say that a cognitive representation of the external world exists, the child must demonstrate certain behavioral signs of cognition. First, the object must be cognized as a permanent object that exists outside the child and that continues to exist even when the child does not perceive it. Secondly, the child must distinguish between properties of the object and its spatial relations. Properties such as size, weight, color, etc., are unchanged when the object is moved around, whereas its spatial position is changed by movements. The independence of these two kinds of properties is required for the object to have permanence. Thirdly, the child must have some knowledge of movements in space. It is very important for him to know that locomotions in space and also turning movements of an object around an axis are reversible, and that any movement can be reversed. Also, he must recognize that, to find an object, he does not need to take the same path it did to reach its present location. If the location is known, any path to that point will locate the object.

Fourthly, the various senses—vision, touch, etc.—must be integrated so that they give the person information about a single external world. Fifthly, the child must have recognized that objects and movements occur outside of himself, and he must distinguish between the movements in the external world, which he observes, and his own movements, which are adapted to the world. It is obvious, as soon as we think of it, that it must not be easy for the child to distinguish between the actions that have external effects, such as hitting, moving, etc., and the actions that have no effect, such as looking or listening. Lastly, and this may be the same as the fourth, the child must have some cognition of himself in this space that he cognizes. He must be one of the objects in his cognitive map.

Piaget has described the stages in the infant's development of cognition of the external world and has described the parallel developments of cognition and goal-directed behavior.

STAGES 1 AND 2   During the first two stages of infancy, which correspond to the period before the child is able to reach for a visually perceived object, none of these criteria for a cognitive map is met. The permanence of perceived objects is best investigated by studying the child's reaction to the disappearance of an object. During this period the child does not search for an object that is gone, nor does he anticipate where it might have gone. At best, he continues to feel or look at the place where it disappeared—*i.e.,* he continues doing what he was doing at the time it disappeared. During this period, there is some integration of the senses. The child learns to look at an object that is making a noise; he can tie together tactual sensations from the hand, kinaesthetic sensations from limbs, and tactual sensations from the mouth. He can put what he touches into his mouth and suck it.

This is not yet space or object perception, but it is the beginning of them. When the same object is involved in two different schemata, or behavior patterns, so that it is touched by the hands and also sucked, the child gets two sources of information about it. Gradually this recognition that something fits into all the various schemata leads to its being unified into an object, but this does not happen for some time.

The fact that the infant cannot distinguish between causing an event and merely observing it (this is implied by his being unable to recognize its being external to his own actions) means that the child feels, in a way, omnipotent. Psychoanalysts (Fenichel, 1945) have pointed to this early feeling of omnipotence in children. It is not omnipotence in the sense that an adult might feel that he was so powerful he could make anything happen. The adult would see himself as outside the event and causing it. The child does not distinguish the external objects from his own actions that involve them. Thus, his omnipotence is perhaps better described as failure to distinguish between what he can cause and what he cannot.

STAGE 3   Moving on now to stage 3, corresponding to the period between the acquisition of visual motor prehension and the ability to engage in goal-directed means-end behavior, we find that the various senses are much better integrated than before. This is one of the characteristics signified by visually guided reaching for an object. This same behavior also puts the child in the position to observe the relationship between two objects rather than merely the relation of an object to his own actions.

Secondary circular reactions (see p. 303) imply the same thing. The child produces a causal sequence in the external world and is able to reproduce it. This attracts his attention to the external events and makes him more sensitive to them. Secondary circular reactions are also part of stage 3 of infancy.

The child in stage 3 still does not search for an object that has disappeared, but he does show some behavior patterns which indicate that he is beginning to conceive of an external object. Piaget describes Jacqueline's behavior when she holds an object that is slowly pulled away from her. If this process causes the hand to follow the movement of the object, then when she finally loses contact with it, she may continue groping along the trajectory she has already begun. If, however, the object is jerked away rapidly or made to disappear by screening it, there is no search for it. Similarly, the eyes may follow a falling object in the first part of its fall. If this movement is begun, then when the child loses sight of it, he continues the downward movement of the eyes and eventually may rediscover the fallen object. This depends, however, according to Piaget, upon the eye movement's or the hand movement's having been initiated by the moving object. The searching is merely an extension of the activity that was going on at the time the object disappeared.

The child also shows an advance in another respect. If the object is not hidden completely by a screen, but is left so that a tiny portion protrudes, the child can at this stage recognize it and retrieve the partially hidden object. When it disappears completely, however, it is not recovered. It is not that the child's search fails; he does not even miss the object, as the following striking observation shows (Piaget, 1954):

At the age of 6 months and 19 days, Laurent was whimpering and fussing because it was just before a meal. When Piaget showed him his bottle, Laurent immediately began to cry lustily. Now Piaget repeatedly hid the bottle, either under a table or behind his hand. As soon as the bottle was out of sight, Laurent stopped crying; as soon as it reappeared he began to cry once more. Each time there was calm as long as the bottle could not be seen. After he had been teased this way several times, Laurent became very angry. His anger was in a sense a response to the frustration even though his motive to have the bottle disappeared when the bottle was invisible. If he had in any way cognized the bottle under the table, his behavior would have been quite different, as illustrated by the effect of making only part of the bottle disappear. When Piaget partly covered the bottle, Laurent's cries remained strong; if anything, they increased in strength.

Further observations show clearly the peculiar situation that exists in the child's cognition at this time. Laurent is unable to turn the bottle around if the nipple is invisible. As long as the nipple can be seen, he is quite capable of rotating it to get the nipple to his mouth, but if he sees only the bottom of the bottle, he does not turn it around but tries to suck from the bottom. Similarly, he recognizes the bottle no matter which part of it protrudes from under the cloth; it does not need to be the nipple in order to set off the crying. Thus, Laurent recognizes that the bottle is to suck and he wants it. If the nipple is visible at all, he recognizes that it is there and he must suck; but, if the nipple cannot be seen, he then sucks the bottom as though he does not recognize that the bottle has a nipple or that a nipple is necessary for effective sucking.

STAGE 4; SEARCH FOR ABSENT OBJECTS   As well as failing to attribute permanence to objects, the infant in stage 3 does not recognize the paths an object may follow. He acts as though the only movement an object could make is in the direction of the child's movement at the time it disappeared. In stage 4 we observe true searching behavior when an object disappears. This corresponds to the period when the child puts two behavior patterns together in a means-end relationship. At this time the child's search for a vanished object is, in a sense, halfway to a full understanding of disappearing objects.

The procedure in one of Piaget's observations can be described as follows: The object is hidden at point *a*—i.e., it is put out of sight at that point but the action is visible to the child. The child then searches for it at *a* and finds it. Now the object is hidden at point *b* before the child's eyes. Although the child has continued to watch the object and has seen it disappear at *b,* he immediately looks for it at point *a* (Piaget, 1954).

> At 0:10(3) Jacqueline looks at the parrot on her lap (a toy parrot). I place my hand on the object; she raises it and grasps the parrot. I take it away from her and before her eyes, I move it away very slowly and put it under a rug 40 centimeters away. Meanwhile, I place my hand on her lap again. As soon as Jacqueline ceases to see the parrot, she looks at her lap, lifts my hand and hunts beneath it. The reaction is the same during three sequential attempts.

Here we see a conflict between repeating the behavior that was previously successful and searching for the toy where it was last seen.

STAGE 5   In the next stage this conflict is resolved. The child attributes permanence to the object, which means that he looks for it at the place where it last disappeared rather than at places where it has previously been found. We must recognize that looking in the customary place for an object is well-adjusted behavior, if one has not observed it put somewhere else.

Along with the achievement of true searching behavior we find that the child's understanding of possible movements of the object is much enlarged. At this time the child can do such things as throwing an object in back of him in one direction and turning around in the other direction to look for it. He can follow the trajectory of an object and look for it where it probably came to rest. Part of the information for such an adjustment may come from one sense modality and part from another; there is an integration of the various modalities.

The Appearance of True Cognition

This is not the end of development during infancy. The final step, according to Piaget, is stage 6, marked by the achievement of a cognition that contains representations of absent objects, events that no longer exist, events that represent possibilities but were never observed, or events that would produce desired effects if they were carried out. In other words, the child is capable of memory, of imagination, of pretending, of hypothesizing about an unknown event, of planning events and foreseeing effects. This cognition takes place only at the level of action and only under simple circumstances, but it nevertheless represents quite an achievement.

Let us look at the evidence for these statements about children in the sixth stage of infancy, which usually occurs close to the age of eighteen months.

DEFERRED IMITATION How can we find evidence for the cognitive picturing of past events? This implies more than recognizing familiar objects, more than profiting by past experience, more than repeating a past action to produce the same effect. One type of evidence for the cognitive picture of a past event is the existence of deferred imitation. If the child can imitate a model after the model is no longer present, Piaget argues that the guidance for the behavior must come from a cognitive picture, a mental image of the model.

PRETENDING Pretending appears for the first time in this same period of childhood. The play behavior that occurs earlier in infancy consists of repeating schemata or behavior patterns after they have been mastered, because such patterns are interesting or fun. When the schema is repeated in an inappropriate context but with the recognition that it is inappropriate, then pretending has occurred. For example, Jacqueline had a ritual about going to sleep. It was a schema that was evoked by the situation of going to bed. In stage 6, Jacqueline performed this going-to-sleep ritual in a play situation when she was not going to sleep. That it was not merely a mistake was indicated by the fact that she did it in a playful way, having fun with her pretense. To pretend implies a cognitive representation of a pattern that is copied outside of situations where it is recognized to be appropriate.

RECONSTRUCTION OF AN INVISIBLE EVENT A third line of evidence of the development of cognition in this period of life is the child's ability to conceive of a movement that was unobservable but that might have happened. For example, Piaget tried the following experiment when Jacqueline was eighteen months and sixteen days old: First, he put a ring in his hand and showed it to her. Then he closed his hand upon it. She opened his hand to find the object with a great deal of enjoyment.

Now, he placed the ring in his left hand, pressed his left hand against his right hand and extended both closed hands to Jacqueline. She searched in his left hand, did not find the ring, and said, "Ring, ring, where is it?"

On the next trial, however, and thereafter, she was not content to look in the hand where the ring had been hidden. She looked there first, but then looked in the other hand to find the ring. Now Piaget put the ring in his hand and then his hand into a beret lying on the table. Then he took his closed hand out of the beret. It took Jacqueline a number of trials to discover the possibility that the ring was left in the beret rather than kept in the hand. Later, she performed much more complicated searches when the closed hand was put under several different objects so that there were a number of possible locations of the hidden object.

INSIGHTFUL PROBLEM SOLVING Finally, let us examine the problem solving that becomes possible once the child is able to picture cognitively nonexistent happenings. The result is an insightful solution to problems without having to try out every possible action to see what its consequence will be.

The following observations show how Laurent at stage 6 discovered how to use a stick as a tool for retrieving objects (Piaget, 1952). The history of Laurent's eventual insight into the use of a stick as a tool goes back to the beginning of stage 3. At that age he sometimes shook the stick, sometimes rubbed it against the side of his crib, and once he accidentally hit a suspended toy with it. He immediately repeated the action, but despite all Piaget's efforts, Laurent could not learn that schema consistently. Later he could use a stick to hit objects, but during stages 4 and 5 he never used the stick as a tool to pull something toward him or to push it away. Jacqueline and Lucienne learned to use the stick as a tool during stage 5, but Laurent did not do so. He hit aimlessly with it and pushed it around with his finger, but did not use it as a tool.

At the age of 12 months, 5 days, Laurent was amusing himself with a small cane. He was obviously much surprised to observe the relationship between movements of one end of the cane and movements of the other end. He moved the cane in various directions, letting the free end drag and watching its movements intently. Still, however, he did not use the stick as a tool.

When he was 14 months, 25 days, he had mastered other relations which are at the same level of difficulty but still could not solve stick problems. Finally, when he was 16 months, 5 days old, Piaget placed a crust of bread in front of him but out of his reach. To the right, Piaget placed a stick. Laurent, who was seated at a table, first tried to reach the bread directly. Then Piaget placed the stick directly in front of him, but not so that it touched the bread. Laurent again looked at the bread, then at the stick, then seized the stick and guided it toward the bread. Unfortunately he had picked it up near the middle so that it was too short to reach the object. He put it down again and tried fruitlessly to reach the bread directly. Then he picked up the stick by one end—we cannot know whether it was by intention or by accident —and drew the bread toward him by the stick. At first he merely touched the bread, then pushed it to the right, and finally drew it in.

Conceptual Thinking in the Preschool Period

A review of the characteristics of stage 6 in infancy might lead us to believe that the infant has little farther to go. He is able to solve problems through mental experimentation without the necessity for actually discovering solutions through trial-and-error procedures. He is able to recognize objects when he sees them from different points of view; he is able to perceive the relationships among external objects, such as the relation between an object and its support. In many ways his behavior fits all the criteria of maturity described in Chapter 2.

But this is true only under very limited conditions. The preschool child, despite the fact that he is past stage 6, does not show all the characteristics of maturity. The following characteristics mark a preschool child's behavior as being less mature than an older child's.

Egocentrism with Respect to Remote Objects

Although the preschool child can respond to objects outside of his immediate environment and can even copy models whose presence is not communicated by cues, the range of objects to which he can respond is still relatively limited. While he can recognize in behavioral terms the different aspects of objects, so that each object has an individual identity, he does not show the same recognition of distant objects.

We have seen that the infant nearing the age of two can recognize his bottle or a toy even when he sees it from a variety of angles. This ability seems to depend upon two conditions: first, the object must not be very remote; secondly, it must have been observed in a variety of situations in which its identity has been confirmed by actual manipulation. The baby has turned the toy around and discovered quite directly that the same toy looks different from different angles.

When this same problem is presented in more abstract terms, as when Piaget (1948) asked children whether a mountain would look different from a different point of view, he found that children of four and five years had no appreciation of the fact that the mountain would look different from the opposite side. The mountain is much more remote than the bottle or toy and it cannot be quickly turned around, so its different aspects are not easily revealed. In order to apply to the problem of the mountain the principles implicit in turning a toy around to see the other side, the principles themselves need to be explicitly recognized and abstracted from any specific concrete situation.

Representation Limited to Concrete Objects

This discussion of the ability to be detached from one's egocentric point of view leads directly to the second general characteristic of the preschool child that differentiates him from older and more mature children. The objects in the young child's environment are concrete. The mental representations of which he is capable are those that are classifiable as images or mental pictures of a situation. The older child and the adult, however, can also conceive of such abstractions as "all odd numbers" or "justice." This change in the character of mental representation is well illustrated by an experiment performed in Piaget's laboratory (1950).

Three beads are strung on a wire that is fastened at both ends and mounted on a board that can be lifted and moved around. The wire goes through a tube, or tunnel, so that when the beads are moved from one end to the other they can all be hidden by the tube. The beads have been placed on the wire in the following order: red, yellow, and blue. They are all moved into the tube and the child is asked to draw a picture of them as they would look in the tube. This is to reinforce his memory of the order of the colors. Then he is asked which color will be the first to come out of the tube if the beads are pushed on through the tube, emerging at the other end. Nearly all preschool children are able to make the correct prediction.

Then the beads are pushed back in the tube and the child is asked in what order they will come out if they are pushed back through the tube so they emerge from the same end from which they entered. It is more difficult for the child to recognize the fact that they will come out in the opposite order. Piaget reports that children of less than four years are unable to solve this problem.

If the child solves this second problem correctly, the experiment is repeated after the entire board on which the wire is strung is turned through a 180° angle while the beads are in the tube. Then the child is asked in what order they will emerge if they are pushed out of the tube in either direction. Some of the children are unable to solve this problem. A child may feel that since the red one came out first on the first trial and the blue one on the second, now it is the yellow one's turn to come out first.

Even if the child can predict correctly the result of one reversal, he may be unable to generalize. If he answers the third problem correctly, then the board is reversed more and more times, one half turn, one full turn, one and one half turns, and so on. Finally the child is asked which would come out first if the board were turned around thirteen times or forty-two times. The difficulty in imagining the result of many turns demonstrates the limitations of the child's mental representations.

It seems likely that the child can imagine the balls in the tube and then in his imagination turn the tube around to obtain a prediction of the effect of one reversal. Then he may even be able to continue the revolution in his imagination until he can predict a full turn. This intuitive approach is, however, limited. It becomes very difficult to keep these revolutions straight for four or five or twenty reversals. In order to obtain the correct prediction for large numbers of reversals, it is necessary to appreciate in some way that any number of full turns is equivalent to no turn at all, and that any odd number of half turns is equivalent to one half turn. Thus, there has to be some representation of the abstraction, *any number of full turns*. This conceptual ability, according to Piaget's results, occurs only after the beginning of school age.

Logical Thinking in the Preschool Period

One question concerning the thinking of children that has been answered differently by different psychologists is whether the child is pre-logical in his thinking or is logical enough in his reasoning but is so hampered by his lack of information that his logical thinking frequently results in the incorrect answer.

In order to understand this question we must look first at some of the properties of logical thinking. It is quite possible for logical thinking to be inaccurate and for illogical thinking to result in an accurate conclusion. It is, for example, completely logical to conclude that because all laboring men are Democrats, because Democrats vote for the Democratic candidate, and because there are enough laborers to hold the balance of power, therefore, the Democratic candidate will be elected. The trouble with such a conclusion is not that it is illogical but that the premises are inaccurate. On the other hand, it is illogical to reason that: a brick falls to the ground; a brick is an object; a piece of iron is an object; therefore, a piece of iron will fall to the ground. The accuracy of the conclusion does not mean that the reasoning is logical.

COGNITION OF A CLASS OF EVENTS   Let us look at a very simple example of child's thinking. At the age of thirty months Jacqueline and her father went on a walk each day to look at some slugs (worms) that were of great interest to her. Piaget asked Jacqueline one morning whether or not they would see a slug today. She answered, "Yes, because it is not sunny." The next morning she responded to the same question with, "No, because it's sunny." Slugs, like angleworms, actually do appear more frequently on cloudy days or after a rain. These answers of Jacqueline's could be arrived at by a very logical procedure. We see slugs on all cloudy days; today is cloudy; therefore, we shall see slugs today. In order for her to follow this line of reasoning, she must in some way be able to recognize the fact that this cloudy day is a member of a "class" that includes all cloudy days.

Now, it is not necessary for her answer to have been arrived at through a recognition of class membership that requires that the individual be able to conceive of a class containing a number of separate events. If we look back to the experiment of Watson that showed how Albert, a child of eleven months, learned to fear furry objects (see p. 74), we recall that the experimenter made a loud noise that frightened the baby at the moment when he was shown a white rabbit. After a few such experiences Albert showed fear of rats, rabbits, even white pieces of fur. We are justified in saying that the similarity of the various objects was sufficient for them all to evoke the same response. It was not necessary for Albert to conceive of "the class of white furry objects," in order to respond as he did.

Jacqueline might have been expecting slugs in much the same way that Albert was afraid of white objects—because of the similarity between this cloudy day and the other days on which slugs were found. Even so, considerably more maturity is required than was necessary for Albert's behavior. One way we might check, therefore, upon whether Jacqueline was reasoning logically or responding on the basis of mere similarity would be to study her response to a class of objects that are not all alike.

COMPARISON OF WHOLE AND PART   Piaget (1952) reports an experiment, not on Jacqueline, which shows some of the problems that arise when children are asked to consider the relationship between the members of a class and the class as a whole. He places about twenty beads in a box. Each bead is a wooden one and the subject agrees that they are "all made of wood." Most of these beads are brown, but a few of them are colored white. In terms of classes there is a class of "wooden beads" that includes all of the beads. The members of this class are not all alike, but are in turn divided into two classes, brown beads and white beads. Now the child is asked, "In this box which are there more of, brown beads or wooden beads?" Up to the age of seven, according to Piaget's results, the children nearly always say that there are more brown ones than wooden ones. Why? "Because there are only two or three white ones." Piaget then questions the child further, along the following lines: "Are all the brown ones made of wood?"—"Yes"—"If I take away all the wooden ones will there be any left?"—"No, because they are all made of wood."—"If I take away all the brown ones, will there be any left?"—"Yes, the white ones." Then the original question is asked again, "Which are there more of, the brown beads or the wooden ones?" Again the answer, "The brown ones—because there are so few white ones."

Piaget explains this curious behavior by saying that the child is unable to consider simultaneously the brownness that distinguishes the two colors and the woodenness that constitutes the basis for the whole class. When the child focuses on one of the subclasses, the brown beads, he cannot simultaneously compare it with the whole class, wooden beads, which includes the subclass itself.

A similar problem arises when preschool children must recognize that they can be in a city and at the same time in the state in which the city is located. Such statements as, "We are *not* in Wichita, we are in Kansas," are very commonly heard from preschool children. Then, if the child is informed that he can be in Wichita and at the same time in Kansas because Wichita is a city in Kansas, the next time the argument may be, "We are not in Kansas, we are in Wichita." Somehow, the idea of being included in a class that is in turn a part of a bigger class demands a double reference and a shifting frame of reference that is hard for the child to understand. It is important to note, however, that the child may be able to respond correctly to the same type of problem if the terms are more familiar and immediate. Thus, the child may be able to say that he is in his house and his house is in Wichita, even when he cannot clearly grasp the more remote relationships of inclusion. Such apparently inconsistent behavior indicates, however, that he does not have a general understanding of inclusion to which he can refer when the city and state problem is explained.

In some cases it is quite clear that the child considers the members of a class to be all the same object. When Jacqueline went for a walk before the one described above, she was looking for slugs, but actually she was looking for "the slug." "There it is" she cried when she spied one. Then when she came upon another about ten yards up the road she said, "There's the slug again." Her father asked her if it wasn't another one. They went back to look at the first one. "Is it the same one?"—"Yes."—"Another slug?"—"Yes."—"Another or the same?" The question meant nothing to Jacqueline.

We can see from this description how difficult it is to decide just how the child is thinking. But we can make some sort of a guess about which situations will facilitate accuracy of judgments and which ones will be difficult for the child. If there is identity of an object, a person or animal or thing, then the different properties of that object do not need to be put into the form of a logical relationship of classes in order to be used effectively. The child who recognizes his father getting off the train and anticipates being picked up may actually be responding to some cue like the brown hat his father wears. This conclusion, if reproduced logically, would be quite difficult. If he had to cognize explicitly the conclusion that "all men wearing a brown hat will pick me up" he would find it very difficult, because "all men wearing a brown hat" is an abstract class. Yet the brown hat may identify his father at a distance.

Another factor facilitating correct judgment is similarity of members of a class. When the qualities of objects that make them members of the same logical class are also qualities that make them superficially similar, accurate predictions are easier than when dissimilar objects must be encompassed in the same logical class.

FOCUS ON ONE ASPECT OF A PROBLEM   We have seen in the experiment with wooden beads the difficulty that the child gets into because he tends to focus upon only one aspect of a situation. This effect can be further seen in the following episode that occurred in a school for six- and seven-year-olds (Isaacs, 1933):

> The children were "going to have a wedding" and there was much talk as to whether Priscilla would marry Frank or Dan, who are the two rivals for her affection.—Frank said, "You can't marry Dan, because daddy must be bigger than mommy." They argue about this and appealed to Mrs. I. as to whether "daddies are always bigger than mommies." She said, "Well, let's ask everyone about it," and we asked each child in turn whether his mommy or his daddy was the bigger. The others all agreed that "daddies *must* be bigger than mommies." Dan then said, stamping his foot, "Yes, you see, I *shall* be bigger than Priscilla."

Here the logic should proceed from the premise, men are bigger than their wives, to the minor premise, Dan is not bigger than Priscilla, to the conclusion, Dan cannot marry Priscilla. Dan was, however, centered upon what he wanted in the situation; so for him the reasoning—if it was reasoning at all—went, I shall marry Priscilla, men are bigger than their wives, so I shall be bigger than Priscilla.

Three examples from Piaget's (1951) observations of his own children will serve to illustrate the discussion further:

> At 2:10(8) J. had a temperature and wanted oranges. It was too early in the season for oranges to be in the shops and we tried to explain to her that they were not yet ripe. "They're still green. We can't eat them. They haven't yet got their lovely yellow colour." J seemed to accept this but a moment later, as she was drinking her camomile tea, she said: "Camomile isn't green, it's yellow already—Give me some oranges."
>
> At 2:1(13) J wanted to go and see a little hunchbacked neighbor whom she used to meet on her walks. A few days earlier she had asked why he had a hump and after I explained she said, *"Poor boy, he's ill, he has a hump."* The day before J had wanted to go and see him but he had influenza, which J called being "ill in bed." We started out for our walk and on the way J said, *"Is he still ill in bed?"*—No, I saw him this morning, he isn't in bed now.—*"He hasn't a big hump now."*
>
> At 2:4(27) in the bathroom. *"Daddy's getting hot water, so he's going to shave."*

Returning now to the question of whether the reasoning of children follows different rules of logic from those of adults, we can find support for both positions in the preceding examples.

Supporters of the second point of view might well argue that Dan's reasoning about his marrying Priscilla was not defective in logical structure, but reflected merely that Dan made his major premise that he would marry Priscilla. Given that assumption, his logic was faultless. Or in the example of the oranges and camomile tea, it might be argued that the child makes the assumption that oranges and camomile tea *must* be the same color. Supporters of the logicalness of childhood thought argue that the fact that they are the same color is known to the child, but that his assumption that they *must* be the same color is due to ignorance. Furthermore, supporters of the position that childhood logic is the same as adult logic can point to examples such as the reasoning that "Daddy is going to shave," as examples of perfectly logical thought in familiar situations.

In what sense, then, is the reasoning employed in these examples different from adult reasoning? The fact that it is inaccurate is obvious, but it seems difficult to explain in terms of lack of information. Jacqueline had the information at her disposal that the hunchback had his hump even when he was not ill in bed. The situation in which she first pronounced him ill provided the information. That she did not use the information is certainly possible, but in this case a more mature child would have found the information sufficient and he would have used it.

The problem, then, is to account for the sort of errors that the child does make, and also to account for the fact that he makes no errors in many situations that require reasoning. The distortion in these errors can be seen to derive from the child's being bound to some aspect of the situation that is immediate and that frequently is of great interest. Dan wanted to marry Priscilla; this motivation distorted the whole structure of the situation. The more mature person would have seen the entire structure, including the major premise, in the objective properties of the situation, regardless of his motivation. His perception of the real world would enable him to withstand the pressure of the motivation that focused his attention on the goal.

The lack of motivational focus is shown in the example of the reasoning about shaving. Jacqueline was here disinterested, and, furthermore, it seems likely that she was anticipating the act of shaving without any especial logic. The reasoning that would have been necessary to deduce shaving would have, in fact, been incorrect. Father does not always shave every time he draws water into the basin.

Whether, aside from the distortion due to focusing on one aspect of a situation, the thinking of the child is logical depends upon just what is meant by logical. It is certainly as logical as many an adult's decisions in which he does not explicitly reason from premise to conclusion. When the child is asked to reason explicitly under controlled conditions he seems unable, at this age, to do so. The story of the brown and white beads illustrates this point. Explicit reasoning demands the cognitive representation of the abstract principles of logic, divorced of any specific content. If this be accepted, then the child at this level of maturity cannot reason. If, however, the correct prediction of results in a concrete situation, which might have been arrived at by logical deduction, is a reasoning process, then the child does reason, and does it quite frequently.

EGOCENTRISM IN ADULT THINKING Furthermore, it is important to point out that adults also can become ego-centered and can make precisely the same sort of errors as the child. The reasoning about the hunchback failed to recognize that there are different kinds of illness and that recovery from one of them does not mean recovery from all of them. The same sort of error is shown in an assumption by an adult that the consequence of an act that is most significant to the receiver of the action is the one that was intended by the actor. It is psychologically possible to conclude that because the Bureau of Internal Revenue does not permit the working mother to deduct the expenses of a maid to take care of the house, the bureau is opposed to married women working. The various other reasons for not permitting such deductions—its enforceability and the loss of tax revenue—are not so clearly perceived, and the interpretation that the working wife makes of this situation may be focused upon the consequences of such a rule for her.

Another example similarly illustrates focusing upon only a limited part of a situation. The college student who in his last semester needs three *C*'s and a *B* in order to graduate receives his grades one at a time. The first grade is a *C*; the second grade is a *C*; the third grade is a *C*; the fourth grade is a *C*. He cannot graduate! What happens? The student feels convinced that it is the instructor in the *last* course who kept him from graduating.

Logical Rules as a Conceptual Schema

How does a knowledge of the principles of logic function in ordinary behavior? The various concrete examples show that the child is presented with certain data or information from the external world. Jacqueline heard the water running. She had certain knowledge that was relevant. On the basis of the knowledge she constructed a cognitive picture of her father shaving. In each concrete case, the child reached a conclusion about the external world on the basis of information, guided by certain logical assumptions. In order for the child to be logical, these assumptions do not need to be verbalized or communicable or even conscious. They do have to be applied to the proper situations and applied correctly. These tacit assumptions that interact with information to produce a cognition are called conceptual schemata by Piaget. If they are to be applied to any sort of situation in which logic is relevant, they must be abstract—*i.e.,* not limited to one specific type of problem.

The Child's Conception of Number

Shifting to another example of a conceptual schema, Piaget and his colleagues have studied the child's behavior with regard to the ideas of quantity and number. First, let us see what tacit assumptions we make whenever we employ the concept of a quantity.

THE CONCEPT OF QUANTITY   We do not describe something in terms of quantity unless we think of the material as something that can be added and combined. We speak of the total weight or total volume of an object. We think of the total number of objects, the total amount of money. But we do not think of the total speed of two cars or the total temperature of the United States. Temperatures and speeds cannot be combined into a total as numbers are, although under special conditions speeds can be added.

The combinatory property is not the only assumption underlying the concept of quantity or number. In addition, we assume that any change of objects or material that does not add something to it or take something away from it leaves the quantity unchanged. If there are ten objects, the number is not changed by moving them about into different patterns, or by clustering them in one big group or many little groups. In other words, certain operations leave a quantity unchanged, although other operations change the quantity. A further assumption is that the number does not depend upon the order in which the objects are counted.

These assumptions constitute the properties of the abstract concept of number. They are: (1) the whole equals the sum of the parts (combinativity); (2) rearrangements leave the quantity unchanged. Now, only some properties of objects have these qualities. Squareness of a pattern, for example, is not something which can be added up, it is not unchanged by rearrangements, and we do not know what the total squareness of something would mean.

We want to see how the child develops such a concept. But we must notice that an error does not necessarily mean that he does not have such a concept. This concept of number or quantity can be applied to an inappropriate property of an object, or it can fail to be applied where it is appropriate. We occasionally hear someone speak of the total amount of sin in the world. Perhaps sin fits the properties of number and quantity, but it seems unlikely. So, to discover the child using the concept of number incorrectly does not necessarily mean he never uses it correctly. If, however, we can find no evidence that he uses it correctly, we may be justified in saying he has not yet developed it.

INVARIANCE OF TOTAL NUMBER Piaget and his colleagues (1952) have performed several experiments to test whether children of various ages recognize these properties of number in simple situations. In one experiment, for example, the child is given a number of vases and a number of flowers. He is asked to arrange a flower in each vase. Then the flowers are bunched together, the vases are spread out over a wide area, and the child is asked to say whether there are the same number of flowers and vases. Children under four tend to say that there are more vases than flowers if the vases are spread out and the flowers bunched, but to say the reverse if the flowers are spread out and the vases bunched. In another experiment the child is shown two jars of liquid. He agrees that there is the same amount in each jar. Now the liquid in one jar is poured out into several smaller jars, but none of it is lost. The child of four will probably say that there is no longer the same amount of the two liquids. It is unpredictable whether he will say the one or the other has more, but he will not usually say they are equal.

These experiments point to the possibility that the child of four does not have any concept of number or quantity that has the properties we have assigned to the concept quantity. It is difficult to be sure of this, because there is always the possibility that the child does not understand the questions. When he says there are more vases than flowers, he may mean that they cover more space. That is probably what he does mean, but the problem is whether he has any concept that is equivalent to the usual concept of number—*i.e.,* an additive property unchanged by bunching or clustering. In these experiments the experimenters tried various ways to be sure that the child knew what was called for. If there were beads in question, he would be asked which would make the longer string. If there were liquids, he would be asked who would have the most to drink. They tried to translate the questions into real-life situations in which the concept of number would be significant in determining behavior.

INVARIANCE OF OTHER TOTALS One series of experiments reported by Piaget (1953) shows that the concept of quantity appears earlier with respect to certain properties than with others. He shows the child two balls of clay of the same size. The child agrees they are the same. Then he squashes one into the shape of a pancake and asks which of the two has the most clay. Younger children tend to think the squashing changes the amount of clay, but children about the age of seven recognize that the amount of clay was unchanged. Then Piaget asks about the volume of the clay. Which one occupies the most space? This is harder. He found that children can recognize the constancy of the amount without necessarily recognizing the constancy of the volume, and to recognize that the weight had not changed was even more difficult.

So we see that the concept of quantity or number is not something that appears suddenly in all areas. It seems likely that the child at first is unable to distinguish the property of quantity from other properties of an object, so he cannot see that nothing is changed when the ball is flattened into a pancake. Gradually he discovers first one and then another concrete example of the concept, but he does not necessarily recognize the concept in other situations. Finally he develops an abstraction that is a set of principles applicable to a wide variety of situations. Then he has the concept of number as a concept. It may still happen, however, that he applies it incorrectly on some occasions, and fails sometimes to apply it when it is appropriate.

We could see this same process in other concepts. Piaget has investigated the development of the concepts of speed, movement, shape, and probability in this same fashion. These show comparable patterns of development. In this way, the child gradually acquires, usually by the age of eleven, the usual repertoire of concepts about time, space, speed, number, shape, etc. which are common property in our culture.

Language Development

Function of Language in Infancy

In the development of conceptual thought, language plays a very significant role. Talking begins before the end of infancy, but the early words that the child uses cannot be considered words in the usual sense. They are not representations or signs of events, but rather vocalizations that are evoked by an object. We can perhaps understand this distinction if we consider the difference between using the word *boy* in reference to a young male and the word *Boy!* in an exclamation of surprised joy. The words infants use are not all exclamations of emotion, but, like exclamations, they do not refer to the object that is the usual meaning of the word. In order for words to function as signs or representations of external objects, the child must be able to distinguish the sign from the thing it signifies and at the same time recognize the relation between the sign and what it indicates. Such ability seems not to occur before the end of infancy.

Language schemata are like other schemata. They appear early in the child's life in his vocalizations and become integrated into the same sorts of circular reactions as does motor behavior. To listen, to vocalize while listening to his own voice, to imitate sounds that he hears: these are the schemata of infancy. The child will, in play, repeat syllables over and over again, just as he playfully repeats other schemata.

Somewhere near the age of one year the child will ordinarily use some syllable in a consistent fashion under the appropriate stimulus situation. "Mamma" or "ba-ba" frequently occur in this way. This is the first word. There is no evidence to show that for the child at this stage the pronunciation of a word is any different from making a movement. The word as a sign of an object implies his ability to maintain some sort of mental representation of the object, action, or situation that the word signifies. Before that can occur, the child must have developed the appropriate ability.

This fact does not mean that words have no function before they take on the truly sign qualities of language. They do have a function. They can be expressive, differentially expressive, so that the parent by interpretation of what these sounds mean can behave more adequately toward the child. They mean something for the parent, even though, for the child, they are symptoms of some internal condition rather than words. As such, they can become so highly specific that they seem almost to serve as a communication from the child to the parent. The specific sound he makes when he feels bladder tension might be merely expressive and still mean to the parent that it would be wise to take the child to the bathroom.

On the other hand, if he is sufficiently mature, saying this word to his mother might be, for the child, a means of getting to the bathroom. Even such a use of language does not imply that the word represents an object or external event. It can be merely a means to an end like other means-end behavior.

At a still more mature level, the child's use of the same expression may be a deliberate communication to the parent that describes an objective fact and at the same time serves as a means to satisfy the child's motive. Before his language to the parent can have these characteristics, the child must be fairly mature.

Since a word can be a schema or a part of a schema that is activated by an appropriate situation, the child may be able to make the appropriate verbal response to a number of objects before he knows that the word means the object. The procedure by which this occurs has been described by Holt (1951). The child sees the object, hears the sound of the word made by the parent, and hears his own voice. If he imitates the parent, then he may learn to make that sound when he sees the object. This is a laborious sort of learning process and it is significant that the child's vocabulary does not increase very rapidly during infancy.

Language as a Sign

As soon as he discovers, however, that words have meaning and that for every object there is a word, then his vocabulary increases rapidly. It is during the third year of life that this tremendous expansion of language usually takes place. It is at this time that the child is continually asking the names of objects.

When the child is ready to use signs, he can use words. Because he can use words, he finds the language a pre-established system of signs that have highly significant influences upon the sorts of things that are conceptualized. To some extent the words must reflect the structure of the external world, but, in other respects, the words impose a structure upon the external world. A tree, for example, is a unitary object; it is differentiated from the external world and in a sense compels the recognition of it as a separate unit. Furthermore, the similarity among trees is probably clear enough that it is quite natural that the word for tree should develop.

There are many such cases, but there are also many distinctions among objects that are never appreciated because no word describing them exists, and there are many possible classifications that are neglected because of the lack of language. Many of the difficulties of translation from one language to another lie in the fact that the differentiations in the two languages do not exactly correspond.

It should also be pointed out, however, that even in the absence of convenient words, many distinctions are made. The Eskimos have many different words for snow, which distinguish among the different kinds of snow that are important to them. There are not these verbal differentiations in English, but children distinguish, nevertheless, between snow that is good for sledding or skiing and snow that is good for snowballing.

The word for an abstraction is very convenient because it gives the abstraction a concrete handle. Since one of the problems of behaving toward an abstraction is its lack of cognitive representation, the word may serve as the representative. Consider, for example, some of the words that describe the ability to cause other people to do what one wishes them to do. The terms *power, influence,* and *control* all describe this ability in a general way. This concept is more easily used because there is a word for it. It would be good, in fact, if there were even more verbal distinctions in this area than there are. There ought to be words for at least three kinds of control. One should describe the ability to make other people do what one wants regardless of whether or not they wish to. Power and control have this general flavor. A second word could denote the ability to delude other people into thinking they wish to do what one wants them to do. The third could indicate the ability to point out to other people the consequences of their behavior so that they will discover that they really want something which they had not known they wanted. In some cases this will be what one wants them to do. The difference between the second and third kinds of influence has been pointed out by numerous writers, but it is frequently ignored in thinking about democracy in the family or in industry. If there are words for these varieties of influence, we would perhaps not discover so often that what a parent tacitly means by democracy in the home is giving the child the freedom to decide voluntarily to do what the parents want him to. Some such parents do not conceive of the possibility that the child's dissenting opinion might be right.

The semanticists—those people who study the science of the meanings of words—are concerned about another problem of words that represent highly abstract conditions such as democracy, Communism, Christianity, etc. Because these words are easily grasped verbal handles, the word may come to have a life of its own, independent of its meaning.

Communism, for example, once had a meaning that was fairly definite. This meaning implied many things about a Communist: his wish to overthrow capitalism, by force if necessary; his support of the interests of the laboring man; his desire for a classless state; etc. The word has come to have such a power that to support one of the policies supported by Communists is taken by many people to justify the label of Communist.

Such reasoning is not unlike Jacqueline's tacit assumption that the two symptoms of "illness," being in bed, and being a hunchback (see p. 349), must go together. Such logic is fostered by the existence of a single word having different meanings and is further fostered by the strong emotionality engendered by the term Communism in our present society.

Summary

This chapter has been devoted to an analysis of cognition in childhood. First, we have seen the difficulty in trying to construct the infant's picture of the world. We do know, however, that he is less able to discriminate than is the adult. Furthermore, there is evidence to show that the infant requires nearly a year and a half before he has what can properly be called a cognitive map. Before that time, he does not integrate the evidence about an object from the various sense modalities; he does not conceive that objects have existence even when they are not perceptible to him; he does not distinguish between the properties of objects and their spatial position.

After infancy the cognitive development of the child consists largely of the development of conceptual schemata. At the end of infancy he can exhibit behavior that follows simple logical rules, but he cannot make the logic explicit or follow the same rules in complex situations that cannot be met by a simple behavioral adjustment. During the preschool and early school age the child gradually develops such conceptual schemata as the rules of logic and the assumptions underlying the use of numbers.

There are various difficulties preventing the development and correct use of such logical schemata. One difficulty is the limited generality of the early schema. The child may understand in a specific concrete situation the invariance of a total when the parts are rearranged but fail to recognize the general applicability of the schema. A second difficulty lies in the child's being so bound to his own point of view that he cannot be detached enough to recognize the objective logical relations among the elements of a problem.

The course of development of these conceptual schemata is from the specific to the general. The child first recognizes relationships in one situation, then gradually generalizes until finally it becomes an abstract schema. Even after that point, logical errors may be made because he applies the wrong schemata to a specific problem.

14

Child Behavior and the
Problems of Development

MODELS OF CHILD BEHAVIOR

REVIEW OF PERSONAL CHARACTERISTICS

THE PROBLEM OF DEVELOPMENT

DEVELOPMENTAL PROCESSES

SUMMARY

NOW WE HAVE COMPLETED our survey of child behavior. The purpose of this chapter is to review briefly the picture of child behavior that has been gradually forming in the preceding chapters and to relate this picture to the problems of child development that will occupy us for the remainder of the book.

Models of Child Behavior

We have used the model of mature behavior presented in Chapter 6 as the theme of discussion. This is a model of deliberate, voluntary, goal-directed adult behavior, but it is not a realistic picture because not all adult behavior is deliberate, voluntary, and goal-directed. Now we shall fill in the model with the details that have been added in the later chapters and put alongside this model some of the other behavior mechanisms that appear in the course of the child's development.

Model of Infant Behavior

A model of behavior in early infancy can be depicted as in Figure 14.1. We have seen that there are two kinds of behavior of the neonate—restless mass activity and specific responses to specific stimuli. Restlessness has been described in terms of the concept of tension. The specific responses, somewhat more complicated, include fixed responses, such as the knee jerk, eyeblink, and grasp response, and stimulus-guided responses. When the baby turns his

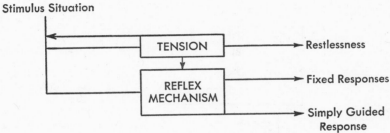

Fig. 14.1   Model of infant behavior.

head in the direction of the tactual stimulation of his face or when he follows a moving light with his eyes, his response is guided by the stimulus. The arrows in Figure 14.1 leading from tension back to the other mechanisms indicate that tension results not only in restless behavior but also in an increased sensitivity to stimuli, a lowered threshold of reflex activity, and an increased susceptibility to rise in tension.

The child by the middle of infancy has acquired some additional fixed responses and some additional forms of guided behavior, but there is no definite way to establish whether the child of six months can have motives that are distinguishable from behavior. The general state of excitement, indicated by tension, has differentiated by this time into some definite emotions like distress and anger, each associated with identifiable patterns of behavior that express these emotional states. These patterns are called *expressive behavior*. These emotions are not yet tied to motives directed toward the source of the instigation.

Behavior at the End of Infancy

By the end of infancy we can depict child behavior diagrammatically as in Figure 14.2. Cognition is present, although its scope is narrow by comparison with cognition at a later stage. The cognitive picture contains suggestions that instigate motives, cues that guide behavior, and external impositions. At

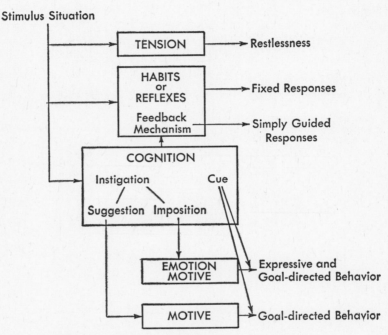

Fig. 14.2   Model of behavior at the end of infancy.

this level of maturity impositions instigate both emotions and associated motives, which in turn appear overtly in the form of expressive behavior and goal-directed behavior. The arrows from cognition to fixed responses and to guided responses indicate that some of these automatic responses are evoked by complex stimulus patterns mediated through cognition as well as by simple immediate stimuli.

Later developments, in so far as they can be pictured in the model, consist of the development of various control mechanisms that determine which motives are realized in an overt attempt to gratify them. There are also many changes within the model that are difficult to picture. Cognition becomes broader, as we saw in Chapter 2. If we measured the frequency of the use of the control mechanisms in the child's life, we would find that as he matures more and more of his behavior becomes goal directed and less of it is mediated through fixed responses. It is true, nevertheless, that a great deal of adult behavior is automatized—*i.e.,* it was once cognitively guided but has become habitual. We would also find that the goal-directed aspects of emotional behavior become more prevalent than the purely expressive aspects. It is not

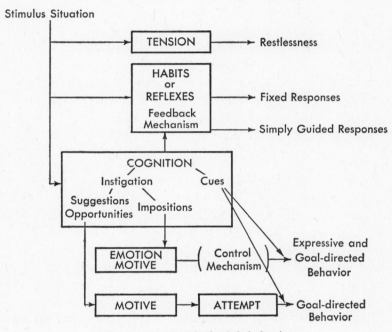

Fig. 14.3   Model of adult behavior.

easy to indicate this fact in Figure 14.3. It is also difficult to put into diagrammatic form the increased resistance to emotional stress that was described in Chapter 5.

Adult Behavior

A model of adult behavior includes all of these mechanisms, as shown in Figure 14.3. This model incorporates as one behavior mechanism the original model of voluntary behavior presented in Chapter 6. It is the most complex and differentiated behavior mechanism and describes that portion of adult behavior which is deliberate, planned, and goal directed.

Review of Personal Characteristics

We have left out of all of these pictures the personal characteristics of the child. These personal characteristics, such as need, ability, or cognitive schema, describe the properties of the person that determine his response to external stimulus situations. Maturity itself is such a characteristic, and maturity is indicated by the increasing differentiation of the model. The other personal characteristics we have discussed have been only labelled, not explained. If they were truly understood, they would be, like maturity, an integral part of the model rather than merely tagged-on names.

The personal characteristics can be grouped under the aspects of the model to which they refer. Thus, there are some characteristics that are primarily concerned with cognition, some with motive, some with attempt, some with emotion, and some with goal-directed behavior. This classification is not completely rigid, because some characteristics are involved in more than one part of the model. Abilities, for example, are primarily relevant to the selection of the means to the goal, but they are also involved in cognition and in the selection of the goal.

Beginning with the characteristics primarily related to cognition, we see that the neonate may have especial sensitivities to one or another kind of stimulus. By the end of infancy, when we first have clear evidence of cognition, the child's cognition depends partly upon his understanding of the objective nature of the world, partly upon his knowledge about that world. With later development knowledge increases tremendously, and, as we have seen in Chapter 13, the child develops many conceptual schemata that structure his cognitive map.

Needs are the characteristics primarily related to motives. In early infancy some activities seem to be pleasurable and reinforce learning. Later we find susceptibilities to specific emotions. By preschool age these have become related to motives tied to the emotions and have been called general needs. By the end of infancy the child has the beginnings of both attitudes and objectives, but the attitudes go through a great deal of later development before they fit the usual adult picture of an attitude. The objectives become more enduring and are directed toward long-range rather than short-range goals. The needs related to conformity and compliance develop primarily after infancy, during preschool and the early school years.

The characteristics associated with goal-directed behavior are abilities. As we have seen in Chapter 11, there is no agreement upon what abilities there are or upon how they develop. It is obvious, of course, that they increase throughout childhood as the child becomes able to perform successfully more and more activities.

The Problem of Development

This, then, is a highly oversimplified picture of the behavior of children. The problem of development concerns specifically the development of these personal characteristics of the child. Children meet the same objective situations as adults; the differences between the behavior of the two depend upon the differences in their characteristics. Maturity is obviously the most important of these. The problem of explaining development is, therefore, the problem of explaining changes in maturity and other personal characteristics.

Hypotheses about Development of Criminal Behavior

We can get an overview of the problem by considering a practical problem that society faces—criminality. We spend millions of dollars each year in the prevention, detection, and punishment of criminal behavior. Why do we have criminals? Let us first analyze criminal behavior from the point of view of a theory of behavior rather than as a problem of development. Some crimes result from temptation—an opportunity to gain something is apparently so good that its being against the law and dishonest does not inhibit the behavior—or the motive may be to retaliate. In many cases the criminal behavior occurs under great emotional stress. To treat criminality solely in terms of a theory of behavior is to change the environment. If people were never subjected to frustration or stress, if they were never instigated to retaliation, if the consequences of breaking the law were more obvious and more inhibiting, criminality would decline; but this would not be feasible. It would require more policemen, more courts, more convictions, more jails. It is just these things that make criminality so expensive to the country. The solution for which criminologists are looking depends upon finding the causes of delinquent behavior in the past life of criminals and learning how to change the characteristics of criminals so that they no longer respond to situations in a criminal way.

Some criminals are extremely impulsive. A delinquent may simply succumb to any temptation. One delinquent gang that stole a car to take a joy ride did not even look to see whether it had gas and ran out of gas in three blocks; then they stole another car, drove it across a state line, and became subject to federal prosecution. They exhibited very poor judgment, quite regardless of their morality. What factors lead to this characteristic of immaturity and bad judgment?

Other criminals are able people. They have foresight, they plan carefully, they exercise good judgment. But they have antisocial values. They obtain power or wealth for themselves. Furthermore, they are apparently not bothered by anxiety or guilt for their crimes. What sort of factors might lead to this pattern of personal characteristics?

Still other criminals seem to hate the world and other people. They do not engage in crime because it gains them wealth or because of any other of the usual ulterior motives. Instead they act as though they were taking revenge on organized society; they operate against laws and injure other people in much the same spirit as others may be altruistic and kind. What sort of developmental factors could be responsible for this turning inside out of ordinary motivation?

There is one extreme position, now not very popular, which holds that criminality is inevitable in some people. The need to become criminal is born in them. This view maintains that criminality is inherited and that it is essentially unchangeable, just as a person's blood type or fingerprint pattern is unchangeable. These people cite as evidence the appearance of criminals in many different cultures and many different historical periods. They point to the development of criminality in people who are apparently very well brought up. They point to the fact that in any home, no matter how bad, not all but only some of the children become criminal.

At the other extreme are those people who maintain that criminality is completely a result of learning. We have essentially taught people to be criminals by the way we rear them. According to this point of view, any person could have been prevented from becoming criminal by the proper upbringing. There is evidence to support this view also. In some homes children are required to steal or are at least rewarded for bringing home the fruits of robbery. Some gangs require thievery. In some prisons young prisoners are taught the skills of the trade by more experienced operators in crime.

One need not adopt either point of view; few do, in fact. Criminality and delinquency are often seen as the resultant both of some inevitable developmental process and some environmental experiences. Sometimes a mixture of heredity and environment is formulated—so much heredity plus so much environmental influence. By training we could exert some influence in development and reduce the probability of the person's becoming a criminal, but there might be an unchangeable characteristic that would make him likely to take up criminal activities.

A more likely and common view of the heredity-environment issue is that the two interact. Perhaps the impulsive criminal represents a boy whose low intelligence is partly a function of his heredity. He is susceptible to many sorts of temptation unless he has incorporated a strong set of moral values. A love for adventure and high courage might predispose a person to become a criminal in some environments but predispose him to be a war hero in other environments and a successful competitor in certain lines of business. According to this view we cannot add up heredity and environment or ask what percentage is due to one and what percentage is due to the other.

Even these are not the only alternatives; it is well to see how many different patterns of causation might exist. Some people argue that certain characteristics are likely to develop but that they can be prevented if the environmental influences occur early enough, before the hereditary predisposition has become fixed. One good example of this is the influence of certain physiological deficiencies. A congenital lack of thyroid secretion has serious effects upon the development of intelligence. The individual lacking thyroid becomes a "cretin"; one of his symptoms is feeblemindedness. This can be completely prevented by providing the individual with thyroid in his diet, provided that it is done so at an early age. The adult cretin, however, cannot improve much in intellectual status through thyroid. Similarly, the dangers that accompany the birth of an Rh+ child from an Rh— mother (these indicate characteristics of the blood) can be reduced by a massive transfusion of blood so that the effects of the mother's antibodies are removed. This must take place early, however, or the damage may be irreversible.

The fact that influences may become irreversible after a certain age does not hold merely for those influences that depend upon heredity. A poor environment may be injurious when the child is an infant and produce irremediable effects if allowed to continue beyond a certain age. We shall see that there is evidence that the institutional care of infants may have this sort of irremediable effect if it continues until the child is three years of age. There may be other factors that have more impact at other ages when the child is, for some reason, especially susceptible.

The problem of development is, then, a very complicated one. It is very easy to oversimplify it and to ask the wrong questions about the background factors that lead to such adult characteristics as criminality or mental disease or musical talent or social creativity or altruism. If we cling too closely to the practical problem and try to find how the childhood of criminals differs from that of nondelinquents or how their ancestry differs, we may become involved in a problem that is too complicated to be solved in a sweeping fashion. An alternative strategy for scientists is to concentrate upon learning about the various processes of development. Once we know the possibilities, we can ask the proper questions about the origins of adult personality.

Developmental Processes

The purpose of this section is to suggest a number of processes that bring about changes in a person's characteristics. These are all hypotheses; for some of them there is considerable evidence that will be discussed in detail in later chapters. First, we shall describe some of the processes that seem to function independently of the person's experience. Some of these, called processes of maturation, lead to a higher maturity level, whereas others do not necessarily result in greater maturity. Then there are processes that describe the impact of experience upon the individual's characteristics, his needs, abilities, knowledge, and other traits. Some of these are called learning; others can be related to the usual processes of learning if we accept certain theoretical positions; and others are dynamic processes that do not fit the usual picture of learning. For example, it may be that an experience can initiate or start up a process that then proceeds under its own steam as though it were a maturation process. This is called stimulus-induced maturation. Another process is a hypothesized effect of deprivation upon the later development of needs.

Growth and Maturation

PREDICTABILITY OF INDIVIDUAL DEVELOPMENT   One of the most striking features of human development is its predictability. This predictability can be exaggerated, but still there is a truly remarkable uniformity in the developmental sequences of different children. The course of development of motor skills, for example, is so constant and the sequence of appearance of various patterns of motor activity is so invariant that it can be used as a prognostic test for future growth. Even when there are individual differences in the rate at which this development occurs, there is likely to be very little change in the order of appearance of the various patterns.

Gesell, more than most psychologists, has emphasized and demonstrated the relative constancy in the order of appearance of different abilities. Figure 14.4 shows the appearance of a few illustrative items of behavior in the development of the average child. These items deal entirely with behavior that occurs spontaneously when the child is supine, i.e., lying on his back. Each line of the graph represents a different item of behavior. The graph shows the percentage of infants at each age level who show this type of behavior. The line connecting the dots (●) shows the percentage of children at

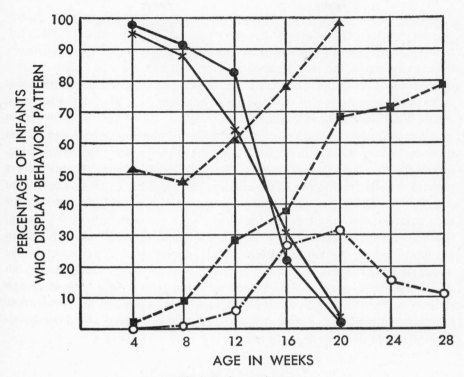

Fig. 14.4 Consistency in the appearance of (supine) behavior patterns. (After A. Gesell, in L. Carmichael, *Manual of Child Psychology*, p. 350)

various ages who, when lying on their backs, kept their heads predominantly rotated to either side rather than unturned. Notice how sharply the predominant rotation of the head declines. At twelve weeks more than 80 percent of the children show it, whereas four weeks later only 20 percent show such behavior. The prevalence of the fencing position of the hands (the *x*'s in the graph), which is associated with the tonic neck reflex (see p. 82), shows a very similar drop because the two items, rotation of the head and fencing position of the hands, are parts of the tonic neck reflex.

Notice that the frequency of a predominantly open position of the hands (■) increases sharply and the frequency of mutual fingering of the hands (O) goes up sharply to a peak and then falls. This graph shows the consistency among children in the time of appearance of specific items of behavior. The orderliness of the growth process is further emphasized by the fact that the order of the appearance of these items is consistent even in children who are generally accelerated or retarded.

Some further indication of the stability of the intellectual growth of individuals may be seen in Figure 14.5, which shows, for five children, the increase of intelligence test scores with age. A perfectly straight line would indicate that the intelligence of the child, relative to other children, is constant and that his test scores are completely regular and predictable. As can be seen from the figure, all of the individual lines are approximately straight, although each child shows some deviations. These data are typical of what has been found in other studies of individual stability of development (Bayley, 1940; Honzik, 1938).

The conclusion to be drawn from such data is that there is considerable stability of the individual patterns of development. Certainly the consistency is sufficiently marked that it must be explained by any theory of development. The individual does not learn to talk or lose egocentricity or develop abstract thinking in a random, chance way. The development of any of these characteristics may be predicted fairly well if one knows the general trends of the whole population. On the other hand, the stability of individual growth curves must not be overstated. Predictability is not complete by any means. Let us, however, examine the reasons that might explain the considerable stability that does exist.

This conformity in the development of children is the most solid basis for the assumption of a maturational process. The growth of the abilities of the child seems—to some extent at least—an unfolding of innate potentialities. Such consistency of development is very difficult to explain in terms of the child's experiences.

MATURATION AS GROWTH OF ABILITY   Sometimes maturation is taken to mean that certain sorts of behavior must necessarily develop at certain ages. The stage of negativism, for example, is sometimes seen as a necessary stage of development. Children must be negativistic at the age of three. It is important to recognize that maturation does not imply that certain *behavior* must occur at certain ages. The abilities of children may mature, and it may be inevitable that children become able to recognize impositions and to resent them, but the actual negativistic behavior is partially under the control of the environment. If the environment does not present impositions to the child,

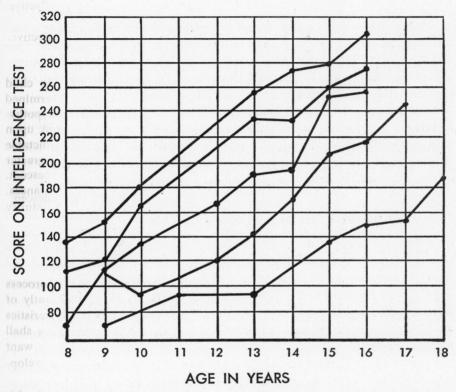

Fig. 14.5 Individual growth curves in intellectual ability. (After F. N. Freeman and C. D. Flory, *Soc. for Research in Child Devel. Monog.*, No. 2, 1937)

he will not be negativistic. Strictly speaking, the maturation process describes the ability of the individual, not his behavior. How this ability affects overt behavior depends upon a variety of other factors, such as his needs and the environmental situation.

Maturation may sometimes not be evidenced directly by the growth of ability. In some cases it seems that the result of maturation is a greater readiness to learn an ability. For example, reading readiness is partially a result of maturation. Even if it were completely predictable, however, the child would not automatically develop the ability to read. He would develop the readiness to learn to read. When the readiness had developed, the child could be taught to read, but if he were not ready, training would be ineffective. All of these processes will be described in fuller detail in Chapter 15.

Other Internally Determined Changes

Since we have made maturity a central concept in describing child behavior, we should reserve the term *maturation* for an internally determined developmental process that brings about greater maturity. We have hypothesized that this process is internally determined, not solely dependent upon experience. There are other processes and changes that are equally predictable but that should not be called maturation because they do not lead to greater maturity. One example is the sudden sexual development of the adolescent. This is a predictable change that occurs in a wide variety of circumstances. It is a part of growing up, but it does not necessarily lead to greater maturity as we have used the term.

Factors in Adjustment That Do Not Increase Maturity

Although some of the developmental changes involve a growth process that is internally determined and proceeds to some extent independently of the experiences of the child, many of the changes of the child's characteristics depend upon his childhood experiences. In Chapters 17, 18, and 19 we shall discuss these processes that depend upon experience. At this point we want merely to enumerate them and to show how they fit into the general development of the child.

Some of the changes that come through experience are important for his adjustment to his environment, but they do not result in any basic increase in maturity. For example, a boy of eight moved to a new town. In exploring the neighborhood he came across a group of boys playing softball. After watching for awhile he was invited to play, and on his first time at bat he made a good hit. As he stood on first base he was aware that his ability had impressed the other boys. As the pitcher prepared to pitch he took a lead off first. Suddenly several players on the other team pointed to him and yelled, "You're out!" Despite his protests he was out, because in his town the boys followed the rule that in softball the man must stay on his base until the ball leaves the pitcher's hand.

As a result of this painful experience the boy learned something that was quite important for his adjustment in so far as playing softball was concerned. Yet it could hardly be said that he had matured as a result of the new information he acquired. He could have understood the rule without the experience. There are many such bits of knowledge, information, and other learning that resemble this item of information in that the behavior after the learning cannot be seen to be more mature than the behavior before it.

If we think about the general characteristics of maturity we can see that none of them describe, in specific, concrete terms the behavior pattern of the mature person. The mature individual knows more about his environment than the immature person. He is better able to understand and to adjust to the concrete circumstances of his specific environment. He can discover the reasons for the things that happen to him, and he can appreciate the consequences of his actions upon the environmental objects with which he deals. He can understand the point of view of other people. In other words, maturity makes it possible to achieve a better adaptation and adjustment to the realities of the world, but there are no specific beliefs, attitudes, habits, or values that invariably characterize maturity. If we examine some of the changes in personal characteristics, we see that many of them describe the adjustment of the person to his specific environment. These changes obviously depend upon his experience in that environment.

HABITS   Habits are behavior sequences that proceed more or less automatically once they are stimulated (see p. 316). In the individual's use of language, for example, phrases come to be automatically selected and used. One does not decide to say "he doesn't" rather than "he don't"; it just happens. Such a habit reflects the specific grammatical rules of the language which the child has learned. In motor activity many skills, such as tying shoelaces and walking, seem to be nearly automatic behavior sequences. These habits specifically reflect the environment to which the individual has been adapted and can be used by an observer to determine the environment from which he comes.

Huck Finn's disguise as a girl was penetrated by the woman who tossed him a ball (Mark Twain, 1885). He clamped his knees together to catch it, whereas a girl would have spread her knees apart. This habit is adjusted to the presence or absence of a skirt. One of the difficult tasks in learning to become a spy is—according to the best spy fiction—to acquire the automatic habits and mannerisms that characterize one's pretended nationality. In England, the spy must keep his fork in his left hand while eating; in America, he must shift it to the right hand after the piece of meat is cut.

At the same time we can see that to learn to eat one way rather than the other does not imply greater maturity. Habits may require a certain maturity to be learned, but the learning does not itself result in increased maturity. Habits are, therefore, one example of a personal characteristic that is a specific acquisition determined by the demands of the environment but nevertheless independent of maturation.

KNOWLEDGE   Another way that the individual becomes adapted to the specific characteristics of his environment is in his body of information. Each of us knows facts and has beliefs that depend upon the environment in which he has lived. Our knowledge would unquestionably have been different had we lived in a different environment. Although it requires more maturity to learn some kinds of information than other kinds, the acquisition of information itself does not raise the maturity level of behavior. Information is a second specific adaptation to the environment in which one lives.

VALUES   Beliefs and habits are not the only characteristics that reflect the external world; some of the needs and the values of the individual must also agree with those of his culture if he is to avoid open conflict. The process by which the individual comes to be a representative of his culture has been called "socialization." It is not necessary to be exactly like everybody in the culture to be socialized. Nevertheless, some values, needs, and attitudes are sufficiently common in the culture that there is a higher degree of similarity among members of the same culture than among representatives of different cultures.

In Western culture, for example, it is expected that people will be competitive. The need to be best is very common. To give a prize for the best performance is a standard procedure for making people work harder to achieve their maximum potentialities. When teachers in the Indian reservation schools attended by Zuni children used this same technique of motivation, they found to their surprise that Zuni children felt hesitant about being best. If the teacher said, "Let's see who is first to finish his problem," she might observe the children deliberately going slowly in order not to be first. The child who excelled felt ill at ease and was resented by the rest.

Thus it can be seen that the individual gradually acquires characteristics that reflect his own environment and his own culture. Some of these characteristics are habits, beliefs, needs, and values.

Relation of Maturation to Learning

We have spoken of these characteristics as though they never contributed to maturity. Sometimes, however, the acquisition of a habit or of some information may lead to more maturity. We might take as an example learning to manipulate simultaneously the accelerator and the clutch in driving a car. To acquire this ability requires some growth. Most people when they first learn to drive do not have these two activities sufficiently coordinated to make a smooth start. Such developments as this bring maturity. It may be that such problems induce a maturation process; we shall speak of this as stimulus-induced maturation. At the same time that the individual is developing this new skill, he is acquiring a habit, a specific adjustment to the clutch and accelerator of the car upon which he learns. When he changes cars he may have to change his habitual pattern slightly; if the new car does not have a clutch pedal he may have to change his habit markedly. This second change does not require any new growth. He has the skill and coordination to manipulate the accelerator and clutch in various ways, although he has to learn the specific combination for each new car.

We can see similar examples in many aspects of childhood. The child who learns not to touch the glassware in the cupboard may be maturing in the sense that he is developing the ability to control his impulses. At the same time he is learning the rules of his own home. In another home there might be no rule against touching glassware, but some other demand that serves the same purpose. We must recognize, of course, that this demand could not induce the necessary maturation unless the child were in general mature enough to be able to learn self-control.

Thus, in real life the processes of maturation and the acquisition of habits, knowledge, or values are all inextricably intertwined. We perhaps cannot find even one situation that can be described solely by one of these factors. Nevertheless, it is useful to separate maturation from learning.

Specific Learning

With this introduction to the general problems, we may proceed to the more specific discussion of learning. The understanding of the conditions of learning and the development of a theory of learning have occupied the energies of a great many psychologists. We shall review in Chapters 17 and 18 the experiments on learning in children and shall examine in Chapter 22 one of the most important learning theories relating to child development. Perhaps as a result of the great interest in learning theories, some people assume that learning is the only mechanism by which experience may affect behavior. If it is not inherited, it must be learned, they argue.

Actually learning, as it has been studied, is a quite restricted effect of experience on behavior. It is limited largely to the specific process of acquiring a behavioral pattern that has been consistently rewarded. Some learning may not seem to be rewarded, but in most cases the subject is at least told whether his performance is right or wrong.

Such learning is undoubtedly very important in this society. The parent teaches the child many skills; the entire school system is geared to inculcate in the child a variety of specific knowledge and skills. Furthermore, the results of a learning experience are not limited to the behavior pattern that was rewarded; the individual may use this behavior pattern in other situations than the one in which he learned it. Learning one skill may make it easier to learn a similar or related skill; it may even develop a general ability. The training of specific athletic skills may develop an all-round athlete. We do not know as much as we should about the diverse effects of training.

Other Effects of Experience

Even with these diverse consequences of learning there are still effects of experience that are difficult to include under learning. For example, one hypothesis that is currently being intensively studied is that the loving care of the young infant is important for his developing a love for people, a sense of trust, and optimism. He is not necessarily being taught to be optimistic by being loved.

The individual may be more susceptible to learning experiences that are gratifying and relaxing. Some general experiences may bring about a state of well-being in the way that eating good food brings about a state of good nutrition. This state may then have marked effects upon how the person responds to a variety of other experiences.

Another illustration of an experience that may affect development, but not through learning, depends upon the fact that learning one skill may make it more likely that the person is put in a position to learn others. This may come about through the nature of the environment. A mother may object to her boy's learning to play pool—not because skill at pool is bad but because she is afraid it will put him in bad company where he will learn undesirable behavior. For another example, association with a botanist may arouse a boy's interest in plants so that he learns much more from his hikes than he did previously.

Still another hypothesis about the effects of experience deals with the consequences of deprivation. Some people believe—and there is some evidence to support it—that if a child is deprived of something he likes, he will want it intensely and never get enough of it when he grows up. Children from concentration camps, in which they were always hungry, frequently hoard food later even when they can have all they want. Just the opposite hypothesis —that if people become used to not having something, they no longer miss it and lose interest in it can also be supported by evidence. We shall look at the evidence for these two hypotheses later.

Summary

In summary, then, we can see that there are some effects of experience that are usually thought of when we speak of learning. If we consider only these when we look at the consequences of experience on development, we are likely to miss important effects. We must, therefore, think of the effects of experience in a very broad sense.

This preview of the problems of development is, in effect, an outline of the rest of this book. First we shall examine the processes underlying development, maturation, learning, and the changes of needs. Then we shall look specifically at the parent-child relationship and its effects on the personality of children. Then we shall examine the two major theories of personality development—general behavior theory and psychoanalytic theory—and examine some of the evidence for them. Finally, we shall try to summarize and integrate all these findings into a tentative theory of personality development.

PART TWO

Development

IN

Childhood

15

Maturation

HEREDITY AND ENVIRONMENT

MATURATION AND LEARNING

STIMULUS-INDUCED MATURATION

SUMMARY

IN THIS CHAPTER we shall try to understand the process of maturation that underlies the very great similarity among the patterns of development of different children. It is this uniformity of development which is the mainstay of the theory that the maturational sequence is fixed—that development is merely the unfolding of a predetermined sequence of steps. Although we shall not accept the theory as a whole, we shall recognize the necessity for assuming some maturational process.

We reviewed in Chapter 14 some of the evidence of similarity in the development of different children. We saw that the sequence of appearance of motor abilities is so constant that it can be used as a test for an individual child. We saw in Chapter 11 that the development of walking, grasping, and crawling was constant enough that it could be described in a series of steps. The development of conceptual schemata and other sorts of development also are consistent among children, although the constancy is not perfect.

Opinions concerning the reasons for this orderliness of development have been divided into two opposite camps, with many people, as usual, attempting to take a middle ground or to resolve the differences between the two extremes. One extreme opinion attributes the orderliness to some sort of predetermined pattern that unfolds during the course of development. The determinants of the pattern have been generally ascribed to heredity, although there are other possible factors that might produce such a predetermined pattern. Because this point of view is supported by the finding that development is orderly, those who maintain this position point to and emphasize the stability of individual development and try to explain away deviations. Because tests are not completely reliable, some of the deviations may be attributed to the tests used.

Those workers who have tried to deny completely that a maturational factor predetermines the developmental sequence have explained the similarities in the development of different children by showing the communality of their environments. It is quite true that children in our culture are exposed to many of the same pressures and opportunities and that some similarity in development should be expected because of that factor. Since a too-great uniformity in development would be difficult for these workers to explain, they tend to point to the demonstrable differences in the development of different children. In other words, they look at the differences rather than the similarities of the growth curves in Figure 14.5 (see p. 368).

Heredity and Environment

Almost inevitably the proponents of these two opposing points of view have also disagreed strongly upon the relative importance of heredity and environment in the determination of the characteristics of human beings. Because this controversy is so entangled with the problems of maturation, we must look at the heredity vs. environment debate. We shall find, however, that to put the question in terms of heredity or environment clouds the issues. The point of view which we shall try to establish is that the most fruitful line of investigation into the problems of developmental psychology does not lie in an attempt to establish the relative importance of heredity and environment.

Comparison of Identical and Fraternal Twins

A good way to begin is to examine one of the best of the typical studies on heredity and environment. An almost ideal method for investigating the relative influence of heredity and environment on the development of an ability is to study indentical twins who have grown up in different environments. The method of such experimentation is to study the similarity between identical twins who have been reared in a common environment, contrasting the findings with those obtained upon two other groups. First, identical twins who have been reared in different environments are contrasted with those reared in the same home. Second, pairs of unrelated children who have been reared together like twins are contrasted with twins. For statistical purposes it is desirable to include also a group of unrelated children reared in different environments. The design for such an experiment, with one example of results, is shown in Table 5, p. 382. Such a study is almost ideal because identical twins have precisely the same heredity. Theoretically it would be better if such twins could be separated at conception so that the common uterine environment could not influence the results, but such an experiment lies at present in the realm of science fiction.

The measure to be obtained for each of the four groups is some index of the similarity of the pairs of children in a specific classification. If it were found that, regardless of whether the children were twins or unrelated, those reared together were more similar than those reared apart, such results would establish the fact that environment makes a difference. If it were found that, regardless of whether they were reared together or apart, twins were more alike than unrelated children, the evidence would prove the existence of a hereditary factor. The evidence might support both of these hypotheses—*i.e.,* identical twins reared together would be most alike, unrelated children reared apart would be least alike, and the other two cells would show intermediate values of similarity. In one such study by Newman, Freeman, and Holzinger (1937), fraternal twins were used instead of unrelated children. (Fraternal twins have a less similar heredity than identical twins but a more similar heredity than unrelated children.) Their findings on height and mental age are summarized in Table 5.

In this experiment the correlation coefficient was used to measure similarity. A coefficient of 1.00 indicates complete similarity. The height of identical twins, whether raised together or apart, resemble each other very closely—*i.e.,* the coefficient is almost 1.00. Identical twins, even when raised apart, are more similar in this respect than fraternal twins raised together. Mental age was found in this experiment to be more affected by environment, although the experiment strongly indicates that similarity of heredity as well as similarity of environment tends to result in a similarity of mental age. In this case, therefore, the effects of heredity were more marked than those of environment in respect to height, but less in respect to mental age.

Such a conclusion is not very satisfying because it holds only for this specific experiment. There is no reason to suppose that the maximum effects of either heredity or environment are being tested. If unrelated children rather than fraternal twins had been used for the experiment, the correlation coefficients in the second row of the table would be much lower and the apparent effects of heredity would be much more marked. On the other hand, had the separated twins been raised in completely different cultures rather than in different homes within the same culture, then the coefficients in the second column might have been much lower and the apparent effects of environment would be more marked.

TABLE 5*

SIMILARITY OF TWINS REARED TOGETHER OR SEPARATELY

Similarity of Identical Twins Reared Together	*Similarity of Identical Twins Reared Apart*
Height $r = .98$	Height $r = .97$
Mental Age $r = .92$	Mental Age $r = .64$
Similarity of Fraternal Twins Reared Together	*Similarity of Fraternal Twins Reared Apart*
Height $r = .93$	Height $r =$ no data
Mental Age $r = .83$	Mental Age $r =$ no data

There is no way the experimenters could equate the difference in environments with the difference in heredities represented in the study. It may seem meaningless even to ask whether two different cultures represent environments that are more or less different than is the heredity of unrelated children of the same race. Although such a question is meaningless, it must be answered if any conclusion about the relative strength of heredity and environment is to be scientifically determined. Such studies as the one we have reported can demonstrate that the effect of either heredity or environment is not negligible. The hypothesis that either factor has no effect can be tested and either proved or disproved by such experiments. For quantitative statements beyond that conclusion, the experiments are of dubious value.

Even if such an experiment were possible, it would be legitimate to question its significance. How would such information, if it could be obtained reliably, be used, and what theories would it support? For studies in eugenics it might be useful. People who advocate selective breeding of humans and sterilization of the unfit would find such studies important.

For the understanding of the process of child development, however, it is hard to see just what would be the contribution of such an experiment. Even for the purely practical questions of training mental defectives or pro-

* From H. H. Newman, F. N. Freeman, and K. J. Holzinger, *Twins: A Study of Heredity and Environment*, University of Chicago Press, 1937.

viding stimulating environment for bright children, the relevant experiments are those dealing with the modifiability of development, not with the relative effects of heredity and environment. Once it has been established that neither heredity nor environment is negligible, the question loses much of its significance for child development. It can be safely assumed that for very few psychological characteristics will either factor, heredity or environment, be equal to zero.

Studies on Phenylketonuria

This argument does not imply that all studies of genetics are fruitless. In fact, we could profit greatly if we adopted the point of view of geneticists. Their efforts are directed toward the discovery of the *mechanism* of hereditary causation. Their approach to the problem can be illustrated by the research on a condition called *phenylketonuria* or *phenylpyruvic oligophrenia,* which can be diagnosed by means of a chemical test revealing the presence of phenylpyruvic acid in the urine. The studies of the pedigrees of the afflicted patients reveal a hereditary factor (Snyder, 1946). It is associated with a severe mental deficiency, and it has been found to be present in about one-half of one percent of the mental defectives in one hospital. It has been shown that the presence of phenylpyruvic acid in the urine stems from the fact that in the metabolic chain of reactions the enzyme necessary for oxidizing phenylalanine is missing. Consequently, the substance that should be used up in this reaction is not consumed but, instead, collects until it finally is excreted in the urine. How the effect upon mental functioning takes place is not known: possibly the metabolism of the brain is starved by the absence of what should be produced by the missing step, possibly the excess phenylalanine that should be destroyed by the missing step acts as a sort of poison, or possibly there is a more indirect relationship.

Penetrance

The contrast between these two types of studies is striking. Each one referred to is a well-conducted experiment, but the two illustrate quite different points of view. The first is concerned with measuring the amount of genetic influence. The second is concerned with explaining the process by which the genetic factor leads to the appearance of various symptoms. The fact that genes do not always lead to the same symptoms is expressed in the field of genetics by the concept of *penetrance.* The penetrance of a genetic condition is measured by the percentage of people with the proper genes for the condition who actually exhibit the condition. Penetrance may be 100 percent, as in the case of blood groups; 10 percent is the estimated penetrance of diabetes.

A penetrance of 100 percent signifies that the condition is completely predictable if the genes are known to be present. A low penetrance means that even if the genes associated with the condition are present, the probability of the symptom's actually occurring is still quite low. Such an index does not measure the relative importance of heredity and environment. Suppose that the penetrance of phenylketonuria were 100 percent. This still would not measure the importance of heredity in feeblemindedness, because phenylketonuria is not the only kind of feeblemindedness, and it would not necessarily be true that all cases of phenylketonuria have this single genetic cause. A statement of 100 percent penetrance merely indicates that when this cause is present, it inevitably leads to the consequent symptoms. The factors that keep the penetrance of a genetic condition low may be environmental, or they may be other genetic characteristics of the individual.

To the extent that we are interested in understanding the processes of the development of personality, it is the second type of experiment rather than the first that contributes significantly to our knowledge. Unfortunately we are not as yet in a position to carry out the second type of experiment as adequately as we might wish, but such experiments mark the path leading to a theoretical explanation of development because they attempt to elucidate the mechanisms underlying development. It is important to note that the significance of the research on phenylketonuria is not, due to its physiological character, but to its intent. Psychological experiments can and frequently do have this same sort of intent, but it seems that the controversy about the relative importance of heredity and environment has continued unduly long in social science to the detriment of a real understanding of the processes by which hereditary and other developmental factors bring about psychological characteristics.

Maturation and Learning

Another issue that has been central to the field of child psychology for many years is entitled *maturation vs. learning*. Experiments on maturation and learning have taken the form of discovering how much the developmental sequence of an individual may be modified by special intensive training or unusual impoverishment of environmental opportunity.

Significance of Problem

We shall examine the evidence on this question quite carefully, because it is much more directly related to the important practical questions of child development than is the study of heredity and environment. The outcome of these studies may provide us eventually with the answers to very significant questions. Should mental defectives be given expensive training in the attempt to bring them to the point where they can adjust to society outside an institution? Perhaps some such patients are treatable and others not. If so, how can they be diagnosed? This area of research stems directly from the analysis of the modifiability of development.

A very different practical question depending upon the same body of information is the timing of subject matter in education. Some people feel, for example, that children ought not be taught to read until they reach the third grade, because the usual first-grade child has not matured enough to learn to read. Some people have advocated that arithmetic be postponed until quite late, so that it will not be learned by rote but rather through a real understanding of the processes. Such questions as these cannot be answered until we know more about the relationship between the maturation process and the special experiences of the individual.

Before turning to the discussion of the experiments on maturation and learning, we should notice that the abilities that develop through a maturation process are not necessarily inherited. The development of an ability might, for example, be initiated by an experience whose after-effects influence the developmental process even after the experience itself is over. After a look at some of the experiments and observations on the modifiability of development, we shall return to a consideration of the nature of this maturation process.

Evidence on Maturation and Learning

STUDIES IN CO-TWIN CONTROL   The evidence that points to some sort of maturational process is, first and foremost, the general consistency of similarity of growth among different people. If despite the differences in the environment of different children they show a highly consistent pattern of development, there must be some sort of developmental process that is not easily modified by special environmental circumstances. Another type of study that has given convincing evidence of some predetermination of development is called the method of *co-twin control.* Gesell and Thompson (1929), for example, studied the modifiability of developmental patterns by giving one of a pair of identical twins special training on such activities as climbing stairs and building structures with cubes. Twin *T* (for trained) was given daily practice over a six-week period, whereas the control twin *C* was given no opportunity to practice these activities. After *T* had been trained for six weeks, *C* was then given two weeks' training. The results of this study are typical of others also. When *C* was first allowed to perform any of the activities in which *T* was trained, she did better than *T* had done on her first attempt six weeks earlier but not as well as *T* was doing at the moment. In the two-week period of delayed training, *C* improved almost as much as *T* had in six weeks (see Figure 15.1). At this time the stair-climbing behavior of the two children was nearly identical.

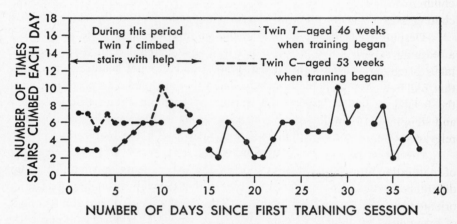

Fig. 15.1 Comparison of the development of a specially trained child with that of her untrained twin. (After A. Gesell and H. Thompson, *Genet. Psych. Monog., 6,* 1929, 1-124)

In other words, the training does improve performance—*i.e.,* the trained twin does improve more rapidly than the untrained twin. The performance of the untrained twin does not remain stationary, however; it improves somewhat without any special training. If training is introduced at a later age it is more effective than a similar training period at the earlier age. The older child is a faster learner than the younger.

In some experiments the training itself seems to be of almost no value. McGraw (1940), in another experiment on twins, toilet-trained one twin during infancy. Despite the fact that the other twin received no special training, the performance of the two at eighteen months was indistinguishable.

One difficulty that must be faced in reaching a proper interpretation of these experiments is the definition of training. In most of the experiments, training includes only those experiences that are actual attempts to perform the activity that will later be tested. Such a definition is too limited, but it is easier to recognize than to rectify the error.

Growth is not something that goes on completely isolated from all environmental conditions. At the very minimum the environment must be sufficient to support life. Illness and malnutrition have been shown to modify the maturation process by temporarily slowing physical and behavioral development (Todd, 1938). Yet such evidence of environmental influence can hardly be interpreted to mean that the developing behavior patterns are necessarily learned. To reduce it to an absurdity, eating is necessary for the developing of stair climbing because the child must eat to live and dead children do not climb stairs; yet nobody feels inclined to say that while the child eats he is learning to climb stairs.

Despite the fact that not every experience necessary for development is a learning experience, it is quite as inappropriate to argue that no learning takes place outside the situation in which it is tested. It is generally admitted that children may learn from experiences that are similar to those in which the behavior will be tested. Thus, the experience of C in walking around and stepping on mounds or stools might well be thought of as training that is relevant for stair climbing even though she did no actual stair climbing.

THE EFFECTIVENESS OF TRAINING AT VARIOUS AGES If the two concepts of maturation and learning are to be distinguished, it seems that the important difference between them is in their temporal course. Maturation is somehow oriented to elapsed time, whereas learning is a process that is oriented in terms of experiences that occur in time.

Two experiments in animal development illustrate the interrelation between time and experience. In the first one, performed by Carmichael (1926) to study the development of swimming in salamanders, tadpoles were anaesthetized by dissolving an anaesthetic in the water. Under this light anaesthetic they continue to develop normally in so far as observable physical structure is concerned but engage in no behavior. When one group of salamanders is anaesthetized at the age just before swimming activity begins to be displayed and a control group is allowed to remain in ordinary water, it can be shown that the effects on the later development of swimming in the first group depend upon the length of time it is anaesthetized. With short periods of anaesthetization (several days), the lack of experience in swimming activities has no consequences. The experimental animals seem to be able to swim as well as did the control group as soon as they recover from the anaesthetic. The loss of the several days of behavioral practice has no effect. Matthews and Detweiler (1926) have shown, however, that if the anaesthetic is continued for longer periods, the behavior does not develop in a typical fashion, and with immersion of more than thirteen days the swimming behavior remains very feeble even though the animal continues to live.

Similar results were obtained in an experiment on pecking in chicks (Shepard and Breed, 1913; Bird, 1925). Newly hatched chicks cannot peck very accurately, but after a short time in the yard their pecking accuracy

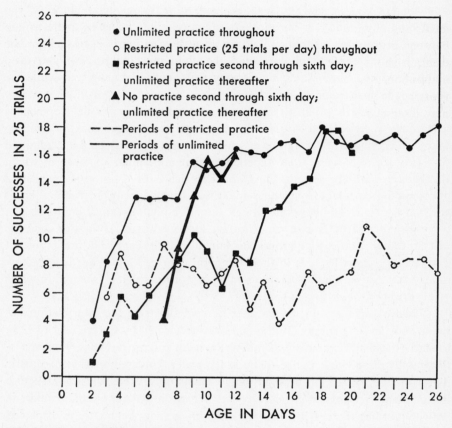

Fig. 15.2 Development of pecking in chicks after a period of impoverishment. (After Charles Bird, *Ped. Sem., 32,* 1925, 68-91)

improves markedly. This improvement in pecking skill may be used to study the effects of experience. The control chicks are allowed to peck from the time they are hatched, but the experimental groups are kept in the dark and fed with an eye dropper for various lengths of time before they are allowed to try to peck. The trend of the results is that chicks kept in the dark for one to five days mature somewhat even in the dark. Their performance upon the first attempt to peck is more accurate than was that of newly hatched chicks, but it is not as efficient as the pecking of chicks who have spent the intervening time in the light. Furthermore, there is some evidence that after they are allowed practice they improve more rapidly than did the newly hatched chicks when they first began to practice pecking. If, however, the experimental chicks are kept in the dark for more than two weeks, they never do learn to peck even after being offered ample opportunity to practice (see Fig. 15.2).

SUMMARY OF RESULTS We can summarize the results of these experiments and observations in the diagram in Figure 15.3 showing the interaction between practice and age of the organism in the development of a skill. The diagram shows that within limits practice may substitute for maturation, or maturation for practice, but that unless there is sufficient maturation practice is extremely inefficient, and that without practice the ability which has matured may disappear.

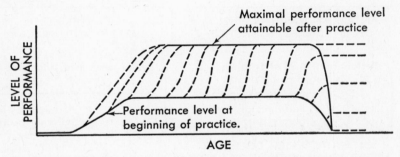

Fig. 15.3 Interaction of age and practice in the development of an ability.

The figure shows two curves that grow and then decline. The lower of these represents one aspect of maturation, the skill displayed by the organism upon the first trial. The behavior of the organism without any previous practice is shown by the lower curve. This curve increases with age up to a peak, indicating that the first performance of the behavior will become more skillful with age without any practice, but only up until a certain age. After that the skill of the organism will decrease if he has had no previous practice. Eventually the organism will ease its ability, as did the chicks who were kept from pecking for two weeks or the salamanders who were kept anaesthetized for thirteen days.

The upper curve of the diagram shows the maximum performance of which the organism is capable after optimal practice. We can think of the dotted lines extending from the lower curve to the upper as learning curves. If practice is begun at the time *a* shown on the diagram, the first performance will be indicated by the height of the lower curve. The dotted learning curve that begins at that point shows the increase of the skill with practice until it reaches a maximum indicated by *b* in the diagram. The upper curve shows the maximum skill that may be obtained if the practice is begun at the time indicated by the lower end of the learning curve. The learning curves become steeper in the middle of the diagram, indicating that learning that is begun later is more efficient than learning that is started early.

The maximum level of performance is seen to decline if the beginning of practice is withheld for too long a period, and with a sufficiently long impoverishment the organism becomes entirely unable to acquire the skill.

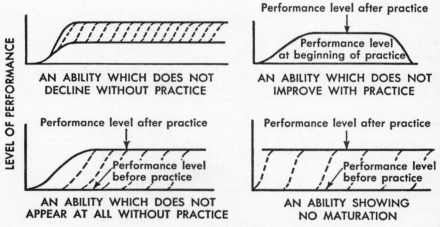

Fig. 15.4 Four patterns of development of abilities.

A diagram of this complexity is required to describe the results obtained in the experiments on pecking in chicks or Gesell's and Thompson's study of twins *T* and *C*. For specific skills the shapes of these curves would certainly differ, and the relations between the lower and upper curve would not always be the same. Figure 15.4 shows some examples of the possible curves. At the upper left we see the curves for an ability that does not decline even if not practiced. Some skills probably show that characteristic. At the upper right we see the situation found in the experiments on swimming in salamanders. The lower and the upper curves are identical. Whatever ability existed did not require any practice to be demonstrated. The maximum performance is the same as the first. The lower-left figure shows the growth of skill in understanding a language. Unless the individual has some practice with a language, his first trial shows no understanding at all. In other words, the lower curve is zero. Nevertheless, he does show an improvement in the efficiency of learning the language, as illustrated by the steepness of the learning curves. The height of the lower curve and the steepness of the learning curves *both* indicate maturation. At the lower right we see the situation if a skill did not depend at all upon maturation. The initial performance and the efficiency of learning would not change with the age of the individual. There are probably no such skills, but there may be.

Stimulus-induced Maturation

Children not infrequently find music lessons very interesting for awhile, but after a few months the daily practice becomes quite boring. Parents sometimes use the allegory of the ball of twine to concretize their insistence upon daily practice. They tell the child that if you are winding up a ball of string you must carefully wind it one wind at a time. If you let it drop even once, so much of it unwinds that it takes you a long time just to make up what has been lost. Music lessons are the same, they say. You must practice every day or else you will have to spend your time just making up for lost ground.

Fortunately the allegory is not entirely true. If a child takes a vacation from his music over the summer or over Christmas holidays it sometimes comes as a great surprise that he seems to be better after the holiday than before. He may be a little rusty at first, but he rapidly surpasses his preholiday performance. William James expressed this finding in the phrase that we learn to ice-skate in summer and swim in winter.

Statement of Hypothesis

The significance of this fact and the many others like it is that it suggests that the development of skills may depend upon the passage of time even if the skill is one that would not have developed through the usual maturation process we have just discussed. We found that time was an important factor in the development of abilities, but the time was considered to begin with the birth of the child. Whatever maturation occurs has been thought to depend upon the processes of development that are common to all children.

What the effect of rest periods in the course of learning suggests is that some developmental processes may be initiated or induced by environmental stimulation—that by practicing the cornet for several months a developmental process is started. This developmental process then shows all the properties that we have found in maturation.

This hypothesis—that what is usually called learning is sometimes actually a maturation process stimulated by some environmental event that challenges the individual—is called the hypothesis of *stimulus-induced maturation*. The name was formulated by Hilgard (1948) who, together with his students, has investigated the possibility of such learning. The notion itself was first suggested by Wheeler (1929).

According to the hypothesis, stimulating environmental events can initiate a growth process that takes place in time. The result of such growth is that the organism is more mature when, after a rest period, it again faces the situations that originally stimulated the growth.

If such a hypothesis is adopted, it would be reasonable to suggest further that the sensitivity and responsiveness of the organism to stimulation and challenge depend in large part upon the level of maturation that the organism has already attained. A further implication of the point of view is that some of the normally expected abilities of the adult in any culture depend upon the occurrence of such stimulus-induced maturation. The culture normally induces the maturation of special abilities that are required in that culture. Because of this dependence upon stimulus-induced maturation, an impoverishment of the environment that strips it of its challenging characteristics deprives the organism of an opportunity to mature. The result is a retarded child or an adult with unrealized potentialities.

Examples of Stimulus-induced Maturation

There are many examples of such stimulating and maturing experiences. The function of a good teacher is assumed to be primarily the stimulation of growth and maturation, not merely the providing of answers and techniques. The following experience of Helen Keller illustrates the kind of experience that is ordinarily thought of as stimulating. The quotation is from a letter by Miss Keller's teacher, Miss Sullivan (Keller, 1903).*

Helen has taken the second great step in her education. She has learned that everything has a name and that the manual alphabet is the key to everything she wants to know. . . .

We went out to the pump-house and I made Helen hold her mug under the spout while I pumped. As the cold water gushed forth, filling the mug, I spelled "W-A-T-E-R" in Helen's hand. The word coming so close upon the sentence seemed to startle her. She dropped the mug and stood as one transfixed. A new light came into her face. She spelled "W-A-T-E-R" several times. Then she dropped on the ground and asked for its name and pointed to the pump and the trellis and

* From *The Story of My Life,* by Helen Keller. Copyright 1903 by Helen Keller, reprinted by permission of Doubleday and Co., Inc.

suddenly turning around she asked for my name. . . . All the way back to the house she was highly excited and learned the name of every object she touched, so that in a few hours she had added thirty new words to her vocabulary.

Stimulus-induced Maturation in Motor Skill

The most direct sort of evidence on the hypothesis of stimulus-induced maturation can be obtained from the study of the learning of specific skills. The process of learning a motor skill will be studied to determine whether the same pattern of factors operate in such learning as operate in the development of other abilities with age. If the factors of time and practice have the same pattern of interrelationship in the learning of a skill over a short period of time as they have in the development of an ability over a long range of time, the hypothesis of stimulus-induced maturation will be supported, because these specific skills are clearly dependent upon practice. The central point of the discussion is, therefore, the relationship between elapsed time and practice trials in motor learning.

As we pointed out earlier in the chapter, the improvement that occurs over a long rest implies that something goes on during the dormant season. It has been a striking experience to many a person to come back to some activity after a long rest, expecting to be rusty and unskilled, only to find that with a relatively small amount of practice his skill seems even greater than it was before the rest period.

These results resemble the ones that we found in the study of maturation. The child, merely through growing older, is maturing so that his performance is better than it would have been earlier. The only difference between learning during rest periods and maturing before training has begun is that the improvement over the rest period depends upon having practiced before the rest period. If this improvement during rest is to be called maturation, then it is maturation that is begun by some sort of training—in other words, stimulus-induced maturation.

The first recorded psychological studies in this area dealt with the effect of massed practice as opposed to practice spaced over an extended time interval. If, for example, twenty repetitions of an act of skill are to be permitted, it has been found that more efficient learning almost always results when these trials are spaced over a long period of time than when the twenty trials are crowded into a short time period.

Some process apparently goes on during the rest period that results in improved performance. One possibility is that fatigue or a similar interference builds up when the trials are closely clustered and that with a time interval this fatigue effect is dissipated; the individual becomes rested and performs better than he did on the last of the massed trials. Such an effect can certainly occur. Another possibility is that practice initiates a growth process that continues even after the practice is stopped and results in continued improvement of performance. Which of these interpretations best fits the data can be considered in the light of the following experiment by Bell (1942).

He used a pursuit rotor task. A piece of metal was fastened to a revolving disc similar to a phonograph turntable. The task of the subject was to keep a stylus in contact with the piece of metal as the disc revolved. As long as the stylus stayed in contact with the metal, a clock was activated so that the success of the subject could be measured by the total time his stylus was touching the metal target during the one-minute trial. There were twenty

TABLE 6*

SUMMARY OF EFFECTS OF REST PERIODS ON LEARNING

Group	Rest Period	Score on Trial No.							
		1	5	6	7	15	16	17	20
A	1 min. after each trial	51	215	251	271	422	442	455	450
B	10 min. after trial No. 5	63	222	300	327				440
C	1 hr. after trial No. 5	60	219	274	321				450
D	6 hr. after trial No. 5	55	220	286	344				480
E	24 hr. after trial No. 5	56	211	281	331				470
F	30 hr. after trial No. 5	62	220	283	323				460
G	10 min. after trial No. 15	46	217			402	443	455	460
H	1 hr. after trial No. 15	55	221			397	399	439	450
I	6 hr. after trial No. 15	64	216			394	365	418	440
J	24 hr. after trial No. 15	56	223			418	399	440	460
K	30 hr. after trial No. 15	61	217			395	385	430	460

trials of one minute each separated by rest periods of one minute. At two points in the process, after the fifth trial or after the fifteenth trial, the experimenter introduced longer rests for certain groups of subjects.

There were eleven groups in all, a control group and two sets of five experimental groups each. For one set of experimental groups the rest was introduced between the fifteenth and sixteenth trials; for the other set the rest period came after the fifth. For one group in each set of five, the rest period was ten minutes, for another, one hour; for another, six hours; for another, twenty-four hours; and for the fifth in each set the rest was thirty hours. The results are shown in Table 6.

Regardless of how many trials came before the rest period, a ten-minute rest produced more improvement than the standard one-minute rest of the

* H. M. Bell, "Rest Pauses in Motor Learning as Related to Snoddy's Hypothesis of Mental Growth," *Psych. Monog.*, 54:243 1942.

control group. This was a temporary improvement; there was no evidence of a permanent effect. There was no evidence that the ten-minute rest made the subject better able to profit from further practice, as indicated by the gain from trial No. 6 to 7, or 16 to 17.

For longer rests there is a marked difference depending upon whether rest comes early or late in the learning process; there are gains if the rest comes early and losses if it comes late. And there is an indication but no reliable evidence that the early long rests, especially the six-hour rest, have permanent effects in that the final performance after twenty trials is improved. The losses suffered during the late rest periods are made up. For these longer rest periods there is always a considerable gain between the first and second trial after a rest, possibly to be interpreted as an increased sensitivity to learning experiences.

The fact that these effects occur over a six-hour rest period suggests that the process going on during that rest is not merely recovery from fatigue in the usual sense of the word. The effect of the ten-minute rest, on the other hand, is quite reasonably interpreted as recovery from fatigue because the interval is not long and because the effect operates in the same way both early and late in the course of learning.

If what is going on during the longer rest periods is interpreted as a stimulus-induced growth process counterbalanced by forgetting, then the following statements can be made about this maturation process: (1) The amount of such growth and the length of time it is effective depends upon whether it occurs early or late in the learning process. (2) It has an upper time limit, *i.e.,* the rest period can be too long. (This is illustrated in other studies on the problem.) (3) It is reflected not only in changes appearing immediately after rest, but also in increased sensitivity to further practice, as shown in the rapid improvement between trials No. 6 and 7, or 16 and 17. This combination of characteristics resembles so closely the general maturation process as revealed in the studies of the effect of age upon susceptibility to practice that it may be taken to support the hypothesis that this sort of motor learning includes a growth process that is automatically initiated by practice.

One of the important problems involved in the hypothesis of stimulus-induced maturation is the proper definition of the stimulating effect of the environment. Hilgard (1948) and his coworkers have examined the hypothesis that the improvement is strictly proportional to the amount of elapsed time after the beginning of practice, but they found that such a simple hypothesis did not fit the data. In Bell's experiment, for example, the final scores are much more nearly proportional to the amount of practice than to the elapsed time.

If, then, the hypothesis of stimulus-induced growth is to be accepted, it will be necessary to investigate the stimulating effect of various numbers of trials to see whether the data can be accurately predicted.

Another sort of evidence from such a learning experiment that would support the hypothesis that it was actually a maturation process would be the finding that the actual behavior early in the learning showed the qualitative symptoms of immaturity, whereas the final behavior was more mature. In some kinds of motor learning we can see the behavior become more mature as the skill increases. In the discussion of differentiation (see p. 82) we spoke of the lack of differentiated finger movements in the beginning pianist. With more time and practice these movements come to be more differentiated and independent of each other. In many examples of motor learning we can observe similar qualitative changes in the performance as the skill increases. There have been, however, no experimental studies that have established such a change during the learning of motor skills. The distinction between that learning which is really maturation and that which is merely the accumulation of information would be made clearer if it could be shown that the behavior before and after the acquisition of information does not differ in maturity, whereas in the process of stimulus-induced maturation the behavior does change in the direction of later maturity. This distinction will be assumed in the next few chapters, which discuss the characteristics of learning.

Stimulation

If the hypothesis of stimulus-induced maturation is tenable, it becomes very important to examine the concept of stimulation itself. We have already used the word *stimulation* in Part I of the book to denote any sort of patterned stimulus situation. Such stimulation was postulated to produce tension in the organism. A certain kind of stimulation was defined as an instigation. Such a situation also produces tension, and, in the case of the prolonged exposure to such situations occurring in frustration, the tension can mount to uncontrollable heights, producing a variety of reactions. The concept of stimulation employed up to this point suggests some parallels to the sort of situation that in everyday language is spoken of as stimulating.

In this everyday language, a stimulating situation, if it is not too severe, generally carries the connotation of being challenging. In other words, it presents the individual an attractive goal that is not too easily reached but yet is attainable. It is recognized as producing tension but not a too-severe tension. In some way this slightly uncomfortable state is an essential part of a challenge. A too-comfortable state of affairs is unstimulating and produces lethargy. A too-severe challenge is so frustrating that it has deleterious consequences and does not produce growth. A challenge that is almost too severe to be met can overtax the organism and leave no room for development.

Following the general conceptualization of the first part of the book, stimulation is now hypothesized to induce maturation or growth under certain conditions. The proper conditions cannot be more adequately defined than to state that some medium level of tension is optimal. Since stimulation is not a completely undifferentiated process, it is quite conceivable that as a focused stimulation is motivating, so a motive that is not immediately satisfied produces a special sort of growth directed in some sense toward the satisfaction of that motive. Presumably each trial on a problem is stimulating because during it the individual is actively motivated. There may be a growth response to any generalized type of stimulation—for example, the child's playing with many different shapes, hearing the mother's voice, and seeing many colored objects. Such a question must be answered by research.

Regardless of the way in which situations stimulate growth, it must be true that the characteristics of a challenge depend upon maturity. What is challenging to the infant need not be challenging to the older child, and perhaps in our culture the child inevitably meets a predictable series of challenging situations. In psychoanalytic theory the existence of certain prescribed states of maturation is postulated, but they are also described as challenges. Weaning, toilet training, etc., pose problems for the child that he must solve. It may be that because of the maturity level at which these events occur, the challenge they present to the child is fairly consistent from one child to another. If the challenge is not presented, then the child does not grow, or if the challenge is too great, fixation on that level of development can occur (see pp. 552f.). This is what psychoanalysis tells us, and in this respect it agrees with our hypothesis. Whether or not childhood is as dominated by these specific challenges as psychoanalysts seem to believe is a question that will be examined later.

Summary

In this chapter we have analyzed the process of maturation. First, we distinguished between the question of heredity versus environment and the contrast of maturation and learning. By an analysis of two experiments on heredity and environment, we have tried to show that unless we look for the mechanisms underlying heredity, knowledge about its importance is not very significant.

The studies of maturation and learning can be fit together into a single consistent pattern. Maturation occurs over time. It has two sorts of effects: one to increase the efficiency of performance and the other to increase the efficiency of learning. Of these, the second is probably the more basic. Elapsed time, whether or not it includes practice, is accompanied by improved performance, although not as much improvement as if the time had been spent in practice. In many activities, however, there must be some practice of a skill before a certain point in time if the maturational potentialities are to be realized. If practice is withheld too long, permanent decrease in ability is produced.

In the last part of the chapter we examined the evidence for a process of stimulus-induced maturation. The common experience of improving over a rest period suggests that practice may initiate a maturation process that continues during rest intervals. In one experiment we saw some evidence for such a process. In the next chapter we shall see whether these hypotheses about maturation, practice, and stimulus-induced maturation are borne out by evidence on the development of intellectual abilities in children.

16

Environmental Stimulation and the Development of Abilities

EFFECTS OF SPECIAL ENVIRONMENTAL STIMULATION
UPON INTELLECTUAL DEVELOPMENT

STUDIES ON EFFECT OF IMPOVERISHED ENVIRONMENT

STUDIES OF EFFECTS OF NURSERY-SCHOOL
ATTENDANCE UPON I.Q.

THE EFFECTS OF INSTITUTIONALIZATION IN INFANCY

SUMMARY

WE HAVE DEVELOPED, in the last chapter, the concept of maturation. Two hypotheses stemming from this concept are that stimulation results in growth and that long deprivation of stimulation may lead to retardation and permanent defect. These two hypotheses have been advanced with respect to the important human characteristics of intelligence and sociability. In this chapter we shall review the controversies that these two hypotheses have produced and examine some of the evidence bearing on them. First we shall study the effect of environment on intelligence.

Effects of Special Environmental Stimulation upon Intellectual Development

At various times in recent years some groups of workers in the field of child psychology have claimed that the intellectual abilities of children can be markedly changed by providing them with a highly stimulating environment. These claims have in every instance been met with strong, vehement denials. Perhaps more harsh words have been exchanged by psychologists over this issue than over any other in psychology. For this reason it is important to analyze the problem carefully and to point out the precise consequences of the hypotheses.

Implications of Changes in Intelligence Test Scores

Let us first assume that no such phenomenon as stimulus-induced maturation can occur, that environmental stimulation has no effect on intellectual development. We shall consider the changes in intelligence test scores that might be expected under this assumption. Then we can see what additional changes depend upon the assumption that the development of abilities may be induced or retarded by environmental stimulation or impoverishment.

DEPENDENCE OF TEST ITEMS ON EXPERIENCE It has always been recognized that the score on an intelligence test is not a foolproof measure of intellectual ability. Ever since the tests have been available there have been parents who coached their children on the items in the intelligence test so that the children obtained spuriously high scores. This is possible because of the fact that many of the items in an intelligence test depend upon the acquisition of specific bits of knowledge and information. For example, the following items form a part of the Stanford-Binet test: "What makes a sailboat move?" "What is an *eyelash*?" "What does *roar* mean?" "How are a baseball and an orange alike and different?"

These questions depend partly, although not solely, upon information. The child who has seen sailboats, has sailed in one, and has played with a model sailboat would know why they moved at an earlier age than a child who had never had anything to do with sailboats. It is possible to teach a very young child the answers to items that he would not normally be expected to answer until a much older age.

An intelligence test consists of a battery of such items. The measured intelligence of the child, the I.Q., is the number of these items which he passes compared with the number which the average child of his age is expected to pass (see p. 270). If so many of the test items depend upon learned information, we might be inclined to think that the test could not measure intellectual ability, but only training. Such a conclusion is not true, however, because the child is unable to acquire some information at an early age. Although knowing what moves a sailboat does depend upon learning, the child of three or four can hardly understand the answer. He is not able to learn this information under normal conditions, and therefore his having this knowledge implies two things: first, that he is able to acquire this information, and, second, that he has had an opportunity to do so.

If the test is to be a valid measure of ability, the information that is necessary must be so commonly available that the child acquires the information as soon as he is able to do so—*i.e.,* the opportunity to have this knowledge must be equal for all children. Then their acquisition of it and use of it reflects their abilities rather than the opportunities to which they have been exposed. Equality of opportunity is a prerequisite for the validity of the test as a measure of ability.

The psychologists who design intelligence tests are well aware of this fact. Terman and Merrill (1937), who have designed and standardized the revision of the Stanford-Binet test, included in their sample children from all parts of the country, from all social classes, from homes of various racial and national origin. They used as the standardization group—*i.e.,* the group of children on whom the test was first tried and whose results determine what items the average child is expected to pass—a small replica of the population of the United States.

No care in standardization can, however, entirely equalize the opportunities of all children. If a child is specifically taught the answers to the test items, he may learn them and get a high score, but it will not reflect the general level of his information. Even if he is not specifically coached, but lives in a home where the necessary information is easily available, his scores will reflect his opportunity. On the other hand, children from a different culture or from an atypical subculture may not have had the usual opportunity to acquire the answers to the test items.

Thus, there is evidence that children from communities with very poor educational opportunities, such as canalboat children in England, show drops in I.Q., especially after they reach school age (Gordon, 1923). Backwoods children in the United States show a similar phenomenon (Asher, 1935; Chapanis and Williams, 1945). Children whose contact with the world is hampered and not compensated for—children with unrecognized poor vision, for example—are likely to have low I.Q.'s. Whether current intelligence tests are very sensitive to this sort of artifact is a highly debatable issue. It has been claimed by Allison Davis (1948) on the basis of his research that the usual tests are "middle-class oriented" and do not apply very well to the experiences of lower-class children.

Since obviously an environment can present information in ways that are more or less clear, it must, therefore, be possible to do a better than average job of teaching a child the facts common in our culture. Such training will help him get a high test score. It would be very surprising, therefore, if it were not possible to raise as well as lower intelligence test scores through environmental stimulation. This fact does not mean that the child's ability is increased, but only that the maximal ability of the child is realized in test performance.

DEPENDENCE OF TEST SCORES ON ABILITY   Although it is important to recognize the fact that mental test scores are dependent upon the exposure of the child to an environment that is not too different from that of the standardization group, it is equally important to recognize that the I.Q. is more than a measure of the experiences the child has encountered. Before he can get test credit, he must have learned something from these experiences, and what he learned from them is dependent upon how intelligent he is. Since the tests are designed ideally to measure the maximal ability, it is much easier for environmental impoverishment to produce a low test score than for environmental enrichment to produce an unusually high test score. There is an upper limit to what the child could learn under the best of circumstances because of the limits of his ability. There is almost no lower limit that could not be reached if his environment were sufficiently different from that of the usual American child. To obtain a valid test of children in another culture it is generally necessary to develop tests that are suited to that culture.

DEPENDENCE OF TEST SCORES ON MOTIVATION   We have said that intelligence testing is dependent upon the opportunities provided by the environment and upon the ability to acquire information and use the knowledge thus provided. There is another factor underlying the behavior of the child in the test situation that must be included—his motivation and needs. The examiner is always concerned with the child's interest and motivation during the test. If the child becomes bored, if he does not try to answer the questions as best he can, the examiner is dubious of the validity of the obtained score.

Motivation and needs may also enter the picture in a more general way. The child's general interests partly determine what he will absorb from his environment. He will pay attention to the aspects of his world that are of especial interest to him and will tend to ignore those things that are of no concern. The ability to which we refer in maturation is not intended to include his interests. The child's interests may keep some of his ability from being realized, but we wish to exclude these motivational factors. The tests are designed to include a wide range of items that tap a number of interests, so that a child with one especial interest does not have an especial advantage, but it is very difficult to find a test for the intellectual ability of children who do not have any intellectual interests.

The effect of motivational and personality factors need not be this specific. Freedom from anxiety, for example, should allow the child to capitalize on his opportunities and should also make him less susceptible to shyness and reticence in the test situation.

Importance of Permanence of Changes in Test Scores

None of these considerations of the accuracy of test results bears upon the question of whether it is possible for environmental stimulation to increase or decrease intellectual ability or for environmental impoverishment to stultify it. If we accept the hypothesis of stimulus-induced maturation or retardation through impoverishment, then we must search for evidence that the ability of the child may be changed by environmental stimulation. According to such a hypothesis, the changes that occur in a rich environment are more than merely the efficient teaching of information and knowledge upon which test results depend. The hypothesis asserts that the changes that take place are deeper, more basic, that the child's intelligence is raised. Stimulation does not produce a child who merely knows more and can solve problems better. Impoverishment, on the other hand, can produce a child who is stunted and insensitive.

In the light of the factors previously discussed, we can see the difficulty of demonstrating stimulus-induced maturation from a study of the effect of special stimulation upon intelligence test scores. We would have to control the interests of children who were in stimulating or unstimulating homes. It would be almost impossible to find a home that provided the child with a wealth of intellectual opportunities but did not stimulate intellectual interests, or to find a home that was impoverished intellectually and did stimulate intellectual interests.

We must, therefore, depend upon the permanence of the effects of an environment to demonstrate stimulus-induced maturation. If, after a child has left an especially stimulating environment, he continues to acquire information and skill more rapidly than is normal for him, we cannot attribute his score to the knowledge he acquired in the enriched environment. We must assume that the stimulating environment made him more receptive and sensitive in new learning situations. This is at least one variety of increased intellectual ability.

Studies on Effect of Impoverished Environment

One systematic attempt to study the effects of deprivation upon the development of ability was carried out by Dennis and Dennis (1936). They studied the development of two children whose first year of life contained an absolute minimum of social contact and minimal opportunity to practice any activity. The experimenters entered the room only for the physical care of the children; the children never left the nursery room. The room itself was very bare of stimulation. It had no toys, no decorations, and no windows except a skylight. The infants were not rewarded or punished for anything; they did not see each other except during the time they were lifted from their beds for care. Physical health was, however, carefully maintained. Even though the children lived under these extreme conditions, there was only slight retardation by comparison with the average, and this could not be definitely attributed to the treatment. The children's maturity in most types of behavior was not outside the range that occurs among normal children. The development of only three types of activity was exceptionally retarded: visually directed reaching, sitting alone, and standing with support. There was sufficient retardation in these skills to suggest that their development requires something more than the mere passage of time. The experimenters found, however, that the children promptly learned these activities upon the initiation of a training program. In other words, no permanent stunting of development was observable.

A more extreme impoverishment of the environment of the child would hardly be possible to create experimentally. There are studies, however, that suggest the consequences of more severe impoverishment.

Scientific studies of the rare natural experiment in which children are without human companionship for a period of their life may throw some light on the question. There have been several cases of such children—called *feral children*—who were removed from all human companionship for a period during childhood (Gesell, 1941). Some of them were thought to have been reared by animals, as were the fictional characters Tarzan or Mowgli, but there is little evidence to support such a contention. When these children are found they run very skillfully on all fours. They have no language. They show no signs of civilization. Naturally their development is retarded by normal standards. What is more important, however, is that they develop more slowly than normal children even after they return to civilization. In no case has such a child ever become a normally intelligent adult.

The validity of these studies on feral children who developed without human companionship has been seriously questioned. One of the factors that make them much less useful than they would otherwise be is that in no case are there any records of the child before his isolation. In fact, there have never been any records to prove when the isolation did actually begin. Skeptics argue that if the child had been as stupid as he seemed, he could never have lived under the severities of the wild life. It has been suggested, therefore, that they are abandoned children who were feebleminded and that they had probably not been abandoned long. There is nothing in the data to disprove such contentions or to prove them. The only argument to be advanced is that in the absence of good evidence incomplete evidence must be evaluated for what it is worth. If it is important to make some hypothesis concerning the possible permanent consequences of prolonged impoverishment, then the present evidence, poor as it is, suggests that there can be such stunting of development if the period of impoverishment is long enough and severe enough.

These studies have illustrated increasing degrees of impoverishment of the environment. The general conclusion to be drawn is that it is certainly possible to restrict the environment so completely that temporary retardation occurs. Perhaps under long severe impoverishment permanent stunting of development will occur. On the other hand, the developmental sequence is not easily modified, and some maturation process seems necessary to account for the data.

Studies of Effects of Nursery-school Attendance upon I. Q.

An extensive study of the consequences of nursery-school attendance, reported by Wellman (1940; 1943), is summarized below. It is especially important to note the permanence of the effects of nursery-school attendance reported in this study. If there are permanent effects, it is not possible to explain the results by assuming that the special environment merely provided the child with more opportunity to learn. He does not learn the answers to eight- or nine-year intelligence-test questions while he is in nursery school. If his performance at eight or nine or later is affected by nursery-school attendance, the effect must come about through a change of ability or interest or personality that is relatively long lasting. This study by Wellman and others is quoted because it is one of the few that contain evidence bearing upon the permanence of the effects of nursery-school experience.

The results in Figure 16.1 show the average I.Q. of children when they

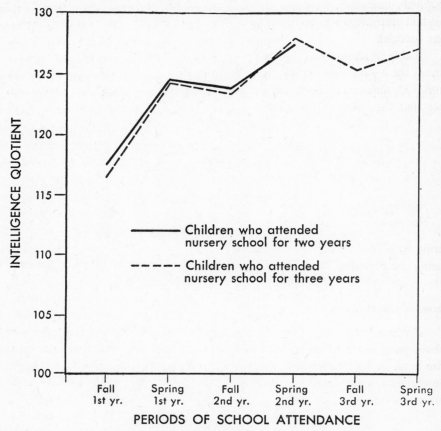

Fig. 16.1 The average I.Q. of nursery-school children at various points during their attendance. (From Beth L. Wellman, in Nat. Soc. Stud. Educ., *Thirty-ninth Yearbook,* Part II, 1940, p. 383. Quoted by permission of the Society)

first enter nursery school and after various periods of attendance. Each line represents a single group of children tested successively. A relatively small group was tested for three years. This group and some others were tested for two complete years; their results are shown in the line extending over a two-year period. Finally quite a large group attended one year; their results are shown in the shortest line.

Changes During Nursery-school Period

The results indicate an increase in I.Q. from the beginning to the end of each academic year. When children are tested in June and again in the following fall, after the summer vacation from nursery school, the I.Q. has dropped somewhat, but not to the level of the previous fall. There is a residual improvement left even after the decline over the summer is taken into account.

Table 7 shows the results of comparing children who attend nursery school for a year with those who do not. In the fall the two groups have the same I.Q. and are of the same age and socioeconomic level. The results indicate that the children who attend nursery school have a higher I.Q. in the

TABLE 7*

AVERAGE I.Q. OF MATCHED GROUPS IN FALL AND SPRING

	N	I.Q. Fall Test	I.Q. Spring Test	Change
Nursery-school Children	34	120.1	127.1	+7.0
Non-nursery-school Children	34	120.0	116.1	−3.9

spring than do the matched children who have not attended any nursery school during the period.

Permanence of Effects

Table 8 shows the results of testing children who had attended nursery school many years before the tests were administered. The authors of the study wish to show the semipermanent effects of nursery-school attendance. Again, the children attending nursery school are matched with children of the same socioeconomic level and intelligence who did not attend nursery school.

The interpretation of these results is not easy. The actual facts obtained

TABLE 8

INTELLIGENCE OF NURSERY-SCHOOL AND NON-NURSERY-SCHOOL CHILDREN IN LATER YEARS†

	N	Initial I.Q.	Percentile Score A.C.E. High-school Test	Initial I.Q.	Percentile Score College Entrance
Nursery-school Children	29	117.3	88.1	122.8	83.9
Non-nursery-school Children	29	116.8	78.3	120.1	71.9

* Beth L. Wellman, "Iowa Studies on the Effects of Schooling," in *Thirty-ninth Yearbook,* Part II, National Soc. Study Education, Public School Pub. Co., 1940, p. 385. Quoted by permission of the Society.

† *Ibid.*, pp. 395, 396.

have been criticized on the grounds that the tests were inadequately given or that the statistics were improperly computed. This is no place for an evaluation of such criticisms. Certainly the experiments were not performed any more inadequately than many other experiments that are accepted as providing valid information.

Interpretation of Findings

Assuming, however, that the facts are true, the interpretation is still not entirely clear. The critical question is whether or not all these effects can be attributed to the nursery school. Although the groups were matched, at the beginning of the experiment, for intelligence and socioeconomic factors, they could not be very adequately matched on the basis of the amount of stimulation provided by the home. By and large, it is true that homes which are stimulating and accelerating are the homes which send children to nursery school. This is one symptom of a stimulating home. The fact that the I.Q. dropped over the summer does seem to indicate that some of the effect was due to nursery school. Home stimulation does not take a summer vacation. Whether the residual effect is a permanent one due to the nursery school alone or to the entire environmental background of the children is difficult to decide. In either case, however, the ability of some sort of environmental factor to change the score on intelligence tests is supported.

When the data of the last table are inspected, this difference in interpretation is much more significant. If the effect of stimulation is conceived of as something that can be permanent, it is very important to control the environments of the two groups of children after the end of the stimulating experience. If, therefore, it could be assumed that the two groups had the same environments between the end of nursery school and the time of the tests in high school, the evidence would be strongly in support of the long-lasting consequences of stimulation. Unfortunately, such an assumption cannot be made. If the homes from which these children came were initially different in their stimulation, they would in all probability continue to be different. Therefore, the advantage of the nursery-school group in high-school intelligence tests may be due to the fact that they continued to live in a stimulating environment, not the fact that they at the age of four to six attended a nursery school.

Finally, we should point out that even if the effects are permanent they need not be the result of change of intellectual ability. They may be the result of changing interests or attitudes or changes in general personality factors. Such a possibility does not affect the social importance of the findings if they are confirmed, but it makes the evidence much less significant for the hypothesis of stimulus-induced maturation of intellectual ability.

When these experiments have been repeated by other research workers, the results have not been confirmed. Of eight studies on the effect of nursery-school attendance on I.Q., Wellman's and one other found sizable changes. Some of the others found effects that were so small that they could not be used as valid evidence. The majority of investigations has not found any change in I.Q. that is large enough to be significant.

It is certainly unjustified, therefore, to expect that merely from attending nursery school a child will show a marked change in intelligence. Perhaps some kinds of nursery-school training or perhaps nursery-school training for some children will have real effects. What blocks us here, as earlier, is that we do not know enough about development and the factors affecting it to attempt to stimulate intellectual development in any but a haphazard way.

If we actually knew the process we might be able to obtain results comparable to those found in chicks. All of the indications of studies on human development, however, point to the fact that the human organism is remarkably resilient to general deprivation, so that long and severe impoverishment would be required to produce the widespread and gross impairments that are required for statistical reliability on intelligence tests. We could hardly expect such resilience in the face of impoverishment and, at the same time, marked improvement in I.Q. through something that occupies such a small part of each day as nursery-school attendance. There is, incidentally, good evidence that nursery-school experience does affect the child's interpersonal relations, even if not his intelligence.

In summary, we can conclude that the evidence for temporary retardation of intellectual development through environmental deprivation is excellent. The possibility of permanent defect is not so clear, but not unlikely. The difficulty of raising the I.Q., even temporarily, is greater than the difficulty in lowering it, but the possibility of doing so seems reasonably likely, although we cannot be sure that I.Q. is always raised by nursery-school experience. The permanence of the effects of nursery school on intellectual ability is the most questionable of all, but the possibility of permanent effects through more significant experience is not ruled out.

The Effects of Institutionalization in Infancy

Let us turn now to the study of the effects of social deprivation upon the development of social adjustment. This line of research began with the observation of some of the behavior syndromes in institutionalized children. Such symptoms as extreme dullness and apathy, or else hyperactivity, seemed from casual observation to be unusually frequent in institutional populations. These observations led to the formulation of an empirical study that compared the behavior of institutionalized children with those cared for individually.

Investigations of various aspects of this problem have been undertaken by a number of people—Levy (1937), Ribble (1945), and Bowlby (1951). Of such studies the two examples that have been selected are those by Rene Spitz (1949) and by William Goldfarb (1943; 1944).

Development During Infancy

The studies of Spitz compare the behavior of children in two sorts of institutions, one of which is called the "Nursery" and the other called the "Foundlinghome." The two institutions were similar in many respects: the children were admitted soon after birth; housing was excellent; food and physical hygiene were satisfactory in both institutions. The important differ-

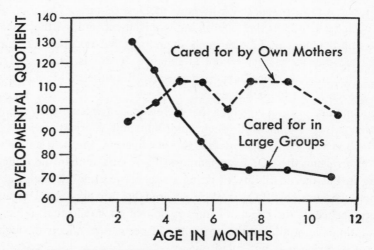

Fig. 16.2 The developmental quotient of children cared for by their own mothers and in large groups. (After R. A. Spitz, *Child Devel.*, 20, 1949, 145-155)

ence between the two institutions for the purpose of Spitz's studies was the fact that in the Nursery each child was cared for by his own mother, whereas in the Foundlinghome the children were cared for by overworked nursing personnel. The fact that one nurse might have charge of as many as eight to twelve infants gives the reader some idea of the impersonal treatment in the Foundlinghome. In each institution there were children of various ages, and since each child had been admitted shortly after birth, the age of the child was also a measure of the time spent in the institution. Figure 16.2 shows the average "developmental quotient" at various age levels in the two institutions. Notice that the development during only the first year of life is covered by the data. The developmental quotient represents a measure similar to the I.Q., except that the items are designed to reveal six segments of personality and the test is used as a measure of the behavior that appears in early infancy. The striking feature of Figure 16.2 is the fact that in Foundlinghome the quotient steadily declines with age, whereas in Nursery it remains relatively constant. These findings resemble those reported earlier on the trend of I.Q. in older children who lived in impoverished environments.

Even more dramatic than the developmental quotients is the comparison of the mortality rates of the two institutions. In a five-year period during which 239 children were observed for one year or more, not a single child in the Nursery died. During a two-year period there was a mortality rate of 37 percent in Foundlinghome. Of this almost 30 percent died in the first year of life. These striking and dramatic differences must, however, be carefully analyzed. One of the factors that must be controlled is the comparability of the children who were admitted to the two institutions. If children admitted to the Foundlinghome were less healthy, the mortality rate cannot be attributed solely to the institutional treatment. Such a control is not so vital for the study of developmental quotients as for mortality, because each child serves as his own control in the study of the developmental quotient—*i.e.*, each child's developmental quotient is compared to his own previous test score. The results indicate an actual decline of the developmental quotient in Foundlinghome.

Permanence of Effects of Separation from Mothers

There are differences in the way different mothers cared for their babies in the Nursery. One of the events that sometimes occurred was that the mother was separated from her child for some length of time. Spitz reports that when this separation occurs during the last quarter of the first year, the child may lose his alertness and responsiveness. He becomes unhappy and depressed, sometimes to the point of panic. The child may show such symptoms as prolonged screaming, crying, and convulsive trembling (Spitz, 1950). During the period of separation the developmental quotient declines. Spitz finds that if the separation lasts less than five months, the decline is remediable; the child quickly regains his former developmental quotient after the mother's return. For a longer period of separation, however, the process seemed to be irreversible during the time Spitz followed the child's development. The results are shown in Table 9.

Although these studies are very suggestive, we must interpret them cautiously. Many factors are impossible to control in such a comparison of institutions whose regimes were established to meet their own needs rather than to serve as experimental situations for a scientific study. Since the direction of these results coincides with other studies of the effect of impoverishment on development, they can probably be trusted, but repetitions are needed. It should not be surprising if upon repetition less dramatic results were obtained. Such an expectation is based upon the results frequently obtained from a repetition of a pioneer study under slightly different conditions and with larger samples.

TABLE 9*

DECLINE OF THE DEVELOPMENTAL QUOTIENT UPON SEPARATION
FROM THE MOTHER AND ITS RECOVERY AFTER HER RETURN

	Change in D.Q.	
Duration of Separation	*During Separation*	*After Return*
Less than 3 mo.	−12.5	+25
3 mo. to 4 mo.	−14	+13
4 mo. to 5 mo.	−14	+12
More than 5 mo.	−25	− 4

Later Development of Children Institutionalized During Infancy

The research of Goldfarb resembles that of Spitz in that he is comparing children who were institutionalized from early infancy until the age of three with another group of children who were living in foster homes during that period of life. But Goldfarb studied both groups after the institutionalized children had been placed in foster homes and allowed to adjust to foster-home life for at least three years. The institutional group was reared in an institution from early infancy until the age of three and then placed in foster homes. The children of the foster-home group had been placed in their homes in early infancy and had stayed in that home or in some other foster home thereafter. Thus the more permanent consequences of such institutionalization can be investigated. Goldfarb studied three age groups: one was approximately seven years of age at the time of the investigation; the second was about eight and one-half; and the third was composed of adolescent children. The same criteria were used to select all three pairs of groups.

PROBLEM BEHAVIOR The general result of Goldfarb's study is that children whose early childhood is spent in the impersonal environment of an institution are definitely handicapped, at least up to adolescence. For ex-

* Rene Spitz, "The Role of ecological factors in emotional development in infancy," *Child Development*, 20, 1949, pp. 145-156.

ample, they consistently exhibit more problem behavior than the control group. Table 10 summarizes several such findings of Goldfarb's studies. The three groups are equated in age, sex, and time under care, but differ in the type of care during the earliest years. The numbers in the table represent the average number of items checked on a list of problem behavior that was filled out for each child. All of the differences between the two groups are statistically significant.

When some measure of maturity, such as the I.Q. or the score on the Vineland Social Maturity Scale, is used as a basis for comparing the two groups, the differences between them are striking. On both scales the foster-

TABLE 10*

INCIDENCE OF PROBLEM BEHAVIOR

Age	Average Number of Items of Problem Behavior	
	Institutional Children	Foster-home Children
6 yr., 9 mo.	6.0	3.5
8 yr., 6 mo.	5.0	2.5
12 yr., 3 mo.	6.5	1.9

home group is almost at the norm for the general population, whereas the institutional group is seriously retarded. This difference is statistically highly reliable.

In trying to obtain a clear picture of the qualitative characteristics of the difference between the two groups, it is useful to look at some of the specific sorts of problem behavior that are most characteristic of the institutional group. Although they show more problem behavior of almost every variety, the items on which there are the largest consistent differences are *restlessness* and *hyperactivity*. Some of the other items on which there are reasonably consistent differences between the two groups are *temper displays, poor school achievement, craving for affection,* and *inability to concentrate.*

APATHY   It is especially instructive to examine the behavior of the two groups on a frustration test. This test, devised by Brown (1939), was given only to the adolescent group. The subject is told to stay behind a certain line drawn on the floor. Outside of this area, standing on the floor, is a telephone with the receiver off the hook. Near it is a low table littered with objects. The subject is instructed to put the receiver back on the hook without touching the floor beyond the boundary line. Nearly all subjects solve this problem after a short time by leaning on the table to put the receiver back on the hook.

* Wm. Goldfarb, "Infant Rearing and Problem Behavior," *American J. Orthopsychiat., 13,* 1943, 249,

Then the subject is told there is a second solution that he must discover. From this point on the experiment can be called frustrating because there is no second solution.

After five minutes' trial, the experimenter tells the subject, "The second solution is much harder. Nearly everyone gets the first answer but a little less than half get this one." The purpose of this remark is to introduce a competitive element into the situation in order to see how the child responds to such a factor.

After another five minutes the child is interrupted to answer some questions and is engaged by the experimenter in a general conversation. If the child does not spontaneously return to the task within three minutes, he is reminded that he has not finished it yet. If this reminder does not induce him to return, he is directed to return to the task. A similar interruption occurs again five minutes later and once again after another five minutes. The behavior of the child during these interruptions is scored for the strength of his need to resume the task.

The analysis of the behavior of the children in the two groups indicates that it is difficult to involve the institutional children in the test. More of them show a syndrome labeled *apathy* than do the foster-home children. This syndrome is derived from four findings. First, the foster-home children show a significantly greater readiness to resume the unsolved task after interruptions. Secondly, the child's involvement in the task can be measured by the extent to which it evokes tension and restlessness. Whereas 87 percent of the institutional children showed no increase in tension, only 27 percent of the foster-home children were psychologically so uninvolved. Thirdly, the extent to which the child puts pressure on himself to find the second solution can be estimated by the observer. Whereas 27 percent of the institutional group are rated indifferent, none of the foster-home group is so rated. At the other extreme, only 7 percent of the institutional group were believed by the experimenter to feel that they "must" succeed in finding the second solution. In contrast, 47 percent of the foster-home group show so intense an aspiration. Fourthly, perhaps the most striking symptom of the relative apathy of the institutional group is in response to the statement about the difficulty of the problem for most children. None of the institutional children shows that he is affected by such a statement, whereas 87 percent of the foster-home children show some rise in aspiration under the effect of the competitive factor.

This pattern of behavior, comprising *restlessness, hyperactivity,* and *inability to concentrate,* yet no rise in tension symptoms when put into a frustrating situation, does not seem very coherent. The *craving for affection* and the *poorer school behavior* of the institutional group shed some light on the dynamics of the behavior. The picture of the institutional group seems to be one of anxiety about love and affection, great involvement in interpersonal relations, but no interest in problems for their own sake. The threat of not being loved seems to be so prominent that the only possible behavior is a direct overt demand for love. The foster-home children need love also, as do we all, but they are secure enough to be interested in other activities and do in fact attain love and respect through realistic activity.

INTERPRETATION OF FINDINGS   That the two groups of children differ markedly is well established by these studies; the nature of the difference is clearly indicated. Any skepticism about the validity of the findings cannot be directed to the failure to establish differences. There might be some question, however, about the comparability of the children between the ages of one and three. The decision not to place an institutional child in a foster home was certainly not made for the purposes of the experiment. Some reasons for not placing institutionalized children in foster homes have nothing to do with the child, but in other cases the failure to place the child does reflect some personal characteristic. Whether the retardation or problem behavior of the children was one of the factors that kept them institutionalized for three years before they were placed in foster homes is an important question. Such a question might be difficult to answer in retrospect, and it illustrates again the difficulties that beset the path of the investigator who tries to establish accurately the consequences of various psychological factors upon human behavior and personality.

Summary

In this chapter we have seen the resilience of the child in unstimulating environmental conditions and also we have found that his development may be stunted by impoverishment that continues over a long enough period and at a critical time. The resistance of different abilities to environmental influence probably varies, and the resistance is probably greater at some periods of life than at others. In general, these data lend credence to the general formulation of maturation as described in Chapter 15, but they do not prove the hypothesis suggested in that chapter. In the course of later chapters we shall see some alternative explanations of some of these data.

17

The Acquisition of Habits

PAVLOV'S EXPERIMENT

FACTS OF THE CONDITIONING PROCESS

THEORIES CONCERNING THE CONDITIONED RESPONSE

ROLE OF CONDITIONING IN INFANT DEVELOPMENT

THE ACQUISITION OF HABITS AFTER INFANCY

SUMMARY

A MAN ONCE returned after many years to the high school that he had long ago attended. At the time of his graduation he had given the valedictory address. In the many years since, he had hardly thought of the speech and could certainly not have remembered more than a little of it. When he returned to the school, however, and stood on the stage where he had practiced and given the oration, the words suddenly returned to him. He could repeat the speech almost verbatim. The re-establishment of the many stimuli surrounding his first learning the speech helped evoke the responses that he had learned so long ago.

That behavior may depend upon re-establishing the circumstances under which it once occurred has been noted for many years. The fact that one idea can bring to mind another idea with which it has been frequently associated was for several centuries the basis for a complete psychological theory, the doctrine of association of ideas.

Pavlov's Experiment

In more recent years the concept of association has been modified, but in the description of conditioning the essentials still remain. Conditioned responses were first extensively investigated by Pavlov, a physiologist studying the process of digestion, who became interested in the so-called psychic factors in digestion. He wondered why the digestive processes were activated not only by the actual presence of food in the mouth and in the stomach, but also merely by the sight of food. In order to investigate this process, he devised a method of measuring the amount of saliva secreted. Then he presented food to a dog, and at the same time he rang a bell (Pavlov, 1927). The dog salivated, of course, when the food was presented. Pavlov discovered that after a number of repetitions of the paired presentation of bell and food, the bell, even when presented by itself, was sufficient to evoke the salivary response. He called this phenomenon a *conditioned reflex,* but its name has been changed to *conditioned response* in order to avoid any connotation that the underlying mechanism is the equivalent of a neurological reflex.

This discovery by Pavlov stimulated a tremendous amount of research and theorizing by psychologists who saw in the conditioned response a possible explanatory mechanism for all kinds of human behavior. In our thinking about the conditioned response, it is important to distinguish three possible interpretations of the phrase. First, it is an experimental fact that has been repeatedly demonstrated. It is possible for a stimulus situation (the conditioned stimulus) to evoke new responses (the conditioned response), ones that it previously could not evoke, by repeatedly presenting it along with another stimulus (the unconditioned stimulus) that has a well-defined response (the unconditioned response).

A second meaning of conditioning is theoretical. *Conditioning theory* is a theory about the nature of the response that is evoked in such situations. Psychologists who believe in *conditioning theory* have hypothesized that the response is an automatic habitlike response automatically evoked by the appropriate stimulus. Their opponents have hypothesized that the conditioned response is the behavior of an organism who has learned to "expect" the food.

Thirdly, conditioning is also associated with the belief that all human behavior can be conceptualized as patterns and sequences of conditioned responses that have been learned through a repetition of the pairing of stimuli and responses. Because some of the important theories about the development of behavior in the child are based upon these notions, we must examine briefly the relevant facts and theories in the field of conditioning.

Facts of the Conditioning Process

In order to understand the factual findings about conditioning, it is important to have a clear picture of the terminology in which the findings are couched. The food in Pavlov's experiment is called the *unconditioned stimulus*. It is the stimulus to which there is a pre-established response. This response—salivation in Pavlov's experiment—is the *unconditioned response*. The bell in Pavlov's experiment is the *conditioned stimulus*. After the repeated pairing of the conditioned and unconditioned stimuli, the conditioned stimulus evokes a response that is the *conditioned response*. Numerous factual findings have been clarified through careful experimentation. Some that are relevant to our discussion are described below.

Course of Conditioning and Extinction

The usual development of a conditioned response may be observed in the experiments of Marinesco and Kreindler (1933) in their study of children fifteen to thirty months of age. Each child had an electrode that could give him a weak electric shock, strapped to his foot or hand. The shock itself lasted twenty seconds, and the conditioned stimulus, the sound of a metronome, preceded it for a period of fifty seconds. When the shock itself was present the child showed restless movements of the arm or leg. When these restless movements appeared consistently to the sound of the metronome alone, before the actual shock was applied, conditioning had taken place. The conditioning does not appear immediately after the pairing of the metronome and shock. It requires a number of trials, about twelve in this experiment, before the movements are evoked by the metronome alone. This gradual appearance of the conditioned response is typical of conditioning experiments.

After the response has been conditioned, the experimenter may *extinguish* it by presenting the conditioned stimulus a number of times without the shock. If the metronome is sounded but no shock follows, the conditioned response to the metronome gradually disappears. This process is called *experimental extinction*. How long it takes to extinguish a conditioned response depends upon a variety of factors, but in general extinction is like conditioning in reverse. One phenomenon that may occur if the individual is given a rest after the response has been extinguished is *spontaneous recovery*. Upon the first few trials in the next session, the conditioned response may reoccur despite the fact that no further reinforcement has taken place during the rest.

Similarity of Conditioned and Unconditioned Response

When the experimental work on conditioned responses was first begun, the process was pictured as a substitution of the conditioned stimulus for the unconditioned stimulus in a simple reflex. The bell substituted for the food. If this were true, the conditioned and unconditioned responses would be identical. They have been shown not to be identical, however, in many experimental situations. The unconditioned eyeblink after a puff of air, for example, is a quick reflexlike jerk, whereas the conditioned eyeblink is a slower gradual closing of the eyelid (Hilgard and Marquis, 1940). It is true, however, that in the classical conditioning experiments the two responses are very similar.

In a somewhat different sort of experiment, *instrumental conditioning* (Hilgard and Marquis, 1940), the difference between the learned response and the response to the original stimuli may be very great. Instrumental conditioning exists whenever the response that is learned has consequences upon the unconditioned stimulus. If, for example, in Marinesco and Kreindler's experiment described above, the shock were administered through a plate on which the foot rested, then the restless activity would move the foot away from the plate and cause the shock to disappear. Now, if the metronome preceded the shock, the child could prevent the shock from happening if he merely moved his foot before the electricity is turned on. This would be quite different from the original experiment in which the shock occurs whether or not the foot moves.

The simplest type of instrumental conditioning is the establishment of an avoidant response that prevents an unpleasant stimulus from occurring. This preventive response may under some conditions be completely different from the response that occurs to the unconditioned stimulus. In one experiment, for example (Morgan, 1900), chicks were presented with caterpillars that had a bad taste. At first the chick pecked eagerly at the caterpillar, picked it up, and then, when it discovered how the insect tasted, spit it out. After several such trials it did not peck at the caterpillar at all. Here the learned response is not to peck. This is a quite different response from spitting the caterpillar out—the unconditioned response in this case.

In many examples of instrumental conditioning, the learned response is not even one that previously existed. A new response is actually acquired by the learning process. The method of teaching the organism in such experiments is to reward the correct response and to punish the incorrect response. In these studies it is customary to use a different terminology. The stimulus which comes after the response of the organism and which rewards or punishes it is said to be the *reinforcement*. In the chick experiment, for example, the caterpillar is the conditioned stimulus. The avoidant behavior, withdrawing from or not pecking, is the conditioned response, and the bitter taste—or rather the absence of the bitter taste—that follows the response is the reinforcement.

Secondary Conditioned Responses

Another fact of considerable importance for understanding the attempts to explain child behavior in terms of conditioning is the existence of *secondary conditioned responses*. If a conditioned response has been well established —for example, the bell-salivation response of the dog—it is possible for the conditioned stimulus in the original reaction to act as the unconditioned stimulus in the establishment of a second-order conditioned response. Thus, if after the conditioned salivation to the bell is well established a light is consistently persented with the bell, the light alone comes eventually to evoke the salivation response. This can occur even if in no case has the light ever been presented when the dog actually receives food.

Another experiment points to the use of the secondary conditioned response as an explanation for more complex behavior. This experiment by Wolfe (1936) was performed on chimpanzees. They were first taught how to obtain food from a vending machine. If a token was inserted into the machine it delivered a grape. Now it was found that the chimpanzees would perform other tasks, solve problems, or learn activities when rewarded with the tokens alone. The chimpanzee could distinguish among blue chips that were worth two grapes, white chips that were worth only one grape, and brass chips that had no value. In many ways the chimpanzees treated the tokens in the way we treat coins.

Second-order conditioned responses have also been established in experiments on children. Marinesco and Kreindler, for example, obtained second-order conditioned responses in their experiment (1933). After the metronome was well established as a conditioned response, it could in turn be paired with some other stimulus, such as a light. During the second-order conditioning the light would precede the metronome sound, and in this trial the shock itself would not appear. The light, therefore, was never actually paired with the shock itself. In the trials the experimenter would occasionally reinforce the conditioned response to the metronome—*i.e.,* he would sound the metronome and follow it by the actual shock. This was necessary to keep the original conditioned response from being extinguished. On these trials, however, the light would not be presented at all. In no case were the light and shock paired. Yet the light, because of being repeatedly paired with the metronome that evoked a conditioned response, eventually was able to evoke the conditioned restless movements.

Stimulus Generalization and Response Generalization

Another empirical finding from conditioning experiments, which must be reviewed if we are to understand the attempts to account for everyday child behavior in terms of conditioning, is *generalization.* Pavlov found in his experiments that, early in the course of conditioning, the animal was likely to show a conditioned response to any one of a number of stimuli. If the door slammed just about the time the bell ordinarily occurred, the dog might begin to salivate to that stimulus.

Gradually, with more conditioning, the response came to be specifically evocable by the bell alone. Even so, there was still some generalization of the response. If, instead of a bell, a tone of a certain pitch was used as the conditioning stimulus, it was found that sounds of slightly different pitches evoked the conditioned response, although less intensely than the pitch used in the conditioning portion of the experiment.

We have already seen in Watson's experiment on conditioning fear reactions in Albert, an eleven-month-old child (see p. 74), that he found a similar generalization of the conditioned response to other stimuli. The conditioned stimulus in his experiment was a white rat. After the child had become afraid of the rat, he was also afraid of many other similar objects— small white animals, white pieces of fur, and the like. Jersild and Holmes (1935) report in their study of fears of children that one child, after being frightened by the hoot of an owl in a zoo, was afraid of the canary at home.

These cases of generalization are called *stimulus generalization.* The conditioned response is evoked by other stimuli than those which were specifically conditioned. There may also be *response generalization* in which other responses than those evoked by the unconditioned stimulus may appear in the course of conditioning. In the experiment by Marinesco and Kreindler, for example, the child, in response to the metronome, might move his whole body restlessly, including all four limbs. With further conditioning the restless movements became localized to the single limb that was going to be shocked.

Theories Concerning the Conditioned Response

We have reviewed the empirical facts that have been established in the many experiments on the conditioned response. These findings and the fact that they may occur in experimental studies of children can hardly be contested. The interpretation of these findings is, however, not so clear. Let us turn now to two alternative explanations of the conditioned response.

The Nature of the Conditioned Response

There are two distinct points of view, the cognitive theory of conditioning and a noncognitive theory. According to cognitive theory the response of the organism depends upon two steps: first, the perception or cognition of the environment, which is a representation of the external world; secondly, the guidance of behavior by this representation toward the cognized goal.

If we apply such a view to the conditioned response we see that the pairing of the conditioned and unconditioned stimuli leads the individual to expect the unconditioned stimulus when the conditioned stimulus occurs. After the dog has observed the bell and food together a number of times, the sound of the bell makes him expect food. His behavior is then guided by that expectation. In this case he looks toward the food dish, he salivates, he pricks up his ears and shows eagerness. If the conditioned stimulus leads him to expect something bad, such as a shock, he behaves appropriately to this expectation. He is restless and whines, and if there is a way to prevent the unconditioned stimulus from occurring he does so.

In summary, the cognitive theory of conditioning hypothesizes that the conditioning process builds up an expectation of the unconditioned stimulus. The behavior that then results is guided by that expectation and directed toward whatever goals exist at the moment. There is evidence for this last point, incidentally, in the findings that animals may not show a conditioned response that is dependent upon food stimuli if at the moment they are not hungry.

The noncognitive point of view about conditioning assumes that the conditioned response is an automatic, habitual, reflexlike behavior that is evoked by the conditioned stimulus and that can be explained without assuming any cognition, expectation, or goal-directed behavior.

The point of view that will be advanced in this discussion is that the results in a so-called conditioning experiment depend upon various circumstances and especially upon the maturity of the individual. Because the ability to have an expectation demands more maturity than is possessed by the young infant, we believe that some conditioning is a process of coupling a stimulus to an automatic response. This results in a fixed response released by a stimulus. This sort of learning can occur very early in the child's life.

Wenger (1936) showed, for example, that the eyeblink of newborn infants could be conditioned. In his experiment the unconditioned stimulus was a flash of light into the eye of the baby. The conditioned stimulus was a tactile vibratory stimulus applied to the foot three seconds before the flash of light. One of the difficulties in these experiments is that young infants may make such a general response to the conditioned stimulus itself that the presumed unconditioned response may be involved. In this experiment, for example, Wenger applied the vibratory stimulus to a control group of six nine-day-old infants. On about 30 percent of the trials, this group showed some eyelid responses along with other activity to the vibratory stimulus. The effects of conditioning were clear, however. Those babies who had experienced the pairing of the vibration and the light responded to the vibratory stimulus alone in 58 to 74 percent of the trials by the time they were nine days old. He concluded that it is possible to condition newborn infants, but that the process is not as stable as it is with older children.

The acquisition of fixed responses can continue throughout life. When the child is mature enough to display the behavior characteristic of cognition, a conditioning experiment may not, however, produce a fixed response. By that time, the child is capable of cognizing the conditioned and unconditioned stimulus and recognizing the relationships between the two. How his behavior is cognitively guided and how he responds to the conditioned stimulus depends upon many other factors. One of the findings of experiments in this field is that older children and adults frequently make poor subjects in conditioning experiments. One explanation that has been advanced is that such people are not "willing" to be conditioned. The difficulty in conditioning older subjects may, in some cases at least, be explained if we assume that they are exhibiting cognitive learning.

An experiment of Dernowa-Yarmolenko (1933) illustrates this point. This experimenter conditioned approximately 1000 children between the ages of eight and nineteen years. Each subject was told to raise his hand when the examiner did so. The examiner then tapped on the table with a pencil and after two seconds raised his hand. This procedure was repeated ten times and a conditioned response was assumed to be established if the subject consistently raised his hand when the pencil was tapped but before the experimenter's hand was raised. The older subjects showed fewer such "conditioned responses" than the younger.

This was an experiment that might produce a conditioned fixed response in some organisms, but for these subjects between the age of eight and nineteen years, there was almost certainly cognitive learning. It seems highly unlikely that the subjects failed to recognize that the tap of the pencil preceded the hand raising. The behavior was, however, also determined by the goal of the subject. The instructions had said to raise the hand when the experimenter did so. Anticipatory hand raising was like "jumping the gun." Since the younger subjects were more impulsive and less controlled than the older ones, they "jumped the gun" more frequently. Consequently, the appearance of an anticipatory conditioned response decreased with age because there was cognitive learning and goal-directed behavior rather than the more primitive conditioning.

In summary, both the cognitive and noncognitive view of what is learned in a conditioning experiment may be accurate under special conditions. The nature of the learned behavior under the usual conditions of conditioning depends upon the maturity of the organism and perhaps other conditions as well. The process of cognitive learning and the similarity between noncognitive and cognitive learning will be discussed more completely in the following chapter.

The Process of Conditioning

One controversy concerning the nature of the conditioned response has been discussed. There is another difference of opinion among psychologists concerning the factors that produce conditioning. The theory of *stimulus contiguity* states that the necessary factor for conditioning is the contiguity of the conditioned and the unconditioned stimulus. On the other hand, the *reinforcement* theory states that the only necessary factor for producing conditioning is the consistent occurrence of a "reinforcing state of affairs" following the conditioned response.

The idea of stimulus contiguity was developed to describe the original conditioning experiments, such as those of Pavlov. We have already seen that, in a strict sense, stimulus substitution is not appropriate because the conditioned and unconditioned responses are not identical. Nevertheless, they are very similar to each other, and this similarity is a fact that must be explained. When applied to the classical conditioning experiment, the stimulus contiguity theory suggests that through contiguity of the two stimuli the conditioned stimulus becomes able to evoke a response that is very similar to the original response to the unconditioned stimulus.

The importance of stimulus contiguity is much more seriously questioned when instrumental conditioning is considered. Especially when the effect of the learned response is to prevent the "reinforcement" from occurring, it is difficult to picture the situation as a repeated pairing of the two stimuli so that the response to the one is transferred over to the other stimulus.

Role of Conditioning in Infant Development

The facts about conditioning experiments are well established, and the results of experimental studies of the infant indicate that even very young babies can learn a conditioned response. The question now is the importance of conditioning in the actual development of infants. If we think back over the various observations of infant behavior that have been reported, we can see that several different kinds of learning occur. One is the extension of a schema so that it is evoked by stimuli that did not evoke it before. A second is the creation of a new schema that is a fixed response, as when the child repeats an action that has just resulted in some interesting happening. A third, more complex sort of learning is the development of simple guided responses, as when the child learns to put his thumb in his mouth from any position, or learns to reach for and grasp an object.

Extension of Schema

We have seen many examples of a child's learning to respond in a familiar way to a new stimulus. One of the earliest is his beginning to make sucking movements when he is being prepared for nursing. This process seems to be well described as conditioning through stimulus contiguity. It is almost a complete parallel to the classic conditioning experiments performed by Pavlov. Later, the child shows sucking movements as soon as he wakes up from a nap. Here, also, the parallel to conditioning is obvious. The time interval between waking up and nursing is longer than the interval between meal preparations and nursing, so the conditioning should be more difficult to establish. This fits well the finding that the second learning occurs later than the first.

We also find obvious parallels to stimulus generalization in the spontaneous behavior of infants. Jacqueline first acquired a secondary circular response by jiggling her legs in the crib when a doll stopped swinging. Later, she showed the same response to the stationary doll even when it had not been swinging. The similarity of the two stimuli is clear, and the extension of the response to the stationary doll seems like stimulus generalization. When we try to apply these principles to the further extensions of the schema, we have more difficulty tracing the process. When she performed this leg jiggling in front of a jack-in-the-box, the similarity is not obvious, but in the absence of any evidence to the contrary, we might postulate a gradual extension of the schema from a suspended doll to all dolls, especially dolls that had just stopped moving. The jack-in-the-box fits such a description.

One of the important developments is the detachment of the schema from its original stimulus. By the time the child is in stage 4, he can run through his repertoire of schemata when presented with any new object. This is even more difficult to envisage in terms of stimulus generalization, but if we had observed the process even more carefully than Piaget did, we might trace out the extension of the reaction to a broad class of stimulus objects.

Role of Perceptual Units

In order to point up the similarities between conditioning and cognitive learning, which we shall discuss in Chapter 18, we want to show that all examples of the extension of a schema can be included in a single mechanism, whether the extension takes place through stimulus contiguity or through generalization. In either case, the new stimuli that are added to the stimulus already evoking the schema are in a perceptual unit with it. We showed earlier in the discussion of maturity (see p. 60) that many of the child's perceptions and behavioral responses are governed by the principles of field organization. One principle is that stimuli that are close to each other, spatially or temporally, or are similar to each other, tend to become a single perceptual unit. Applying this notion to conditioning, we can see that if a schema is established to one stimulus, other stimuli that are in the same perceptual unit will become able to evoke the response.

We see, therefore, that stimulus contiguity and stimulus generalization are frequently illustrated in the development of the infant in his natural habitat as well as in controlled experimental situations.

Formation of New Schemata

We can also see illustrations of reinforcement learning in infant behavior. The clearest examples are the creation of new schemata that are secondary circular reactions. It seems obvious that the basis for the infant's repetition of a behavior pattern when it produces some striking result is that the result reinforces the learning. In the most striking examples only one repetition is apparently required to establish the learned behavior, but this does not contradict the principles of reinforcement learning. Probably we can find other examples in which more than one repetition is required to bring about learning.

The behavior of the child in developing a pattern of guided behavior also closely resembles the behavior of an animal or child in an experiment on learning through reinforcement. The description of the very young baby with an object in the palm of his hand is a case in point. At first he grasps it only when it is in the palm of his hand. Then, later, he happens to touch some object with part of his hand; he cannot grasp it, but his hand movements change character. His hands continue to wave but they remain in the region of the handkerchief. Since his restless movements are confined to this small region he soon touches the handkerchief with the palm of the hand and grasps it. The result of a number of such experiences is that whenever the child's hand touches an object, he is able to shift his hand position and grasp the object. He performs this action consistently and accurately.

Such behavior certainly looks like instrumental conditioning. The grasping of the object rewards the child and as a result his behavior is changed so that the behavior evoked by touching the hand becomes adapted to produce the grasping that reinforces the behavior. We have already seen that this behavior leads to the assumption that grasping, sucking, and the like are rewarding experiences (see p. 181). These particular rewards have not been studied experimentally, although other forms of interesting behavior have been used as rewards. Monkeys will solve simple mechanical problems for no ulterior reward. Music and interesting sounds have been used as reinforcements for learning.

The behavior of the infant in learning to grasp an object or to suck his thumb resembles the behavior of an animal in acquiring a new skill through reinforcement, but it is not easy to trace the details of the process. It is not clear just what behavior is actually reinforced. We cannot see in the random movement of the infant the behavior that finally emerges once the skill is learned. Reinforcement describes best the selection of one specific response out of a pre-existing repertoire of responses. It is more difficult to see how the process works when the result of learning is a new skill or ability. In some studies, however, the learned response has been shown to be a repetition of a chance action. Regardless of these questions, there is no doubt that rewarding the successful performance of an activity helps the child to learn to do it well.

The Acquisition of Habits after Infancy

During infancy we find very little evidence for the existence of cognition or cognitively guided behavior. The main behavior mechanisms are fixed responses to releasing stimuli and simple guided behavior controlled by some simple, immediately perceptible stimulus. We have hypothesized that these patterns of behavior are acquired through a conditioning process.

After infancy, the child begins to exhibit cognitively guided behavior. In the next chapter we shall describe cognitive learning, the process by which cognitively guided behavior is learned. Not all behavior that is learned after infancy is cognitively guided, however. New habits are formed after infancy. Presumably they are formed in much the same way as before, although the unconditioned and conditioned stimuli may be much more complex.

If there are two mechanisms of learning, it is important to know the conditions that favor the one and the conditions that favor the other. The detailed discussion of this problem must be deferred until the next chapter, but we can anticipate some of the discussion here. The important condition that must be fulfilled before cognitive learning can take place is cognitive clearness of the situation and the availability of the necessary repertoire of behavior patterns that are under voluntary control.

We discussed in Chapter 13 the meaning of cognitive clarity. The various parts of the situation must be distinguished from each other and their relationships to each other must be perceived. Some situations that are very complicated or very hazy are often not cognitively clear.

Some behavioral responses are not under voluntary control, such as reflexes, the detailed motions within a motor pattern, and emotional reactions. These suggest the situations in which learning is likely to be noncognitive and to follow the general principles of conditioning and reinforcement learning. This would suggest that many of the new motor skills of the child are not cognitively learned. Throwing a baseball, making a slip knot, skipping, or shooting a marble are probably learned in much the same way that the infant learns to reach for an object, although some individuals approach such tasks in an intellectual cognitive fashion. Learned emotional reactions are probably not cognitively guided. Because we usually are not cognitively clear about interpersonal relations, it seems likely that social tact, persuasiveness, and other complicated social behavior patterns are not cognitively learned. Learned behavior that is exhibited while the person is asleep is not cognitively guided.

Use of Conditioning in the Treatment of Enuresis

It is interesting, in the light of this last point, to note that conditioning methods have been effectively used to teach a child to wake up when his bladder tension becomes high. One of the problems of the enuretic child is that he stays asleep when the symptoms of bladder tension would wake up a non-enuretic child. Consequently, he wets his bed. Mowrer and his coworkers (1938, 1939) have devised an apparatus to wake up the child as soon as he begins to urinate. There are two electrodes separated by dry cloth that establish an electrical connection as soon as the urine wets the cloth. This connection awakens the child by ringing a bell, or disturbing his sleep in some other way. In this way, the child learns to wake up and get up when the symptoms of bladder tension are strong, so that after the period of conditioning he no longer needs the bell. He wakes up when he needs to go to the bathroom. This does not solve all the problems of enuresis, but it is a real help to the enuretic child. Of thirty-five cases on whom this technique has been used, thirty-four stopped wetting their beds within eight weeks. This experiment is interesting also because it suggests that the mechanism by which the child perceives bladder tension and voluntarily goes to the toilet during the daytime does not operate when he is asleep. He must, apparently, have a separate automatic mechanism for awakening to this specific stimulus even though he sleeps through other disturbing stimuli.

Razran (1936) reports that it is much easier to obtain conditioned responses in adult subjects when the subject is engaged in some other activity and is paying little attention to the conditioning stimuli or to his conditioned response. This also suggests that cognitive clarity facilitates cognitive learning.

Summary

Habit formation, either of the fixed-response variety or of the simple feed-back system that can guide behavior, is an important learning process both in infants and in older children. We have suggested that this is the only mechanism of learning during infancy, but that later in life cognitive learning resulting in changes in cognitively guided behavior may occur.

We have surveyed the findings from conditioning experiments on children to show that they are capable of being conditioned. The free behavior of infants furnishes many illustrations of conditioning through stimulus contiguity or through reinforcement. We have also seen that stimulus generalization is common. Finally, we have looked at the role of noncognitive learning in older children. Learning motor skills, learning responses to very complicated unclear situations, and learning while asleep or while occupied with some other activity all seem to be examples of noncognitive learning after infancy.

18

Cognitive Learning

A FEW YEARS AGO there were very few people who could tell the difference between a male and a female day-old chick. It was quite an important distinction to make because if the hatchery could sell a batch of baby chicks with the assurance that they would all develop into hens, it could command a much better price for them than if it had to sell a batch of chicks whose composition of pullets and cockerels was unknown. Consequently, the man who could discriminate pullets from cockerels was a very useful person.

There were some few people who could separate pullets from cockerels reliably, but the trouble was that they did not know how they did it. Such an expert could look at a day-old chick and know that it was a pullet, but he couldn't say how he knew. The method of teaching this skill was quite simple but very slow. The expert who could make the discrimination would begin to teach a student by handing him a chick and saying, "This one is a pullet." He would then hand him another and say, "This one is a cockerel." After awhile he would have the student try to make the discrimination. If the student guessed right—and at this stage it felt just like guessing—he was told that he had been right. When he made a mistake he was informed of that. Eventually, after many, many trials, the student began to be right more often than he was wrong, but he did not know how he could tell the difference any more than his teacher could. He was "getting the feel" of the problem. With enough practice the student could become an expert also and be able to tell the difference with very few mistakes.

This is a good example of adjustive behavior that is not cognitively guided. The process by which it is learned is noncognitive learning. It depends upon reinforcement of the correct responses until finally the correct discrimination appears automatically without the individual's knowing why. Sexing of day-old chicks is no longer an intuitive process of this sort. Instead there are tests for the sex that may be described verbally and applied by any person. The basis for the judgment is clear. The discrimination is now cognitively guided and the process by which it is acquired is cognitive learning.

The Improvement of Cognitively Guided Behavior

The model of behavior presented in Chapter 6 is a model of cognitively guided behavior. It presupposes that the individual has a repertoire of behavior patterns under voluntary control. Furthermore, these patterns of schemata are independent of each other so that the individual may at will combine them in any sequence or in any combination that is not prevented by physical reality. He cannot, of course, raise and lower his arm at the same time, but he can combine raising one arm with lowering the other.

When a person of this maturity faces a problem, his task is not to learn to perform the necessary actions but rather to discover what actions will lead him to his goal. In order to know what actions do lead to his goal he must obtain an accurate cognitive picture of the situation. Cognitive learning, then, consists of refining, completing, and correcting his cognitive map. Learning consists in obtaining information and interpreting it correctly so that his understanding of the problem situation is clear. The process by which he adds to or corrects or clarifies his cognitive picture is cognitive learning.

It may happen that when he has an accurate cognitive picture he discovers he cannot perform the behavior required because he has not learned that skill or because he does not have it under voluntary control, or perhaps because it is impossible. He now faces a different problem. To learn a new skill is not cognitive learning, although it may take place more rapidly if the person is cognitively clear about what his action ought to be.

Description of Cognitive Learning

Learning through Observation

In its clearest form cognitive learning is learning through observation about the relations among objects in the external world. In one of Piaget's observations (1951), Jacqueline said, "Daddy is running the water, he is going to shave." She had discovered from her observations that the first behavior was a good indication of the second. Since she did nothing about the fact, it seems likely that she learned it merely through observation, not because any behavior of her own was rewarded.

The child sees his sister mark in his new book. When he sees another of his books marked in, he accuses his sister of doing it. He may not be completely justified in his accusation, but he is showing the effects of cognitive learning, nevertheless. The child observes that his teacher keeps a friend in after school because he made three mistakes in spelling. When he himself makes three mistakes, he expects that he will be kept in and feels appropriately apprehensive or angry or repentant. There are, obviously, innumerable such examples of acquiring knowledge through the observation of happenings in which we do not participate.

Behavior Designed to Produce Information

Even though we actually take part in the situation, the learning may still be described as cognitive learning. When we feel the cloth in a new suit, sample a new kind of cooky, test out an electrical repair job by seeing whether the light goes on properly, we are actively producing results; we do so for the purpose of gaining information about the external world, not because we want to produce the result. We are not learning to turn on the light or we may not even want the light to be on, but we are behaving in a way that will provide cognitive information.

Even when we are actually learning some new skill we may approach it cognitively. We may say, in effect, "If I take this path, what will happen? Suppose I now try this path." In other words, we are learning the relation between our own behavior in a situation and its consequences.

Cognitive learning can thus be seen to depend upon the perception of relations between one part of the external world and another, between one action and another, or between one's own action and its effects. When the relationship is easily perceived or cognized, the learning takes place rapidly and the task is simple. When the relationship is very difficult to discover, then the learning takes a long time.

Factors Which Make Cognitive Learning Easy

When two objects or actions are strongly unified by the various perceptual unit-forming factors (see p. 62), the relationship between them is easily learned. It is simple to learn that a light switch turns on a light because the two actions occur in such close temporal proximity. If after the switch was thrown, it took thirty minutes for the lights to go on, we would have considerable difficulty in learning the relation between the two phenomena. The fact that all light switches look very much alike makes it easy to discover how to turn on the lights in a new house. We can apply what we learned in other situations. If the lights sometimes went on when the knob of the radio was turned, sometimes when the bottom step on the stairs was stepped on, sometimes when the window blind was pulled down, it would require a major research effort to learn how to turn the lights on in every new room.

Perceptual Units in String Problems

Richardson (1932) presented a number of string problems to children. In these problems one string out of a group is attached to a goal object, and the child tries to obtain the goal by pulling the correct string. In Figure 18.1 a number of the problems are diagrammatically presented, in order of increasing

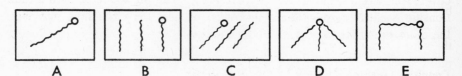

Fig. 18.1 The effect of unit formation on the difficulty of string problems. (After H. M. Richardson, *Genet. Psych. Monog., 12*, 1932, 230)

difficulty. We can see that the clearness of the unit formation between the string and the goal and also the unity between the close end of the string and the far end makes the first problem quite easy and the last one quite difficult. In the first problem only one string has any marked perceptual unit formation with the goal object. In the second all of the strings have a clear perceptual relationship, but only one of them has any real causal relationship.

Repetition as a Unit-forming Factor

Another factor besides proximity and similarity has been shown to be very important in conditioning—namely, repetition of the pairing of the response and the reinforcement, or the pairing of the conditioned and unconditioned stimulus. Repetition is not one of the unit-forming factors that were discussed earlier, but we recognize that it can be one.

In some cases, especially when the unit is complex, cognition of the relationship may depend upon repetition of the unit, even in the perception of spatial units. In the two lines of Figure 18.2, for example, the same pattern

Fig. 18.2   The factor of repetition in unit formation, showing how the repetition of a pattern makes it more easily perceivable.

occurs. This pattern appears only once in the first line, whereas in the second line it is repeated several times. In the second line the tendency for this pattern to form a perceptual unit is very clear, whereas in the first line there is almost no tendency for it to form a psychological unit. Notice that the other unit-forming factors are kept relatively constant. In each case the given pattern is segregated from the rest of the line by a greater distance than occurs anywhere within the pattern. It can also be seen from Figure 18.2 that a simpler pattern, such as ● ● ●, appears unified even without repetition. The enhancing effect of repetition upon unit formation is more striking for complex patterns than for simple ones.

Thus, one property of cognitive learning is that relationships can be discovered among objects in the external world. The discovery of such a relationship is affected by the same factors of contiguity and similarity that affect the more primitive, noncognitive learning processes.

Cognitive Learning Through Testing Hypotheses

In general, cognitive learning requires maturity. But one kind of cognitive learning, the formulation and testing of hypotheses, requires even more maturity. If the child is sufficiently mature, he may actively seek to discover the relationships among events in the external world by formulating a hypothesis about a relationship and testing it through special observation or behavioral experiment. Hypothesis testing is not the basis of all cognitive learning; the relation can be apparent without any active search. Complex relationships that would never have been recognized otherwise may, however, be discovered through hypothesis testing. Deliberate search for a certain kind of relationship enhances the probability of finding it—provided it is present.

For a child to discover by himself that a switch downstairs can turn on the light in the upstairs hall, he has to throw the switch and then go upstairs and see that the light is on; then he returns downstairs, switches off the switch, and goes upstairs to see that the light is off. He is likely to repeat this procedure a number of times. It is hard to say whether the repetition is necessary for him really to satisfy himself about the fact or whether it is merely the exercise of a newly discovered relationship. But notice that in this process there is a sort of contiguity between the light turned on upstairs and the switch turned on downstairs. It is a remote sort of contiguity, probably noticeable only because the child deliberately experimented to see what happened.

The effect of deliberate search can also be illustrated in visual figures. In the conglomeration of dots shown in Figure 18.3 no units stand out very

Fig. 18.3 The effect of a hypothesis on perception of groupings, showing how the pattern ●● ● ●● is easily seen once you search for it.

clearly. If, however, the figure is searched to see whether it contains the pattern ●● ● ●●, it is not difficult to find. Or to take a slightly more complex example, the pattern of dots in Figure 18.4 looks relatively meaningless, and it is quite difficult though not impossible to discover what systematic arrangement is present. If, however, one approaches the problem with the hypothesis that the dots are the intersections of two sets of imaginary lines, then it is not hard to find the system. The formation and the testing of hypotheses greatly increase the probability of discovering a complex relationship that fits the hypothesis.

The deliberate search for a specific hypothesized relation has a disadvantage in that it reduces the probability of discovering some other relationship that is present but that does not fit the hypothesis. Thus an active attempt to make a situation cognitively clear may actually prevent one from being able to respond to it adequately in an intuitive fashion. The active analysis may, if it is on the wrong track, blind the individual to relationships that would be obvious if he were to adopt a more passive attitude.

Despite the fact that active testing of hypotheses may lead to error, such an attitude requires maturity because it demands attention. By paying attention to those properties of the stimulus configuration that are relevant to the hypothesis, the individual becomes more sensitive to such properties. Atten-

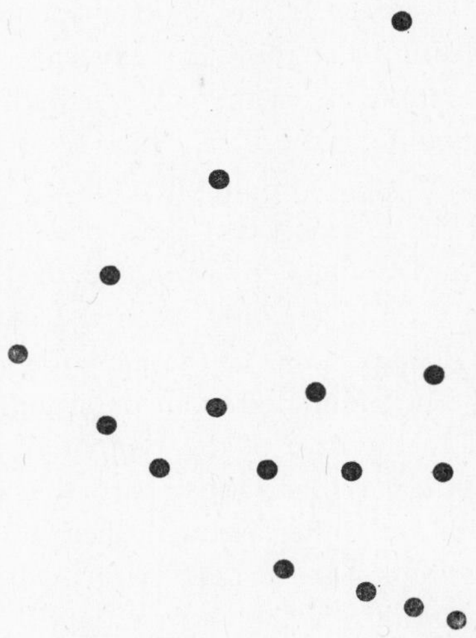

Fig. 18.4 The importance of a hypothesis in understanding complex situations.

tion, although it is only poorly understood, is itself a characteristic of relative maturity because it demands that the individual be sufficiently independent of the irrelevant unit-forming factors in the situation to override them or to ignore them.

The Conditions upon Which Cognitive Learning Depends

Now that we have examined a number of examples of cognitive learning and the external factors that make it easy or difficult, we can return to the formulation of the conditions required for such a process to occur.

DIFFERENTIATED COGNITION In order for the individual to learn the relation between two external objects, it is obvious that his cognition must be sufficiently clear and differentiated to perceive the two objects as distinct and separate. If for any reason the individual were so immature that his perception lacked any sharp distinctions, it would not be possible for him to show cognitive learning. We know the perceptions of very young children are quite vague, and we can find situations for adults as well in which the situation is perceived so diffusely that separate objects are not differentiated from each other.

When, for example, an untrained person listens to a symphony orchestra, he fails to differentiate all the sections—the brasses, woodwinds, strings, etc. Consequently, it may happen that one theme consistently shifts from the clarinet to the bassoon section without that consistent relationship being apparent to the listener. The trained musician, on the other hand, because he hears the sections in a more differentiated way, may find such a consistent shift very obvious and clear. In another realm, skillful observers may perceive in a group discussion the clear existence of subgroups and thus learn how one subgroup affects another. A less skillful observer may perceive the discussion as an undifferentiated sequence of remarks. Any factor that makes the cognition of a situation undifferentiated makes cognitive learning difficult and causes the learning that does take place to resemble noncognitive learning.

Another way to formulate this first condition is to say that cognitive learning can occur only when the individual is capable of some object constancy. The portions of the incoming stimulation that relate to a single object must be differentiated from the totality and related to the appropriate causal object. In the case of the symphony, the totality of sound must be differentiated into parts, and those parts that come from the bassoons must be identified with each other and with the bassoon section.

SEPARATION OF COGNITION AND ACTION   A second condition for cognitive learning is the separation of cognition from action (see p. 91). In cognitive learning the observation of the external situation leads to knowledge concerning it that may be used to guide behavior but is not inextricably tied to behavior. The fact that cognition is separate from action means that the individual learns what the situation is like and then decides what to do. In conditioning, on the other hand, it is the behavior that is learned. With the acquisition of a conditioned response, the response follows automatically upon the presentation of the stimulus situation. Cognitive learning requires, therefore, a sufficient separation of cognition from action to permit cognitive guidance of behavior.

ANTICIPATION IN COGNITION   A third condition necessary for cognitive learning, at least cognitive learning through hypothesis testing, is the ability to have an expectation—i.e., sufficient maturity to be able to anticipate the consequences of actions and to recognize impending events. Such an expectation can be relatively vague and undifferentiated, as when we have a vague anxiety or dread without a cognitively clear basis for it. Or, on the other hand, it can be a scientific prediction stemming from cognitively clear observations and principles. The infant whose entire psychological world is in the present is not capable of cognitive learning in this sense.

To summarize, then, we can see that cognitive learning, in the sense in which we have used it, depends upon a differentiated perception of the world, upon object constancy, upon ability to anticipate the future, and upon the separation of cognition from action. These conditions do not hold for the very young infant, nor do they hold for all the behavior of the adult. In situations that are very confused or, as we shall see later, in which there are emotional reasons preventing cognitive clearness, the adult's learning may be of the more primitive variety.

Learning Social Rules and Social Roles

One important area in which the differences between cognitive and non-cognitive learning are important is in learning the rules of society that form such a large part of socialization.

We saw earlier (see p. 211) that in any culture there are customary ways of behaving that people are more or less coerced into following. These social rules differ from physical laws in that they are not so clearly indicated by the perceptible cues in the situation. Furthermore, they do not operate so consistently—*i.e.,* the consequence of breaking a social rule is not so predictable as the consequence of violating a physical law. Because of this, social rules are more difficult to learn. For example, children have to learn when to talk and when not to talk; they must know how loudly it is proper to talk. One must be quiet in church; one is free, on occasion, to talk but not to yell in school; on the playground any volume is appropriate; at a football game yelling is the preferred tone of voice. These rules are not obvious. They are by no means so obvious as the fact that one cannot walk through fences, and are probably more difficult to learn than that one should not poke his finger inside an electric-light socket.

The organization of social rules can best be described in terms of the roles of people in different settings (see p. 212). The minister has a certain role in society. In specific settings, church service for example, the rule prescribes the appropriate behavior.

Some social rules are the same for nearly everybody regardless of his role. The individual can count upon such rules; they can be learned once and for all. Rules about killing are almost uniform in our culture, although there are circumstances that mitigate or justify a killing. In a more stable culture than ours, there are likely to be many universal rules and taboos. Other social rules apply only in certain defined situations and depend upon the role of the individual. The behavior of chairing a meeting is appropriate only when the individual is in the role of chairman. When he is in a similar situation but in a different role, different behavior is appropriate.

Importance of Cognitive Clarity of Rules

This difference among rules has implications for cognitive clarity. When a rule is universal, flexibility is not required. The individual is never under pressure to decide what to do and what not to do with regard to an inflexible rule. For such a rule, cognitive unclearness is no disadvantage. Since the most important behavioral characteristic of cognitive unclearness is its reducing the flexibility of adjustment (see p. 327), it is less significant when the social rule requires no flexibility.

The rule concerning exposure of the body make a good example of a cognitively unclear rule that is obeyed by most people, but not through cognitively guided behavior. In the discussion of various social rules (see p. 213) we saw that this rule is focused on motivation. It is wrong to want to exhibit one's body, but exposure itself is not seriously condemned if it occurs through some other motivation, such as wanting to go swimming.

The behavior of most people in relation to bodily exposure shows a fairly accurate intuitive grasp of this rule, but it certainly is not cognitively clear. Our behavior in this area is generally governed by feelings of shame and guilt that automatically arise. The lack of cognitive clarity is shown also in the fact that curious inconsistencies arise. There was a man once who liked to go to the beach and did not feel exposed in a swimming suit, but he did not like to wear his suit underneath his clothes because it embarrassed him to take off his trousers in public even though the swimming suit was underneath.

Similarly, someone may be shocked to see young people on the beach wrap towels around their waists because this hides the fact that they have suits on—makes them look as though they do *not* have suits on, in fact— and yet does not provide enough coverage to be respectable except in a swimming suit.

These examples show that the core concept, to avoid deliberate exhibitionism, is not cognitively clear; if it were, the feelings would not arise. The embarrassment of the man who did not like to take his trousers off in public stems from the superficial similarity of this act to the taking off of one's trousers at home, where such an action should be private.

Because these feelings are not cognitively clear, they show considerable rigidity under changing circumstances. If we were to move to another culture or join a nudist camp, recognizing cognitively that different proprieties exist there, we would still have to get over gradually the feeling of embarrassment at being exposed.

Thus, we see that social rules and customs may be cognitively clear or they may be cognitively unclear. The task of the next few sections is to point out some of the conditions in learning social rules that bring cognitive clarity. We can hypothesize that a social rule is likely to be cognitively unclear under any of the following four conditions: (1) if the child is too immature to be cognitively clear about what he learns; (2) if the rule is taught in an arbitrary way without explanation or rationale; (3) if a rule is inconsistently enforced; (4) if the rule is taught in such a way that anxiety, shame, and guilt are aroused and the child represses the motives that are unacceptable. Let us examine now each of these conditions.

Maturity of the Child at the Time a Rule Is Learned

Because, as we have seen, the very young child is not capable of cognitive learning, it is to be expected that any social rules that are inculcated at a very early age will, if learned at all, be learned in a noncognitive way.

Here we see the interaction of maturity and learning. If the socialization of some specific behavior is begun too early it is ineffective. If it is begun slightly later, we have seen from various experiments (see p. 384) that learning is relatively inefficient. Now, in addition, we can see that such learning is noncognitive, and consequently the learned behavior is less clear, less flexible, and less cognitively guided.

We might choose as an example learning to stay clean and to be neat. The toddler is not very tidy. He dumps toys on the floor, becomes distracted by something else, and goes off leaving them lying. If he is attracted into a dirty place, the fact that it is dirty or the fact that he has on clean clothes is of no psychological significance. If the mother is upset by this messiness of the child, she may begin to teach him to pick up his toys and to stay clean. Each concrete case of messiness will be commented on; the child will be punished by being made to clean up his toys before he starts something new. He may be punished still more severely if he forgets to do so. Spilling milk at the table will be treated similarly. The immature child may not see these various actions that are rewarded or punished as examples of a single principle. To see the relation of all the concrete examples of cleanliness to the general principle is to be cognitively clear. Because the child is not able to recognize the general principle of neatness, he may receive punishment that he cannot understand. He does not recognize every new example of neatness and does not connect it with previously learned rules. These incomprehensible actions of the parent may make the child anxious about dirt. Unlike the adult who is motivated to clean a dirty room for some clear reason, the child may feel anxious or uneasy when he becomes dirty. If such a pattern of learning is well established, it may be quite rigid and unamenable to realistic considerations. One child who was very thoroughly taught to be clean and neat actually became rather panic stricken when he found a speck of dirt on his coat. He seemed to feel that any dirtiness was bad. Dirtiness was for him an absolute black or white sin. He felt this way despite the fact that his mother tried to reassure him that tiny specks of dirt were not so important as he made them out to be.

This discussion may have given the impression that all training that is begun before the child is cognitively clear about his actions must produce disastrous neurotic results. This is not true. Much of the attempted training of very young children has no effect at all. In other cases the first learning may be noncognitive, but with increased maturity the child comes to understand the reasons underlying the social rule. In still other cases the lack of cognitive clarity does no damage.

The rigid inculcation of a cultural standard is unfortunate only when the child must later change his standards either because the standard changes with the role the child has or because the standards of his own home environment are not typical of those he will find in the wider world into which he will eventually emerge. In a stable culture in which standards and expectations remain constant from one generation to another, lack of cognitive clarity about the basic rules of the society may be no problem because there is no reason to be flexible. In our rapidly changing culture, on the other hand, those standards that are not cognitively clear may be the source of serious maladjustment.

Rationality of Disciplinary Practices

One factor that may bring about cognitively unclear learning is, as we have seen, the immaturity of the child at the time the learning occurs. A second factor has to do with the way the discipline is applied.

When psychologists teach rats to solve problems or run mazes, they are forced to teach them in a very arbitrary way. The rat is given an opportunity to take either of two choices and suddenly receives a shock. There is no way to tell the rat the reason for the shock.

Children may be taught in the same way as rats, but fortunately the child is almost always told what he did that was wrong. His attention is directed through words to the relevant aspects of the situation. Even the most taciturn parent is likely to say something to the child, such as, "Don't touch that stove," when he reprimands him. He does not merely give the child a whack with no explanation whatsoever. There can obviously be all degrees of clarification, from the minimum just described to the parent who explains that the stove is hot and holds the child's hand close enough to it that he feels the heat without being burned. The purpose of explaining a rule is to make it clear to the child what the rule is and how it is related to some underlying principle that justifies it.

Although a clear explanation of the reason for a rule tends to produce a better understanding of it, other factors may prevent the explanation from being effective. An explanation cannot function very effectively if the child is too immature to understand the rationale that is explained to him. Sometimes parents spend fruitless effort trying to explain the reason for a rule when the child is too immature to understand it. In most cases, however, an explanation makes it easier for the child to be cognitively clear about the rule. Such explanations tend in addition to prevent the child from seeing the rule as the whim of the parent. This consequence is not, however, related to cognitive clarity and will be discussed later (see p. 446).

Consistency of Discipline

A third characteristic of the parent's disciplinary practices that influences the clarity with which a rule is learned is the consistency of the teaching. Psychologists and other students of child development have frequently pointed out the importance of being consistent with a child. He should not be coddled on one day for behavior that is punished on another. Similarly, it is important that the different authorities in the child's life—his mother, father, grandparents, nursemaid, and baby-sitter—should follow the same rules and enforce the same regulations.

One of the effects of inconsistency is that it makes the achievement of cognitive clarity very difficult. If no single underlying principle can be perceived behind the various actions of the parents, the only way the child can form a clear picture of the conditions under which a rule holds is to learn which person in what mood has what rules. This is a difficult problem and we have already seen that people tend to behave intuitively when they face situations that are too complicated to be clearly understood. Inconsistent reinforcement does not interfere with a conditioning process as much as it does with a process of cognitive learning. Consequently, the child may develop a consistent behavior pattern under inconsistent training, but it will develop slowly and then it will be quite rigid and unchangeable because it is not cognitively clear.

Experimental results from conditioning experiments support the hypothesis that inconsistent reinforcement makes learning more resistant to extinction. Humphreys showed this in his experiments on conditioning the eyeblink response (1939). If a puff of air strikes the eye, the eye involuntarily blinks. The air puff is the unconditioned stimulus and the blinking the unconditioned response. Humphreys conditioned this response to a light. Just following the flash of light came the puff of air. After several repetitions of this pairing, the conditioned eyeblink was established; the eye blinked when the light stimulus was presented. Humphreys used two groups of subjects. For one group the light was consistently reinforced; each time it was presented the air puff invariably followed. For the other group there was inconsistent reinforcement; sometimes the light stimulus was followed by the puff of air, but sometimes it was not reinforced in this way. The reinforcements in the second group occurred on one half of the trials, but they were randomly distributed—i.e., on no trial could the subject predict whether the light would be reinforced or not.

Humphreys found, surprisingly enough, that the conditioning proceeded equally rapidly in both groups. When, however, he compared the two groups with regard to the rate of extinction of the conditioned response, he found that the inconsistently reinforced response was much more resistant to extinction. It took many more extinction trials, during which the light was never followed by the air puff, to extinguish the subjects' habit of blinking when the light came on.

The resistance of an inconsistently reinforced response is not due entirely to its being unclear. We can see that even with complete cognitive clarity, a random pattern of reinforcement produces learning that is more resistant to extinction than learning produced by a regular pattern. If we know that some action will produce a desirable reward some of the time, but not all of the time, then a failure to receive the reward on one or two occasions will not contradict the hypothesis that the action will sometimes be rewarded. It takes many failures to convince one that the action will never again be rewarded. Not all the rigidity that comes from the inconsistent training, therefore, is due to the fact that it is noncognitive.

Training that Induces Repression

A fourth condition of learning can be seen to reduce the cognitive clarity of a social rule. In the discussion of repression (see p. 258) we learned that repression is an insensitivity to stimulus situations that for one reason or another evoke dangerous motives. In this context we can see that some sorts of disciplinary procedures might lead to repression of the child's motives and in this way to cognitive unclearness.

One of the important discoveries of psychoanalysis is the effect of repression upon an individual's behavior. One young Jewish boy had received very rough treatment while he lived in Germany. His resentment and hatred came into conflict with many other feelings and principles. He finally came to the United States. He reported a very curious feeling of having occasionally an immediate intense dislike for certain people without any logical reason. After careful observation he discovered that these people were tall, blond, Nordic-looking young men. His behavior might be seen as the result of cognitive unclearness. First, it was unclear in that it was a baseless feeling of dislike that came over him automatically, not like the dislikes we all experience that are based upon certain recognized characteristics of the other person. Secondly, his response was to a superficial cue. To be tall, blond, and Nordic may in Germany be statistically highly correlated with having anti-Semitic feelings, but if this boy's cognition were clear, and the basis for his dislike conscious, he would respond with dislike to people who he found were anti-Semitic, regardless of their size and coloring, and he would not dislike people who were friendly toward Jews, despite their similarity to his childhood persecutors.

In a similar way child-rearing practices such as shaming and induction of guilt and anxiety may induce repression of motivation and can lead to behavior that is understandable to the trained observer but cognitively unclear to the person himself. For example, a boy who was dominated by his father but who was forced to repress his resentment might become antagonistic to anyone in a position of authority whether or not he was domineering.

To summarize this section, we can say that if the child's unsocialized motives are disciplined in such a way that they produce guilt and anxiety they may be repressed. If so, the resulting socialized behavior will exhibit the diffuseness, the rigidity, and the occasional inappropriateness characteristic of behavior that is not cognitively guided.

We have discussed four kinds of learning situations that may result in the child's learning social rules in a cognitively unclear fashion: (1) learning while still immature; (2) learning in situations in which the relationships between the discipline and the action that provoked it are unclear—i.e., discipline that is not explained to the child; (3) inconsistent discipline; and (4) discipline that tends to produce repression of the motives that are being socialized. The first three of these hypotheses provide a theoretical explanation for the common-sense advice of psychologists and educators who recommend delaying training until the child can understand a rational disciplinary policy and consistency of training. The fourth is also reflected in common-sense advice to parents to discipline the child's behavior without making him feel that he is an unworthy or guilty person—i.e., to make him feel that he is a good and worthwhile person who has misbehaved rather than that he is a bad and unworthy person.

Cognitive Learning of Interpersonal Relations

One of the results of a cognitively clear understanding of a situation is that it is communicable. This implies that when the child's learning is cognitively clear, the effects of rewards and punishments depend greatly upon how they are verbally interpreted to him. We can see an important illustration of this fact in the effect of different sorts of discipline upon his cognition of the source of the rules that he is expected to obey.

The child's response to socialization depends upon whether he sees the parent as the source of the rules or whether the parent appears to be merely the interpreter of the rule—*i.e.,* a person who is telling the child what the world is like but who does not take responsibility for the rule's being what it is.

Child psychologists, when asked for advice about disciplining children, sometimes recommend that the parent should make the consequence of the child's action stem from reality rather than from the parent, and that the parent should, if possible, give commands in an impersonal way. He may in effect say to the child, "I tell you to do this" or he may in effect say, "I am giving you the information that reality demands that you do this." In the first case he makes himself the source of the action, the person responsible for the command. In the second he puts himself in the role of a person who merely communicates or transmits the demands of the real world. He takes no responsibility for it.

The difference between these two ways of exerting control can be followed through most clearly if we assume that the situation is cognitively clear to the child. How will his experience in the home, if it is cognitively clear, affect his attitudes toward the parent and how will it create more general needs affecting behavior outside the home? The preschool child is certainly not cognitively clear about his relations to his parents, but we can come to understand his behavior better by first assuming that there is no unclearness. Then we can see how the lack of clarity modifies our conclusions.

One way that the parent may avoid being the source of the rule is to explain the reasons for it. If he convinces the child that he would be wise to go to bed early because he is going to get up early in the morning, the parent does not force the child to go to bed. If the child is mature enough to understand the reason, a rational explanation may ease disciplinary friction.

In many cases the parent wishes the child to obey a request that is not easily explained in clear logical terms. Nursery-school teachers have a technique for putting rules in an impersonal way without actually explaining them. Instead of saying, "Don't throw sand," the teacher may say, "The sand stays down." Instead of saying, "Don't put your jacket there," she may say, "Jackets belong on the hooks, don't they?" Instead of, "You must go to bed now," the parent might say, "The clock says it is getting near bedtime." In each of these examples the adult shifts his request from a personal to an impersonal form. Instead of being the source of the rule the parent becomes the informant only. Even the simple use of "We don't do that, do we?" has this effect.

Sources of Rules in a Democratic Group

These devices may in some cases be no more than tricks, but an essential part of democracy in the home is to substitute reasons for rules whenever possible. Lewin, Lippitt, and White, in order to study the effects of democracy, created three different group atmospheres in several clubs of school-age boys. The ostensible purpose of the clubs was to do craft work of various kinds. The experimenters kept extensive records of the behavior of the boys who played in these different social atmospheres. At times during the experiment the leaders were shifted around so that the effect of change of atmosphere could be studied. The three social climates created in this experiment were authoritarian, democratic, and laissez-faire. We shall report the results of the experiment later, but the rules the experimenters used to establish the three kinds of atmosphere show clearly that democracy is not so much a lack of control as a control guided by reality. Table 11 shows the criteria used to create the three atmospheres.

The second and fourth criteria, especially, reveal the attempt of the democratic leader to interpret reality rather than to dictate rules. The first and third point to other aspects of democracy, the substitution of individual autonomy where possible and the transfer of power from the leader to the group as a whole. We see that when the parent makes himself the source of the controls upon the child, he is following an authoritarian technique; when he merely communicates to the child the rules that exist he is following a democratic technique.

If these practices are merely techniques, they are likely to fail. If the parent is really expressing his own wishes, he may pretend that they are objective rules, but he faces the chance that the child will ask to be convinced. The child may say "Johnny gets to go to a movie on school nights." The parent, unless he gives in, must now say, "I don't care what Johnny gets to do, you cannot go." Then the parent has made himself the source of the rule—and in fact he is the source of the rule.

As the example indicates, the differences between the authoritarian or democratic parent appear most clearly in the way prohibitions, orders, and punishment are structured. Most parents, democratic and authoritarian alike,

TABLE 11*

CRITERIA FOR DIAGNOSING A LAISSEZ-FAIRE, AN AUTHORITARIAN, AND A DEMOCRATIC ATMOSPHERE

Laissez-faire (No control)	Authoritarian (Maximum control) (Leader is source)	Democratic (Moderate control) (Leader interprets reality)
1. Complete freedom for group or individual decision without any leader participation.	All determination of policy by the leader.	All policies a matter of group discussion and decision, encouraged and assisted by leader.
2. Various materials supplied by leader, who made it clear that he would supply information when asked. He took no other part in work discussions.	Techniques and activity steps dictated by the authority, one at a time, so that future steps were always uncertain to a large degree.	Activity perspective gained during first discussion period. General steps to group goal sketched, and where technical advice was needed the leader suggested two or three alternative procedures from which choice could be made.
3. Complete nonparticipation by the leader.	The leader usually dictated the particular work task and work companions of each member.	The members were free to work with whomever they chose and the division of tasks was left to the group.
4. Very infrequent comments on member activities unless questioned, and no attempt to participate or interfere in the course of events.	The denominator was "personal" in his praise and criticism of the work of each member, but remained aloof from active participation except when demonstrating. He was friendly or impersonal rather than hostile.	The leader was "objective" or "fact-minded" in his praise and criticism and tried to be a regular group member in spirit without doing too much of the work.

* Ronald Lippitt and Ralph K. White, "The Social Climate of Children's Groups," in R. G. Barker, J. Kounin and H. F. Wright (ed.), *Child Behavior and Development*, McGraw-Hill, 1943.

do not express positive approval of the child in a way that emphasizes their role as mediators of the culture. When he caresses the child, the parent is expressing his own feeling, and when he sympathizes it is his own sympathy. When he does something nice for the child he generally does it because of his own wish to be kind. On relatively rare occasions, he says, "I don't think there is anything wrong in that" or, "That seems like a good idea," conveying the idea that there *is* a right and wrong against which the parent is checking the child's behavior. Most of the positive feelings expressed are the parent's own, both in his own eyes and those of the child.

Consequences of Authoritarianism

Let us turn now to the consequences of these different ways of structuring parental action. The consequence of being the source of action rather than the communicator or mediator of an action stems from the fact that the feelings of resentment, gratitude, contempt, or admiration are directed to the source of action.

When a parent makes himself the source of control, the child is encouraged to direct his feelings toward the parent and to behave in an appropriate manner. Probably no parent can avoid being viewed as a source of action, because in many cases he actually is. The authoritarian parent, however, emphasizes his personal authority. Consequently, an authoritarian policy will increase the child's resentment when the parent is frustrating and enhance his gratitude when the parent is cooperative with his purposes. Secondly, it makes the child more sensitive to the parent's feeling toward him, because he views the parent's prohibitions as expressions of hostility and permissive actions as symptoms of friendliness. Thirdly, it encourages the child to identify with the parent because it puts the parent in a position of prestige and power.

RESENTMENT OF AUTHORITARIAN PARENT It is the negative reactions that differentiate most clearly between the authoritarian and democratic home. Punishment is usually more severe in the authoritarian home than in the democratic one, and children raised in an authoritarian punitive home are likely to feel hostile and resentful.

The punitive parent also punishes expressions of hostility. Thus, he increases the child's resentment, but on the other hand he reduces the tendency of the child to show his hostility. The result, if there were cognitive clarity, would resemble the situation when any of us must submit to a dictatorial boss. We hate him but obey. As soon as possible we leave the situation, try to get out from under his control. If we ever obtain any power over such a person, we are inclined to take revenge. We certainly do not deliberately copy his actions or his beliefs; if anything we are inclined to believe the opposite.

SOURCE OF RULES IN POSSESSIVE HOMES In a possessive home (see p. 502) as well as in a punitive one the parent's behavior structures the situation so that the parent is the source of the actions that influence the child. Whenever the possessive parent's anxiety about the child controls his behavior, parental rules are direct expressions of his wishes. One important difference between the authoritarian home and the possessive home is that more of the actions in the possessive home are warm and friendly to the child; therefore the child's feelings are more likely to be friendly than hostile.

Another important difference is the use of "visible suffering" in possessive homes. When the parent suffers from the child's behavior, he personalizes his relation to the child, even though at the moment he is the victim rather than the source of action. Such parental behavior focuses the child's perceptions upon the effect of his actions on the parent rather than upon the objective consequences of his behavior in the real world. Possessive homes, therefore, like authoritarian ones, tend to create attitudes and feelings about the parent at the expense of beliefs and attitudes about the objective world.

OBEDIENCE IN ABSENCE OF PARENT Another consequence of perceiving the parent as the source of the rules or as the personal victim of the child's action is that the child's obedience is dependent upon the possibility of being discovered by the parent. When a parent wishes his child to stay away from a hot stove, he informs the child that the stove is hot, that it will burn him if he touches it. If the child accepts this fact, he will continue to believe that the stove is hot even if the parent is not around. If, however, the parent were to say, "Don't touch that stove" and limit his explanation to that statement, the child might perceive the behavior solely in terms of its interpersonal consequences. If he did so he would have little reason to inhibit his impulse to touch the stove unless the parent were on the scene.

To summarize, perceiving the parent as the source of rules directs the child's feelings toward the parent and makes his obedience dependent upon the parent.

This discussion of various methods of social control illustrates the importance of the context of learning, especially the verbal context, upon the child's cognition and consequently upon his behavior. In actual fact the child is not cognitively clear about many of his punishments and rewards. In such a case he will be likely to blame the parent even if the parent tries to make it clear that he is interpreting the external reality. Many a child has become angry at the parent who tries to explain that he cannot make it stop raining or he cannot stop a skinned knee from hurting. Nevertheless, and especially as the child grows older, the way the enforcement of rules is phrased becomes increasingly important in determining the child's emotional response to the parent.

Role of Maturation in Cognitive Learning

Let us return now to another problem in cognitive learning—the role of maturation. We have seen that if the cognitive map is clearly structured, cognitive learning is possible. Such learning fills in the gaps in the map and makes it more nearly complete. It is possible, however, for the cognitive map to become clear through experiences. The situation may be only vaguely understood at first, but after one has had experience with it and has attempted to behave appropriately in it, it may become cognitively clear. This process is not merely one of acquiring new information or knowledge. It is a process that results in more maturity.

Time for Incubation in Problem Solving

The similarity between the development of cognitive clarity and other sorts of maturation is indicated by the fact that the passage of time may be required. The need for a period of *incubation* in problem solving has been mentioned by a number of creative thinkers who tried to describe how they came to make important intellectual discoveries. Frequently the inspirations are sudden; they are preceded, says Poincaire (1914), by several days of fruitless effort. They seldom come immediately at the end of such a period of effort but are more likely to appear suddenly after a period of rest, perhaps upon awakening or in the middle of some apparently irrelevant occupation. Graham Wallas (1926) described the four stages of creative thought as *preparation, incubation, illumination,* and *verification.* It is the first two that concern us here, because they form a good description of the process of maturation. The problem is set and struggled with for a period. This stimulation initiates a growth process that takes place over a period of time. After the growth has occurred, the solution then appears, perhaps quite suddenly. Frequently when it is discovered it seems so obvious that the person can hardly believe he could not think of it before.

Let us now look at the conditions under which this maturation or growth of cognitive clarity takes place. Such growth occurs most strikingly and consistently when the individual actively tries to clarify his understanding of a vaguely understood situation. When faced with an unclearly cognized situation there are thus two different ways that the learning may occur. The individual may learn an adjustment to it on a noncognitive basis without any increase in cognitive clarity. Or he may try to bring about an increased cognitive clarity by searching for relationships and by formulating hypotheses to be tested. If he succeeds, some maturation has occurred and his understanding is cognitively clearer than it was before.

Individual Differences in Importance of Cognitive Clarity

Different people in the same situation may, because of personality differences, learn in different ways. One person may always try to "get things straight in his mind," whereas another may behave more intuitively. Some children seem to know how to take teasing; their feelings are not hurt, and they laugh it off. For them a "teasing" stimulus situation almost automatically evokes a different response from that evoked by true hostility. For other children, this distinction is more difficult. They tend to respond to teasing as well as to true hostility with anger and retaliation. Such a child may learn to be a good sport by a sort of intellectual process. He clarifies in his own mind the fact that the presence or absence of hostility of the other person is the essential difference between teasing and true aggression. With this guide, he can behave appropriately and come to have the appropriate feelings as well. The cognitive process is not so obviously detached and intellectual as we have made it seem. Nevertheless, the latter child can sometimes actually put into words the essential principle of this simple interpersonal relation, whereas the former may have no cognitive understanding of teasing.

In coping with the problem of a rebellious child, one mother may "muddle through." She will at first be very antagonistic to the child. This makes him angry; there are stormy scenes. Gradually she sees his point of view; her own attitudes change in the process. Now she is no longer so antagonized by the behavior that previously made her angry. Her values have changed. The child has also changed, and the problem is relieved. Throughout this process, neither mother nor child may ever clarify, in a cognitive sense, the issue between them.

Another mother may approach this problem by trying to analyze her own feelings and the child's. She may discover that she is applying to the child the standards of her own childhood. This, she can recognize, is not entirely realistic. She relents somewhat but decides on a policy of firm kindness on the issues that seem really important. She tries to make it clear to the child which are the important issues. This process may, like the less cognitive one, lead to a real adjustment.

Both mothers reach a similar behavioral solution, although not the identical one. One mother achieves it through a relearning of feelings and impulses, the other through cognitive clarification. In real life nobody ever adjusts through cognitive clarification alone, and probably nobody ever adjusts without some cognitive clarification. People differ greatly, however, on the extent to which they seek cognitive clarity.

The person who strives to be completely rational tries to make all his behavior cognitively guided, trusting nothing to intuition. He can succeed only by attaining a cognitively clear and correct picture of each situation he faces. If he succeeds he achieves a more flexible, communicable understanding. A clear and accurate picture of a complex situation, however, may be extremely difficult to achieve. In such a situation a more diffuse, intuitive approach may be more effective.

Factors Facilitating Cognitive Clarification

In general it is true that the clearer a situation is to begin with, the easier it is to clarify further the aspects that are still vague. The already clear aspects give something on which to base hypotheses and to reach out to a further understanding. The situation that is most difficult to clarify is one in which the elements themselves are undifferentiated. If a layman peers down the throat of a child looking for evidence of disease, he does not know what to look for. It looks like a red throat; that is all he can say about it. The doctor has this stimulus situation organized; he has names for the various symptoms that can exist and he can see more differences in the appearance of throats than can the layman.

For the same reasons it must have been difficult to understand the meteorological significance of clouds. Although we now have them classified in a way that has functional meaning, there are so many different kinds of clouds and so many varieties not conforming to the well-established types that it must have been difficult to know which kinds to classify together. In science this step is called the definition of the variables of a problem. Until the variables are defined it is very unlikely that hypotheses will be fruitfully tested. This definition of variables is equivalent to differentiating the various objects in the situation.

In general, then, simple situations are easy to clarify and complex undifferentiated ones are difficult to clarify. So it is no surprise that the more complex judgments that people make—judgments about artistic merit, diagnosis of disease, judgments in clinical psychology, judgments about social policy, prediction of the stock market—are all areas in which considerable intuition is required. In situations that are very difficult to clarify, the most efficient procedure is to acquire the proper intuitive judgment and to be satisfied not to understand clearly the reasons for the judgment. All of us must behave this way some of the time and we must trust our judgments to be valid in such complex situations.

We have spoken only of the external factors that lead to noncognitive learning rather than cognitive clarification and consequently to an intuitive understanding rather than a cognitively clear picture. Other factors depend upon the personality of the individual and his past history and upon the interaction of various emotional factors with cognitive ones.

The Automatization of Cognitively Guided Behavior

The only examples of automatic behavior that have been considered thus far in this chapter were achieved noncognitively. In order to complete the picture we should recognize the process by which behavior that was at first cognitively guided later becomes habitual. This process is called *automatization.*

Playing the piano and typing are excellent examples of behavior that is at first cognitively guided. The beginner decides to strike each separate key; he may think carefully about where it is located. Gradually the location of the keys becomes habitual. In typing, a whole word is read and typed off without any further decision. In piano playing, chords and phrases are automatically played in the proper sequence.

Like other sorts of behavior that are automatic rather than cognitively guided, habits are not flexible in the face of changed circumstances. It would not make much difference if the keyboard were changed when the typist is just learning, but the skillful typist would be hopelessly lost. Much more efficient typewriter keyboards have been designed, but to change the automatic habits of thousands of typists seems such an impossible task that the new keyboards have not been well received.

With respect to flexibility then, automatized habits are just like any other fixed response. There is one important difference, however, stemming from the fact that the habit was once cognitively guided: namely, that the cognitive guidance can be reestablished. When we first drive a car without a clutch, we may find ourselves stamping on the nonexistent clutch pedal, but each time we do so its absence reminds us of the changed situation. We know what to do as soon as we stop to think. This is different from the situation arising if the expert at sexing day-old chicks were to be given a batch of ducks or some other species unlike the chicks he was accustomed to. He could not reestablish a cognitively clear picture because he never had one. He would have to relearn his intuitive feeling for pullets and cockerels.

Summary

In this chapter we have discussed the problems of cognitive learning. Cognitive learning, because it depends upon the existence of cognition, becomes important in the periods following infancy. It consists of acquiring information about the external situation by observation, by test behavior designed to reveal information, by trial-and-error behavior, or by hypothesis testing. Once the situation is cognitively clear and accurate, the individual knows what to do to attain his goal. He may or may not have the skills that are necessary to carry out his plan, but the acquiring of skills is not part of cognitive learning.

The situational factors that make cognitive learning easy or difficult closely resemble the factors that make conditioning easy or difficult. If two objects or events are in a clear perceptual unit, their relationship is easier to discover than if they are separated by space or time or dissimilarity. Cognitive learning is, therefore, a logical extension of noncognitive learning.

As we have seen in earlier discussions, cognitive clarity allows a more flexible adjustment to changing circumstances, and a cognitively clear situation can be verbally described. For these reasons cognitive learning can occur through verbal instruction.

We have examined two problems of social behavior that are illuminated by the concepts of cognitive learning. First, cognitive learning of social rules differs in clarity from noncognitive learning. The rules that demand flexibility obviously are the ones that require cognitive clarity. Some of the conditions that hamper the cognitive learning of a social rule are: (1) too-early training, (2) enforcement without explanation, (3) inconsistent enforcement, and (4) enforcement that produces shame or guilt. A second problem in social relations illustrates the significance of the verbal context of the enforcement of rules when the child is cognitively clear. By the way he enforces the rules the parent may structure the child's cognition so that the parent is seen as the source of the rule, or he may appear to the child to be an interpreter of external reality. These two methods of enforcement correspond roughly to the democratic and autocratic methods of control. The effect of being the source of the rules is that the parent is the object of whatever resentment or hostility the rule arouses.

Another problem of cognitive learning is the role of maturation. The situation may be cognitively unclear at first but become clearer. This occurs in many cases of problem solving, and we can see similarities between problem solving and the process of maturation. The importance of letting the problem incubate has been stressed by many people who have described their methods of thinking.

Finally we saw that cognitively guided behavior may become habitual through automatization. The result is a fixed habit with the same rigidity of any other fixed response except that when it requires change the individual can re-establish cognitive guidance, whereas he could not do so if the activity had not at one time been cognitively guided.

19

The Development of Needs

TWO DEVELOPMENTAL PROCESSES have been described thus far—maturation and learning. As we saw in the general discussion of development in Chapter 14, there are many effects of experiences that cannot be readily described in terms of the usual conception of learning. The purpose of this chapter is to discuss some of the ways in which needs change over time, and the effect of various sorts of experiences upon the individual's motivation.

First, we shall look at some of the ways in which needs and motivation may change over short periods of time (*e.g.,* fading of needs or increase in the strength of needs through psychological involvement). Some of these same changes may also occur over longer periods of time, especially the influences of childhood experiences on needs throughout life. We shall examine the effect on the sensitivity to an instigation of continuous exposure to that instigation over a long period. Perhaps it may desensitize the individual and destroy the need, or it may continually stimulate the individual and make the need stronger and stronger. Then we shall observe that activities which were originally means to goals may become goals in themselves, and that activities which were originally goals may become means to a more ultimate goal. Finally, we shall discuss the development of attitudes and the adoption of needs and values from other people.

Factors Changing Needs over Short Periods

Frequently needs are conceived to be permanent enduring characteristics of the person lasting a lifetime. Although some needs are enduring, others are more short-lived. There are changes in needs that last only a very short time. Needs may be created in ten minutes and last only a half an hour.

Fading of Strength of Needs

When a mother reminds her child to be sure to hurry home that afternoon because he has a music lesson, she hopes that she is creating a need in the child so that when school is out he will be motivated to take his music lesson. The strength of such needs seems to fade with time. A reminder half an hour before the time to go to the music lesson is more likely to be effective than a reminder three or four hours before.

It is not easy to see just why this should be so, because even during a half-hour interval the child's mind is not continuously occupied by thoughts of his music lesson. Once he begins to think about other things, then it is not obvious why he should be reminded of or spontaneously recall his music lesson more easily during the first half hour than during the tenth half hour. He has not forgotten in the sense that he is unable to recall it. In this case it seems that the probability of remembering the existence of the music lesson decreases with time. How badly he wants to take music lessons may influence his memory, although people forget appointments that they seriously want to remember. On the other hand, it is certainly true that we are more likely to remember appointments that we do wish to keep than those which we would prefer to avoid.

Not only may the remembering of an intention fade with time, but the strength of the motive that is evoked by the memory may also fade with time. We have probably all had the experience of being interrupted in the middle of an interesting novel. We lay it down reluctantly and leave it for a time. If within the next hour or the next day we again have an opportunity to read, we may eagerly pick up the novel to finish it. If, however, something prevents any resumption for several weeks, it is not uncommon to find ourselves no longer especially interested in the book. Even when we see it and think about the fact that it is unfinished, the eager anticipation is gone.

Time alone, therefore, may under some conditions—we do not know clearly just what conditions—result in the loss of strength of a need so that the previous motive is no longer recalled easily and even if recalled may not be re-evoked very intensely.

Psychological Involvement

The fading of needs during a period when no relevant motive is evoked is countered by the creation, strengthening, or concretizing of a need by periods of active motivation. A boy may go out of the house on a Saturday morning looking for someone to play with. At that moment it is perhaps not important just who the playmate is. He finds a friend and they begin to play. After an hour or so, the friend has to leave to get a haircut. The boy now is stricken; he is no longer satisfied with any one of a number of friends, but instead demands only that one. In the course of the hour's play, the boy's goal became much more concrete and specific than it had been earlier. His interest became focused upon those aspects of the play for which nobody else could be a substitute for the original friend.

EXPERIMENTS ON INTERRUPTION OF ACTIVITIES This process of psychological involvement has been subjected to experimental investigation by Ovsiakina (1928). She found similar results in both adults and children. The subject is asked by the experimenter to perform some activity, chosen so that it would not be especially interesting in its own right—e.g., filling in the squares of a sheet of coordinate paper to make a checkerboard, or copying a table of figures. After the subject was well along in the task, he was interrupted. Sometimes the interruption was apparently an accident, perhaps an unexpected call for the experimenter. Sometimes the experimenter deliberately interrupted the subject. After the interruption, which might last a few minutes or half an hour, the subject was placed in a position where, if he spontaneously wished to, he might resume the interrupted activity. The resumption was not requested by the experimenter; in fact, in some cases it was specifically prohibited. When the interruption was apparently accidental, there was a resumption or a tendency toward resumption in 100 percent of the cases.

When the experimenter deliberately interrupted the activity, giving the impression that it had been a mistake to begin it or that the experimenter no longer wanted it done, there was resumption or at least a tendency to resume the activity in 82 percent of the cases.

It attempting to explain this resumption it is very difficult to see how the subject was at first motivated by anything but a desire to comply with the experimenter's instructions. These were people who had agreed to be subjects in the experiment and who consequently followed instructions and did what they were told. It is also difficult to see how the subjects discovered in the activity anything which, had they seen it at first, would have made it intrinsically interesting and exciting. It seems much more reasonable to assume that through becoming embedded in doing the task, they became psychologically involved. This specific task developed motivation of its own; this motivation created a need that lasted through the interruption and that sensitized the subject to opportunities to complete the interrupted task. In some cases this need became so strong that it led them to disobey the experimenter's prohibitions.

Two implications of these experiments are important: that psychological involvement can set up a motive to perform an action that originally existed only as means to an end but that becomes an end in its own right, and, secondly, that needs can be created by this same involvement.

EASE OF INVOLVEMENT Further experimentation has shown that it is not equally easy to obtain involvement in all tasks. It makes a difference whether or not the task itself is really uncongenial. It makes a tremendous difference whether the individual, when he is interrupted, interprets the interruption as a failure to succeed or as interruption from the outside. If it is seen as a failure, personal adjustments are likely to produce marked effects upon the willingness to resume (Rozenzweig, 1933). In Ovsiakina's experiment the interruption was structured so that it would come from the outside.

It also makes a difference whether the interrupted task is one which has a clearly defined end goal or whether it is a continuous task, such as putting pegs into a very large board or making a chain of paper clips with an apparently endless supply of clips (Ovsiakina, 1928). As would be expected, the more clearly structured the task so that it has a definite end, the more involvement occurs.

SIGNIFICANCE OF PSYCHOLOGICAL INVOLVEMENT In these experiments and examples only short-term and superficial needs have been developed through psychological involvement in a task. The process is of considerable importance, however, as one of the mechanisms by which the child comes to develop needs that adapt him to the culture in which he lives. The process will be discussed in more detail later, but one example at this point will suffice to point out the social significance of psychological involvement. Many children do not have definite occupational aims. They may enroll in certain kinds of classes or take certain kinds of jobs not through any intrinsic attractiveness of that specific job or course but because it is required of them or urged upon them by social pressure. If a boy is offered a job in a library, for example, he may be interested only in the income that the job will bring, but he may, through exposure to it, become involved in it. He may develop an interest in it and as a result become a librarian. Mere involvement is certainly not the only factor operating in such a process; he may find that library work contains opportunities that would have motivated him from the first except that he did not know they existed in the profession of a librarian. Nevertheless, psychological involvement is certainly one of the factors that leads him to his ultimate vocational choice.

Satiation

We have discussed fading and involvement as factors that lead to changes of needs. A third sort of change comes through the repetition of an activity over and over again. Even though it was once highly motivated, such activity may become satiated through repetition and in the end be very distasteful (Karsten, 1928). In other words, satiation is the process of reducing the strength of a need through repetition of the goal activity over and over again. One of the essential characteristics of experiences that produce satiation is their repetitiveness.

If an experimental subject is asked to perform repeatedly some task—usually some simple routine one—his behavior goes through various stages before he is finally so satiated with it that he refuses to perform any more. One of the characteristics of his behavior during the process of satiation is his deliberate variation in the response. If the task, for example, is drawing moon faces, his early drawings are fairly standard and uniform and much like the model. As he becomes satiated, he begins to vary the drawings; some are big, some are small, some are very sloppy, some are meticulously done, some have smiles, some have frowns; adornments and elaborations may be added to some of the drawings. Finally he refuses to go on.

This process of satiation can be conceptualized in terms of the reduction in the strength of the need until it finally becomes negative, a dislike instead of a like. What was once an opportunity, although in the case of moon faces not a very exciting one, finally becomes an imposition and a burden and eventually forces withdrawal.

SATIATION IN CHILDHOOD   There are many examples of satiation in child behavior. The child will under many circumstances become bored more easily than the adult. Such routine activities as sanding woodwork, practicing scales on an instrument, or sitting still in the car on a long trip are tiring to the child. He satiates more quickly on such activities than the adult, and in addition he has less ability than the adult to continue despite satiation. Thus the child is easily bored with repetitive activity.

In other kinds of activity, however, the child seems almost insatiable. In many of the simple games adult play with children, such as pat-a-cake or "This is the way the ladies ride," the adult is bored long before the child. We know some of the factors that contribute to the insatiability of some of these childhood activities, although there is still much to be understood about them. Perhaps the most important factor is that these activities are more difficult and therefore more interesting for the child than for the adult. For the adult the possibilities of ticktacktoe are quickly exhausted. For the child they are constantly being discovered. The child, therefore, is no more likely to be satiated with this simple game than the adult is with chess. As long as the complete potentialities of the activity are not known, then each repetition is a new experience. In some activities knowledge gradually exhausts the potentialities; in others knowledge continually reveals new potentialities. To the ordinary listener it may be the same old composition, whereas to the concert pianist every new rendition of a well-loved piece of music is a new experience.

Another reason for the readiness of the child to repeat some of his activities interminably is the fact that he is living more in the immediate present than is the adult. In order for something to be repetitive and boring it must be recognized as having been repeated for many times, and it is especially satiating when the individual sees the activity extending on and on into the future. If he can somehow divorce himself from his past and future and be embedded merely in the present, then monotony cannot occur, psychologically speaking. The adult may occasionally get into such a state when he becomes fascinated by watching successive waves roll up on the beach, or an animated electric sign go through its routine again and again. The child, whose attention is captured more easily than the adult's, may find himself thus caught up by some repetitive activity more frequently than the adult.

We should notice also that activities may become insatiable not because they capture attention completely but because they become so automatic as to demand no attention at all. We do not become satiated with putting one foot in front of the other despite all the walking we do. It is not uncommon for an employee doing a highly routinized job to feel very satiated with it at first, but gradually he seems to be able to do it automatically in a detached way so that the activity is no longer boring. Automatization removes the activity from the class of motivated behavior.

We have discussed in this section three factors that change the strength of needs. The first was the passage of time. Many needs fade unless the relevant motives are occasionally activated. The second was psychological involvement, which is the increase in the strength and the concretizing of a need when the individual becomes psychologically embedded in an absorbing activity. The third factor is satiation.

Changes of Needs over Long Periods

Continuous Exposure to Instigation

When we study the effect of childhood experience upon the motivation and needs of later life, we meet a very curious paradox. Sometimes, for instance, it seems that if a person is dominated and ordered about throughout childhood, he later becomes a weak, dependent person who is unwilling to take responsibility. On the other hand, the reaction of some people to being dominated over a long period of time is to become very domineering and authoritarian when they have the opportunity.

This same paradox may be found in many sorts of needs. In the experiments by Goldfarb, for example (see p. 412), we saw that one of the consequences of being reared impersonally in an institution might be the development of a craving for love that was so strong that it defeated the child's attempts to obtain it realistically. On the other hand, Bowlby (1951) has found that the results of separation from the mother and loss of personal love during infancy may be the development of a person who is incapable of forming a close attachment and loving another person. The paradox is nowhere better exemplified than in the various experiments on the sucking need in infancy.

Investigations of the Sucking Need in Infancy

These investigations stem from a perennial question about the relative desirability of breast or bottle feeding of infants. A century ago, nearly all babies were breast fed, although perhaps by a wet nurse rather than the mother herself. With the development of methods of maintaining a sterile supply of milk and the knowledge of the essential nutriments that a baby's food should contain, it seemed as though the old-fashioned breast feeding should be allowed to die out. Scientifically adjusted formulae, tailored to fit the requirements of the individual child and kept free from the many unknown germs and infections of the mother, appeared to be a food supply much preferable to the mother's milk.

For a time bottle feeding rapidly increased. Then it was claimed that the bottle-fed babies were not psychologically as healthy as breast-fed babies. Some studies were made in an attempt to prove this assertion or to disprove it, but the results were very ambiguous, probably because bottle feeding may be done in many different ways, coldly or warmly, impersonally or tenderly— and for that matter, so may be breast feeding.

Finally one specific question within the general issue was clearly formulated. Does the infant have a "sucking need" that if not gratified will produce evidences of frustration and other kinds of sucking, such as thumbsucking?

SHORTENED PERIODS OF SUCKING   Two studies bearing on the need for sucking will be reported, one on animals by Levy (1934) and one on cup feeding in infancy by Sears and Wise (1950). Levy, who is primarily responsible for formulating the hypothesis of a sucking need in a clearly testable form, became convinced that such needs exist because of his clinical observations of infant behavior. Levy observed that babies whose mothers had an abundant supply of milk finished feeding quite rapidly with a minimum of sucking, whereas the children of other mothers whose milk supply was not so copious required more sucking to obtain a meal. Levy observed that the first group of infants was more likely to show thumbsucking than the second. In order to control conditions more effectively, he used nursing pups for his experimental subjects. One group of pups nursed from a bottle that had a large hole in the nipple so that with a small amount of sucking the pup received sufficient food. The pups in the other group nursed from a bottle with a small hole in the nipple so that a longer period of sucking was necessary for them to become satisfied. In this way the satisfaction of hunger was controlled, but the duration of sucking varied. In all other respects the two groups were treated alike. He found that the pups who had obtained food with a minimum of sucking were more likely to chew slippers, furniture, and other things than were the pups who had a prolonged sucking experience as a part of feeding.

MOVEMENT RESTRAINT   The plausibility of the hypothesis of a need for sucking is further strengthened by evidence for a similar sort of a need that is frustrated by movement restraint. Levy found in this modality also that similar symptoms occurred in human infants and in animals. Institutionalized babies who are kept in a crib are observed to show rhythmic weaving movements not unlike those observed in horses kept in small stalls without sufficient opportunity for free movement (Levy, 1944). Chickens kept in small pens, Levy found, showed a typical behavior symptom, the "head shaking tic," which occurred less frequently if the hen was kept in a larger cage and almost disappeared when the hens were turned loose in the chicken yard. One further experiment lends additional support to the basic contention. Hunt (1941) found that depriving young rats of a portion of their food supply resulted in food hoarding in the adult rats.

Such a body of confirmatory evidence forms a respectable and solid support for the hypothesis of such needs as "sucking needs" and "movement needs."

AGE OF WEANING The study of cup feeding undertaken by Sears and Wise (1950) was the result of a fortunate accident. It happened that a certain group of pediatricians had advised some mothers to feed their infants from a cup at a very early age. They had found that infants could, in a fashion, drink from a cup and that cup feeding had one advantage over bottle feeding in that the mother was compelled to hold the baby on her lap and devote considerable attention to it in order to accomplish the desired end. With the modern labor-

TABLE 12*

RELATION OF AGE OF WEANING TO DISTURBANCE AT WEANING

Age of Weaning	Number of Cases	Degree of Disturbance				Percentage Showing Minimum Disturbance
		3	2	1	0	
Early	10	0	0	0	10	100%
Middle	18	1	1	2	14	78%
Late	52	7	9	12	24	46%

saving devices for holding the bottle at the proper angle it is possible to give even a young infant a bottle without much parental attention.

Such a situation constituted a ready-made experiment because these infants had had a minimum of sucking experience in connection with eating and might be expected, therefore, to show behavior analogous to those that Levy found in pups and in babies whose mothers' abundant milk supply gave them sufficient nourishment in a short time. Sears and Wise were able to collect data on three groups of children, those who were weaned early, practically at birth, those weaned during the middle part of the first year and those weaned to the cup late in the first year. They measured two aspects of the behavior of infants: the degree of disturbance at the time of weaning, and the frequency and severity of thumbsucking at the age of two and a half years. The results are shown in Tables 12 and 13. In Table 12 the degree of disturbance at the time of weaning is rated on a scale from 0 to 3. The table shows the number of infants in each group who showed various degrees of disturbance.

* R. R. Sears and G. W. Wise, "Relation of Cup Feeding in Infancy to Thumbsucking and the Oral Drive," *Amer. Jour. Orthopsychiat.*, 1950, *20*, 123-138.

In Table 13 is shown the percentage of children who suck their thumbs at some time, and the severity of thumbsucking at the age of two and one half years. The final column shows the percentage with minimal severity of thumbsucking at age two and one half.

None of these differences is dramatically significant, but in general the data point to the conclusion that late weaning is associated with more rather than less disturbance at weaning and no less thumbsucking at the age of two and one-half years. With regard to weaning disturbances the early-weaned children seem to show the least disturbance at the time of weaning.

Sears and Wise interpret their findings within the framework of general behavior theory, which will be described in detail in Chapter 23. They argue that the sucking habit was reinforced by the fact that it was followed

TABLE 13*

RELATION OF AGE OF WEANING TO THUMBSUCKING

Age of Weaning	Percentage Showing Thumbsucking at Some Time	Severity of Thumbsucking at Age 2½			Percentage with Minimal Severity at Age 2½
		2	1	0	
Early	70	1	3	6	60
Middle	61	2	2	14	78
Late	69	14	22	26	50

by relief from hunger. The children who were weaned early had had the least reinforcement of the habit; therefore, the habit would not be strong; therefore, they would show less disturbance over having to give it up than would children who had had the habit reinforced for a long period of infantile nursing. Although the data do not entirely support this contention, the trend of their data supports the hypothesis.

COMPARISON OF LEVY EXPERIMENT WITH SEARS AND WISE STUDY   When the results of these two investigations of sucking are put side by side, we are in the not uncommon position of needing to reconcile experiments that at first glance seem diametrically opposed. It is important to recognize a difference in the situations studied by Levy and by Sears and Wise. In Levy's observations the infants and the pups were stimulated to suck at every feeding. They were subjected to the external stimuli that evoke sucking behavior. In the experiment of Sears and Wise the infants who were weaned early were

* R. R. Sears and G. W. Wise, "Relation of Cup Feeding in Infancy to Thumbsucking and the Oral Drive." *Amer. Jour. Orthopsychiat.*, 1950, *20*, 123-138.

never afterwards stimulated to suck except as they might accidentally get a thumb or some object into the mouth.

In the earlier discussion of thumbsucking (see p. 181), it was suggested that the thumbsucking need depended upon the previous existence of sucking. Thumbsucking developed out of sucking. In the Levy experiment there was no lack of sucking stimulation on which to build a psychological sucking need. Once the need is established through nursing, then the hypothesis that the child may become sensitive to other opportunities to suck is not unexpected. When the child is weaned very early, however, it might be questioned whether the creation of a sucking need were possible. If sucking behavior shows the same characteristics as pecking in chicks (see p. 388), the lack of stimulation of the sucking response might be expected to result in the absence of well-established sucking behavior and the absence of the need to suck.

There is even some slight support for this hypothesis in studies of movement restraint. A child kept in a crib in a nursery is able to move about as freely as he wishes until he is able to crawl. Then the crib is restraining. At the same time he is probably stimulated to move toward many distant objects. The restraint is then frustrating. If he were never allowed to move around freely, the development of the movement need might be prevented. There is incidental evidence in regard to this which can be found in observations upon children who are kept in a papoose board throughout infancy. Such infants are reported to enjoy the restraint of the bindings and to hesitate to leave them. Even if the child were kept in a crib but were not stimulated to move toward objects outside of the crib, he might not show signs of frustration. In the study by Dennis and Dennis (see p. 404), the child was kept in a crib and the room was kept barren of stimulating objects. Although Dennis and Dennis (1938) do not specifically mention in their observations that the children failed to show the symptoms of movement restraint reported by Levy, they do not mention any such behavior.

This interpretation of the findings of Levy and of Sears and Wise cannot be said to be clearly supported by the observations of any of these experiments, but it offers a possible line of investigation that might reconcile the differences between the two experiments. Regardless of how we may try to understand these experiments, there seem to be two sorts of processes going on. One will be called adaptation to stimulation. The other is need accentuation through exposure to instigation.

Adaptation and Habituation

Most people feel—with considerable justification—that children are disorderly creatures, unrestrained by social custom. It is sometimes surprising, therefore, how conservative children can be about routines. One little girl became adjusted to the routine of taking a bath before dinner in the evening, eating in her robe and slippers, having a visit with her parents after dinner, and then going to bed. When on one occasion it would have been much more convenient for her to eat her dinner first, then take a bath, she set up a highly indignant outcry. It was not "right" for her to take a bath after dinner. It seems very difficult to find anything other than custom to justify her protests. It appeared to her parents that she missed nothing and gained nothing merely by changing the order of the activities. Adults sometimes feel the same sort of conservatism. Some people, for example, are so accustomed to attending movies only in the evening that when for some reason they attend in the afternoon, they feel a definite uneasiness and dissatisfaction when they emerge from the theater to find daylight outside.

This habituation is the acquisition of a customary way of behaving from which any deviation seems not only unusual but actually improper. It has its counterparts in processes of adaptation that may occur before birth, or in lower forms of life. Adaptation seems, in fact, to be a general rule for all living tissue. A stimulus that, when it is first applied, results in some active response will after repeated applications gradually lose its potency to evoke a response.

PHYSIOLOGICAL ADAPTATION   In some cases this process of adaptation is incorporated in the physiological mechanism in a specific way. The eye, for example, shows adaptation to light. If the light is strong, several changes occur that make the eye less sensitive; one of these is the familiar contraction of the pupil so that less light actually strikes the retina. In other cases the adaptation is not mediated through such a specific mechanism.

If a loud sound is produced close to the abdomen of a pregnant mother, the fetus can be shown to respond by an increased heart rate and more active movements. If the sound is maintained continuously for a period of several minutes, the fetus partially adapts. Its heart rate slows, its activity decreases, and it shows less responsiveness.

If the sound that evokes these fetal responses is applied every day, the initial response each day becomes gradually less intense. This is somewhat different from the process of becoming less responsive to a continuous stimulus. The fetus seems to have become so adapted to the sound that it is no longer so stimulating as it once was.

SENSORY ADAPTATION   When this desensitization occurs in a simple sense modality, especially if its physiological mechanism is known, it is called *sensory adaptation*. Sensory adaptation is the term used to describe the fact that we do not feel a ring on our finger or a wrist watch on our wrist when it is there constantly. We often do not realize that it is missing until we notice its absence in some other way. The speed of adaptation to odors is well known. Farmers rapidly lose their feeling that a barn smells different from the outside world; chemists no longer notice the laboratory smell; people who live near stockyards may adapt even to that odor. Similarly, people seldom realize the peculiar taste of the water in the town in which they live, even though a stranger may feel that it tastes very bad indeed.

When a similar desensitization process takes place to more complex stimulus situations, the term *habituation* is generally considered more appropriate. Sights that were once strange and noticeable lose their impressiveness through habituation to them. Social attitudes that seem peculiar or even wrong when one is first exposed to them may gradually, through habituation, come to be accepted as normal and customary. "Familiarity breeds contempt" is a proverbial description of the process of habituation.

Thus far the process of habituation has been described merely as a desensitization to stimulation. It is also a common result of habituation that the situations to which one has become habituated may acquire the characteristic of being "proper" or "right" rather than being merely neutral. The water to which we have become accustomed may actually taste better than the water in other cities.

CREATION OF NEED THROUGH HABITATION   Since a customary behavior may seem "right," a deviation from a customary pattern of behavior can be perceived as an imposition. If so, it evokes a motive to re-establish the situation to which one has become accustomed. Krugman (1943) performed an experiment in which subjects were exposed to a certain kind of music for a long period of time. Gradually, they began to show a liking and appreciation for it and sometimes to prefer it to other varieties of music that they had originally liked better. Many people discover that the scenery, the food, the music, and the customary handling of birthday and holiday occasions to which they became accustomed in childhood keep their attractiveness after the individuals have grown. These continue to seem more attractive than the patterns of behavior that have a more recent origin. The process of habituation can, in this fashion, establish a need that in later life is at the root of motivated behavior.

We have seen that grasping, sucking, looking, listening, and other repeatable or circular responses seem to become foci in the behavior of the young infant about which new behavior patterns develop. In the discussion of learning we wondered how such behavior could reinforce a conditioned response. Perhaps it is through habituation that they become satisfying and thus capable of reinforcing behavior (see p. 181).

We have seen another example of the importance of habituation in the child's fear of strange people, places, and happenings. The young infant's love for his mother and the other familiar people in his life seems to be based primarily upon their being familiar. As the child grows older, love for other people certainly comes to involve more than mere habituation. It can, however, be the basis for the young infant's preference for his mother.

Some aspects of the child's reactions to his mother are unquestionably based upon habituation. One mother, for example, was accustomed to end every episode of diaper changing with a loving pat on the baby's buttocks. She was hardly aware that this was her habit because it had never evoked any response in her own babies. When, however, she changed the diaper of a neighbor's baby she was shocked at the outcry produced by her pat.

We can now describe habituation in more formal terms. One of the effects of stimulation may be the evocation of motives. If the stimulating situation is properly structured, it may instigate motivated behavior. If through adaptation or habituation the stimulating character of a situation changes so that it is no longer so psychologically stimulating or tension producing as it once was, then the motives that such a situation once produced may no longer be so strongly evoked.

We have mentioned several times that the new abilities which the child has just acquired are often repeatedly exercised but that gradually the new skill becomes less exciting to the child. This may be partly due to the fact that the child has become habituated to the new activity.

To summarize, habituation or adaptation is a process which underlies the fact that upon the repetition of a situation we gradually become desensitized to it. Through habituation a motivating situation may lose its power to motivate. Habituation may even result in an actual preference for the customary state of affairs, so that the individual is motivated to re-establish it when the custom is disturbed. Thus, habituation is one process by which new needs may be created.

Accentuation of Needs Through Repeated Instigation

If habituation is one result of exposure to stimulation, the development of an intense dislike and a strong desire never to experience such stimulation again may be another possible outcome. For every child who grew up on a farm and could never be contented in the city, we can probably find a child whose lonesome childhood life on the farm made him run to the city and avoid the country for the rest of his days.

HOSTILITY FOLLOWING AUTOCRACY   One experimental study showing how external prohibition and repression of behavior may build up a strong hostile need was performed by Lippitt and White (1947). These experimenters established a number of boys' clubs. They wished to study the effect of three sorts of leadership—democratic, autocratic, and laissez-faire—upon the behavior of the boys in the clubs. We have already reported this experiment in connection with the source of control. We recall that the autocratic leader ordered the children around, assigned them to jobs, assigned partners, and supervised actively every step of the task of making masks (which was the activity carried out in the club meetings).

The experimenters found, first of all, that there might be two opposite reactions to autocracy. Some clubs became apathetic and passive; others be-

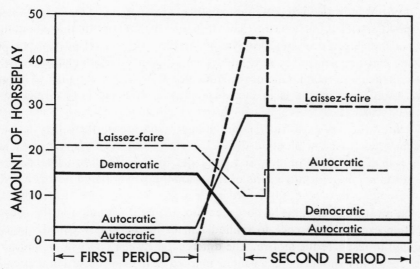

Fig. 19.1 The effect of change of group atmosphere on aggression and horseplay. (After R. Lippitt and R. K. White, in T. N. Newcomb *et al.*, *Readings in Social Psychology*, pp. 315-330)

came hostile and rebellious under pressure. This relates to the fact that dominance may instigate either submission or resistance.

But what is more interesting is the behavior of the clubs when the leadership was changed. Figure 19.1 shows the change in the amount of hostility and horseplay in various clubs when the atmosphere was shifted. Notice especially that the apathetic clubs suddenly burst into forbidden behavior when the atmosphere was shifted from autocracy to democracy. It seems that the apathy was—at least in some children—a result of inhibition of expression of anger and hostility. The feeling and motivation were evoked continuously by the autocratic leadership, but the expression of the hostility was continuously forbidden. Under these conditions, the need was accentuated so that when the opportunity to be hostile was presented, the boys were strongly motivated to be hostile.

Factors Determining Whether Habituation or Accentuation Will Occur

We have seen that continuous exposure to a situation may result either in its acceptance, perhaps even in its becoming preferred, or on the other hand, in the accentuation of the motivation that it initially instigates. The most important issue is how to predict which will happen. There is relatively little evidence that bears on this question, but on the basis of our everyday experience we can formulate some hypotheses.

STRENGTH OF INSTIGATION   First, it is probably important how strongly the situation instigates some motivation. If the situation repeatedly presents stimuli that are neutral or only mildly instigating, then adaptation is more likely than accentuation. One of the strategies of dictators who plan to impose restrictions on a people is to introduce them slowly and gradually. If they were imposed all at once, they might incite rebellion; but if they are begun gradually with mild restrictions in unimportant areas, then they can be gradually increased without instigating overt resistance.

It is a corollary of this first principle that deprivations are easier to adapt to than more positive sorts of frustration in which the motive is actively instigated and then blocked. In order for a deprivation to be frustrating, the person must keep in mind his lost pleasure. If there is nothing in the present situation except its absence to remind him of it, the impoverished situation may fail to instigate the motive. The difference between deprivation and positive frustration should be even more marked if the person is immature. As we saw in the Levy and Sears experiments (see p. 463), Levy studied situations in which the child had learned to enjoy sucking and was prevented at each meal from gratifying his motivation. This was an instigation. By frustration of the instigated behavior through a too-short period of sucking, the need was accentuated. In the Sears experiment, the deprivation was probably not an instigation for the young infants because they had not learned to like sucking; and after weaning, the sucking motivation was not repeatedly instigated. It was more nearly pure deprivation.

Note that even though deprivation may be less frustrating than blocking an active motive, its consequences may be even more serious. In some cases it is the very fact that the child adapts to a deprivation that is the serious consequence. Thus, to adapt to an impersonal environment and to become indifferent to being loved is a more serious consequence than to be strongly instigated by an impersonal environment and to develop an unreasonable craving for love, although both consequences are serious enough.

THE IMPORTANCE OF FRUSTRATION OF THE INSTIGATED MOTIVE   In most of the studies we have reported in which accentuation of needs occurred, the situation not only instigated a motive but frustrated it. Suppose a child were repeatedly provoked into being hostile and angry and allowed to express his hostility freely and openly. Suppose another child were equally provoked but never allowed to express his anger or to behave in a hostile fashion. The second child would be provoked, and, in addition, his motivation would be frustrated. What we need to know is whether the second child's hostility would be more likely to be accentuated and more strongly accentuated than the first child's hostility.

All of our everyday experience suggests that the prevention of expression of an instigated motive accentuates the motivation and probably accentuates the need. It probably sensitizes the person to further instigation.

Although our everyday experience suggests strongly that preventing the expression of a motive may accentuate it, there is less unanimity in our common-sense ideas about the consequence of repeated instigation of a motive when the motive is then gratified. Some people would feel that the acting out of the motivated behavior would "get it out of his system" so that the person would not show any effects of the experience. Others would argue that such a person becomes accustomed to experiencing the motive, and thus becomes more readily and easily motivated than before. Still others would feel that the instigation would gradually lose its instigating character through habituation. Perhaps under certain conditions any one of the three might occur. More research is needed to elucidate the various possibilities.

One factor affecting strength of needs has been shown to be repeated or continuous exposure to the stimuli that might instigate the motivation. We have seen that sometimes such exposure brings habituation, sometimes accentation; and we have looked at some of the factors that probably play a role in determining which effect exposure will have.

Change of Needs Through Shifting of Means and Ends

When an action is learned through reinforcement, the action may not be cognized as a means to obtain the reward. This is the typical result of non-cognitive learning. When the means and end are not distinguished, or when they are not seen as even being related, means may acquire attractive characteristics merely through the fact that they are reinforced. On the other hand means may become repugnant merely through their association with bad consequences.

Cognitive Unclearness of Reinforcement

A child may like a cake icing so avidly that when he has an opportunity he gorges himself. If as a result he gets sick, perhaps re-experiencing the taste of it along with the nausea, he may ever afterward find the food nauseating. One of the methods that has been tried as a cure for alcoholism is to give the alcoholic whiskey mixed with an emetic so that it produces nausea. The individual may in this fashion become so conditioned that drinking whiskey nauseates him. A simple conditioning mechanism does not produce these results if the consequences are clearly separated from the means. It would be very difficult, probably impossible, to make a four-year-old dislike candy by punishing him every time he ate it. Even if through such treatment he learned not to eat candy, he would not necessarily dislike the taste of it. The difference between receiving punishment for eating candy and being nauseated through eating too much of it lies in the degree of separation of the eating and the consequences. When the child becomes sick from overeating, the taste of the food becomes almost inextricably tangled with the unpleasant feeling of nausea, whereas the taste of the food and the more external punishment are kept separate. Thus we can see that activities may acquire the attractive or repulsive characteristics of the consequences to which they lead if the differentiation between the action and its consequence is cognitively unclear.

It may seem that the situation just described, in which the learned behavior is not distinguished from the reinforcement or the reinforcement is not cognized at all, is rare in ordinary life. We like to think that we know the reasons for our actions. Actually, the situation may be quite common. The instigation of a motive resembles in many ways the releasing of a fixed response. We do not decide to be motivated; it just happens to us. We feel a requiredness about the motivation that we seldom question. It is this lack of control over what we are motivated to do that makes us describe such motives as impulses. We sometimes feel powerless in the face of these motives, or we must struggle strongly to control them.

Unconscious Motives

In a good many cases our motives may have an adaptive function that is not obvious to us any more than the reinforcement behind a conditioned response is obvious to the infant who is conditioned. We saw in the last chapter that social rules might be learned noncognitively, so that the individual feels required to behave in a certain way in a variety of situations without ever realizing that all of these diverse actions form an understandable pattern. The pattern of behavior regarding exposing the body was used as an illustration.

Whenever the individual shows a pattern of behavior which consistently brings about the same result, but which the person himself is not aware of, we see an example of what psychoanalytic theory calls an unconscious motive. If a person, without realizing it, consistently gets into fights with his friends, if all his personal relations deteriorate, we can say he is unconsciously hostile. The person himself may feel that each quarrel arose for a different reason. In one case, he lost a friend by standing up for principles; in another case, his friend criticized him behind his back. The observer suspects that there is an unconscious motive because of the appearance of the same result over and over again, indicating the presence of goal-directed activity (see p. 79).

The term *unconscious motive* may not be a very happy one to describe the man's behavior because it gives the impression that he has a complete cognitive map that is unconscious. As we have seen, however, behavior that is not cognitively guided differs from cognitively guided behavior in other respects than being unconsciously motivated. It is less flexible; it is not changed by verbal instructions; it appears to the subject himself as involuntary behavior, or as an impulse that forces itself on him. Furthermore, it is actually less effective than cognitively guided behavior in achieving its reinforcing adaptive result because it is released by stimuli that are not completely reliable indicators of the reinforcement, whereas guided behavior is governed by the goal itself.

Unconscious motivation provides another mechanism for the development of needs. If a pattern of behavior is reinforced and if the relation between the behavior and the reinforcement is not cognitively clear, then the behavior pattern, once it is learned, is automatic and involuntary. In simple involuntary actions, such as contraction of the pupil of the eye, the conditioned response occurs without any feeling of wanting or not wanting to perform the action. We can, however, think of a motive as a response also. The result of reinforcement of a complex behavior pattern may be a conditioned motive. Under the proper stimulus conditions, the individual feels the impulse. The conditioned stimulus in other words, functions as an instigation to a motive. In describing the behavior of the person, we can say he now has a need sensitizing him to that instigation. The reinforcement has played a role in developing this need, but it does not play a role in the instigation of the motive.

We can illustrate this distinction with a hypothetical example. Suppose that we were listening to a lecturer. If some diabolical psychologist had arranged that five seconds after the lecturer used any prepositional phrase denoting time—such as "in the morning" or "at three o'clock"—we all received a shock, at first the shock would come as a senseless thing. What led to the shock would not be obvious. If we were able to solve the problem and realize that a temporal prepositional phrase was the cue, then we would hear each such phrase, cognize the approaching shock, and take appropriate action. This would be a case of cognitive learning.

Even if we did not solve the problem cognitively, it might still happen that we would gradually develop a sensitivity to temporal prepositional phrases. Every time one was used, we would feel anxious or perhaps have an impulse to get up. Consciously we would not even recognize the relation of the impulse or anxiety to the stimulus. We would merely have curious pangs of anxiety that came at apparently random intervals. This would be an unconscious motive, in contrast to the conscious one which would occur if we realized the significance of the temporal prepositional phrase.

It is important to recognize that the lack of cognitive clarity is essential in the formation of this sort of need. If the relation between the behavior and the reinforcement is cognitively clear, the so-called conditioned stimulus is a sign of the reinforcement. It becomes an instigation after the person recognizes that it is a sign that the reinforcement can be achieved, but it instigates a motive whose goal is the reinforcement. The learned behavior is cognitively guided and is a means to the goal. The behavior itself now has none of the properties of an impulse or a motive, but merely those of a means to an end.

Needs Through Psychodynamic Processes

When we begin to explore the ways in which these needs can change, we enter into the exceedingly complex problems of psychodynamics. Unconscious motives can result from repression, from immaturity, from child-rearing methods. Many of them are laden with emotion so that they activate defensive processes. Attempts to clarify the individual's cognitive picture may meet with resistance. Further repression may occur to protect already existing repressions. Defenses may build up against defenses. Psychoanalytic investigation of personality has shown us how complex the needs and changes in needs may be, but we do not yet have the information to work out the conditions bringing about the various patterns of change of needs. This is the area of the development of psychodynamic defenses, which has received very little careful research.

Orderliness in the Developmental Sequence of Needs

We have discussed a number of processes by which needs may change over time. They may fade or disappear through habituation. They may become accentuated; new needs may appear through psychological involvement or through increased cognitive clarity. Despite all these mechanisms that describe changes in needs, it seems that, in our culture, there is a certain orderliness in the appearance of needs throughout childhood. The infant is certainly more concerned with sucking and mouthing objects than is the usual five-year-old. Jealousy and concern with exclusiveness in friendship appear during the preschool period. Sexual curiosity tends to appear in the preschool period rather than later. Psychoanalytic theory, as we shall see in Chapter 22, hypothesizes a quite rigid sequence of needs in the development of all children. This orderliness may not be so great as psychoanalytic theory presumes, but the development of needs is certainly not a completely haphazard random affair.

Predisposition of Needs

There are, in fact, three reasons for the expectation that needs appear in a certain order. The first reason is that the possession of a need leads to behavior that may predispose the individual to develop one need rather than another. The second reason is that the increasing maturity of the child is an orderly process. This maturational development may be reflected in the sequence of needs. Thirdly, the culture may impose its socialization pressures in an orderly fashion. For this reason all the children within one culture may tend to show the same needs at the same age.

We can see the first of these factors operating in the development of thumbsucking, which develops historically out of sucking on the breast or bottle (see p. 181). As we have seen, thumbsucking is not necessarily an expression of the same need that makes the child suck the bottle, nor does it serve as a substitute for it. Its appearance after meals and when the child is relaxed points to its being an independent source of pleasure. Nevertheless, it would not occur except for the fact that the infant sucks early in his life. It is an outgrowth of sucking. Furthermore, it has certain qualitative characteristics that reveal its historical origin.

The development of shyness is another example of the way that one need may predispose a child to develop another. If a child is shy and retiring, he spends much of the time by himself. This isolation makes it unlikely that he will develop some of the social needs, such as aggressiveness or social tact. The same retirement makes him more likely to develop some intellectual needs, such as reading or scientific curiosity, which can flourish in isolation. There is nothing certain about either of these predictions. Scientific interests can develop in a very sociable youngster and an isolated child may not develop scientific interests, but there is likely to be a correlation between the two.

Change of Needs Through Maturation

Superimposed on this tendency for one need to lead to another is the fact that the child grows more mature. Some sorts of needs require more maturity than others. Altruistic needs, for example, require more maturity than selfish ones, because they demand the ability to take another person's point of view. Gratitude requires more maturity than resentment (see p. 195). Abstract needs, such as autonomy or independence, require more maturity than concrete needs, such as wanting an allowance (see p. 29). We have seen in Chapter 8 that different sorts of needs appear at different age levels.

If the child is in a home that puts certain consistent pressures on him, his increasing maturity may bring with it a sequence of needs, each one more mature than the previous one but all dealing with the same general issue. The child who, through fear, tries to avoid making his parent angry becomes sensitized to the symptoms of anger. Because of this sensitivity, he notices anger in other people. By noticing symptoms of anger, he is presented with opportunities to tease or to be a peacemaker. He is also threatened with dangers that a less sensitized child would never perceive. If he feels weak in the face of these dangers, he may become placating toward other people as well as his mother. He may, with maturity, develop a need to be a peacemaker. He may have ethical convictions that anger does no good. Thus, out of a concrete limited need, a mature abstract need may develop. Such a need shows signs of its historical origin but is, nevertheless, a genuine need, not merely a disguised form of the need that was historically the beginning of the developmental sequence.

In psychoanalytic theory, this sort of process is assumed to go on constantly (see p. 546), although the theory does not explain it in the same terms in which we have. Thus, general curiosity is seen to develop out of one of its concrete manifestations, sexual curiosity; cleanliness is seen to stem from cleanliness in toilet training. We shall see further examples in Chapter 22.

Orderliness of Cultural Pressures

We have seen thus far two sources of an orderly developmental sequence of needs. A third source of orderliness is the fact that in any culture the child is subjected to certain types of socialization pressure at certain times. Although children are weaned at different times in different cultures, in any one culture weaning tends to occur at approximately the same time in the lives of all the children.

Thus, in any culture, there is a common pattern of social pressures upon all children. Every child is taught to control his hostility at approximately the same time; if this period comes after the beginning of training for independence, the entire culture is subjected to these two sorts of pressures in the same order. There is actually very great uniformity even in the details of socialization. In our culture toilet training follows weaning. Then comes training in the control of hostility and of sexuality. Independence training occurs slightly later. Training in actual skills comes later yet (*e.g.,* reading and arithmetic in the first grade). So consistent a pattern of social influences must tend to produce a consistent pattern of needs.

In summary, we have found three bases for an orderly development of the personality. The first is the fact that one need predisposes the child to develop another. The second is that increasing maturity tends to produce a series of increasingly mature needs that all bear on the same general issue. The third is the regularity of social pressure within a single culture. The interaction of these three factors permits a wide variety of developmental patterns. Whether they actually work out in the way the theory postulates must be determined by further research.

Creation of Attitudes Toward People

The child's environment is not composed merely of goals and means to goals. The events that happen to a child are not always the result of his own actions. Not only do we cause changes in our environment, but also our environment is changed by some other agency. Even when we are trying to reach some goal of our own, we may require the help or benevolence of someone else who is put in the position of being able to help or hinder our progress toward a goal.

Out of these experiences with objects that we use as tools to achieve our goal and with people who may aid us, hamper us, or impose on us, we develop attitudes toward these objects in our environment. We tend to have a sentimental attachment for the house we live in, the bicycle we rode to school for years. We also tend to be fond of some people, to dislike others, to be contemptuous of others, and so on through the list of possible attitudes.

The task of this section is to discuss the way these attitudes develop.

An obvious yet important fact is that our feelings toward people are quite different from our attitudes toward inanimate objects. An object that serves us well is valued as a good tool, but only as a tool. When it fails to function it is thrown away without regret and usually without anger toward it for not living up to our expectations. Our attitudes toward inanimate objects are not invariably so detached and impersonal—we may have a sentimental attachment to an inanimate object—but as a general rule we treat objects in a utilitarian way.

Our attitudes toward people are different. When a person serves us well we like him for it, even when he is not immediately benefiting us. People who have lost their usefulness are not thrown away like a burned-out light bulb. When people disappoint us, on the other hand, when they frustrate us, we become angry at them, and our anger continues after the actual harmful act is completed.

The fact that attitudes toward people last longer than the actions that cause the attitudes indicates that they are governed by the characteristics we perceive in other people. A friendly attitude toward another person is a response to perceiving his friendly attitude. His friendliness is exhibited in his behavior, but his characteristic of friendliness does not stop as soon as his overt expression of it stops. Consequently, we feel friendly toward him even when his behavior is not obviously friendly, as long as it does not contradict our belief in his friendship.

The development of attitudes in the mature person, therefore, is partly a process of discovering the characteristics of other people. Children's attitudes are more changeable than adults' and more dependent upon the actual behavior of the other person, but they stabilize with maturity.

Attitudes not only result from contacts with other people, but they also affect our interpretation of the behavior of other people. One's experience and attitudes may prevent the possibility of discovering contradictory evidence or may color one's interpretation of another's attitudes so that valid judgment is difficult. Thus, a dislike and feeling of hostility stemming from one incident may prevent further contact and provide no way for the attitude to change. Or the dislike may make us interpret overtly friendly actions as being selfishly motivated.

By no means all attitudes develop from actual experience with the object of the attitude. Children may form attitudes on the basis of hearsay, from the opinions of friends, and most strongly from the opinions of their parents. Once an attitude of liking and respect for someone has developed, then the opinions of such a person are believed and his attitudes and values are frequently taken over. We have already discussed the role of identification in the acceptance of the values and attitudes of other people (see p. 224). We have also seen that the attitudes of children gradually conform more and more to the attitudes of our culture (see p. 229). Later, we shall look at some of the antecedents for specific attitudes and values.

Summary

This chapter has been concerned with various processes that bring about changes in needs, attitudes, and values through childhood experience but that are not well described as learning. First, we have looked at some of the ways needs may change over short periods of time—fading of needs through time, satiation of needs through continuous gratification, and increase of needs through psychological involvement. Then we looked at some of the processes occurring over a long period of time. Continuous exposure to stimuli may continually instigate motivation and result in an accentuation of needs, or it may lead to adaptation and habituation with a disappearance of a need. We have also seen how through increase or decrease in cognitive clearness, needs may change so that means become ends, or ends means.

20

Parent Behavior

THE ROLE OF PARENTHOOD

REJECTING BEHAVIOR

EMOTIONAL INVOLVEMENT

EMOTIONAL DETACHMENT

THE DEMOCRATIC PHILOSOPHY

SUMMARY

IN PART II of this book we have been discussing some of the developmental processes in children: conditioning, cognitive learning, maturation, habituation, accentuation of needs, and others. There are two tasks remaining before us. One is to consider the empirical data that describe the specific effects of various antecedent conditions upon the personality of the individual who emerges from these experiences. The other task is to present some of the important current theories of personality development, especially psychoanalytic theory and general behavior theory, to both of which we have made occasional reference previously.

We shall first discuss the empirical data relating antecedent conditions, especially the characteristics of the home in which the child is raised, to the personality characteristics that he exhibits. In order to do this, we must digress slightly to discuss parent behavior itself, to understand its roots in the interaction of the parent and child within a culture, and to examine some of the patterns of parent behavior that commonly occur in our culture.

The Role of Parenthood

We described earlier the way that society is organized into positions, each of which has certain rules of behavior that go with it (see p. 211). The person who fills the position is permitted certain types of behavior; other behavioral patterns are expected of him; and some types of behavior are forbidden to him. Parenthood is one such position in our society.

Roles may be assigned to people in various ways: some of them are adopted voluntarily; others are automatically acquired. Parenthood in our society is not entirely voluntary, but on the other hand it is not a role which any person must necessarily accept. No one is forced to enter marriage, although there are strong psychological reasons that may effectively force some people to want to be married. Although a couple is not forced to have children, there are social pressures for married people to have children. In addition, of course, there may be accidental pregnancies which the married couple tried to prevent.

Factors in the Selection of the Role of Parent

The selection of a role, when the individual is free to select it or reject it, involves many factors. Because of the fact that it forms a psychological unit of associated behavior patterns, a role may be inviting for one reason despite the fact that some of the other expected patterns of behavior are very distasteful. The mother may look forward to having a baby because she pictures a cuddly, warm little human who will love her. The idea of herself holding a baby in her arms makes an attractive picture. She may recognize the fact that having a baby means getting up at two o'clock in the morning, but the picture of herself getting out of a warm bed on a cold morning when she is tired and sleepy does not figure nearly so prominently in her anticipations as do the pleasanter aspects of motherhood. Therefore, she may, despite the fact that she looks forward to being a mother, find the role a disappointing one. Or, as is more usually the case, she finds unexpected rewards as well as unexpected burdens in the role of parent and therefore continues to be happy with her lot.

The decision to select a role seldom considers all the realistic factors in proper proportions. It cannot be made in a cognitively clear fashion like the decision to buy a refrigerator. Nevertheless, it may be made with a fairly realistic appreciation of what it entails, or it may be made in a very confused fashion. The woman may be very ignorant of the realities of motherhood, especially if she has not grown up with younger siblings. The many assets and liabilities of family life have to be experienced to be appreciated fully.

Even if the problem is not one of mere ignorance, the decision to have children may be made in a confused way. One single factor may have so much emotional impact that it blocks out the perception of all the rest. Children may be seen as a duty, as a means of keeping up with the Joneses, as a relief from loneliness, or as a source of love.

People whose decision to have children is reached in a realistic way are likely to be happy in their choice, but it is certainly true that many other people actually enjoy their families once they arrive. There are so many unforeseeable contingencies that the decision to have children is best based upon one's intuitive judgment of whether it would be satisfying rather than upon any calculation of the odds on both sides.

Prescriptions of the Parental Role

PROTECTION AND SUPPORT OF CHILDREN   As in all roles, certain behaviors are demanded of the parent. Economic support and maintenance of the physical welfare of the children are probably the clearest demands upon parents in our culture. Desertion is forbidden, and any sort of evasion of the responsibility for supporting the children is frowned upon. The parent should provide the child with good food and with adequate clothes; he should take care of the child's health and nurse him during illness.

Emotional support of the children and training them into the ways of this society are also demanded of the parent. A mother is supposed to love her children and be available to comfort them in time of trouble; she should give them the support to meet new situations bravely. Mother love is almost taken for granted, as though it automatically occurs whenever a woman becomes a mother. Not to love one's children is viewed as unnatural by many people in this culture. Fortunately, individuals in the culture know that it is impossible to rear children without becoming angry at them occasionally; so mothers can sometimes talk frankly about their short tempers or their pet peeves and can console each other that Johnny will outgrow his passion for splashing bath water all over the room. The irritating qualities of children do not seem to be culturally recognized. Impatience with children is tolerated; mother love is demanded.

SOCIALIZATION OF CHILDREN   To discipline children, not to let them run wild, to teach them the difference between right and wrong, to send them to school on time, to know where they are and what they are doing: these are further requirements of the parental role in our culture. The mother who gives in to every whim of the "spoiled brat" is disapproved just as much as the mother who does not love her children. The exact content of the training that the child should receive and the exact method of carrying out the training are not so prescribed as are the results of the training. Although a mother of a spoiled child may be disapproved for not punishing him, the mother who never spanks the child is not ordinarily the subject of criticism if the child behaves himself.

The cultural expectations of the child at various ages constitute in themselves definitions of the cultural expectations of the parents. These cultural expectations have not been subjected to careful scientific investigation; they probably vary within the culture from one subgroup to another. We can see from casual observation, however, that a child who still nurses from a bottle at the age of four is thought of as babyish and his parent comes in for censure. There are ages beyond which childish activities such as undressing in public, eating with fingers, sex play, talking out loud during prayer, and walking off with toys from the ten-cent-store counter are disapproved. Such activities are in a sense always disapproved, but they are tolerated in the young child because they are seen as childish and not indicative of a person who has "gone bad." If such behavior appears in an older child, it is treated more seriously. It is a reflection on the adequacy of parental training.

In this discussion of the role of the parent in our culture, we have not distinguished between the role of the father and that of the mother. The mother is in general charged with the major responsibility in all these areas, although the father is supposed to assist, especially when the child becomes older and especially in the area of discipline.

Having described to some extent the demands of the parental role in our culture, we turn now to the satisfaction with which the parent can meet these cultural demands. The various patterns of parent behavior will eventually be seen as patterns of adjustment of the human personality of the parent to the demands of the culture in dealing with the personality of the child.

Satisfaction and Dissatisfaction with the Parental Role

HARMONY OF ROLE WITH PARENTS' NEEDS   The demands that the culture makes of parents and the behavior that is expected of parents may or may not harmonize with the needs of the parent as an individual. If, for example, a parent likes to be nurturant, to take care of other people, to be responsible for their welfare, and to make them feel happy and contented, then such a person finds the parental role satisfying in many ways. Such needs seem especially designed for the parent of the young child.

There are other needs that are not difficult to coordinate with the duties of parenthood. Most sorts of professional needs of a father are compatible with fatherhood; some professional activities that can be carried out in the home and that do not demand regular hours can be successfully combined with the duties of the maternal role even when the child is very young.

But other needs of the individual may be incompatible with parenthood. A problem of adjustment that all parents, especially mothers, must face is the integration of their adult life and its patterns of satisfaction with the different responsibilities and satisfactions of parenthood. A mother may feel that she must sacrifice all her own private life for her child. She may do so willingly, and dedicate her life to her children. She may, on the other hand, feel that she is forced to do so. Other mothers keep a portion of their time for their own lives, although the mother of a young child may feel herself fortunate if she gets a "maid's night out." What actually occurs in a specific case depends upon all the circumstances involved—the demands of the child, the personality of the mother, the financial position of the family, and other such factors. Some parents, without actually leaving the home to seek their own satisfactions, may adopt a policy of sending the children to bed early so that they may have an evening to themselves; they may adopt the policy of having the children eat separately so that they may enjoy dinner in their own adult fashion.

The behavior of the parent must change with the age of the child if it is to continue to meet the cultural prescription of the role. The early life of the child demands much more constant physical care and attendance than do the older years. The older child, on the other hand, requires more social interaction, tact, and judgment than does the infant.

It is probably true that the basic potentiality for satisfaction in parenthood increases as the child grows older. Even though adolescence is proverbially a difficult age, adolescent children are more adultlike than they were earlier in life. Since a person has perforce developed a more or less adequate way of interacting with his contemporaries, and since, as we discussed in Chapter 1, the adult is more readily understood than is the child, it seems reasonable that the possibility of a satisfying interpersonal relationship with a child is enhanced as he becomes more nearly adult. In other words, the adjustment that a mother must make to an infant is much more divorced from her prematernal social adjustment than it would be if children were born adolescent. Parents may, however, become accustomed to the adjustments that a young child necessitates and be unable to treat the adolescent as a near-adult despite the fact that he is capable of taking considerable responsibility.

Not only do the demands on the parent vary with the age of the child, but they depend a great deal upon the characteristics and personality of the child. Some children are defective, mentally or physically. The culture does not make much allowance for the fact that such children require much more care and attention than the normal child. Such children are likely to be felt as burdens. Other children are active, vigorous, and resistant to socialization. They require more time and care if the social rules of society are to be successfully inculcated. Other children have very great potentialities or talents. There is pressure on the parent to help the child realize his talent.

WARMTH Regardless of the specific reasons for satisfaction, if the parent finds his role gratifying, he is basically an acceptant and warm parent. His motivation encourages him to spend time with the child, to find the necessary sacrifices not difficult ones, to accept his responsibilities without too much conflict, and to love the child.

If, on the other hand, the parent finds his professional career frustrated and his social life restricted, if he finds that the complete responsibility for the life of another person entails great anxiety, if the dirty menial labor is sufficiently irksome and distasteful, he will probably reject the child. By this is meant that he will be strongly motivated to avoid the responsibilities of parenthood, to reduce to a minimum his contact with the child, and to dislike the child who is the source of all these frustrations.

These are bald and stark descriptions that are grossly oversimplified. For most parents life with baby is no bed of roses, but neither is it an unredeemed frustration. For them, parenthood has its good and bad aspects. At times they feel warm and acceptant; at other times they are convinced that children should be kept in a barrel and fed through a tube. The atmosphere of most homes varies somewhere between constant wholehearted acceptance and continual cold rejection. It may be casual or reasonably warm, or perhaps it veers toward the "let him take care of himself" atmosphere. Furthermore, it fluctuates with numerous factors—the amount of sleep the mother had on a specific night, the orneriness and cantankerousness of the child this day, and whether father is off having a good time or is around to help with the dishes.

Another factor must be recognized in this picture. The social expectation for a parent in our culture is that a mother love her children. The absence of mother love is viewed as unnatural. Thus, parents never express their negative feelings toward the child as freely as their positive feelings. Not only do they inhibit overt expression of rejection, but most parents feel guilty if their conscious feeling of rejection becomes strong. Fortunately, most parents can accept and talk about their annoyances with their role; our culture does not demand a completely unrealistic sweetness toward children. Still, there is very real guilt if the mother does not feel that she genuinely loves her children. This guilt can produce its own set of adjustments; for this reason some parents have developed defenses to prevent such feelings of guilt and anxiety, and to prevent the appearance of the rejectant behavior that would be natural in a person who is saddled with an unrewarding burden.

This discussion may have given the impression that the personality of the parent is a fixed characteristic—that in so far as the parental role happens to fit the personality, the parent is satisfied and warm, but that when it does not fit, he rejects the child. We should remember that personality may change. The parent may find the first infant a burden, but enjoy the second. The parent may have wanted a boy but find that a girl is a satisfying child also. The satisfactions of parenthood can be acquired through the various methods of creating needs that were discussed earlier (see p. 463). Dissatisfactions may also mount. Some mothers accept with good grace the period of confinement of early childhood. They look forward to being freed of it, but accept it gracefully without resentment. If, however, another child comes along, the prospect of once more going through the same period may be unacceptable. Thus, the warmth of the parent's feelings toward a child may change through a wide variety of circumstances. Warmth is no fixed unchangeable property of the parent-child relationship.

Rejecting Behavior

What are the behavioral consequences of these various feelings of satisfaction and dissatisfaction with parenthood? Since the consequences of rejection on the behavior of the parent are probably more obvious than those of acceptance, it will be convenient to outline first the patterns of rejectant behavior.

Neglect

The obvious reaction to finding the child burdensome is to have as little to do with him as possible. The parent through self-control may inhibit this natural impulsive reaction, or because of personality defenses he may not perceive the child as burdensome. Let us, however, look first at the simple cases of overt rejection.

The most extreme form of avoidance of parenthood is, of course, open abandonment of the child, but very rarely does any parent go to such an extreme. There are legal and social obstacles to such a course, and, in the large majority of parents, internal obstacles as well. The parent believes it is wrong to avoid taking care of his child even though he does not find it much fun.

Short of this complete abandonment, the most overt expression of rejection is to neglect the child, perhaps not in terms of physical care, but in having as little personal interaction with him as possible. Such a parent might be expected to hire a nurse for the baby if it is economically feasible. He might utilize various labor-saving devices to reduce the labor involved in taking care of the child. It would be expected that aside from the routines the baby would spend much of his time alone in his crib. We should point out that these behaviors might stem from other factors than rejection—a house full of other children, perhaps. Some parents may use all the labor-saving methods they can so that they have time to enjoy the baby in pleasanter circumstances than when changing his diapers.

Dictatorial Policy

When the child is older the demand for physical care lessens. Now, if the parental role is unsatisfactory, the source is likely to be the social interaction between parent and child. We can see that the desire to reduce social interaction with the child would tend to make the parent dictatorial. The parent must make decisions about the child; he will be asked questions. The response of the parent who does not want to enter into the situation is to make some snap judgment in a final fashion. "No, you cannot go to the movie, now leave me alone," or "Do whatever you want to, but get out of the kitchen," are answers which reveal the fact that at the moment the child's demands are burdensome. Every parent has felt this on some occasion; the rejecting parents are those who feel this interaction to be an imposition and intrusion whenever it occurs.

A rejecting parent, despite the fact that he tends to be dictatorial about decisions, is not likely to go out of his way to fasten rules on the child. The child may actually have a great deal of freedom as long as he does not intrude upon the parent. The areas of interaction are likely to be arranged in an authoritarian fashion to fit the convenience of the parent. In other areas the child may make his own decisions by default.

Hostility

There can be in our culture no complete avoidance of interaction. Therefore the parent who finds his life with the child burdensome may view every interaction as an imposition. The consequence may be to arouse actual hostility toward the child as well as to evoke the motivation to withdraw from the interaction. The child is a constant frustrating irritant. The hostility that the parent feels may, more or less frequently, overcome his desire to avoid interaction. Suppose, for example, that a father has just arrived home and picked up the paper. He does not have to be a consistently rejecting parent to find this moment of peace and relaxation very precious. His child begins to "pester" him because from the child's point of view his arrival stimulated various motives. "Daddy, will you fix my doll? Her arm came off." "Daddy, look at my spelling paper," and so on. If the parent under this barrage of interruptions becomes angry, he may respond to some such request as, "Daddy, may I go over to Jackie's house?" with a "No!" Actually, to give the permission would get the child out of his way for a little while, but he may be so irritated that he punishes the child by refusal of his request. If the parent frequently displays this intentionally frustrating behavior, the home may be called an actively hostile rejecting home in contrast to the previously described passive neglectful rejecting home.

Rejection as a Policy

It should be apparent that these incidents used to illustrate rejecting behavior can occur in any home and do probably occur in all homes. It is only when such behavior is the rule that the home may legitimately be called rejecting. Rejection is almost never a truly planned policy of neglect or hostility; it is the atmosphere created when a parent continually finds that the behavior demanded of him is a burden and the little incidents of everyday life are irritating. He responds to them individually as impositions. The total effect of such rejecting behavior in one incident after another may resemble the behavior that would result from a cognitively clear dislike of the child, but in most cases the dislike itself is not actually present.

Parent Behavior Scales

Baldwin, Kalhorn, and Breese (1945) have published descriptions of various patterns of parent behavior in two different forms. The first is a more standardized quantitative description based on a battery of thirty Parent Behavior Rating Scales developed first by Champney (1941) and then utilized by Baldwin, Kalhorn, and Breese to describe the parent behavior of the parents who cooperated in the research program of the Fels Research Institute. This research institute is engaged in a longitudinal research program, studying a group of children from before birth to maturity. The homes are periodically visited and the behavior of the mother is rated on the scales. The

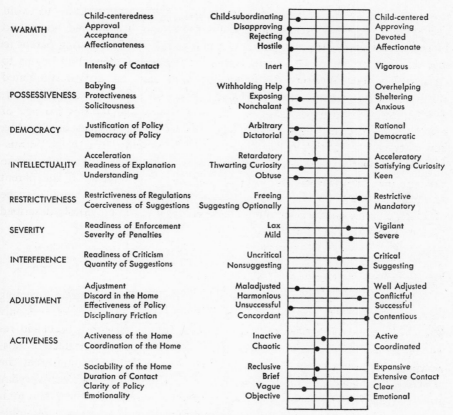

Fig. 20.1 Passive-neglectful parent behavior. (After A. L. Baldwin, J. Kalhorn, and F. H. Breese, *Psych. Monogr.*, 58:268, 1945)

rating is made on the basis of a detailed description of the variables as given on the actual rating sheet and as described in publications by Champney (1941) and by Baldwin, Kalhorn, and Breese (1945; 1949).

In Figure 20.1, the scales are grouped into syndromes of related variables. These syndromes can be used as somewhat coarser variables than the detailed ones that make up each syndrome. Thus, the first group, which can be labeled *warmth,* corresponds fairly well to the warmth variable as we have described it, except that in the parent-behavior profile parent *behavior,* not parent motivation, is rated. Defensive behavior is, therefore, described according to its manifest characteristics, not in terms of the basic satisfaction of the parent with the child.

The average profiles of the two types of rejecting homes, the actively

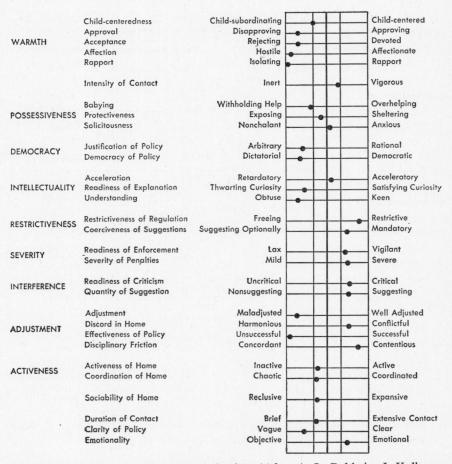

Fig. 20.2   Actively hostile parent behavior. (After A. L. Baldwin, J. Kalhorn, and F. H. Breese, *Psych. Monogr.,* 58:245, 1945)

hostile one and the passively neglectful one, are shown in Figures 20.1 and 20.2. The following two excerpts from case descriptions describe one home of each sort. They are quoted from a monograph by Baldwin, Kalhorn and Breese, and were written to illustrate the central features of rejection.

Sam Dugan: Passive Rejectance

The Dugan home is soberly industrious, almost puritan in its quality. Married in their teens, both parents have a farm background and setting up as farmers was, for them, a logical and unquestioned step. Both parents are staid, conservative individuals, solemnly intent on life as a business. In their struggles to get ahead both have had to work extremely hard, but their ideology goes beyond this—work is not a means but an end in itself, and most recreation can be chalked off as a frivolous use of time. Both are so firmly entrenched in the pattern of values laid down by generations of industrious forebears, the general "farm culture," that an outsider finds it hard to believe they really are so young—still in their twenties—rather than the settled, middle-aged couple their attitudes would indicate. If there is conflict, restlessness, an urge to see the world in a different perspective than that given by a small Markham County farm, it is so deeply repressed and hidden as to go unrecognized even by the Dugans themselves.

Their acceptance of the isolation and hard work afforded by the farm life they have chosen is in part a reflection of their own reclusive and rather anti-social temperaments. Mrs. Dugan, in particular, was probably termed shy as a girl. Now a mature woman, she can only be described as cold, hostile, suspicious. Little companionship is evident in the marriage; there is hardly more interaction between husband and wife than between either one and a stranger. Work is divided according to the traditional farm pattern—the man to the barns and fields, the woman to the house and child training—with little mutual interchange of experience beyond routine informational conversation.

In this setting, child bearing is as natural and unquestioned as the farm work itself, a matter not of choice and planning, but of custom, even duty. Thus, Sam, who was born within a year, was "accepted" as an inevitable part of their marriage even though the Dugans have no fondness for children as such. They found little recompense in enjoyment for the burden of fitting his schedule and demands into an already overcrowded work program. Parental policy, therefore, had to set rigid boundaries, require a minimum of contact with the child, and let the parents off in the easiest fashion commensurate with their obligation to the child, so that they could devote themselves to the more important work waiting for them.

This type of handling is evident even in Sam's infancy. Accounts of fondling the baby or playing with him are rare. A visitor reports that, at eleven months, "his mother was dressing him at the kitchen table, holding him on her lap like a small baby and thrusting him into his clothes." No opportunity was given for any degree of self-help because that would have been time consuming. At the same age, on the other hand, he was already being given sharp slaps to teach him not to get into things. The home has been highly accelerational in those areas where the mother's goal is to be able to leave the child alone without worrying about him; at the same time, more help is given than the child needs if doing so will save time and effort.

Over and above the attempt to conserve time and energy in the handling of the child, Mrs. Dugan is unduly restrictive and autocratic. An example from a time-sample recording made on an early home visit is illustrative: (17 months) "He saw my book and dove for it, jabbering unintelligibly. He slapped at my book and his mother said, 'Don't do that.' He took my ankle in his hand and his mother told him not to do that. He went over to the couch and pulled at a pillow, to which his mother said, 'Now leave that alone.' He came over to me and pulled at my pen and buttons. His mother pulled him away." Mrs. Dugan's vigilant severity in this instance seems unnecessary, if her only motivation is to conserve energy. Probably it reflects an active resentment and hostility.

As Sam grew older and could more nearly be trusted to conform, the relationship became more inert with Mrs. D ignoring his activities until a disciplinary crisis would arise. The fact that Mrs. Dugan rarely forestalls a crisis by acting ahead of time can, in part, be attributed to her lack of attention to the child—there is practically no interaction between her and Sam *except* when he has done something irritating or "wrong." This aloofness is evident in the following anecdote from a report of a visit made when Sam was three: "He had one period of giggling which lasted several minutes and was renewed with a rather forced note once or twice subsequently. His mother did not enter into his giggling, but on the other hand she made no attempt to stop him and waited until it disappeared." This visit was made shortly after the birth of Sam's first sib, and the mother reports that the only time she had seen Sam exhibit real jealousy was when the maternal grandparents visited. "They have held Sam a good deal more than his parents do; when his grandparents hold the baby, Sam shows real jealousy and strives in various ways to get their attention." (Visitor's report of mother's comments.)

Lack of interaction is evident in other areas than discipline too. Sam's speech development was slow, and after he did begin to talk his language was markedly distorted. Another visitor reports: "Mrs. Dugan said that she and his father could understand him, but that most people could not. They make no attempt to correct his speech." It is as if once bare communication had been established, no matter how faulty, they felt their responsibility was at an end. There is a general disinterest in Sam's inner life, what he thinks, feels, how he's reacting. One home visitor reports that over a period of two years or so, she never heard Mrs. Dugan so much as ask Sam what had happened at school that day. In the school area, as in others, Mrs. Dugan's only concern is with success or failure, conforming conduct or troublesome mischief. When Sam was having difficulty with spelling, she dutifully drilled him at home, demonstrating a "what can you expect?" attitude, and some irritation at the extra time entailed.

Again it seems that Mrs. Dugan's behavior is too extreme to be accounted for solely in terms of a minimum expenditure of effort. She now seems unnecessarily aloof and disinterested, just as formerly she seemed unnecessarily vigilant and restrictive. Both probably reflect the same underlying hostility.

Aside from the psychological isolation it provides, the home is not severely restricting at this point. Arbitrary standards for conduct have been laid down, but so long as Sam conforms to those standards his behavior is not too closely scrutinized—the parents have neither the time nor the interest. The independence this has fostered, plus a desperate seeking for affection and attention and demands for status of one sort or another, have made his school record one of near-delinquency, although at home he is just conforming enough to escape the "problem" classification. By identification with gangs, he has found the affection and status which he misses at home, but there is no reason to suppose that a redirection of his behavior into socially acceptable channels is not possible. So far as Sam himself is concerned, however, help in the redirection of his energies will have to come from teachers or other interested adults—his parents are as unperceptive of his problems now as they were in their own behavior which created the problems.

Betty McKane: Active Rejectance

Mrs. McKane is fundamentally a selfish, egocentric woman who evaluates events and people in terms of the extent to which they contribute to her own satisfaction. She is one of nine children, who takes childbearing and raising a family as a matter of course but is fundamentally irritated by children. When Betty was six months old, Mrs. McKane remarked: "I hate to sit and hold her. I don't care to hold babies . . . for some reason or other I never did."

As an individual, Mrs. McKane is aggressive, dominant, given to expressing her opinions fervently, with a vigorous bob of the head punctuating each pronouncement. She indulges herself with a lot of sleep, enjoys evenings off at the "Y" with other women, seems to seek rather a "bachelor-girl" existence, with which her husband and children must interfere as little as possible. She suffers no pangs of conscience in modifying her home, her children's behavior or her husband's mode of life to suit her own convenience and tastes.

Though Mrs. McKane would probably be unable to verbalize a philosophy of the parent's role, she nevertheless has certain cast-iron attitudes which she is uninhibited about expressing and unquestioning in applying. In describing her own behavior she is completely matter-of-fact, even righteous, and rarely makes an effort to rationalize or justify her policies. She is utterly obtuse and insensitive to other people's needs, completely lacking in understanding of or sympathy for "the child personality."

For Mrs. McKane the model child is the quiet, unobtrusive one. She attains this goal in two ways—by imposing on the child rigid standards of behavior which become habitual, and by meeting immediate situations with arbitrary commands. Throughout, there is a note of suspicion, as if the mother believed that her whole disciplinary policy would collapse unless constantly reinforced by fresh commands. She is thoroughly pessimistic of what might result from Betty's initiative. The measures taken to insure obedience (severe tone, harsh words, sarcasm, etc.) are as caustic as those many parents use as punishment after the fact. This strictness is not as much evidence of Mrs. McKane's concern for the children's well being as it is a reflection of her own desire to secure herself from annoyance and irritating conflicts.

If Betty eats an ice cream cone, her mother says: "I suppose you're going to spill that down the front of your dress?" If Betty is sent upstairs to take a bath, Mrs. McKane says: "I suppose you're going to leave those dirty clothes all over the floor when you're through." If Betty starts out the door, she says: "I suppose you're going to leave the screen open and let every fly in town into this house." Always it is taken for granted that Betty, left to her own volition, will do something that is irritating to the mother or contrary to the accepted standards of the home. In the words of the family doctor, "Mrs. McKane is much too strict with the girls; she would like it if they would sit on a chair and do nothing." Another observer writes: "The mother would prefer that her children be altogether inactive, or so inhumanly good that no effort on her part is necessary."

Although Mrs. McKane's behavior can perhaps be accounted for in terms of her self-indulgence, her eternal vigilance seems to require considerably more energy than is necessary to produce a docile, well-disciplined child. She seems to go out of her way to be frustrating, caustic and unpleasant to Betty.

Second only to the severity of the atmosphere is the inconsistency of policy. "Nonsense" that may draw down severe punishment one time may on another occasion be laughed off, depending on Mrs. McKane's mood; she indulges in rough joking horseplay with the children when *she's* feeling good, but when the mood passes she flares up with sudden anger and clamps down on the girls with heavy-handed parental authority. This irrational and whimsical treatment leaves the children with only a hazy concept of what behavior is actually sanctioned.

The amount of babying, sheltering, solicitousness, etc.—expressed directly to the child or implicit in parental policy—is too extreme in Mrs. McKane's case to be representative of the rejecting group. This anxiety is probably a function of her own maladjustments and irrational fears. She will not let her older daughter, age twelve, go to the store alone, for instance, because "a man might get her"— Mrs. McKane herself has given considerable evidence that fear of ravishment is practically a phobia with her. Even though this solicitousness is atypical of the rejecting group, it shows again how Mrs. McKane's own peace of mind is the determining factor in her handling of the children. She protects her daughter rigorously from certain imagined or real dangers that are, to her, genuine and threatening, at the same time that she exposes them all, and Betty particularly, to traumatic psychological experiences, e.g. she threatened to break up the home and take the children with her if her husband didn't get transferred to the day shift. She is so lacking in understanding, so obtuse from the psychological view point, that she simply doesn't perceive what is significant.

During Betty's preschool years Mrs. McKane's treatment was an illogical and haphazard succession of warm indulgence, strict discipline, and anxious solicitude. After Betty was six, however, the warmth disappeared and the picture is now more generally one of cold indifference and dislike alternating with heated conflict. From this time on the mother is rated as being extremely rejecting and hostile toward the child.

In reaction to this vigorous and constricting policy Betty has steadily become withdrawn, shy and stubbornly resistant, in a passive fashion, to adult authority. At school her decorous and superficially docile behavior cannot be criticized, but in any situation which demands a response she retreats into an almost inaudible, "I don't know." Her bewildered, discouraged teacher says: "I just can't get at her—nothing seems to reach her."

Guilt Feelings about Rejecting Behavior

Many parents who on occasion rebuff the advances of the child because they are tired, preoccupied, anxious, or desirous of solitude feel guilty about such incidents. They see the child as having come to them with love, only to be rebuffed. The parent feels he has hurt the child. He may somehow picture the child as an unloved little waif who is all the more deserving of love because of being rejected. He may through this motivation make it up to the child, perhaps by being indulgent, perhaps by planning some period of activity together with the child. Often this works out very well, especially if the parent is sensitive to what the child wants. Most well-adjusted households have such periods of family play and other periods in which the children are left on their own.

The danger of such guilt-stimulated love and sympathy for the child lies in the possibility that when the parent is ready for a sentimental tête-à-tête the child may want to play baseball with his gang or read comic books. Children have their desire for solitude, too. If the parent can recognize it, he can put off the joint activity until a more convenient time or he can give the child his choice in the matter and be ready to accept the child's right to reject him. The parent may, however, feel hurt by the child's reaction. We want the people toward whom we feel sympathy to be properly grateful when we do something kind for them. Thus it can happen that guilt feelings promote behavior which is rejected, which in turn gives the parent the psychological justification for being angry with the child.

What we have been describing as a minor superficial incident is a kind of reaction formation to feelings of rejection. When such a reaction formation becomes more pervasive, we find that such parents show great tenderness for the child and great ego involvement. As we shall see in the discussion of possessiveness, such positive feelings together with ego involvement lead to leniency, fear of harm to the child, and a demand that the child return this love and respect. If the child does not readily return it or conform to the pattern of rules that such love prompts, the parent may experience a return of hostility toward the child, this time more easily justified, for the child has become more than a mere burden. He is now a disobedient, disrespectful, and unloving child.

Finding a child disobedient and unloving justifies resentment. This introduces us to another sort of defense against guilt—namely, to justify the rejection so that it no longer evokes guilt feelings. This attribution of blame to the people toward whom we feel hostile is a defense mechanism called "projection."

The possibility of projecting hostility onto the child depends upon his age. It is necessary for the child to be viewed as a responsible person before he can be blamed for his bad actions. Although not impossible, it is usually difficult to become angry at an infant. Even when he does things that are frustrating or when his care is burdensome, he is, in our culture at least, considered irresponsible. He may be trained, and even punished as a part of that training, but until he is viewed as a free agent, it is difficult to be hostile toward him. The child in our culture begins to be treated as though he were responsible for his actions somewhere around the age of two or three. It is after this age, therefore, that resentment against the child is more probable. Since children do many things that we would ordinarily resent in an adult, it is not difficult for the parent who is so inclined to find justification for resentment in the behavior of the child.

Another result stemming from guilt feelings may be that the parent does not feel free under any circumstances to reject the child's advances. He feels compelled, in order to avoid guilt feelings, to give up his own activities whenever the child wants it. He can hardly fail to feel resentment at these intrusions —which in turn stimulates more guilt feelings. Eventually the parent may come to the point where he feels that the child is wrong or thoughtless to make so many demands of him. Thus, the parent's freedom of action is constricted by guilt feelings or anxiety so that he is forced into overdoing the good things that protect his conscience. Then he relapses into unreasonable resentment that is equally unjustified.

It is especially unfortunate when a parent who really does enjoy and love his child comes to feel guilty because of a too-literal acceptance of some of the good advice of child psychologists, such as "Love is all-important." Love is all-important, but love need not make the lover into a slave—thus the soundness of the advice to parents to trust their impulses. Doing what comes naturally frequently works out for the best.

The wisdom of this advice is especially clear in those intellectual homes in which the policies of rearing children are carefully planned in terms of "the book." By devoting himself to the scientific care and rational treatment of the child, the parent can protect himself against guilt feelings. Yet this sort of scientific care, if it is not supported by love and affection, can become very cold and inconsiderate. Most rational methods of dealing with human beings need to be well tempered by good humor, common sense, and good judgment. In many homes it is only too apparent that the parent has more regard for his theory of child development than he does for the child as a person.

Thus, if the parent-child relationship is basically unrewarding and unsatisfying to the parent, the consequences, if openly expressed, are likely to be neglect and resentment. If these are prevented through defensive measures, the parent may perceive the child to be at fault. If he adopts a different defense, the parent may display quite the opposite sorts of behavior, but generally to excess and untempered by the usual good sense of warm parents.

Emotional Involvement

Turning now to the discussion of warm parent behavior, we shall see that there are more ways of being a warm parent than of being a cold one. Although there is only one basic pattern of rejection, there are two quite different patterns of warmth that are unlike in the extent to which the parent is ego-involved in the child's behavior.

In order to make this clear we must examine some of the natural psychological consequences of being in love. These "natural" consequences are those reactions toward the people we love that occur directly and impulsively. They are outlined more fully in Chapter 8, in which the characteristics of love at different levels of maturity are discussed. To love someone is to want him to be happy and safe. Loving someone implies a certain emotional involvement in his behavior and his happiness. If someone we love does something shameful, we find it hard to believe. It may, if sufficiently gross, be sufficient to turn us against him, but more generally it makes us ashamed of him and for him. We ourselves are likely to have certain feelings of shame.

Sensitivity to Loved One

To love someone makes us vulnerable. The things he does are important to us, and therefore he can do things that hurt us, that make us proud, or that make us happy. Because we love a person, his actions have more psychological potency and affect us more than if we do not care for him. It is this vulnerability of the person in love which makes it difficult for some people to fall in love. To fall in love is to be left open to possible hurt as well as to possible joy. For some people it is safer to remain aloof.

When, however, we do fall in love we are, willy-nilly, more sensitive to the behavior of the one we love. It is only natural, therefore, to try to protect ourselves by exerting what influence we can to keep the loved one from doing things that would hurt us. We react more violently to his behavior than to the behavior of a stranger. Thus, it is frequently true that we become more angry with the people we care for than with strangers. We can ignore strangers, leave them alone; their opinions are not our concern; but we cannot ignore and be insensitive to the people whom we care for and respect. It is, of course, a tragic possibility to be bound to someone so closely by love that it is impossible to break that bondage even if it becomes obvious that the person does not deserve respect or affection.

Love for a Child

Parental love for a child is not identical to loving one's wife or husband, but the two do have much in common. The difference lies mainly in the fact that the feeling of love toward a young child is accompanied by the perception that he is less responsible, that he is more influenced by momentary moods than an adult, and that the bad things he does are more frequently mistakes than misdemeanors. Most parents can accept with a certain equanimity the violent declarations of the young child that "I don't love you any more," when he has been disciplined or forbidden to do something he wants. And parents do not ordinarily feel as ashamed if a young child does something bad as they would if an older person had done it.

Lack of Trust

On the other hand this same recognition of his immaturity makes the parents anxious when they must trust the child in situations in which the child's decisions can have serious consequences. To let the child walk to school by himself, braving the traffic, requires more courage than to let an adult walk around town by himself. Parents are quite justifiably uneasy when their child overhears some confidential information, because he finds it difficult to keep a secret.

There are other areas in which parents may feel ashamed of their children even though the child is not responsible. The parent may have high standards that make him ashamed even of the usual childish escapades. Or the parent may be ashamed when his child does not walk or talk or learn to read until later than the average child. Just as shame is evoked by our defects, whether or not we are responsible for them, so may the parent's shame be evoked by his child's apparent defects. His response may be an unrealistic frantic eagerness for the child to excel.

Another factor that frequently contributes to the parent's feeling of shame or guilt at the child's actions is the sensitivity of the parent to the cultural norm. The culture, as represented by relatives, friends, and neighbors, perceives the involvement of the parent and child and attributes much of the behavior of the child to parental teaching. The parent does carry much of the responsibility for the behavior of his child, but at times these cultural expectations may be quite unrealistic. The degree of disapproval of sex play, noisiness, disrespect, and neighborhood depredations is culturally determined and frequently is not reasonable.

Dictatorial Policy

Because of the mother's emotional involvement in her child's behavior, she naturally wants to encourage him to do the things that will make her proud and to discourage the things that make her ashamed. Thus, she protects him against possible dangers, against bad influences, and against failure—especially public failure. Emotional involvement with the child predisposes the parent to watch him constantly and prevent misdemeanors. It predisposes the parent to be *possessive* toward the child and to treat him as though he were a mere tool and agent of the parent rather than as though he were an independent person.

Merrill (1946) has shown experimentally how possessiveness is evoked. She has shown that mild criticism of the child increases a mother's tendency to become more directive and critical. Merrill observed through a one-way screen the behavior of a mother-child pair in two standardized play situations. For the control group, the second situation was merely a repetition of the first. Each mother in the experimental group, however, was individually told after the first session that the child had not realized his full capacities in the play period. The mothers in the control group did not, on the average, change between the sessions. The experimental mothers, however, showed statistically significant increases in the following variables: directing the child's activity, interfering with the child's plans, criticizing his performance, and structuring changes in his activity.

Possessive Parent Behavior

Merrill found, however, that some mothers were much more sensitive than others to these critical remarks. Everyday observation indicates that in some homes possessiveness is a continual occurrence that needs no special stimulation to evoke it. It is difficult for the possessive parent to accept a child who has his own ideas and who expresses the hostility that children must on occasion feel toward the parent. These expressions have the effect of hurting the possessive parent's feelings, and arousing his conviction that the child is ungrateful.

Whenever the parent is hurt by the child and expresses that fact to the child, he is, deliberately or not, using the technique that was described as "visible suffering" (see p. 195). Because the emotionally involved parent actually is hurt by signs of the child's ingratitude, and because his involvement reduces his self-control, he is very likely to express openly his unhappiness and disappointment over the child's behavior. In some cases this expression is so overdramatized and occurs so readily that it resembles a deliberate technique, like the refined fainting of the proverbial Victorian lady. In most cases, however, it is merely the overt expression of the way the possessive parent actually feels. Deliberate or not, it is one of the most potent kinds of influences on the child, and, as we have seen, contains the seeds for much later unhappiness.

Because he is hurt or disappointed in the child, the possessive parent may perceive hostility in the child's behavior. Such a perception is not always unreasonable, because some child behavior is overtly hostile toward the parent and is intended to hurt. The child may revenge himself for those parental restrictions that he considers deliberate attempts to make him unhappy.

Even when the child's behavior is not overtly hostile and is only a demand to be independent, the possessive parent can easily perceive it to be hostile and resentful. When a possessive mother says about some specific piece of disapproved behavior, "You mean you went out with that boy even though you know how badly it makes me feel," or "You mean that smoking (or whatever is the issue) is more important to you than I am?" then it is easy to see that the parent will perceive hostility in the child's continued efforts to do what he wants.

Just what happens in such cases depends upon many specific circumstances. The parent-child relationship may be violently disrupted and the child overtly rejected by the parent; the parent may accept the behavior with continued recriminations. The independent behavior may sometimes impress on the parent that he has been unduly possessive, and he can suddenly accept the child as an independent person even when he was unable to do so gradually. But we should not forget the probability that parental disapproval of a specific incident is well founded. In this case, it is most unfortunate that parental possessiveness has driven the child to rebel on an issue on which he really needs parental guidance. Also, we should not forget the possibility that the parental possessiveness may make the child himself so ego-involved in the parent-child relationship that he will never be able to rebel and gain his independence.

An example of a possessive parent is described in the following case study and parent-behavior profile (see Fig. 20.3) from Baldwin, Kalhorn, and Breese (1945):

Shirley Ann Harper: Possessiveness

From Shirley Ann's birth, indulgence and child-centeredness have been the central features of the Harper household. When Shirley was two and a half months old, the home visitor reports: "Mr. and Mrs. Harper have apparently lost all objectivity in dealing with the child.

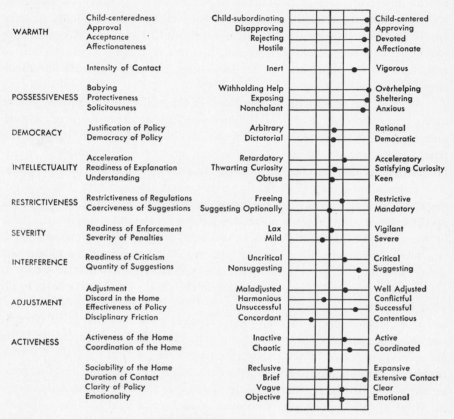

Fig. 20.3 Possessive parent behavior. (After A. L. Baldwin, J. Kalhorn, and F. H. Breese, *Psych. Monogr.*, 58:268, 1945)

Their treatment of her is a succession of lavish kisses, affectionate conversation, and considerable handling, almost mauling. Baby talk abounds, even when Shirley is not present." In all of her social contacts, Mrs. Harper's description of Shirley Ann is liberally sprinkled with such saccharine phrases as "Shirley is our life," "She's my little sweetheart," or, proudly, "At school she's really a teacher's little helper." At the time of the birth of the second child, Mrs. Harper had the delivery at home, saying, "I'd much rather go to the hospital but I just couldn't stand to be away from this little dumpling."

Even in disciplinary situations Mrs. Harper finds it necessary to temper her severity with indulgent sympathy because, as she says, "punishment just about breaks Shirley's little heart." When Shirley was two, we have this report: "Mrs. H's request are all on an emotional level, usually given to baby-talk. When the mail came, Mrs. Harper let

Shirley have it on the condition that she would not tear any of the letters. Shirley proceeded to tear the letters open. Mrs. H. finally took them away from her, then commiserated with her when she began to cry."

Next only to the Harpers' rapture over the "bundle from heaven" they have produced comes their concern with molding this property into an utterly nice, utterly proper child. At three months Shirley was being broken of thumbsucking; at ten and a half months, we find this behavior: "The baby imitated everything that her mother did . . . once, inadvertently, Mrs. H. forced air out of her lips, and Shirley did that too. At first Mrs. H. was amused, then she became worried, saying that she did not want Shirley to have the habit." Muss and clutter are forbidden and from the very earliest age Shirley was subjected to intense restriction as to how many toys she could have out at a time and to rules about picking up one thing before going on to the next.

This imposition of adult standards of propriety, neatness, orderliness, reaches into the area of "free play" too, of course, since little of Shirley's life may be conducted according to her own initiative or taste. Another visitor reports: "Mrs. H. remarked to me with some despair after she had fruitlessly tried to get Shirley to arrange the blankets on her doll in correct order (sheet, blanket, quilt, and spread), 'How old do they have to be before they learn to do things *right*?' " The proprieties which Mrs. Harper attempts to din into the child vary from good manners at the table, including saying grace, to a subservient respect for her elders; this old-fashioned, rigorous philosophy of the docile child who is to be seen but not heard conflicts continually, of course, with the rapt adulation of the parents. Their approval is intense, their punishment half-hearted and full of sympathy for "the poor little thing."

The combination of indulgence and insistence on social graces leads to an extremely restricting form of protectiveness. Throughout infancy Shirley was kept in a condition of "surgical asepsis." When she was three, for example, she had a special doll to take to bed that she couldn't play with at any other time because it was kept laundered, fresh and supposedly germ free. Her social life is similarly kept free from possible taint. Very few outsiders are permitted more than the most casual relationship with Shirley, all being found "bad for her" in one way or another. The paternal grandfather has all but been forbidden the house, for instance, because he persisted in "spoiling" Shirley Ann (laughed when she sucked her thumb, kept her from a nap to entertain her, etc.); children are uniformly not good enough to play with her—they are dirty, infectious, bad-mannered or contaminating in some other way. A Country Day School was handpicked to exert the proper guidance on Shirley and to set a high moral tone. . . .

Naturally enough, Shirley has been thoroughly protected from information about sex. During Mrs. H.'s second pregnancy, Shirley was instructed to "pray to Jesus" every night for a baby brother or sister. Day-to-day routines are handled equally obliquely. The interviewer reports, when Shirley was three and a half: "Shirley is not accustomed to seeing her father completely undressed, perhaps never has. He usually bathes when she is asleep and if it is 'necessary' for him to take a bath while she is up, Mrs. H. usually entertains her some place else." All in all, Shirley's days are spent in cotton batting, a protective covering carefully kept in place by a mother vigorous and alert to shelter her child from the most ordinary of life's difficulties.

Though in reality Shirley is far from being a docile, conforming child, she stays well enough within the limits imposed by the parents to assure a safe margin of approval. Disciplinary crises are rare, but small mischievous types of disobedience are common enough to warrant continual suggestions and nagging. An interviewer summarizing a conversation with Mrs. Harper wrote: "The general impression of the home is that Shirley is the apple of the eye; she has a secure place, but is handled with old-fashioned strictness about routines and 'niceness,' is being brought up 'properly.' I felt that Shirley was on to this and could manage her parents skillfully, crying, loving, being cute, good, independent, etc., within the well-defined discipline limits, and that she is far more dominating and sure of herself, more indulged and self-centered than her parents suspect. I had the feeling that Shirley was well in command of the situation and was keeping her parents happy."

Emotional Detachment

A Philosophy of Child Rearing

We have seen that possessiveness is the natural impulsive response to being in love with someone, especially when the loved one is seen as incapable of good judgment and when we are judged by society upon how well the loved child conforms to social rules. Counteracting these possessive tendencies is the parent's conviction about the proper way to rear a child. A philosophy of child rearing, whether it is explicit or implicit, is certain on some occasions to run counter to these natural impulses. The person who feels that punishment is the only consequence that children understand will not like to punish a child who commits a crime through misunderstanding; yet his philosophy may command him to punish. The parent who believes that a child must make mistakes and suffer the natural consequences will find it difficult not to spare him the sorrow of error.

To carry out any philosophy requires self-control at times. In this sense any philosophy requires maturity of the parent. He looks forward to the consequences of his treatment upon the child's development or future happiness and is guided by those consequences rather than by his momentary feeling.

Such self-control is more easily maintained if the parent, while loving the child, can still maintain some emotional detachment. If he refrains from feeling personally involved in the child's behavior, if he does not personally feel extremely anxious when the child is taking some risk or mortified when the child does something wrong, it is easier for him to use his best judgment in deciding upon a wise course of behavior. He is at the same time better able to appraise realistically the child's actual ability to solve problems, to meet dangers, and to behave responsibly.

This dimension, ranging from emotional involvement to emotional detachment, is the second basic variable of parent behavior. The emotionally involved parent is very likely to be possessive. The emotionally detached parent is able to follow some philosophical convictions about parent behavior and child rearing. Just what convictions he follows are not predictable from either his warmth toward the child or the extent of his emotional detachment, although some philosophies are more difficult than others to follow consistently.

Respect for a Loved One

We have already seen that loving a person makes us want him to be happy. We are motivated to procure for him the things that we consider good for him. One interesting development with maturity is the way that we change our conception of what is "good" for the loved one. At first the child seems to procure for the loved one the things he himself wants—he assumes that other people want the same things he wants. The person who detests Limburger cheese may find it impossible to believe that somebody else likes it. "You can't like that old smelly stuff," he may say.

At a later maturity level, we may not assume that other people's wishes are the same as our own, but we may feel that we know better than the loved one what is good for him. Underlying such an assumption is the belief that the other person is incapable of good judgment. If we believe he will be sorry about his choice, we may be tempted, through our love for him, to provide him with what we think will make him happy rather than what he wants at the moment.

When we accept his motives as valid we show that we "respect" him; that we grant him his freedom of choice and limit our control to attempts to point out to him the reasons we fear his wishes are unwise. We try to provide him with true information and try to clarify his cognitive map, but we let him make his own decisions. It is this final release, implying as it does the acceptance of the loved person as capable and mature, which is difficult for parents, especially for possessive ones.

Respect for the validity of the wishes of other people need not imply that we do not care what happens to them. If we love someone, we sorrow at his unhappiness, whether or not it was his own fault and whether or not we foresaw the consequences of his judgment. There is emotional detachment, however, in our granting him the right to make mistakes. In our treatment of young children, we have good reason to doubt the validity of their wishes. The objective parent can, however, judge the risk involved in the child's making a mistake, and he can recognize areas in which to grant the child freedom. He can recognize the necessity for helping the child develop the willingness to take responsibility. In other words, the child must also accept his own wishes as valid; this is what is meant by accepting the responsibility for his own actions.

Scientific Democracy

This emotional detachment may be so extreme that the parent is not concerned with how the child's mistakes may affect his happiness. Such parents are warm in the sense that they do not try to avoid the demands of child care or begrudge the child the time required to explain things to him or to counsel him, but they may be so concerned to follow the tenets of their philosophy that they lose sight of the consequences on the child.

Those parents who slavishly follow an ideology and are completely guided by the logical deductions to be made from its cognitively clear principles should be called ideological democratic parents. They accept the principles of democracy—self-determination of action, rational discussion of reasons for behavior, and noncoercion of other people except through such discussion. These intellectualizing democratic parents apply the principles with almost no attempt to see whether such practices make sense in a concrete situation.

In order to behave this way, it is necessary at times to run counter to almost all the natural impulsive tendencies that arise from one's affection for the child. It seems probable, therefore, that such parents are afraid to trust their feelings and impulses or that they really do not at all like the child as a person. The results are likely to be the same in either case. This sort of blind adherence to a few principles that cannot be considered to offer a complete guide to social behavior has unfortunately convinced many sensible people that democratic parent behavior and progressive education are idealistic and impractical. The following case is not at the extreme but illustrates many of the points mentioned above. Figure 20.4 shows the parent-behavior profile for the home (Baldwin, Kalhorn, and Breese, 1945).

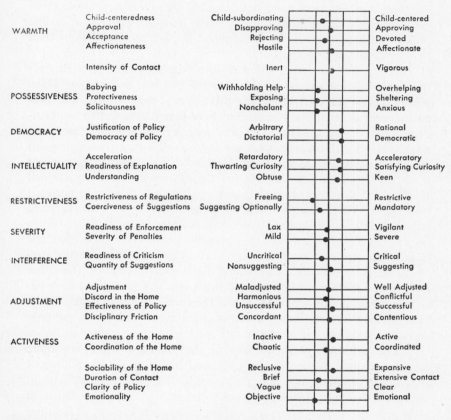

Fig. 20.4   Scientific democracy in the home. (After A. L. Baldwin, J. Kalhorn, and F. H. Breese, *Psych. Monogr.*, 58:268, 1945)

Dale Jameson: Scientific Democracy

The close relationship between democracy in the home and the intellectuality of the parents appears in a chemically pure form in the Jameson home. . . . The parents, both graduates of the department of education of a large state university, with training in modern theories of child care, are liberal in their social philosophy and consider it a duty to themselves, to their children, and to society to express their democratic philosophy in the home. Coldly and scientifically, although with unusual insight and intelligence, they have applied the theories of democratic management to the problem of raising Dale. Mrs. Jameson, particularly, in her effort to make each decision the "correct" one has suppressed her natural feelings and spontaneity in dealing with the children. She seldom acts impulsively but instead checks her own policy against the dictates of "the book" before venturing to act. Far brighter, however, and more realistic than the average young mother who relies on scientific testimony, Mrs. J. does maintain a flexible policy and is guided less by specific text-book recommendations than by a broad set of principles.

The particular constellation of forces in Mrs. J.'s personality almost require that she adopt this scientific method of handling Dale. Frustrated in her own desire for prominence, achievement and personal popularity, she simulates the hard-boiled intellectual sophisticate. This pose on the one hand protects her from becoming emotionally involved with other people, and on the other hides her feelings of inferiority. When Dale was born, Mrs. J. felt that she had been given a second opportunity to achieve her desired goals. She is determined that Dale shall have the assets which she feels are lacking in her own personality. The consequence of such an identification with the child would ordinarily be extreme emotionality and overindulgence. But in the case of Mrs. Jameson this is impossible for three reasons: First, she is unwilling to let herself become so emotionally involved with anybody; second, such behavior would be frowned upon by the other enlightened mothers of her set; and third, she recognizes that such behavior would almost certainly defeat the ends she has in mind. In the light of these factors, her attitude of scientific objectivity is the only workable solution.

The workings of democracy in the Jameson home are quite cleverly adapted to the children's age and capacities. With children of preschool age, methods which are obviously democratic are difficult to apply. At this level democracy consists of giving the child a choice in all possible situations, allowing him the maximum amount of freedom which is compatible with his safety and the rights of the other members of the household, and more fundamentally, recognizing and respecting him as an individual even though he is inarticulate, immature, and irrational from the adult's point of view. In these respects, the Jameson home is thoroughly democratic. When he was five, Dale was voicing his opinion as to the menu, whether he should play indoors or out, stay at home or visit the neighbors, have a nap or stay up and play. Beyond the routine schedule, almost every decision during the day relating to immediate issues or plans for activities was child-determined.

Nor were Dale's choices subjected to subtle adult coercion. If Mrs. Jameson wished to influence or modify Dale's activity, she approached the matter directly and openly, rather than by manipulating Dale's decisions into parentally approved channels. If Dale's presence was felt to be an intrusion, for instance, he was not sent away on some conjured up errand which would keep him out of sight and busy for a while but was instead told frankly that this was an adult situation in which he would not be interested. This policy of directness was and is an expression of the Jameson's belief that Dale had a right to know when he was frustrated and why. The same techniques have been used as Dale has become older. In addition, the "family council" method (cf. L. Rampion case) has been adopted to handle Dale's school age adjustments in democratic fashion.

Just as characteristic of the Jameson home as its democracy has been the refusal to baby or protect Dale. Mrs. J., for instance, refrains from pampering the children even when they are ill and tries to make the period in bed as dull and boring as possible so that they will be motivated to get well. When at the age of three Dale retreated to the house scratched and bloody after an encounter with a cat, he met a cool and unsympathetic response from his mother. "You must have been teasing it," was all she would say.

Behind this aloofness there is probably more than a calculated objectivity. Mrs. Jameson seems psychologically incapable of expressing warmth and affection. Friendly physical contacts have always been predominantly of the rough-house, wrestling type rather than fondling or gentle cuddling. Companionability on an intellectual level, however, between Dale and his mother has never been lacking nor stilted. Mrs. J., can register genuine enthusiasm and interest in Dale's creative efforts and intellectual attainments. She is responsive and stimulating in these areas. It is only when warm, emotional affectionateness is demanded of her that she seems unable to respond; at such moments she is likely to become brusque, clipped in her speech, and inhibited.

To complete the picture of the intellectual *democratic* home, Mrs. Jameson is extremely acceleratory in her treatment of Dale. A policy of providing Dale with every opportunity for experimentation, exploration and drill in useful activities was instituted when he was a baby and has continued unabated. When D. was a small infant just starting to crawl, Mrs. J. would hide toys from him in unlikely places with the idea of training him in the coordination of eye and hand and improving his reasoning ability. When D. was two or three he was taught to use the dial telephone, to answer it, to give and receive messages. When books were read to him incongruities were pointed out and he was encouraged to comment and criticize. All questions were given grave consideration, answered in language which he could comprehend and the explanation reinforced until he had mastered the point. He was urged to ask about the meanings of words he heard in conversation or reading and to fit these words into his own vocabulary; language was considered a tool, and he was encouraged to make sharp and precise use of it. In addition to providing this facilitating environment, Mrs. Jameson has been very anxious for Dale not only to become competent but to excel other children in the neighborhood. Finding Dale very responsive to acceleratory measures, Mrs. Jameson has pushed him on to the straining point in her determination that Dale shall reach the heights which she herself has never been able to achieve. Not content with furnishing Dale an accurate speech pattern to copy, Mrs. Jameson demanded perfection. Dale pronounced his final consonants with a conclusive thud long before other children were out of baby talk. When Dale spontaneously became interested in reading and writing at the age of five, Mrs. Jameson was not content merely to foster the interest by encouragement but set standards of excellence beyond the abilities of the average second grader. Her intellectual ambitions for Dale are so great that the values of the family are centered on rational intelligent behavior. "It's bad and you shouldn't do it" has been entirely replaced by "only *stupid* people behave like that."

Dale is perhaps the most obviously precocious child in the study. The maturity of his speech, as evidenced in pronunciation, content, and manner of expression, has been so strikingly advanced as to focus considerable attention on him. The richness of his imagination and the originality of his play made him stand head and shoulders above other children in the nursery school, and in his grade school group. The tenacity and thoroughness with which he explores an interest is illustrated by these items; interested in baseball, he learned the batting averages of all the important players in the major leagues; caught in the fervor of war games, he can identify by number all the U.S. plane models.

Even more striking than his precocity, however, has been his violent, uninhibited aggressiveness toward society. Fearing neither man nor beast, he seeks no quarter and gives none. He will kick, bite, and scratch his teachers, his relatives, and even innocent bystanders with the same ferocity that most children reserve for playmates. His over-aggressiveness, particularly its unreasonableness—he is as likely to respond aggressively to a friendly overture as to a disciplinary attempt —seems to indicate a positive need to be defiant and to rebel. This need, born probably of his insecurity and lack of emotional warmth in his relations with his mother and fostered by the permissive atmosphere of the Jameson home, bids fair to lead Dale into seriously anti-social behavior. The prognosis has been much improved, however, since D's school entrance by the fact that he wants to be popular and is. Now that he is finding that his non-conformity seriously de-

tracts from his social acceptability he is beginning to modify his behavior toward a more realistic balance of conformity and freedom.

In contrast, there are parents who accept the general principles of
democratic procedures, but who do so with good judgment, modifying them

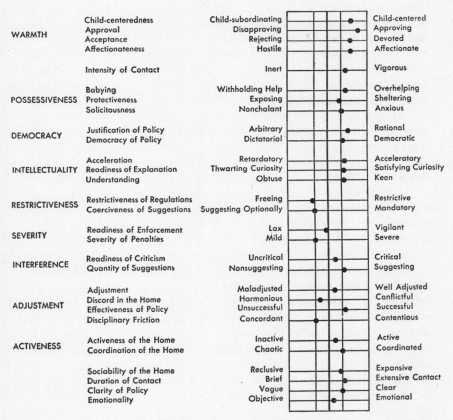

Fig. 20.5 Warm democracy in the home. (After A. L. Baldwin, J. Kalhorn,
and F. H. Breese, *Psych. Monogr., 58*:268, 1945)

to meet the circumstances of the specific case and having in mind constantly
what is the best thing for the child and for the family rather than what is the
"democratic" thing to do. This is illustrated by the Rampion home (Baldwin,
Kalhorn, and Breese, 1945) and by the parent behavior profile in Figure 20.5.

Leonard Rampion: Warm Democracy

The Rampion household represents a rather happy combination
of those factors judged by the authors to be productive of a "good

environment" for a child. The parents themselves are well-adjusted, vital, outgoing; they enjoy children as such, and their own children as individuals. They show a healthy balance between the type of psychological detachment which allows them to appraise the child objectively and a warm emotionality that permits them to exhibit their devotion without embarrassment or artificiality. The child occupies his proportionate place in the household as a full member of the family group, and is neither catered to nor ignored.

Mrs. Rampion herself is a healthy "farm-woman" type of person, sturdily built, stable, kindly and good humored. She was a professional woman before her marriage, and possesses to a remarkable degree qualities of tolerance and patience. With a keen sense of humor she embellishes the most mundane situations, making life interesting and flavorful for her family. She is alert and interested in community life, contributes generously of her time and services for a variety of groups and causes. Liberal in her political philosophy, she is a genuinely democratic person in the home and in the community.

The maturity Mrs. Rampion exhibits in her personal life and in her general attitudes is also displayed, naturally enough, in her behavior toward the children. Respecting them as individuals, she makes a conscious and conscientious effort to maintain an emotional distance, a detachment giving objectivity to her appraisal of them. An incident which reveals her imperturbability in the area of sex behavior is equally illustrative of her ability in general to see the children's behavior in perspective. "There is some possibility that Leonard masturbates, although Mrs. R. does not know definitely. He likes to stick out his penis and run around the house. Bobby is disgusted with the performance, Carol and Bud think it funny. Leonard also likes to rub himself on a toy horse which the children play on. 'He's very sexy,' Mrs. R. remarked. She had no emotional reaction to it, seemed casual and straightforward about the situation. It is definitely not a problem in her mind."

Her philosophy of non-intervention is further illustrated by the following incident: "The three children were playing well together. Once Carol got too near a ladder the boys were balancing. Mrs. R. called out the window for Leonard to watch her. She remarked that she hated to do it, and only resorted to warnings when she could foresee serious injury." If anything, the parents are too loath to intervene. In their determination to stay out of the children's disputes they sometimes allow an undue amount of social pressure to be exerted upon the unfortunate culprit who incurs the disapproval of his siblings.

The Rampions, more than any other family in the study, have explicit and formalized techniques for expressing their democratic philosophy of child care. Family council is traditional, with full and equal membership being accorded each child as soon as he can meet the requirement of repeating verbatim and explaining the motion before the group. The agenda may consist of matters ranging from the question of who shall wash and who shall wipe the dishes to the decision as to whether Mrs. R. should take a job offered her. The council convenes at the request of any member, and customarily handles the arbitration of all disputes. For example: "A situation has recently arisen in the Rampion family which is significant in that it shows the technique of settling difficulties among members of the family. While Bobby was combing his hair upstairs, Leonard 'dibbsed' on the wishbones from two chickens. Bobby was furious when he found what L. had done, said that it was unfair because one could never dibbs on more than his share, that he never had done it, etc. As a matter of fact, Bobby had done it more than any of the others. The two argued about it far into the night. Both Mr. and Mrs. R. kept out of the argument, hoping, however, that Leonard would stick to his guns and that Bobby's fallacy in argument would be brought out by him. The night of my visit Bob had called a family council to settle the question, said that he would abide by the council's decision. Mrs. R. said that she was going to bring up the fact that Bobby was the prize dibbser unless the other children mentioned it first."

In spite of the formality of democratic government and in spite of the emotional distance which the Rampions maintain, the home atmosphere is not bleak or forbidding. The warm tone so evident in the family's relationships characterizes their attitudes toward one another. Without a great deal of fondling or other overt symbols of affection the parents convey to the children their deep devotion.

It should be emphasized that the Rampion home is not "perfect" nor even optimum in its effect on the child—so far as we can, at present, evaluate the optimum. Mrs. Rampion faces the usual run of disciplinary crises, feeding problems and general reversals that come to most mothers, though she handles such situations with more than average patience and understanding. In this democratic atmosphere Leonard is, at present, making an excellent social adjustment, although his development in the past has illustrated some of the difficulties peculiar to such a closely knit and satisfying family structure. On the one hand his home background has been so encompassing in its satisfactions that Leonard found the outside world, by comparison, somewhat dull and uninteresting. His social adjustment during the preschool years was marked by shyness and withdrawal. At the same time, Leonard has suffered from his failure to meet the high standards of the Rampion household. He has been the most irresponsible and lazy of the children and, as a consequence, has been subjected to tremendous pressures, not from the parents as much as from his siblings. As a result, he has suffered from rather severe feelings of inferiority which have only been alleviated by his quite remarkable popularity in school. Under the flattering admiration of his classmates, his talents for leadership and organization have blossomed until, at present, he is making a good adjustment.

Analysis of the cases falling in the *democratic* group makes it increasingly evident that neither a democratic philosophy nor democratic techniques applied in the training of the child can provide an automatically optimum environment. Parental goals are as important as the techniques used in attaining those goals, and healthy personalities in the parent are a prerequisite for a healthy child. Adequately applied, these techniques *may* facilitate the production of a child who is an independent human being, secure in his relationships, able to appraise himself and his environment, and capable of self-direction and attainment. But these goals of the democratic method can be defeated by the parent who warps the child's personality in some other way, the parent whose own misapplied devotion and confined viewpoint restrict the child's growth and freedom or the parent who, by his own withdrawal and detachment, makes the child insecure and uncertain in his goals and relationships.

The Democratic Philosophy

These democratic homes probably constitute the largest group of parents in our society who are consistently following some philosophy. In our culture at the present time, the most prevalently taught philosophy of parent behavior is the democratic one. Self-demand schedule, lenient toilet training, giving children the reasons for policy, self-determination where feasible: these are the practices currently emphasized and encouraged by educators, psychologists, social workers, pediatricians, and other professional leaders.

Whether such an emphasis be good or bad, it is the current emphasis. As we shall see later, its validity is by no means established, but the profession, including the present author, is committed to the conviction that democracy is a sound policy for parents. It is to be expected, in the light of this analysis, that democracy is found largely in homes that are exposed to this philosophy. Thus, there is a clear relation between democracy in the home and parental education (see Fig. 20.6).

If a parent has any explicit philosophy, it is in our culture probably a democratic one. This is not to say that there are not other policies that are accepted by their adherents with equal sincerity, and that likewise demand emotional detachment. It is not possible to show that democratic parent behavior follows automatically from emotional maturity; such a statement is almost certainly untrue. The democratic philosophy must be deliberately chosen; the basis of such a choice must be found in the situation and values of the person making it.

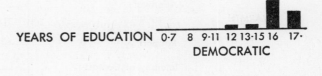

YEARS OF EDUCATION 0-7 8 9-11 12 13-15 16 17·
DEMOCRATIC

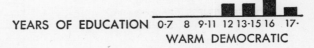

YEARS OF EDUCATION 0-7 8 9-11 12 13-15 16 17·
WARM DEMOCRATIC

Fig. 20.6 The educational level found in various types of homes. (After A. L. Baldwin, J. Kalhorn, and F. H. Breese, *Psych. Monogr.,* *58*:268, 1945)

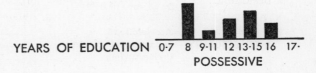

YEARS OF EDUCATION 0-7 8 9-11 12 13-15 16 17·
POSSESSIVE

YEARS OF EDUCATION 0-7 8 9-11 12 13-15 16 17·
PASSIVE-NEGLECTFUL

YEARS OF EDUCATION 0-7 8 9-11 12 13-15 16 17·
ACTIVELY HOSTILE

Although emotional maturity does not, ipso facto, demand democratic procedures on the part of the parent, it is true that the practices growing out of the democratic philosophy do necessitate a large measure of emotional detachment. If the parent has decided that a general atmosphere of self-determination is wholesome for the child, then he must let the child undergo some hazards. He cannot protect the child from every conceivable danger. The child must have an opportunity to make mistakes. The democratic parent may well try to prevent the child from continually undertaking too-difficult tasks, but he must at times be strong enough to withhold his help and see the child fail because of it. Most difficult of all, he must let the child present his side of controversies and the parent must be willing to be convinced if the child's position is sound.

He will behave this way some of the time, perhaps much of the time, but

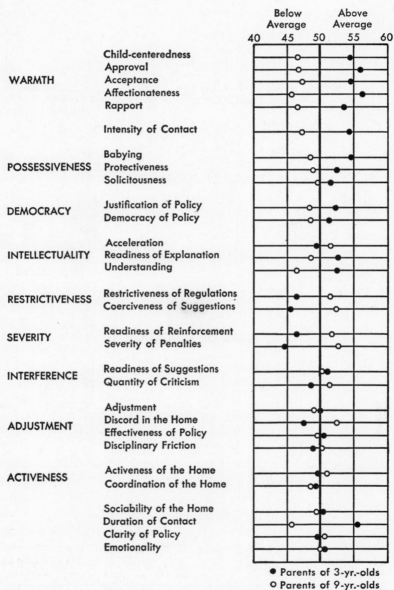

Fig. 20.7 Differences in parent behavior toward 3- and 9-year-old children. (After A. L. Baldwin, *J. Personality*, 15, 1946, 149-165)

there will always be lines beyond which he will not permit self-determination. Rules such as those about crossing streets will prevent the young child from getting into complicated situations that are potentially too dangerous to permit

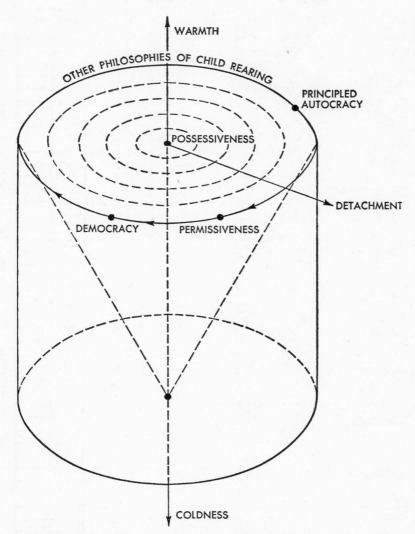

Fig. 20.8 The relationship among three aspects of parent behavior: (1) warmth, indicated by height; (2) detachment, indicated by distance from the vertical axis; and (3) philosophy of child rearing, indicated by the various points around the edge of the top of the cylinder. The cone within the cylinder indicates the region within which most parents fall. Most cold parents tend to follow similar child-rearing practices, whereas warmth may be expressed in a great variety of ways.

a mistake. Just where the lines are drawn is a matter of good judgment. The decision must take into account the maturity of the child, the complexity of the situation, its danger, and the psychological fortitude of the parents.

The democratic philosophy is easier to follow when the child is young than when he is older. The very young child cannot really participate in a democratic group. To allow a self-demand feeding schedule is one of the few democratic techniques of infancy. When the child is two or three, he can be coaxed and wheedled into conformity with the parents' wishes—some of the time. At that age he is not skillful in presenting his own view and he is suggestible. As he grows older, however, he becomes able to offer better and better arguments for his position. Here is the spot where democracy in the home begins to pinch. Another problem in letting older children guide their own behavior is the increased seriousness of the possible consequences of their making a mistake. A fall from a chair is usually a trivial episode, but a bicycle accident can easily be serious, and a car wreck on a social date can very possibly be fatal. Therefore, it is not surprising that the number of children having democratic parents declines between the ages of three and nine. Figure 20.7 shows the results of such a study (Baldwin, 1946).

Summary

In summary, these main dimensions of parent behavior might be conveniently diagrammed in a sort of three-dimensional figure, in which the main axis is warmth, as shown in Figure 20.8. The relative uniformity among cold parents is shown by the way the figure comes to a point at the low end of the warmth axis. The behavior that is close to the warmth axis represents the natural consequences of warmth, the impulsive tendencies that follow from loving the child. At the top end of the warmth axis, therefore, is possessiveness. The distance from the axis indicates the amount of detachment. All varieties of behavior are possible if the parent is relatively detached, depending upon what philosophy he has. These different philosophies—democratic, patriarchal, and others—are represented around the circumference of the circle.

21

Impact of the Home

STIMULATION OF MATURATION

INCULCATION OF SOCIAL NORMS

A STUDY OF THE HOME BACKGROUND
OF DELINQUENTS

CONSEQUENCES OF POSSESSIVENESS

NEED FOR LOVE

SUMMARY

THE CHAPTER ON PARENT BEHAVIOR, although something of a digression from
the main theme of these chapters, was a necessary one if we are to understand
the consequences of parent behavior upon the personality development of the
child. Having described the most important patterns of parent behavior, let us
now examine the effect of these various patterns of parental and home environment upon the child and his development.

Some of the consequences of the home environment may be ascribed to
the home's stimulating maturation. Some other consequences may be described
in terms of the needs whose development the home encourages. Others are
best discussed in terms of the child's understanding and knowledge of the
world in which he lives.

521

Stimulation of Maturation

One of the consequences of institutionalization of children, as reported by Spitz (see p. 410) and also by Goldfarb (see p. 412) is the general retardation of development. Thus, it would seem that one of the consequences of a home environment might be the stimulation of maturational processes. We have seen in the earlier discussion of stimulus-induced maturation that the stimulating effect of experiences is not easy to define; perhaps if we look at some studies of I.Q. change in different kinds of homes we can see more clearly what sort of environment is stimulating.

Relation of Parent Behavior to Child's I.Q.

There have been several studies of the intelligence of children from various kinds of homes. Champney (1940) studied the changes of intelligence-test scores of children between the ages of one and five. Those homes in which the I.Q. increased most during the period were compared to those in which the I.Q. did not increase. A similar study is reported by Baldwin, Kalhorn, and Breese (1945) who studied changes in I.Q. over a three-year period (see Figure 21.1). The results of the two studies lead to the same conclusions.

INCREASES IN I.Q.   Homes showing large gains in I.Q.—which, however, average only eight or ten points—are those marked by the following three characteristics: warmth, freedom of exploration, and acceleratory pressure from the parent. These findings might be anticipated from the general principle that maturation is stimulated when the child meets challenges that are not too severe.

If the parent allows the child considerable freedom, his wanderings inevitably put him in contact with challenging situations. He may become interested in climbing onto the sofa, in trying to get a marble out from behind the bookcase, in trying to fit a jar top onto a jar, in pouring water into a narrow-necked bottle. All such activity is challenging and encourages the development of abilities.

Warmth is, however, an important adjunct to freedom. Some of the things the child tries to do are too difficult for him. A completely frustrating task does not stimulate growth as much as one that the child can solve with effort. The child who is allowed complete freedom may become frightened when he finds himself at the top of the slide or when his curiosity leads him to poke his finger into a set mouse trap. The warm, loving parent protects his child against serious dangers, comforts him and helps re-establish his confidence after some fright, and helps him to solve problems that are too difficult for the child to conquer by himself.

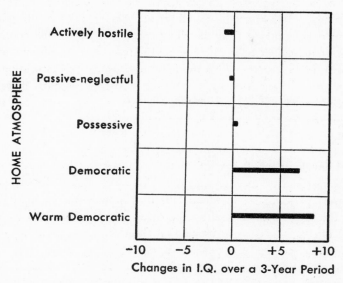

Fig. 21.1   Change of I.Q. in various home atmospheres. (After A. L. Baldwin, J. Kalhorn, and F. H. Breese, *Psych. Monogr.*, 58:268, 1945)

Acceleratory pressure, the third factor in increasing I.Q., is, of course, the deliberate attempt on the part of the parent to teach the child activities that are precocious. A deliberately acceleratory parent sets challenges that the child would not otherwise face until a later date.

I.Q. CHANGES IN REJECTING HOMES   In the light of these findings we can understand that the different patterns of parent behavior may result in more or less stimulation of maturation. The rejecting homes, for example, offers little acceleratory pressure. Rejecting parents do not, in general, try to provide their children with stimulating toys; they do not send them to nursery school; they do not put pressure on them to walk early. In some areas, especially those in which the child's learning a skill would relieve the mother of a burden, rejecting parents may try to accelerate development, but their acceleratory efforts are not extensive. Rejecting homes are neither especially free nor especially restricting. The parents make no undue effort to restrict the child, but neither do they show any special tolerance for the child's explorations. Finally, rejecting homes contain but little warmth. On the whole, therefore, rejecting homes do not stimulate maturation. In the Baldwin, Kalhorn, and Breese study the average I.Q. change in rejecting homes was slightly downward, a small insignificant decrease.

I.Q. CHANGES IN POSSESSIVE HOMES   Possessive homes show a different pattern. They are warm but frequently so protective that the child's explorations are seriously hampered. The parent is afraid the child will be hurt, or he is intolerant of the child's bumbling explorations. Possessive homes, because of their orientation toward the social norm, may be very acceleratory with regard to the obvious social signs of precocity such as walking, talking, toilet training, reading, manners, and the like. The total effect is not much different, as far as intellectual maturation is concerned, from the effect of rejection. In the study mentioned above (see Figure 21.1), children from possessive homes showed an insignificant increase in I.Q. over a three-year period.

I.Q. CHANGE IN DEMOCRATIC HOMES   The democratic home stimulates intellectual development. It is warm but also allows freedom. There is usually a considerable acceleratory tendency, which does not ordinarily take the form of overt pressure to be precocious but appears rather in the parent's providing the child with a wealth of special opportunities and experiences. Baldwin, Kalhorn, and Breese found that the average gain in I.Q. in democratic homes over a three-year period was eight points (see Figure 21.1). It is worth noting that the intelligence and educational level of the democratic parents are above average. The I.Q. of the children is above average and also increases more than the average.

Relation of Parent Behavior to Other Abilities

Findings from another study of child behavior in the free-play situation of a nursery school show similar consequences of the various home environments (Baldwin, 1948; Baldwin, 1949). Those aspects of nursery-school behavior that may be taken to reflect skills and abilities show the consequences of the neglect that is characteristic of the rejecting home, the stifling in the possessive home, and the freedom of the democratic home. Children from possessive homes show, on the average, less originality, planfulness, and curiosity than children from other sorts of homes. The children from possessive homes are especially marked by their low scores on large-muscle skill and their high scores on physical apprehensiveness. On these last two variables children from rejecting homes are not especially different from the average. In small-muscle skill, which it seems possessive parents would be likely to encourage and foster, the children from possessive homes are not sufficiently below the general average to be very noticeable.

Inculcation of Social Norms

One of the effects of the child's home environment is to stimulate or retard his maturation. A second set of effects is closely related to the parent's attempt to teach the child the social rules of the culture, to teach him to conform to them, and to inculcate the values that the parents believe are important.

Cognitive Clarity of Norms

The parental behavior that is intended to produce these effects differs widely from one home to another. One dimension of variation is related to the cognitive clarity of the rule that is finally taught to the child. We have already discussed the types of parental discipline that result in cognitive clearness or unclearness as an illustration of cognitive and noncognitive learning (see p. 441). Reviewing that section briefly, we recall that early training, arbitrary discipline, inconsistent discipline, or disciplinary techniques that depend on the production of shame, anxiety, or guilt all have the effect of making the child's conforming behavior cognitively unclear.

In still an earlier section dealing with the child's acceptance of the values of the people he admired, we saw that different sorts of values may be transmitted to the child, depending upon whether the child's understanding of his attitude toward the parent and his perception of the parent's values is cognitively clear or unclear (see p. 224). The acceptance of cognitively clear belief systems, such as social, political, or scientific beliefs, depend upon the child's accepting these beliefs because he accepts the parent's opinion as correct. This, in turn, depends upon his attitude toward the parent. Attitudes and values that are not clearly formulated may be transmitted through mere exposure and may be adopted by the child without any realization that they come from the parent and without his accepting the validity of the parental attitudes.

Child's Cognition of the Source of Rules

Still another dimension of parental discipline previously described is the location of the source of the rules that the child must obey (see p. 446). We saw that some parents discipline the child in such a way that they are the apparent source of the restrictions, benefits, and punishments that the child experiences. This is a disciplinary procedure employed by many autocratic parents and especially by possessive parents. It has the general effect of directing the child's gratitude and resentment toward the parent and focusing the child's attention upon the interpersonal consequences of his behavior—whether it angers or hurts the parent—rather than upon the total effect of his behavior on the external world. A parental policy of interpreting external reality to the child that puts the source of the rules in the external situation tends to have the opposite consequences.

Conformity vs. Spontaneity

Another important consequence of the parent's disciplinary policy is its effect upon the spontaneity of the child's behavior. This effect is, in general, correlated with the total amount of control exerted over the child, especially when he is young.

Some parents put good behavior and conformity so far ahead of everything else that they sacrifice everything for it. Other parents feel that although conformity is important, they must not sacrifice the child's spirit to achieve it. They want their children to be spontaneous, curious, and independent. They feel that the child who is too severely disciplined may lose his initiative and freedom.

Despite the fact that parents differ in their goals, there is not so much difference in objectives as there is in the behavior of their children. Even the most lenient permissive parent probably feels on occasion that his child is boisterous, unthinking, and disrespectful, that he does not show sufficient conformity. The lenient parent may feel that this stage must be endured and not suppressed, but he hopes that the behavior will be short lived and quickly modified. On the other hand, the parent of the child who becomes very upset when he gets a little dirty probably feels that the child ought not to be so concerned about a little bit of dirt, even though the parent himself thinks that cleanliness is next to godliness.

In terms of socialization, the most significant effect of control is to produce overt conformity. The parent who clamps down upon the child's misbehavior succeeds in stamping it out—at least during the time the parent is close by.

Actually severe control over the child has more widespread consequences than merely to enforce obedience to the parent. Baldwin (1948) has investigated the behavior of four-year-old children who come from homes in which there is severe control. He found that such children show less disobedience, aggression and nonconformity in nursery school. At the same time they show less curiosity, planfulness, sociability, and the like. It seems that, as far as the four-year-old is concerned, control suppresses many kinds of spontaneous behavior, the constructive as well as the antisocial.

A Study of the Home Background of Delinquents

One of the most obvious failures of socialization is the delinquent child. He may be conforming to some set of social rules—in areas where the delinquency rate is very high, he is probably conforming to the rules of his peer group—but in the areas of most serious delinquency not all children accept the values of the gang rather than the parents.

The following study by Sheldon and Eleanor Glueck of the factors underlying delinquency has been carefully controlled to study the factors in delinquency when the general social economic conditions are held constant. Because it is already well established that juvenile delinquents frequently come from lower economic levels and from the slum population, the authors made no attempt in this study to verify that fact.

Procedure of Study

Sheldon and Eleanor Glueck (1950) collected records of 500 persistently delinquent boys and matched each delinquent boy with a nondelinquent boy who was approximately the same age, who had the same general intelligence level, who came from the same sort of underprivileged neighborhood, and who had the same racial and national background. Since the importance of the economic factors is well established, the Gluecks concentrated their efforts on studying the factors which make some boys who live in slum areas susceptible to the dangers of such neighborhoods whereas others remain immune. In other words, they compared boys who were equally exposed to poverty, to older delinquents, and to other such influences. They sought to determine what made some boys become delinquent under these circumstances whereas others do not.

Each boy in the group of 500 pairs was studied exhaustively. His grandparents were investigated; his immediate family was observed, studied, and interviewed; his school record was carefully sifted. The boy himself was given psychological tests, medical examinations, and a psychiatric interview; a careful appraisal of his body build was included. More than 400 different variables were used to describe each boy.

General Personality Factors

Because the central purpose of this chapter is to discuss the effect of early childhood experiences upon later personality development, the findings on the home background and early childhood of delinquent boys will be presented in more detail than the other aspects of the personality of delinquents. Some description of the general personality factors is, however, important. The following summary statements concerning the personality of delinquents are selected and quoted from the authors' report (Gleuck and Gleuck, 1952).

> . . . a significantly higher proportion of the delinquents than of the nondelinquents are characterized by feelings of not being recognized or appreciated and by feelings of resentment. However the delinquents as a group have an appreciably lower incidence of certain handicapping emotional attitudes—feelings of anxiety or insecurity, helplessness and powerlessness, fear of failure and defeat.

> . . .

> As a group the delinquents are markedly less cooperative in their relations to those with whom they are closely associated; a substantially greater proportion of them have conscious or unconscious hostile impulses; they are more suspicious of the motives of others; they are more destructive; and more of the delinquents than of the nondelinquents are armed with an exaggeratedly defensive attitude toward life.

> . . .

> In much greater proportion than their nondelinquent counterparts, they are defiant and ambivalent toward, and/or less submissive to, authority. . . . They are definitely more impulsive and less self controlled.

The research also showed some differences in the pattern of intellectual abilities, although the cases had been matched on the general level of the I.Q. It was also found that the delinquents were more likely to have a mesomorphic body build, whereas the nondelinquents were more likely to have an ectomorphic body build. Mesomorphy, a term used by Sheldon (Sheldon, Stevens, and Tucker, 1940) in the description of body build, indicates a solid muscular build. Ectomorphy indicates a lankier, more fragile body build.

Parent-Child Relations

When the home environments and early histories of these two groups of boys are compared, striking differences are found in the stability of early home life, the warmth of interpersonal relations within the family, the degree of supervision and control of the child's behavior, and the rationality of disciplinary methods. The nondelinquent boys are found to come from homes more consistently characterized by these variables than are those of the delinquent boys.

Tables 14, 15, and 16 summarize the results. In each table the tabled

TABLE 14
AFFECTIONATENESS IN THE HOMES OF DELINQUENT AND NONDELINQUENT BOYS*

Parent Toward Child

	Delinquent		Nondelinquent	
	Mother	*Father*	*Mother*	*Father*
Overprotective	24.4%	†	15.2%	†
Warm but not over-protective	47.7%	40.2% †	80.4%	80.7% †
Indifferent	21.2%	42.0%	3.4%	16.0%
Hostile, rejective	6.7%	16.9%	1.0%	3.3%

Child Toward Parent

	Delinquent		Nondelinquent	
	Mother	*Father*	*Mother*	*Father*
Attached	64.9%	32.5%	89.8%	65.1%
Indifferent	4.6%	16.5%	.2%	5.6%
Hostile	2.2%	11.8%	.6%	2.8%
Noncommittal‡	28.3%	39.2%	9.4%	26.5%

value is the percentage of the 500 boys in the group who came from homes characterized by the various listed descriptions. The boy's relationships with his mother and with his father are computed separately.

Interpretation of Findings

This retrospective history of delinquent boys avoids some of the pitfalls that endanger the interpretations of such studies, and the authors of the research are very careful not to claim any oversimplified explanation of delinquency. They feel, however, that their research has supported some of the current theories of the consequences of parental rejection, especially when it

* Adapted from Tables XI, 13, 14, 15, 17, S. Glueck and E. Glueck, *Unravelling Juvenile Delinquency,* The Commonwealth Fund, New York, 1950.

† Only a few cases of overprotection were found for the fathers. They are included in the figure for warmth in the report of the study.

‡ The boy in the interview was unable or unwilling to express any feeling toward his parents.

is combined with a generally lax supervision and inconsistently severe punishment for some offenses.

At the same time, the research points to the existence of some factors in the personality of the boy which predispose him to become delinquent if other factors appear in the proper constellation. These factors might be assets to the

TABLE 15
DEGREE OF CONTROL IN THE HOMES OF DELINQUENT AND NONDELINQUENT BOYS†

| | Delinquent | | Nondelinquent | |
	Mother	Father	Mother	Father
Lax	56.8%	26.6%	11.7%	17.9%
Overstrict	4.4%	26.1%	1.6%	8.7%
Erratic	34.6%	41.6%	21.1%	17.9%
Firm but kindly	4.2%	5.7%	65.6%	55.5%

TABLE 16
METHODS OF CONTROL IN THE HOMES OF DELINQUENT AND NONDELINQUENT BOYS*

| | Delinquent | | Nondelinquent | |
	Mother	Father	Mother	Father
Physical punishment	55.6%	67.8%	34.6%	34.7%
Deprivation of privileges	46.5%	24.9%	45.2%	26.2%
Threatening or scolding	46.9%	32.2%	37.0%	31.5%
Reasoning	16.4%	11.3%	28.2%	24.4%
Appeal to pride	9.7%	3.7%	9.4%	6.0%
Discipline left to the other parent	3.9%	8.8%	1.8%	12.1%

boy under some conditions. Personality factors in some of the nondelinquents point to the possibility that children may fail to be delinquent because of anxiety and fear. This same fearfulness might be expected to hamper other activities demanding courage, initiative, and willingness to take risks. In other words, some children fail to become delinquent not because they have accepted the values of our society but because they are afraid of punishment. Contrariwise, delinquents may be brave, at least in certain situations; it is not pure myth that some delinquents become war heroes.

* Adapted from Table XI, 22, S. Glueck and E. Glueck, *Unravelling Juvenile Delinquency,* The Commonwealth Fund, New York, 1950.

† Adapted from Table XI, 23, S. Glueck and E. Glueck, *Unravelling Juvenile Delinquency,* The Commonwealth Fund, New York, 1950.

Consequences of Possessiveness

The antisocial behavior of the delinquent can be seen to be correlated with several signs of rejection in the home: severe punishment, lack of supervision, etc. A different sort of antisocial behavior has been found by Levy (1943) to appear in children who are overprotected. Levy's term *overprotection* certainly includes the pattern we have called possessive in Chapter 19. He finds a sizable proportion of possessive mothers so indulgent that their children are the typical spoiled children. Another large minority are very submissive and obedient at home.

Levy found disobedience, tantrums, excessive demands on other people, and domineeringness to be important features in the behavior of the over-indulged children. The behavior pattern of the dominated and overprotected was just the opposite: obedience to authority, submissiveness in school, timidity and withdrawal among peers. In many cases there was a focus upon intellectual interests; school work was generally satisfactory, and an intense interest in reading was not uncommon. Anxious and fearful children seem to be one predominant product of possessive homes. There are several reasons for this. One important reason is that the possessive parents are themselves anxious. As a consequence of his ego involvement in the child, the parent's control is likely to take the form of warning against danger coupled with statements that he is worried, "Don't climb on the banister. You might fall and break your leg. It worries me to see you take such risks." If we recall the description of Mrs. Harper (see p. 504), we can see that much of her efforts were directed toward protecting the child from danger.

The consequence is that the child does perceive the outside world to be full of risk and danger. Not only is the child from the possessive home made anxious about the external world, but he is also subjected to the parent's visible suffering and thus is prone to feel guilt-stricken about his misdemeanors.

There is considerable empirical evidence for the statement that possessiveness in the home environment of a child tends to make him fearful and apprehensive. Baldwin (1949) found that physical apprehensiveness was much greater in children from possessive homes than from either democratic or cold rejecting homes. Other signs of anxiety and fearfulness may be found in the lack of originality, creativity, and curiosity found by Baldwin, Kalhorn, and Breese (1945) in children from possessive homes. This empirical evidence confirms an opinion frequently voiced by clinicians about the consequences of overprotection.

Relation of Anxiety to Hostility

Among clinical observers of children there is a widely held opinion that hostility and anxiety go together. Children who are hostile tend also to be anxious—perhaps, as some people believe, because they fear retaliation or perhaps for some other reason. The empirical evidence for this hypothesis is, however, difficult to find. Although we have all on occasion seen people become very anxious after they have gone too far in their hostility, it is not usual to see hostility and fearfulness appear overtly together.

The bullying child illustrates the way in which anxiety and hostility may be joined. He is overtly blustering and shows clear hostility, but he may, if resolutely resisted, prove to be bluffing. He is really easily frightened, and the hostility is only a defense.

If a child displays this same mechanism but carries his hostility far enough that he does not back down in the face of a fight, his hostility may provoke fear, which is a dangerous need. The defense against this is hostility, which in turn makes the child more fearful of the consequences of his hostility and so on around and around the vicious circle. In such a case the fearfulness would not be at all apparent. Frequently the anxiety that is said to be linked with hostility is not apparent. For this reason it is difficult to establish empirically whether or not such a pattern of defenses is a common one. Sometimes we too easily assume that because a person is unnecessarily hostile he must be anxious underneath.

Anxiety and Lack of Limits

Another hypothesis frequently put forth by observers of child behavior is that anxiety may stem from too much freedom (Jersild, 1954). According to this line of reasoning, children fear the consequences of their own impulsiveness. They may recognize that under the provocation of a strongly motivating situation, they will be unable to control themselves.

We can see illustrations of this pattern in everyday life. When children are left on their honor, they sometimes show how anxious they are about their self-control by the way they resolve to live up to their agreement. When the parent returns they are very proud of their success yet very relieved that the ordeal is over. It seems, therefore, that children really like the parent to set limits even though they fight against them. They find it more comfortable to let the parent enforce the rules than to accept the responsibility for enforcing the rules themselves.

For this reason the "naughtiness" of children with a new person is frequently described as "testing the limits." If the adult sets no limits, the child, according to the hypothesis we are describing, becomes anxious at the consequences or the possible consequences of his behavior. He cannot help trying more and more extreme pranks until finally the adult does set a limit. Thus in some cases it seems as though too few restrictions upon the child make him anxious. In this pattern, as in the previous one, the anxiety is not usually obvious; therefore, it is difficult to obtain empirical evidence for it. In the light of the general theory we have been developing, anxiety about the lack of restrictions should be greatest if the parent punishes the child after his misdemeanors but does not establish clear rules to prevent them from occurring.

Need for Love

The final variety of need to be discussed here is the need for affection, attention, and love, displayed by a desperate clinging to adults, by trying to become teacher's pet, and by distress at being separated from mother. We have already seen one example of such behavior in the discussion of Goldfarb's experiments (see p. 412). The children raised in an institution showed in some cases excessive demands for affection. They wanted so strongly to be liked that they could not seem to become psychologically involved in other activities.

A craving for love is one of the two reactions that have frequently been described as resulting from rejection. A parent who treats his children coldly may evoke hostility from them, or rejection may produce exactly the opposite reaction, the overt seeking of affection. The possibility of exactly opposite responses to the same situation has, by now, become familiar to us. This pattern of evoking love by withholding it is at the root of a frequent feminine wile—playing hard to get. By appearing disinterested she can whet the affections of the man in whom she is interested, provided he is already motivated. The frustration of his affectionate motives motivates him more strongly than ever.

If, however, the young lady plays her disinterested role too convincingly or for a too prolonged period, she may find that her once interested young man is changed. He may be hostile to her, bored with her, or attracted in another direction. Children are usually caught more securely than even the most faithful lover. They may cling and openly beg for attention. Lafore (1945) found, for example, that parents who made the fewest affectionate

TABLE 17

SUMMARY OF INVESTIGATIONS OF IMPACT OF PARENT BEHAVIOR ON CHILD PERSONALITY

Type of Home	Type of Child Behavior Associated with It
Rejective	Submissive Aggressive* Adjustment difficulties Feelings of insecurity* Sadistic Nervous Shy, stubborn Noncompliant
Overprotective, babying	Infantile and withdrawing* Submissive* Feelings of insecurity* Aggressive Jealous Difficult adjustment* Nervous
Dominating parent	Dependable, shy, submissive, polite, self-conscious, uncooperative, tense, bold, quarrelsome, disinterested
Submissive parent, permissive	Aggressive*, careless*, disobedient*, independent*, self-confident*, forward in making friends*, noncompliant
Inharmonious	Aggressive* Neurotic Jealous* Delinquent* Uncooperative
Defective discipline	Poor adjustment* Aggressive Jealous Delinquent Neurotic
Harmonious, well-adjusted	Submissive Good adjustment

* These findings are reported by several investigators. (Adapted from M. J. Radke, *The Relation of Parental Authority to Children's Behavior and Attitudes,* University of Minnesota Press, 1946.)

TABLE 17—(*Continued*)

SUMMARY OF INVESTIGATIONS OF IMPACT OF PARENT BEHAVIOR
ON CHILD PERSONALITY

Type of Home	Type of Child Behavior Associated with It
Calm, happy, compatible	Cooperative*
	Superior adjustment
	Independent
Child accepted	Socially acceptable
	Faces future confidently
Logical scientific approach	Self-reliant
	Cooperative
	Responsible
Consistent strict discipline	Good adjustment
Child given responsibilities	Good adjustment
	Self-reliant
	Security feelings
Parents play with child	Security feelings
	Self-reliant

advances to their children received the largest number of such advances from them. Such children were found in this study to be insecure.

This suggests that although the dictatorial policies and frustrating actions of rejecting parents tend to produce hostility, their lack of affection for the child may provoke a craving for love. It seems likely that when the two types of parent behavior, hostility and rejection, appear together the hostility probably outweighs the craving for affection.

In less hostile homes, which are marked by coldness and lack of affection but not by active hostility, the child is quite likely to develop a craving for parental attention and affection. Institutions represent just such a pattern of deprivation of active affection without the hostility toward the child that is displayed in some rejecting homes.

We might also assume, from the discussion of maturation, that the motivation to be loved might have to be developed before the withholding of it would create an intense craving for love. It seems likely that if children were really ignored from birth, they might never show such a craving for affection. This hypothesis has not been tested.

We have discussed the home conditions that might lead to the development of three kinds of needs—hostility, fearfulness, and a craving for affection. These have illustrated some of the general principles of the formation of needs as well as indicated some of the concrete consequences of parent behavior.

Table 17 presents a summary of the findings of a large number of studies of the effect of different patterns of parent behavior upon child personality and behavior. The starred items are those findings confirmed by several investigators. The table is taken from Radke (1946), with some additions to bring it more nearly up to date.

Summary

We have in this chapter seen some of the various ways that home environment may affect child development. First, it may affect the maturation process, accelerating or decelerating it in special areas of skill. Maximal growth occurs in an environment that provides freedom, emotional support, and positive encouragement to be mature.

Secondly, the parent's disciplinary policy has various effects upon the child, some of which were discussed in earlier chapters. It may affect the child's cognitive clearness about social rules; it may affect the object of the child's feelings aroused by the rules; it may affect the type of attitudes, beliefs, and values that the child accepts from the parents. The amount of control over the child, especially during the preschool period, affects the spontaneity of the child. Children who are required to be obedient to rules are likely, during the preschool age, to be less spontaneous and creative than the child who is allowed more freedom, but the freedom does result in more antisocial behavior. Many of these principles are illustrated in the study of the home environments of delinquent boys reported by the Gluecks.

Then we discussed the factors in the home that have been found to be related to the anxiety and fearfulness of the child. Possessiveness is one pattern of parent behavior tending to produce fearfulness. We also discussed the hypothesis that anxiety and hostility go together, and that lack of clear limits may make the child anxious.

Finally, we discussed the craving for love, and found that it is most common in rejecting homes. We saw, however, that rejection may sometimes result in the opposite reaction—ignoring the rejecting parent.

22

Psychoanalytic Theory of
Personality Development

IN THE DISCUSSION of child development we have now reviewed some of the basic concepts of learning and maturation and have examined some of the empirical evidence relating the experiences of childhood to the personality of the child. We have discussed parent behavior and the relationship between home environment and the personality of the child.

Now we come to the task of integrating all these findings and theoretical ideas into some coherent point of view about the development of the personality. One serious attempt to provide a detailed theory of child development is represented by psychoanalytic theory. We have mentioned various aspects of psychoanalytic theory in earlier discussions on the concept of tension reduction (see p. 185) and the idea of repression (see p. 258). In many other places we have described concepts that were originally developed within psychoanalytic theory but that have been taken over by various other points of view. Identification, for example (see p. 569), is such a concept.

We have already seen, therefore, some of the basic ideas of psychoanalytic theory and examined them in the light of other theoretical ideas or in terms of empirical research findings. Here we shall examine in a systematic fashion the coherent theory of child development proposed by Freud. Then we shall examine one of the currently popular outgrowths and modifications of the theory. Finally, we shall try to integrate many of these concepts with the general theoretical position that has been developed throughout this book.

Freudian Theory

Sigmund Freud began his professional career as a medical doctor in Vienna. His research interests lay in physiology. Early in his career, however, he became interested in one type of psychiatric patient—the hysteric. Hysteria is relatively rare nowadays, but during the last century there were numerous patients who showed some pattern of hysterical symptoms, such as blindness, paralysis, lack of touch sensations in some part of the body, or other apparently bodily symptoms. The puzzling thing about these patients was that no organic defect could be found, and under the appropriate conditions they could be shown to be capable of responding in a way that would be impossible if the defect were real.

After Freud became interested in such patients his interest in psychiatry spread; he began to develop a theoretical point of view about psychiatric disorders and later about normal personality. He early came to the belief that the cause of these disorders can be traced back to the childhood of the patients. Consequently he was led to a theory of child development, which was, however, largely based upon his experience with maladjusted adults. He did analyze some children, and his followers have observed many children, either in the course of therapeutic treatment or for research purposes. Through these observations the foundations for the psychoanalytic theory of personality development have been strengthened.

In order to be clear about the psychoanalytic conceptualization of personality development, we must first outline some of the basic concepts of the theory, especially the theory of instincts and the functional division of the personality into the id, ego, and superego (Freud, 1949). Then we can survey the developmental process—psychosexual development, as it is called in the theory—and the mechanisms of fixation and regression that describe how the developmental process may go awry.

Instincts and Their Vicissitudes

The infant engages in many activities. As we saw in the description of infancy, he may be found sucking his thumb, sucking on the breast, looking at objects, listening, moving about, etc. According to psychoanalytic theory the cause of these activities is instinctual. These are the activities that are from the infant's point of view enjoyable in their own right. They are not means to anything, they are just fun to do.

LIBIDO   How are these activities energized, Freud asked himself. What makes them occur? His answer was the instinct, an energy source. This energy is the motor for all human behavior during infancy and later. The behavior of the young infant is the natural, spontaneous, uninhibited outlet for this instinctual energy. All later behavior patterns are believed to be outlets for this energy. It is diverted away from its natural outlet because of the fact that the impulsive behavior of infancy is unrealistic.

Wishes may not always be immediately satisfied. Delay of gratification may lead, in the long run, to greater gratification. Some types of gratification are prohibited by society; other types are strictly regulated. These pressures upon the child from the external world lead to the diversion of instinctual energy from its original primitive activity into other types of activity that are permitted by society or are realistically possible. Thus, for example, nursing is not permitted in adult life. The energy that activated the nursing during infancy must be redirected. Some of it presumably appears in the form of ordinary eating; some may appear as chewing on the end of a pencil, smoking cigarettes, chewing gum, and the like.

As the child grows up, his instinctual energy finds outlets in many different activities, directed toward a wide variety of objects. Some of the changes in outlet are the result of motivation, others the result of external pressure. The complexity of these diversions of energy, shifting of objects, and substitution of activities leads to the term *vicissitudes of the instincts*.

The activities that are the manifestations of these instincts are so numerous and varied in their nature that it seems as though the basic energy must be something very general and nonspecific. In Freudian theory this basic energy, called *libido,* is nonspecific in the sense that it can energize any sort of activity, but it is relatively specific in that its natural expression is sexual.

This libido is the energy source for all social behavior. At least, this was the position Freud held at one time. Later he conceived of a second energy source, the death instinct, which underlies destructive behavior, aggression, and hatred. Many psychoanalysts do not, however, accept the hypothesis of a death instinct but cling to the earlier formulation. In any case the libido is the important instinctual energy for the theory of child development.

LIBIDO AND SEXUALITY   One of the aspects of Freud's theory that aroused especial antagonism among his readers was the statement that the basic libidinal energy is sexual in nature. Sexuality or the libidinal instinct was, for Freud, not sexuality in the common meaning of the word. It involves the pleasure the child obtains in nursing, in the activities of his bowels, in looking, in curiosity and exhibitionism, as well as in sexual activity in the narrower sense.

It is quite true that much of the infant's activity is earthy and unsocialized. It would not be acceptable in polite society. At the time Freud formulated his theory, the existence of such uncivilized pleasures during childhood was not recognized by psychiatrists and psychologists, but by now the existence of childhood sexuality is widely acknowledged. It is commonly recognized that children will on occasion engage in bathroom talk, will openly peer at people who are undressed, will masturbate and engage in other sexual activity.

Even if this activity is recognized to exist, it is not obvious that all other social behavior stems from sexuality. Freud was led to such a belief by the fact that all the patients he treated showed sexual maladjustment. He was also impressed by the types of fantasies that patients said they experienced. The patient in psychoanalysis is instructed to say whatever occurs to him while he lies on the couch in the analyst's office. He is to inhibit no idea, regardless of how crazy, stupid, gross, crude, or illogical it seems. It is not easy to let one's ideas flow freely and without inhibition, but when the patient is able to do so, the free associations that he reports are often raw and crude. He may report the fantasy of commanding millions of men or being wildly acclaimed by row upon row of admirers kneeling at his feet—as in *The Secret Life of Walter Mitty*. Or the patient may report images of cannibalism, sex organs, crude sexual perversions, or gross sensual distortions, such as a vagina with teeth.

The frequent appearance of such images in the free association of patients led Freud to the belief that at the root of any behavior, if we trace it back far enough, we shall find sexuality. By no means all of the patient's conversation with the analyst concerns sexual behavior; much of it has to do with feelings of inadequacy or hostility or pride in everyday life. Sexual topics are, however, not uncommon.

The emphasis upon sexuality is one of the points upon which some non-Freudian psychoanalysts disagree with the more orthodox. Horney (1939) has pointed out that a personal maladjustment may inevitably have its effects upon the individual's sex life without necessarily being the result of a sexual maladjustment. Other analysts seemingly accept the sexual descriptions of behavior without being really concerned with the theoretical implications of the terminology. The aggressive woman who seems compelled to rob her men friends of their initiative and freedom of choice, and to mold them to suit herself is, for example, sometimes called a "castrating woman." This is not a bad metaphorical description; she is trying to take away the traits and attitudes that proverbially belong to men in our culture. Some psychoanalysts seem satisfied to use the term castration in this metaphorical sense. Freud used the term as more than a metaphor. He meant that the woman unconsciously wants to castrate men, to take away their male sex organs.

It is difficult to evaluate the validity of this belief in the sexual root of all activity without witnessing the behavior of patients as the analyst does. Many psychoanalysts argue that the evidence they see would convince any unbiased person if he could actually witness it. This may be true, but it is not impossible that some of the interpretations propounded by analysts have been guided more by the theory they hold than by the evidence they see.

DEFENSE MECHANISMS   Turning now from our examination of the nature of libidinal energy, we can take a look at the mechanisms by which this energy is diverted from its original aim to other aims. These are the various defense mechanisms. We have already discussed several of them—repression, reaction formation, and substitution (called displacement in Freudian theory). Under the pressure of social standards or external reality, the libidinal energy may be bottled up and allowed no expression. This is repression. Only a portion of the energy can be so handled; repression is never entirely successful. The energy may be turned into the directly opposite aim—love for hate, celibacy for sensuality, altruism for selfishness. This is reaction formation as it is conceived in Freudian theory. Or the energy may be diverted from one aim to another which is similar to it but less unacceptable to society. This is displacement, or substitution. One such mechanism may be piled on top of another; the energy may be displaced, then repressed, then break out in a substitute activity that is not socially and personally acceptable. There may then be a reaction formation, transforming that substitute activity into its opposite.

Neurotic and psychotic symptoms are the results of such complicated defenses, and defenses against defenses. The symptom is the final outlet of the libidinal energy, but usually it is a very inadequate outlet, offering little satisfaction. Thus the neurotic does not really gain genuine satisfaction from his symptoms because so much of the energy is repressed and has no real outlet. At the same time the neurotic's outlets are in some way tied so closely to the original aim that they may themselves be socially unacceptable. Yet the neurotic seemingly cannot find any outlet that is genuinely satisfying yet still socially productive and useful.

SUBLIMATION   The difference between neurotic symptoms .and the behavior of well-adjusted individuals is expressed in terms of Freudian theory by saying that the normal person has *sublimated* his libidinal instincts. *Sublimation* is in some ways a defense mechanism like substitution or reaction formation. The man who makes a profession of tearing down buildings may be sublimating his hostility. The movie star may be sublimating exhibitionism —which is basically sexual exhibitionism.

Sublimation is different from substitution, however, in that such activity is socially valued and it is "desexualized." Just how this desexualization can happen is not at all clear, but it is the intent of the theory to point out the fact that a sublimated activity is not a second choice. It is not an activity that is the best substitute the individual can find for the sexual activity he craves. Instead, if there is real sublimation, the activity becomes a genuine goal in its own right; it is truly satisfying not as a substitute but for itself. Yet at the same time it is an outlet for the libidinal energy. These two properties seem logically contradictory; that is what makes the theory unclear. Yet the phenomenon to which the Freudian theory points is very significant. There is something genuine about a sublimation that is not true of a substitution. We shall return to this point later with an alternative explanation for the difference.

To summarize, the basic instinctual energy, according to Freudian theory, is the libido. This is sexuality, although broader in meaning than in the usual usage of the term. The behavior of the individual serves as an outlet for this libidinal energy. The original aim of the instinct may be lost and the manifest behavior be the result of the various defense mechanisms, of which repression, reaction formation, and displacement are only a few. If the new aim becomes genuine and truly satisfying and at the same time socially valued, it is a sublimation.

Ego, Id, and Superego

The mechanisms that accomplish these defenses, the structure within which this libidinal energy operates, is sometimes described as the topography of the personality. In this mechanism there are three systems: the *id,* the *ego,* and the *superego.*

THE ID   The id is conceptualized as the source of the instinctual energies. Sometimes it is personified as a "little man" who wants to do the things that would directly and immediately gratify the instincts. Such behavior would serve as a full direct outlet for the instinctual energy. The metaphor of the "little man" suggests itself because of the diversity of outlets that the energy seeks. To take various pathways to a goal resembles the striving of a person to do what he wants in the face of numerous obstacles, giving up one path but seeking another, sometimes being satisfied with less than complete gratification.

Another phenomenon that suggests the idea of the "little man" is the commonly experienced feeling when we struggle against our own impulses. The child does not want to go to bed, but once he is mature enough he knows he ought to and he takes himself to bed against his own desires. Or if the impulse wins out, he stays up against his own best judgment. This inner struggle, which is sometimes clearly conscious, resembles the struggle of two different people. Freud conceived that all behavior represents such a struggle, except that in most cases the whole conflict is unconscious. We would be so aghast, argued Freud, at the grossness of the impulses we struggle against that we cannot bear to know that we even have such impulses. Therefore, the entire conflict, the impulse and the counter-reaction, is repressed and made unconscious.

Freud did not, of course, really mean that little men inhabit our personalities but only that the systems within the personality are distinct from each other and that each may have wishes that it tries to realize. It is difficult to convey the kind of conflict that Freud believed to exist among these systems of the personality without personifying them. We shall, therefore, refer to them as if they were people, remembering that the description is metaphorical.

The id is impulsive. It is the source of the activities that gratify instinctual urges. It changes, as we shall see, as the child matures, but it is a primitive, unthinking, irrational, source of behavior whose aim is to gratify the instincts directly, fully, and openly. It is almost wholly unconscious.

THE EGO The ego is the system that is formed as the child becomes aware of realistic factors. It involves the perception of the external world, and thus it recognizes the realistic barriers that prevent immediate impulse gratification. Freud speaks of the ego as being under pressure from the id to gratify the instinctual urges. Under this pressure the normal ego develops all of the characteristics that we have in this book called maturity. Maturity and ego-strength are different terms for describing similar characteristics of an individual.

According to Freudian theory, this maturity serves to provide the individual with the greatest possible ultimate instinctual gratification. The ego may delay gratification because immediate gratification would lead to even more frustration, whereas delayed gratification may be safe. The ego may choose between two activities in terms of which provides, ultimately, the most gratification. This choosing in terms of ultimate goals rather than immediate impulses has been described as value constancy. The purpose of all these delays, choices, and machinations is, however, maximal instinctual gratification. Freud was committed to the assumption that all of man's activities were ultimately selfish and egocentric, although he did in fact speak much of the ability of the mature, well-adjusted person to love warmly and tenderly rather than selfishly and ruthlessly. According to his theory, however, the warmth always has an ulterior purpose of instinctual gratification.

THE SUPEREGO Freudian theory postulates still another system within the personality. This is the set of social rules, mores, and values with which the individual identifies. He identifies with his parents and to some extent with other important people in his life, and therefore he accepts and takes in uncritically the rules in which they believe. These rules are not perceived as external factors governing behavior; therefore, they are not part of the ego system.

Such a social rule might be solely a matter of ego adjustment if the individual had no sympathy with it, did not accept it, but, nevertheless, had to adjust to it. An explorer may be very careful not to violate the taboos of the culture in which he temporarily lives. This is not because he accepts the taboo or believes in it, but merely because it is realistically unwise and impolitic to antagonize the members of the culture who do believe in the taboo.

The rules that one accepts, however, are in the superego. The superego is an internalized agency that punishes the individual by making him feel guilty when he violates its mores. It corresponds to the conscience in everyday language, except that many of the rules and conscience pangs are unconscious. They are unconscious because they prohibit behavior that the individual cannot conceive he has any impulse to do. We find it hard to believe that we have cannibalistic impulses which are prohibited by the superego. If we do have such an impulse, it is unconscious, and so is the rule against it.

The superego is, from the point of view of the ego, an external pressure whose demands must be integrated with the realities of the external world before satisfactory outlets for instinctual urges can be discovered. In the theory, therefore, the superego does not function like the ego, but is instead another external factor to which the ego must make an adjustment. Thus the ego is like a person who is urged on by the id to satisfy certain needs and who must do so as best he can in the face of the realistic barriers in the outside world and the prohibitions incorporated in the superego.

RECONCILIATION OF ID AND SUPEREGO DEMANDS The behavior of the individual is the ego's solution to this conflict. The problem-solving process is continually guided by anxiety, which is the sign, so to speak, that the behavior is unsatisfactory. If the individual is impelled toward behavior that would lead to danger or to violation of social rules, he feels anxious. The ego has solved its problem when the anxiety has disappeared.

Because he depends upon anxiety for a cue, the individual may be free from anxiety without necessarily achieving maximal realistic instinctual gratification. Neither does the individual need necessarily to be socially useful in order to be free from anxiety, although it is generally true that people who are not valued by society and who are not finding a real outlet for their instinctual urges are likely to be anxiety ridden.

Thus far we have seen that, in terms of Freudian theory, the behavior of the individual is directed toward the gratification of instinctual urges and that this process must take place through the mediation of the ego, which is faced with the restrictions of the real world and the imperatives of the superego. Now we shall see how this system changes as the child grows up.

Psychosexual Development

The libidinal drive, even when it is uninhibited and fully expressed, does not always manifest itself in the same way. According to psychoanalytic theory libido in the early infant has as its aim sucking and oral activity. Then during the second year the aim changes so that anal activities form the important symptoms of libidinal urges. Finally genital activity becomes the aim of the libido.

This change is a maturational one. According to Freud it unfolds without being affected seriously by environmental influences. It follows its own timetable. Psychosexual development is, for Freud, like biological growth. He even speculated a little about possible biochemical mechanisms underlying the libidinal changes that occur during psychosexual development.

Freud's assumption of a relatively unchangeable maturational psychosexual development is one that has been questioned by many other analysts. As an alternative hypothesis it has been suggested that the shift from the oral to anal stage comes when weaning is completed and toilet training begins. In other words, cultural or environmental factors may be at the root of the orderliness of psychosexual development. No orthodox analysts, however, question the existence of such an orderly development.

ORAL STAGE   The traditional name for the first stage of psychosexual development is the oral stage because during that time the infant's most important source of pleasure and gratification is stimulation of the oral areas—the mouth, lips, cheeks, and tongue. The young infant spends a large proportion of his waking life in oral activity. We have seen that sucking may become an activity that is engaged in for its own sake, as in thumbsucking or in mouthing other objects. When the infant explores an object, he almost always puts it in his mouth.

At first the important oral activity is sucking and is relatively passive. The child does not grab objects when he is very little; he may suck them avidly but only when they come into his mouth. For this reason the oral stage is divided into two parts, an early passive receptive oral period and a later active aggressive oral period in which biting is the main activity.

Does the sucking and other oral activity of the child bear any relationship to later personality? Psychoanalytic theories agree that it does. They are in general agreement about the personality characteristics to which orality is related, but they do not agree upon the mechanism by which these effects are produced.

The instinctual gratification of the early oral stage is passive, receptive, and centered at the mouth. The result of oral activity is incorporation of outer material into the body; gratification depends upon the beneficence of and gratuities from the external world. In psychoanalytic theory, all of these features of the activity of the infant during the early oral period are important. The difficulty of being passive and patient under some conditions and active and aggressive under other conditions is a universal problem. The problem of being dependent upon others is also universal. The well-adjusted adult must be willing to receive benefits from others without feeling that the world owes him a living.

The behavior of the child during the early oral period and the degree to which his instinctual urges are gratified during early infancy results, according to psychoanalytic theory, in one or another type of solution to these universal human problems involving passivity, receptivity, incorporation, and trust of other people. As evidence the analysts usually point to the clinical findings on people whose adult problems seem to stem from a maladjustment during this period. There is accessory evidence, however, in the metaphors of our culture. Passive receiving of stimuli is called "drinking in." Completely controlling the life of others, especially through possessive parental love, is called "swallowing those one loves." These figurative phrases, say the analysts, are not accidents. They reflect the unconscious oral element in the behavior which is being described.

The later oral period begins when the child acquires teeth; teething frequently leads to weaning because nursing becomes painful to the mother. Even if teething does not result in weaning it may provoke punishment from the nursing mother. According to the theory, weaning results in hostility toward the mother. The aim of the period is biting and active aggressive incorporation of other people. It is a period of being deprived by the environment. The child faces his first important human problem, acceptance of deprivation.

Here again the analysts view these concrete problems of infancy as representations or prototypes of the universal problems of human relationship. The way they are solved in childhood determines how corresponding problems will be solved in later life; and if the child cannot solve them, he may continue on through life trying fruitlessly to solve these universal problems in an unrealistic way.

The child may never learn to accept deprivation; he reacts to each new deprivation with a hostile predatory grabbing of the wanted object or with hostile attacks on the frustrator. The oral root of the behavior may be reflected in the use of "biting" sarcasm; the individual may have oral aggressive mannerisms, such as chewing his nails, biting through pipe stems, or grinding his teeth.

Another pattern that may develop from frustration of these oral drives is the identification of food with love. Some parents express their love for their children by stuffing them with food, and with presents and gifts. Love is something to be given. The result of this identification of food with love may be a person who reacts to frustration by going on an eating binge or by showering himself with gifts. The person feels that he deserves these gifts because he is frustrated. He views every frustration as something's being withheld, which can be offset by something's being given.

BASIC TRUST   The most fundamental personality characteristic that stems from the oral stage is, according to Erikson (1950), a basic trust or mistrust of the world. The adult who possesses this basic trust is one who operates on the tacit assumption that situations will never be more than can be managed, that they will be of a piece with the stable known world. Furthermore, he assumes that people will not be unreasonably hostile or undependable. In a sense he approaches each situation expecting good from it; its hostility, danger, or undependability has to be demonstrated. This is a stark contrast to the person who expects bad from every new situation and to whom the kindness and dependability of people must be demonstrated. Trust is basically a global undifferentiated attitude, a contentment and confidence which stems from a deep assumption that life is pleasant and will not become unmanageable.

We should be careful not to misunderstand the term *trust*. First, it does not imply unrealistic optimism, although it is not incompatible with an irrational trust. It is, rather, a readiness to be optimistic. Secondly, it is reflected as much or more in the willingness to enter into new situations, the acceptance of responsibility, and the collaboration with other people as it is in the explicit statement that "I trust people," or in a rose-colored optimism. A feeling that the world is undependable makes one unwilling to try the new, to take responsibility or to depend on others. Thirdly, even though trust presumably stems from the first year of life, the year-old child does not trust in the same way that an adult does. In the year-old child trust is more unrealistic, less differentiated, less cognitively clear, is less a trust of other people as differentiated from the impersonal world than it is a lack of withdrawal from the new. We might conceptualize the psychological world of the one-year-old as being either an unsafe place with certain islands of security, or on the other hand as being a safe place with certain delimited areas of danger. These two correspond to mistrust and trust.

Two kinds of experience presumably affect the trust of the individual. The first is the general atmosphere of contentment or of unhappiness that pervades the first year of life. A child who is constantly under tension is not able to establish the stable relationships necessary for trust. In order to be mistrustful he need not clearly believe the world cannot be trusted; a chronic state of tension and restlessness may merely prevent him from learning about the dependable things of the world.

The second sort of experience that might affect basic trust is the existence of challenges in the environment to direct his attention outward, to build up stable behavior patterns toward external stimulation, and to establish contact with the real world. Erikson argues that the experiences of eating and weaning are crucial in the development of trust.

ANAL STAGE   Following the period in which the instinctual gratifications are primarily centered in the oral region, Freud postulated that the anal regions next become libidinized—i.e., endowed with gratifying sensations. He argues that the act of defecating is pleasurable, that the distention produced by the presence of fecal matter in the colon may be pleasurable. During the anal stage this type of gratification is very important.

Whether this focus upon anal pleasures comes inevitably with a certain age or whether it is tied to the process of toilet training is a matter upon which psychoanalysts may disagree. They agree, however, that in our culture the anal stage does begin during the latter part of the second year and continues approximately to the age of three.

As in the oral stage, the activities of the anal period have many concrete features that represent certain types of universal problems. Toilet training emphasizes withholding of feces or urine until the proper time and place; then the proper behavior is to expel this material. The pressures may have various foci. The parent may emphasize punctuality—the child should defecate or urinate when put on the toilet seat. He may be put there at regular intervals and expected to perform each time. If he fails to have a bowel movement during one day, the worried mother may give him an enema to induce it.

Sometimes the enema is structured as a punishment, sometimes as a medicine. In other homes, the emphasis may be put upon cleanliness. The child should not soil or wet himself. Regularity in toilet habits in such a home means withholding until he gets to the toilet, but there may be little emphasis upon the positive act of defecating on schedule.

What universal problems are epitomized in the earthy tasks of toilet training? Cleanliness and neatness is one. Punctuality is another. More important, according to Freud, is the way that defecating is seen as giving something to the parent. The demands on the child make him see the feces as somehow valuable and defecating as the giving of a gift. Thus, if the child pictures the feces as valuable, withholding is a form of stinginess.

The child's treatment of feces suggests another kind of aggressiveness and hostility—namely, expelling, squashing, destroying. The toilet-training process, or some other factor during this period, produces hostility so regularly that it is not unusual to hear the anal stage called the anal-sadistic stage. One basis for the hostility is probably that the impositions of the parent during toilet training are structured so that the parent is the clear source of the imposition.

Erikson's (1950) formulation of the basic problem of the anal period is the development of autonomy. During this period the muscular development of the child has freed him from the physical necessity of being carried around. He is able to get around by himself. The control over the anal sphincter is another type of independent muscular activity. The anal period, therefore, epitomizes the achievement of autonomy or the failure to achieve it. There are two opposite social modalities represented in the acquiring of well-trained bowels, holding on and letting go. Erikson suggests that holding on can be destructive and cruel, or it can become a pattern of taking care of other people. He also suggests that letting go can turn into a letting loose of destructive forces or it can become a relaxed "to let it pass" and "to let be."

One consequence of the toilet-training conflict can be the "anal character" described by Freud. This type of person is marked by the triad of traits: stinginess, orderliness, and obstinacy. The fact that these traits do tend to appear together in the same person has been confirmed by a statistical analysis of personality traits (Sears, 1936). That the origin of such a syndrome lies in the anal period of development is believed by the psychoanalysts on the basis of their clinical experience.

EARLY GENITAL STAGE Following the period when anal sensations are the predominant source of pleasure and when holding in or letting go are the chief modes of action, the child enters the genital stage, in which the primary source of libidinal satisfaction is the genital region. The genital period, however, is a long and complicated one. It begins during the late nursery-school period but has a short life—at least in our culture. It ends temporarily about the beginning of school and reappears only with the onset of adolescence. The preschool genital period is called the early genital stage. Following this is the latency period during the elementary-school years. Adolescence ushers in the late genital stage.

The early genital stage is the period of the *Oedipus complex,* according to the psychoanalytic theory of psychosexual development. This pattern of emotional relations involves—at least for the boy—a love for his mother and feelings of rivalry with his father. Its name recalls Oedipus, who killed his father and married his mother. For the girl the developmental process is more complicated, but eventually comes to include rivalry with the mother for the love of the father.

The Oedipus pattern develops from the fact that during early childhood the mother is the central person in the life of the child. Upon her he showers his affection. Her absence is most disturbing to the young child; her return is most vociferously greeted. This relationship, like all of the young child's relationships with objects, is narrow and monopolistic. There are thus many occasions in which the child sees the father as intruding upon the mother-child relationship.

During the genital stage the child becomes interested in sex. He becomes interested in the difference between the sexes, he watches other people undressing. He wants to know how babies are born. These sexual interests certainly occur, although we may doubt whether they form the primary source of gratification for the child. He is also interested in marriage and he may say that he is going to marry his mother. He may say this whether he is a boy or girl. Later, when he has the social customs more clearly in mind, he may say he is going to marry the parent of the opposite sex.

All of this, according to Freudian theory, is merely the conscious outcropping of a much more intense and more obviously sexual set of unconscious feelings and fantasies. According to the theory, all children have some idea, often vague and distorted, of the nature of the sexual relationship between the parents. It is this pictured relationship with the parent of the opposite sex which the child comes to want. Such a goal is doomed to frustration by the rule against incest, by the power of the parental rival, and by the biological immaturity of the child.

In the child's unconscious these factors result in the fear of castration. The boy fears the father will castrate him; the girl, because she lacks a penis, fears she has been castrated or that she is defective.

This fear of castration is the force behind the repression of all these incestuous dreams which the child has during this period. Consequently the Oedipus complex dies away, leaving as sublimations of its urges the identification of the boy with his father or the girl with her mother. This is a reaction formation against the previous hostility toward the rival and is at the same time, according to Freudian theory, a taking over of the characteristics of the successful rival in order to become more loved by the parent of the opposite sex.

With this identification with the parent comes the development of the superego. The superego is conceptualized in psychoanalytic theory as the wants and values of the parent with whom the child identifies. The formation of the superego, depending upon the Oedipus complex, is the primary basis for the socialization of the child and his taking over the cultural values through identification with the parent.

This description of the complexities of the early genital period has been oversimplified. There is possible, within the framework of the Oedipus complex, rivalry for either parent and love for either parent by a child of either sex. To some extent all these possibilities are realized in any individual, although the dominant theme is the one described above.

These concrete problems of the preschool period obviously involve a number of universal problems that must be resolved. Jealousy and rivalry arise in many situations outside the purely sexual realm. Some individuals feel hurt or take it as an insult if any friend of theirs does not enter into an exclusive relationship. The problem of dealing with a more powerful person toward whom one is hostile must be faced on occasion by all of us.

Perhaps the most fundamental problem raised is that of initiative. Erikson sees this period as one in which the child for the first time chooses a goal. The earlier period is marked by a struggle for autonomy from the parent; this one deals with the consequences of a more positive choice of a love object.

The preschool child, in Erikson's words, is "on the make." If this be taken in a more general sense than the sexual one, it means attracting another person, gaining some control over him, taking the initiative in establishing a satisfying interpersonal relationship. To outgrow this egocentric type of relationship is to develop a respect for the other person and for oneself which is compatible with a relationship between equals.

One may gain possession of another by open conquest or aggressive action. This is the pattern which in our culture is masculine. The pattern of ensnaring or enticing others into one's power is usually meant when we say a girl is "on the make." When these are outgrown, the sublimation of the male pattern appears in the form of outgoing sociability, making the first move, going more than half way in establishing a social relationship. The sublimation of the feminine pattern is to be lovable and endearing. It is obvious that for good adjustment both men and women must possess both qualities to some degree.

LATENCY PERIOD   The period of latency following the resolution of the Oedipus problem is the last one we shall discuss, since we are concerned with the preadolescent development of the child. During this period, according to Freudian theory, the libidinal urges are repressed. The child is thus left free to develop his ego-strength in dealing with the external world.

This period, corresponding roughly to the school-age period, is the time when the child most eagerly investigates the real world, acquires learning, is intensely curious, uses new tools, acquires new skills. Many of these activities are viewed in Freudian theory, as sublimated desexualized forms of activities which once were tied to libidinal urges. Curiosity, for example, once was curiosity about sexuality, about parental sex relations, about the difference between boys and girls. Now it is desexualized, appearing as interest in how things work, what other cultures are like, what happened in the past. If the previous libidinal curiosity had not occurred, this sublimated curiosity would not have developed. If, on the other hand, the sexual curiosity had not been frustrated and punished, the interest would not have spread to nonsexual interests. Or, as a third possibility, if the sexual curiosity had been too harshly treated, curiosity as a whole might be repressed and the child might not have an interest in the mysteries of the real world because the uncovering of anything hidden would be anxiety provoking.

The realistic orientation of the school-age child is described by Erikson (1950) as the development of industry. The problem of the latency period is learning to become industrious and through industry to acquire competence. The failure to solve this problem—which is frequently the result of a previous failure to solve the earlier problems of development—leads to incompetence and inferiority.

Fixation and Regression

We have seen that Freudian theory pictures the development of the child as a series of stages during which one type of libidinal pleasure is uppermost, during which one social modality—incorporation, letting go, initiative, etc.—is predominant, and during which one sort of love object is likely to be prominent. Each of these stages presents some universal problem which the child must face. The way he solves it or his failure to solve it then affects his behavior whenever he meets that same universal problem in some other guise.

Two factors are prominently mentioned as reasons for the failure to solve the problems posed at any stage. One is a constitutional factor. One type of pleasure may for some biological reason be excessively attractive or unattractive, or the child may lack the ego-strength to solve a problem. A second factor is environmental. Through either excessive indulgence or undue harshness, a stage may be made too attractive to be given up or too difficult to bear. Thus, if toilet training is too severe, the child may return to the oral stage; or if anality is too generously indulged, the child may return to that stage in the face of mild frustration.

The failure to solve a problem posed by one of the stages of development may result in either of two consequences, *fixation* or *regression*. If the child remains at one developmental stage, continues to get pleasures from the activities of that stage, and employs the social modality of that stage, he is said to be *fixated* on it. His psychological development has not gone beyond that period of life. If, however, the child in the face of problems at one developmental level returns to a source of pleasure and social modalities that he had previously given up, then he is said to have *regressed* to the stage at which these pleasures were normal.

Rarely if ever is there a complete fixation or complete regression. Partial fixation and regression may be described in terms of the concepts of psychoanalytic theory. Part of the libido may find outlets in the immature activity of an early developmental stage, but the rest of it may find its outlet in more mature emotional activity. This mature behavior is not very satisfying because only a part of the individual's libidinal energy is utilized in this fashion. In other respects, perhaps only in fantasy, he functions at an emotionally immature level. A boy may, for example, never have solved his Oedipus complex. He may still unconsciously be in love with his mother. He can on the surface be tender to her, care for her, and express this love in socially acceptable ways. He may hide or repress the resentment he feels toward the father or toward other people who are important to his mother. In some sense he has gone beyond the early genital stage, but basically he has not done so. Some incident—such as the death of his father and remarriage of his mother, or her death, or his falling in love with a contemporary but feeling unfaithful to his mother—may break his fragile adjustment and lead to an overt neurosis.

This is the usual pattern of neurotic growth. The individual meets some problem of childhood that is never really solved. But he continues to make a superficial adjustment until later in life some period of stress or some incident precipitates a more open regression to the stage at which he had been partially fixated.

When such fixation or regression occurs, it does not mean that the individual acts just like a child of the appropriate age level. Regression to the anal stage does not make a person act like a two-year-old in all ways. It means that his behavior is focused upon the types of libidinal gratification of the two-year-old and that his social relations show the characteristics of letting go and withholding, the anal picture of hostility, and the other symptoms of disguised anal gratification.

Summary and Conclusions of Freudian Theory

We have seen how the Freudian theory of personality development is put together. Some of it has undoubtedly seemed bizarre and strange. Psychoanalysts say this is because we have repressed the memories and fantasies that would make us recognize the validity of these psychoanalytic propositions.

Nevertheless, psychoanalysis, because of its apparent strangeness, has been condemned by many people without any serious attempt to evaluate it or even to understand it. In the culture that saw its birth there were many blind spots. Childhood sexuality was almost unrecognized in medical fields. Certainly it is impossible to watch a child grow up without witnessing many incidents of sexual behavior. Another fact is that sexuality plays a role in almost all maladjusted behavior. The therapist does not have to probe very deeply or make many symbolic interpretations in order to find in his patients sexual deviation, guilt about sexuality, sexual incompetence, and lack of sexual satisfaction. The theory cannot be dismissed as ridiculous or profane, and fortunately it no longer commonly meets such a reception.

On the other hand, the fact that Freud pointed to real aspects of behavior that were commonly denied by his contemporaries does not imply that he arrived at the correct theory concerning them. Freud built a theory of human behavior on which the science of psychology has fed for fifty years. If his theory is evaluated in terms of its fruitfulness in stimulating research and new ideas and in modifying the thinking of an entire science, there is hardly a greater one. Nevertheless, it may be all of these things and still be inaccurate.

Two types of criticisms have been most frequently leveled against the theory: first, the emphasis upon sexuality; secondly, the ignoring of the cultural factors in personality development. That sexual factors appear frequently, perhaps universally, in child development and maladjustment cannot be denied. When such factors are found, Freudian theory makes them the root of the problem. The sexual aspect of behavior is accepted as undisguised, genuine motivation, and the nonsexual aspects are conceived to stem from the sexual. Repression is assumed to account for the failure of overt sexuality to appear as important as it really is. Although there is good evidence for repression, it does not support the theory that the sexual is primary. Neither does overt child behavior justify the emphasis on sexuality, although it does point to the existence of infantile sexuality. The findings within the analysis of patients form the main empirical support for the importance of sexuality in personality and these findings are themselves questioned by psychotherapists of other varieties. Because of these factors many psychologists and psychiatrists do not accept the hypothesis of the primacy of sexuality.

A second criticism of Freudian theory has been its failure to give sufficient importance to cultural factors. As the theory was first formulated, all such phenomena as the Oedipus complex, the anal stage, or the latency period were believed to be biologically inevitable. Our recently acquired greater knowledge of other cultures does not support these beliefs. In some cultures, in which the uncle plays the role of the disciplinarian, hostility is expressed against the uncle, despite the fact that in Freudian theory it is the sexual relation between the father and mother which is at the root of the hostility (Malinowski, 1927). In some cultures there seems to be no latency period (Mead, 1928). In cultures, in which toilet training occurs very late, the anal stage, if it exists, has very different characteristics from those in western culture.

Because of such criticisms as these, a neo-Freudian point of view has been developed by Horney and other psychoanalysts who accept a somewhat different picture of personality development.

The Theories of Karen Horney

Karen Horney (1937, 1939, 1945, 1950) sees child development as a maturational process leading to full realization of his capabilities. There is an actual force toward growth which, if not hampered or impaired, leads toward the continual unfolding of the individual's potentialities. This assumption is made also by other psychologists (Rogers, 1942; Goldstein, 1940). The fact that the child continues to develop under a large variety of circumstances suggests that we may do no better than to let the child develop unhampered. Only if we interfere with this maturational process are we likely to harm the child.

Basic Anxiety

According to Horney the interference that lies at the root of neurotic development is a lack of love. When the guardians of the child are so enveloped in their own strivings that they do not give the child their love and do not perceive him as an independent human being, they produce in him a profound insecurity. Their handling of the child may be authoritarian, overindulgent, possessive, or inconsistent, but its importance lies in whether it evokes *basic anxiety* in him. The child who feels alone and helpless in an unsafe, hostile environment suffers basic anxiety.

This anxiety puts the child under undue pressure to relieve it. Just how he must act to relieve it depends upon the specific pressures of the environment, as well as upon his temperament. His behavior, however, tends toward overemphasis upon one of the three modes of interpersonal relations described earlier (see p. 193).

Three Types of Social Action

Horney has developed the theory of the three types of social action: moving toward others, withdrawing from others, or acting against others. All of these types of action are appropriate in certain circumstances. In the normal personality all three appear. In the neurotic personality there is a distortion in favor of some one of these basic social modalities at the expense of the other two. So a child may, under pressure of his anxiety, try desperately to win the love of others—*i.e.,* to move toward other people. He cannot stand up for himself in the face of hostility because it makes him too anxious. He cannot withdraw to take counsel with himself; he needs love too badly. So he develops a lopsided behavior pattern that contains too much ingratiation and placation and too little autonomy. Other children under the same basic anxiety may develop other patterns if the specific circumstances differ slightly.

This solution never, according to Horney, provides any real solution. It leaves the individual lacking in self-confidence and security. His behavior is defensive. He continually runs into problems demanding other types of behavior of which he is incapable. He feels alone, weak, and inferior. Because of these feelings he urgently feels the need to be better than others. He forms an idealized picture of perfection that gradually takes over his behavior. Horney calls this self-idealization a comprehensive neurotic solution.

Self-idealization

Now the individual demands perfection from himself and at the same time demands from others the treatment that he would expect if he were his idealized image. He may be hurt if someone he met only once a year ago does not immediately recognize him when they meet a second time. This feeling of being hurt contains a tacit assumption that he is so important that everybody should remember him after one contact. On the other hand he is hurt and depressed by being thus forgotten. If he were as important as he assumes, he would not need to be remembered. His being hurt shows the weakness that underlies the behavior.

Depending upon the specific pattern of self-idealization that the individual displays, he may show any of a number of different neurotic trends, as Horney calls them. They are all marked by a driving ambition for external success, although it may not be reflected in realistic endeavor. A common trend is the need to triumph vindictively over others.

We are interested here in the developmental theory proposed by this variant of psychoanalytic theory rather than in the specific neurotic patterns. We see that Horney's language is quite different; some of the basic concepts are different; especially we notice the absence of a libido theory. In predicting the consequences of any one pattern of home environment, however, this theory does not differ so much from Freudian theory as its language suggests. It is a different theoretical formulation of the same facts of child development that Freudian theory explains. It emphasizes the same phenomena. Both theories, for example, would predict that too much harshness toward the child or too much indulgence tends to lead to a neurotic pattern of development. Both theories tend to express in conceptual terms the same intuitive understanding of personality development that an understanding therapist achieves through his years of experience with patients and their troubles.

Discussion and Critique of Psychoanalytic Theory

Constancy of Basic Needs

One of the fundamental assumptions of psychoanalytic theory is the constancy of basic needs. All behavior is an outlet of instinctive energy; most of the significant social behavior is an outlet for libidinal energy. Thus, the explanation of behavior in psychoanalytic theory consists largely in showing how it is an expression of libidinal energy. In contrast to this point of view, we have listed in Chapter 18 a number of ways that needs may change. The appearance of new needs and the disappearance of old needs is assumed to go on continually. This is certainly a basic theoretical difference between psychoanalytic theory and the conceptualization we have been developing.

In the face of a difference like this between two points of view, it is important, first of all, to discover why the theories make the assumptions they do. What facts led Freud to assume that adult behavior was motivated by the same needs that had existed since infancy? One fact was his finding a historical continuity from childhood behavior to adult behavior. He could trace back the steps in the process from miserliness in adulthood to retention of feces in childhood. A second fact was the detectable qualitative resemblance between the two sorts of behavior, the withholding aspect of each of them. A third consideration, in the opinion of this author, was a tacit assumption that the organism was somehow like a boiler under pressure, and that behavior uses up or releases the pressure. This analogy made it very easy to picture the process by which one outlet of energy, if it were blocked off, could result in the development of another outlet. In terms of releasing pressure, any two outlets of the same size are equivalent. Freud had plenty of evidence that superficially different behavior patterns could be related to each other. This hydraulic analogy provided a neat theory of the process. A fourth factor is, perhaps, that psychoanalysts have dealt largely with neurotic people for whom it can truly be said that their entire life is consumed in finding first one and then another adjustment to the same basic problem. The permanence of childhood needs is perhaps much clearer in neurotics than in non-neurotic adults.

The picture of needs we have been developing can account for many of these same facts. We saw in Chapter 18 that an orderly sequence of needs might appear in the course of a child's development. If the development of thumbsucking is taken as an example once more, the continuity between nursing and thumbsucking is clear. The resemblance between the two behavior patterns is obvious. One does develop historically out of the other. Yet, we are not required to assume that they are expressions of the same need.

Sublimation

In terms of the concepts of Chapter 18, there might be two courses of development, one being the development of new needs related to previous ones and in a sense stemming from childhood needs, but still new ones. Thus, we saw that shyness might conceivably lead to the development of intellectual interests in solitary pursuits. These interests may in turn make the individual more secure about his own ability and may motivate him to seek the company of certain people. Thus, the adult who emerges may not be obviously shy, or his shyness may be present on occasions but constitute no serious problem.

On the other hand, shyness might predispose the individual to a different development. If the child were shy and forced into solitude but spent his isolation in vainly wishing for companionship, he might not accept his retirement and find satisfying activities compatible with it. He might build a dream world of companions; he might resent other children for not making friends with him and develop slyly hostile behavior. He might merely remain frustrated, tense, and insecure. Such a child's future behavior might truly be a continuation of the same old conflict between shyness and sociability which he struggles vainly to solve.

These two different developments stemming from the same characteristic suggest that the first is the type of development called sublimation in psychoanalytic theory and the second is the result of fixation.

Sublimation, it will be recalled, is a mechanism by which libidinal energy finds an outlet that is socially acceptable and genuinely satisfying. Other behavioral symptoms are different from sublimation in that they are merely disguises for infantile libidinal drives or defenses against them.

We saw in our discussion of Freudian theory that the distinction between sublimation and substitution was difficult to explain in terms of the theory. Viewing normal development as a sequence of needs, each of which is truly independent of the preceding one, makes it much easier to describe the difference between sublimation and substitution.

If a new need develops, it is not a substitute for the need that preceded it. It is genuinely satisfying in its own right, just as a sublimated expression is supposed to be. Such a new need may reflect its historical root, as solitary pursuits reflect shyness. In other words, we may be able to tell out of what need it developed. In this regard, the concept of a developmental sequence of needs has a real advantage over the psychoanalytic formulation of sublimation. What Freud called sublimation may be conceived of as the development of a new need out of an old one.

Fixation and Regression

When a new need does not develop out of the frustrations of an earlier one to provide the individual with a genuine source of satisfaction, then the later expressions of the need fit the psychoanalytic picture of defense mechanisms, and we can consider them as fixations.

Let us examine for a moment the reasons that might prevent the need from being superseded or modified by the need that could normally follow it. The first possibility is that maturation is stunted. Either through too little challenge in the child's life or through too much challenge, the maturity required to comprehend the later abstract forms of the present concrete needs might be lacking. This line of thinking is already familiar from the previous discussion of maturation.

Another situation that might prevent the development of subsequent needs is a too-strong present need. The effect of a very strong need is to keep the individual almost continually motivated. A man who must constantly work desperately to make enough money is not likely to develop his potentialities in the areas of art and music. The same conclusion would follow if the need were not realistically founded. Similarly, a child who is constantly focused on obtaining love may not be able to develop the usual intellectual and social needs. We saw an example of this in Goldfarb's study (see p. 412).

An individual with one overpowering need is so sensitive to opportunities and threats that almost every situation evokes his central all-encompassing motivation. The state of motivation focuses him upon means for satisfying his motive, but desensitizes him to aspects of the situation that are irrelevant to the present motivation. Since it is through involvement in the irrelevant aspects of a situation that new needs may arise, this is just the pattern of sensitivity which would tend to prevent the individual from developing a new and broader need. He would be very sensitive to the possibilities of new means to the same goal, or to possible substitutes for the goal, but not to an entirely new goal. We can see the result in personality development. The individual develops new patterns of behavior related to already existing needs. Depending upon the specific need, he may develop defenses against it or substitutes for it. But his behavior will be tied to the old need, and the normally expected new need will not develop.

The psychoanalytic description of such a person is very accurate. His behavior is a constant attempt to satisfy a few basic needs on the developmental sequence. For such a person the terms *fixated* or *regressed* are very appropriate.

Significant Childhood Experiences

The present view of personality development also captures some of the other significant contributions of psychoanalytic theory. One of the most important features of Freudian theory is that it hypothesizes the significance of the concrete experiences of childhood for later personality. By picturing a developmental series of needs, all relating to the same general problem but showing increasing maturity, this same continuity between childhood and adulthood is maintained.

At the same time such a conceptualization permits flexibility in development. A need for autonomy might develop from its historical origin in toilet-training behavior. If the parent were autocratic about toilet training, he might provoke a rebelliousness in the child. Most parents who are autocratic about toilet training continue to be autocratic in later situations in which the child's independent action is at stake. Therefore, the rebellious personality pattern initiated during toilet training might be realized through these later experiences.

If, however, the toilet-training issue were a special problem to the parent and his behavior in other situations were not consistent with his toilet training practices, then the potential personality that began during toilet training would not be realized. Instead, some other sequence of needs would occur. The theory points to the fact that it is not specific experience but the climate of the home that is important. This fact has been stressed by numerous child psychologists.

At the same time there can be critical periods in which experiences are much more influential than in other periods. The beginning of a developmental series is more critical than any other point. The first experience the child has in achieving autonomy is more influential than his seventy-fifth experience. Because toilet training is, in our culture, one of the first concrete situations in the child's life that involves autonomy, it is an especially important period for the development of autonomy. It does not predetermine but it does predispose later developments.

As Erikson points out, the first year is especially critical because basic trust is developed during that period. A continuous state of high tension and unrest during this period may retard the child's perceiving a stable world with permanent objects in it. It may prevent a stable attitude toward the mother. Such a consequence may in turn modify the entire series of needs that are built on this historical foundation.

The view we are now examining contains the possibility of a change in the developmental course at any time, but emphasizes the relatively great importance of the early experiences in channeling personality development.

Summary

In this chapter we have seen the Freudian theory of development of the personality and one variant of it. There are numerous others, generally not differing from the original theory as much as Horney's does.

Freudian theory is based upon the concept of libidinal energy, which is released through various kinds of behavior. If one outlet is blocked, other outlets are sought. The activity that directly expresses the libido changes with the maturational level of the child. It goes through the various stages: oral, anal, early genital, the latency period, and the late genital period of adolescence. At each of these stages the individual has one primary source of gratification, a few primary social modalities, and one type of love object. If the problems faced at one level are not solved, the individual is fixated, wholly or partially, at that level. Or he may react to frustration by regressing to an earlier level of gratification.

Horney does not have so complex a theory. It differs fundamentally in its lack of emphasis on libidinal drives and on the importance she gives to the social environment. The fundamental problem in Horney's theory is basic anxiety. This leads the child to a lopsided pattern of behavior and gradually to an unrealistic idealization of the self which Horney picturesquely calls the search for glory.

Finally, we have seen that the ideas we have been considering about the development of needs contradict Freudian theory in one of its most basic assumptions, but this contradiction is not radical. The essential characteristics of psychoanalytic theory can be captured without assuming that all adult behavior is an expression of a single or very limited set of basic instinctual drives.

23

Personality Development According to General Behavior Theory

GENERAL BEHAVIOR THEORY

DERIVED NEEDS AND MOTIVES

A STUDY OF CHILDHOOD ANTECEDENTS
OF AGGRESSION AND DEPENDENCY

ANXIETY AND GUILT

POSITIVE AND NEGATIVE FIXATION

DISCUSSION AND CRITIQUE OF GENERAL
BEHAVIOR THEORY

A SECOND COHERENT APPROACH to the problems of personality development is represented in the developments stemming from the work of Hull (1943). Although Hull himself was almost exclusively concerned with the analysis of the learning process, some of his colleagues and students have developed and extended his theoretical conceptions in an attempt to build a theory of personality development and personality dynamics. Naturally enough in a movement of this sort, different workers have gone in different directions and have proposed different modifications of the basic model.

563

General Behavior Theory

The basic model is a reinforcement theory of conditioning (see p. 424). Any response to a stimulus which is reinforced—*i.e.,* which results in a reduction in drive—becomes learned, so that when that stimulus is repeated the reinforced response is more likely to occur than it was on the previous occasion. The known factors about conditioning, stimulus generalization, secondary conditioning, and the like are assumed in the basic model. In addition, the theory assumes a few biological drives, such as hunger, thirst, etc. These drives produce stimuli (see p. 185) that are reduced when the appropriate satisfaction is obtained. Ingestion of food results in reduction of hunger. It is this drive reduction that reinforces learned responses to stimulus situations.

It has proved necessary to add another assumption to general behavior theory in order to encompass the hostile behavior of human beings. Aggression does not seem to be limited to situations in which it clearly reduces some biological drive. Therefore in general behavior theory there is a specific assumption that *frustration instigates aggression.* Aggression is not the only consequence that frustration may have, and the aggression may in turn be prevented from occurring overtly, but one of the invariable consequences of a frustration is an instigation to be aggressive. Thus, aggression is seen as having the status of a drive which is evoked by frustration and is lowered by being aggressive. At the same time, it has some properties of a habit in that the aggressive response is evoked by any stimulus that represents the frustrating agent. This hostile response can, through generalization, be evoked by stimuli that are similar to the frustrator. It can also be inhibited by lack of reinforcement, or incompatible habits can be strengthened through reinforcement, so that the hostility is not expressed toward a person who is invulnerable and has power enough to punish hostile behavior. We shall understand this assumption better in the light of the applications of the theory to specific problems.

Derived Needs and Motives

One of the most perplexing problems in child development is the reason for the development of the various patterns of needs and motives that govern so much of the adult's life. In view of the fact that the infant does not seem to need popularity, social approval, self-esteem, or aesthetic appreciation, we must build a theory to explain how such needs come to be important.

In general behavior theory the explanation is suggested by the findings from the studies on secondary reinforcement. The hypothesis of secondary reinforcement states that any stimulus that is consistently associated with the reduction of a drive can gradually acquire the ability to serve as a reinforcement. The stimulus thus becomes a "secondary reward."

Development of Dependency

A good example of this derivation in general behavior theory is found in the development of dependency. The key person in the early dependency of the child is the mother. The mother is a stimulus pattern that is consistently associated with the reduction of the child's drives—*i.e.,* she relieves his hunger, she changes him when he is wet and cold, she relieves him of some of the pains he feels. Thus, she becomes a secondary reinforcement. After the conditioning process is well along, the child will stop crying when his mother picks him up, even before he is actually relieved of his hunger or pain. In other words, her mere presence acquires reward value for him and acts like relief from a drive. In strange situations that are frightening, her presence satisfies him even though she does nothing but pick him up and remain close to him. Because the mother's presence has the same effect on the child as drive reduction, her presence can reinforce new behavior patterns that do not in themselves lead to any reduction in biological drives. He can learn to cry for his mother, for example, because crying is a type of behavior that is reinforced by her answering the baby's cries.

Permanence of Derived Needs

There are many problems hidden in this statement. If we look back at the experiment illustrating secondary reinforcement, in which apes learned to work for tokens that could later be used in a vending machine to get food (see p. 420), we see that the tokens reinforced the learning, but only as long as they could be used in vending machines to obtain food. The rewarding effects of a mother's presence seem to last much longer after she no longer provides relief from primary drives than the experiments would suggest. There is another problem as well. Many kinds of activity, such as walking, talking, reaching, etc., are instrumental to gratifying basic motivation. Yet not all these activities become secondary drives in the way that dependency and aggression do. Similarly, many sorts of objects, such as inanimate tools, are useful in obtaining goals. But not all objects providing a means to a goal become valued for their own sake. The theory must, therefore, contain some hypotheses that distinguish between the activities which become secondary drives and those which do not.

Criterion for Development of Secondary Drive

There is not complete agreement among behavior theorists about what is necessary for the development of secondary or derived drives. One hypothesis suggested by Whiting (Sears, Whiting, Nowlis, and Sears, 1953) is that drives depend upon both reinforcement and punishment of the activity. If an activity is always reinforced but never punished, it becomes an instrumental activity usable whenever the appropriate stimuli and drive are present, but it never becomes a drive in itself. Walking, talking, reaching, and most of our instrumental actions have this sort of history, says the theory. If, however, an activity is sometimes rewarded and sometimes punished—but, as we shall see, not too severely punished—it becomes a drive. This seems at first glance a very peculiar hypothesis, but it is really another attempt to describe a fact that we have noted before. Frustration can increase the motivation; repeated instigation of a motive which is then frustrated can accentuate the need; imposition instigates resistance to the imposition. We obviously must admit this fact to our theories; in behavior theory it is introduced here. We shall see evidence for it shortly.

The same hypothesis can be described in another way. Punishment creates pain. This is a potent drive which is gratified by the ending of the pain. The most common way to teach rats is to shock or hurt them unless they make the correct response. The absence of shock or the cessation of shock on the correct path reinforces learning. Now, the anticipation of shock or expectancy of it can also serve to motivate learning. Miller (1948) put an animal in a box with two compartments. After a short time the animal was given a strong shock in the first compartment, and it rapidly learned to go to the next compartment to escape the shock. Now, however, the animal was afraid of the shock compartment whether there was any shock present or not. It ran to the safe compartment of the apparatus and would even learn to perform various actions that were necessary to open the door to the safe area. All of this learning was motivated by the fear of the shock area, even though during that time the animal never received a shock in it.

Thus we see that punishment of an action not only fails to reinforce it, but also creates an expectancy of pain. This fear can serve as a drive. It is evoked by stimuli that have become associated with pain and is reduced by escape from those stimuli. So if the child's crying for mother or seeking her attention is punished, he may become fearful in situations that evoke such behavior—*e.g.,* being alone. Nurturant behavior from the mother relieves the child of this fear or anxiety even if it does not actually relieve a more primary drive. In general, this means that secondary drives are readily established whenever a situation has become associated with punishment so that it arouses fear or anxiety. This drive is reduced by any behavior that relieves the anxiety.

The Aggression Drive

Two important secondary drives that develop in all children are aggression and dependency. We have seen how dependency develops. The development of aggression follows the same principles, but its course depends upon the child's perceiving pain or hurt in other people. In general behavior theory (Sears, Whiting, Nowlis, and Sears, 1953) aggression is seen to develop because the child discovers that by hurting other people he can secure compliance to his wishes. The success of aggression reinforces it. This is at first merely instrumental aggression—*i.e.,* hurting others in order to obtain some goal—but this behavior is not only reinforced but punished. Therefore, aggression, like dependency, becomes a drive as well as a learned instrumental action. It seems likely that the aggressive drive develops later than the dependent drive because the cues that the other person is in pain are more subtle and varied than are the cues that the other person is friendly and nurturant.

A Study of Childhood Antecedents of Aggression and Dependency

Having seen some of the theoretical ideas underlying the development of dependence and aggression, we should now look at some of the empirical evidence that has emerged from studies of the relationships between child-rearing practices and these behavior patterns in the nursery-school child (Sears, Whiting, Nowlis, and Sears, 1953). A group of 40 mothers were interviewed about the details of their child-rearing practices. Some of these practices were current ones, the mother's behavior with her nursery-school child. Others were concerned with what she had done when the child was a baby. These latter were, of course, retrospective. On the basis of these careful interviews the experimenters rated each of the mothers on a large number of separate scales that could be combined into twelve major scales relating to frustration during infancy, current frustration, nurturance during infancy and at the time of the interview, and punitiveness. Punitiveness is a measure of the severity of discipline and amount of maternal punishment of the child, generally in response to aggression on the part of the child.

The child was being studied at the same time in a variety of ways. First the nursery-school teacher was asked to rate the child on various symptoms of dependence toward adults and toward children, independence in the sense of initiating and carrying out activity by himself, identification (which means imitating or emulating parent or teacher), and aggression. The child was also studied by direct observation of nursery-school activity. The number of instances of various sorts of dependent and aggressive behavior in a fixed period of time was counted. Finally, each child was introduced to a standardized doll-play situation, involving a family of mother, father, boy, girl, and baby dolls and a crude doll house equipped with toy furniture. The child was permitted to play with these dolls for four fifteen-minute sessions. His play behavior in this situation was recorded and judged in terms of various sorts of aggression.

Infant Frustration and Dependency

The first important finding is that among this sample of children the amount of dependent behavior is related to the extent that dependence is frustrated during infancy. Children who were weaned severely tended to be the most dependent on the teacher in nursery school. Toilet-training frustrations, on the other hand, were unrelated to dependency in nursery school. According to the theory, dependence should be related to gratification of nurturance as well as frustration of nurturance, but the relation does not appear in this study. The experimenters suggest that all children among this sample receive enough reinforcement of dependent behavior so that the differences in frustration are the important ones introducing individual differences. In a group including extremely non-nurturant parents or institutionalized children the importance of reinforcement might be clearer. Since nursing frustration rather than toilet-training frustration is related to dependence, the experimenters suggest that the crucial period for dependence is the last part of the first year of life and is especially connected with feeding. This prediction is exactly what would be derived from psychoanalytic theory, even though the basis of the prediction is quite different.

Current Frustration and Dependence

The relation of dependent behavior to the current level of frustration and punishment is much more complicated. The empirical findings are that for boys there is a positive correlation between punitiveness of the parents (frustration in the home) and dependent behavior; but just the opposite relationship holds for girls. This reversal of relationships for the two sexes has become such a common finding in these studies that it is now almost expected.

In order to explain these differences the experimenters develop an elaborate theory—too elaborate if this were the only finding that required it. As we shall see, however, other findings later require a similar sort of theoretical model.

The first assumption to be made is that the strength of drive that is formed from the combination of reinforcement and punishment depends upon the severity of the punishment. Whereas a mild punishment or a threat of one may only strengthen the motive that is frustrated, a very severe punishment may inhibit behavior completely. The severity of punishment required to inhibit action may depend upon the strength of the motive. This hypothesis overlaps to some extent an earlier one we have discussed regarding the effect of tension level upon the directedness of behavior. Moderate tension permits directed adaptive behavior; very high levels result in restless un-directed behavior. So the theory now hypothesized is that the combination of reinforcement and moderate frustration or punishment establishes a drive of maximum strength. Too much or too little frustration results in a weaker drive.

Now, a second assumption is that girls are more susceptible to punishment by their mothers than are boys. This in turn depends upon the assumption that girls are more identified with their mothers, whereas boys are more identified with their fathers. Thus, when a mother punishes her daughter, the punishment has greater psychological impact than when she punishes her son; it is more likely, therefore, to inhibit than to accentuate the motivation. We shall see other evidence that is generally supportive to this assumption, but first let us see how all this leads to an explanation of the empirical findings.

Putting these two assumptions together, let us suppose that the effect of frustration upon the strength of drive is represented by the curve in Figure 23.1. Now, if punishment by the mother were more severe for girls than for boys, then the sample of girls in this study would fall toward the right-hand end of the curve. In this region of the curve, the more punishment, the less drive. The boys, on the other hand, are less affected by being punished, so they would fall along the left-hand end of the curve. Within this region, the more punishment, the more drive. This corresponds to the empirical finding.

This same argument holds as well for aggression as for dependency. Therefore it is gratifying to discover that there is the same empirical reversal of relationship between punitiveness of the home and amount of aggression in boys and girls. The more punitive the mother, the more aggressive the boys. For girls there is a clear relation showing that moderate punitiveness is related to high aggression, whereas low or high punitiveness leads to less aggressive behavior.

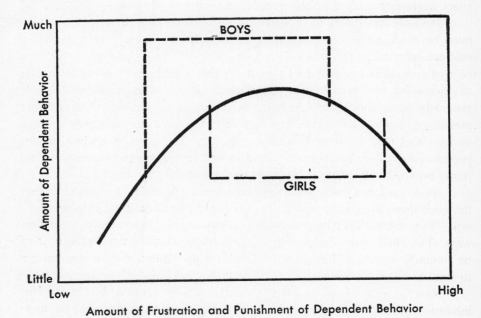

Fig. 23.1 A possible explanation for the relation of frustration to dependence. (After R. R. Sears, J. W. M. Whiting, *et al.*, *Genet. Psych. Monog., 47*, 1953, 135-234)

In other respects, however, the findings on aggression do not exactly match the findings for dependency. There is no clear relationship between any sort of infancy experience and aggression in nursery school. If there are any tentative findings they relate to severity. of toilet training rather than severity of feeding frustration.

Aggression in Doll Play

Now let us turn to the findings of aggression as exhibited in the doll-play situation (Sears, 1950). Some of the aggression in doll play is overt aggression of the child toward the dolls and the toys. The child may throw the toys around, step on them, etc. Then, secondly, there may be aggression in the dramatic play that the child enacts. He may pretend that the father falls into the fireplace and is burned up. He may enact the mother punishing a child for disobedience. All of this is aggression, but probably it does not have the same meaning. Some of the aggression in doll play may represent aggression that the child would like to indulge in but cannot; some of it may re-enact aggression that he actually displays in the home or school; some of it may enact aggression that has been directed toward him.

GENERALIZATION OF GRATIFICATION AND INHIBITION   Some assumptions must be made in order to analyze such complex behavior. The hypotheses that are most frequently made in general behavior theory rest upon the concept of generalization (see p. 421). If a child is frustrated and is instigated to aggression by his parents, the presence of the parents themselves will gradually come to instigate aggressive behavior. At the same time the parents punish aggression, so that the aggressive behavior which they instigate is more or less inhibited. Thus, there are two response tendencies instigated by the parents—aggression and fear of punishment. These operate in opposite directions; usually the fear is greater than the aggression.

Having learned these responses in the home, the child also tends to make the same response in situations that are similar because of stimulus generalization. The teacher in nursery school is similar to the parents in many ways. The child who is motivated to be aggressive toward his parents may be similarly motivated toward the teacher, or his inhibition may also spread to similar stimulus objects.

Now we make a second assumption that is well supported by data. The inhibition or anxiety does not spread so far as does the positive instigation. It resembles the earlier situation (see p. 51) in which we discussed the approach and avoidance tendencies toward an object that is both rewarding and punishing. The avoidance tendencies drop more sharply than the approach tendencies.

When this same picture is translated into the present situation, we find that the child may be inhibited from being aggressive toward his parents, but he may be aggressive toward his teacher. The aggression is not so high as the inhibition when the stimulus object is the original instigator, but toward a dissimilar object the aggression may be higher than the inhibition. The effect of making the inhibition stronger is to push out the crossing point of the two curves (see Figure 23.2) so that the stimulus may have to be quite different from the original object before overt aggressive behavior can be discerned.

RELATON OF PUNITIVENESS TO AGGRESSION IN DOLL PLAY   Sears (1950; 1951) has reported on investigations of the aggressiveness of preschool children in a doll-play situation and has related this play behavior to the parental frustration of the child. If frustration produces aggression, then the most frustrated child should be the most aggressive. Parental control is frus-trating; therefore parental control should produce aggression. If this were the sole factor, children from very repressive homes would be extremely hostile. At the same time however, the parental control may be directed

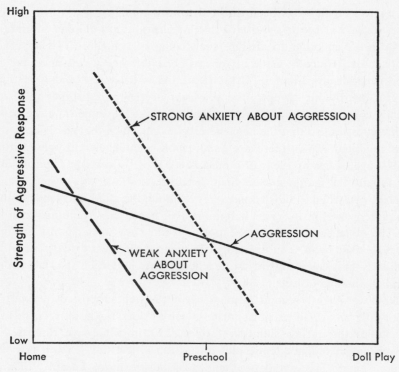

Fig. 23.2 Mechanism underlying displacement of aggression. (After R. R. Sears, J. W. M. Whiting, *et al., Genet. Psych. Monog., 47,* 1953, 135-234)

against the child's expressions of hostility. The actual behavior of the child is therefore conceived as the consequence of the degree of frustration and the extent to which the parent punishes expressions of aggression. This pattern is called *punitiveness.*

Figure 23.3 shows the aggressiveness of three groups of children observed in free play in a nursery school and in a doll-play situation. The first of the three groups comes from homes that are low in punitiveness, *i.e.,* punishment of the child. The second group of children comes from moderately punitive homes, and the third group comes from homes that are highly punitive.

In the nursery-school situation, the children from moderately punitive homes show the most aggression. Sears believes that the low aggressiveness

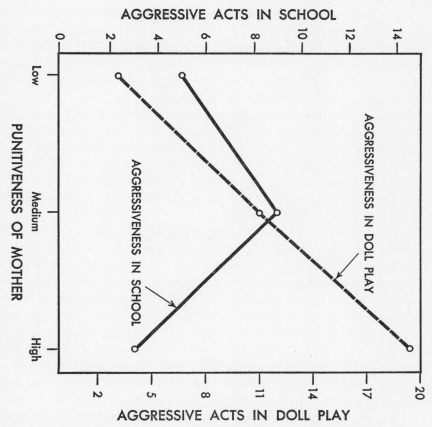

Fig. 23.3   Relation of aggressiveness to punitiveness of the home. (After R. R. Sears, *Amer. Psych., 6,* 1953, 476-483)

of children from nonpunitive homes is a result of the fact that they are subjected to very little frustration. Consequently little aggressiveness is evoked. The low aggressiveness of the children from highly punitive homes is presumably due to their fear of punishment for being aggressive.

The aggressiveness in doll play of the children from the three varieties of homes support this same interpretation. In their doll play the children from highly punitive homes show more aggressiveness than do either of the other two groups. Sears believes that the fear of punishment does not show enough generalization to cover the doll-play situation and so aggressiveness is permitted to appear.

Let us examine this interpretation more closely. The children are frustrated in the home; thus, their aggressiveness would normally appear in the home situation. The parent evokes an aggressive response. Why, then, does the child show aggressiveness in nursery school where the parent is not present? According to general behavior theory he does so because his conditioned response to the parent is generalized (see p. 421). Other stimuli that resemble the parent evoke the same aggressiveness. Thus, the teacher evokes it. The other children also evoke it, although less so because they are less like the parent than is the teacher.

Similarly, the inhibition of aggressiveness is evoked by the parent. This inhibition operates through arousing anxiety and is also generalized. It is evoked, Sears argues, in the nursery-school play group because the stimuli there are sufficiently like the parent. In doll play, however, the aggressiveness is evoked and the inhibition of the aggressiveness is not evoked. In other words, the aggressive response generalizes to a wider range of stimuli than does the inhibition of aggressiveness.

EFFECT OF PUNISHMENT OF AGGRESSION IN DOLL PLAY   There is evidence to support the hypothesis that the punitiveness of the experimenter can affect the expression of aggression in doll play. An experimental and a control group were each studied during four sessions. During the second session the children in the experimental group were reproved every time any of the doll characters behaved aggressively in the dramatic play. "Now, John, you know nice boys don't do things like that." On each of the last three sessions the children of the control group, who were never reproved, showed more aggressive play than did the experimental group. The difference in aggressiveness was especially marked during the third session, coming as it did immediately after the experimental group had been reprimanded.

Thus, we see evidence that aggression in doll play can be a valid symptom of the motive to be aggressive in real life which is too strongly inhibited to be openly expressed. This is the usual interpretation put upon doll-play activities when they are used as a clinical tool.

Anxiety and Guilt

As we have seen, the development of anxiety, according to general behavior theory, arises from the fear of pain. When the child is punished, it hurts. His response to this pain includes many different kinds of behavior:

crying, muscle tension, withdrawal, and the like. Suppose that the father does all the punishing; he is then consistently associated with punishment. Like the animal in the shock box, the child may come to respond to his mere presence with some of the same behavior that accompanies punishment itself. The actual pain is not evoked, but some of the emotional responses to pain may be evoked even though no pain is present.

Anxiety

According to general behavior theory this pattern of internal expressive responses appropriate to a painful situation, when it occurs in the absence of the pain stimuli, is what we call fear or *anxiety* in ordinary language.

Anxiety has some of the characteristics of punishment itself, and the relief of anxiety can serve to reinforce behavior just as does the relief from pain. In the study of instrumental conditioning, in which the animal learns to stay away from a charged grid, the effective mechanism in the learning is assumed to be the relief from anxiety. The stimuli that are consistently associated with the shock evoke anxiety. The withdrawal response removes those stimuli and this relieves the animal of anxiety. This relief reinforces the withdrawal.

When the child is put in a situation that has been associated with punishment, he becomes anxious, he shows some of the behavior expressive of anxiety, and he will learn to perform the patterns of behavior that relieve him of the anxiety. Anxiety-producing situations are the result of secondary drive.

Guilt

Guilt is another characteristic that has been investigated by workers within the framework of this general theory. Guilt can be viewed as merely one form of anxiety. As we saw previously, stimuli associated with punishment evoke anxiety. One of the stimuli consistently associated with punishment is the forbidden act. Gradually, the evocation of anxiety about punishment comes to depend less and less upon the actual conditions that make punishment probable, and eventually the mere contemplation of a forbidden action can by itself evoke anxiety.

Suppose, for example, that a child has been punished for teasing the cat. He may learn to be anxious about the punishment in advance of its application. The cat yowling or the parent advancing with a grim expression may evoke anxiety. Eventually the mere thought of teasing the cat or the sight of the cat may evoke anxiety even though the child has done nothing to deserve punishment.

This anxiety evoked by the forbidden act, altogether separated from the probability of detection and punishment, is guilt. When guilt is thus aroused, the individual relieves or prevents guilt feelings by preventing himself from behaving in a forbidden fashion.

Relation of Guilt to Anxiety

A more elaborate hypothesis has been developed to predict the presence of guilt. It has been proposed by Whiting and Child (1953) that guilt is not just any anxiety provoked by the contemplation of a forbidden act. Rather, it is a special variety of anxiety emerging from a specific type of punishment at the hands of specific people—namely, the fear of loss of the love of the people on whom the child has come to depend. Thus, they conceive guilt to be a form of anxiety that specifically requires that the child has developed dependence upon the parent or some other agent. Guilt is the anxiety evoked by situations that threaten this dependent relationship. Furthermore, it can be called guilt only when the forbidden act by itself, disassociated from any actual threat of punishment, is sufficient to evoke the anxiety. If this hypothesis is accepted, then the guilt feelings of the boy who teased the cat would occur only if the punishment he had received for the act had been loss of love. If the parent had punished him very impersonally or if the cat had punished him by scratching him, he might feel anxious when he considered teasing the cat but he would not feel conscience-stricken.

Positive and Negative Fixation

The concepts of secondary drive and reward have been developed by Whiting and Child in a series of hypotheses concerning the different effects to be predicted if a pattern of behavior is learned under the influence of reward or if it is learned under the motivation to escape anxiety.

We can make this problem somewhat more concrete. Whiting and Child are concerned with the problem of socialization of the child. Children are not immediately at birth forced to behave like adults. With regard to their manner of eating, for example, children are permitted to obtain food by nursing for a period of time. This is not the adult way of obtaining food, but it is permitted. During this period the behavior that obtains food is being repeatedly reinforced. Therefore sucking and nursing gradually acquire secondary-reward value. The mere act of sucking becomes rewarding even when it does not lead to reduction of hunger, just as the presence of the mother becomes rewarding in an earlier example. This period is called by these authors the "period of indulgence."

After a while—the exact time varies from one culture to another—the child is taught to eat in an adult fashion. This learning may take place slowly, gently, and gradually. He may be given opportunity to eat solid foods; he may be praised and caressed when he does eat in the culturally approved fashion; yet throughout all this time he may be permitted to nurse whenever he wants to. Under these conditions the shift from the infantile to the adult manner of eating takes place because the adult method is more satisfying and rewarding than the infantile method.

In other cultures the weaning of the child may be quite differently handled. It may be an abrupt process, a sudden removal of the breast and bottle. The child's attempts to nurse may be punished. A bitter substance may be painted on the mother's breast. He may be starved into eating from a spoon or cup or eating solid food. Under these conditions the shift from the infantile to adult method of eating may take place under the threat of punishment. Under a severe regime the adult method is the only way to avoid punishment, but under the gentler regime the adult method is made more satisfying to the child than his infantile behavior. The gentle method of weaning the child produces, according to Whiting and Child, *positive fixation*. The more punitive method produces *negative fixation*.

What are the consequences of positive and negative fixation? The result of positive fixation is, according to the authors, that the child continues to get reward value from the behavior patterns that are so fixated. In this case, eating activities give the individual much satisfaction. Oral activities like sucking, even if non-nutritional, are satisfying. All aspects of eating, even weaning, have been accompanied by satisfactions. Such a person might be a gourmet who intensely enjoys the experience of eating, or the person who responds to frustration and disappointment by going on an "eating jag." Such people use eating as a satisfier or pacifier as well as a method of obtaining nourishment.

Negative fixation, on the other hand, should result in a great deal of anxiety connected with eating and oral activities. Food stimuli and other reminders of eating have been associated with being hungry, being punished, and being frustrated. Therefore, they should evoke a secondary drive, anxiety or guilt. Such people should be expected to treat eating as an unpleasant necessity, to bolt down their food without tasting it, to be finicky about food, and perhaps worried about indigestion.

Cross-cultural Study of Positive and Negative Fixation

Whiting and Child (1953) tested the validity of these hypotheses by observing whether the members of those cultures that wean children suddenly and violently reveal their anxiety connected with food by theories that illness is caused by something one eats.

This is an example of cross-cultural research. We should digress a moment to take a look at this research tool. If we want to study the effects of child-rearing practices upon personality development, two procedures suggest themselves. The most common method consists of studying a group of children from our own culture who come from homes in which a variety of different sorts of child-rearing practices are found. An alternative procedure is to study the way children are reared in various cultures and to relate these child-rearing practices to the personality characteristics of the children or adults in that culture. Thus, if neglect of children is normal in one culture and loving care is normal in another, and if the two cultures are otherwise sufficiently alike to be comparable, then the differences in the adult personalities that are typical of the two cultures might be attributed to the difference in the methods of caring for children. This conclusion is strengthened if other pairs of cultures that are comparable except for the pattern of neglect show the same differences in adult personality. One assumption that is made in such a study is that the adults in the culture were reared in the same way in which they are bringing up their children. Although this assumption is clearly untenable for our own culture, it is a reasonable assumption for a more stable culture.

A cross-cultural study of the effects of childhood experiences has certain advantages over studies within a single culture. One is that a larger variety of child-rearing practices exists among the hundreds of societies in the world than can be found in a single society. The second is that these practices are normal within each society, whereas many of the extreme patterns would be deviant if they occurred in our own culture. We might confuse the effect of the practice with the effect of its deviancy.

The big obstacle in the way of cross-cultural research is the lack of comparable information from enough different cultures. Fortunately, however, such studies have become much more feasible now that a file of information upon many different cultures has been established at Yale University. Observations upon cultures have been especially difficult to study because the material is scattered in the books and articles and records of anthropologists, explorers, naturalists, diplomats, and travelers. These are in many languages, and much of the information in them needs support and confirmation, which may exist in some other study. It has been the task of the Human Relations Area Files to collect such scattered material, abstract it, classify it in some systematic way, and make it available for use.

Procedure of Study

Whiting's and Child's studies of positive and negative nxation utilized these files. They selected seventy-five cultures on which there is sufficient information to make some sort of rating on a battery of variables concerning childhood experience and child-rearing practices and also sufficient information to make some evaluation of the consequences of these practices on the culture.

The conceptualization of socialization adopted by Whiting and Child has already been described (see p. 216). They conceive socialization to be training toward culturally approved social behavior. This training may come early or late, after a period of *initial indulgence*. During the period of initial indulgence the child is allowed to behave in a natural infantile way. A second descriptive variable is *severity of socialization*. When the time comes for socialization to occur, it may be done gently or harshly. These cultural characteristics are rated for each culture. The research also determines the age of onset of socialization, the frequency and intensity of various techniques of socialization, and the importance of various socializing agents—*e.g.,* parents, relatives, nonrelatives, and specialists (schoolteachers, for example).

Whiting and Child selected as the cultural characteristic to relate to these socialization practices the theories held in the culture to account for illness and the recovery from illness. The reasons for using this aspect of the culture were both practical and theoretical. Good personality descriptions of adults from direct observation would be the ideal material for a cross-cultural study, but not many of the studies of cultures have furnished such descriptions. The beliefs about illness have, however, attracted the attention of many field workers. Such information is available in quantity and quality. This is the practical reason for selecting this belief system for study.

At the same time there is reason to believe that theories about the causation of illness reflect the personality of the members of the culture. Their beliefs cannot be very realistic because most primitive cultures do not have the information that permits their theories of illness to be oriented in reality. Even when their therapeutic practices are successful, the theory of their operation is not realistic. Whiting and Child conceive, therefore, that the cultural theories about illness may be taken as a sort of projective test, an index for the culture. If some sort of activity were strongly anxiety-provoking, one might predict that it would be perceived as a cause of illness. If, on the other hand, some type of activity were comforting and anxiety-reducing, it might well be incorporated in the therapeutic procedures of the culture.

Whiting and Child study five systems of behavior: oral, anal, genital, aggressive, and dependent. Psychoanalytic theory suggests that these are significant drive systems in infancy, and their resolution has important consequences for the adult personality. For each drive system the authors rate the initial indulgence and the severity of the socialization. Next they rate the importance of these activities in the theories of illness and the theories of therapy. If within the culture there is a belief that some illness is caused by eating something, then that society is classified as one for whom an oral explanation of illness exists. If urine or feces is seen as the material responsible for some illness, then it is called an anal explanation. It would be quite possible for all of the explanations to exist in a single society; one theory might be held for one disease, another theory for another disease.

Some of the classifications of theories as oral or anal might not be obvious to the layman, but they are classifiable on the basis of psychoanalytic theory. For example, the belief that illness results from the patient's failure to perform some ritual is classified as anal because of the psychoanalytic hypothesis that an emphasis upon ritual stems from conflict over toilet training. This hypothesis stems from the fact that toilet training is often made into a ritual which is scheduled and requires the child to play his part.

Negative Fixation

Whiting and Child test a number of hypotheses; five of them will be presented. The first is the hypothesis of negative fixation (see p. 577). This states that those systems which are severely socialized result in anxiety and are expected to be incorporated in the theories of illness in the society. Table 18 indicates the result of the findings. The societies were grouped on the basis of presence or absence of a particular theory of illness. The average severity of socialization for that system of behavior was calculated for each group. If the severity of socialization is greater for the societies in which the corresponding theory of illness is present than in those in which it is absent, the hypothesis is supported. Concretely, there were sixteen societies without any oral theory of illness and twenty-three societies with such an explanation. The average severity of weaning in the first group was 8.94 on a scale from 0 to 20. The average severity of weaning in the second group is 12.22. This difference is very significant, statistically speaking, and supports the hypothesis. The results for other systems of behavior are not so clear or so significant, but they are in the same direction.

Positive Fixation

The second, the positive fixation hypothesis, states that behavior that is initially very satisfying through a long period of indulgence will tend to be incorporated in the therapeutic practices of the society. The results are generally negative. There are some small differences in the predicted direction, but others in the opposite direction. In only two cultures were sexual practices

TABLE 18

RELATION BETWEEN SOCIALIZATION ANXIETIES AND EXPLANATIONS OF ILLNESS: MEAN DIFFERENCES*

Societies where Corresponding Explanation of Illness is	Average Rated Socialization Anxiety in each System of Behavior				
	Oral	Anal	Sexual	Depend-ence	Aggres-sive
Present	12.22	12.10	12.21	13.38	14.82
Absent	8.94	11.00	11.21	11.71	10.80
Statistically significant?	yes	no	no	yes	yes

believed to have specific therapeutic value; in these two societies there is very high indulgence of childhood sexuality. For this drive system the findings were significant.

Antecedents of Guilt

The last three hypotheses to be reported deal with the childhood practices that are related to guilt. The aspect of the theory of illness taken to indicate guilt is the belief that the patient is responsible for his illness. In some societies illness is conceived to be primarily the fault of the patient; in others it is conceived to be accidental or due to the hostility of some outside agent.

In terms of general behavior theory (see p. 566), guilt is hypothesized to be a form of anxiety. On this basis, then, it might be expected that those societies with the severest socialization practices would create the most anxiety and guilt, and in these societies, therefore, would be found the belief that the patient is responsible for his own illness. The study found support for this hypothesis. Societies that are rated above the average on belief in the patient's

* J. M. W. Whiting and I. L. Child, *Child Training and Personality,* Yale University Press, 1953.

responsibility for illness tend to be the societies that are above the median on average socialization anxiety for all systems of behavior. The correlation coefficient is $+.29$, a low but still significant correlation supporting the hypothesis. It was found that oral and aggressive anxieties were more closely related to patient responsibility than the other systems.

Another theory as to guilt held that it is due to anxiety over the loss of love of the person on whom the child is dependent (see p. 565). In this case three predictions can be made. Guilt should depend upon establishment of dependence through initial nurturance; it should be most severe where loss of love is the threat used to induce conforming behavior from the child; it should be most severe when the parents function as the socializing agents. The results indicate that initial nurturance is not related to the patient-responsibility theory of illness. There is evidence, however, that societies tending to use love-oriented techniques of punishment do have higher ratings on the acceptance of patient responsibility for illness. There was no evidence, however, that the societies in which the parents are the most important agents of socialization are the ones that have the most guilt, as measured by patient responsibility. The difference is in the predicted direction but not significant.

One objection to such cross-cultural studies of socialization is that they cannot distinguish cause from effect. In the Whiting and Child study, for example, the data would support a theory that the abrupt weaning of children leads to an oral theory of disease or that the causation goes in the reverse direction. We might imagine that a culture with anxiety about eating would tend to put pressure on the child to eat in an approved and safe way. Realistically the causation does not go in either one direction or the other in a stable cultural pattern. It is entirely likely that the socialization practice results in anxiety which in turn reinforces the socialization methods. The result of such a complex process is a syndrome in which the various symptoms fit together in a sensible way, but in which it is not possible to say which one is the primary cause and which ones are the effects. Such a condition does not make the discovery of a syndrome less valuable.

Discussion and Critique of General Behavior Theory

Role of Maturation

Just as in the case of psychonalytic theory, the conceptualization we have been developing in this book agrees closely in many points with general behavior theory. Many of the ideas in this book are in fact taken from the theory. One of the most striking differences between general behavior theory and the one presented in this volume is the use of a concept of maturation. General behavior is an uncompromising learning theory, and its proponents have never been interested in or have found it necessary to assume any maturation process. This may be because they have never tried to predict some of the results of experiments cited in Chapter 15 on maturation; or it may be because maturation can be eliminated as a concept in child development. Only the future can tell.

Role of Cognition

A second difference between general behavior theory and the point of view we have presented is in the amount of stress laid on motives and on cognition. We have adopted practically all the principles of conditioning in so far as they apply to habits and to simple guided behavior. We have, however, made an important distinction between cognitively guided behavior and the simpler behavior mechanisms. Furthermore, we have made a distinction between cognitive learning and learning through stimulus contiguity or reinforcement. As we have seen, this distinction does not deny the effectiveness of reward in motivating a person to solve a problem through cognitive learning.

In none of the research presented in this chapter stemming from general behavior theory has any use been made of cognition or motivation as we have used these concepts. Other writings by workers in the tradition of behavior theory seem to describe cognition as a response to a stimulus, and a motive as a response to a stimulus. These responses are internal and do not directly result in overt behavior, but they can be thought of as responses that can be reinforced, extinguished, inhibited, and generalized just like any other response. This is an interesting way of formulating the problem and may well prove to be fruitful.

Two Strategies of Theory Building

The philosophy of scientific strategy held by general behavior theorists is to get along with the absolute minimum of concepts. They generally restrict their activities to a limited area and do not try to build a theory which is intended to encompass all behavior. Instead, they try to predict the behavior they have studied and by this process gradually enlarge the scope of the theory. Other theorists prefer a large vague theory which is all-encompassing and proceed to refine it to fit the details of specific experiments. These are two ways that science can progress. Each has its assets and each has its liabilities. The broad theory may never become specific; the narrow theory may concentrate more and more effort on a better explanation of insignificant behavior. Probably the choice between the two depends more upon the personality of the scientist than upon the requirements of the subject matter.

24

Recapitulation

WE HAVE COME to the end of the road. Beginning with the contrasting behavior of children and adults, we have analyzed descriptions, examined experimental research, explained the mechanisms of child behavior at various levels of maturity, and reviewed the common-sense notions of parents and teachers, all in an attempt to discover and to understand the processes of child development. Let us glance back at these various concepts to see how they all fit together into a pattern, and to take an over-all view of what has been accomplished.

The Neonate

The newborn infant has two behavior mechanisms. First, stimulation produces tension. Tension, if it is not too strong, makes the infant responsive to stimuli that evoke reflex behavior. If the tension level is too high, a focused response is impossible and only general restless behavior occurs. Second, the infant is equipped with a number of specific behavioral response patterns that are evoked by the appropriate stimuli. Some of these are self-stimulating. When they are activated, they either repeat themselves or bring about a stable result, such as grasping. Others, such as the knee jerk, occur but do not re-stimulate the mechanism. The first variety are the bases for important future developments.

Developments from the Reflex

Both the tension mechanism and the circular reaction undergo changes in the course of development. Let us first consider the changes that take place in the reflexlike process. First, the execution of the behavior itself seems to

585

become gratifying to the infant, and it becomes the reinforcement for a learning process. He learns to bring about the conditions that establish or prolong the reflex activity. For example, he learns to put his thumb in his mouth to stimulate sucking. At the same time, the infant learns to recognize situations that result in this sort of gratification. He begins to respond by sucking to the preparation for feeding. The first of these learning processes illustrates learning through reward or reinforcement. The second illustrates conditioning through stimulus contiguity. Both of these learning processes can be repeatedly observed in child behavior.

Then the child becomes interested in new activities. Not only his own reflex activities, but interesting external events become pleasurable and re-inforce a learning process that enables him to re-establish interesting external events. Piaget calls them secondary circular reactions. Again the learning process seems to be thorough reinforcement, although in some cases the learning takes place in one trial.

In some of these activities the stimuli that evoke the behavior can also guide the behavior toward the goal. Some guided behavior toward immediate goals occurs in the behavior of neonates, and other similar behavior patterns develop quickly. Most of these simply guided behavior patterns are physical movements in space: reaching for an object, or putting the thumb in the mouth, or hitting an object. In other cases of infant behavior, the stimulus that evokes the behavior cannot serve as a guide. In this case, the behavior is fixed and predetermined, at least until the organism matures enough to guide be-havior through a more complex cognitive process.

An important development occurs when the infant first connects two behavior patterns into a sequence in which one is a means to an end and the other is the goal activity itself. The ability to use many different behavior pat-terns as means to ends and to use the same behavior pattern as a means to many different goals is one important characteristic of mature behavior.

Another important development occurs when the child becomes able to vary his behavior deliberately. Instead of repeating the habit exactly or taking advantage of some accidental variation, the child modifies his behavior. This ability gives him more accurate control and permits him to invent new solu-tions to problems.

Development of Emotional Behavior

Along with this behavioral development, we also can observe an emo-tional development. The tension of early infancy is a sort of undifferentiated excitement. Gradually, various emotions become differentiated from each other and each expresses itself in a certain form of overt behavior—*e.g.,* distress is expressed by crying. Some of these are important in the development of social behavior. Distress, for example, differentiates into fear and anger. These emotional states come to be related to the motive to escape and to attack. Interpersonal attitudes, such as love, hate, and fear, develop and come to have their mature significance.

Development of Cognition

During this same time, cognitive development is proceeding. Maturation is probably a necessary condition, but through experience with various sorts of behavior patterns that deal with the same object, the child gradually comes to recognize the properties of objects, to appreciate the fact that they may exist even when he does not perceive them, and to discriminate between those of his actions that affect the external world, such as hitting, grasping, reaching, and walking, and those that are merely information-getting, such as looking and listening. He must also recognize the difference between his moving toward an object and an object's moving toward him.

All of this takes place in a simple way by the end of infancy. The child is able to solve some problems without trying out all the various solutions. He is able to pretend, imagine, and visualize invisible events.

Varieties of Learning

On the basis of these behavioral symptoms, we can assume that the child has a cognitive map of the external world. With the appearance of cognition, new mechanisms of behavior and new learning processes emerge. Cognitively guided behavior is possible to the extent that the child's cognition is clear and his repertoire of behavior patterns is under voluntary control. The new learning process to go along with cognitively guided behavior is cognitive learning, or the building of a more accurate and complete cognitive map. We can see that cognitive learning is in some sense an outgrowth of noncognitive learning, because of the similar effects of such external conditions as stimulus contiguity or similarity upon both learning processes. These conditions make cognitive learning easy, just as they make conditioning and stimulus generalization easy. Reinforcement (now it might better be called reward) of correct behavior also plays a role in cognitive learning, but not the same role it played in learning habits through reinforcement. The child may solve a problem that demands cognitive learning in order to obtain a reward. The reward motivates behavior and keeps the child involved in the problem that requires cognitive learning.

Cognitive and Noncognitive Mechanisms of Behavior

From this point on in the child's life, two different behavior mechanisms may operate. Behavior may be an automatic reaction to stimuli, or it may be cognitively guided. These are probably only extremes of a continuum, but we can describe them as though there were two distinct kinds of behavior. Cognitively guided behavior is based on clear cognition and has the following characteristics: (1) It is voluntary and deliberate. (2) It is flexible and adjustable to new circumstances. (3) The factors controlling it and guiding it are conscious. (4) The content of the cognitive picture is verbally communicable to other people. (5) The cognitive picture and cognitively guided behavior may be changed by verbal instruction.

Various factors in the socialization of a child may affect the clearness of his reasons for behavior. If he is not mature enough, he cannot be cognitively clear or his behavior cognitively guided. If he is rewarded and punished arbitrarily without being told why, he is more likely to learn a behavior pattern that is not cognitively guided. If he is rewarded and punished inconsistently, his learned behavior is less likely to be cognitively guided than if his discipline is consistent. If he is disciplined in such a way as to induce repression through the production of anxiety, shame, or guilt, this repression reduces cognitive clearness.

Later cognitive development brings cognitive clarity about remote relations, more abstract characteristics of the environment, the more difficult problems of interpersonal relations, and various conceptual schemata, such as concepts of number, space, and time. These function in producing an accurate cognitive map.

Through this developmental process, both learning and maturation processes interact. In many different areas, perhaps in all, the best formulation of the interaction between maturation and learning is that maturation results in an increased sensitivity to learning experiences. It increases the ability to learn skills, establish conditioned responses, solve cognitive problems. In some cases, the mature organism can learn in one trial or solve a problem immediately. In other cases, such as in developing automatic habits or acquiring masses of information, a learning process is essential. We have assumed that a maturation process may be induced by stimulating problem situations.

Development of Needs

We have looked at a number of processes that describe changes in needs. First, a need may fade through the passage of time, or it may become satiated through continuous gratification of the motive. Needs may also diminish in strength or disappear through habituation or adaptation to a situation that was once mildly instigating. Through habituation, a situation that was once neutral or even unpleasant may become normal or even preferred.

Needs may also come into existence. Many sorts of experiences are interesting and are repeated if the individual is free to do so. These needs are usually short-lived. More permanent needs may be developed through psychological involvement. The individual may engage in an activity for one reason but become so involved in it that he continues to engage in it even after the original reason has disappeared. We have also seen that needs may be accentuated through continuous exposure to an instigation, especially if the individual is not permitted to gratify the motive that is repeatedly aroused.

We have also seen that needs may change through an increase or decrease in cognitive clarity. By discovering the reason for actions that have been blindly learned, one may change his behavior from being an end in itself into being an instrumental action or a means to a goal. Just the opposite may occur also. Either through automatization or through repression a cognitively guided behavior pattern toward a clearly cognized goal may become an automatic response in which the individual has no awareness of a goal or any feeling of volition. Such a change also makes the behavioral pattern less flexible and adjustable.

Through maturation, the child may display an orderly sequence of needs, all perhaps having to do with the same general area of human activity—e.g., how to deal with authority. The need of the young child will be limited and concrete, but it may predispose him to develop a series of more and more generalized needs, until in the adult we can see a generalized personality adjustment pattern. We can find other bases as well for an orderly sequence of needs in development. One is the orderly imposition of socialization pressures in any particular culture.

Impact of Environment on Child

In describing the environment of the child and its impact upon him, we must consider first its effect upon maturation. We have accepted in this discussion the hypothesis that maturation may be accelerated or retarded or even initiated by environmental stimulation, as well as through an inherent growth process. We have seen that freedom and security and deliberate training may all contribute to the stimulation of maturation processes.

The second and probably the most important impact of the environment on the child is the inculcation of social rules and social roles. Two important processes underlie socialization: training through reward and training by example. Each of these may be more or less cognitively clear. Probably early socialization is entirely through reward and punishment. Identification, which is the basis of training by example, may depend upon previous patterns of reinforcement. In any case, one important achievement of the socialization process is the development of a need for conformity or compliance. Not all socialization occurs through this need, and in the process of internalization, we see that the same behavior may come to represent the individual's own need rather than his compliance to an external pressure or a sense of duty.

A third impact of the environment, especially the home, upon the child comes through the parent's emotional reactions to the child as a person, and to the role of parent. We have analyzed parent behavior in terms of three variables: warmth, emotional involvement, and parental ideology.

Building a Theory of Child Development

Finally, we have examined two major theories of personality development: psychoanalytic theory and general behavior theory. These two are, to some extent, different only in the language they employ, but at some points they are contradictory. The conceptualization formulated in this book has much in common with both of them, especially general behavior theory. It differs from them in important respects. In some cases it seems to describe child behavior better than either.

But the facts of the matter are that no theory, at the present time, is even close to adequate. There are gaping holes in every theory. Usually, the holes are covered over with some label, but ignorance is never dispelled by merely naming it. The function of theories of child behavior and development at the present time is to stimulate more research, to suggest new experiments, and to challenge new theory builders to fill in the gaps or perhaps redesign the whole theoretical structure. If we succeed in stimulating this sort of investigation, we have helped build the foundation for an adequate theory of child behavior and development.

Bibliography and Author Index

The numbers in boldface type following each entry refer to pages in this volume on which the specified material is either quoted or cited.

Adler, D. L., 1939. "Types of Similarity and the Substitute Value of Activities at Different Age Levels." Unpublished Ph.D. dissertation, State University of Iowa. **248.**

Allport, F. H., 1924. *Social Psychology*. Houghton Mifflin. **324.**

Ames, Lois B., 1937. The sequential patterning of prone progression in the human infant. *Genet. Psych. Monogr., 19,* 409-460. Reprinted by permission of the Journal Press. **289, 290.**

Anderson, C., 1940. "The Development of a Level of Aspiration in Young Children." Unpublished Ph.D. dissertation, State University of Iowa. **150.**

Anderson, H. H., and H. F. Brandt, 1939. Study of motivation involving self-announced goals of fifth-grade children and the concept of level of aspiration. *J. Social Psych., 10,* 209-232. **150.**

Angyal, A., 1941. *Foundations for a Science of Personality*. Commonwealth Fund. **142.**

Arnold, M. B., 1942. A study of tension in relation to breakdown. *J. Genet. Psych., 26,* 315-346. Reprinted by permission of the Journal Press. **83, 84.**

Arsenian, Jean M., 1943. Young children in an insecure situation. *J. Abn. and Soc. Psych., 38,* 235-249. Reprinted by permission of American Psychological Association. **153-154, 191.**

Asher, E. J., 1935. The inadequacy of current intelligence tests for testing Kentucky mountain children. *J. Genet. Psych., 46,* 480-486. **401.**

Baldwin, A. L., 1946. Differences in parent behavior toward three- and nine-year-old children. *J. Personality, 15,* 143-165. Reprinted by permission of the Duke University Press. **518, 520.**

———, 1947. Changes in parent behavior during pregnancy: An experiment in longitudinal analysis. *Child Devel., 18,* 29-39. **199.**

———, 1948. Socialization and the parent-child relationship. *Child Devel., 19,* 127-136. **524, 526.**

———, 1949. The effect of home environment on nursery school behavior. *Child Devel., 20,* 49-62. **524, 531.**

Baldwin, A. L., J. Kalhorn, and F. H. Breese, 1945. Patterns of parent behavior. *Psych. Monogr., 58,* No. 268. Reprinted by permission of American Psychological Association. **490-497, 503-506, 509-517, 522, 523, 531.**

Baldwin, A. L., J. Kalhorn, and F. H. Breese, 1949. The appraisal of parent behavior. *Psych. Monogr., 63,* No. 299. **491.**

Baldwin, B. T., and B. L. Wellman, 1928. The pegboard as a means of analyzing form perception and motor control in young children. *J. Genet. Psych., 35,* 387-414. **73.**

Barker, Roger G., T. Dembo, and K. Lewin, 1941. Studies in topological and vector psychology, II: Frustration and regression: An experiment with young children. *University of Iowa Studies in Child Welfare, 18,* No. 1. **95, 242.**

Barker, R. G., J. Kounin, and H. F. Wright, 1943. *Child Behavior and Development.* McGraw-Hill.

Barker, Roger G., and Herbert F. Wright, 1952. *Dutton Thurstone.* Privately printed. Quoted with permission of the authors. **21.**

————, 1955. *Midwest and Its Children: The Psychological Ecology of an American Town.* Row Peterson. **120.**

Bayley, N., 1935. The development of motor abilities during the first three years. *Soc. for Research in Child Development Monogr.,* No. 1. Reprinted by permission. **292, 293, 369.**

Bell, H. M., 1942. Rest pauses in motor learning as related to Snoddy's hypothesis of mental growth. *Psych. Monogr., 54,* No. 243. Reprinted by permission of American Psychological Association. **394.**

Bender, L., and P. Schilder, 1936. Aggressiveness in children. *Genet. Psych. Monogr., 18,* 400-525. **190.**

Beyrl, F., 1926. Über die Grösserauffassung bei Kindern. *Zeitschrift Psychol., 100,* 365. Reprinted by permission of A. Barth. **42.**

Binet, A., and T. Simon, 1908. Le développement de l'intelligence chez les enfants. *L'Année Psychologie, 14,* 1-94. **269.**

Bird, Chas., 1925. The relative importance of maturation and habit in the development of an instinct. *Pedagogical Seminary, 32,* 68-91. Reprinted by permission of the Journal Press. **385.**

Blatz, W. E., and D. A. Millichamp, 1934. *The Development of Emotion in the Infant.* University of Toronto Studies in Child Development, No. 2.

Bott, H., 1928. Observations of play activities in a nursery school. *Genet. Psych. Monogr., 4,* 44-88. **206.**

Boutonier, J., and P. Henri, 1946. La peur et l'angoisse chez les enfants et les adolescents aveugles. *J. de Psychologie Normale et Pathologique, 39,* 341-349. **189.**

Bowlby, John, 1951. *Maternal care and mental health.* World Health Organization Monogr., No. 2. **410, 463.**

Bridges, K. M. B., 1932. Emotional development in early infancy. *Child Devel., 3,* 324-341. Reprinted by permission of the Society for Research in Child Development. **71, 158.**

Brown, J. F., 1939. Reactions of psychiatric patients in a frustrating situation. *Bull. of Menninger Clinic, 3,* 44-64. **410.**

Brown, Judson S., 1940. "Generalized Approach and Avoidance Responses in Relation to Conflict Behavior." Unpublished Ph.D. dissertation, Yale University. **51, 52.**

Brunswik, Egon, 1928. Zur Entwicklung der Albedowahrnehmung. *Zeitschrift Psychol., 109,* 40-115. **43.**

————, 1930. Über Farben- Grössen- und Formkonstanz in der Jugend. XI Kongr. *Bereit für Experimentelle Psychologie.* **42.**

Buckingham, B. R., 1931. New data on the typography of text books. National Society for the Study of Education, *Thirtieth Yearbook,* Part II. **26.**

Bühler, C., 1930. *The Mental Development of the Child.* Harcourt, Brace. **140.**

Bühler, C., and H. Hetzer, 1927. Das erste Verständnis von Ausdruck im ersten Lebensjahr. *Zeitschrift Psychol., 107,* 50-61. **73, 157.**

————, 1935. *Testing Children's Development from Birth to School Age.* Farrar and Rinehart. **140, 277.**

Carmichael, L., 1926. The development of behavior in vertebrates experimentally removed from influence of external stimulation. *Psych. Rev., 33,* 51-58. **387.**

Cattell, Psyche, 1942. *Measurement of Intelligence of Infants.* The Psychological Corporation. **277.**

Champney, H., 1940. Unpublished manuscript. **522.**

————, 1941. The measurement of parent behavior. *Child Devel., 12,* 131-166. **491.**

Chapanis, A., and W. C. Williams, 1945. Results of a mental survey with the Kohlmann-Anderson intelligence tests in Williamson County, Tennessee. *J. Genet. Psych., 67,* 27-55. **401.**

Child, I. L., and I. K. Waterhouse, 1952. Frustration and the quality of performance, I: A critique of the Barker, Dembo, and Lewin experiment. *Psych. Rev., 59,* 351-362. **97.**

Criswell, J. H., 1939. A sociometric study of race cleavage in the classroom. *Arch. Psych., 33,* 235. Reprinted by permission. **204-205.**

Crudden, 1948. Reported in Werner, 1948. **89.**

Davis, E. A., 1937. *The Development of Linguistic Skill in Twins, Singletons with Siblings, and Only Children from Age Five to Ten Years.* Institute of Child Welfare Monogr. No. 14, University of Minnesota Press. **296.**

Davis, W. Allison, 1948. Socialization and adolescent personality. National Society for the Study of Education, *Forty-third Yearbook.* **401.**

Davis, W. A., and R. J. Havighurst, 1946. *Father of the Man.* Houghton Mifflin. **217.**

Deiter, J. B., 1954. "An Investigation into the Nature of Subception." Unpublished Ph.D. dissertation, University of Kansas. **240, 328.**

Dembo, T., 1931. Der Ärger als dynamisches Problem. *Psychol. Forsch., 15,* 1-44. **248.**

Dennis, W., 1934. A description and classification of the responses of the newborn infant. *Psych. Bull., 31,* 5-22. Reprinted with permission of American Psychological Association. **132.**

————, 1951. Presidential address. Division of Childhood and Adolescence, American Psychological Association. **75.**

Dennis, W., and M. G. Dennis, 1936. Infant development under conditions of restricted practice and a minimum of social stimulation: A preliminary report. *J. Genet. Psych., 53,* 149-157. **404.**

Dernowa-Yarmolenko, A. A., 1933. The fundamentals of a method of investigating the nervous system as revealed in overt behavior. *J. Genet. Psych., 42,* 319, 338. **423.**

Engel, R., 1928. Reported in Woodworth, 1938.

Erickson, E., 1950. *Childhood and Society.* Norton. **547, 549, 552.**

Escalona, S., and P. Bergman, 1949. Unusual sensitivities in very small children. In *The Psychoanalytic Study of the Child,* Vol. III. **180.**

Escalona, S., M. Leitch, and others, 1953. *Early Phases of Personality Development: A Non-normative Study of Infant Behavior. Soc. for Research in Child Development Monogr.,* No. 54. **180, 184.**

Fajans, S. E., 1933. Erfolg, Ausdauer, und Activität beim Saugling und Kleinkind, *Psych. Forsch., 17,* 268-305. Reprinted by permission of Springer Publishing Co. **241, 283.**

Fales, E., 1940. *Genesis of Level of Aspiration in Children from One and One-Half to Three Years of Age.* Reported in C. Anderson, 1940. **150.**

Farber, M. L., 1945. Imprisonment in topological and vector psychology, III: Imprisonment as a psychological situation. *University of Iowa Studies in Child Welfare, 20.* **257.**

Fenichel, Otto, 1945. *The Psychoanalytic Theory of Neurosis.* Norton. **338.**

Fernberger, S. S., 1950. An early example of a "hidden figure" picture. *Am. J. Psych., 63,* 448. Reprinted by permission. **58.**

Freeman, F. N., and C. D. Flory, 1937. Growth in intellectual ability as measured by repeated tests. *Soc. for Research in Child Development Monogr., 2,* No. 2. Reprinted by permission. **368.**

Freud, S., 1900. *The Interpretation of Dreams.* Translated in *The Basic Writings of Sigmund Freud,* Modern Library, 1938. **258.**

————, 1949. *An Outline of Psychoanalysis.* Norton. **538.**

Gates, G. S., 1923. An experimental study of the growth of social perception. *J. Ed. Psych., 14,* 449-461. **74.**

Gesell, Arnold, 1928. *Infancy and Human Growth.* Macmillan. **277.**

————, 1940. *Wolf Child and Human Child.* Harper. **404.**

————, 1946, 1954. Ontogenesis of infant behavior. In L. Carmichael, ed., *Manual of Child Psychology.* Wiley and Sons. Reprinted by permission. **83, 88, 267.**

Gesell, A., and Frances L. Ilg, 1942. *Infant and Child in the Culture of Today:*

The Guidance and Development in Home and Nursery School. Harper. **146, 163, 198.**

————, 1949. *Child Development: An Introduction to Human Growth.* Harper. **233-235, 255.**

Gesell, A., and H. Thompson, 1929. Learning and growth in identical infant twins: An experimental study by the method of co-twin control. *Genet. Psych. Monogr., 6,* 1-124. Reprinted by permission of the Journal Press. **386.**

Glixman, A. F., 1949. The recall of completed and incompleted activities under varying degrees of stress. *J. Exp. Psych., 39,* 281-295. Reprinted by permission of American Psychological Association. **260.**

Glueck, Sheldon, and Eleanor Glueck, 1950. *Unraveling Juvenile Delinquency.* Cambridge, Mass., Harvard University Press. Copyright, 1950, by The Commonwealth Fund, New York. Reprinted by permission of the publishers and The Commonwealth Fund. **527, 529, 530.**

————, 1952. *Delinquence in the Making.* Harper. Reprinted by permission. **528.**

Goddard, Henry H., 1919. *Psychology of the Normal and Subnormal.* Dodd, Mead. **36.**

Goldfarb, William, 1943. The effects of early institutional care on adolescent personality. *J. Exp. Ed., 12,* 106-129, 309-310. **410.**

————, 1943. Infant rearing and problem behavior. *Am. J. Orthopsychiatry, 13,* 249-265. **410.**

Goldstein, K., 1940. *Human Nature in the Light of Psychopathology.* Harvard University Press. **555.**

Goodenough, F. L., 1931. *Anger in Young Children.* University of Minnesota Press. **158.**

Gordon, H., 1923. *Mental and Scholastic Tests among Retarded Children: An Inquiry into the Effects of Schooling of Various Tests.* Educational Pamphlets of the Bureau of Education (London), No. 44. **401.**

Gottschaldt, K., 1926. Erfahrung auf die Wahrnehmung von Figuren. *Psychol. Forsch., 8,* 261-317. **60.**

Gough, H. C., D. B. Harris, W. E. Martin, and M. Edwards, 1950. Children's ethnic attitudes in relation to certain personality factors. *Child Devel., 21,* 83-91. **204.**

Gould, R., 1939. An experimental analysis on "level of aspiration." *Genet. Psych. Monogr., 21,* 3-115. **149.**

Green, E. H., 1933. Friendship and quarrels among preschool children. *Child Devel., 4,* 302-307. **160, 190.**

Greenberg, P. J., 1932. Competition in children: An experimental study. *Am. J. Psych., 44,* 221-248. **163.**

Griffiths, Ruth, 1954. *The Abilities of Babies.* University of London Press and McGraw-Hill. Reprinted by permission. **285-288.**

Gross, M. M., 1946. The effect of certain types of motivation on the honesty of children. *J. Ed. Research, 40,* 133-140. **232.**

Halverson, H. M., 1931. An experimental study of prehension in infants by means of systematic cinema records. *Genet. Psych. Monogr., 10,* Nos. 2, 3. Reprinted with permission of the Journal Press. **288-289.**

————, 1931. A further study of grasping. *J. Gen. Psych., 7,* 34-63. Reprinted with permission of the Journal Press. **289.**

Hartshorne, H., and M. A. May, 1928. *Studies in the Nature of Character,* Vol. I: *Studies in Deceit.* Macmillan. **232.**

Head, Henry, 1921. *Studies in Neurology,* Vol. II. Oxford University Press. **311.**

Heider, Fritz, 1953. "Theory of Interpersonal Relations." Unpublished manuscript. **33, 45, 66-67, 142, 193, 197.**

Heiss, A., 1930. Zum Problem der isolienenden Abstraktion. *Neue Psychologische Studien* (ed. F. Kreuger), *4,* 285-318. **64-65.**

Henle, M., 1942. An experimental investigation of dynamic and structural determinants of substitution. *Contributions to Psychological Theory, 2,* No. 3. **248.**

Hilgard, E. R., 1948. *Theories of Learning.* Appleton. **392, 395.**

Hilgard, E. R., and D. G. Marquis, 1940. *Conditioning and Learning.* Appleton. **419.**

Hilgard, J. R., 1951. Learning and maturation in pre-school children. In W. Dennis, ed., *Readings in Child Psychology.* Prentice-Hall.

Holmberg, Allan M., 1950. *Nomads of the Long Bow: The Siriono of Eastern Bolivia.* Smithsonian Institution, Institute of Social Anthropology, Publication No. 10. **217.**

Holt, L. P., 1951. Unpublished manuscript. **234, 355.**

Homans, George, 1950. *The Human Group.* Harcourt, Brace. **66.**

Honzik, M. P., 1938. The constancy of mental test performance during the preschool periods. *J. Ed. Psych., 24,* 417-441, 498-520. **369.**

Horney, K., 1937. *The Neurotic Personality of Our Time.* Norton. **555.**

————, 1939. *New Ways in Psychoanalysis.* Norton. **540, 555.**

————, 1945. *Our Inner Conflicts.* Norton. **193, 555.**

————, 1950. *Neurosis and Human Growth.* Norton. **555.**

Howells, T. H., 1938. Factors influencing honesty. *J. Social Psych., 9,* 97-102. **232.**

Hull, Clark, 1938. The goal gradient hypothesis applied to some "field force" problems in the behavior of young children. *Psych. Rev., 45,* 271-299. **51.**

————, 1943. *Principles of Behavior—An Introduction to Behavior Theory.* Appleton. **563.**

Humphreys, L. G., 1939. The effect of random alternation of reinforcement on the acquisition of conditioned eyelid reactions. *J. Exp. Psych., 25,* 141-158. **443.**

Hunt, J. McV., 1941. The effects of infant feeding-frustration upon adult hoarding in the albino rat. *J. Abn. and Soc. Psych., 36,* 338-360. **464.**

Irwin, O. C., 1930. The amount and nature of activities of newborn infants under constant external stimulating conditions during the first ten days of life. *Genet. Psych. Monogr., 8,* No. 1, 1092. **82.**

———, 1941. Research on speech sounds for the first six months of life. *Psych. Bull., 38,* 277-285. **87, 294.**

Isaacs, Susan, 1930. *Intellectual Growth in Young Children.* Harcourt, Brace. **95.**

———, 1933. *Social Development of Young Children.* Harcourt, Brace. Reprinted by permission. **348.**

James, William, 1890. *Psychology.* Henry Holt. Reprinted by permission. **317, 335.**

Jensen, Kai, 1932. Differential reactions to taste and temperature in newborn infants. *Genet. Psych. Monogr., 12,* 361-479. Reprinted by permission of the Journal Press. **99, 100.**

Jersild, Arthur T., 1954. *Child Psychology.* Prentice-Hall. **532.**

Jersild, A. T., and F. B. Holmes, 1935. Children's fears. *Child Devel. Monogr., 20,* 358. Reprinted by permission of Teachers College, Columbia University. **152, 189, 421.**

Jersild, A. T., and F. V. Markey, 1935. *Conflicts between Preschool Children.* Teachers College, Columbia University. **160.**

Jersild, A. T., and R. J. Tasch, 1949. *Children's Interests.* Teachers College, Columbia University. **206-207.**

Jones, H. E., 1949. *Motor Performance and Growth.* University of California Press. **293.**

Jones, H. E., H. S. Conrad, and L. B. Murphy, 1939. Child development and the curriculum. National Society for the Study of Education, *Thirty-eighth Yearbook.* Public School Publishing Co. **233.**

Jucknat, M., 1937. Accomplishment, level of aspiration and self-consciousness. *Psychol. Forsch., 22,* 99. **149.**

Judd, C. H., 1908. The relation of special training to general intelligence. *Ed. Rev., 36,* 28-42, **328.**

Kardiner, A., 1945. *The Psychological Frontiers of Society.* Columbia University Press. **217.**

Karsten, A., 1928. Psychische Sättigung. *Psychol. Forsch., 10,* 142-254. **461.**

Keller, Helen A., 1903. *The Story of My Life.* Copyright 1903 by Helen Keller. Reprinted by permission of Doubleday and Co. **392.**

Klein, R., 1932. Die Authorität als eine Form der sozialen Beeinflussung. *Zeitschrift Kinderforschung, 39,* 248-299. **145, 155.**

Klimpfinger, S., 1933. Die Entwicklung der Gestaltkonstanz vom Kind zum Erwachsenen (Untersuchungen über Wahrnehmungsgegenstände, ed. by E. Brunswik), *Archiv f. d. gesamte Psychol., 88.* **43.**

Kohler, W., 1924. *The Mentality of Apes.* Harcourt, Brace. **240, 320.**

Kounin, Jacob S., 1941. Experimental studies of rigidity, I: The measurement of rigidity in normal and feeble-minded persons. *Character and Personality, 9,* 251-272. Reprinted by permission of Duke University Press. **84-86.**

Krugman, H. E., 1943. Affective responses to music as a function of familiarity. *J. Abn. and Soc. Psych., 38,* 391-395. **469.**

Lafore, G. G., 1945. Practices of parents in dealing with preschool children. *Child Development Monogr.,* No. 31. Teachers College, Columbia University. **533.**

Landis, C., and W. A. Hunt, 1939. *The Startle Pattern.* Rinehart. **152.**

Lazar, M., 1937. *Reading Interests, Activities and Opportunities of Bright, Average, and Dull Children.* Contributions to Education, No. 707. Teachers College, Columbia University. **207.**

Lazarus, R. S., and R. A. McCleary, 1951. Autonomic discrimination without awareness: A study of subception. *Psych. Rev., 58,* 113-122. **328.**

Leitch, M., and S. Escalona, 1949. *The Reaction of Infants to Stress.* Reprinted from *The Psychoanalytic Study of the Child.* International University Press. **97.**

Leuba, C., 1933. An experimental study of rivalry in young children. *J. Comp Psych., 16,* 367-382. **164.**

Levy, D. M., 1934. Experiments on the sucking reflex and social behavior of dogs. *Am. J. Orthopsychiatry, 4,* 203-224. **464.**

―――, 1937. Primary affect hunger. *Am. J. Psychiatry, 94,* 643-652. **410.**

―――, 1937. Studies in sibling rivalry. *Research Monogr. of American Orthopsychiatric Assoc.,* No. 2. **255.**

―――, 1943. *Maternal Overprotection.* Columbia University Press. **531.**

―――, 1944. On the problem of movement restraint; tics, stereotyped movements, hyperactivity. *Am. J. Orthopsychiatry, 14,* 664-671. **464.**

Lewin, K., 1935. *Dynamic Theory of Personality.* Trans. by D. K. Adams and K. E. Zener. McGraw-Hill. **102, 243, 322.**

Lewin, K., T. Dembo, L. Festinger, and R. R. Sears, 1944. Level of aspiration. In J. McV. Hunt, ed., *Personality and the Behavior Disorders,* Vol. I. Copyright 1944. Reprinted by permission of Ronald Press. **149.**

Lewin, K., R. Lippitt, and R. White, 1939. Patterns of aggressive behavior in experimentally created social climates. *J. Social Psych., 10,* 271-299. **470-471.**

Ling, B. D., 1941. Form discrimination as a learning cue in infants. *Comparative Psych. Monogr., 17,* No. 2. **337.**

Linton, R., 1939. In Kardiner, 1945. **217.**

Lippitt, R., N. Polansky, and F. Redl, 1950. An investigation of behavioral contagion in groups. *Human Relations, 3,* 319-348. **224.**

Lippitt, R., N. Polansky, and S. Rosen, 1952. The dynamics of power. *Human Relations, 5,* 37-64. **224.**

Lippitt, R., and R. K. White, 1947. An experimental study of leadership and group life. In T. N. Newcomb and E. L. Hartley, eds., *Readings in Social Psychology*. Henry Holt. Reprinted by permission. **323, 470-471.**

———, 1943. The social climate of children's groups. In R. G. Barker, J. Kounin, and H. F. Wright, eds., *Child Behavior and Development*. McGraw-Hill. Reprinted by permission. **448.**

Lissner, K., 1933. Die Entspannung von Bedürfnissen durch Ersatzhandlungen, *Psychol. Forsch., 18,* 218-250. Reprinted by permission of Springer Publishing Co. **246-247.**

Lorenz, K., 1952. *King Solomon's Ring*. Trans. by M. K. Wilson. Crowell. **317.**

Luchins, A. S., 1942. Mechanization in problem solving: The effect of *Einstellung. Psych. Monogr., 54,* No. 248. **253.**

McGraw, Myrtle B., 1935. *Growth: A Study of Johnny and Jimmy*. Appleton. Reprinted by permission. **291.**

———, 1940. The neuro-muscular development of the human being as exemplified in the achievement of erect locomotion. *J. Pediatrics, 16,* 580-590. **289.**

———, 1940. Neural maturation as exemplified in achievement of bladder control. *J. Pediatrics, 16,* 580-590. **386.**

———, 1943. *The Neuro-Muscular Development of the Human Infant*. The Columbia University Press. Reprinted by permission. **291.**

MacKinnon, D. W., 1938. Violation of prohibitions. In H. A. Murray, *Explorations in Personality: A Clinical and Experimental Study of Fifty Men of College Age*. Oxford University Press. **196.**

McNemar, Quinn, 1942. *The Revision of the Stanford Binet Scale*. Houghton Mifflin. Reprinted by permission. **90.**

Malamund, W., and F. E. Lindner, 1931. Dreams and their relationships to recent impressions. *Arch. Neurology and Psychiatry, 25,* 1081-1099. **260.**

Malinowski, B., 1927. *The Father in Primitive Society*. Norton. **555.**

Marinesco, G., and A. Kreindler, 1933. Des reflexes conditionnels, I: L'organization des reflexes conditionnels chez l'enfant. *J. Psych. and Normal Pathology, 30,* 855-886. **418, 420.**

Maslow, A. H., and B. Mittelmann, 1941. *Principles of Abnormal Psychology*. Harper. Reprinted by permission. **259.**

Matthews, S. A., and S. R. Detweiler, 1926. The reaction of amblystoma embryos following prolonged treatment with chloretone. *J. Exp. Zoology, 45,* 279-292. **384.**

Maudry, M., and M. Nekula, 1939. Social relations between children of the same age during the first two years of life. *J. Genet. Psych., 54,* 193-215. **158.**

Mead, Margaret, 1928. *Coming of Age in Samoa*. In *From the South Seas*. Morrow. **555.**

Meili, Richard, and Erick Tobler, 1931. Les mouvements stroboscopiques chez enfants. *Archives de Psychologie, 23*. **88.**

Merrill, B., 1946. A measurement of mother-child interaction. *J. Abn. and Soc. Psych., 41,* 37-49. **502.**

Michotte, A., 1946. La perception de la causalité. In *Études de psychologie,* Vol. 6, J. Vrin. Librairie Philosophique. **63.**

Miller, N. E., 1944. Experimental studies of conflict. In J. McV. Hunt, ed., *Personality and Behavior Disorders,* Vol. I. Copyright 1944. Reprinted by permission of Ronald Press. **52.**

———, 1948. Studies of fear as an acquirable drive, I: Fear as motivation and fear reduction as a re-inforcement in the learning of new responses. *J. Exp. Psych., 38,* 89-101. **566.**

Morgan, C. L., 1900. *Animal Behavior.* Arnold. **419.**

Mowrer, O. H., 1940. An experimental analogue of regression with incidental observation on reaction formation. *J. Abn. and Soc. Psych., 35,* 56-87. **249.**

———, 1950. *Learning Theory and Personality Dynamics.* Ronald Press. **257.**

Mowrer, O. H., and W. M. Mowerer, 1938. Enuresis—a method for its study and treatment. *Am. J. Orthopsychiatry, 8,* 436-459. **429.**

Murphy, L. B., 1937. *Social Behavior and Child Personality.* Columbia University Press. **164, 174.**

Newcomb, T. M., 1950. *Social Psychology.* Dryden Press. **211.**

Newman, H. H., F. N. Freeman, and K. J. Holzinger, 1937. *Twins: A Study of Heredity and Environment.* Copyright 1937. Reprinted by permission of University of Chicago Press. **381-382.**

Nice, M. M., 1925. A child's attainment of the sentence. *J. Genet. Psych., 42,* 216-244. **296.**

Ovsiakina, M., 1928. Die Wiederaufnahme von unterbrochener Handlungen, *Psychol. Forsch., 11,* 302-382. **459, 460.**

Parten, M. B., 1932. Social participation among preschool children. *J. Abn. and Soc. Psych., 27,* 243-269. Reprinted by permission of the American Psychological Association. **229-230.**

Pavlov, I. P., 1927. *Conditioned Reflexes.* Trans. by G. V. Annep. Oxford University Press. **417.**

Piaget, Jean, 1926. *The Language and Thought of the Child.* Harcourt, Brace. Reprinted by permission. **329-331.**

———, 1928. *Judgment and Reasoning in the Child.* Harcourt, Brace. Reprinted by permission. **53-55.**

———, 1929. *The Child's Conception of the World.* Trans. by Joan and Andrew Tomlinson. Harcourt, Brace. **53, 75.**

———, 1930. *The Child's Conception of Physical Causality.* Trans. by Marjorie Gabain. Harcourt, Brace. **54, 75.**

———, 1932. *The Moral Judgement of the Child.* Harcourt, Brace. **34, 54.**

———, 1950. *The Psychology of Intelligence.* Trans. by Malcolm Pearcy and D. E. Berlyne. Harcourt, Brace. **55, 344.**

———, 1951. *Play, Dreams, and Imitation in Childhood.* Trans. by C. Gattegno and F. M. Hodgson. Norton. Copyrighted. **223, 311, 323-324, 349, 433.**

————, 1952. *The Child's Conception of Number.* Trans. by C. Gattegno and F. M. Hodgson. Routledge. **47, 342, 346.**

————, 1952. *The Origins of Intelligence in Children.* Trans. by Margaret Cook. Copyright 1952. Reprinted by permission of International University Press. **31, 47, 77, 181, 299-314, 352.**

————, 1953. *Logic and Psychology.* Manchester University Press. **353.**

————, 1954. *The Construction of Reality in the Child.* Trans. by Margaret Cook. Basic Books. Reprinted by permission. **39, 339-340.**

Piaget, Jean, and Bärbel Inhelder, 1948. *La Représentation de l'espace chez l'enfant.* Presses Universitaires de France. **53, 344.**

Pintner, R., and L. Brunschwig, 1937. A study of certain fears and wishes among deaf and hearing children. *J. Ed. Psych., 28,* 259-270. **189.**

Poincaire, H., 1914. *Science and Method.* Trans. by F. Maitland. Nelson and Sons. **451.**

Queyrat, Fr., 1920. *Les Jeux des enfants.* Reported in Werner, 1948. **75.**

Radke, M. H., 1946. *The Relation of Parental Authority to Children's Behavior and Attitudes.* University of Minnesota Institute of Child Welfare Monogr. Series, No. 22. Reprinted by permission of University of Minnesota Press. **534-536.**

Razran, G. H. S., 1936. Attitudinal control of human conditioning. *J. Psych., 2,* 227-237. **429.**

Redl, Fritz, 1949. The phenomenon of contagion and shock. Effect in group therapy, p. 315. International University Press. Reprinted by permission. **67.**

Reed, Margaret, 1952. "Some Effects of Frustration When the Goal Is Not Cognitively Present." Unpublished Master's thesis, University of Kansas. **242.**

Révész, Géza, 1922. *Über audition colorée.* Reported in Werner, 1948. **91.**

Reynolds, M. M., 1928. *Negativism of Preschool Children.* Contributions to Education, No. 288. Teachers College, Columbia University. **145.**

Ribble, M. A., 1943. *The Rights of Infants: Early Psychological Needs and Their Satisfaction.* Columbia University Press. **410.**

Richardson, H. M., 1932. The growth of adaptive behavior in infants: An experimental study of seven age levels. *Genet. Psych. Monogr., 12,* 230. Reprinted by permission of the Journal Press. **434.**

Rogers, C. R., 1942. *Counseling and Psychotherapy: Newer Concepts in Practice.* Houghton Mifflin. **555.**

Rosenzweig, S., 1933. The recall of finished and unfinished tasks as affected by the purpose with which they are performed. *Psych. Bull., 30,* 698. **460.**

Russell, R. W., 1940. Studies in Animism, II: The development of animism. *J. Genet. Psych., 56,* 353-366. **75.**

Russell, R. W., and W. Dennis, 1939. Studies in Animism, I: A standardized procedure for the investigation of animism. *J. Genet. Psych., 55,* 389-400. **75.**

Rust, M. M., 1931. *The Effect of Resistance on the Intelligence Scores of Young Children.* Child Development Monogr., No. 6. Teachers College, Columbia University. **145.**

Scheerer, Martin, and Maurice Huling, 1952. Unpublished research. **36.**

Scupin, Ernst, and Gertrud I., 1907. Reported in Werner, 1948. **75.**

Sears, R. R., 1936. Experimental studies of projection, I: Attribution of traits. *J. Social Psych., 7,* 151-163. **549.**

————, 1950. Relation of fantasy aggression to interpersonal aggression. *Child Devel., 21,* 5-6. **190, 570-571.**

————, 1951. Effects of frustration and anxiety on fantasy aggression. *Am. J. Orthopsychiatry, 21,* 498-505. **571.**

————, 1951. A theoretical framework for personality and social behavior. *American Psychologist, 6,* 476-483. Reprinted with permission of American Psychological Association. **573.**

Sears, R. R., E. Maccoby, H. Levin, *et al.,* 1952. Unpublished study. **219, 220.**

Sears, R. R., M. H. Pintler, and P. S. Sears, 1946. Effect of father separation on pre-school children's doll play aggression. *Child Devel., 17,* 219-243.

Sears, R. R., J. W. M. Whiting, V. Nowlis, and P. S. Sears, 1953. Some child rearing antecedents of aggression and dependency in young children. *Genet. Psych. Monogr., 47,* 135-324. Reprinted by permission of the Journal Press. **566-567, 570, 572.**

Sears, R. R., and G. W. Wise, 1950. Relation of cup feeding in infancy to thumb sucking and the oral drive. *Am. J. Orthopsychiatry, 20,* 123-128. Reprinted by permission of authors and the Journal. **464-466.**

Senden, M. von, 1932. *Raum- und Gestaltauffassung bei operieten Blindgeborenen von und nach der Operation.* Barth. **336.**

Sewall, M., 1930. Two studies of sibling rivalry, I: Some causes of jealousy in young children. *Smith College Studies in Social Work, 1,* 6-22. **200.**

Sheldon, W. H., F. F. Stevens, and W. B. Tucker, 1940. *The Varieties of Human Physique.* Harper. **528.**

Sheperd, J. F., and F. S. Breed, 1913. Maturation and use in the development of instinct. *J. Animal Behavior, 3,* 274-285. **385.**

Shinn, Millicent W., 1909. *Notes on the Development of a Child, Vol. I.* Reprinted by permission of The University Press, Berkeley, Calif. **39, 92.**

Shirley, Mary M., 1933a. *The First Two Years. A Study of Twenty-five Babies' Intellectual Development.* Institute of Child Welfare Monogr., Series No. 6. Reprinted by permission of University of Minnesota Press. **24.**

————, 1933b. *The First Two Years. A Study of Twenty-five Babies' Personality Manifestations.* Institute of Child Welfare Monogr., Series No. 7. University of Minnesota Press. **188.**

Slaght, W. E., 1928. Untruthfulness in children: Its conditioning factors and its setting in child nature. *University of Iowa Studies in Character, 1,* No. 4. **232.**

Sliosberg, S., 1934. A contribution to the dynamics of substitution in serious and play situations. *Psychol. Forsch., 19,* 122-181. **248.**

Smith, M. E., 1926. An investigation of the development of the sentence and the extent of vocabulary in young children. *University of Iowa Studies in Child Welfare, 3,* No. 5. **25, 295.**

Snyder, L. H., 1946. *The Principles of Heredity.* Heath. **385.**

Spitz, René, 1949. The role of ecological factors in the emotional development of infancy. *Child Devel., 20,* 145-156. Reprinted by permission of the Society for Research in Child Development. **409, 410, 412.**

Spitz, R. A., and K. M. Wolf, 1946. The smiling response: A contribution to the ontogenesis of social relations. *Genet. Psych. Monogr., 34,* 57-125. **156, 191.**

Staples, Ruth, 1932. The responses of infants to color. *J. Exp. Psych., 15,* 119-141. **73.**

Stendahl, 1830. *The Red and the Black.* **252.**

Sullivan, Anne: See Keller, 1903.

Terman, L. M., and M. A. Merrill, 1937. *Measuring Intelligence: A Guide to the Administration of New Revised Stanford-Binet Tests of Intelligence.* Houghton Mifflin. Reprinted by permission. **270-274, 401.**

Thompson, G. G., and J. E. Horrocks, 1947. A study of the friendship fluctuations of urban boys and girls. *J. Genet. Psych., 70,* 53-63. Reprinted by permission of the Journal Press. **202.**

Thurstone, L. L., 1938. *Primary Mental Abilities.* University of Chicago Press. **275.**

Thurstone, L. L., and T. G. Thurstone, 1946. Tests of primary mental abilities for ages five and six. Science Research Associates. **282.**

Tinbergen, N., 1951. *The Study of Instinct.* Clarendon Press. **317.**

Todd, T. W., 1938. The record of metabolism, imprinted on the skeleton. *Am. J. Orthodontics and Oral Surgery, 24,* 811-826. **387.**

Twain, Mark, 1885. *Huckleberry Finn.* **371.**

Updegraff, Ruth, 1930. The visual perception of distance in young children and adults: A comparative study. *University of Iowa Studies in Child Welfare, 4,* No. 4. **73.**

Valentine, C. W., 1946. *The psychology of early childhood.* 3rd ed. Methuen. **224.**

Vernon, P. E., 1950. *The Structure of Human Abilities.* Wiley, **280, 282.**

Volkelt, H., 1926. Fortschritte der Experimentellen Kinderpsychologie. *Bericht u. IX Kong. f. Exp. Psychol.* Reprinted with the permission of Gustav Fischer, publisher. **64-65.**

Wagner, I. F., 1937. The establishment of a criterion of depth of sleep in the newborn infant. *J. Genet. Psych., 51,* 17-59. **99.**

Wallas, Graham, 1926. *The Art of Thought.* Harcourt, Brace. **451.**

Watson, J. B., and R. Raynor, 1920. Conditioned emotional reactions. *J. Exp. Psych., 3,* 1-4. **74, 346.**

Weiss, L. A., 1934. Differential variations in the amount of activity of newborn infants under continuous light and sound stimulation. *University of Iowa Studies in Child Welfare, 9,* 9-74. **101.**

Wellman, B. L., 1940. Iowa Studies on the effect of schooling. In Intelligence: its nature and nurture, Part II. National Society for the Study of Education, *Thirty-ninth Yearbook.* Reprinted by permission. **405-407.**

Wellman, B. L., I. M. Case, I. A. Mengert, and D. E. Bradbury, 1931. Speech sounds of young children. *University of Iowa Studies in Child Welfare, 5,* No. 2. **295-296.**

Wenger, M. S., 1936. An investigation of conditional responses in human infants. *University of Iowa Studies in Child Welfare, 12.* **223.**

Werner, Heinz, 1948. *Comparative Psychology of Mental Development.* Rev. ed. Follett. Reprinted by permission of the author. **89, 92-93, 117, 129, 312.**

Wertheimer, Max, 1923. Untersuchungen zur Lehre von der Gestalt, II. *Psychol. Forsch., 4,* 301-350. **62.**

West, James, 1945. *Plainville, U.S.A.* Columbia University Press. **220.**

Wheeler, R. H., 1929. *The Science of Psychology.* Crowell. **392.**

Wheeler, R. H., and T. D. Cutsforth, 1931. The synaesthesia of a blind subject. In R. H. Wheeler, *Readings in Psychology.* Crowell. **91.**

Whiting, J. W. M., 1941. *Becoming a Kwoma: Teaching and Learning in a New Guinea Tribe.* Yale University Press. **218.**

Whiting, J. W. M., and I. L. Child, 1953. *Child Training and Personality.* Yale University Press. Reprinted by permission. **216, 576, 581.**

Witkin, H. A., *et al.,* 1954. *Personality through Perception: An Experimental and Clinical Study.* Harper. Reprinted by permission. **61, 124.**

Wolfe, J. B., 1936. Effectiveness of token rewards for chimpanzees. *Comparative Psych. Monogr., 12,* No. 60. **420.**

Wolowik, A. B., 1927. Über die gegenseitige Wirkung der Schmerz und Nahrungsreflexe bei Kindern. *Jahrbuch Kinderheit, 115,* 185-193. **99.**

Woodcock, Louise P., 1941. *Life and Ways of the Two-Year-Old.* Basic Books. Reprinted by permission. **7, 10, 60, 321.**

Woodworth, Robert S., 1938. *Experimental Psychology.* Henry Holt. Reprinted by permission. **179.**

Wright, Herbert F., 1937. The influence of barriers upon strength of motivation. *Contributions to Psychological Theory, 1,* No. 3. Duke University Press. **147.**

Zambrowski, B. Barbara, 1951. "A Study in Childhood Egocentricity, as Revealed by Piaget's Test." Unpublished Ph.D. dissertation. New School for Social Research. **75.**

Zeigarnik, B., 1927. Über das Behalten von erledigten Handlungen. *Psychol. Forsch., 9,* 1-85. **260.**

Zietz, Karl, 1931. Reported in Werner, 1948. **91.**

Subject Index

Authors cited in the text are listed in the Bibliography and Author Index, pages 591-604.

hostility—(*Cont.*)
and frustration, 470-471
and jealousy, 197-201
parental, 490
sex differences in, 190
and sibling rivalry, 199-201
(*see also* aggression)
hypothesis testing, and cognitive learning, 435-437

I.Q. (*see* intelligence quotient)
id, 542-543
identification
and cognitive clearness, 225
and conformity to social rules, 224-225, 551
and development of attitudes, 479-480
illness, concept of, 579, 581
imitation
age differences in, 323-325
and conformity to social rules, 223
deferred, 341
immaturity (*see* maturity)
imposition
definition of, 142
and emotion, 143
methods of meeting
resistance, 144-145
unstructured, 143
withdrawal, 144
impulsiveness
immaturity and, 49
tension and, 103-104
incubation, in problem solving, 451
independence of function, 81*ff.*
and acquisition of new behavior patterns, 81
adaptability and, 81
in co-satiation experiment, 84-86
as criterion of differentiation, 71
and flexibility, 87
of goal selection and goal-directed behavior, 116-117
lack of, mass activity and, 82
and rigidity of behavior pattern, 82
and tension, 83
indignation, 263
infancy
behavior patterns in, 132-137, 184-185, 300-313
cognition in, 335*ff.*
cognitive map in, 359

infancy—(*Cont.*)
conditioning in, 423, 425-427
and deferred imitation, 341
depth perception in, 73
distractibility in, 20
effect of institutionalization during, 409-415
effect of separation from mother during, 411-412
effects of tension in, 99*ff.*
end of
activity level at, 20
characteristics at, 19-20, 360
fear in, 152
goal-directed behavior in, 19
love in, 191
memory test in, 140
model of behavior in, 359, 360
object concept in, 337-343
and omnipotence, 338
play in, 310
prehension in, 19, 134, 288
pretending in, 341
psychoanalytic theory of, 184-185, 545-548
response to concealed objects in, 29, 341, 343
selectivity in social responses in, 179-180
sensitivity to stimulation in, 179-180
talking in, 20
vision in, 18, 35, 72-73
insight (*see* problem solving, insightful)
instigation, 118*ff.*, 472
and challenge, 146*ff.*
and distraction, 243-244
function of in model of human behavior, 118-121, 360-361
and imposition, 141-164
and reciprocation, 155*ff.*
reduction of, 242
by adjustment to fear, shame, and guilt, 257
by encapsulation, 243
instinct, 539-542
instinctive behavior, 117, 316-317
institutionalization, effect of
on development, 409-415
on infant mortality, 411
intelligence, 269*ff.*
constancy of, 270, 368, 401-413
criticism of, 278-279
general, 129, 269*ff.*